Athletes and Coaches of Summer

MACMILLAN
PROFILES

Athletes
and Coaches
of Summer

Macmillan Reference USA
an imprint of the Gale Group
Detroit • New York • San Francisco • London • Boston • Woodbridge, CT

Copyright © 2000 by Macmillan Reference USA, an imprint of the Gale Group

Macmillan Reference USA
1633 Broadway
New York, New York 10019

Gale Group
27500 Drake Rd.
Farmington Hills, MI 48331-3535

Library of Congress Catalog Card Number: 00-103787

ISBN 0-02-865493-5
Printed in the United States of America
10 9 8 7 6 5 4 3 2 1

Cover design by Berrian Design

Front cover, clockwise from top: Muhammad Ali, Babe Ruth, Mia Hamm, Tiger Woods. All photos used with the permission of Corbis.

Contents

Preface

Macmillan Profiles: *Athletes and Coaches of Summer* is a unique reference work featuring 193 profiles of male and female athletes of note. The biographies of these athletes, who excel in the spring and summer sports of baseball, golf, horse racing, auto racing, boxing, tennis, and track and field, provide a starting point for student research in social studies, world cultures, and history. The articles describe the struggles, triumphs, and perseverance of the greatest athletes of our time while providing information about their early years and personal development.

Sports has become a pivotal part of American and world culture and history, and Macmillan Reference USA recognizes the need for reliable, accurate, and accessible biographies of notable figures within that framework. In *Athletes and Coaches of Summer,* the majority of the biographies are new and were commissioned to supplement entries from original sources, which include Macmillan's award-winning reference materials for libraries across the world. In fact, it is likely that several of the encyclopedias on the shelves in this library were published by Macmillan Reference or Charles Scribner's Sons.

The goal of *Athletes and Coaches of Summer* is to present an exciting introduction to the life and times of athletes from American and world history who have, through hard work and talent, become the best in their field. Students will be drawn to the focused, determined nature of these characters and, along the way, learn a great deal about history. Carefully researched and prepared by well-respected scholarly writers, these biographies are uplifting and informative. The article list was based on the following criteria: relevance to the curriculum, importance to history, and representation of as broad a cultural range as possible.

As we made the articles selections for this volume, we were forced to make some difficult choices, but we feel that these biographies represent a broad cross-section of international athletes, both male and female. After long discussion and debate, we also decided to include race horses in the volume; their strength, power, and speed contribute as much to the sport of horse racing as do the jockeys who ride them to victory. Finally, the article list was refined and expanded in response to advice from a lively and generous team of librarians from school and public libraries across the United States.

FEATURES

Athletes and Coaches of Summer is the thirteenth volume in the **Profiles Series.** To add visual appeal and enhance the usefulness of the volume, the page format was designed to include the following helpful features:

- Time Lines: Found throughout the text in the margins, time lines provide a quick reference source for dates and important events in the life and times of these athletes

- Notable Quotations: Found throughout the text in the margins, these thought-provoking quotations are drawn from interviews, speeches, and writings of or about the person covered in the article. Such quotations give readers a special insight into the distinctive personalities of these great men and women.

- Definitions and Glossary: Brief definitions of important terms in the main text can be found in the margin. A glossary at the end of the book provides students with an even broader list of definitions.

- Sidebars: Appearing in shaded boxes throughout the volume, these provocative asides relate to and amplify topics.

- Pull Quotes: Found throughout the text in the margin, pull quotes highlight essential facts.

- Suggested Reading: An extensive list of books and articles about the athletes covered in the volume will help students who want to do further research.

- Index: A thorough index provides thousands of additional points of entry into the work.

ACKNOWLEDGMENTS

This work would not have been possible without the hard work and creativity of our staff in New York and in Farmington Hills. We offer our sincere thanks to all who helped create this marvelous work.

Macmillan Reference USA

Aaron, Henry "Hank"

FEBRUARY 5, 1934– ● BASEBALL PLAYER

Henry Louis Aaron grew up in relative poverty in Mobile, Alabama. The third of eight children born to Herbert and Estella Aaron, he developed an early love for baseball, playing whenever possible on vacant lots and, later, at municipally owned, though racially restricted, diamonds in his neighborhood. He played semipro ball for the Mobile Black Bears before signing a contract in 1952 with the Indianapolis Clowns of the American Negro League. Aaron quickly attracted the attention of major league scouts, and in May 1952, he signed with the Boston Braves of the National League. The Braves sent him to their Northern League farm club in Eau Claire, Wis., where he won Rookie of the Year honors. In 1953, Aaron and two other black ball players were selected to integrate the South Atlantic League by playing for the Braves' Class A farm team in Jacksonville, Fla. In 1954 he was elevated to the Braves' major league

1934 Aaron is born in Mobile, Alabama.

1952 Aaron joins the Indianapolis Clowns, Negro American League.

1954 Aaron joins the Milwaukee (later Atlanta) Braves.

1974 Aaron hits 715th home run, breaking Babe Ruth's record.

"Hank made everything look easy. Mays did everything with flair, but he never made the perfect throws to the cut-off man the way Hank did. Hank was just so smooth about everything. He was the best all-around player I ever saw."

Lew Burdette, Braves pitcher

club, which had moved to Milwaukee the previous year. Aaron rapidly became one of the mainstays for the Braves, both in Milwaukee and, from 1966 to 1974, in Atlanta, leading the Milwaukee club to World Series appearances in 1957 and 1958 and a world championship in 1957, and Atlanta to the National League championship series in 1969. In 1957, he was named the National League's most valuable player. In 1975, after 21 seasons with the Braves, Aaron was traded to the American League's Milwaukee Brewers, where he completed his playing career in 1976.

The most celebrated highlight of Aaron's major league career came on April 8, 1974, when he eclipsed the career home run record of Babe Ruth by connecting off the Los Angeles Dodgers' Al Downing at Fulton County Stadium in Atlanta. The home run, his 715th in the major leagues, climaxed a very difficult period in Aaron's life as he confronted various forms of abuse, including racial insults and death threats, from those who did not want an African American to surpass Ruth's mark. "It should have been the happiest time of my life, the best year," Aaron has said. "But it was the worst year . . . So many bad things happened. . . . Things I'm still trying to get over, and maybe never will. Things I know I'll never forget."

Aaron's lifetime record of 3,771 base hits ranks behind only those of Pete Rose and Ty Cobb, and he is the all-time leader in home runs (755), runs batted in (2,297), extra-base hits (1,477), and total bases (6,856). His 2,174 runs scored tie him for second place (with Ruth) behind Cobb. These credentials, established over a 23-year career, easily earned "Hammerin' Hank" induction into the Major League Baseball Hall of Fame at Cooperstown, N.Y., in his first year of eligibility, in 1982.

Following his retirement as a player, Aaron returned to the Braves as director of player development and later was promoted to a vice presidency. In this capacity, he has been one of the most outspoken critics of major league baseball's sparse record of bringing minorities into executive leadership positions both on and off the playing field. In addition, he is a vice president of Turner Broadcasting Company and maintains a number of business and charitable interests in the Atlanta area. ◆

Agassi, Andre

APRIL 29, 1970– ● TENNIS PLAYER

Born in Las Vegas, Nevada, on April 29, 1970, Andre Agassi has become one of the biggest stars of the tennis world. His powerful game—along with ever-changing clothing and hairstyles as well as lively on-court behavior—has spawned legions of fans in an era of technically proficient, but rather dour and business-like, professional tennis. The same characteristics also draw detractors, however, who have criticized Agassi for supposedly putting more effort into his style than into the substance of his game. But it cannot be denied that Agassi has greatly enlivened professional tennis and drawn the public to the sport.

The man who is sometimes to referred to as the "rock star of tennis" (and, in his earlier years as a professional player, as the "bad boy of tennis") is the youngest of four children. Rita, Phil, Tami, and Andre were born to Betty and Mike Agassi. Mike, an Olympic boxer, grew up in Iran and immigrated to the United States in 1952. There, he became fascinated with tennis—the game became an obsession, and Mike was determined that his children were going to be champions.

Betty and Mike moved west from Chicago, Illinois, so that the family could play tennis outdoors all year long. The family landed in Las Vegas, and Mike set about trying to mold the youngsters into tennis pros. They would practice an hour in the morning before school and three hours afterward. Mike did all their training, using a court at a nearby casino. All of the children worked

Andre Agassi backhands a return shot.

1970 Agassi is born in Las Vegas, Nevada.

1986 Agassi begins professional play.

1992 Agassi wins his first Grand Slam title.

1994 Agassi wins the U.S. Open.

1996 Agassi wins an Olympic gold medal in men's singles.

hard to please their father, but it was Andre who had the deepest yearning to do what it takes to become a success in the professional tennis world. He began to win more and more tournaments in his age group.

As his innate talent and desire to succeed became more evident, the family's tennis focus shifted to Andre (probably much to the relief of his siblings, who had long suffered under the stress of trying to meet their father's grand expectations). At age 13, Andre was sent to live and train at the Nick Bollettieri Tennis Academy in Bradenton, Florida. Andre's talent was so striking that he was eventually given a full scholarship to attend.

Agassi hated being so far away from home, and his off-court behavior at the Bollettieri Academy reflected this, but he vastly improved his game. He was challenged there by all of the other extremely talented young players who attended the school. The players would go to regular classes in the morning, then work on their tennis all afternoon.

In May 1986, just two days after he turned 16, Agassi turned professional. His brother, Phil, traveled with him everywhere, managing his career and helping him adjust to his new life. It was not an easy transition for Andre. He often behaved badly on the court, throwing tantrums and being rude to spectators, officials, and other players. Still, in his first season as a pro, he managed to reach number 91 in the world rankings.

His second year as a pro, Agassi improved both his behavior and his results. He still did not capture any of tennis's important Grand Slam events—Wimbledon, the U.S. Open, the French Open, and the Australian Open—but he moved up to number 25 in the rankings and also increased his earnings. He achieved this at the same time that he flouted the unwritten dress code of professional tennis. Instead of wearing sedate white clothes, Agassi often wore wildly colored clothes and shoes. His hair was likely to be dyed platinum and cut in a Mohawk.

In 1988, Agassi started winning tournaments, winning six of the seven tournaments in which he reached the finals. He collected more than $800,000 in prize money, and he signed contracts for commercial endorsements that brought him millions more. He was ranked number three in the world.

In 1989, Agassi fell back in the rankings a bit, to number seven, but in 1990 he rebounded, to fourth. That year, Agassi finally made it to the finals of two Grand Slam events—the U.S. Open and the French Open—though he did not win the tournaments. He also played on the winning U.S. Davis Cup team.

In 1991, he reached the finals of the French Open but, after a rain delay, lost to fellow American Jim Courier, a rival since Agassi's days at the Bollettieri Academy. Depressed, Agassi began overeating, and within months he gained 25 pounds. When he played at Wimbledon, he bowed to the officials' insistence that all players wear white (but he kept his long blonde hair flowing). His added weight slowed him down, however, and he was eliminated in the quarterfinals. Two months later, he was trounced easily at the U.S. Open. Agassi fell to number 10 in the rankings.

Agassi was discouraged, but not beaten. He pulled himself together, lost weight, and improved his physical conditioning. Gradually his superb game was back in evidence, and he won his first Grand Slam title in 1992 on the grass courts at Wimbledon. His fans went wild as Agassi, overcome with joy, fell to the grass weeping.

That year, Agassi also participated in another winning Davis Cup team, but he lost in the quarterfinals at the U.S. Open. That loss was a sign of things to come.

The year 1993 was not Agassi's best. He fell to 24th in the rankings and, in December, underwent surgery to repair tendinitis. His right wrist had been bothering him for some time, and it was increasingly causing him problems on the court.

The surgery was successful, and in 1994 Agassi played so well that he vaulted all the way to number two in the world rankings—his best showing thus far. He finally won the U.S. Open, a moment of sheer triumph that every American player strives to achieve. Agassi's good fortune continued through 1995, when he reached the finals of 11 tournaments and won 7 of them, including the Australian Open. For 30 weeks, he was ranked number one in the world. The lone sour note came when he was not able to collect a second U.S. Open win, losing in the final round to Pete Sampras.

Agassi played for the U.S. team in the 1996 Olympics, held in Atlanta, Georgia, and became the first American man to win the gold medal in Olympic singles since 1924. Aside from the Olympics, however, it was not Agassi's best year on the courts, and he began a losing streak that continued into 1997. His world tennis ranking plummeted, bottoming out at an astonishing 141st in November 1997. However, happiness in Agassi's personal life that year offset his professional setbacks when he wed actress Brooke Shields, who frequently attended his matches. In

"I've realized my dreams of winning a Grand Slam tournament. If my career was over tomorrow, I got more than I deserved, than I could ever ask for."

Andre Agassi

In 1999, for the first time ever, Agassi finished the season ranked as the number one men's tennis player in the world.

1998 Agassi's game returned to form and he made up some lost ground, climbing back into the top 10. Many observers felt that, despite the comeback in the rankings, Agassi's tennis still seemed uninspired.

In 1999, however, Agassi played with passion and completed his stunning comeback. Fit and trim, as well as newly divorced from Shields, Agassi returned to tennis entirely focused on his game and quickly captured two Grand Slam titles—the French Open and the U.S. Open. The win at the French made him only the fifth man to win all four Grand Slam events in a career. For the first time ever, he finished the season ranked as the number one men's tennis player in the world. Agassi was back on top of the tennis world, adored by fans and recognized equally for his talent, heart, and newfound maturity.

Agassi started 2000 right where he left off in 1999, winning the year's first Grand Slam event, the Australian Open. In the previous 12 months, Agassi had won three of the four Grand Slam events and finished second at the final one (Wimbledon). That put him in the company of legends—not since Rod Laver did it in 1969 had a man reached the final match of four straight Grand Slam tournaments.

Agassi is deeply involved in charity work. In 1994, he founded the Andre Agassi Charitable Foundation, which helps at-risk youth in Las Vegas. He stays in shape, on-court and off, with the help of coach Brad Gilbert (since 1994) and trainer Gil Reyes, and is in close contact with his family and childhood friends. Sometime in the summer of 2000, Agassi was expected to marry girlfriend and fellow tennis legend, Steffi Graf. Agassi maintains a home in Las Vegas. ◆

Akers, Michelle

FEBRUARY 1, 1966– ● SOCCER PLAYER

Michelle Akers has accomplished the formidable task of becoming a hero to millions of women thanks to her skills in a sport that few Americans know much about—soccer. A founding member, guiding spirit, and on-field star for the U.S. Women's National Team, she has overcome physical and emotional setbacks to help lead the United States to two women's World Cup titles (1991 and 1999). Her lofty accomplishments include a mark of 104 goals in 146 appearances (second only to Mia Hamm's 111 goals in 179 matches); the first endorsement contract ever signed by a woman soccer player (with Umbro in 1991); and FIFA's highest honor, the Order of Merit, awarded to Akers on June 7, 1998, for her distinguished record of achievement. In the words of Hank Stenbrecher, general secretary of U.S. Soccer, "She's the most powerful force to exist in women's soccer. No one was ever more domineering on the field and off-field. She is such a voice, pushing people to pay attention to the women's game."

Before the rise of Michelle Akers, there was no major women's soccer in the United States. She played in the U.S. Women's National Team's first game 14 years ago and scored the squad's first goal in a 2–2 tie with Denmark on August 21, 1985, in Jesolo, Italy. But the decade preceding that was one of hard work and fierce dedication to a sport that enjoyed very little of the peer-group allure that it has since attained among young students. Akers recalls that as a child she was a "typical tomboy" with fierce competitive instincts that her mother tried to channel constructively by steering Michelle into a soccer program when she was eight years old. It was not love at first sight. "We lost a lot at first, and I begged my mom to let me quit. She refused." But thanks to her mother's persistence, Michelle hung on a while longer and "fell in love with the game," harboring adolescent dreams of becoming a "pro soccer player in Europe."

Despite an array of teenage tribulations—coping with her parents' divorce and, in her words, "skipping school, dating older guys, experimenting with drugs, lying"—Akers remained focused enough on her soccer talents to attain local stardom as a three-time All-American at Shorecrest High School in Seattle. She received a soccer scholarship to the University of Central Florida just after soccer became a varsity sport in the wake of Title IX, a federal law that mandated equal funding for men's and women's athletic programs. In her sophomore year, 1985, she became a member of the first U.S. Women's National Team, traveling with the squad to its inaugural international competition in Italy, where the Americans were far outclassed by the more experienced European squads, losing three and tying one of their four matches.

The trip was a sobering reminder of how far the U.S. team had to go to close the competitive gap with its international rivals. Akers returned to the United States and redoubled her

"I usually play harder than anyone else on the field, and that gives me an advantage. But I don't play for awards. I play because I love the game and I love to compete."
Michelle Akers

1966 Akers born on February 1.

1985 Akers becomes a charter member of the U.S. women's national soccer team.

1991 Akers plays in the World Cup in China: scores both goals for U.S. in victory over Norway.

1994 Akers is diagnosed with Epstein-Barr ("chronic fatigue") syndrome.

1996 In the Atlanta Olympic Games, Akers drills game-tying penalty kick in semifinal against Norway; the U.S. wins gold.

training efforts, emerging as the finest women's soccer player in the country. She was a four-time All-American at Central Florida and became the UCF record holder for goals and assists. Her outstanding play earned her the prestigious Hermann Award in 1988. Her marriage to Roby Stahl, one of the best men's soccer players in the United States, seemed a further indication of her all-out dedication to the game.

Akers's unremitting perseverance and formidable athleticism set a high bar for the Women's National Team, which had set its sights on the first women's World Cup competition scheduled for 1991 in China. Some skeptics wondered if the U.S. team would even qualify. They not only surmounted that hurdle, but they went on to amaze the world, charging ahead to five consecutive victories and earning a spot in the finals against Norway. It proved to be a superb, taut match, deadlocked at 1–1 with three minutes left when Akers scored the winning goal, clinching the first American championship in soccer since 1862. Her brilliant performance in the World Cup spurred her to international fame, a lucrative endorsement contract, and a place on a professional women's team in Sweden, the Tyreso Football Club. In 1992 she scored the most goals of any soccer player, male or female, in Sweden. She was also the leading scorer during the U.S. Olympic Festival in 1993.

Underlying these heady accomplishments was a gnawing sense of alarm over the persistent fatigue that increasingly had plagued her since the World Cup victory. It was not until 1994 that physicians finally diagnosed her condition as Epstein-Barr syndrome, a kind of viral infection that induces chronic fatigue. By the end of that year, the illness had relegated her to the sidelines. She described her ordeal to a reporter: "Every day I felt as if I had just flown to Europe, not gotten any sleep or anything to eat, gotten right back on the plane, flown on to the U.S. and then trained. When it was bad, I couldn't sit up in a chair. All I could do was lie in bed. At night I sweated so much I went through two or three T-shirts. And the migraine headaches pounded. Boom! Boom! Boom!"

Akers's physical trials were compounded by the end of her marriage in 1995, which proved to be the first step in a process of personal renewal that eventually restored her confidence and her health. Spurred by a spiritual awakening, she adopted a rigorously healthy diet and training regimen that brought her back to playing form just in time for the 1996 Olympics, the first games at which soccer was scheduled as an official competition.

She started all five matches in the Olympics and dramatically rescued the U.S. team from elimination by scoring a critical tying goal on a penalty kick in America's 2–1 victory over Norway in the semifinals. The Americans then went on to a 2–1 gold-medal win against China.

Still grappling with bouts of chronic fatigue, Akers took most of the following year off from the game to recuperate from knee surgery. She rejoined the U.S. National Team in a match against Sweden on October 30, 1997, as the Americans began their long-term tune-up for the 1999 World Cup. By the time the finals began in July 1999, Akers had again rebounded to become a critical component in the Americans' attack as they hurtled toward a confrontation with China in the finals at the Rose Bowl in Pasadena, California.

In a thrilling U.S. final victory decided by penalty kicks, Akers put forth a heroic effort. In the words of Steven Goff of *The Washington Post*, "In perhaps the most courageous performance of her 14-year international career, Akers was the foundation of the Americans' defensive effort against China's dangerous attack." The U.S. coach, Tony DiCicco, said, "The fans were treated today to witnessing one of the greatest women athletes in history—a true champion leaving it all on the field, fighting for her teammates. Michelle Akers inspires me, and I know she does the same for everybody on the U.S. team." ◆

> *"People are sick of seeing me get hurt, but that's who I am. I take big risks. Sometimes I fall flat on my face, but I also get some mountaintop moments."*
> Michelle Akers in
> *Sports Illustrated*

Ali, Muhammad

JANUARY 17, 1942– ● BOXER

Muhammad Ali was born Cassius Marcellus Clay, Jr. in Louisville, Kentucky in 1942. He began boxing at the age of 12 under the tutelage of Joe Martin, a Louisville policeman. Having scant interest in school and little affinity for intellectual endeavors, young Clay devoted himself wholeheartedly to boxing. He showed great promise early on and soon developed into one of the most impressive amateurs in the country. He became the National Amateur Athletic Union (AAU) champion in 1959 and in 1960, and also won a gold medal in the light-heavyweight division at the 1960 Olympics in Rome. As a result of his boyish good looks and his outgoing personality—his poetry recitations, his good-natured bragging,

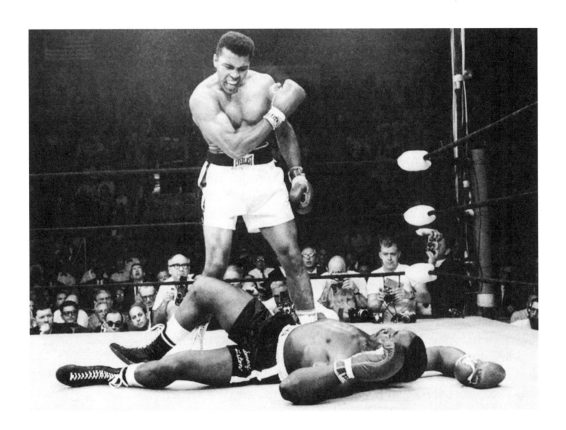

Muhammad Ali poses
triumphantly over Sonny
Liston in 1964.

and his undeniable abilities—Clay because famous after the
Olympics. Shortly after returning from Rome, he turned professional and was managed by a consortium of white Louisville
businessmen. Carefully nurtured by veteran trainer Angelo
Dundee, he accumulated a string of victories against relatively
mediocre opponents and achieved a national following with his
constant patter, his poetry, and his boyish antics. At 6' 3" and a
fighting weight of around 200 pounds, he astonished sportswriters with his blazing hand and foot speed, his unorthodox style of
keeping his hands low, and his ability to avoid punches by moving his head back. No heavyweight in history possessed Clay's
grace or speed.

On February 25, 1964, Clay fought as the underdog for the
heavyweight title against Sonny Liston. Liston, an ex-convict,
was thought by many to be virtually invincible because of his
devastating one-round victories against former champion Floyd
Patterson. An air of both the theater of the absurd and of omi-
nousness surrounded the bout in Miami. Publicly, Clay taunted
and comically berated Liston. He called him "the Bear," ha-
rassed him at his home, and almost turned the weigh-in cere-

mony into a shambles as he seemingly tried to attack Liston and appeared on the verge of being utterly out of control. Privately, however, Clay was seen with Malcolm X and members of the Nation of Islam (NOI). Rumors circulated that he had joined the group, which advocated black nationalism and self-defense. Soon after, it was discovered that he had been secretly visiting NOI mosques for nearly three years and that he had indeed become a friend of Malcolm X, who sat ringside at the Liston fight.

Clay beat Liston fairly easily in seven rounds, shocking the world by becoming heavyweight champion. Immediately after the fight, he announced that he was a member of the NOI and that his name was no longer Cassius Clay but Muhammad Ali. The response from the white press, white America, and the boxing establishment generally was swift and intensely hostile. The NOI was seen, largely through the rhetoric of Malcolm X, its most stylish spokesman, as an antiwhite hate group. (When Malcolm X broke with the NOI, shortly after the Liston fight, Ali remained loyal to Elijah Muhammad and ended his friendship with Malcolm X.) Following his public conversion to Islam, Ali was publicly **pilloried**. Most publications and sports journalists refused to call him by his new name. Former champion Floyd Patterson nearly went on a personal and national crusade against the NOI in his fight against Ali on November 22, 1965, but Patterson later became one of the few fighters to defend Ali publicly during his years of exile. Indeed, not since the reign of Jack Johnson was the white public and a segment of the black population so enraged by the opinions and life of a black athlete.

After winning his rematch with Liston in Lewiston, Maine, on May 25, 1965, in a bizarre fight that ended with Liston apparently being knocked out in the first round, Ali spent most of the next year fighting abroad, primarily because of his unpopularity in the United States. Among his most important bouts during this period were a 15-round decision over George Chuvalo in Toronto, a sixth-round knockout of Henry Cooper in London, and a 15-round decision over Ernest Terrell in Houston. While Ali was abroad American officials changed his draft status from 1-Y (unfit for Army services because of his low score on Army intelligence tests) to 1-A (qualified for induction). Many saw this change as a direct response to the negative public opinion concerning Ali's political views and the mounting war in Vietnam. Ali refused to serve in the Army on the grounds that it was a vi-

pilloried: an individual or group being publicly punished or scorned as a result of particular actions or beliefs by that individual.

"With the exception of Martin Luther King, no black man in America had more influence than Ali during the years when Ali was in his prime."

Thomas Hauser, biographer

1942 Ali is born Cassius Clay in Louisville, Kentucky.

1960 Ali wins the light-heavyweight gold medal at Olympics in Rome.

1967 Ali refuses induction into armed forces; his boxing title is stripped and his license is suspended.

1971 "The Fight of the Century": Frazier wins 15-round unanimous decision against Ali.

1978 Ali retires for the final time, with a 56–5 record.

1996 Ali lights torch inaugurating Summer Olympics in Atlanta.

olation of his religious beliefs. (Elijah Muhammad, leader of the NOI, had served time in prison during World War II for refusing to serve in the armed services.)

In 1967, Ali was convicted in federal court of violation of the Selective Service Act, sentenced to five years in prison, and immediately stripped of both his boxing title and his boxing license. For the next three and a half years, Ali, free on bond while appealing his case (which he eventually won on appeal to the U.S. Supreme Court), was prohibited from boxing. Still, Ali had inspired black athletes to become more militant and more politically committed. Medal-winning track stars John Carlos and Tommie Smith gave a clenched-fist salute during the playing of the National Anthem at the Olympic Games in Mexico City in 1968, and Harry Edwards became one of the more outspoken leaders of a new cadre of young black athletes whom saw Ali as a hero.

By 1970, with public opinion decidedly against the Vietnam War, and a growing black influence in several southern state governments, Ali was given a license to fight in Georgia. He returned to the ring on October 26 to knock out Jerry Quarry in the third round. Although he was still a brilliant fighter, the nearly four year lay-off had diminished some of Ali's abilities. He took far more punishment in the ring during the years of his return than he had taken before. This was to have dire consequences for him as he grew older.

In the early 1970s Ali fought several of his most memorable matches. On March 8, 1971, he faced the undefeated Philadelphian Joe Frazier in New York City. Frazier had become champion during Ali's exile. The 15-round fight, which Frazier won in a close decision, was so fierce that both boxers were hospitalized afterward. Many have speculated that this fight initiated Ali's neurological deterioration. In July of that year Ali won the North American Boxing Federation (NABF) heavyweight title by knocking out Jimmy Ellis in 12 rounds. His next major boxing challenge came in March 1973, when Ken Norton captured the NABF title from Ali in a 12-round decision. Ali regained the title six months later with a 12-round decision over Norton. In January of the following year, Ali and Frazier staged their first rematch. This nontitle bout at Madison Square Garden ended with Ali victorious after 12 hard-fought rounds. Ali finally regained the world heavyweight title in Kinshasa, Zaire, on October 30, 1974, when he knocked out a seemingly indestructible George Foreman in eight rounds. To counter Foreman's awesome punching power, Ali used what he called his "rope-a-dope" strategy, by which he leaned back against the ropes and covered his head, allowing Foreman to tire himself out by throwing many punches. The next year, Ali and Frazier faced off one last time in what Ali dubbed "The Thrilla in Manila." Both boxers received tremendous punishment during this bludgeoning ordeal. Ali prevailed, however, when Frazier's trainer refused to let the boxer come out for the 15th round.

During the 1970s Ali was lionized. No longer seen as a race demon, he virtually became a national icon. He appeared in movies—including the film *The Greatest* (1977), based on his autobiography of the same name (1975). Like Jackie Robinson and Joe Louis before him, Ali played himself in the film—he also appeared in television programs and in commercials. He was one of the most photographed and interviewed men in the world. Indeed, Ali even beat Superman in the ring in a special issue of the comic devoted to him. Part of Ali's newfound popularity was a result of a shift in attitude by the white public and white sportswriters, but part of it was also a reflection of Ali's tempered approach to politics. He became a great deal less doctrinaire in the political aspects of his Islamic beliefs and eventually embraced Wallace D. Muhammad's more **ecumenical** form of Islam when the NOI factionalized after the death of Elijah Muhammad in 1975. Finally, as befitting a major celebrity, Ali had one of the largest entourages of any sports personality in history, resembling that of a head of state.

On February 15, 1978, Ali again lost the title. His opponent this time was Leon Spinks, an ex-Marine and native of a north St. Louis housing project. Spinks fought in only eight professional bouts before he met Ali. Ali, however, became the first heavyweight in history to regain the title for a third time when he defeated Spinks on September 15 of the same year.

In 1979, Ali was aged and weary; his legs were shot, his reflexes had slowed, and his appetite for competition was waning as a result of the good life that he was enjoying. Ali retired from the ring at that time, only to do what so many other great champions have so unwisely done, namely, return to battle. His return to the ring included a savage 10-round beating on October 2, 1980, at the hands of Larry Holmes, a former sparring partner who had become champion after Ali's retirement. His next fight was a 10-round decision lost to Trevor Berbick on December 11 of the following year. After the Berbick fight, Ali retired for good. His professional record stands at 56 wins, 37 of

"Man, I hit him with punches that'd bring down the walls of a city. Lawdy, Lawdy, he's a great champion."

Joe Frazier about Ali, after their "Thrilla in Manila" fight, 1975

ecumenical: a general extent of influence; encompassing, including, or representing a variety of religious persuasions.

which were by knockout, and 5 losses. He was elected to the Boxing Hall of Fame in 1987.

During Ali's later years, his speech became noticeably more slurred, and after his retirement he became more aged: moving slowly, speaking with such a thick tongue that he was almost incomprehensible, and suffering from attacks of palsy. There is some question as to whether he has Parkinson's disease or a Parkinson's-like deterioration of the neurological system. Many believe that the deterioration of his neurological system is directly connected to the punishment he took in the ring. By the early 1990s, although his mind was still sound, Ali gave the appearance of being a good deal older and more infirm than he actually was. He found it difficult to write or talk, and often walked slowly. Despite this, he is living a full life, travels constantly, and seems to be at peace with himself. ◆

Allen, Mel

FEBRUARY 14, 1913–JUNE 16, 1996 ● SPORTSCASTER

"Going, going, gone!" and "How about that!" are the two most famous of the many signature phrases coined by Mel Allen, one of the pioneers of modern sports broadcasting. From the early 1940s to the mid-1960s, Allen's was the nation's dominant sportscasting voice, heard not only on the local radio and TV broadcasts of the New York Yankees but also on Fox Movietone newsreels and on annual radio and TV network coverage of the most important sporting events. Allen's broadcasts include 20 World Series, 24 baseball All-Star Games, five Rose Bowls, and two Sugar Bowls.

Allen was born Melvin Avrom Israel in Birmingham, Alabama, on February 14, 1913, the first of three children of Julius and Anna Israel, both Russian immigrants. Mel's earliest years were spent in Johns, Alabama, where his father owned a general store. After the store closed, Julius Israel owned stores in other small towns and then became a traveling shirt salesman, during which time the family moved through several Alabama towns and briefly to Greensboro, North Carolina. A precocious student with a special zeal for sports in general and baseball in particular, Allen entered high school when he was just 11 and still managed to put in some time on the varsity squads in basket-

From the early 1940s to the mid-1960s, Allen's was the nation's dominant sportscasting voice.

ball, football, and baseball. On a visit to relatives in Detroit one summer, he even sold soda at Tiger Stadium just so he could see major league baseball games.

After graduating from Birmingham's Phillips High School at age 15, Allen enrolled at the University of Alabama, where he played intramural sports and became sports editor of the student newspaper while studying speech and political science. After receiving his B.A. degree in 1932, Allen entered the University of Alabama law school, from which he graduated in 1936. Struggling to make ends meet during the early years of the Depression, Allen eventually won a teaching fellowship in the speech department in his senior year of college, a job that led to his appointment as public address announcer for Alabama football games. In that capacity Allen developed a close relationship with the university's renowned football coach, Frank Thomas, who was supportive of Allen's early broadcasting ambitions.

Allen got his first radio exposure covering Alabama football for a Birmingham station, which happened to be an affiliate of the bourgeoning Columbia Broadcasting System (CBS). Allen's work was heard by the manager of CBS's southeast station group, and when Allen joined some fraternity brothers for a vacation in New York in December 1936, the CBS manager urged Allen to audition for an opening on the national announcing staff. Allen beat out 23 other applicants and moved to New York, appeasing his puzzled parents with the promise that he would try out broadcasting for one year just for the experience and then return to Alabama to practice law. He never returned.

After a name change from Melvin Israel to Mel Allen (at the behest of CBS executives), Allen quickly established himself as an appealing and versatile on-air personality, announcing everything from dance-band broadcasts and quiz shows to newscasts and sporting events. It was in the last that Allen's talents stood out in sharpest relief. In 1939, for example, CBS sent Allen up in a plane to cover the Vanderbilt Cup auto race. When rain forced a cancellation of the race, Allen filled the air time with absorbing, improvised accounts of local boat races and tennis matches, a feat of broadcasting savvy that won Mel a special commendation from CBS and a permanent assignment in the CBS Sports department.

Allen's first major baseball job was doing color commentary for the 1938 World Series. In 1939 he got his first regular job in major league baseball as the assistant announcer on Yankee and

1913 Allen is born Melvin Avrom Israel in Birmingham, Alabama.

1938 Allen lands first major baseball job: color commentary at World Series.

1946 Allen becomes chief broadcaster for the New York Yankees.

1977 Allen begins narrating *This Week in Baseball.*

1996 Allen dies in Greenwich, Connecticut.

Giant home games. He became the chief announcer the next season, a position he held until he entered the army in 1943. Already a popular sportscaster, Allen was a valued contributor to the Armed Forces Radio Service, where he figured prominently on the *Army Hour* program during World War II.

After his army discharge in 1946, Allen became the chief broadcaster for the home and road games of the New York Yankees, whose dominance of postwar baseball helped to make Allen one of the most famous and popular figures in sportscasting. Already well established as "The Voice of the Yankees," Allen also excelled in a variety of choice network assignments that brought his resonant baritone, distinctive cadences, and descriptive powers to a national audience (including 12 years as chief announcer for NBC TV's coverage of NCAA football). A leading TV critic of the day wrote that Allen and his renowned colleague Red Barber (the voice of the Brooklyn Dodgers) were distinguished by "complete impartiality, a great zest for detail, and a thorough knowledge of baseball." In the words of Richard Sandomir of *The New York Times*, "Mr. Allen's voice, distinctly Southern but a perfect fit for the Bronx, became synonymous with baseball's rhythms, its lazy summer afternoons, chilly Octobers and shadows creeping over Yankee Stadium's greensward. He was everything a sportscaster should be: quick, smart, descriptive, and exuberant."

Allen's fortunes took a downward turn in the early 1960s in the face of mounting career pressures and health problems. Throughout the 1963 season Allen had been having intermittent problems with his voice, and during the final game of the 1963 World Series, he completely lost his voice in the last inning and had to be replaced on the air by the Dodgers' Vin Scully. He then missed two weeks of the 1964 season with persistent minor health problems. His **iconic** stature in the business notwithstanding, the Yankees dropped Allen at the end of the 1964 season, giving no official reason for the move. They replaced him with Phil Rizzuto as their featured World Series broadcaster that year. Allen's network duties at NBC Sports also came to an end in 1964, as did his long tenure at Fox Movietone News, which shut down its newsreel operation that year.

Allen sought to retain a foothold in major league broadcasting, working for the Milwaukee Braves in 1965 and the Cleveland Indians in 1966. After Allen's season with the Indians, however, his broadcasting career went into gradual decline until 1977, when he signed on as the narrator of Major League

iconic: description of a person or thing given great deference and largely uncritical respect. An icon is a person who has reached legendary status.

Baseball's popular weekly highlights show, *This Week in Base-ball*. Thanks to this nationally syndicated show, Allen's voice once again became a familiar backdrop to summer, and his career gathered renewed momentum. Allen's comeback was further propelled that summer when he and Red Barber became the first broadcasters inducted into the broadcasting wing of the Baseball Hall of Fame. The following year the Yankees' owner, George Steinbrenner, hired Allen to call 40 Yankee games a summer on cable TV (a position he held until 1985), to host the syndicated *Yankees Magazine* TV show, and to make personal appearances for the club. He held the latter two positions until his death at his home in Greenwich, Connecticut, on June 16, 1996.

When told of Allen's death, Steinbrenner said, "Mel Allen meant as much to the Yankees tradition as legends like Ruth, Gehrig, DiMaggio, and Mantle." Reflecting on Allen's flair for imparting the dramatic peaks of a game, a writer called him "the Homer of homers. . . . Night after night, October after October, Mel Allen composed the epic poem of baseball's Homeric age." ◆

Andretti, Mario

FEBRUARY 28, 1940– ● RACE CAR DRIVER

One of America's most successful racing drivers, Mario Andretti was voted Driver of the Year three times (1967, 1978, and 1984), more than any other driver. He also achieved distinction in a wider variety of venues than any of this contemporaries: midgets, IndyCar, Formula One, sprint cars, sports cars, dirt-track cars, and even drag racing.

One of three children of Alvise Louise and Rina Andretti, Mario was born in Montona, Italy, on the Istrian peninsula. His father lost his property during World War II, after which Istria became part of Yugoslavia. In order to remain citizens of Italy, the family moved to Lucca, where Alvise took up work in a toy factory and applied for visas to the United States.

During their years in Lucca, Mario's father took him and his twin brother, Aldo, to see the Mille Miglia, a 1,000-mile cross-country car race. The young Mario was captivated by the daring panache of Italy's great Alberto Ascari. As Andretti later re-

Mario Andretti was voted Driver of the Year three times (1967, 1978, and 1984), more than any other driver.

Mario Andretti celebrates another Indy Car victory.

called, "He was my idol, and I guess that's where my love of racing first started." Mario and Aldo enrolled in a course in auto mechanics and also joined a program to train young race drivers. After a fatality during a race, however, the program closed, and Alvise forbade his sons from entering any more races. They persisted on the sly, however, telling no one but their uncle, a priest who was bound to secrecy.

When the family's visas finally came through in 1955, the Andrettis moved to Nazareth, Pennsylvania, where the father found work in a textile factory. Mario began high school there but soon dropped out to pursue his racing ambitions. He took a job as a car mechanic, and with two years' worth of savings, he and his brother bought and rebuilt a used Hudson Sportsman. In the next three years, Mario drove the Hudson to 20 victories in regional stock car races. Aldo fractured his skull in 1959 and pulled back from racing for a year, although he did eventually return and raced until 1969, when another racing injury forced his retirement. Mario stayed with racing the whole time, however, even at the cost of breaking with his father (they reconciled in later years).

Andretti got married in 1961, and his wife encouraged him to pursue his dream. He quit his garage job and joined the United Racing Club (URC), racing sprint cars in regional eastern competitions for the next year. In 1963, his first year driving midgets on the American Race Drivers Club (ARDC) circuit, he won 11 races. His fearless driving captured the interest of Clint Brawner, a highly regarded mechanic and car designer for Dean Van Lines, which became Andretti's official sponsor. Dean Van Lines's sponsorship gave Andretti the resources he needed to compete effectively in racing's top rung, the United States Auto Club (USAC), which Andretti joined in 1964.

In his rookie season Andretti ranked third in the USAC Sprint Car division and placed in the top 10 in six races. The following year he moved up from the Sprint division and won his first Champ Car race, the Hoosier Grand Prix. Then came the premier event in American auto racing, the Indianapolis 500, where Andretti won the Rookie of the Year with a third-place finish. By the end of that impressive season, he had won the first of his four Champ Car national championships (1965, 1966, 1969, and 1974).

After earning the Champ Car title again in 1966, the restless Andretti set out to conquer the stock car world as well, racing in events sponsored by the National Association for Stock Car Auto Racing (NASCAR). Amazingly, he succeeded immediately by winning NASCAR's prestigious Daytona 500 in 1967, averaging 149.926 miles per hour in his Ford. The following year he took on his first U.S. Grand Prix Formula One race at Watkins Glen and was off to a promising start when clutch trouble forced him out of the race. Andretti placed second on the IndyCar circuit in 1967 and 1968, but recaptured the crown in 1969, the year he won his only Indianapolis 500. His first Grand Prix win came in South Africa in 1971; Andretti drove a Ferrari to victory. He cast an even wider net in 1974, when he won the USAC dirt track title and was barely nosed out for the Formula One crown.

For several years thereafter, Andretti attempted an ambitious balancing act while racing in several circuits—Champ Car, Formula One, Formula 5000, and Can-Am racing—with disappointing results and only intermittent victories. From 1975 to 1981 he focused his energies on the Formula One Grand Prix circuit; in 1978 Andretti reached a career peak, winning six races and becoming the second (and to date, the last) American to win the World Driving Championship (WDC). He remains the only driver to have won both an IndyCar championship and the WDC.

After returning to IndyCar racing in 1982, Andretti needed only two years to capture his fourth championship. Although he never recaptured the Indy 500, he came within a hair's breadth in 1981, when Bobby Unser appeared to have beaten him by eight seconds; the next day Unser's victory was annulled and handed to Andretti because of a passing violation by Unser. Four months later, however, an appeals panel returned the crown to Unser, punishing him with a $40,000 fine instead. Andretti's final flourishes of glory on the IndyCar circuit came in 1987 when he claimed a second-place finish in the Indy 500 and his fourth IndyCar season championship.

1940 Andretti is born in Montana, Italy.

1967 Andretti wins the Daytona 500 and is named Driver of the Year.

1969 Andretti wins the Indianapolis 500.

1978 Andretti wins the Formula One championship and four CART titles; he is named Driver of the Year.

1984 Andretti is named Driver of the Year for the third time.

Andretti's lifetime total of 52 IndyCar victories places him second only to A. J. Foyt, and Andretti is the all-time leader in pole positions (67). His lifetime IndyCar earnings—$10,887,392—are the fifth-highest in history. In 1991, when Andretti ranked seventh in the IndyCar championship point standings, the title went to his son Michael, while his nephew, John, finished in the top 10.

A member of the Indianapolis 500 Hall of Fame, Mario Andretti retired from racing in 1994 and now keeps busy with a variety of business interests. He and his wife, Dee Ann, still live in Nazareth, Pennsylvania. ◆

Arcaro, Eddie

FEBRUARY 16, 1916–NOVEMBER 14, 1997 ● JOCKEY

A legend among twentieth-century jockeys, Eddie Arcaro compiled a daunting record in big-money races during his 18-year career. But he was without peer in horseracing's summit of prestige, the Triple Crown. Arcaro attained a record 17 victories in those races: five in the Kentucky Derby (a record shared with Bill Hartack), a record six in the Preakness, and tied for a record six in the Belmont Stakes (also held by Jimmy McLaughlin). He was, moreover, the only jockey to have ridden two Triple Crown-winning horses—Whirlaway and Citation.

George Edward Arcaro's key qualification for racing glory was already evident in his birth weight of three pounds. In his adult prime he stood at five feet, two inches and weighed 114 pounds. Born in Cincinnati, Ohio, on February 16, 1916, he grew up longing to be bigger and stronger. He said, "I remember the only thing I really hungered for as a kid was [to be] the size to play baseball. When the other kids would choose up sides for a game, I was always left over, and I think that's why I went for racing."

Arcaro's racing ambitions were almost derailed when he was 12 years old, when he was involved in a severe sledding accident that ripped his thigh and required 40 stitches. But Eddie rebounded quickly, his sights set on the track. At 14 he left school to take a job as an exercise boy at a stable, and he rode his first race at the age of 15, on May 18, 1931, finishing sixth

> *"Once we got clear there wasn't the slightest doubt in my mind. I just leaned over and told Whirly, 'Let's get running.' That's what he did. He came right through without drawing even one deep breath."*
>
> Eddie Arcaro after the Belmont Stakes, 1941

at Bainbridge in Ohio. It took him 45 more mounts to claim his first victory, atop Eagle Bird at Agua Caliente in Mexico on January 14, 1932.

In a career strewn with serious injuries—he claimed to have suffered more than 50 spills—one of the worst occurred early on, in 1933, when a tumble during a race fractured his skull, broke his nose, punctured his lung, and sent him into a three-day coma. Sidelined for three months, the indefatigable racer made a full recovery and, undeterred, solidified his reputation over the next two years, earning his first shot at the Kentucky Derby in 1935, when he rode Nellie Flag to a fourth-place finish. His next Derby mount came in 1938, when he rode Lawrin to the first of his six victories at Churchill Downs.

Eddie Arcaro celebrates a Triple Crown win.

In 1941 Arcaro rode Whirlaway to his first sweep of the Triple Crown. He recalled, "Whirlaway was the most exciting horse I ever rode. Whirlaway had that habit of tearing out on the turns, and [I had] seen him run some terrible races."

In 1942, given the choice between Shut Out and Devil Diver for the Kentucky Derby, Arcaro chose Devil Diver and ended up finishing sixth. In the Belmont Stakes he switched to Shut Out and rode him to victory. In the fall of that year Arcaro had an altercation with a Cuban jockey named Vincent Nodarse and was punished with a year-long suspension. Reflecting on the incident years later, Arcaro said, "It was the best thing that ever happened to me. It gave me time to think and take stock of myself."

Rebounding quickly from this setback, Arcaro returned to his winning ways but didn't score his next Triple Crown victory until 1945, when he won two titles atop two different horses: Hoop Jr. at the Kentucky Derby and Pavot at the Belmont Stakes.

In 1948 Arcaro was offered the chance to ride Citation at the Kentucky Derby after the horse's designated jockey, Albert

1916 Arcaro is born in Cincinnati, Ohio.

1941 Arcaro wins his first Triple Crown, on Whirlaway.

1948 Arcaro wins his second Triple Crown, on Citation.

1961 Arcaro retires with 4,779 victories.

1997 Arcaro dies at age 81.

Snider, disappeared on a boating trip. Arcaro guided Citation to victories in the Derby, the Preakness, and the Belmont Stakes, earning his second Triple Crown. Arcaro donated half of his Derby winnings to Snider's widow. He ended that year with winnings of $1,686,230, a record at that time.

Over the following decade Arcaro's victories and riches continued to mount, but at a progressively slowing pace. He won the Preakness in 1950 and 1951, and in 1952 he piloted Hill Gail to a Derby victory and One Count to first place in the Belmont Stakes. In 1955 Arcaro rode Nashua to second place behind Swaps in the Derby and then went on to capture the Preakness and Belmont with Nashua, although Swaps did not enter those races. Nevertheless, the rivalry between Nashua and Swaps led to a $100,000 all-or-nothing race, won handily by Arcaro atop Nashua.

By the time Arcaro was inducted into the racing Hall of Fame, his peak years were behind him. Arcaro's final victory in a Triple Crown race was his 1956 Preakness win atop Fabius, the son of Citation. His final run of victories came with Kelso, a magnificent performer that Arcaro rode to 12 victories in 14 races. "I believe Kelso was the best horse I ever rode," Arcaro said.

After riding in a race on November 18, 1961, the 45-year-old Arcaro announced his retirement, having amassed 4,779 victories, total earnings of $30,039,543, and 554 stakes, the last a record that stood until surpassed in 1972 by Willie Shoemaker.

During his retirement Arcaro did television commentary and was a public relations consultant for the Golden Nugget Casino. He died on November 14, 1997, at age 81. ◆

Armstrong, Henry (Jackson, Henry, Jr.)

DECEMBER 12, 1912–OCTOBER 22, 1988 ● BOXER

Born in Columbus, Mississippi, Armstrong was the 11th of 15 children of farmer-butcher Henry Jackson, Sr., and his wife, America (Armstrong). The family later moved to St. Louis, where Armstrong graduated from high school. Henry adopted his mother's maiden name when he began to box. He achieved a boxing record of 58–4 as an amateur, and turned pro in 1931. The 5′ 5 1/2″ fighter won the world featherweight championship on October 29, 1937, with a sixth-round knock-out of Pete Sarron. Then he dethroned welterweight champion Barney Ross on May 31, 1938, and lightweight champion Lou Ambers on August 17, 1938, both by 15-round decisions. He is the only boxer ever to hold three world championships simulta-neously. Armstrong resigned his featherweight crown in No-vember 1938, having never defended it. He lost a rematch with Ambers on August 22, 1939, and thereafter mainly fought as a welterweight, although he lost a ten-round decision to middle-weight champion Ceferino Garcia in 1940. Armstrong at one time won 46 straight bouts, including 27 consecutive knock-outs, which earned him the nickname "Homicide Hank." He lost his welterweight crown on October 4, 1940, decisioned in 15 rounds by Fritzie Zivic. Zivic knocked him out in their Madi-son Square Garden rematch on January 17, 1941, drawing a record indoor crowd of 23,190.

Armstrong retired in 1945, with a record of 144–21–8–1 (including 97 KOs among the 144 victories) with over $1 mil-lion in purses. Thereafter he was involved in a Los Angeles nightclub, and in 1951 he became an ordained Baptist minister, working as an evangelist and running the Henry Armstrong Youth Foundation to fight juvenile delinquency. The movie *King Punching* is based on his life. An autobiography, *Gloves, Glory and God*, was published in 1956. He became director of the Herbert Hoover Boys Club in St. Louis in 1972. Armstrong was elected to the Boxing Hall of Fame in 1954. ◆

1912	Armstrong is born Henry Jackson, Jr. in Columbus, Mississippi.
1937	Armstrong wins the world featherweight championship.
1938	Armstrong wins welterweight and lightweight championships; wears three crowns simultaneously.
1945	Armstrong retires with 144–21–8–1 record.
1954	Armstrong is elected to the Boxing Hall of Fame.
1956	Armstrong publishes his autobiography, *Gloves, Glory and God*.

Armstrong, Lance

SEPTEMBER 18, 1971– ● BICYCLIST

On October 8, 1996, bicyclist Lance Armstrong an-nounced that he had choriocarcinoma, a rare and lethal form of testicular cancer that had spread to his brain and lungs. Doctors gave him a 50 percent chance of sur-vival. Yet after only 18 months of chemotherapy treatments and aggressive surgeries to remove a testicle and lesions on his brain,

Lance Armstrong after a winning ride.

"*Sport is a way of life and life is a sport. The only one keeping score should be you.*"

Lance Armstrong

he was miraculously declared-cancer free. Armstrong returned to competition in 1998, and in 1999 he became only the second American to win bicycling's most prestigious race, the Tour de France.

The tenacious Armstrong was born September 18, 1971, in Plano, Texas. An only child, he attended Bending Oaks, a small private High School in Dallas. He began competing in the "Iron Kids" triathlon program, and in his teens, he was a particularly good swimmer. Armstrong went on to become a two-time National Sprint Triathlon Champion. The triathlon is a grueling competition that combines swimming, biking and running in succession.

Armstrong's triathlon career ended when a representative of the U.S. Cycling Federation saw him on a bicycle and convinced him to concentrate on just that sport. At the age of 17, while still in high school, he began training with the Junior National Cycling Team. After competing in the Junior World Championships in Moscow, Armstrong signed with Suburu-Montgomery, a pro/amateur racing team. That year, he won the U.S. National Amateur Championship.

Armstrong was a member of the U.S. National Team in 1991 and 1992, and showed early hints of his competitive fire. Bicycling is a team sport, and most of a team's members, known as "domestiques," try to control the pace, riding ahead to create a draft that helps another team member conserve his energy for a final sprint. In 1991, riding for the U.S. National Team, Armstrong, still an amateur, was asked by a coach to hold back so another, more popular pro rider could win an Italian race. Armstrong refused and won the race without the help of his team's domestiques, even though fans littered the road with tacks to slow him.

Following a 12th place finish in the 1992 Olympic road race, Armstrong turned professional, and in his first professional event, the 1992 San Sebastian Classic, he came in 111th, a last place finish. Eighty riders had not finished the race, and Armstrong, 30 minutes behind the leader, was expected to quit too. The race foreshadowed the refuse-to-quit attitude that would carry him through his ordeal with cancer.

Soon after, Armstrong signed with Motorola, the top U.S. cycling team at the time. He helped lead the team to a No. 5 world ranking in 1993, winning races with a confident and aggressive style. Stage racing is a grueling test of physical conditioning. Pro races often take several weeks, and have dozens of stages covering 2,000 miles or more over mountainous terrain. The Tour de France, for example, has stages through the French Alps, where exhausted riders pedal up steep slopes, climbing stretches that rise 3,000 feet or more in only a few miles. Armstrong made his mark in 1993, winning a stage in the Tour de France, and winning the World Championship in Oslo, Norway. He was only 21 years old.

Over the next three years, Armstrong had trouble living up to his early success, although he won America's premier cycling race, the Tour DuPont, in 1995 and 1996. Two days after teammate and friend Fabio Casartelli died in a 50-plus mph downhill crash, Armstrong also took a stage in the 1995 Tour de France. Overcome by emotion, he broke away from the pack, pedaling hard to the stage victory. As he crossed under the finish banner, he closed his eyes and raised his head and hands to the sky.

After a strong early 1996 season, many predicted Armstrong to win the Tour de France. Bicycling is a sport dominated by Europeans, and only one American, Greg LeMond in 1986, 1989 and 1990, had ever won the Tour, which was established in 1903. Armstrong was forced to drop out in the sixth stage with bronchitis. He disappointed again in the 1996 Olympic road race, finishing only 12th. At the end of the 1996 season, after signing a new contract with the French team Cofidis, Armstrong realized something was wrong when he began coughing up blood.

While undergoing debilitating cancer treatments in late 1996 and 1997, Armstrong was unable to endure his six-hour-a-day training schedule but he was given approval to ride up to 50 miles a day to stay in some sort of shape. That maintenance paid off when he beat the disease and shocked the cycling world by staging a comeback in 1998. Armstrong signed with the U.S. Postal Service Team, but after several early season races, he left the sport to contemplate his future. He thought about retiring.

1971 Armstrong is born in Plano, Texas.

1993 Armstrong wins a stage in the Tour de France; wins World Championship in Oslo, Norway at 21.

96–97 Armstrong undergoes treatments for cancer.

1999 Armstrong becomes only the second American to win the Tour de France, at an average speed of 24.9 mph.

Armstrong
began 1999 with
his focus on the
2,306 mile Tour
de France.

After a short time away, he returned and attacked the sport with the same perseverance and drive he had in the past. Toward the end of the season Armstrong won two European stage races, the Tour of Luxembourg and the Rheinland Pfalz in Germany. He finished fourth in the 1998 World Championships.

Armstrong began 1999 with his focus on the 2,306 mile Tour de France. On July 4, 1999, the first day of his first Tour since abandoning the 1996 race, Armstrong won the short prologue stage, smashing five-time tour champion Miquel Indurain's course record. In the next stage, he lost the "maillot jaune," or yellow jersey worn by the race leader, to the only other racer who would wear it. Armstrong retook the jersey in a stage-eight time trial and never lost it again, holding it through the taxing stages in the mountains. He became the second American to win the race, dominating the fastest Tour ever with an average speed of 24.9 mph.

When not riding, Armstrong has devoted much of his life to helping others diagnosed with cancer. He lives and continues to train in Austin, Texas. His Lance Armstrong Foundation raises money to fund research grants to study cancer, and provides support and help to those affected by the disease. ◆

Ashe, Arthur Robert, Jr.

JULY 10, 1943–FEBRUARY 6, 1993 ● TENNIS PLAYER

Born in Richmond, Virginia, Arthur Ashe traced his lineage back 10 generations on his father's side to a woman who in 1735 was brought from West Africa to Yorktown, Virginia, by the slave ship *Doddington*. Ashe's mother, Mattie Cunningham, also of Richmond, taught him to read by the time he was four. She died when Arthur was six, one year after giving birth to her second son Johnnie. Ashe, who was frail in his youth, was forbidden by his father, a police officer in Richmond's Department of Recreation and Parks, to play football on the segregated Brookfield playground adjacent to the Ashes' home. Instead, young Ashe took to playing tennis on the four hard courts of the playground. By the time he was ten, Ashe had attracted the keen eye of Dr. Walter Johnson, a Lynchburg, Virginia, physician and tennis enthusiast who had previously discovered and coached Althea Gibson, the first black woman to win Wimbledon.

Ashe's father and Dr. Johnson were both stern disciplinarians who insisted that Ashe cultivate self-discipline, good manners, forbearance, and self-effacing stoicism. These qualities would characterize Ashe throughout his entire life and, even in the midst of the most turbulent social conditions, would define him as a man of reason, conscience, integrity, and moral authority. His cool disposition enabled him not only to survive, but to distinguish himself in an overwhelmingly white tennis environment.

In 1960, Ashe was awarded a tennis scholarship to UCLA, where he earned All-American status. Two years after Ashe graduated with a business degree, he became the first black man to win one of the preeminent Grand Slam titles, accomplishing that as an amateur and U.S. Army representative at the U.S. Open of 1968. Numerous titles would follow, highlighted by Ashe's place on three victorious Davis Cup squads and the addition of two more Grand Slam titles, one at the Australian Open in 1970, and the other, his biggest triumph, at Wimbledon in 1975.

Arthur Ashe returns a shot during competition at Wimbledon.

Throughout those years, Ashe devoted considerable time and energy to civil rights issues. In 1973, after three years of trying, he secured an invitation to play in the all-white South African Open. Although his participation was controversial, it personified Ashe's lifelong belief in constructive engagement— an attitude that he abandoned only on one noteworthy occasion in 1976, when he joined in the call for an international embargo of all sporting contact with South Africa.

In 1979, at age 36, Ashe suffered a heart attack, which forced him to have bypass surgery and retire from tennis. Nevertheless, over the ensuing years he served as the U.S. Davis Cup captain (1981–1985), worked as a journalist and television commentator, and served or helped create various foundations, ranging from the American Heart Association to the United Negro College Fund to his own Safe Passage Foundation.

Eighteen months after undergoing a second heart operation in 1983, Ashe learned that he had contracted the AIDS virus through blood transfusions. He immediately set to work on his definitive three-volume history of black athletes in America, *A Hard Road to Glory* (1988). Forced by the national newspaper *USA Today* to reveal that he was suffering from AIDS in April 1992, Ashe worked as an activist for the defeat of AIDS until he died of the disease in February 1993. ◆

Ashford, Evelyn

APRIL 19, 1957– ● TRACK AND FIELD ATHLETE

Born in Shreveport, Louisiana, Evelyn Ashford did not run competitively until her senior year of high school, when she ran on the boys' track team because the school had no team for girls. Ashford won a track scholarship to the University of California at Los Angeles in 1975. The following year she finished fifth in the 100-meter dash at the Montreal Olympics, and her 400-meter relay team finished seventh. Although she dropped out of UCLA in 1979, UCLA women's track coach Pat Connolly continued to train her, and Ashford won the 100-meter dash at the 1979 World Cup, becoming the top female sprinter in the world. Her dream of winning a gold medal in the 1980 Olympics was thwarted, however, when the United States decided to boycott the 1980 Olympics in Moscow.

After this disappointment, Ashford considered dropping out of track and field altogether. But with her husband Ray Washington as her coach, she won the women's 100-

meter dash at the 1981 World Cup. In the 1984 Los Angeles Olympics, Ashford won the 100-meter dash and anchored the winning 400-meter relay team. The recognition she gained with her Olympic gold medals included promotional work for such large international corporations as American Express and Mazda.

In 1986, Ashford won the 100-meter dash in the 1986 World Cup, ran the fastest 100 meters of the year, and was ranked number one for the year. In 1988 she competed in her third Olympics, and won a silver medal in the 100-meter competition and a gold medal as part of the winning 400-meter relay team. In 1992, at the age of 35, Ashford competed in the Barcelona Olympics, where she won her fourth Olympic gold medal as the lead-off runner in the 400-meter relay. In June 1993 she retired from track and field competition. ◆

1957 Ashford is born in Shreveport, Louisiana.

1984 Ashford wins Olympic gold medals in the 100-meter dash and the 4 x 100 relay.

1988 Ashford wins Olympic gold in the 4 x 100 relay and a silver medal in the 100-meter dash.

1992 Ashford wins Olympic gold medal in the 4 x 100 relay.

Austin, Tracy

DECEMBER 12, 1962– ● TENNIS PLAYER

Born in the affluent southern California community of Palos Verdes on December 12, 1962, Tracy Austin has often been described as a "tennis prodigy." She started playing as a young girl, and in 1977, soon after her 14th birthday, Austin won her first title at the Avon Futures of Portland, Oregon. Although she still retained her amateur status at the event by refusing any prize money, she became the youngest person to ever win a professional tournament.

Later that year, while still an amateur and unseeded, Austin became the youngest player ever to play in the prestigious Wimbledon tournament at the All-England Tennis Club. Also in 1977, she managed to beat back formidable competition to reach the quarterfinals of the U.S. Open. The tennis world had been put on notice that a new star was on the scene. In 1978, Austin was ranked among the top 10 players in the world. When she represented the United States in Wightman and Federation Cup tournaments, she became the youngest woman ever to do so.

Austin won her first major tournament, the Italian Open, in 1979, triumphing over Chris Evert. In so doing, Austin broke Evert's string of 125 consecutive victories on clay courts. True success in the tennis world is achieved when a player wins one

1962 Austin is born in Palos Verdes, California.

1977 At 14, Austin becomes youngest to play at Wimbledon.

1979 Not yet 17, Austin defeats Chris Evert to win the U.S. Open.

1980 Austin becomes the youngest player ever ranked number one in the world; is named Women's Sports Foundation's Sportswoman of the Year.

1992 Austin is the youngest player ever inducted into International Tennis Hall of Fame; publishes her autobiography, *Beyond Center Court*.

"The only person I've seen who has come close to my determination was Tracy. She was tough. I could see it in her eyes."

Chris Evert on Tracy Austin

of the four events that make up the Grand Slam: the U.S. Open, Wimbledon, the French Open, and the Australian Open. Austin won her first Grand Slam event, the U.S. Open, in 1979—again defeating Evert for the win. She was just three months shy of her 17th birthday, the youngest person to accomplish such a win. The Associated Press named her Female Athlete of the Year.

In 1980, Austin was ranked number one in the world, setting yet another "youngest" record, this time as the youngest player ever to achieve the top spot. That year, she was honored as the Women's Sports Foundation's first ever Sportswoman of the Year. As she entered the 1980s, Austin experienced continued success. She remained in the top 10 for six consecutive years, from 1978 to 1983. And, Austin achieved yet another "first": she earned $1 million in career prize money—the youngest player, male or female, to have achieved that milestone.

With her quick, intuitive game, Austin excelled at doubles tennis as well as at singles play. In 1980, she and her brother John won the Wimbledon mixed doubles title, the only brother/sister team in history to do so. That year, however, Austin began having significant back pain, caused by sciatic nerve damage. Austin had to stop playing for a full eight months, and the problem would eventually lead her to give up competing professionally.

Austin plowed forward, however, and returned to the tennis circuit. At the 1981 U.S. Open she made it to the finals, where her opponent was the powerful Martina Navratilova, who took the first set easily, 6–1. But Austin, always a keen competitor, rallied to win the next two sets and the match, winning hard-fought 7–6 tiebreakers in each set. The exciting match thrilled tennis spectators around the world.

Austin's physical problems soon returned to haunt her, however. In late 1982, her back began bothering her again, putting severe constraints on her game. A shoulder injury made playing even more difficult. In mid-1983, Austin retired from professional tennis, unable to vanquish these particular foes. During her brief career on the courts, she had won approximately 30 singles titles and $2 million in prize money.

Austin has remained in the public eye as an articulate and insightful tennis commentator, usually for women's matches; and since 1978, she has hosted an annual celebrity tennis event for underprivileged children. In 1989, Austin was in a terrible car accident that broke her leg and nearly took her life. But she was soon back in the swing of things. In 1992, Austin was honored with yet another "first," as the youngest person ever to be inducted into the International Tennis Hall of Fame. Today, Austin lives in Rolling Hills, California, with her husband, Scott Holt, and their two sons, Dylan and Brandon. ◆

Azzi, Jennifer

AUGUST 31, 1968– ● BASKETBALL PLAYER

Born and raised in Oak Ridge, Tennessee, Jennifer Azzi began playing basketball when she was just four years old, launching a career that has been one of extraordinary accomplishment. While starring on the Oak Ridge High School basketball team, Azzi was heavily recruited by major colleges. Her talent on the court earned her a full scholarship to Stanford University in California, where she played a key role in the Cardinal's domination of women's collegiate basketball in the late 1980s. During her four years as a guard at Stanford, Azzi led her team to a 101–23 record, two Pacific 10 conference championships, and three appearances in the NCAA tournament. Along the way she set Stanford and Pac-10 career records for three-point field goals made (191) and for three-point shooting percentage (.452).

Jennifer Azzi celebrates Stanford's 1990 NCAA title.

Throughout her collegiate career Azzi garnered many awards. She was named to the Kodak All-America team in 1989 and 1990 (the only junior selected in 1989) and won both the Wade Trophy and the Naismith National Player of the Year Award her senior year. She was named All-Pac-10 first team in 1988, 1989, and 1990, and in 1989 and 1990 she was

1968   Azzi is born in Oak Ridge, Tennessee.

1990   Azzi is named MVP of the NCAA Final Four and is the Naismith National Player of the Year.

1995   Azzi is a founding member of National Women's Basketball League; joins San Jose Lasers.

1996   Azzi wins an Olympic gold medal.

named Pac-10 Player of the Year. But the highlight of Azzi's collegiate career was her senior year, when Stanford compiled a 32–1 record and won an NCAA championship. Azzi was named the most valuable player in the 1990 NCAA Final Four and most valuable player in the West regional.

Azzi also had a prolific career playing for the United States in international competition. From 1987 to 1998 she played on 14 different USA Basketball teams that compiled a combined record of 127–14. In the 133 games in which she played Azzi scored 800 points, shooting nearly 47 percent from the field and over 44 percent from three-point range. Some of her other statistics were equally impressive: 276 assists, 177 rebounds, 106 steals, and a free-throw shooting percentage of almost 86 percent. Highlights of her international career include a gold medal in the 1996 Olympics, gold medals at the World Championships in 1990 and 1994 (to go with a bronze in 1998), and a gold medal in the 1990 Goodwill Games. In all, Azzi-led international teams competed for 11 medals and won 10. About her wide-ranging experience she said, "Facing a lot of adversity, playing in different countries, with the national team, different leagues, there's been a lot of change—that makes you grow up."

Like many women who starred at the collegiate and international levels at that time, Azzi wanted to pursue a professional basketball career, but her only option was to play in Europe. In Italy, France, and Sweden, she enjoyed the same level of success that marked her college years. During the 1995 season with Arvika Basket in Sweden, she averaged an impressive 31 points per game. During this time, opportunities for women basketball players in the United States began to emerge with the formation of the American Basketball League (ABL). At a Stanford Athletic Hall of Fame dinner in 1995, Azzi met with Gary Cavalli, the co-founder of the ABL, who pitched the idea of a women's pro basketball league to her. Azzi was excited about the idea, and when the league began play in October of that year, she was a member of the San Jose Lasers and one of the founding members of the league. Unfortunately, 11 games into the season, Azzi dislocated a shoulder, putting her out of action for the rest of the season. Never one to waste an opportunity, she used her newfound free time to talk to high school, community, and business groups; conduct interviews; lead free basketball clinics for girls; and serve as a positive role model for young athletes, particularly through the Jennifer Azzi Basketball Camp for girls. In 1996 she was named one of the March of Dimes' Female Athletes of the Year.

After recovering from her shoulder injury, Azzi went on to become one of the dominant players in the ABL. She was named captain of the 1996–97 Western Conference All-Star team, and in 1998 she made the All-ABL first team and was among the league's leaders in both scoring and **assists**. When the ABL disbanded and the Women's National Basketball Association was formed, she was drafted fifth by the Detroit Shock. In 1997 Azzi was selected as one of the "core" members of the USA Basketball Women's Senior National Team to compete in the 2000 Olympics in Sydney, Australia. But unfortunately for her fans, Azzi later left the team, deciding she had taken on too much in an already hectic life.

Coaching may be in Jennifer Azzi's future once her playing days are over. "One of my strengths as a player [has been] helping teammates, and I just love to see people improve and get better. I love the game, and think that [coaching] might be a good fit down the road." ◆

assist: action of a team athlete who passes a ball or puck to a teammate who then scores a goal, or makes a putout; statistical measure utilized to recognize such actions.

Bailey, Donovan

DECEMBER 16, 1967– ● TRACK AND FIELD ATHLETE

Until mid-1999, when new American superstar sprinter Maurice Greene broke Donovan Bailey's 100-meter dash world record of 9.84 seconds, Bailey was universally considered the World's Fastest Human. And the brash Canadian sprinter, though now 32 years old, is scarcely ready to peacefully yield the title to the younger man. "Think what you want, but I'll be ready next year in Sydney," he says. "I'm fully prepared to win the gold medal once again in the 100-meters no matter who's showing up."

Donovan Bailey was born in Manchester, Jamaica, but moved to Canada at age 13. Bailey grew up in Oakville, Ontario, where he attended Queen Elizabeth Park High School. Though he was first introduced to track and field in grade school in Jamaica—and was considered extremely talented almost immediately—for a long time Bailey viewed track as merely a hobby. After graduation he attended Sheridan College, where he majored in economics and also starred as a forward on the basketball team. Armed with his college degree, Bailey went on to build a successful career as an independent marketing consultant and stockbroker in Toronto, still considering track nothing more than a diversion. In 1990, though, Bailey started to train under the direction of Erwin Turney but still "didn't really start to take track seriously," he says, until he began working with Don Pfaff in 1995. Indeed, though he had already won a World Championship relay gold (1993) and ran a world-class 10.03 in the 100-meter race the previous year, Bailey simply exploded during the 1995 season. After breaking

> *"I'm not trying to do what Ben [Johnson] did, or undo what Ben did in Seoul. My name is Donovan Bailey."*
>
> After breaking the 100-meter dash world record, 1996

1967 — Bailey is born in Manchester, Jamaica.

1993 — Bailey wins World Championship relay gold medal.

1996 — Bailey breaks 50-meter indoor world record; at the Olympics, he sets a world record for 100-meter dash. Bailey also records the fastest-ever human speed: 27.1 mph.

Achilles tendon: the tendon joining the muscles in the leg calf to the bone of the heel; a particularly common area of injury in athletic competition.

the Canadian record at the LSU Alumni Gold Meet (9.92 seconds), Bailey won the Canadian Nationals in a stunning 9.91 over favored Bruny Surin. Bailey then won the 100-meter gold medal at the World Championships at Goteborg, Sweden, in 9.97, while anchoring Canada's 400-meter relay team to the gold medal (38.31) as well.

But all of Bailey's accomplishments were just a warm-up for 1996. That year he broke the 50-meter indoor world record (5.56 seconds) in Reno, Nevada, then proceeded to totally dominate the Atlanta Olympics, setting a stunning world record of 9.84 seconds in winning the 100-meters then, once again, anchoring the Canadian relay team to the gold. Bailey's explosive speed and smooth finish were best witnessed by the fact that among all the 100-meter finalists in Atlanta, he was measured to have the slowest reaction time at the start (0.174 seconds). Yet in that race, he recorded the fastest ever measured speed for a human being (27.1 mph).

Unfortunately, Bailey couldn't maintain his momentum. Though he won the much-hyped "World's Fastest Human" match race against Michael Johnson (Johnson was injured and did not finish the race), the event left a bitter taste in his mouth. After the 1997 World Championships, a frustrated Bailey left coach Pfaff to work with Loren Seagrave in Atlanta—but in the fall of 1998, he was back with Pfaff. Still, Bailey managed to have a good season: he won the Canadian Nationals and several Grand Prix events (Rio de Janeiro, Paris) but, bothered by a mystifying inconsistency, finished a horrible 7th in the Goodwill Games. He also failed to get his time under 9.90.

Then, in September '98, Bailey suffered a complete rupture of the **Achilles tendon** while playing basketball. Rehabilitating with his customary intensity, he came back perhaps too soon. As a result, his 1999 season was a disaster: He lost race after race, and was forced to watch Maurice Greene break his hard-won world record. Worse still, Bailey's Canadian archrival, Bruny Surin, had a banner year in 1999, tying Bailey's 9.84 Canadian record and creating a major controversy over which sprinter should anchor the Canadian relay team at the Olympic Games.

"I simply wasn't fully healthy—so, yes, I admit I embarrassed myself the way I was running this year," Bailey admitted later. "But I gained a lot of mental preparation from it all. I know what I have to do. I'll see Mr. [Maurice] Greene in Sydney [for the 2000 Olympic Games]." ◆

Banks, Ernie

JANUARY 31, 1931– ● BASEBALL PLAYER

Known perhaps as well for his sunny demeanor as his prodigious home runs, Ernie Banks became such a beloved character in Chicago that his name became synonymous with the team he played for, earning him the endearing nickname Mr. Cub.

Ernest Banks was born in Dallas on January 31, 1931, the second of 12 children. Banks was a gangly child who preferred basketball and football to baseball. Banks' father, a semi-pro catcher turned grocer, bought his son a glove for his 10th birthday, but had to bribe his son to play catch. In high school, Banks played softball—his segregated school in North Dallas did not offer baseball—and began to display some of the skills he inherited from his father. At the age of 17, he was invited to barnstorm with a semi-pro baseball team, the Amarillo Colts, around the South and Midwest. At a game in San Antonio, Banks caught the eye of Negro League great "Cool Papa" James Bell, who was scouting for the Kansas City Monarchs.

Bell convinced the Monarchs to sign the young shortstop, and Banks joined the team after graduating high school. Shortly thereafter, however, Banks was drafted by the army. Stationed in Germany, Banks played ball to pass the time and refined his game. After two years in the service, Banks rejoined the Monarchs.

Jackie Robinson had broken Major League Baseball's **color barrier** in 1947, and in the early '50s teams began scouring the Negro Leagues for new stars. Legendary showman Bill Veeck, the owner of the St. Louis Browns, had his eye on Banks, but couldn't afford the Monarchs' asking price. Veeck told Cubs general manager Wid Matthews about Banks, and in September of 1953 the Cubs bought the rights to Banks for $15,000. The 22-year-old Banks showed up at Wrigley Field with no mitt and was promptly issued a book on how to play baseball. In 10 late-season games, Banks displayed enough promise to show he belonged in the major leagues.

The next season as the Cubs starting shortstop, Banks enjoyed a standout rookie campaign, hitting .275 with 19 homers and 79 runs batted in (RBI). He played every inning of every game. Though he was somewhat clumsy in the field, his power

> *"It's a great day for a ballgame. Let's play two."*
> Ernie Banks

color barrier: the unofficial policy of segregation in Major League Baseball that barred nonwhites from competing until 1947, when Jackie Robinson broke the barrier by playing for the Brooklyn Dodgers of the National League.

1931 Banks is born in Dallas, Texas.

1958 Banks is named National League Most Valuable Player; leads league in home runs.

1959 Banks wins his second MVP; first National Leaguer to win the Most Valuable Player award in back-to-back seasons.

1977 Banks is inducted into the Baseball Hall of Fame.

at the plate began winning over the fans. At 6–1, 185 pounds, Banks didn't have a classic slugger's frame. Even though short-stops were usually the lightest hitters on teams, Banks possessed lightning-fast wrists that let him hit for power because he could wait until the last second to swing at pitches.

The next season, Banks had a breakout campaign, belting 44 homers—including a major-league record of five grand slams—and 117 RBI. That year Banks also made the first of 13 All-Star Game appearances.

That year also marked the start of a remarkable six-season span that would see Banks hitting more homers than superstar sluggers Mickey Mantle, Willie Mays, and Hank Aaron. In 1958, Banks was named the National League Most Valuable Player (MVP) after leading the league in homers (47, still a record for shortstops) and RBI (129). The award made Banks the first player to win the award from a ball club with a losing record (the Cubs finished in fifth place). As an encore in 1959, Banks hit 45 round-trippers and drove in 143 runs to win another MVP award, becoming the first National League player to win back-to-back honors.

By the end of the decade, Banks had also managed to overcome his deficiencies in the field. In fact, he improved enough to win the Gold Glove, awarded for outstanding fielding, in 1960. Injuries, however, soon began to take a toll on Banks and in 1962 he moved to first base, a less-demanding position. Though his numbers slipped in the 1960s (he last hit over .300 in 1959), Banks' remained a fan favorite for his clutch hitting and indomitable spirit, as he toiled for a perennially losing team.

In 1969, his 17th season, it seemed that Banks' dream of playing in a World Series was finally going to come true. At the age of 38, Banks drove in 106 runs, but the Cubs ended up collapsing late in the season, losing the **pennant** to the upstart New York Mets. The next season, Banks became the ninth player at the time to reach the 500-home run plateau, hitting his milestone round-tripper off Pat Jarvis of the Atlanta Braves on May 12 at Wrigley Field. Banks retired in 1971 at the age of 40 with 512 home runs, tied for 13th on the all-time list. He served as a Cubs coach for a season and then worked as roving minor league instructor and in the club's front office.

Mr. Cub joined baseball's immortals in the Baseball Hall of Fame in 1977, his first year of eligibility. In 1999, Banks was named to Major League Baseball's 30-man All Century Team

pennant: a flag symbolizing a sports championship; mostly associated with Major League Baseball and the champions of the respective American and National Leagues.

and was picked by the readers of *Baseball Digest* as the 24th top player of the twentieth century.

Today he remains an active good will ambassador for both the Cubs and the game of baseball. ◆

Beamon, Bob

AUGUST 29, 1946– ● TRACK AND FIELD ATHLETE

B ob Beamon's place in the history of track and field was preserved by a single moment, making him different than other track legends like Jesse Owens and Carl Lewis, who made their names by consistently winning events over many years. On October 18, 1968, at the Olympic Games in Mexico City, Mexico, the 22-year-old Beamon didn't just break the world record for the long jump, he shattered it, beating the previous world record by 1 foot, 9 3/4 inches. It was a feat that stunned the sports world, and it forever placed Bob Beamon's legend beside more consistent track performers like Owens and Lewis. His jump of 29 feet, 2 1/2 inches, not only made him the first 29-foot long jumper, it made him the first man *ever* to jump farther than 28 feet. His record stood for more than 20 years. Beamon himself would never again produce a jump anywhere near the stunning leap.

Beamon was born August 29, 1946, in Jamaica, New York, a neighborhood in New York City. His mother died from tuberculosis when he was an infant, and as a youngster Beamon was often in trouble. Jamaica was a rough neighborhood, with street fights and gang membership a normal way of life for teens. Beamon's salvation was his great athletic ability, and it provided his ticket to a better life. Although Beamon started out as a basketball player, a coach at his high school realized Beamon was even better at track, and encouraged him to stick to it. Beamon worked hard, and eventually developed near world class speed of 9.5 seconds for the 100-yard dash.

Beamon attended North Carolina A&T to be near his sick grandmother, but after she died, he transferred to the University of Texas at El Paso, a school with a considerably better track program. There, he worked on his speed and long jumping method, perfecting an approach in which the jumper continues his running motion in the air all the way through his jump. It

> *"I've met long jumpers who told me, 'You're the one who killed our event.'"*
>
> Bob Beamon in Red Smith's, "To Reach the Unreachable Star," 1971

1946   Beamon is born in Jamaica (Queens), New York City.

1968   At the Olympics in Mexico City, Beamon shatters long-jump world record by almost two feet.

With his knees to his chest, Beamon kept sailing, almost to the end of the long jump pit.

was an unpolished style, and coupled with his tall, gangly 6 foot, 3 inch frame, it made him look awkward compared to other jumpers. Beamon had great speed and explosive spring in his legs, but he often fouled by stepping over the line and onto the board. A jumper must take off from behind the board to avoid fouling. Three fouls cause disqualification.

Despite his often erratic performance, Beamon had an excellent 1968 season heading into the Olympics. Prior to Mexico City, Beamon's best jump had been a wind-aided 27 feet, 6 1/2 inches. His best jump performed within the maximum allowable tailwind was 27 feet, 4 inches, just shy of the world record. But in his qualifying jumps, he fouled twice, almost disqualifying himself for the finals at the Olympics.

Oddly enough, it was Beamon's competition, Ralph Boston, who helped Beamon ensure his place on the Olympic team. Boston, who had won the gold medal in the long jump in the 1960 Olympics, and the silver medal in the 1964 Olympics, was considered the favorite to win. Before Beamon's last attempt at a qualifying jump, Boston told him to relax and to take off a foot before reaching the line if necessary, to make sure not to foul. Beamon followed the advice, and barely qualified for the finals with a jump of 26 feet, 10 1/2 inches.

The long jump finals began with three jumpers fouling. As Beamon, the fourth jumper, prepared, the tailwind dropped to 2 meters per second, the maximum allowed for a record. He got terrific speed on his approach, taking 19 strides down the runway. He eased up perfectly on his last step, taking off behind the board. When his feet left the track, he achieved a tremendous height of six feet above ground. With his knees to his chest, Beamon kept sailing, almost to the end of the long jump pit. He knew he had broken the world record, but only after it was measured at 29 feet, 2 1/2 inches, did he realize the magnitude of his accomplishment. He broke down in tears, kneeling with his hands on his head. The competition was effectively over, even though no other competitor had yet registered a qualifying jump.

To add some perspective to Beamon's leap, consider that Jesse Owens jumped 26 feet, 8 1/4 inches in 1935, a record that held up for 25 years. Between 1960 and 1967, the record was broken or tied eight times by the United States' Boston and Soviet jumper Igor Ter-Ovanesyan, but it increased only 8 1/2 inches. In one jump Beamon pushed the record another 1 foot, 9 3/4 inches. Another jump of even 28 feet wasn't recorded until 12 years later. His mark held up for almost 23 years, until the United States' Mike Powell jumped 29 feet, 4 1/2 inches in 1991.

Critics pointed out that the maximum allowable tailwind had aided Beamon, and that the lightning fast track in the Olympic Stadium had already produced several record-breaking performances. The high altitude of Mexico City, which sits 7,350 feet above sea level, was also a big advantage, because thin air benefits jumpers. But Beamon's defenders were quick to point out that the other competitors, including the co-world record holders Boston and Ter-Ovanesyan, jumped under the same conditions and didn't come anywhere near Beamon's performance.

After the Olympics, Beamon never again came close to his record-setting jump. He had lost his scholarship at Texas El-Paso for participating in a boycott of a meet against Brigham Young University, a school many blacks thought guilty of racial discrimination. Hampered by injuries, he barely competed the next few years, failing to make the 1972 U.S. Olympic team. He competed in a professional track tour for a year, consistently jumping 25 and 26 feet, respectable for most, but well below the unmatchable standard he had set for himself. He eventually left the sport entirely, earning a degree in sociology from Adelphi University. Today Beamon is a professional motivational speaker, and has a talent for abstract art. He is enshrined in the National Track and Field Hall of Fame and the Olympic Hall of Fame. ◆

> *"I had the feeling my first jump was a good 27 feet. . . . 'You did 29 feet,' [Ralph Boston] told me. I could hear the crowd roaring, but I couldn't get it through my head."*
>
> Bob Beamon in Red Smith's, "To Reach the Unreachable Star," 1971

Bench, Johnny

DECEMBER 7, 1947– ● BASEBALL PLAYER

No conversation about the greatest catchers in the history of Major League Baseball would be complete without mentioning Johnny Lee Bench. In fact, to many, the conversation would end right there. Bench revolutionized the catcher's position and set a standard of excellence that today's catchers still strive to achieve.

Born on Dec. 7, 1947, in Oklahoma City, Oklahoma, Johnny was the third of four children of Ted and Katy Bench. A two-sport athlete in high school (baseball and basketball), Bench dreamed from childhood about playing in the Major Leagues. His father

1947 Bench is born in Oklahoma City, Oklahoma.

1968 Bench is the first catcher to win Rookie of the Year.

1970 Bench wins his first Most Valuable Player award (second in 1972).

1989 Bench is inducted into the Baseball Hall of Fame.

Bench proved as valuable behind the plate with the glove, winning the Gold Glove as baseball's top defensive catcher.

worked with him, developing his catching techniques. One of the drills, intended to develop arm strength, involved him throwing 254 feet, double the distance from home to second base—the longest throw for a catcher—from a catcher's crouch.

Bench impressed the Cincinnati Reds enough that they chose him in the 1965 amateur draft. He wouldn't stay in the minors long.

He made his Major League debut with the Cincinnati Reds at age 19, on August 28, 1967. The next season, he came up to the major leagues for good. The confident Bench boldly predicted that he'd be the first catcher ever to win the Rookie of the Year Award. Then he made that prediction a reality by hitting .275 with 15 homers and 82 RBI, while catching a rookie record 154 games.

Bench proved as valuable behind the plate with the glove, winning the Gold Glove as baseball's top defensive catcher. It would be the first of 10 straight for him. He also boasted a cannon of an arm and made no bones about the fact that he could throw out any opposing base stealer. Bench quickly developed a reputation as a superb handler of pitchers and a master of calling a game. His approach to catching pitches was also unique, as he set up in his crouch with his throwing hand behind his back, protecting it from dangerous backswings and unpredictable foul tips. His technique has become the norm in today's baseball at all levels.

Bench was a key component of an up-and-coming Reds squad that would dominate baseball throughout the 1970s and earn the nickname "The Big Red Machine." Teamed with the likes of Pete Rose, Joe Morgan, Tony Perez, Ken Griffey and George Foster, and managed by the fiery Sparky Anderson, Bench and the Reds ushered in a new era of winning baseball in Cincinnati. The Reds, who had finished in 7th place in 1966, won the National League's Western Division in 1970 and would finish first in five of the next seven years, reaching the World Series four times and winning it twice.

In 1970, Bench won his first Most Valuable Player Award (MVP), hitting 45 homers and driving in 148 runs. He won his second MVP Award in 1972, blasting 40 home runs and driving in 128 runs, both major league highs. But in both years, the Reds lost in the World Series, first to the Baltimore Orioles, then the Oakland Athletics.

In 1975, the Reds again got to the World Series. But this time, they brought home a championship, beating the Boston

Red Sox in seven games in one of the most memorable Series in baseball history. The Reds won it all again the next season, sweeping the New York Yankees. Bench took center stage in 1976, earning Playoff MVP honors by hitting a blazing .533 in the Series, with two homers and six RBIs, including the Series-clinching home run. Just as important, Bench threw out Yankees base-stealer extraordinaire Mickey Rivers in the first game of the Series, intimidating New York into never attempting to steal another base the rest of the Series.

Bench called it a career following the 1983 season. Over his 17 years, the seemingly indestructable catcher set an endurance record by catching at least 100 games in 13 seasons. He was a 14-time All-Star, and set the Major League record for home runs by a catcher with 327 (a record that has since been broken by Carlton Fisk).

Bench was inducted into the Baseball Hall of Fame in 1989, his first year of eligibility, getting 431 votes of 447 ballots cast, an astounding 96.42 percent of the vote (seventh-best all-time, third-best at the time).

Although Bench retired from the game of baseball as a player, he still has not left the game entirely. He hosted a kids' show called "The Baseball Bunch" in the mid-1980s and he is currently a broadcaster on the CBS Radio Network and on WLWT in Cincinnati.

He also is a scratch golfer, who plays on the Celebrity Golf Association Tour, as well as in numerous charity golf tournaments. He hosts the Kroger Senior Classic, which benefits the Johnny Bench Scholarship Fund and the Kroger Scholarship Fund. Bench also is a much-sought-after motivational speaker. ◆

"Jimmy Connors plays two tennis matches and winds up with $850,000, and Muhammad Ali fights one bout and winds up with five million bucks. Me, I play 190 games—if you count exhibitions—and I'm overpaid?!"

Johnny Bench on his $175,000 salary, 1975

Berra, Yogi

MAY 12, 1925– ● BASEBALL PLAYER

Lawrence Peter "Yogi" Berra holds a special place not only in the storied history of the New York Yankees and in the hearts of Yankee fans, but also to fans of the game of baseball. The Hall of Fame catcher for the powerhouse Yankees of the late '40s, '50s, and early '60s, Berra was unique, whether at the plate swatting a bad pitch, receiving a good pitch from

Yogi Berra applies the tag on an opposing base runner.

"You give 100 percent in the first half of the game, and if that isn't enough in the second half you give what's left."

Yogi Berra

the superb Yankees staff, or fielding a question from a curious reporter.

Born in St. Louis, Missouri, on May 12, 1925, Berra, the son of Italian immigrants, got his nickname from a childhood friend who believed Berra resembled an Indian man in a movie about a snake charmer. Growing up, Yogi dreamed of playing for his hometown St. Louis Cardinals, and at age 17 tried out for Cardinals General Manager Branch Rickey. Rickey had just signed Yogi's friend Joe Garagiola for $500 and offered Berra $250 to play with the Cardinals. Berra turned the offer down. Despite Rickey's alleged claim that Berra would "never make anything more than a Triple A ballplayer at best," Yankees scout Leo Browne signed Berra for $500.

In 1944, at age 18, Yogi joined the Navy. He served during World War II in North Africa and Italy and was part of the invasion force at Omaha Beach on D-Day. When he came back to the states, the Yankees assigned him to their minor league team at New London, Connecticut. New York Giants manager Mel Ott offered the Yankees $50,000 for Berra's contract, but the Yankees turned him down. They would be glad they did. After a short stint with the International League's Newark Bears in 1946, Yogi got the call to the major leagues late in the 1946 season. He would never see the minors again.

Berra was always a superb hitter and he was notorious for being a "bad-ball" hitter. No pitch was too high or too low for Yogi to hit and hit far. Over his career, Yogi hit for a .285 average, with 358 home runs (at the time the most ever by a catcher) and 1,430 runs batted in. To help improve his defense, the Yankees hired their legendary catcher from the '20s and '30s, Bill Dickey, to work with him. It didn't take long before Berra became a top-notch defensive catcher. Yogi would go on to play in 15 straight All-Star Games, and he won three league Most Valuable Player Awards (1951, '54 and '55). He was a key part of the Yankee dynasty of the late '40s and early '50s that appeared in 10 World Series in 12 years, winning eight of them, including five in a row from 1949 through 1953.

Yogi was at his best in the Fall Classic. He played in 14 World Series, winning a record 10 times, and setting numerous other records, including most games by a catcher, most hits, most times on a winning team, most at-bats and most doubles. He also holds the distinction of hitting the first pinch-hit home run in World Series history, doing so in the 1947 Series.

Berra was famous for his talking behind the plate and for his pranks to distract opposing batters. But his most famous talk came when he spoke to the press, and his unique observations off the field soon became as famous as his ability on it. Sayings like, "It's deja vu all over again," "When you come to a fork in the road, take it," and "The future ain't what it used to be" are well known Yogi-isms.

Yogi ended his playing career in 1963, but stayed in the game by becoming manager of the Yankees in 1964. That season he led the Yankees to 99 wins and an American League pennant. But he was forced out after the Yankees lost the World Series in seven games to the St. Louis Cardinals. In 1972, Yogi received the ultimate honor, being elected to the Major League Baseball Hall of Fame in Cooperstown, New York. His induction class included Lefty Gomez, Will Harridge, Sandy Koufax, Early Wynn, Ross Youngs, and Negro League legends Josh Gibson and Buck Leonard. That same season, his No. 8 was retired by the Yankees.

1925 Berra is born in St. Louis, Missouri.

1946 Berra joins the major leagues with the New York Yankees.

1947 Berra produces the first pinch-hit home run in World Series history.

1951 Berra wins his first Most Valuable Player award (also in 1954 and 1955).

1964 Berra becomes manager of the Yankees.

"Little League baseball is a very good thing because it keeps the parents off the streets."
    Yogi Berra

The following year, Yogi again found himself managing in New York, but this time it was with the Mets of the National League. Yogi's Mets rallied around the cry, "You gotta believe," and came from last place in September to win the National League East. The Mets then beat the favored Cincinnati Reds in the League Championship Series and gave the defending World Series champion Oakland A's all they could handle before losing in a tough seven-game series. Yogi was fired by the Mets during the 1975 season, but was immediately rehired by the Yankees, this time as a coach.

Berra was named manager to begin the 1984 season. The team finished in third place, with an 87–75 record. The following season, Yankees owner George Steinbrenner fired Berra after only 16 games, replacing him with Billy Martin. Heartbroken, Yogi declared that he would never return to Yankee Stadium as long as Steinbrenner owned the team.

After serving from 1986 to 1992 as a coach with the Houston Astros, Berra retired from baseball. He returned home to northern New Jersey to spend time with wife, Carmen. Their three children would carry on the Berra name in the world of professional sports, as Larry played in the Mets **farm system**, Tim played for the NFL's Baltimore Colts, and Dale played for the Yankees (while Yogi was there in '85) and the Pittsburgh Pirates.

farm system: network of teams affiliated with major league clubs which develop younger players' skills and abilities at minor league levels until they are deemed ready for major league play.

On Oct. 8, 1997, Carmen, Yogi and the Friends of Yogi, Inc., opened the Yogi Berra Museum and Learning Center in Montclair, N.J., on the campus of Montclair State College. The museum overlooks the home of the Northern League's New Jersey Jackals, fittingly named Yogi Berra Stadium. Yogi seemed content with his life, spending time with Carmen (his wife of 50 years), working in the museum, and running his own annual charity golf tournament.

Finally, on Jan. 5, 1999, Steinbrenner visited the Berra Museum seeking to make amends. He apologized to Yogi, calling his feud with him "a monumental mistake on my part." Yogi accepted Steinbrenner's apology and agreed to come back to Yankee Stadium.

On April 9, 1999, despite a steady rain, Yogi Berra returned to the Bronx for the Yankees' home opener. The crowd stood and cheered for several minutes as Yogi took the mound and threw the ceremonial first pitch. It was an emotional reunion as Yankee fans welcomed Berra home. As Yogi might have put it, "With all that rain, there wasn't a dry eye in the house." ◆

Biondi, Matt

OCTOBER 8, 1965– ● SWIMMER

Swimmer Matthew N. Biondi was born on October 8, 1965, in Moraga, California. As a child, he was a good swimmer—but not a brilliant one. That would come later. Through love of the sport and persistent hard work, he eventually excelled to the point where he won 11 Olympic medals, including six golds. Today, he is hailed as one of the two greatest American male swimmers (along with Mark Spitz) ever.

As a child in California, Biondi practiced diligently at several local swim clubs. He enjoyed the intense focus and persistence that swimming requires. But he was not particularly comfortable in formal competitions, as they made him nervous. He tended to concentrate on one step at a time, entering first local competitions, then state meets. (His first national meet was, amazingly enough, in the Olympic Trials for the 1984 Summer Games.)

After high school, Biondi attended the University of California at Berkeley. He swam on the UC Berkeley swim team, of course, but also became co-captain of the university water polo team. He was so good at water polo that at one point he was advised to concentrate on that sport rather than swimming. Biondi, however, found the two sports to be complementary; swimming is an individual sport that requires endurance and self-discipline, while water polo is a team sport that is superb for physical conditioning and for building interpersonal skills.

At the 1984 Summer Olympic Games, held in Los Angeles, California, Biondi won a gold medal in the 400-meter freestyle relay event. He also began racking up other accolades and achievements. In 1985, for example, he was named Swimmer of the Year and given the Phillips Performance Award. He set world records twice in the 100-meter freestyle. In 1986, Biondi was named U.S. Olympic Committee (USOC) Sportsman of the Year. He also set another world record in the 100-meter freestyle.

Biondi was unusually big for a swimmer—6 feet 6 inches, and 200 pounds—but with his powerful stroke and exceptional endurance, he glided through the water with seemingly little effort. In the Olympic Trials held six weeks before the 1988 Summer Games in Seoul, South Korea, Biondi set a world record

1965 Biondi is born in Moraga, California.

1984 At the Olympics in Los Angeles, Biondi wins gold medal in the 400-meter freestyle.

1986 Biondi is named Sportsman of the Year by the U.S. Olympic Committee (also in 1988).

1988 At the Olympics in Seoul, Korea, Biondi sets a world record in the 100-meter freestyle; of seven medals, five are gold. He also sets world records in the 50-meter and 100-meter freestyle.

Olympic Swimming

Like many events, swimming has changed dramatically since the first modern Olympic competition in Athens in 1896. Today, swimmers compete in climate-controlled 50-meter pools; in 1896 swimmers in the 1,200-meter freestyle jumped off a boat into the icy, turbulent waters of the Mediterranean Sea, and the winner later confessed that he was worried more about surviving than winning the race. Some of the events have changed, too. In 1896 there was a 100-meter event for Greek sailors; underwater and obstacle events debuted in 1900 but quickly disappeared. Women began competing in 1912.

Today both men and women compete in 16 events. Freestyle races cover 50, 100, 200, and 400 meters; additionally, women compete in an 800-meter and men compete in a 1,500-meter freestyle event. Butterfly, breaststroke, and backstroke races each cover 100 and 200 meters. Individual medley events in which swimmers use each of the four strokes in different legs of the event are held at 200 and 400 meters. Relay races include the 4 x 100 freestyle, the 4 x 200 freestyle, and the 4 x 100 medley (with each of the four swimmers in the medley using a different stroke). Eight swimmers compete in the final of each event, with individual swimmers in the shorter races (50, 100, and 200 meters) advancing in heats to the final round and the fastest swimmers in the preliminary rounds of the relays and the longer events advancing directly to the final round.

Olympic swimming is governed by tight rules. Swimmers often shave their bodies to reduce resistance, but they are not allowed to use any kind of grease to help them slide through the water, nor are they allowed to wear swimsuits that increase buoyancy. Further, swimmers are automatically disqualified for a false start. Swimming competitions are often decided by fractions of seconds, prompting the development of sophisticated technology for measuring times. Pressure plates at the starting blocks register when swimmers take off, and a pad on the wall at each end of the pool registers when the swimmer touches it during turns or at the end of the race.

> *"Persistence can change failure into extraordinary achievement."*
>
> Matt Biondi

(48.42 seconds) in the 100-meter freestyle. For the Olympics themselves, Biondi hoped to match the accomplishment of Mark Spitz, who at the 1972 Olympic Games in Munich, Germany, had won seven gold medals and set seven world records in seven races.

At the Seoul Games, Biondi came close to meeting that lofty standard. He collected seven medals, including five gold. Biondi won individual gold medals in the 50- and 100-meter freestyle events, and he was part of the winning 400- and 800-meter freestyle relay teams and the 400-meter medley relay team. He took an individual silver in the 100-meter butterfly race, and a bronze medal in the 200-meter freestyle. It was the highest medal count of any athlete at the Games.

His performance at Seoul made Biondi a huge worldwide star. Over the next several years, he continued his hot streak. He was again named USOC's 1988 Sportsman of the Year and set world records in the 50-meter and 100-meter freestyle. Along with Janet Evans, another Olympic great, he was named Swimmer of the Year. At the 1992 Summer Olympics, held in Barcelona, Spain, Biondi won the silver medal in the 50-meter freestyle event. As a member of the 400-meter freestyle and 400-meter medley relay teams, he also picked up two gold medals.

After the 1992 Games, Biondi retired from competition, having won 11 Olympic medals. The medals are on display at the National Italian-American Sports Hall of Fame in Arlington Heights, Illinois. He gives generously of his time, speaking in public to help motivate children to take up swimming, which he believes is a fine way to build character. He says that the accomplishment he most values, along with his swimming, is his relationship with his wife. ◆

> *"It's the path getting there that counts, not the cheese at the end of the maze."*
>
> Matt Biondi
> after winning
> seven Olympic
> medals
> (five gold) at
> Seoul, 1988

Boggs, Wade

JUNE 15, 1958– ● BASEBALL PLAYER

Despite the many accomplishments during his 18 years in baseball, Wade Boggs will be remembered vividly for three things: Riding a police horse after winning his first World Series with the New York Yankees in 1996; kissing home plate after homering for his 3,000th career hit; and eating chicken.

The superstitious Boggs always made chicken his pre-game meal, and with his .328 career batting average, good for 16th all-time, who could argue?

Boggs began his career with the Boston Red Sox in 1982 and right away his impact was felt. He set a new American League rookie batting mark with a .349 average and finished third in the American League Rookie of the Year voting (Cal Ripken, Jr., won the award). The next season Boggs won his first batting title, with a .361 average.

The Red Sox made it to the World Series in 1986, but lost a heartbreaker in seven games to the New York Mets. It would be 10 years before the mustachioed third baseman would get another chance at a championship.

1958 Boggs is born in Omaha, Nebraska.

1982 Boggs joins the Boston Red Sox; sets American League rookie batting average by hitting .349.

1999 Boggs collects his 3000th hit, which is also a home run—he is only the second man to reach the 3000-hit plateau with a home run.

expansion team: a team which joins a professional athletic association or league well after the group of originally chartered teams was established.

But that didn't stop Boggs from remaining one of the top players in the game. From 1985 to 1996, he was named to 11-straight All Star teams—and he batted .321 in those games. He led the league in batting from 1985–88. He set a new Major League mark by gaining 200 or more hits in consecutive seasons from 1983–89. He set the record for most singles in a season in 1985 with 187.

In 1992, Boggs' average plummeted more than 70 points from the year before, down to a modest .259. Baseball fans were wondering if Boggs' career was on the downswing. The Red Sox granted him free agency after the season and on Dec. 15, 1992, he signed on with the Sox's bitter rivals—the New York Yankees.

Boggs' career was reborn in the Big Apple, as his average shot back up over .300 and he steadily improved his defense at third base. He won the American League Gold Glove in 1994 and 1995, but 1996 brought the crowning moment of his career. After 14 seasons of individual successes, Boggs' team finally gave him the thrill of a World Series ring. The Yankees beat the Atlanta Braves in six games and Boggs celebrated by hopping on the back of a police horse and riding around Yankee Stadium—despite a fear of horses. It was an emotional moment for Boggs and he made the most of it, as it turned out to be his only championship.

On Dec. 9, 1997, Boggs went home. He didn't retire, though; instead he signed with the **expansion team** known as the Tampa Bay Devil Rays, who would begin play in 1998. Although he was born in Omaha, Nebraska on June 15, 1958, Boggs considered himself a native of the Tampa area, having moved there when he was 11-years-old and graduated from H.B. Plant High School and Hillsborough Community College. Boggs said that he wanted to finish his career playing pro ball just a few short miles from his high school baseball diamond.

On Opening Day 1998, Boggs hit the first home run in Devil Rays' history against the Detroit Tigers. He couldn't have scripted a better first game with his hometown team.

Boggs again stamped his place in baseball history on Aug. 7, 1999. One day after his National League counterpart, Tony Gwynn, recorded his 3,000th hit, Boggs joined the elite club himself. And he did it in the most dramatic fashion possible. The man who had hit only 118 home runs in his career belted a 2–2 pitch from Cleveland Indians pitched Chris Haney into the right field stands at Tropicana Field for his 3,000th hit. He pointed to the sky numerous times while rounding the bases in memory of his mother, who died in a car accident in 1986. And as he approached home plate, he knelt down and kissed it. He then got a hug from his wife and son, and his father. Boggs became the only player of the 22 to get 3,000 hits to reach the milestone with a home run.

"When it left the bat, I said, 'Oh, my God, that's a home run, and I'll never get that ball back,' " Boggs said.

But a generous fan did return the ball to Boggs, and he continued his consistent hitting for another month, until a knee injury ended the season for Boggs on September 8. As of the close of the 1999 season, Boggs had 3,010 hits in 9,180 at bats in 2,440 games. He had 1,014 runs batted in and had scored 1513 runs. A batter with a keen eye who was notorious for not swinging until he saw a strike, Boggs walked 1,412 times in his career—compared to only 745 strikeouts. His fielding percentage was an impressive .965.

Boggs is considered a shoo-in for induction into the National Baseball Hall of Fame in his first year of eligibility—which will be five years after his retirement in November 1999, when he accepted a front-office job with the Devil Rays. ◆

> *"When I was six years old."*
> Wade Boggs, in reply to a question about when he knew he would play major-league baseball

Bolton-Holifield, Ruthie

MAY 27, 1967– ● BASKETBALL PLAYER

No one has to tell Ruthie Bolton-Holifield about unselfishness. The hot-shooting guard of the WNBA's Sacramento Monarchs learned that early on—she grew up in a family with 19 siblings.

Alice Ruth Bolton was born on May 27, 1967, in Lucedale, Mississippi, the 16th of 20 children of the Rev. Linwood and Leola Bolton. She preferred to be called Ruthie and can thank her family for helping her find her calling as a basketball player. She chose to play basketball because her siblings did, but for her ability to take her game to a higher level, she owes no one credit but herself and her inner drive.

After starring at McClain High School in McClain, Mississippi, Ruthie took her basketball talents to Auburn University. The Lady Tigers saw unprecedented success in the four years that the 5–9 guard was in their backcourt. Auburn compiled a 119–13 record (a .901 winning percentage), including three straight

Ruthie Bolton-Holifield of the Sacramento Monarchs.

30-win seasons, and won three Southeastern Conference (SEC) championships. The team earned berths in the Final Four each of Bolton's four years and reached the final game in 1989 and 1990. Bolton was named to the Midwest Region All-Tournament team in 1988 and 1989 and to the 1988 NCAA All-Tournament team. She finished her Auburn career ranked third in school history in assists (526) and steals (246), and her success in the classroom equalled her success on the court. She was named to the SEC All-Academic Team in 1988 and 1989. She graduated from Auburn in 1989 with a degree in exercise physiology.

Because the United States did not have professional women's basketball at the time, Bolton went to Sweden to play. She also continued to make a name for herself in the U.S. with her stellar play on the USA National teams.

She starred for the 1990 USA Select team and helped the 1991 World University team win a gold medal by averaging 15.3 points and 4.5 rebounds while dishing out 19 assists, making 14 steals and shooting .320 from three-point range.

The year 1991 was a rewarding one, as Bolton was named the 1991 USA Basketball Player of the Year. That same year she added military experience to her resume by attending officer school (she is currently a first lieutenant in the army reserves) and added Holifield to her last name, by marrying Mark Holifield.

Professionally, the ports-of-call changed for Bolton, but her excellence on the court did not. Whether with Tungstrum (Hungary) or for Erreti Faenza (Italy), Bolton-Holifield was a shooting star—not to mention a passing and rebounding star. Her career took off while she played in Italy. She averaged 25.5 points per game and 6.0 rebounds her first season with Erreti Faenza then, topped those numbers the next season (28.0, 7.1). She even sang with a local Italian group called Antidum Tarantula.

Meanwhile, Bolton-Holifield continued to thrive on the national front, starring on the 1994 World Championship and Goodwill Games teams. After playing one season in Turkey, she came back to play with the USA National team that went 52–0 in pre-Olympic competition, then won Olympic gold at the 1996 Atlanta Games. Though winning the gold was a dream come true, the ever-unselfish Bolton-Holifield put family first and gave her medal to her younger sister, Mae Ola, who had tried out for the team but didn't make it. "She should have played in the Olympics," Ruthie said. "It was her dream, too."

When the WNBA came into existence in 1997, Ruthie Bolton-Holifield signed with the Sacramento Monarchs, and was selected as the first WNBA Player of the Week and named First-Team All-WNBA, with an average of 19.4 points per game, second-best in the entire league.

The 1998 season took a disastrous turn for Bolton-Holifield, as she tore her left **anterior cruciate ligament** in Sacramento's fifth game and missed the remainder of the season. Her surgery (coincidentally performed by Dr. Eric Heiden, a five-time Olympic speed-skating champion) was a complete success, and with typical Bolton determination, she worked her way back and had an outstanding season. She averaged 13.6 points, 4.3 rebounds and 2.4 assists in 1999. Bolton-Holifield represented the Monarchs with the West All-Stars in the first WNBA All-Star Game.

Prior to the start of that game, as she has done before every game over the last four years, Bolton touched her left hand as a tribute to her mother, a gesture that she recalled doing the last time she saw her mother prior to her death in 1995. The gesture

1967 Bolton-Holifield is born in Lucedale, Mississippi.

1988 Bolton-Holifield is named to SEC All-Academic Team (also in 1989).

1991 Bolton-Holifield is named USA Basketball Player of the Year.

anterior cruciate ligament: the front ligament of the two ligaments in the knee which cross one another and help stabilize the joint; this ligament is often injured in athletic competition. "Blowing out the ACL" has become one of the most common phrases in all of sports.

serves as a constant reminder of the power of family and its importance to Bolton, whatever the future may hold for her in basketball. ◆

Bonds, Barry

JULY 24, 1964– ● BASEBALL PLAYER

Barry Lamar Bonds, the left fielder for the San Francisco Giants, is widely considered to be one of the finest all-around players in the history of baseball and perhaps the best of the 1990s. The son of Bobby Bonds, a power-hitting major league outfielder of the 1970s, Barry was born in Riverside, California, on July 24, 1964, the oldest of three children. Bonds's baseball apprenticeship began early in his childhood, when he shagged fly balls at the Giants' Candlestick Park alongside his father and his godfather, Willie Mays. He played his first organized ball in the Little League of his well-heeled hometown of San Carlos, California, and went on to multisport distinction at Serra High School in San Mateo, California, only 20 miles from Candlestick Park. In three high school seasons Bonds batted .404 and was named a prep All-American his senior year.

Declining a $70,000 offer from the San Francisco Giants upon graduating from high school, Bonds accepted a scholarship offer from Arizona State University, a mecca for aspiring diamond stars. While there, Bonds displayed generous quantities of both his spectacular baseball talent (he was an All-American) and the mercurial temperament for which he has become notorious among fans and sportswriters. In the words of Jack Brock, Bonds' baseball coach at Arizona State, "I liked Barry Bonds. Unfortunately, I never saw a teammate care about him. Part of it would be his being rude, inconsiderate, and self-centered. He bragged about the money he turned down, and he popped off about his dad. I don't think he ever figured out what to do to get people to like him."

After Bonds hit 23 home runs in his junior year, he became the first-round draft choice of the Pittsburgh Pirates, and he dropped out of Arizona State to accept their offer. He served only a brief stint with Hawaii of the Pacific Coast League before being called up to the Pirates in 1986. Switching from center

> Bonds's baseball apprenticeship began early in his childhood, when he shagged fly balls at the Giants' Candlestick Park alongside his father and his godfather, Willie Mays.

field to left because of his below-average throwing arm, Bonds impressed despite his .223 batting average, previewing an eye-popping combination of speed and power: he topped all National League rookies in home runs (16), runs batted in (48), stolen bases (36), and walks (65).

Yet Bonds' progress over the next few seasons was disappointing, as reflected in his underwhelming batting average and slugging percentage, respectively—.261 and .492 in 1987, .283 and .491 in 1988, and .248 and .426 in 1989. After a protracted contract wrangle in 1989, the Pirates began to shop the under-achieving Bonds to other clubs, but they were just as wary of him as the Pirates, and there were no takers.

After Bonds lost an arbitration battle with the Pirates after the 1989 campaign, he vowed to redeem his career and confound the naysayers. In the off-season he undertook a rigorous training regimen under the guidance of Pittsburgh's conditioning coach, Warren Sipp, and came to camp in 1990 with a fiery sense of purpose that had been missing since his final year at Arizona State. That season Bonds finally blossomed into one of baseball's finest all-around performers, posting a .301 batting average, a .565 slugging percentage (best in the National League), 33 home runs, 114 runs batted in, and 52 stolen bases. He earned his first Most Valuable Player (MVP) title and the first of seven Gold Gloves for his outstanding defensive skills. Not coincidentally, the Pirates as a whole excelled that year, capturing the National League East title. But Bonds and his teammates Pirates crashed to earth in the League Championship Series, losing to the Cincinnati Reds (that year's eventual world champions) four games to two.

In 1991 Bonds lost another arbitration dispute with the Pirates, settling for $2.3 million rather than his proposed $3.25 million. His simmering frustration over that defeat climaxed in a public, abusive tirade against the team's mild-mannered manager, Jim Leyland, who publicly rebuked his temperamental star, already a major source of friction in the Pirate clubhouse. Although Bonds later apologized, the incident cemented his reputation for belligerence and arrogance.

On the field, Bonds' numbers were strong again in 1991, with the Pirates repeating both as winners of the National League East pennant and losers of the league championship series, this time to the Atlanta Braves, in seven games. Bonds' performance in that series was one of his great disappointments: he batted .148, with one run scored and none batted in. He was

1964 Bonds is born in Riverside, California.

1986 Bonds joins the Pittsburgh Pirates.

1990 Bonds earns first National League MVP (wins again in '92); wins first of seven Gold Gloves.

1998 Bonds becomes first to collect 400 home runs and stolen bases.

*"He makes his liv-
ing running fast
and I make mine
running slow."*

Barry Bonds on
Carl Lewis, 1990

the runner-up in the National League vote for MVP, a result
Bonds attributed—justly, in the eyes of many observers—to the
enmity he had fostered among so many sportswriters.

Unable to afford the now-expensive players they had developed, the attendance-starved Pirates sought to trade
Bonds in the off-season but could not come to terms with the
leading suitor, the Atlanta Braves. Pittsburgh then inked
Bonds to a one-year deal for $4.7 million, the most lucrative
salary in baseball history to that point. Even though sidelined
with injury for three weeks, Bonds earned his hefty paycheck
in 1992, leading the National League in slugging percentage
(.624), runs (109), walks (127), and extra-base hits (75),
spearheading the Pirates' drive to another National League
East crown and earning his second MVP award. The Pirates
once again faced Atlanta in the league championship series,
which they led until the final inning of the decisive seventh
game, when a dramatic Atlanta rally once again sealed Pittsburgh's doom.

A free agent after the 1992 season, Bonds was wooed ag-
gressively by the new ownership of the San Francisco Giants,
which signed the moody slugger to a record-breaking six-year
deal for a base salary of $43.75 million and generous **incentives**
that have added millions more to his paychecks. Bonds' on-
field transition to the Giants was a smooth one; his father was
hired as hitting instructor and his father's long-time friend,
Dusty Baker, was brought on as manager. As part of a potent
lineup that included Will Clark, Matt Williams, and Robby
Thompson, Bonds set a scorching pace early in the season,
cooling only slightly toward the end and ending up with personal bests in all the key batting statistics, including 46 homers
and 129 runs scored. He again received National League MVP
honors, becoming the first player ever to win the MVP three
times in four seasons. Despite winning 103 games, however,
the Giants were edged out of the National League West title
on the last day of the season by the Atlanta Braves.

Although his formidable array of talents have yet to lift the
Giants to a National League West crown, Bonds' steady stream
of superlative seasons has secured his status as the best overall
player of the 1990s; he ranks among the major league leaders in
almost every offensive category for the decade: first in runs batted in (993), second in slugging percentage (.601), first in walks
(1,073), third in home runs (327), and sixth in stolen bases. In
1998 he became the first player ever to reach the 400 figure in

incentive: an inducement
to perform or act in a certain manner; many profes-
sional athletes have
clauses in their contracts
which promise more
money for reaching particular levels of individual or
team achievement.

both home runs and stolen bases (only three other players have even reached the 300–300 plateau). Never the most beguiling of diamond heroes, Bonds nonetheless commands respect for his talent. In the words of an opposing player, "Barry Bonds, to me, is possessed. It's like he rolls out of bed, looks at himself in the mirror, and knows he's the best. You can see it in his eyes. He has the total respect of everyone in the game. He's worth every penny he gets." ◆

Borg, Bjorn

JUNE 6, 1956– ● TENNIS PLAYER

Bjorn Borg was born in Soldertaljie, Sweden, on June 6, 1956. The story goes that the young boy's life course was sealed when his father won a tennis racquet in a Ping-Pong match and gave it to his son. What is certain is that Bjorn had an undeniable talent with a tennis racquet. By his mid-teens, he had made a name for himself in the sport nationally.

By his late teens, Borg was an international tennis star as well. In 1974, he won nine tournament titles, including his first French Open—one of the major annual tennis events in the world. (He went on to win that event a record six times through 1981.)

Borg has a native athletic ability that translated well on the tennis court. Fast, focused, and agile, he wowed legions of professional tennis fans with his ability to retrieve seemingly impossible shots. Along with his brilliant baseline game and consistent play, those skills helped make him the dominant male player in international tennis in the late 1970s and early 1980s. When he was 16,

1956 Borg is born in Soldertaljie, Sweden.

1974 Borg wins the first of a record six French Opens.

1976 Borg wins Wimbledon for the first time (he won again in 1977–80).

singles: in tennis and other racquet sports, singles competition involves one player against another in a match.

doubles: in tennis and other racquet sports, doubles competition involves two players against another pair of players in a match.

Borg was invited to play on Sweden's Davis Cup team; three years later, in 1975, he led the Swedish players to win the prestigious Davis Cup title.

The next year, Borg conquered an even more esteemed venue: Wimbledon, in England. Not only did he win on the grass courts in 1976—he also triumphed in 1977, 1978, 1979, and 1980. When he reached Wimbledon's final round in 1981, however, his winning streak was cut short by another young tennis star, John McEnroe.

It was a momentous occasion for McEnroe, who, like many other professional tennis players, had greatly admired Borg. The Swede's consistent, seemingly flawless game was legendary. Equally famous was Borg's serious presence on the court. He would rarely even smile. In a dramatic tennis era in which histrionics and temper tantrums were not uncommon among tennis stars (most notably McEnroe), Borg's calm, unflappable public demeanor was remarkable.

Whatever unique combination of skills and personal characteristics resulted in Borg's phenomenal success in the tennis world remains a subject of much debate. What is not questioned, however, is his mastery of top-level tennis over a long period of time. Frequently rated the number-one male player in the world, Borg collected an astounding 62 men's **singles** titles and four **doubles** titles. Eleven of his singles wins were in Grand Slam events. He was ranked in the top 10 from 1974 to 1981.

Borg was not without his weaknesses, however. Conquering the fast, hard surfaces at the U.S. Open courts in Flushing Meadows, New York, seemed beyond him. He made it to the finals four times—and lost four times.

Borg may have been calm and polite on the court, but he stubbornly insisted on going about things his own way. He never followed the entire worldwide tennis circuit; he refused, for example, to play the Australian Open, one of the four so-called Grand Slam events (the others are Wimbledon, the U.S. Open, and the French Open). In 1982, the men's tennis council took him to task for taking a four-month vacation. Borg was warned that he would have to play qualifying rounds for every major tennis event that year because he would not participate in the requisite number of tournaments. Instead of folding to the council's wishes, Borg simply took the year off. Apparently he enjoyed the free time, because the next year, at just age 26, Borg decided to retire. Players and fans alike were dismayed; his decision signaled the end of a glorious era in professional tennis.

Grand Slam of Tennis

Every year top pro and amateur tennis players can compete in scores of tournaments throughout the world. For many players, though, these tournaments are warm-ups for the four major events on the tour: the Australian Open, the French Open, the U.S. Open, and Wimbledon collectively, the Grand Slam of Tennis. A player who wins one Grand Slam event catches the world's attention, as Boris Becker did in 1985 when, as a 17-year-old qualifier, he became the youngest man ever to win Wimbledon. A player who wins two or three can claim a place among the sport's elite. A player who wins all four in the same year becomes a legend.

What makes winning all four Grand Slam events such an extraordinary feat is that each tournament makes different demands on its champions. The first of the four, the Australian Open, is played on a synthetic hard court, so the ball bounces off the surface like a rocket. In the French Open in Paris, players slide back and forth on loose red clay, making footwork a key challenge. Then it's off to England and the grass courts of Wimbledon, where players have to fight rain, slippery grass, and tough bounces as the ball comes off an imperfect natural surface whose character can change from day to day. At the U.S. Open in Flushing Meadows, New York, players return to a hard surface (cement) and face the distractions of noisy crowds and airplanes taking off and landing overhead. A measure of how difficult it is to win all four tournaments is the frustration of Pete Sampras, who in 1999 tied Roy Emerson's record by winning his twelfth Grand Slam event and his record sixth Wimbledon title. Sampras, though, has never won the French Open and made it to the final only once.

A select few players have had the versatility to sweep the Grand Slam. American Don Budge did it in 1938, and Australian Rod Laver did it in 1962 and 1969. Among the women, American Maureen Connolly pulled it off in 1953, as did Australian Margaret Court in 1970. The last Grand Slam winner was Steffi Graf in 1988.

Borg still had plenty of options. He had become fabulously wealthy, and no one would say no to the sports hero. He could do whatever he wanted. He owned a successful pro shop and several homes, one in Monte Carlo and one on a small island in Sweden. He was earning approximately $4 million per year in commercial endorsements. He was a huge celebrity throughout the world, and particularly in Europe. He was so popular that the festivities for his 1980 marriage to Romanian tennis player Mariana Simionescu had a "corporate sponsor": A company paid about $200,000 just for the right to photograph the wedding and reception. (The marriage later ended in divorce, as did a second marriage for Borg.)

In the 1990s, Borg resurfaced on the world stage as a player on the "senior" professional tennis circuit, vying for wins against

"Prominent tennis players have been heard to applaud Jimmy Connors because he is colorful, while cocking a snoot at Bjorn Borg because he seldom gives any outward sign of emotion."

Red Smith, "Tantrums on Grass," 1981

such former rivals as Jimmy Connors. ("Senior" is a convenient rather than defining term for this circuit, as many of the participating players are quite young. Borg, for example, is still in his early forties.) The years off from competitive tennis have taken the edge off his game. Nonetheless, the reclusive star's mere participation in an event draws headlines—and fans. ◆

Brett, George

MAY 15, 1953– ● BASEBALL PLAYER

The last modern player to make a serious run at hitting .400 over the course of a season, George Brett was elected to the Hall of Fame in 1999. Along with Mike Schmidt of the Philadelphia Phillies, Brett helped redefine third base as a pivotal offensive position and became the only player to win batting titles in three different decades.

Brett was born in Glendale, West Virginia. His brother Ken, born five years earlier in Brooklyn, NY, blazed his way to the major leagues as a star pitcher and was drafted by the Boston Red Sox in 1966. George was a star shortstop through high school, and was eventually drafted by Kansas City in 1972 to be their shortstop of the future. The Royals were a mediocre fourth place team in 1972, and one of their few bright spots was a slick fielding shortstop named Freddie Patek. Thus, Brett saw some playing time at third base in 1973, the first year of the designated hitter in the American League, and won the starting third base job the next season.

Brett shot to national prominence by only his second full season, leading the league in hits and triples and the Royals to a second place finish behind the Oakland A's in 1975. He added his first batting title the following season, again leading the league in hits and triples, as the Royals won their first division title. His .333 mark that year edged out teammate Hal McRae's avergage on the final day of the season. Meanwhile, Brett's brother Ken was making a name for himself as an effective, if well traveled, starting pitcher. Ken Brett would pitch with varying effectiveness for the Yankees, White Sox, Angels, Twins,

> *"If anyone stays away, my response is this: Those people had no right to ever come to the park, because they aren't true baseball fans."*
>
> George Brett after the 1981 players' strike

Dodgers and Royals before his retirement in 1982; he owns an 83–85 career record.

George Brett, on the other hand, was only getting better. From 1976 to 1978, the Royals won three straight divisional titles, but lost each year in the playoffs to the Yankees. His three successive homers off Hall of Famer Catfish Hunter in the 1978 playoff remains one of the single greatest achievements in postseason history.

Just before the 1980 All-Star break, Brett strained an ankle ligament sliding into second base. He was hitting .337 at the time, and when he returned to the field in July, he mounted a run at becoming the first man since Ted Williams to hit .400. On August 17th, 1980, he went 4-for-4, reaching .400 for the first and only time. Thanks to a late season slump, Brett ended the season at .390, but he also led the league in slugging and on-base percentage. To no one's surprise, he was the unanimous selection for Most Valuable Player. That year, the Royals broke their playoff jinx against the Yankees as Brett homered in Game One and hit an upper deck home run off Goose Gossage to win game three. Although the Phillies, led by Mike Schmidt, beat Kansas City in six games, Brett was dominant at the plate, going 9-for-24 in the Series. Five years later, Brett and the Royals finally won a championship and Brett starred both offensively and defensively. In game seven, he went 4-for-5 and robbed the St. Louis Cardinals of five potential hits.

On July 24, 1983, Brett made history in an entirely different way altogether. With the Yankees leading Kansas City 4–3 in the ninth inning at Yankee Stadium, Brett homered with two outs and a man on to put the Royals in front 5–4. Yankee manager Billy Martin argued that Brett had used too much pine tar; the rule states that a bat may not have **pine tar** more than 18 inches from the knob to the barrel. When the umpires overruled Brett's home run, the passionate Royal blazed out of the dugout in a frenzy that is still remembered as "The Great Pine Tar Incident." The league eventually overturned the umpires' decision and restored Brett's home run.

Brett won another batting championship in 1990, his third over three decades. He retired after the 1993 season with a .305 batting average and 3,154 hits. He spent his entire career with the Royals and is now a member of the Royals front office. ◆

1953 Brett is born in Glendale, West Virginia.

1975 Brett leads league in hits and triples.

1983 Brett is involved in "The Great Pine Tar Incident."

1999 Brett is inducted into the Baseball Hall of Fame.

pine tar: tar distilled from the wood of a pine tree; used on baseball bats to give the batter a better grip on the bat to improve the striking of the ball.

Budge, Don

JUNE 13, 1915–JANUARY 25, 2000 ● TENNIS PLAYER

Born in Oakland, California, John Donald Budge in 1938 became the first tennis player in history to win the coveted Grand Slam—the singles championships of Great Britain, France, the United States, and Australia. Known for his smooth, effortless backhand and powerful serve, he had a rather short but illustrious amateur career.

Budge began learning to play tennis on public courts in California when he was eight years old. The red-haired, freckle-faced youngster preferred football, baseball, and other sports, however, and played no tennis at all from the ages of 11 to 15. In 1930 Budge's family encouraged the tall, lanky, teenager to take up tennis again and enter the California state boys' championship. Budge took up the challenge, practiced hard, and

Don Budge, first to win tennis's Grand Slam.

won, thus winning the first tournament in which he ever competed. With this victory, Budge decided to keep on playing and become a champion.

In 1933 Budge won both the junior and senior championships of California. These victories were followed by the national junior singles championship that same year, which he won by defeating Gene Mako of Los Angeles, who later became his doubles partner. The next year Budge and Mako won the doubles title at the Pacific Coast Sectional Tournament at Santa Barbara, California.

Although ranked only ninth in the U.S. in 1935, Budge was chosen to play for the United States at the Davis Cup tournament. He lost his early matches to English players Fred Perry and "Bunny" Austin, but his later victory over Germany's Baron Gottfried von Cramm secured the U.S. team's participation in the final rounds.

Back in the United States,. Budge and Gene Mako reached the finals of the national doubles championship in 1936, but Budge lost the national singles title to Bryan ("Bitsy") Grant. He also lost at Wimbledon and the U.S. Open that year to Fred Perry, who was ranked number one in the world. However, he did beat Perry at the Pacific Southwest tournament.

A member of the U.S. Davis Cup team again in 1937, Budge won all his matches and helped lead the U.S. to victory, its first Davis Cup since 1926. His win over Baron von Cramm in the finals, after trailing 4 to 1 in the fifth set, was one of the most brilliant games of his career.

Budge became the top-ranked player in 1937 after Fred Perry turned professional. He won the singles title at the U.S. Open and Australian Open and the singles and doubles titles (with Gene Mako) at Wimbledon. Budge also won the U.S. national singles title and the mixed doubles title with Sarah Fabyan. Because of his outstanding achievements Budge was awarded the James E. Sullivan Memorial Trophy as the outstanding U.S. amateur athlete of the year, the first tennis player to ever receive this honor.

Budge had a great year in 1937, but the following year was even better when he astounded the tennis world with his Grand Slam singles victories at Wimbledon, the Australian Open, the French Open, and the U.S. Open. Never before had any player won all four of these tournaments in a single year. Budge also helped the U.S retain its Davis Cup title that year. Between the 1937 and 1938 seasons, Budge had an incredible 92-match,

"He stands tall in the record books. He had a lot of self-confidence as well as one of the game's all-time weapons in his backhand. His backhand was what we called a concluder, the sort of shot people will still be talking about a hundred years later."
Tony Trabert, winner of Wimbledon, the French Open, and the U.S. Nationals in 1955, on Don Budge

1915 | Budge is born in Oakland, California.

1938 | Budge becomes the first player to win all four Grand Slam events within a calendar year.

1964 | Budge is inducted into the International Tennis Hall of Fame in Newport, Rhode Island.

2000 | Budge dies in Scranton, Pennsylvania.

14-tournament winning streak. The Associated Press honored Budge in 1938 by naming him athlete of the year.

Budge gave up his amateur status in 1939 and defeated his former rival Fred Perry in his first professional match at Madison Square Garden in New York on January 3, 1939. On the pro tour that year he defeated Ellsworth Vines, 21 matches to 18, and Fred Perry, 18 to 11. He also beat the aging Bill Tilden 51 matches to 7. Budge won the U.S. pro singles title in 1940 and 1942, defeating Fred Perry and Bobby Riggs.

Budge joined the Air Force in 1942 and put his tennis career on hold until after World War II. During military training he suffered a shoulder injury that reduced his effectiveness after the war. Budge reached the U.S. Professional tournament finals in 1946, 1947, 1949, and 1953, losing the first three to Bobby Riggs and the last to Pancho Gonzalez. Elected to the National Lawn Tennis Association Hall of Fame in 1964, Budge continued to play on the Seniors tour. During the height of his career Budge wrote two books, *How Lawn Tennis is Played* (1937) and *On Tennis* (1939), both of which became best-selling titles.

Budge died in Scranton, Pennsylvania, on January 25, 2000 after suffering a cardiac arrest. ◆

Campanella, Roy

NOVEMBER 19, 1921–JUNE 26, 1993 ● BASEBALL PLAYER

In 1948, the year after Jackie Robinson crossed baseball's color line to become a member of the Brooklyn Dodgers, Roy Campanella joined him in Brooklyn and became the major league's first African-American catcher. Campanella and Robinson were the vanguard of major league baseball's first contingent of black superstars, soon to be joined by Willie Mays, Ernie Banks, and Hank Aaron.

The son of John Campanella, an Italian fruit-stand owner, and Ida Campanella, his black wife, Roy Campanella was born in Philadelphia. His athletic talents were noticed early, and by the time he was 16 he was offered a position with the Bacharach Giants, Philadelphia's black semipro team. After playing with the Giants for only a few weeks, Campanella transferred to the Baltimore Elites, one of the most important teams in the Negro National League, with whom he excelled both defensively and at the plate.

In 1946 he signed a contract with Branch Rickey, owner of the

Roy Campanella at Ebbets Field in Brooklyn.

"You gotta be a man to play base-ball for a living but you gotta have a lot of little boy in you."

Roy Campanella

Dodgers, and after two years in the minor leagues became the Dodgers' second black player. During his 10 seasons with the club, Campanella won three Most Valuable Player awards and set new slugging records for a catcher. He also became the first player to catch at least 100 games for nine straight seasons. A frequent All-Star, Campanella helped lead the Dodgers into five World Series.

An automobile crash after the 1957 season left Campanella partially paralyzed. He fought back from the accident to become a community-service worker and instructor for the Dodgers. He was elected to the Baseball Hall of Fame in 1969. ◆

Canseco, Jose

JULY 2, 1964– ● BASEBALL PLAYER

In many ways Jose Canseco personifies the American dream. Born in Havana, Cuba, on July 2, 1964, Jose (his birth name is Canseco y Capas) and his family moved to Miami when he was nine months old. His father had a mere $50 in his pocket.

Jose showed promise as a baseball player from a young age. He starred for the Coral Park High School baseball team in Miami, where he played with his twin brother, Ozzie. As a senior, Jose hit .400 and was named to the All-Greater Miami Athletic Conference first team. Both Cansecos were chosen in the 1982 Amateur Draft. Jose wasn't chosen until the 15th round, but he was finally drafted by the Oakland Athletics.

Although he hit with tremendous power, Canseco came under heavy criticism for a perceived lack of work ethic and his penchant for striking out (in 1983, he led the Northwest League, whiffing 78 times).

Unfortunately, it took a family tragedy for Canseco to turn things around. In 1984 his mother died, and Canseco missed six weeks of the season. During that time, he contemplated his future and realized he needed to work harder and improve his game.

Canseco returned that season with a new resolve. He led his Modesto team with 15 homers, 73 runs batted in (RBI), hit for a .276 average, and showed an improved batting eye, drawing 74 walks.

The following season, Canseco's new work ethic paid off. He was named Minor League Player of the Year, totaling a combined .328 average, with 41 home runs and 140 RBI for three teams (Double-A Huntsville, Triple-A Tacoma, and Oakland, where he played the season's final 29 games).

A powerfully built combination of raw power and speed, Canseco burst onto the Major Leagues in 1986. With a quick, hard swing, Canseco could hit the ball to all three fields with power. Although, like most home run hitters, he still struck out a lot (175 times in 1986), he walloped 33 home runs, one short of the team single-season rookie record, and knocked in 117 runs, was voted an All-Star, and was named Rookie of the Year. Things would get even better for Canseco and the A's.

In 1987, Oakland finished at .500 for the first time in six years and was about to embark on a three-year run that would see the team win 103, 99, and 104 games, three American League pennants, and a World Series championship.

Canseco factored heavily in that success. He and first baseman Mark McGwire formed a devastating one-two punch in the heart of the batting order, and they became known as the "Bash Brothers," not only for their ability to hit home runs, but for the bashing of forearms when meeting at home plate after homers that became the team's celebratory ritual.

His third full season in the major leagues, 1988, would be historic. Canseco led in home runs (42), RBI (124) and slugging percentage (.569). He also showed great instincts and blazing speed on the base paths, stealing 46 bases, to become the first player in Major League history to hit at least 40 home runs and steal at least 40 bases in the same season. [The "40–40 Club" has since been joined by San Francisco's Barry Bonds (1996) and Seattle's Alex Rodriguez (1998)]. Canseco also became only the ninth player in Major League history to be unanimously voted the American League Most Valuable Player.

Though Oakland made it to the World Series, they lost in five games to the Los Angeles Dodgers. Canseco got only one hit in 19 at-bats in the series, a grand slam in game one that would have meant the margin of victory, had it not been for Kirk Gibson's dramatic ninth-inning home run, which swung the momentum the Dodgers' way.

Despite the World Series loss, the A's rewarded Canseco for his contributions by signing him to a five-year, $23 million contract—at the time the most lucrative contract ever offered to a professional baseball player—prior to the start of the 1989 sea-

1964 Canseco is born José Canseco y Capas in Havana, Cuba.

1985 Canseco is named Minor League Player of the Year.

1986 Canseco enters the major league as a member of the Oakland A's.

1988 Canseco is the first major leaguer to hit at least 40 home runs and steal at least 40 bases in the same season; named American League's Most Valuable Player.

son. A broken hand limited Canseco to only 65 games, but he returned to the lineup and helped the A's return to the World Series. Canseco hit .357, as the A's beat the San Francisco Giants in four straight games to win a world championship in a series best remembered for an earthquake that delayed the conclusion of the Series for almost two weeks.

The 1990 season saw Canseco and the Bash Brothers again reach the World Series. He even got to play with brother Ozzie, who was traded to the A's. But Oakland was swept by the upstart Cincinnati Reds.

In 1991, Canseco tied for the Major League lead in homers (44), while driving in 122 runs. But that season would be his last with Oakland—early in the 1992 season he was traded to Texas. But the change of scenery didn't slow Canseco's production, nor did it limit his popularity with baseball fans.

Canseco's awesome strength and power made him a popular gate attraction. A six-time All-Star, he received the most votes of any American League player for the 1990 All-Star Game. But the attention that he drew with his prolific offense became a double-edged sword, as it brought to light his defensive lapses in the outfield. In addition, several off-the-field incidents further tarnished his reputation.

Despite a nagging back injury, Canseco, with his "all-or-nothing" swing and long, high-arcing home runs, is still one of baseball's most entertaining at-bats. After short stints with the Red Sox and Toronto Blue Jays, Jose signed with the expansion Tampa Bay Devil Rays in 1998. That year, he became the first player to hit 30 home runs with four different teams (Oakland, Texas, Toronto, Tampa Bay), and on April 14, 1999, he hit his 400th career home run. ◆

Caray, Harry

MARCH 1, 1914–FEBRUARY 18, 1998 ● BASEBALL ANNOUNCER

Baseball broadcaster Harry Caray was born Harry Christopher Carabina in a poor section of St. Louis, Missouri, on March 1, 1914. His father died when he was an infant, and his mother when he was just 10 years old. After that time, Harry was raised by an aunt. It was a difficult childhood that he later called "depressing."

Caray played sandlot baseball as a boy, and beginning in his late teens played in several local semi-professional teams. Listening to radio announcers call games, he decided he could do a much better job, finding their style boring. He spent a few years learning the broadcasting business at radio stations in Joliet, Illinois, and Kalamazoo, Michigan. (It was the manager at the Joliet station who encouraged Harry to change his name from Carabina to Caray.)

In 1945, Caray won the job he really wanted, as play-by-play announcer on KMOX-TV and Radio for the St. Louis Cardinals, the team that was his childhood favorite. Caray's exuberant style immediately appealed to listeners. He was a true baseball fan, and his enthusiasm for the game translated well on the air.

Caray broadcast in St. Louis for 29 years and, in the process, became a huge attraction for baseball fans. It was clear to spectators and listeners that Caray was one of them. His lively descriptions of the plays painted a vivid picture for listeners. Not only was he entertaining, but he also called the games as he saw them, without regard to "politics." He lavished praise on players, umpires, and managers when it was merited—and he was just as frank when they messed up, even if they were from the home team. This did not always make him popular with players and managers, but he felt that it was his job to be honest.

Caray broadcast for the Oakland A's in 1970, then went to Chicago, where he spent a decade announcing for the Chicago White Sox. In 1981, he started calling games for the Chicago Cubs. During these years, Caray became a baseball legend unto himself. "Hello again, everybody," he might say. "It's a bee-yooo-ti-ful day for baseball." He became famous for such "Caray-isms" as "Holy cow!" and "It might be, it could be, it is! A home run!" During the seventh-inning stretch, he would call out "A one and a two and a three" and lead the stadium fans in singing

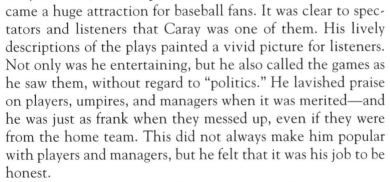

"I've only been doing it for 52 years. I think with some experience, I might get a little better."

Harry Caray, dismissing rumors of retirement, 1996

1914 Caray is born Harry Christopher Carabina in St. Louis, Missouri.

1945 Caray begins as play-by-play announcer on KMOX–TV and Radio for St. Louis Cardinals.

1989 Caray is inducted into the Baseball Hall of Fame.

1998 Caray dies in California.

"Take Me Out to the Ballgame." He was a terrible singer, but the crowds loved it.

Caray's motto was "Live it up, the meter's running." He thought it was very important to have fun, and he certainly did that on the job and off. He might broadcast from the bleachers in a lounger, wielding a fishnet to catch foul balls, drinking beer, and eating hot dogs. He would strip down to his shorts in the hot summer sun and jump into the shower between innings to cool off. His thick, heavy black eyeglasses, gray hair, and generous physique made him instantly recognizable.

In February 1987, Caray suffered a stroke. He received boxes and boxes of get-well letters from fans, whose encouragement he later said helped him to overcame speech difficulties and paralysis resulting from the stroke. On May 19, 1987, he resumed his broadcasts from Wrigley Field. President Ronald Reagan himself called during the game to welcome him back. Fans could not believe it when, in the middle of the phone call, Caray all but hung up on the president when a big play on the field caught his attention!

Caray was well rewarded for his unique style. Not only was he handsomely paid, but he became a national icon, beloved as baseball's most colorful figure. During his tenure in St. Louis, The Sporting News named him "Baseball Announcer of the Year" for seven consecutive years. In 1989, he was inducted into the Baseball Hall of Fame. Caray owned a popular restaurant in Chicago called, of course, Harry Caray's. He was perhaps most gratified, however, by the fact that his son, Skip Caray, and grandson, Chip Caray, followed his lead and became sports announcers themselves.

In his later years, Caray's memory began to falter. The *Chicago Sun-Times* ran an affectionate weekly column in the sports section recounting his mistakes, such as mispronouncing players' names and forgetting the words to "Take Me Out to the Ball Game." (Caray noted that he had been broadcasting for 52 years and wryly suggested, "With a little experience, I might get better.") Despite these lapses, Caray never retired, and he was never pushed aside.

Caray died on February 18, 1998, in California, where he and his wife Dutchie maintained a home. In his honor, his fans gathered outside Wrigley Field and sang "Take Me Out to the Ball Game" one last time. ◆

Chavez, Julio Cesar

JULY 12, 1962– ● BOXER

A hero to millions of adoring fans throughout Mexico, Julio Cesar Chavez is a fierce warrior who was champion in three weight divisions and fought all the top fighters of his day. Born in Culiacan, Mexico, Chavez grew up in a poor environment and turned to boxing at an early age. By the time he was 17, he had turned professional and began a winning streak that would take him to the top of the world of boxing.

A busy fighter, Chavez fought at least 10 times in each of his first three years as a pro (1980–82). In 1984, with a record of 44–0 and 40 knockouts, he took on Mario Martinez for the World Boxing Council junior lightweight championship. For eight rounds, Chavez battered Martinez, using his short, powerful punches to the head and body to win his first professional title. For Chavez, the victory was important because although he was already very popular in Mexico, he was now gaining notice in the lucrative American boxing market.

Over the next three years, Chavez continued to blast his way through the junior lightweight division, defending his title nine times. Many of those defenses were televised as Chavez beat such well known fighters as Roger Mayweather, Rocky Lockridge, and Juan Laporte. In 1987, Chavez moved up in weight and added his second title—the World Boxing Association Lightweight crown—by defeating the hard-punching Edwin Rosario in 11 brutal rounds. Throughout 1988 and 1989, Chavez continued to fight all comers and defend his title. Chavez particularly enjoyed returning for fights in his home country of Mexico, in front of his adoring fans. Often Chavez would fight for less money and against less well-known opponents so that his biggest fans could get the thrill of rooting him on. Once, during a span of just 18 days in 1989, Chavez fought twice in Mexico, once in Tijuana and once in Mazatlan, registering knockouts in both fights.

Still, by 1990, Chavez was internationally recognized as one of the best pound-for-pound fighters in boxing. On March 17, 1990, he helped cement that claim with a stunning 12th-round,

> Chavez particularly enjoyed returning for fights in his home country of Mexico, in front of his adoring fans.

1962 Chavez is born in Culiacan, Mexico.

1987 Chavez wins World Boxing Association Lightweight crown.

1993 In Mexico City, Chavez knocks out Greg Haugen in the fifth round before the largest crowd to see a boxing match live.

come-from-behind knockout win over International Boxing Federation champion Meldrick Taylor. Using his amazing hand speed, Taylor built up a big lead going into the 12th round. But Chavez never gave up and, with only seconds left, he landed a vicious right cross that knocked down Taylor. Referee Richard Steele decided that Taylor could not continue and stopped the fight with two seconds left, making Chavez a knockout winner in one of the most exciting fights of the 1990s.

Continuing to defend his title, in February 1993 Chavez fought in front of the biggest live crowd in history, as he knocked out Greg Haugen in five rounds in Mexico City, in front of a crowd of more than 120,000 wildly pro-Chavez fans.

Seven months later, Chavez stepped into the ring with an amazing record of 87–0 with 72 knockouts to face Pernell Whitaker, a master of defense. After 12 tough rounds, many thought Whitaker had handed Chavez his first defeat, but the judges called the fight a draw. Only four months later, however, Chavez finally suffered his first loss, a 12-round defeat at the hands of Frankie Randell. It was Chavez's 91st fight.

Four months after losing to Randall, the two fought again, this time Chavez was able to regain his title, beating Randall on a technical decision after Chavez was cut by a head butt and was unable to continue the match.

As with all athletes, years eventually take their toll. In 1996, Chavez was challenged by the much-younger Oscar de la Hoya. After four brutal rounds, de la Hoya stopped Chavez on cuts. Chavez continued to fight through 1999, losing a 10-round decision to a journeyman fighter named Willy Wise, dropping Chavez's still-outstanding record to 101 wins, 4 losses, and 2 draws, with 84 knockouts. At 37 years old, it appears Chavez's career as a top fighter is waning. But for his fans, there will always be the memory of the 14 years when no fighter near his weight could defeat the great Mexican warrior. ◆

Citation

April 11, 1945–August 8, 1970 ● Thoroughbred Racehorse

Citation was born on April 11, 1945, at Calumet Farm in Kentucky. The foal's dam, or mother, was the British mare Hydroplane II, his sire the American Triple Crown runner Bull Lea. Although Bull Lea was not a champion racer, he was well bred and had become Calumet Farm's foundation sire. Calumet Farm's owner, Warren Wright, decided to introduce some new blood into the mixing, purchasing Hydroplane II from Lord Derby of England. The mating that produced Citation was inspired: blessed with both exceptional endurance and breathtaking speed, Citation would become one of the greatest American racehorses of all time.

Wright decided to send the beautiful colt to Maryland to be trained by Jimmy Jones and his father, Ben. The Joneses quickly realized that they might have an exceptional champion in the making.

The two-year-old Citation made his first start in a race at Havre de Grace, on April 22, 1947. He won the $4^1/_2$-furlong race by half a length. He was entered in his first stakes race on July 30—the Elementary Stakes at Washington Park. Citation won by two lengths.

Citation floundered in his next outing, the Washington Park Futurity, on August 16, losing to stablemate Bewitch. But he soon redeemed himself with victories in the Belmont Futurity and Pimlico Futurity races.

In his first season, Citation had won eight out of nine races. That was impressive enough, but his second season was no less than spectacular.

The three-year-old Citation triumphed at such distinguished starts as Hialeah Park, the Everglades Handicap, and the Flamingo Stakes. The **thoroughbred** was then taken back to Maryland to be prepared to run in the Triple Crown races—the Kentucky Derby, the Preakness, and the Belmont Stakes—the pinnacle of American racing. Tragedy struck before those races took place, however, when Citation's jockey, Al Snider, was lost in the Everglades during a fishing trip. Trainer Jimmy Jones decided to pair Citation with the legendary rider Eddie Arcaro. Arcaro and Citation made their racing debut at the Chesapeake Trial at Havre de Grace, on April 12, 1948. The new pairing was still immature, however, and Citation lost to Saggy by a length. But that was their only loss. Citation and Arcaro went on to win 15 races during the rest of the year.

They easily rode to victory in the Kentucky Derby, by $3^1/_2$ lengths. Citation powered through the Preakness Stakes, winning by $5^1/_2$ lengths. And at the Belmont Stakes a month later, Citation galloped to a Triple Crown victory by eight lengths. (In between the Preakness and the Belmont Stakes, incidentally, the sturdy Thoroughbred won the Jersey Derby by 11 lengths.) Citation won nine more races in 1948, including a

1945 Citation is born at Calumet Farm, Kentucky.

1947 Citation runs his first race, at Havre de Grace, and wins.

1948 Citation wins the Triple Crown with jockey Eddie Arcaro.

thoroughbred: an English breed of horses kept for racing purposes; originated from crossing English mares and Arabian stallions.

walkover in the Pimlico Special. In his first two seasons, Citation lost only twice. He had earned $865,150 in prize money, near the record.

It had been owner Warren Wright's dying wish that Citation reach the million-dollar mark in prize money. Before Wright's death in 1950, he asked Jimmy and Ben Jones to keep Citation in competition long enough to reach that pinnacle of success. At the start of 1950, Citation had taken $938,630 in earnings. He still had a way to go to crack the million-dollar barrier.

But this meant that the hard-working thoroughbred was kept racing until he was six years old—in retrospect, clearly too long. Toward the end of his racing days, Citation had a series of losses that, perhaps unfairly, diminished his legend. Injuries had kept Citation out of racing in 1949, but he was deemed fit enough to make a start in an allowance race on January 11, 1950. He took the victory by $1^1/_2$ lengths. He made eight more starts that year—but won only one other time. He lost four times to a single horse, Noor.

But the stalwart horse pulled out his final three starts. He triumphed in the Century Handicap and the American Handicap. Citation capped off his career with a victory in the Hollywood Gold Cup. In his last two races, Citation won over his old stablemate, Bewitch. The Hollywood Gold Cup alone brought $100,000 in prize money to Citation, bringing his career earnings to $1,085,760.

Citation was finally retired from racing in mid-1951. At that point the sport's only million-dollar-earner, the beautiful bay was retired to stud at Calumet Farms. He produced several notable offspring, including Fabius, runner-up in the 1956 Kentucky Derby. However, none of his progeny could come close to matching their sire's brilliant career. The stalwart horse died on August 8, 1970, at age 25. ◆

Clemens, Roger

AUGUST 4, 1962– ● BASEBALL PLAYER

For nearly 20 years, Roger Clemens has dominated hitters like no American League pitcher since Walter Johnson. Playing much of his career in tiny Fenway Park during an age when good pitching was scarce and hitting was plentiful, Clemens nevertheless won a record five Cy Young Awards and became the last starting pitcher to win the Most Valuable Player (MVP) award.

Born in Dayton, Ohio, Clemens was drafted out of high school by the New York Mets in 1981 but opted to attend the University of Texas instead. A star pitcher for the Longhorns, the 6′ 4″ Clemens awed scouts with a fastball clocked at over 90 miles per hour and an excellent forkball. He reentered the draft in 1983 and was picked on the first round by Boston. Clemens blew through the minor leagues, and by 1984 he was already in the major leagues as a relief pitcher and spot starter, going 9–4. Unfortunately, his second season was hardly as impressive: Clemens injured his shoulder, and ended up pitching in only 15 games in 1985.

Clemens made a swift recovery, and only two weeks into the 1986 season, on April 29, 1986, he set a major league record by striking out 20 batters in a game. Amazingly, he would match his own record 10 years later as a member of the Toronto Blue Jays. But 1986 was a breakout season for the "Rocket," as he was called, leading the Red Sox to their first pennant in 11 years and winning the Cy Young Award and MVP, thanks to a 24–4 record. The Red Sox would lose to the Mets in seven games that year in heartbreaking fashion.

Clemens rebounded to win the Cy Young again in 1987 and led the Red Sox to the Division title in 1990 with a 21–6 record and a 1.93 **earned run average**. But his brilliant 1990 season was marred by his second inning ejection in a playoff game versus Oakland, a result of Clemens cursing out home plate umpire Terry Cooney. The Red Sox would go on to lose to the A's, and Clemens was severely criticized for losing control at a critical time—he received a five game suspension and a $10,000 fine for his gaffe.

Clemens won his third Cy Young the following season, but beginning in 1993, he suffered through a four-year rough patch marked by mediocre pitching and an underachieving Red Sox team. Many felt Clemens' reign of dominance had come to an end, and following the 1996 season, Clemens surprisingly rebuked a contract offer from the Red Sox and signed with Toronto as a free agent. In his first season as a Blue Jay, Clemens silenced his nay-sayers as he won his fourth Cy Young award and became the first American League pitcher to win the Triple Crown in 51 years, leading the league in wins (21), ERA (2.05)

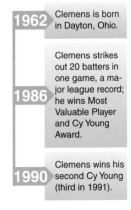

1962   Clemens is born in Dayton, Ohio.

Clemens strikes out 20 batters in one game, a major league record;
1986   he wins Most Valuable Player and Cy Young Award.

Clemens wins his
1990   second Cy Young (third in 1991).

earned run average (ERA): baseball statistic measuring performance of pitchers; calculated by dividing the total of earned runs scored against a pitcher by the total number of innings pitched, then multiplying that number by nine.

and strikeouts (292). Clemens duplicated those feats again in 1998, becoming the first pitcher to win five Cy Young awards. That year, he also set a league record by recording 20 straight victories, three more than the previous record. And after two dominant seasons in Toronto, he was traded to the New York Yankees in 1999 for a package of players including 1998 World Series hero David Wells. Clemens was the winning pitcher in the Yankees World Series-clinching victory.

Clemens owns a career 247–134 record, and is currently ninth on the career strikeouts list. He has the most wins and strikeouts of any active pitcher and with four more good seasons, he could join the elite 300-victory club. A future Hall of Famer, Clemens lives in Houston with his wife and four children. ◆

Clemente, Roberto

AUGUST 18, 1934–JANUARY 1, 1973 ● BASEBALL PLAYER

Baseball star Roberto Walker Clemente was born on August 18, 1934, in Carolina, Puerto Rico, a comfortable suburb of the capital of San Juan that remained his home. His father was the foreman on a sugarcane plantation and his mother ran a grocery store for the plantation workers.

His father planned for Roberto, the youngest in a large family, to become an engineer. But in high school Roberto was such an outstanding baseball player that at age 17 he received a bonus of $500 to play on the Santurce Cangrejeros team in the Puerto Rican League. Clemente played for Santurce for three seasons: the winters of 1951–52, 1952–53, and 1953–54. He hit .356 in his third season.

In the major leagues during the early 1950s, an informal quota on black players still existed, as well as prejudices against Spanish-speaking players. Yet Clemente seemed such an excellent prospect that the Brooklyn Dodgers signed him to play for their Montreal farm club for the 1954 season. Because Clemente was subject to the baseball draft at the end of the season, the Dodgers played him infrequently, hoping that other teams would overlook his great ability. But in November 1954 the Pittsburgh Pirates, entitled to the first draft pick because they had finished last in the National League, selected Clemente. He would play for the Pirates for his entire career.

1961 Clemente leads the National League in batting (again in 1964, 1965, and 1967).

1972 Clemente collects his 3000th hit.

1973 On January 1, Clemente is killed in a plane crash on a mercy mission for earthquake victims in Nicaragua.

1973 Clemente is voted into the Baseball Hall of Fame (five-year waiting period waived).

During his first five seasons beginning in 1955, Clemente hit .255, .311, .253, .289, and .296, a decent but not outstanding record. His career took off in 1960, when he hit .314 and helped the Pirates win the National League pennant and then the World Series against the New York Yankees. For 11 of the remaining 12 years of his career, Clemente hit over .300 for a lifetime batting average of .317. He won the batting championship four times, his highest average being .357 in 1967. Clemente was a line-drive rather than a power hitter. His highest home run total was 29 in 1966 and his career total was just 240, but with the help of his running speed he had 440 doubles and 166 triples during his career. He became known for his ability to hit any pitch within the strike zone and many outside of it, even though many of his swings were awkward.

In right field, Clemente was one of the best outfielders in the game. His strong arm could throw a ball not only at rifle speed but with amazing accuracy. When he was not throwing runners out, he was intimidating them into foregoing the extra base. In addition, his practice of making basket catches at the waist thrilled fans. He won 11 Gold Glove awards.

His overall skills got Clemente to baseball's annual All-Star game 12 times and won him the National League's Most Valuable Player award in 1966. Yet he did not receive the recognition due him until the 1971 World Series between the Pirates and the Baltimore Orioles. His .414 batting average and his participation in key plays during the "fall classic" were essential to Pittsburgh's 4 games to 3 victory and won him the Most Valuable Player award for the Series. (His salary was $100,000 that year.) In September 1972 Clemente became only the 11th player to reach the 3,000-hit plateau.

A humanitarian who worked for the youth and poor of Puerto Rico, Clemente agreed in 1972 to head Puerto Rico's relief effort for Nicaragua, whose capital of Managua had been hit

"He had about him a touch of royalty."
Bowie Kuhn, baseball commissioner, on Roberto Clemente

by a devastating earthquake. On January 1, 1973, Clemente boarded a plane carrying supplies for Nicaragua. The plane crashed shortly after takeoff from San Juan International Airport, and all aboard were killed. Clemente left behind his wife, Vera, and three children. He was elected to the Baseball Hall of Fame later in 1973 when Baseball waived the usual minimum wait of five years after the end of a player's career. ◆

Cobb, Ty

DECEMBER 18, 1886–JULY 17, 1961 ● BASEBALL PLAYER

Tyrus Raymond Cobb was born December 18, 1886 in Narrows, Georgia to 15-year-old Amanda Cobb and William Hershel Cobb. His distinguished lineage included Revolutionary War heroes and two Civil War brigadier generals. In 1893, the Cobb family moved to Royston, Georgia, where like his overbearing father, young Ty developed a nasty personality. Cobb's bitterness was cemented by a tragic incident in 1905, when his mother fatally shot his father, who'd been poking around outside her bedroom window one night. William Cobb reportedly suspected his younger wife of infidelity and climbed the roof porch outside her window. Amanda Cobb mistook him for a burglar.

During his baseball career, Cobb was known as "the Georgia Peach," but it had nothing to do with sweetness. His 24-year career, played mostly as a Detroit Tiger, was characterized by hatred of nearly everyone different from him. That not only included players in opposing uniforms, but also people of other races.

Stories of Cobb's maliciousness and maniacal will to win are legendary. It was rumored that in order to injure opponents, he sharpened his spikes like razors and slid into bases with his feet high. Even more shock-

Ty Cobb perfects his swing.

ing are the stories about his off-the-field racism and belligerence, such as the day he stepped in some freshly poured asphalt while walking in Detroit. When a construction worker, who happened to be black, yelled at Cobb, Cobb slapped the man, knocking him to the ground and leading to a lawsuit that Cobb settled out of court.

Despite his personality off the field, Cobb's place in the Major League Baseball record book argues his having been the most unstoppable hitter of all time. When he retired in 1928, he held more than 90 records, including a .367 lifetime batting average, 12 batting titles (including 9 in a row) and 2,245 runs scored—all records that still stand. Three times Cobb batted above .400. His 892 career stolen bases, including a record 35 steals of home, made him the most feared base runner of his day. His 4,191 career hits was one of baseball's most enduring marks, standing until broken by Pete Rose 57 years later.

In 1907, his first regular season, Cobb hit .350 to win the batting title. It was his first of nine batting titles in a row. His Detroit Tigers won the American League pennant that year, but lost the World Series to the Chicago Cubs in four straight games when Cobb hit just .200.

Cobb batted .324 in 1908 and .377 in 1909 to win batting titles. In 1909, he also led the league with 9 home runs and 107 RBIs, to win the Triple Crown, which is awarded when a player leads the league in batting average, home runs and RBI. In both years, the Tigers won the American League pennant, and in 1908 they again met the Cubs in the World Series. This time Cobb played considerably better, batting .368. The Tigers still lost in five games.

During the 1909 season, Cobb got into a fight with a black hotel manager in Cleveland and slashed him with a knife. Police were waiting in Ohio with a warrant for his arrest as the Tigers traveled by train to Pittsburgh to play the Pirates in the World Series. Anticipating the arrest, Cobb went to the World Series via Canada, and batted only .231 against the Pirates, who beat his Tigers in seven games. Cobb never appeared in another World Series.

His best year was 1911, when he batted .420 to lead the league. He led the league in seven other offensive categories too, including hits (248), runs (147), RBIs (144) and stolen bases (83). Except for the stolen base total, all were career bests for Cobb, who was awarded the American League's first Most Valuable Player award.

1886 Tyrus Raymond Cobb is born in Narrows, Georgia.

1907 Cobb wins batting title by hitting .350 (first of nine consecutive batting titles).

1909 Cobb wins the Triple Crown: he leads the league in batting average, home runs, and runs batted in.

1936 Cobb is one of six original inductees into the Baseball Hall of Fame.

*"He would climb
a mountain to
take a punch at
an echo."*

Arthur "Bugs"
Baer, on Ty Cobb

In 1912, he batted .410 to become the first player to hit .400 or better two years in a row. Despite his success on the field, his uncontrollable rages continued. During one game, he went into the stands and beat up a heckler—a man who was missing one hand and three fingers of the other due to an industrial accident. American League President Ban Johnson suspended Cobb for 10 games. But his teammates refused to play as long as he was suspended. Detroit was forced to field a team of sandlot players who lost one game 24-2 before the real Tigers' players ended their strike.

In 1915, Cobb stole 96 bases, a record that lasted nearly 50 years. His streak of nine consecutive batting titles ended the next year, when Tris Speaker's .386 average beat his .371. In 1921, Cobb became Detroit's player-manager. As a player he remained among the game's best hitters, batting .338 or better the next six years, including a .401 average in 1922. He left the Tigers following the 1926 season, and signed with the Philadelphia Athletics. He batted .357 in 1927 and .323 in 1928, and became the first player with more than 4,000 career hits.

Cobb was one of six original inductees to Baseball's Hall of Fame in 1936, receiving more votes than any of the other original members: Babe Ruth, Honus Wagner, Walter Johnson, Christy Mathewson and Walter Johnson. His shrewdness led to several innovations that changed the game. He started the practice of swinging several bats in the on-deck circle so that one would feel light when he stepped up the plate. During the off-season, he wore lead-weighted shoes, so his legs would feel light after switching to normal shoes at the start of the season. His cunning was not limited to baseball. He bought a great deal of Coca-Cola stock at just over $1 a share, and made a fortune in the stock market. He was reportedly worth $12 million when he died on July 17, 1961 in Atlanta. But only four people from baseball attended his funeral, proof that his malicious play didn't make many friends. ◆

Coe, Sebastian

SEPTEMBER 29, 1956– ● TRACK AND FIELD ATHLETE

Sebastian Newbold Coe, Olympic gold medal winner and one of the great names in the annals of British sport, was born in London, England, on September 29, 1956. He grew up in Sheffield, England, which he considers home.

Coe's career as a world record–setting middle-distance runner took root when he was 12 years old and began running with a local track club, Sheffield's Hallamshire Harriers. As a teenager Coe won school and county championships in cross country and in 1,500- and 3,000-meter races. He enrolled in Loughborough University to study economics and social history and, in 1977, won his first major race as an international competitor, the 800-meters at the European Championships in Spain.

In 1973, when Coe was still in high school, his father—who was also his coach—predicted that his son would shave five seconds off the world 1,500-meter record by 1980. Coe did better than that. Over a period of just 41 days in 1979 he broke not one but three world records—the 800-meter and mile in Oslo, Norway, and the 1,500-meter in Zurich, Switzerland. Coe was the first man in more than 50 years to hold world records at both 800 and 1,500 meters. The following July he set a world record for the 1,000-meter race in Oslo. That win gave Coe an incredible four world records at the same time.

One of the world's great sports stories during the early 1980s was Coe's intense rivalry with fellow Briton Steve Ovett, who also competed in middle-distance races, although the two rarely ran in the same event. They competed against each other for the first time in 1978 in an 800-meter race in Prague, Czechoslovakia, though neither won. Beginning in 1979, Coe and Ovett alternated holding the world record in the mile, beginning with Coe's Oslo time of 3 minutes, 49 seconds (3:49) on July 17 of that year. The following summer, Ovett shaved two-tenths of a second off Coe's record. Then, in 1981, the record toppled in quick succession over a 10-day period in August. On August 19, in a race in Zurich, Coe regained the record with a time of 3:48.53, only to see Ovett reclaim the record on August 26 in Koblenz, Germany, with a time of 3:48.40. Just two days later, in Brussels, Belgium, Coe took the record back with a time of 3:47.33, a record that stood for nearly four years before being broken by another Briton, Steve Cram.

Although that 10-day period captivated the world, the rivalry between Coe and Ovett actually had reached its climax in the 1980 Olympics in Moscow. Coe, the more graceful but reserved runner, was predicted to win the 800-meter; Ovett, the more powerful but gregarious runner, was the pick in the 1,500. The two titans confounded the experts, though. Coe finished in second place in the 800-meters to win the silver, but he rebounded with a strong finish around the final curve to win the

1956 Coe born in London, England.

1979 Coe breaks world records in the 800-meter, the 1,500-meter, and the mile events.

1980 Coe wins the gold medal at the Moscow Olympics for the 1,500-meter.

1984 Coe sets world record for 1,500-meter (and wins gold medal) at the Los Angeles Olympics.

Coe came back in the 1984 Olympic Games in Los Angeles to capture two more medals, setting an Olympic record in the 1,500-meter and winning silver in the 800-meter.

gold medal in the 1,500-meters; Ovett could do no better than third in the race.

Coe continued to topple records in 1981. In addition to his two mile records, he broke the record for the 800-meter in Florence, Italy, with a time of 1:41.73, a record that stood until 1997. In Oslo that same year, he recaptured the record at 1,000-meters with a time of 2:12.18, a record that still stood in late 1999. Over the next two years, his racing career was interrupted by illness, but he came back in the 1984 Olympic Games in Los Angeles to capture two more medals, setting an Olympic record in the 1,500-meter and winning silver in the 800-meter. Coe won his final medals in the 1986 European Championships, taking gold at 800-meters and silver in the 1,500. Once again illness intervened, and he failed to make the 1988 Olympic team. He ran his last competitive race in 1989 and retired from running. In all he won four Olympic medals, two of them gold, and set eight world records during his career.

In 1992 Coe took part in one more race when he ran for and won a seat as a Conservative member of the British Parliament for Falmouth and Camborne. His career in British politics continued in 1994 when he was appointed a Parliamentary Private Secretary and, in 1996, a government whip. In 1997 he was appointed Private Secretary to William Hague, the leader of Parliament's opposition party.

Despite his new career in politics, Coe's interest in sports continued. He was vice chairman of Britain's Sports Council from 1986 to 1989, a steward of the British Boxing Board of Control from 1994 to 1998, and a member of the Sport for All Committee and the International Olympic Committee. He also served as president of a charitable organization that gives disabled children the opportunity to participate in sports by providing them with specially built wheelchairs. In 1991 he was awarded the coveted Order of the British Empire. ◆

Comaneci, Nadia

November 12, 1961– ● Gymnast

"I have no faith in human perfectibility," wrote Edgar Allan Poe. But he never saw Nadia Comaneci perform. At the 1976 Summer Olympics in Montreal, the Romanian gymnast—who was all of 14 years old at the time—earned the first perfect score of 10 at an Olympic gymnastic event and went on to redefine the possibilities of her sport.

In a sport where age 25 is considered "old," youth is the rule rather than the exception. Nadia Comaneci began her gymnastics career at age six. On a school recess one afternoon in 1967, the six-year-old Nadia and a friend were gleefully emulating gymnastic moves on the playground, under the rapt gaze of Bela Karolyi, the gymnastic coach at a nearby sports school. Stunned by her effortless athleticism, Karolyi watched in frustration as Nadia and her friend melted into the throng of students and disappeared. He searched frantically for the youngster. "I knew I would never leave that school until I found them," Karolyi recalled. "I went into each class of that kindergarten looking for them. . . . The third time around I asked each class, 'Who loves gymnastics?' In each class a few of the little girls would raise their hands. But in one class two of them sprang up and shouted, 'We do! We do!' and I had found them. One was Nadia Comaneci. The other one is now a very promising ballerina."

Nadia Comaneci on the balance beam.

Nothing in Comaneci's background seemed to mark her for such a special vocation. The daughter of an auto mechanic and a hospital caretaker, she was born on November 12, 1961, in Onesti, Romania, near the Carpathian Mountains. Nadia's parents eagerly seized on the opportunity for their serious-minded daughter to constructively channel her prodigious energies. Even at that age, she seemed to have the focus of a champion. Her mother recalled, "She was always a very lively child, but she never smiled very often. She was always serious—and emotionally strong. I don't remember seeing her cry." Observing her after her enrollment at his sports school, Karolyi anticipated great

1961 Comaneci is born in Onesti, Romania.

1972 Comaneci wins three gold medals in her first international competition.

1976 At the Montreal Olympics, Comaneci scores an unprecedented perfect 10 on uneven parallel bars; she goes on to earn six more perfect 10's, and three gold medals.

1980 Comaneci wins gold medals in balance-beam and floor exercise at Moscow Olympics.

things for her: "She is intelligent, dedicated, loves the sport, and has a strong spirit; she knows no fear."

Comaneci made her competitive debut in 1969 at age seven, placing 13th at the Romanian National Junior Championship. Karolyi thought it a good beginning, but he kept up the pressure on his budding star. "I gave her a little sealskin Eskimo doll I had bought in Canada when I was on a handball trip," he told a reporter. "I said, 'This is for you—to remind you never to finish 13th again.'" Fired with the ambition to be the best, Comaneci trained ever harder and captured the junior championship in 1970 and won the Romanian title for her age group the next two years. In 1972, in her first international competition, she went up against Olympic contenders from all the Eastern bloc countries and came away with three gold medals. Only 10, she was ineligible for the Olympics despite her dominating performance.

In 1975, the first year in which she was allowed to compete in senior international events, she entered the European championships at Skein, Norway, where she was up against the likes of the Soviet Ludmilla Turishcheva, a five-time European champion. Described by one reporter at Skein as a "13-year-old fragile-looking child . . . all legs and rib cage and no pelvis to speak of," Comaneci made short work of the competition, winning the overall four-event competition and capturing gold medals in long-horse vaulting, the uneven bars, and the balance beam. In the floor exercises she won the silver medal, finishing behind the Soviet Union's Nelli Kim. Her spectacular performance led the European sportswriters and the International Gymnastic Federation to vote her the Sportswoman of the Year for 1975.

Comaneci was ready to unfurl her dramatic skills before all the world at the 1976 Summer Olympics in Montreal. As a warm-up, she competed in various U.S. cities and Toronto in Olympic qualifying events. In the first American Cup competition, she scored the first perfect 10 in American gymnastics history by flawlessly executing a full twist back into a somersault in which she actually topped the inventor of the move, Mitsuo Tsukahara of Japan, who scored only a 9.3 in the event. Her coach commented, "At the American Cup competition she performed for the first time in the history of women's gymnastics a backward double salto, a double flip. And then she finished with a double salto, with a twist. It was remarkable, but for her it wasn't difficult."

When the Montreal Olympics opened in July 1976, the 14-year-old Comaneci was already considered the world's leading female gymnast, and she did not disappoint the capacity crowds and worldwide viewing audience who eagerly anticipated her performance. In her very first routine, on July 18, 1976, she stunned the assemblage with an unprecedented perfect 10 on the uneven parallel bars. Over the next three days of competition, she earned six more 10's and won gold medals for the individual all-around, the balance beam, and the uneven parallel bars.

She returned to Romania a heroine but denies reports that the Communist government quietly lavished riches on her. "When I went back to Romania, in 1976, I had to live like everybody else. I didn't have privileges. I had to stand in lines, and miss out, and be followed by the police. I had no money, no special treatment. It was all rumors."

Despite the difficulties of life in Romania, Comaneci never veered from her quest for excellence, winning the Chunichi Cup in Japan in 1976 and another European championship in 1978. Elena Mukhina of the Soviet Union wrested the world title from her in 1978, but Comaneci recaptured the European championship and the World Cup in 1979. At the 1980 Moscow Olympics, Comaneci captured two more gold medals in the balance-beam and floor exercise and a silver medal in the team competition, despite losing the all-around competition to Elena Davidova of the Soviet Union.

The steely perfection of her athleticism masked emotional turmoil that had built up over years of unrelenting pressure from Karolyi, a master manipulator who put her through eight-hour training days and controlled every detail of her life until he defected to the United States in 1981. Responding to rumors of suicide attempts, Comaneci told a reporter, "I didn't try to die, I drank shampoo by mistake. I didn't get sick, but I got scared, so I went to the hospital and got flushed." Asked about possible drug use, she said, "I never saw any drugs. One time, I had to lose eight kilos in three weeks to compete. It was hard: a crash diet. I ate very little. But I knew I had to do it, so I did. I was dizzy competing, but I was often dizzy."

After retiring from active competition in 1984, Comaneci became an international gymnastics judge for a while and helped to coach the 1984 Romanian Olympic team. In 1989, she defected to the United States, where she spent several directionless years, fitfully trying to make it as a model. In the early 1990s she met the American gymnastic champion Bart

"She has three qualities. The physical qualities—strength, speed, agility. The intellectual qualities—intelligence and the power to concentrate. And Nadia has courage."

Coach Bela
Karolyi on
Nadia Comaneci

Olympic Boycotts

Even though the Olympic Games are dedicated to the spirit of peace and cooperation among nations, they have not been immune from the chronic strife of international politics. The most dramatic and tragic political incursion into the Olympics was the massacre of nine Israeli athletes by Palestinian terrorists at the 1972 games in Munich, Germany. But international conflict has also marred Olympic competition through nonviolent forms of protest, the most prominent being boycotts by one or more nations against the games over Olympic policy or over conflicts entirely unrelated to the Olympics.

The first form of boycott protest over the policies of the International Olympic Committee (IOC) itself was a prominent issue at the 1976 games in Montreal, Canada. African nations led by Tanzania (along with Iraq and Guyana) boycotted the games that year to protest the presence of New Zealand, whose rugby team had recently made a tour of South Africa, a nation then governed by a white supremacist regime. The IOC refused to bar the New Zealanders on the grounds that the travels of various national teams were beyond its control, especially in non-Olympic sports like rugby. Only Tanzania staged a total boycott; the other African nations arrived in Montreal, but when faced the IOC's intransigence, decided to leave before the games began.

The 1979 Soviet invasion of Afghanistan cast a long shadow over the 1980 games in Moscow. The U.S. policy of vigorous opposition to the invasion extended to the American Olympic team, which President Jimmy Carter ordered not to participate in the Moscow games at the risk of revocation of their passports. Because Carter pressured other nations to withdraw from the games as well, participation was a third less than it had been four years earlier. Japan and West Germany were among the absentees that year; Great Britain and Australia formally supported the boycott but did not bar individual athletes from participating. The Western nations have since disparaged the results of the 1980 games, claiming that the level of competition compromised the integrity of the medals.

Still smarting over its snub by the Western powers at the 1980 Olympics, the Soviets returned the favor by organizing a boycott of the 1984 games in Los Angeles (their ostensible reason for not attending was a professed concern over the adequacy of the security arrangements). Although the Soviet bloc nations observed the boycott, a record number of nations participated in the Los Angeles games. Unfortunately, since the absent nations had accounted for 58 percent of the gold medals at the 1976 games, the quality of the competition once again suffered badly. Nevertheless, the 1984 games, the first since 1896 to have been mounted without governmental financial aid, were a popular and commercial success.

Conner; they married in 1996 and are now co-owners of the Bart Conner Gymnastics Academy in Norman, Oklahoma.

Although seemingly happy now, Nadia Comaneci still seldom smiles. As she once said, "I know how to smile, I know how to laugh, I know how to play. But I know how to do these things only after I have finished my mission." ◆

Connor, Bart

MARCH 28, 1958– ● GYMNAST

A native of Chicago, Illinois, Bart Conner began his journey toward an Olympic gold medal in gymnastics at the age of 10, when he discovered that his boyhood fondness for doing headstands, flips, and cartwheels could become a serious athletic pursuit. After Bart's six-week physical education course in the fourth grade, his teacher was so impressed with his natural talents that he took Bart to meet the gymnastics coach of nearby Niles West High School. After a brief audition, Bart found himself working out with the high school team twice a week in addition to working out with kids his own age at the Northwest Suburban YMCA.

Conner's many hours of diligent training at the high school and the Y paid off when, at the age of 14, he won his first national competition, the Amateur Athletics Union (AAU) Junior Olympics. Two years later he placed first at the first United States Gymnastics Federation (USGF) Junior National Championships. By the time Conner graduated from high school in 1976, he had already won the AAU Junior National Championship, the USGF Junior National Championship, and a Co-Championship of the USGF Senior Nationals. He had also been selected for the U.S. Pan Am team and made the U.S. men's gymnastics squad for the 1976 Olympics in Montreal.

Overwhelmed with college scholarship offers, Conner chose Oklahoma University because he "had a gut intuition, an intuition that Oklahoma was where I *wanted* to be. . . . Primarily, I liked the coach at Oklahoma. I had first heard of Paul Ziert when he was training gymnasts at a high school in Chicago." His intuition was borne out as Ziert proved to be a superb, dedicated mentor who shepherded Conner through all the steps—and the many setbacks—on the path to his Olympic triumph in 1984.

Conner's gymnastics training and travels were so demanding that it took him eight years to complete his undergraduate studies at Oklahoma. "Between the '76 Olympics and the '84 Olympics, I trained for and competed in the World University Games in Varna, Bulgaria; the World Championships, in Strasbourg; the World Cup in São Paulo; another World Cup in Tokyo; The Champions All competition in London; the World Championships in Fort Worth; the 1980 American Olympic

> *"Find your F.O.C.U.S.: Find what your talents are; Observe your mentors; Challenge yourself (set goals); Utilize your resources; Strive to make a difference."*
>
> Bart Conner

1958 Conner is born in Chicago, Illinois.

1974 Conner places first at U.S. Gymnastics Federation Junior National Championships.

1984 Conner earns two perfect 10's and wins gold medal at Olympics in Los Angeles.

team trials; the World Championships in Moscow; the World Championships in Budapest; as well as numerous United States and NCAA championships throughout the country," Conner said.

At the peak of his athletic powers in 1980, Conner was poised to achieve Olympic glory in that year's Summer Olympics in Moscow after finishing as the highest scorer in the trials. But on the final day of the trials, he tore his biceps, an injury that would likely have limited his performance at the games. Undaunted by injury, Conner's Olympic hopes were nevertheless blotted out by international politics—President Jimmy Carter announced that the United States planned to boycott the games in protest of the Soviet invasion of Afghanistan.

Despite his disappointment, Conner soon set his sights on the 1984 games, scheduled for Los Angeles. In his words, "In 1981 I was preoccupied with several major competitions, the World Championships, the American Cup, and my responsibilities to my college gymnastics team. The Olympics seemed far away. Then suddenly, in the summer of 1982, somebody casually mentioned something about the Olympics, and it came back to me. '*Good grief! It's just two summers away!*,' I thought." A major preparatory competition was the December 1983 Chunichi Cup in Japan. Conner had just begun his routine on the rings when disaster struck. As he later recalled, "Suddenly, right next to my ear, I heard that sound. A fast, loud rip, like when you yank apart pieces of Velcro. The pain was hot and sharp. My left biceps had ripped off the bone and snapped down my arm like a window shade."

With the help of Coach Ziert and a leading sports therapist, Keith Kleven, Conner enlisted the surgical talents of Dr. Lonnie Paulos in Salt Lake City, Utah. Three days after the surgery he was in Kleven's clinic in Las Vegas to begin a grueling rehab regimen aimed at a gold-medal-caliber performance in the Olympics, then only seven months away. Despite Ziert's apprehensions, by May 1984 Conner felt ready to enter the National Championships in Chicago, which counted 40 percent toward qualification for the Olympic team. On his first event, the floor exercise, he faltered badly and had to withdraw from the rest of the competition. The Olympic coach, Abie Grossfield, was not encouraging: "We don't need Bart if he's not at his best," he said.

With the final trails coming up in June in Jacksonville, Florida, Ziert and Conner returned to Oklahoma for three weeks of relentless training to take a last shot at the Olympics. At the Jacksonville trials, Conner summoned all his determination and strength and just made the team—his sixth-place finish was last among the qualifiers, but he had his ticket to the games in Los Angeles.

Although the level of competition at the 1984 Olympic Games was compromised by a retaliatory Soviet boycott, the U.S. men's gymnastics team still faced formidable competition from the Japanese and the Chinese, who had beaten the Russians at the World Championships earlier that year. Having surmounted a potentially catastrophic injury to barely claw his way onto the team, Conner vanquished all pain and doubt: he demolished the competition on the parallel bars, earning two perfect scores of 10 on his way to a gold medal in that event. He placed fifth in the floor exercise, the highest finish ever for an American up to that time. He also took home a team gold medal.

Through pain, injury, and disappointment, Bart Conner had finally reached the end of that long journey that began with a few boyish headstands at the Northwest Suburban YMCA 16 years earlier. His goals fulfilled, Conner retired from competition after the 1984 Olympics to become a coach and a TV gymnastics commentator. In 1996 he married the star of the 1976 women's Olympic gymnastic competition, Nadia Comaneci, a native of Romania. Today they are co-owners of the Bart Conner Gymnastics Academy in Norman, Oklahoma. ◆

> Conner vanquished all pain and doubt: he demolished the competition on the parallel bars, earning two perfect scores of 10 on his way to a gold medal in that event.

Connolly, Maureen

SEPTEMBER 17, 1934–JUNE 21, 1969 ● TENNIS PLAYER

Had her career not been cut short by an accident, Maureen Connolly might have become one of the finest of all female tennis players. The first woman to win the Grand Slam—victories in the Australian Open, French Open, Wimbledon, and the U.S. Open in a single year—she also became, at age 14, the youngest girl to win the U.S. national junior girls championship.

Born in San Diego, California, Maureen Catherine Connolly loved horses as a child and wanted to take up horseback riding, but her divorced mother could not afford riding lessons. While playing at a playground near her home at age nine, she

Maureen Connolly
attempts a backhand.

"There is nothing like competition. It teaches you early in life to win and lose, and, when you lose, to put your chin out instead of dropping it."
Maureen Connolly

watched people playing tennis and became interested in that as well. After she began playing, local tennis pro Wilbur Folsom noticed her natural abilities and offered to give her lessons. Within only a few months Connolly entered her first tournament and emerged as runner-up.

Soon afterward, Connolly was introduced to Eleanor Tennant, a highly respected teacher who had coached such champions as Helen Wills, Alice Marble, and Bobby Riggs. Tennant helped Connolly develop her talents, and Connolly worked extremely hard—practicing three to four hours each day, five days a week, all year long. Within a short time she had learned to execute her skills superbly, and her efforts paid off handsomely as she began winning tournaments and breaking records. Seeing her play, Helen Wills predicted that she would become national champion.

That prediction came true soon enough. In 1949, at age 14, Connolly won the U.S. National Junior Championship. That same year she also won 56 straight matches. By this time Connolly had been given the nickname "Little Mo" by her fans and the media—an allusion to "Big Mo"—the U.S. battleship *Missouri* —and a reference to her cannon-like drives. The following year, Connolly repeated her singles victory at the junior championships and also won the doubles title as well. Her efforts that year earned her a number 10 ranking among women, making Connolly the youngest person of either sex to appear among the top 10.

Connolly did not defend her title at the junior nationals in 1951; instead, she became the second youngest to win the women's division title, defeating Shirley Fry. Later that year she also became the youngest player at the time to compete on the U.S. Wightman Cup team, and her singles victories helped win the cup that year. Connolly also played on the Wightman Cup team in 1952, 1953, and 1954. During her four years of Wightman Cup play, she amassed records of 7–0 in singles and 2–0 in doubles. In 1952, the U.S. Ladies Lawn Tennis Association recognized her notable contributions to tennis by awarding her its Service Bowl.

Connolly held the number one U.S. ranking from 1951 to 1953, and was the undisputed world leader from 1952 to 1954. She won her first Wimbledon title in 1952 and repeated that victory in each of the next two years. In 1953, at age 19, Connolly also won the U.S. Open, Australian Open, and French Open, becoming the youngest woman to win the coveted grand slam. By the end of her career, she had won a total of three U.S. Opens, three Wimbledons, one Australian Open, and two French Opens. She also earned a spectacular record, winning all but one match between September 1951 and July 1954. During that time the Associated Press named her Woman Athlete of the Year three times in a row.

Just a few weeks after her Wimbledon victory in 1954, Connolly had a tragic accident that ended her tennis playing career. While horseback riding she was struck by a truck, which severely damaged her leg and left her unable to play competitively. The year after the accident she wed Olympic equestrian Norman Brinker. Although unable to play, Connolly taught and coached players. She also promoted junior tennis through the Maureen Connolly Brinker Foundation, which sponsors international team competition for girls 18 years old and younger.

Like her brilliant career, Connolly's life was cut short as well. Diagnosed with terminal cancer in 1969, she died later that year. A member of the International Tennis Hall of Fame (she was inducted in 1968), Connolly was also elected to the Women's Sports Foundation Hall of Fame in 1989. Each year at the U.S. national junior championships, an award named in her honor is presented to the girl who has shown exceptional ability and sportsmanship. ◆

1934 Connolly is born in San Diego, California.

1949 Connolly wins the U.S. National Junior Championship at age 14; "Little Mo" wins 56 straight matches.

1952 Connolly wins the first of three consecutive Wimbledons; she is named the Associated Press Woman Athlete of the Year (also in 1953 and 1954).

1953 At 19, Connolly becomes the youngest woman to win the Grand Slam.

Connors, Jimmy

SEPTEMBER 2, 1952– ● TENNIS PLAYER

With his fiery temperament, feisty attitude, quarrels with opponents and officials, and arrogant behavior on the court, Jimmy Connors gained a reputation in

Jimmy Connors returns a backhand.

his early years as a "bad boy" of tennis. However, his controversial and sometimes notorious behavior could not take away from the fact that he was a truly great tennis player. Connors mellowed in his later years, and his enthusiasm and personality eventually endeared him to his fans.

Born in Belleville, Illinois, Connors was introduced to tennis by his mother, Gloria Thompson Connors, a tennis teaching professional, and his grandmother, Bertha Thompson, who had been a tournament player. He began taking lessons from his mother at age three, and within two years had become quite proficient for a youngster. The first competition he won was at the Southern Illinois Tournament for boys age 10 and under. Between ages 8 and 16, Connors played in every U.S. national boys junior championship, but won only one singles title during that time.

Gloria Connors realized that her son needed another teacher to let him reach his full potential, so the family moved to Los Angeles, California, where Connors began training with pros Pancho Gonzales and Pancho Segura. After graduating from high school, Connors enrolled at the University of California at Los Angeles and won the National Collegiate Athletic Association (NCAA) singles championship in 1971. After only one year in college, Connors dropped out in order to play tennis professionally. When he turned professional Connors immediately became known as a maverick by refusing to join the Association of Tennis Pros (ATP), a newly formed union of male players.

In 1973, Connors' first year on the professional tour, he won his first two tournaments but lost his third, the Washington Indoors, to Stan Smith. At Wimbledon he upset Bob Hewitt in the first round but lost in the quarterfinals to Ilie Nastase. But Connors finished the year with 75 victories (matches, not tournaments), the most among the American males on the tour. The following year he lost in the early rounds at Wimbledon to

Alex Metreveli of the Soviet Union. But Connors bounced back, winning the U.S. Pro Championship by toppling the favorite, Arthur Ashe, in the finals. Connors also reached the quarterfinals of the U.S. Open, which he lost to John Newcombe. Later in the year he beat Arthur Ashe again to win the South African Open.

Controversy erupted in 1974 when Connors was banned from the French Open because he had signed to play in the World Team Tennis league, which the Association of Tennis Pros and French tennis authorities opposed. He entered the other three tournaments in tennis's Grand Slam, however, and won all three, claiming the titles at the Australian Open, Wimbledon, and the U.S. Open. He won both Wimbledon and the U.S. championship with crushing victories over Australian veteran Ken Rosewall. Because he had been denied entry at the French Open, Connors lost a possible chance to win the coveted Grand Slam.

In 1975 Connors lost in the finals of the Australian Open to John Newcombe, who praised his opponent's strong serve. At Wimbledon, Connors faced Arthur Ashe, whom he was suing because of statements made in connection with the controversy over the World Tennis Team league the year before. Many considered this to be a grudge match, and most players and spectators were clearly on the side of Ashe, who won the tournament.

Other players, such as John McEnroe, Bjorn Borg, and Ivan Lendl, began to eclipse Connors in the late 1970s and early 1980s. Nevertheless, he remained a strong competitor and amassed a number of impressive records. Connors won the U.S. Open four more times—in 1976, 1978, 1982, and 1983—and gained a second Wimbledon title in 1982. His victories at the 1982 and 1983 U.S. Open tournaments were against rising star Ivan Lendl, and he gained his 1982 Wimbledon title with an upset victory over the newest "bad boy" of tennis, John McEnroe.

Between 1974 and 1978 Connors won more than 50 tournaments and was ranked number one in the world for five years in a row. The time he spent ranked number one during this period—a total of 263 consecutive weeks—is second only to Ivan Lendl's 269 weeks as number one. In 1984 Connors became the first player to win 100 singles titles. At the U.S. Open in 1989, at the age of 37, he amazed spectators with a fourth-round upset of Stefan Edberg before losing in the quarterfinals. By this time, his attitude had mellowed and he had become a crowd favorite and respected "elder" of the sport.

1952 Connors is born in Belleville, Illinois.

1973 Connors defeats Arthur Ashe to win the U.S. Pro Championship.

1974 Connors wins the Australian Open, Wimbledon (also in 1982), and the U.S. Open (also in 1976, 1978, 1982, and 1983).

1984 Connors becomes the first player to win 100 singles titles.

Perhaps the most extraordinary year in Connors' career was 1991. Troubled by an injured wrist in 1990, he had played only three matches that year and slipped to number 936 in the world rankings. Surgery restored his wrist, and in 1991 he played 14 tournaments, including a phenomenal semifinals finish at the U.S. Open after beating John McEnroe and Aaron Krickstein. At age 39, Connors was the oldest semifinalist at the U.S. Open since Ken Rosewall lost the title 17 years earlier to none other than a 22-year-old Connors himself. Although he lost the semifinals to Jim Courier, and Stefan Edberg won the title, Connors was without doubt the fans' favorite.

Connors continued to impress the fans in 1992 when, on his 40th birthday, he won an early match in the U.S. Open against Jaime Oncins. He ended the year ranked number 83 in the world—a remarkable achievement for a player of his age in such a physically demanding sport. Connors finally retired from professional competition in 1993. He was elected to the International Tennis Hall of Fame in 1998. ◆

Cooper, Cynthia

APRIL 14, 1963– ● BASKETBALL PLAYER

Cynthia Cooper was born on Easter Sunday in Los Angeles, California. One of eight children, she didn't begin playing basketball until she was 16 years old, but when she was named Los Angeles high school player of the year just two years later, she gave notice that she was a talent to be watched. And for nearly two decades basketball fans around the world watched as Cooper grew into one of the most dominant players in the women's game.

Cooper enjoyed an outstanding career as a collegiate player at the University of Southern California, where she played from 1981 to 1984, then in the 1985–86 season. (She left basketball for a year after a younger brother died of stab wounds in 1984.) During her four years her teams compiled a 114–15 record and played in four NCAA tournaments, winning two NCAA titles (in 1983 and 1983) and playing in the 1986 tournament final. In 1982 she earned All-American honors as a freshman, in 1984 she was named to the NCAA All-West Regional tournament team, and in 1986 she was named to the All-Pacific West

Conference first team and to the NCAA All-Final Four tournament team. She ranks eighth among all-time career scorers at USC.

After college Cooper played professional basketball for 11 years in Europe, moving from league to league. It didn't matter what league she played in—she could score anywhere, leading her leagues in scoring 8 of the 11 years. Along the way, she became fluent in Spanish and Italian. During the 1986–87 season she played for Segovia in the Spanish league, and she was named most valuable player in the 1987 European All-Star game. She then moved to the Italian league, where she played for Parma (1987–94, 1996–97) and Alcamo (1994–96). She capped her career in Europe in the 1996 European Cup, in which she was leading scorer (37.5 points per game). European fans enjoyed the fast-paced style Cooper brought to their game.

Cynthia Cooper drives to the basket for the WNBA's Houston Comets.

In the meantime Cooper was a key player for the United States in international competition. She was a member of the gold-medal–winning World Championship and Goodwill Games teams in 1986 and 1990 (sinking 17 of 17 free throw attempts in the 1990 games); the Pan American Games team that took the gold in 1987; the gold-medal–winning 1988 Olympic team in Seoul, South Korea (leading her team with 27 points in the game against the Soviet Union), and the bronze-medal–winning 1992 Olympic team. She ranks fourth among U.S. women in all-time career points scored in Olympic competition with 109, while shooting over 51 percent from the field. She counts winning the 1988 Olympic gold medal and giving the medal to her mother as among her proudest moments.

In 1997 Cooper returned to the United States to join the Houston Comets in the newly formed Women's National Basketball Association (WNBA). Playing at guard, she quickly emerged as perhaps the best player in the league. In the WNBA's inaugural season she led the league in scoring with a

22.2 points per game average, shooting 47 percent from the field and scoring a record 44 points in one game. She led the Comets in six statistical categories and led the team to the WNBA championship. That year she was the only unanimous pick on the All-WNBA team and was a runaway winner of the league's most valuable player award. She was also named Most Valuable Player (MVP) of the league championship series.

As if to prove that these accomplishments were not a fluke, Cooper repeated them in 1998, when the Comets repeated as WNBA champions (and had an incredible 15–0 run to start the season) and Cooper repeated as league scoring leader (22.7), first-team All-WNBA, championship MVP, and league MVP. That year she was named Sportswoman of the Year by the Women's Sports Foundation. During the Comets 26–6 regular season in 1999 she maintained her consistent high level of play, averaging 22.1 points per game (including a 42-point performance against the Utah Starzz, a game she dedicated to her friend and fellow player Kim Perrot, who died that year), shooting over 46 percent from the field, and raising her free throw shooting percentage to over 89 percent. Once again she was the league's leading scorer, and again she was named to the all-WNBA first team and was MVP of the league championship series, which the Comets won for the third year in a row.

Cooper was active off the court as well. A strong motivational speaker, she began a foundation called Building Dreams to help young people focus on and attain their goals. In addition, she worked with General Motors to promote the fight against breast cancer. Cooper also found time to help raise seven nieces and nephews who lived with her in Houston. ◆

Court, Margaret Smith

JULY 16, 1942– ● TENNIS PLAYER

For sheer strength of performance, Margaret Smith Court is considered one of the greatest players in the history of women's tennis, noted especially for her powerful serve and exceptional endurance. The world's dominant female tennis player in the 1960s and early 1970s, Court was the second woman (after Maureen Connolly) to win the Grand Slam of tennis—capturing the singles titles at the Australian Open,

French Open, Wimbledon, and U.S. Open in the same year. Before her marriage to Barry Court in 1967, she went by her maiden name of Smith.

Born in the small town of Albury in New South Wales, Australia, Smith became one of the first Australian tennis greats from outside the nation's major cities. As a young girl, Smith was a bit of a tomboy who enjoyed many different sports, including soccer and cricket. She began playing tennis at age eight after sneaking into a local tennis club with friends to play on its courts. Although caught repeatedly, she nevertheless made a favorable impression on the club owner, Wally Rutter, who decided to make her a member in the club and start giving her tennis lessons when she was 10 years old.

Tennis gradually absorbed more of Smith's attention, especially after former world champion Frank Sedgman took an interest in her and invited her to Melbourne, Australia, to train there. In 1960, at age 18, Smith won her first major singles title at the Australian Senior International Championship, defeating Jan Lehane in the finals. This was also the first of a record 11 Australian singles titles, and the first of seven in a row.

Smith traveled abroad for the first time in 1961. Playing with former foe Lehane as her partner, she reached the doubles finals at Wimbledon, losing to the team of Karen Hantze and Billie Jean King. In singles play she won the All-Comers Championship in Kent, England, but was defeated in the semifinals of the Italian championship and in the quarterfinals of Wimbledon and the French Open.

Smith had a much better year in 1962, winning the Australian, Italian, French, and U.S. Open singles titles, but losing at Wimbledon to Billie Jean King in her first match of that tournament. Despite the loss at Wimbledon, Court finished the year as number one in the world rankings.

In 1963 Smith won her third consecutive Australian Open singles championship, failed to defend her title in the French Open, finally defeated her rival Billie Jean King at Wimbledon, and lost the U.S. Open. In mixed doubles play in 1963, Court won the Grand Slam, winning each of the four major tournaments with her partner, fellow Australian Kenneth Fletcher.

Smith won the singles titles at the Australian, Italian, and German championships in 1964, but lost at the French Open, U.S. Open, and Wimbledon. The following year she won the

1942 Court is born in Albury, New South Wales, Australia.

1962 Court wins the Australian, Italian, French, and U.S. Open singles; ranked number one in the world.

1963 Court wins the Grand Slam in mixed doubles (with Kenneth Fletcher).

1970 Court wins the Grand Slam in singles (only the second woman to do so) with a record of 104–6 for the year.

U.S. and All-England titles, but her game seemed to be deteriorating. In 1966, after losing the French Open to Nancy Richey and Wimbledon to Billie Jean King, she announced that she was retiring. Smith's retirement was not permanent, however. In 1967 she married Barry Court, an Australian yachtsman and wool broker, who encouraged her to return to competition the following year. Although Court lost all four of the major tournaments in 1968, she fought back the following year to win three out of the four—losing only at Wimbledon.

Court began 1970 with a win at the Australian Open. This victory was followed by the singles title at the French Open, where she beat Helga Niessen, and at Wimbledon, where she defeated her former rival Billie Jean King. Many consider the finals match with King at Wimbledon to be one of the greatest ever played by two women. Court followed up her Wimbledon triumph with another win at the U.S. Open against Rosemary Casals. With that victory, Court completed the coveted Grand Slam, becoming only the second woman to do so since Maureen Connolly in 1953.

In 1971 Court failed to win at the Australian Open, French Open, and Wimbledon, which she lost to crowd favorite Evonne Goolagong. After Wimbledon, Court stopped playing for about a year because she was pregnant. She returned to competition in late 1972, but played in only six tournaments that year. Between her return and the spring of 1973, Court won 16 out of 18 tournaments and 78 out of 80 singles matches.

Court's most publicized match of 1973—and certainly one of the most unusual in her career (as well as in tennis history)—was a widely televised one against 55-year old Bobby Riggs, a noted male star past his prime. Court was responding to a challenge by Riggs, who publicly stated that women could not play as well as men and challenged any of the top women players to play against him. Falling prey to nervousness, and thrown off balance by Rigg's slow and eccentric playing, Court lost the match despite the fact that she should have easily won. Riggs, of course, continued to offer the same challenge to other top female players and was soundly defeated by Billie Jean King in front of a television audience of 50 million people on September 20, 1973—four months after his match with Court.

On the world tour in 1973, Court won the singles title at the Australian Open and then faced 18-year old phenom Chris Evert in the finals of the French Open. In a particularly hard-fought contest, Court beat Evert, but the match was a close one.

Later that year Court won her fifth U.S. Open title by defeating Evonne Goolagong. This proved to be Court's last victory at any of the four major tournaments. She continued to compete for a number of years, but many new and talented young players had come on the scene to capture the major titles.

During her career Court amassed an amazing record, including 64 Grand Slam championships in singles, doubles, and mixed doubles. Her titles included five U.S. Open victories (1962, 1965, 1969, 1970, 1973); three Wimbledons (1963, 1965, 1970); five French Opens (1962, 1964, 1969, 1970, 1973); and 11 Australian Opens (1960–66, 1969–71, 1973). She is the only player to achieve a Grand Slam in both doubles (1963) and singles (1970).

Court represented her native Australia six times in the international Federation Cup championships, helping lead the team to victories in 1964, 1965, 1968, and 1971. Between 1961 and 1973, she was ranked number one in the world seven times and was among the top five in the other years. Margaret Smith Court was elected to the International Tennis Hall of Fame in 1979. ◆

Crenshaw, Ben

JANUARY 11, 1952– ● GOLFER

Ben Daniel Crenshaw was born on January 11, 1952, in Austin, Texas. His mother, Pearl, was a schoolteacher. His father, Charlie, a lawyer, introduced young Ben to the game of golf when the boy was in elementary school. Ben showed early aptitude and won his first tournament, the Casis Elementary Open, when he was in fourth grade. He qualified for the Texas state junior tournament when he was 13 and won it two years later. He collected his first national title, the Jaycees Junior Championship, in 1968.

> *"This is a sweet, sweet win. I don't think there'll ever be a sweeter moment."*
>
> Ben Crenshaw at the 1984 Masters

Although Crenshaw was active in many sports during high school, he focused on golf, sometimes playing 36 holes a day. When he was a senior, he finished an impressive 32nd in his first U.S. Open, tying for the low amateur medal. Crenshaw went on to win all but one of the 19 tournaments he entered that year.

Not surprisingly, the promising young athlete was awarded a golf scholarship to attend the University of Texas in 1970.

The Ryder Cup

The Ryder Cup is a biannual match play tournament that pits a team of American golf professionals against a team from Europe. Controversy still shrouds the precise origins of the competition, which evolved in the 1920s from informal British-American matches. One version has it that the idea for a match between American and British professionals originated in 1921 with Sylvanus P. Jermain, the president of the Inverness Club in Toledo, Ohio. Another account credits the concept to James Harnett, the circulation manager of *Golf World* magazine, who sought to boost readership in 1920 by raising the money needed to sponsor a match between golf pros from the United States and Britain. The Professional Golfers Association of America (PGA) did award the funds to Harnett in December 1920 to promote such a tournament.

The precise authorship of the idea notwithstanding, the first unofficial U.S.-British match was held in 1921 in Gleneagles, Scotland, with an American team selected by Harnett, probably with advice from Walter Hagen, an American pro. The British team cruised to a 9–3 victory that year. In 1926 another informal match was held between the Americans and the British at Wentworth, Surrey, at which the Americans suffered an even sounder thrashing, 13^1/$_2$ to 1^1/$_2$. An ardent gallery member at this match was Samuel Ryder, a wealthy British seed merchant who had taken up golf late in life on the advice of his physician and had become a major enthusiast of the game. After the 1926 match, the British pro George Duncan suggested that Ryder sponsor an official competition, and Ryder jumped at the chance. In short order he donated a solid gold cup measuring 17 inches in height and weighing four pounds (it is worth $13,900 in 1999 dollars). He even offered to pay for the prize money: "I will give five pounds to each of the winning players, and give a party afterwards, with champagne and chicken sandwiches." That idea never caught on, but the awarding of the cup did.

The inaugural Ryder Cup match was held on June 3–4, 1927, at the Worcester Country Club in Massachusetts. An American team captained by Walter Hagen dominated the match, winning by seven points. With the tournament's locale alternating between the United States and Britain, the home team won the next four matches until the U.S. team triumphed at Southport and Ainsdale in 1937. Because of World War II, the match did not resume until 1947, when the Oregon fruit grower Robert Hudson subsidized the British team, still hampered by postwar economic stringency. Having crossed both an ocean and a continent to Oregon, the British squad suffered a lopsided defeat, 11–1. Thereafter the Americans owned the Ryder Cup until 1957, when the British finally ended their slump at Lindrick in Yorkshire.

The American team regained the cup in 1959 and retained it for a quarter century, until 1985, by which time the American team was facing an all-European lineup thanks to a 1979 ruling that expanded America's opponents to include all members of the PGA European tour who are residents of a European nation. With a dramatic come-from-behind victory in the 1999 match, the United States now enjoys a 27–7–2 advantage in Ryder Cup competition.

There, after a string of individual and team victories, Crenshaw was named to the 1971 All-American collegiate golf team.

Crenshaw was becoming well-known throughout the golf world and was being compared to Arnold Palmer and Jack Nicklaus. But Crenshaw was reluctant to quit college and turn professional, fearing that his golf career might flop and he would be left without a degree. In the summer of 1973, however, he had achieved so many victories at the collegiate level that he could resist no longer. The decision proved favorable. Within six weeks on the Professional Golfers Association (PGA) Tour, Crenshaw had won $76,749 in prize money. He had also won the admiration of sports fans and fellow competitors alike, as he had not just an impressive game but also a likable, easygoing manner. The 5' 9", 160-pound golfer was nicknamed "Gentle Ben."

The next few years were tough ones for Crenshaw. His mother died of a heart attack in 1974, and his golf game faltered. He missed the cut at the U.S. Open twice and finished 24th at the prestigious Masters tournament.

Crenshaw decided to enlist the aid of golf instructor Bob Toski, who helped him to improve his swing—and his mental attitude. As he told *People* magazine: "I was about five inches from becoming an outstanding golfer—that's the distance between my left ear and my right one."

His new approach to the game worked, and Crenshaw began racking up wins on the PGA tour. He triumphed at the Bing Crosby Pro-Am Open, in January 1976. The following week, he won the Hawaiian Open, breaking the Waialae Country Club's course record. By the end of that year, Crenshaw had taken second place at the Master's and won his first European title, the Irish Open. He ranked second on the PGA's annual money list, behind only Jack Nicklaus.

Crenshaw took first place at a number of championships in the next few years, but he fell short at the four major tournaments on the PGA tour—the U.S. Open, the Masters, the British Open, and the PGA Championship.

Of those tournaments, his failure to win the British Open upset him the most. As an avid and widely respected golf historian, he holds the British Open in awe. The British courses, he told the *Chicago Tribune* on July 18, 1982, are special because "the links courses [in Britain] were created by the interaction of rain, wind, snow, tides, erosion, even sheep and burrowing animals. Here it's man against the elements, golf in its natural state."

1952 Crenshaw is born in Austin, Texas.

1976 Crenshaw wins the Bing Crosby Pro-Am Open, the Hawaiian Open, and the Irish Open.

1984 Crenshaw wins the Master's (again in 1995).

1991 Crenshaw receives the Bobby Jones Award, the U.S. Golf Association's highest honor.

In 1982, Crenshaw hit a slump. He left the PGA Tour in August and turned to his father and friends for advice. They suggested that he had forsaken the swing that was most natural to him, trying instead to conform to a more classic swing model. He decided to do what came naturally and instinctually, and his game improved measurably. He rejoined the tour at the Masters in April 1983, tying Tom Kite for second place and restoring his confidence.

Crenshaw's hard work was rewarded in 1984, when he finally won the prestigious Master's, his first major victory in more than a decade on the tour. But his game soon declined again, perhaps due to personal problems. Crenshaw was divorced from his wife, Polly, in fall of that year, and in late 1985 he was diagnosed with a hyperactive thyroid. With medical treatment, the ailment was brought under control within several months, and Crenshaw started to improve on the golf course as well.

In the years since that Master's victory, Crenshaw has become one of golf's enduring figures. Although he continues to have slumps and high periods, he remains one of the leading money-winners in the sport and is considered to be one of the game's true ambassadors of good will. In 1991, the U.S. Golf Association gave him its highest honor, the Bobby Jones Award. He has won several important matches, including another Master's in 1995. In 1999, Crenshaw received one of his highest honors when he was selected to captain the U.S. team for the Ryder Cup, a prestigious international contest held every two years that pits the top American golfers against the top golfers in Europe in a fiercely contested three-day competition. With Crenshaw leading the cheers, the U.S. team defeated the Europeans, 14$\frac{1}{2}$ to 13$\frac{1}{2}$.

Crenshaw has also started spending more time off the tour, working on his golf course architecture business. His firm, Coore & Crenshaw, has restored and built courses throughout the United States. Crenshaw has been married to Julie Forrest since November 1985. They have three daughters and live in Austin. ◆

Davies, Laura

OCTOBER 5, 1963– ● GOLFER

Golfer Laura Davies was born in Coventry, England, on October 5, 1963. She is esteemed in the sports world as an instinctive player and a great competitor who has managed to stay down-to-earth and approachable even as she has become Britain's leading woman golf pro.

The tall (5′ 10″), athletic Davies credits British golfer David Regan as the person who has most influenced her career. Davies played as an amateur during the early 1980s and quickly made a name for herself. In 1983, she won the English Intermediate Championship. The following year, she captured the Welsh Open Stroke Play Championship and was a member of the Great Britain and Ireland Curtis Cup team. In both 1983 and 1984, Davies triumphed in the South Eastern Championships.

Davies turned professional in 1985. In 1987, she won her first major victory, at the U.S. Women's Open. This accomplishment led the Ladies Professional Golf Association (LPGA) to grant her automatic membership. In 1988, Queen Elizabeth II named Davies a Member of the British Empire (M.B.E.)—one of the highest honors that can be bestowed upon a British citizen—in recognition of her contributions to golf. During the 1990s, Davies was a member of five European Solheim Cup teams. She won several Standard Register Championships as well as two McDonald's LPGA Championships—both events among golf's major tournaments. Davies was named Rolex Player of the Year in 1996, the same year that she won the prestigious du Maurier Classic.

> *"You've got to have fun. Otherwise this would be too much like a real job. Just hitting balls aimlessly is a complete waste of time."*
>
> Laura Davies on her aversion to practice

1963 Davies is born in Coventry, England.

1987 Davies wins the U.S. Women's Open.

1988 Davies is named a Member of the British Empire by Queen Elizabeth II.

1996 Davies wins the du Maurier Classic and is named Rolex Player of the Year.

short shrift: very little attention or consideration given to a particular subject.

As a professional player participating in tournaments all over the world, Davies has established herself as one of the most able women in golf. She is also one of the top money earners. Though she is a powerful and successful player, Davies does not practice much, even before a tournament. She has a natural aptitude for the game and does not hesitate to take risks on the course, qualities that make her a tough competitor.

Davies' long game is her particular strength; when she has faltered on the course, it is usually her putting that has let her down. After a 12-month period in 1997–1998 when she kept missing crucial three- or four-footers, Davies experimented and found that putting with her left hand below the right delivered better results—at least for the time being.

In recent years, Davies has become well known for championing greater promotion and legitimization of women's golf in Europe, which she feels has been given very **short shrift**. She is concerned that up-and-coming women golfers will soon have inadequate competitive venues; in 1998, for example, there were only about half a dozen professional women's tournaments in Europe. She points out that a lack of worthy venues will translate into a dearth of good players.

Davies lives in West Byfleet, England. She enjoys fast cars, gambling, and sports—she maintains a soccer field on the grounds of her estate. ◆

Day, Pat

OCTOBER 13, 1953– ● JOCKEY

A reporter described the jockey Pat Day as "100 pounds of man who makes a living trying to control 1,100 pounds of horse." Although the physics of that relationship sound daunting, it has proved a winning formula for Day, whose mounts have galloped to career earnings of more than $150 million, with Day pocketing about 10 percent of that total.

For much of his career Day was a surer master of horses than of his own life, in which renown and wealth have come at the expense of bouts of alcoholism and despair. It was only after many years of personal turmoil that a sudden conversion to fundamentalist Christianity in 1984 brought Pat Day inner peace and stability.

Born on a cattle ranch in Colorado in 1953, Day was surrounded by animals growing up and from earliest childhood was imbued with a love of horses by his father. As Day later recalled, "I believe I inherited my father's uncanny knack of understanding animals. My father was a tremendous horseman in his own right, and taught me basic horsemanship that has been my foundation. That has helped me tremendously in a roundabout way—being able to understand the temperament of the horse and adjusting to get along with that."

With his ranching background, Day's first professional involvement with horses took him not to the track but to the rodeo circuit through several Western states, where he attained a modest renown in steer-roping and bull-riding contests. Day's short, slight build (four feet, eleven inches and 100 pounds) attracted the notice of racing promoters, who encouraged him to train as a jockey. Intrigued by the fat purses of big-time racing, in 1973 Day set out for an apprenticeship on the California farm of Farrell Jones, a horse breeder. Crestfallen when he discovered that his obligation there seemed tantamount to indentured servitude—several years of training plus labor on the farm for at least one additional year—he skipped out after only a month and landed in Las Vegas, where he was hired to gallop the horses at the Las Vegas Downs track. That job led to a series of odd jobs on the racetrack circuit in Arizona, where Day observed and practiced while waiting for his first chance to ride in a race. That break came late in the summer of 1973, when he won his first race at Prescott Downs.

After several months Day moved to Arizona's biggest racetrack, Turf Paradise in Phoenix. There he soon emerged as the top jockey, earning a shot in 1974 to move on to Chicago's Sportsman's Park, where he again quickly distinguished himself before seizing even bigger, more lucrative opportunities at tracks in Florida and New York.

As his bank account bulged, Day increasingly found himself on the fast track away from work as well, caught up in a frenetic nightlife that included heavy indulgence in drugs and alcohol. His binges cost him his marriage and, for a while, his emotional stability. Day said, "I was a real basket case after my marriage fell apart. I was wanting to blame the race track for my personal crisis, and the race track was not to blame. It was my immaturity and inability to handle my personal affairs."

1953 — Day is born in Colorado.

1982 — Day is named the top national rider.

1984 — Day wins the prestigious Eclipse Award (also in 1986, 1987, and 1991).

1991 — Day is named to the Racing Hall of Fame.

1998 — Day wins his 7,000th victory, only fifth jockey to do so.

Day, who had previously dismissed religion as a crutch for the weak, fell to the floor in tears and vowed to devote his life to God.

Although Day managed to sustain his professional success despite his personal difficulties, he was walking a tightrope. "In retrospect, I see I was there on the brink of destruction," he said. "Everything came so relatively easy, almost as if it was owed to me or I was deserving of it. I had a tendency to be on the cocky and boasting side anyway." With his personal life stabilized after his second marriage in the early 1980s, Day enjoyed a string of fresh successes: he was named top national rider in 1982 and won the prestigious Eclipse Award in 1984, 1986, 1987, and 1991.

But Day's most momentous personal transformation came on the night of January 27, 1984, as he sat in a hotel room, the fire-and-brimstone oratory of the evangelist Jimmy Swaggart pounding at him from the TV screen. Day, who had previously dismissed religion as a crutch for the weak, fell to the floor in tears and vowed to devote his life to God. His conversion was in such earnest that he nearly walked away from the gambling-driven world of the track. "I really struggled with that," Day recalled. His new religious devotion, unflagging to this day, seems to have benefited his professional life. He transferred his main site of operations to Churchill Downs, home of the Kentucky Derby, and has since become the most successful jockey in the history of that fabled arena.

Day's lifetime of outstanding achievement on the track earned him admission to the Racing Hall of Fame in 1991, his first year of eligibility for membership. The following year he added the only key line missing from his resume, a victory at the Kentucky Derby atop the horse Lil E. Tee. In 1994 he enjoyed two more victories on the Triple Crown circuit, riding Tabasco Cat to first-place finishes in the Preakness and Belmont Stakes.

On August 25, 1998, Day's first-place finish atop the juvenile colt Bay Harbor made him only the fifth jockey to attain 7,000 career victories. Contemplating Willie Shoemaker's record of 8,833 wins, Day commented, "I really don't know. I've never been one to say I want to win 7,000, I want to win 8,000. . . . Obviously, my intentions are to win every time I go out there, to do the very best the horse is capable of doing, and the numbers have piled up." ◆

de la Hoya, Oscar

FEBRUARY 4, 1973– ● BOXER

"**G**olden Boy" boxing champion Oscar de la Hoya, whose sterling good manners outside the ring give no indication of how ferocious he is inside it, has the goal of winning seven titles in seven weight divisions— a feat no other boxer has accomplished.

De la Hoya, a third-generation boxer, was born February 4, 1973, in East Los Angeles, California, the second of three children to Mexican immigrant parents. His mother, Cecilia, was a seamstress and occasional singer. His father, Joel, arrived in Los Angeles at 16, and worked as a professional lightweight boxer in the 1960s, before taking a job as a shipping and receiving clerk in the warehouse of an air-conditioning manufacturer. De la Hoya's paternal grandfather, Vicente, was an amateur featherweight in Durango, Mexico in the 1940s.

Oscar de la Hoya grew up in a poor neighborhood plagued by street gangs. Although he didn't join a gang, he often got into fights with gang members. When Oscar was six, his father took him to Pico Rivera Sports Arena to learn to box. In his first bout he knocked his opponent out in the first round. He began working out at the Resurrection, a gym in a former church, at the age of ten. When he was 11, seeing East Los Angeles resident Paul Gonzales win the 1984 Olympic gold medal for boxing gave him dreams of doing the same.

De la Hoya's father asked Al Stankie, the former vice cop who had trained Gonzales for the 1984 Olympic games, to make Oscar a gold medalist too. While competing on the amateur circuit, de la Hoya earned an impressive record of 223 wins to 5 losses—with 153 knockouts. During training, he worked with a private tutor to make up for the school he was missing. His amateur career was bankrolled by Shelly Finkel, a manager who gave Oscar and his father $ 100,000 when Joel de la Hoya asked for help because his wife was dying from breast cancer.

Oscar was very close to his mother. She went without radiation treatments to watch him box in the 1990 Goodwill

"I have felt violent inside the ring. Outside the ring, I want no trouble with anybody. I want peace and tranquillity. I want to be happy and enjoy life."

Oscar de la Hoya
official web site

Oscar de la Hoya delivers a punch.

Games in Seattle (where he won a title), and died later that year at the age of 38. On her deathbed, she asked Oscar to win the gold medal for her at the 1992 Barcelona Olympics. He did as she asked, winning the only Olympic gold medal in 1992 for the U.S. boxing team.

After the Olympics, de la Hoya became associated with the management team of Steve Nelson and Robert Mittleman, who provided more than $1 million to Oscar and his father. De la Hoya made his professional debut on November 23, 1992, in Inglewood, California, flooring opponent Lamar Williams three times in the first round. De la Hoya backed out of a fight scheduled for December 9, 1993, which was to be his New York City debut. Unhappy with his managers, he fired them and became his own manager, eventually connecting with fight promoter Bob Arum's Top Rank organization.

De la Hoya won his first world title in only his twelfth bout as a professional, in March 1994, when he defeated Danish boxer Jimmi Bredahl with a technical knockout for the World Boxing Organization (WBO) junior lightweight crown. That same year, he moved up to the next higher weight class, winning the WBO lightweight crown from Jorge Paez only 39 seconds into the second round.

The following year, de la Hoya beat three-time world junior lightweight champion John John Molina, the toughest and most experienced opponent of his career. Several months later, in May 1995, in what was billed as the largest lightweight unification bout in more than a decade, de la Hoya defeated Rafael Ruelas with an astounding display of power punches, gaining the International Boxing Federation junior lightweight title. Only a few months later, using almost exclusively his right arm because his left was hampered by a back injury, he successfully defended his title against challenger Genaro Hernandez. Three months later, he pummeled Jesse James Leija, the former WBC super featherweight champion, in two rounds.

In 1996, in what was only his second fight in a new weight class, de la Hoya won the WBC super lightweight championship from his boyhood idol, six-time champion Julio Cesar Chavez, in four brutal rounds. De la Hoya defended that title in January 1997 against Miguel Angel Gonzalez, winning a unanimous decision. In April 1997 de la Hoya got his fifth title in four weight classes when he took the WBC welterweight championship from Pernell "Sweet Pea" Whitaker, in what was regarded as a controversial decision. Whitaker is known as a defensive fighter, while de la Hoya was not particularly aggressive in that fight. Critics said that under such circumstances, the fight is usually given to the incumbent. But the judges gave de la Hoya a higher score. It was after that fight that *Ring* magazine judged de la Hoya to be the world's best fighter "pound for pound." Although people were calling on de la Hoya to fight Whitaker in a rematch, de la Hoya defended his new welterweight title against unranked Kenyan boxer David Kamau, knocking him out in the second round. De la Hoya won against Hector "Macho" Camacho on September 13, 1997, in a 12-round decision.

The 5 foot 10 1/2 inch de la Hoya has won world crowns at 130, 135, 140, and 147 pounds. He is noted for fast hand speed, a powerful jab, and an incredible hook. Critics protest that de la Hoya was able to coast early in his career by choosing relative unknowns for opponents. To this charge de la Hoya has responded that he fought weak opponents so he could gain experience in the ring and in the future he will only challenge champions.

De la Hoya is well liked for his charismatic personality and trademark grin, and for encouraging inner-city youth to stay in school and avoid drugs and crime. He contributes money for scholarships to his Garfield High School, from which he graduated in 1991. And as of January 1997 he had spent three quarters of a million dollars to buy an old gym and turn it into an oasis for inner-city youth who aspire to be boxers. In 1997 de la Hoya earned $37 million in prize money, the most any non-heavyweight made in a year in the history of boxing. ◆

Dempsey, Jack

JUNE 24, 1895—MAY 31, 1983 ● BOXER

The night in 1914 that he badly beat George Copelin in Cripple Creek was the first time he fought under the name "Jack Dempsey."

Dempsey's parents called him Harry. He was an 11-pound baby, one of 11 children born to Hyrum and Mary Celia Smoot Dempsey, pioneering parents who took their brood across the Colorado and Utah frontiers while in search of an elusive fortune. Hyrum had been a schoolteacher in West Virginia, and Mary, a no-nonsense Scotch Irishwoman, claimed Utah senator Reed Smoot as a distant relative. Both parents were part Indian and lived on and off welfare and through Mormon charity when farming, ranching, prospecting, and restaurant work could not be found. "You learned to work hard or starve," Dempsey remembered of the family's survival strategy. As a result, he did not go beyond grammar school.

As an adolescent in Lakeview, Utah, Jack shined shoes in a barbershop and was fired for accidentally breaking a comb. The experience fueled his "impatience to grow up." Other indignities followed. He shoveled dung, fed pigs, worked sugar-beet fields, and helped pitch circus tents. By 16 he had joined his older brother Bernie as a coppermine mucker, loading ore 3,000 feet down in Bingham County, Utah, and Cripple Creek, Colorado. Jack sparred with Bernie when his brother launched a brief boxing career as "Jack Dempsey," the name of an Irish middleweight who died the year of Jack's birth. The boy who would become the Jazz Age's Jack Dempsey sprinted against horses to test his speed and endurance. He followed Bernie's example by chewing gum to strengthen his jaw, and he bathed his face in beef brine to look older and meaner.

As "Kid Blackie" he took fights wherever he could get them for purses of $2, $5, and sometimes $10. For five years he rode the rails, living in hobo camps and always looking for a fight. The night in 1914 that he badly beat George Copelin in Cripple Creek was the first time he fought under the name "Jack Dempsey." A series of "crumby" fights followed, in which the untrained fighter fought hoping for "future rewards." Dempsey beat Slick Merrill in Tonopah, Nevada, but lost to Johnny Sudenberg in Goldfield, Nevada. He fought Sudenberg to a draw in Reno, beat the Boston Bearcat in a single round in Ogden,

Utah, and up-ended Sudenberg in the second round of their fight in Ely, Nevada.

Dempsey built a four-foot-high cage and began sparring in it to perfect a stalking crouch that would become his signature in the ring. He intensified his training regimen by running six miles every morning. Three quick knockouts over highly regarded western fighters followed. Denver's Otto Floto and other sportswriters began to take notice. By June 1916 Dempsey felt on the verge of "becoming somebody." He arrived in New York City and toured the sports departments of the various newspapers with new fight manager Jack Price. Damon Runyon of the *American* and Nat Fleischer of the *Press* promoted Dempsey into an exhibition bout on his 21st birthday at the Fairmont Athletic Club in Chicago against ring veteran Andre Anderson. Each fighter decked the other several times in 10 rounds, but Dempsey, always the aggressor, won the decision.

Dempsey's brawling bouts that summer with "Wild Bert" Kenny at the Fairmont and John Lester Johnson in Harlem, where he fought eight rounds with broken ribs, gave a glimpse of Dempsey's extraordinary tenacity. For these fights, he made only $150, which he evenly split with Price. It wasn't enough. A disappointed Price returned to Salt Lake City; a few days later, after sleeping outside in Central Park, Dempsey followed.

On an impulse Dempsey married a piano player from a Commercial Street saloon on October 9, 1916. Maxine Cates from Walla Walla, Washington, was 15 years Dempsey's senior. Hoping to restart his ring career, he was knocked down four times in the first round by "Fireman" Jim Flynn in Murray, Utah, on 13 February 1917 before his brother Bernie threw in the towel. His no-decision bouts against "Handsome" Al Norton and "Fat" Willie Meehan in Oakland seemed to confirm the impression that at age 21, Dempsey was punched out.

After hiring out as a Seattle lumberjack and a Tacoma shipyard worker, Dempsey returned to Salt Lake City in the summer of 1917 after his younger brother Bruce was stabbed to death in a street fight. Maxine did not go with him, returning to saloon life. Broke, tired, beaten down by the fight game, Dempsey resigned himself to washing dishes, mining coal, picking fruit, and digging ditches. But a telegram from 34-year-old John Leo McKernan, an Oakland fight manager known as "Doc" Kearns, offered Dempsey a second start.

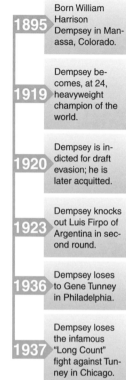

1895 Born William Harrison Dempsey in Manassa, Colorado.

1919 Dempsey becomes, at 24, heavyweight champion of the world.

1920 Dempsey is indicted for draft evasion; he is later acquitted.

1923 Dempsey knocks out Luis Firpo of Argentina in second round.

1936 Dempsey loses to Gene Tunney in Philadelphia.

1937 Dempsey loses the infamous "Long Count" fight against Tunney in Chicago.

Dempsey moved in with Kearns, trained diligently, worked on quickness, developed his left hook, and learned how to finish a fighter. In the six months that followed Kearns craftily built up his protege. A four-round decision over Meehan, twin wins over Kearns crony Norton, and an October 2, 1917 slugfest with "Gunboat" Smith in San Francisco's Mission Park began to attract press attention and crowds. When Dempsey, at six feet, one inch, and 187 pounds, dispatched the "Oklahoma Mastiff," six-foot, four-inch, 235-pound Carl Morris, at San Francisco's Dreamland Pavilion in four rounds on 1 November 1917, Kearns began to believe his hype that Dempsey might be championship material.

Through 1918, Kearns built Dempsey's knockout record to an impressive 60 percent by matching him with one round wonders like Homer Rice, Tom Riley, and Kid McCarthy. Bouts against the better-known Bill Brennan and Billy Miske were fought when Kearns was certain the increasingly confident Dempsey was ready. His real target was **heavyweight** champion Jess Willard, the six-foot, six inch "Pottawatomie Giant," who had taken the title from Jack Johnson in April 1915. Dempsey's knockout of number-one contender Fred Fulton in 18 seconds in the first round on July 27, 1918 in suburban Harrison, New Jersey, brought press pressure for a Willard-Dempsey title fight. Kearns created the Jack Dempsey Revue for vaudeville houses to keep Dempsey's name in the papers, while cultivating through the nation's sports pages the image Dempsey as an impregnable warrior.

A crowd of 20,000 people attended the Independence Day 1919 championship fight in Toledo, many watching in utter amazement as the sneering, stalking, saddle-colored Dempsey knocked Willard to the canvas seven times in the first round. When the badly battered Willard could not come out for the fourth round, Dempsey became, at 24, the heavyweight champion of the world. Kearns immediately capitalized on Dempsey's celebrity status by signing his star to a $15,000 weekly contract to tour the Pantages vaudeville circuit. Hefty appearance fees followed. A West Coast studio, Pathe, planned to star Dempsey in a 15-episode serial, *Daredevil Jack*, but the project was shelved when Dempsey was **indicted** by a federal grand jury in February 1920 for evading the draft. Dempsey's former wife Maxine (they had divorced early in 1919), who charged Dempsey had not supported her during the war, later recanted her testimony and he was acquitted. The negative publicity

heavyweight: a boxing classification determined by weight, usually being at least 198 pounds and without limit.

indicted: to be charged with a crime after the finding of a grand jury.

haunted Dempsey. He had fought for himself, many papers wrote, while other able-bodied men had fought for their country.

Dempsey's July 2,1921 match with French war hero Georges Carpentier, skillfully promoted by Kearns and boxing showman George "Tex" Rickard, produced great crowds at Boyle's Thirty Acres in Jersey City, New Jersey, and boxing's first $1 million gate. Dempsey's 1920 knockouts over Billy Miske and Bill Brennan, two fighters he had fought before, created nowhere near the excitement and drama of the Carpentier match. So taken was the press by pre-fight publicity pitting a great war hero against a reputed American war slacker that "the greatest battle since the Silurian Age," as a Chicago sportswriter described it, appeared to take on international significance. Dempsey's knockout victory over Carpentier and his July 1923 defeat of Tommy Gibbons seemed to solidify his growing reputation as a great fighting machine. It was, however, his ferocious battle with the "Wild Bull of the Pampas," Argentina's Luis Firpo, that left a lasting impression.

A crowd of 88,000 fight fans, including Babe Ruth, Ethel Barrymore, Kermit Roosevelt, William K. Vanderbilt, L. H. Rothschild, and the leading celebrities of the **Jazz Age** crowded into the Polo Grounds in New York City in September 1923 to witness one of the most memorable four-and-a-half minutes in ring history. The oversized Firpo was floored seven times in the first round, getting off the canvas to punch Dempsey through the ropes and onto the press table. A dozen reporters and leading stars on Broadway later claimed credit for hurling the enraged Dempsey back into the ring. The champion tore into his Argentine opponent and in the second round laid him out for good.

The $1 million gate for the Dempsey-Firpo fight reflected the degree to which boxing and Dempsey had become big commodities. In five years Dempsey had fought 39 rounds, totaling just short of two full hours. His total earnings of $1,257,000 during that time prorated to $32,231 a round, $10,744 a minute, $179 a second. For the pleasure of sending Firpo back to Buenos Aires, Dempsey earned $100,000 a minute. "Dempsey worship," sports columnist Ring Lardner wrote, had become "a national disease."

Adoring crowds closed in on Dempsey at every public appearance. He was a star. Men and women paid to shake his hand. Reporters and editors saw circulations soar in the weeks before and the days after a Dempsey title defense. Dempsey was in no hurry to return to the ring. He moved to Hollywood, acri-

"I told you I would knock him out in the first round, and to all intents and purpose that is what I did. He took a lot of punishment in the next two rounds, but was so feeble that I hated to have to hit him."
Jack Dempsey after defeating Jess Willard, 1919

Jazz Age: period in the 1920s in which the national economy was very successful and jazz music first came to prominence in the United States; "The Roaring '20s."

Dempsey knew, however, that the long layoff and soft lifestyle had made him a shadow of his former self.

moniously broke his long professional relationship with Kearns, and married a beautiful, fast-fading, silent film actress, Estelle Taylor, in a highly publicized February 1926 wedding.

The bidding for Dempsey's return to the ring against the lightly regarded Gene Tunney involved Chicago, New York, and Philadelphia promoters. Approximately 2,500 millionaires joined some 120,000 other spectators in paying $2 million to see a visibly slowed Dempsey lose his championship to Tunney in a 10-round decision on September 23, 1926 in Philadelphia's Sesquicentennial Stadium. Listeners in homes, public parks, and storefronts heard the infant National Broadcasting Company's call of the contest. Nearly everyone had difficulty believing their generation's great "fighting machine" had been defeated.

Rumors immediately circulated that Dempsey's pre-fight meal had been drugged by gamblers. Dempsey knew, however, that the long layoff and soft lifestyle had made him a shadow of his former self. He returned gamely to the ring, knocking out future champion Jack Sharkey in the seventh round at Yankee Stadium on July 21, 1927 before a crowd of 72,000. The comeback fight against Tunney at Chicago's Soldier Field on September 22, 1927 produced a record $2.3 million gate and was heard by a worldwide audience that included three of every four adult Americans. It included what many would later regard as one of the most famous moments in the history of sports. Trailing by points in the seventh round, Dempsey momentarily flashed his former brilliance and caught Tunney with a looping left. An avalanche of lefts and rights left Tunney sitting and badly dazed. But instead of going to a neutral corner Dempsey towered over his fallen opponent, and the start of the referee's count was delayed more than six seconds. As a result, Tunney rose to his feet at the count of nine, nearly 18 seconds after hitting the canvas, and held off Dempsey to retain his championship. The fairness of the "long count" would be argued for a generation.

Dempsey no longer needed to fight to make money. His classy acceptance of twin defeats further endeared him to millions. He starred with his wife, Estelle, in *The Big Fight*, a production of Broadway showman David Belasco, and it did good business during the summer of 1928. The death of Dempsey's crony Tex Rickard in January 1929 brought Dempsey back into promoting fights. But the collapse of the stock market, the onset of the Great Depression, a costly divorce, and $3 million in

Florida real estate losses bankrupted the former champ. In 1931, at the age of 36, he embarked on a series of boxing exhibitions designed to build him up for another title shot. A four-round beating by Kingfish Levinsky in Chicago Stadium finally persuaded Dempsey to end the pretense.

Dempsey then married singer Hannah Williams in 1933 and settled into domestic life. They had two daughters. As occasional actor and part-time wrestling referee, Dempsey rode out the **Great Depression** quietly. He made headlines by joining the Coast Guard while in his middle forties during World War II. By that time the cultural memory of Dempsey as slacker had been displaced by affection for a middle-aged boxing legend. In 1943 Dempsey and Williams were divorced.

Dempsey married Deanna Piatelli in 1958 and could be seen most evenings taking a familiar seat at his eponymous Broadway restaurant in midtown Manhattan.

There, he happily greeted the many who came to shake his hand or exchange mock blows beneath the fighting photos of his ring years. Before the restaurant closed in 1974, Dempsey had reconciled with Kearns, been honored by the Boxing Hall of Fame, and been named by the Associated Press as the greatest fighter of the half-century. His 75th birthday, staged at Madison Square Garden in June 1970, saw an outpouring of love for the man many still called champ. ◆

Great Depression: period in the United States between the stock market crash of 1929 and the beginning of World War II; marked by poor economic conditions, high unemployment, and low economic and social confidence.

Devers, Gail

NOVEMBER 19, 1966– ● TRACK AND FIELD ATHLETE

Gail Devers, perhaps the greatest combination sprinter-hurdler in history, was born in Seattle, Washington, on November 19, 1966. The daughter of a Baptist minister, Devers attended Sweetwater High School in National City, California, where the family had moved when Devers was a young girl.

Early on Devers displayed exceptional athletic gifts, at first showing particular aptitude in the 800-meter race. By her senior year in high school, Devers had an astonishing personal best 11.69 seconds in the 100-meter and could run a very swift 14.15 over the low hurdles as well.

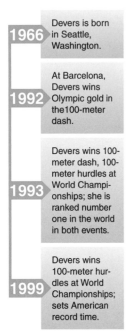

1966 Devers is born in Seattle, Washington.

1992 At Barcelona, Devers wins Olympic gold in the 100-meter dash.

1993 Devers wins 100-meter dash, 100-meter hurdles at World Championships; she is ranked number one in the world in both events.

1999 Devers wins 100-meter hurdles at World Championships; sets American record time.

After graduation, Devers attended UCLA, where she continued to improve dramatically throughout her college years. A sociology major, Devers won no less than nine Pacific 10 Conference titles in just two years of competition. As a freshman, in 1984, she ran an 11.51 in the 100-meter, finishing second in the USA Juniors (as well as sixth in the semifinals of the 100 hurdles). She won a bronze medal in the 100 meters at the junior Pan Am Games and ran the third leg on the gold medal-winning 400-meter relay team.

As a sophomore, Devers improved her best time to an already-world-class 11.19 in the flat sprint and 13.16 in the hurdles. In both events, she finished sixth in the NCAA championships while running a personal record 59.26 in the 400 meters as well. As a junior, she finished fourth in the hurdles in the NCAA championships and fifth in the 100-meter at the U.S. National Championships. She also set a personal record 42–6.75 in the triple jump in 1986.

In 1987, Devers won both events at the Pac 10 Championships. She was second in the NCAA and fourth in the U.S. Nationals in the 100-meter, and she won the gold medal at the Pan Am Games with a time of 11.14 seconds.

Devers' best times were down to an impressive 10.97 and 12.61 in 1988, as she finished eighth in the 100-meter hurdles semifinals in her first Olympic Games in Seoul. However, just as the 20-year old athlete seemed to be on top of the world, tragedy struck. In June 1988, Devers began experiencing terrible migraine headaches. She also experienced dizziness and a temporary loss of sight in her right eye. At first it was assumed that her problems were merely caused by stress, but her condition only continued to deteriorate. Unfortunately, it was a full two years before doctors finally came up with the correct diagnosis for Devers: She had a hyperactive thyroid gland, also known as Graves' Disease. Though she initially tried radiation to combat the disease, the side effects proved too intolerable. Finally, a combination of careful diet and the proper thyroid medication began to bring Devers' disease under control.

Incredibly, after missing two and a half years of competition and being so gravely ill, Devers returned to competition in 1991 and immediately finished second in the 100-meter hurdles at the World Championships—in a personal best of 12.63 seconds, no less. The next year, 1992, was an Olympic year and Devers, toughened by all her travails, was more than ready for the fight. She won the hurdles (12.55) and placed second in the

100-meter in a wind-aided time of 10.82 seconds at the Olympic trials. And that was just a warm-up for the main event.

The finish of the 100-meter final in Barcelona was the closest in the history of the Olympic Games. Devers and the Russian favorite, Irina Privalova, ran almost even for the entire race but the other top contenders, American Gwen Torrence and two Jamaicans, Merlene Ottey and Juliet Cuthbert, all came up in the end as well. It was impossible to tell who won in the razor-close finish until the official announcement, finally, gave the gold to Devers. With the win Devers became the third straight 100-meter Olympic winner in a row who had attended UCLA.

Unbelievably enough, the final in the 100-meter hurdles came to an equally dramatic finish. Devers moved to the front by the fourth hurdle and seemed to be home free with just one hurdle left. But she came up to the final barrier too quickly and, just as she rose to clear it, she glanced briefly to her right. She hit the hurdle with her lead foot on the way up and lost her balance. She scrambled toward the finish line on her hands and knees and, miraculously, still managed to finish fifth.

Devers, now at the very top of her game—won both the 100-meter (10.82) and the 100-meter hurdles (12.46) at the 1993 World Championships. At the end of the year, she was ranked No.1 in the world in both events.

Over the next two years, Devers was somewhat slowed by hamstring problems but came back strong to win her second consecutive Olympic gold medal in Atlanta, in the 100-meter (her time was 10.94) while finishing fourth in the hurdles (12.66). Devers also ran the second leg on the gold medal-winning 400-meter relay team.

In 1997, after winning the World Indoor title in the 60-meter in 7.06 seconds, Devers decided she needed a rest, and she refrained from competition in 1998. She came back strong in 1999, winning the 100-meter hurdles at the World Championships in an American record time of 12.37 seconds while finishing fifth in the 100 meters behind new American sprint sensation Marion Jones.

Currently, Gail Devers is training vigorously under Coach Bob Kersee (husband and coach of track star Jackie Joyner-Kersee) for the 2000 Olympic Games, to be held in Sydney Australia. "I intend to double, running in both of my events," she said. "And, even though I'll be 34 years old by then, I think I have an excellent chance of winning one or both once again." ◆

> *"It's hard to enjoy this [100-meter victory], knowing that someone is trying to destroy the Olympic spirit. But they won't be able to do that unless we let them."*
> Gail Devers after a pipe-bomb explosion in Atlanta, 1996

Didrikson–Zaharias, Mildred "Babe"

JUNE 26, 1914–SEPTEMBER 27, 1956 ● GOLFER, ALL-AROUND ATHLETE

"She is beyond all belief until you see her perform. Then you finally understand that you are looking at the most flawless section of muscle harmony, of complete mental and physical coordination, the world of sport has ever seen."

Grantland Rice on Babe Didrikson

Declared AP's Woman Athlete of the First Half of the Twentieth Century in 1950, Mildred "Babe" Didrikson excelled as both an amateur and professional in nearly every major sport—track and field, basketball, baseball, football, and golf.

Mildred Didrikson (known popularly as "Babe" throughout her career) was born in Port Arthur, Texas, on June 26, 1914, the sixth child of Norwegian immigrants who placed a high value on physical fitness and athletics—her mother had won skating awards in Norway, and her father, Ole Didrikson, had spanned the globe as a sailor before becoming a cabinetmaker. Her early childhood nickname "Baby" evolved into "Babe" when her Babe Ruth-like prowess at hitting home runs became evident in the boys' baseball games in which she participated as an equal. She was also a standout basketball player on the girls' team at Beaumont Senior High School.

While playing in a high school game in Houston, Didrikson impressed the coach of the Golden Cyclone Athletic Club of the Employers Casualty Company of Dallas, one of the country's leading women's basketball teams. Still a senior at Beaumont, she received special permission to travel with the team that spring, studying on her own. Didrikson returned to school in June to take her exams and attend graduation ceremonies.

She was named All-America in basketball for the two years she played on the Golden Cyclone team, which she helped to a victory in the national Amateur Athletic Union (AAU) tournament. Meanwhile, she was also blazing a trail in track-and-field competition: In the AAU tryouts for the Olympic Games in 1932, she won five of the eight events she entered and set four world records in one afternoon. Her astounding first-place score of 30 points outdistanced the 22 point total attained by her nearest rival, an entire *team* of women athletes.

Didrikson's stunning athleticism made headlines at the 1932 Olympics in Los Angeles, where she won two gold medals and set world records in the javelin throw (43.68 meters) and the 80-meter hurdle (11.7 seconds). In all, she set four world marks at the 1932 games, prompting this accolade from the noted sportswriter Grantland Rice: "The Babe . . . is without any question the athletic phenomenon of all time, man or woman."

Still only 19, Didrikson was flooded with professional offers, but she rebuffed them all, wishing to retain her amateur standing. Her one slip, however—a commercial endorsement of a car—resulted in her temporary suspension from the AAU. Rather than accept reinstatement, Didrikson finally did turn pro, penning a syndicated column and appearing as the only woman on two pro sports teams: the All-American Basketball Team and the House of David baseball squad. She pitched an inning for the Brooklyn Dodgers and played for the St. Louis Cardinals in an exhibition game. In one of her pitching stints, she struck out the legendary Joe DiMaggio. She even put together a touring vaudeville act about which she said, "I did the things I knew how to do, like putting the shot, acrobatics, and playing the mouth organ."

But Babe Didrikson still had new worlds to conquer. Her wide-ranging professional ventures had left her with enough money and leisure to dedicate herself to golf, which she mastered with her customary alacrity. She won her first tounament in 1934, and in 1935 she captured the Texas Women's Golf Association title. Barred after that by the United States Golf Association from the amateur circuit, she turned professional and received a lucrative endorsement deal from a major sporting goods company.

For lack of any major women's pro tournaments to play in, Didrikson spent the following year touring with the men's champion Gene Sarazen, playing exhibitions around the world before packed galleries. In 1938 she married the professional wrestler George Zaharias. After five years as a professional, Didrikson rejoined the amateur ranks in 1944 in order to participate in high-profile golf tournaments. The couple took up residence in California, where Babe went into intensive golf training in preparation for her return to the presitgious amateur tour in 1944. She then captured 17 consecutive amateur golf tournaments and, in 1947, became the first American to capture the leading tournament of the day, the British Women's Amateur Championship, in 1947.

Having vanquished the world of women's amateur golf, Babe, along with Patty Berg, cofounded the Ladies Professional Golf Association (LPGA). She was the Women's Open Champion in 1948, 1950, and 1954, the last victory achieved in the

1914 Mildred Ella Didrikson in Port Arthur, Texas.

1932 At Olympics in Los Angeles, Didrikson sets world records in javelin throw and 80-meter hurdle, winning two gold medals; sets two other world records.

1933 Didrikson plays exhibition game with St. Louis Cardinals; strikes out Joe DiMaggio.

1944 Didrikson returns to amateur golf; wins 17 consecutive tournaments 1946–47.

1949 Didrikson co-founds the Ladies Professional Golf Association.

1954 Didrikson wins U.S. Women's open by a record 12 shots.

1956 Didrikson dies in Galveston, Texas.

"My goal was to be the greatest athlete who ever lived."

Babe Didrikson

aftermath of surgery for cancer that was diagnosed in 1953. Babe Didrikson succumbed to the cancer on September 27, 1956, at age 43. ◆

DiMaggio, Joe

NOVEMBER 25, 1914–MARCH 9, 1999 ● BASEBALL PLAYER

"J oltin" Joe DiMaggio was as much a symbol of American history as he was a legend in baseball history. He played the game with a grace and dignity rarely seen in sports, both in his era and today. His 56-game hitting streak in 1941 is one of the most treasured—and, many believe, unbreakable—records in all of sports. It also helped him earn a place on Major League Baseball's All-Century team, announced at the 1999 World Series.

> *"It's mostly a matter of luck. You have to get lucky breaks to run up a long consecutive batting streak. And I got plenty of them."*
>
> Joe DiMaggio referring to his 56-game batting streak, 1941

Born in Martinez, California, on Nov. 25, 1914, Joseph Paul DiMaggio began his career not far from home. He began playing baseball with his brothers in the sandlots of the neighborhood. During the Depression, Joe dropped out of high school to take a job working on the docks. But he knew what he really wanted to do. Two of Joe's brothers, Dominic and Vincent, played baseball for the minor-league San Francisco Seals (both also went on to solid major league careers). Joe's father was a fisherman, but Joe and his brothers saw their futures heading down a different path. In 1932, Joe joined his brothers on the Seals.

In DiMaggio's first full season, 1933, he hit in 61 straight games—a hint of things to come. But DiMaggio would have to cross the country to find his place in history. After his 1935 Seals' season, the New York Yankees brought the young outfielder up to the major leagues.

DiMaggio was an instant hit, playing left field in his first season with the Yanks (he would move to centerfield for the rest of his career beginning in 1937). Despite the pressure of playing in "The House that Ruth Built," DiMaggio calmly batted .323 and had 125 runs batted in (RBI) as the Yankees steamrolled to a World Series title.

DiMaggio immediately inherited the role of team leader from Babe Ruth, who left the Yanks in 1934, and Lou Gehrig, who would retire in June 1939. DiMaggio became the Yankees' heart and soul and was given the title of "Yankee Clipper."

The Yankees captured four straight championships in DiMaggio's first four years, and Joltin' Joe was steadily piling up monumental offensive numbers. In 1939, DiMaggio won his first Most Valuable Player (MVP) award, batting .381 with 30 home runs, 108 runs and 126 runs batted in.

Then came the 1941 season, which will long be remembered in baseball history.

The man who was a hero in New York, and to the Italian community, became a national icon. DiMaggio won the American League MVP award as he led the Yankees to another championship. He batted .351, with 30 home runs and 125 RBI, but none of those numbers mattered. Even Boston's Ted Williams' .406 batting average was completely overshadowed that year by what DiMaggio had accomplished from May 15 to July 17: he hit in 56 straight games, a feat yet to be approached in almost 60 years.

Unfortunately, DiMaggio was not able to build on his successes for very long, as he, along with many other prominent major leaguers such as Ted Williams, was drafted into the U.S. Army for service in World War II after the 1942 season.

DiMaggio returned to baseball in 1946 after his military service. His average dipped below .300 for the first time in his career, but he was soon back in the swing, edging Williams for the 1947 MVP award.

The Yankees won three straight championships from 1949–51. A rookie outfielder for the Yanks named Mickey Mantle began to turn people's heads in 1951. After an unimpressive 1951 season for DiMaggio, he announced his retirement on December 11. He finished his career with a .325 average, 361 home runs, 1,537 RBI and 1,390 runs. He was named to 13 All-Star teams and a three-time MVP, and was elected into the Hall of Fame in 1955.

DiMaggio is as well known for his short marriage to actress Marilyn Monroe, as he is for anything he did on the baseball diamond. They divorced after 10 months of marriage in 1954, but remained close. After her death in 1962, DiMaggio refused to talk about her publicly—and stayed true to this for the rest of his life. Later, Joe became a pitchman for Mr. Coffee, appearing in television commercials and ads for the company. But his mystique as a quiet, unassuming character continued.

1914 DiMaggio is born in Martinez, California.

1933 In his first full season, with the San Francisco Seals, DiMaggio hits in 61 straight games.

1939 DiMaggio wins his first Most Valuable Player award (also in 1941 and 1947); he boasts a .381 batting average.

1941 DiMaggio slugs his way to an unmatched 56-game hitting streak.

1951 DiMaggio retires with .325 career average and 361 home runs.

1955 DiMaggio is elected to the Baseball Hall of Fame.

1999 DiMaggio dies in Hollywood, Fla., at age 84.

During the World Series run of the 1998 Yankees, DiMaggio became very ill with pneumonia. But he recovered and it was hoped that he would be able to throw out the first pitch to his former teammate Yogi Berra at Yankee Stadium on Opening Day 1999. Unfortunately, just a month before that date, DiMaggio health worsened, and on March 9, 1999, America had to say goodbye to Joltin' Joe. Opening Day turned into a memorial service for DiMaggio, and the Yankees wore his number 5 on their sleeves for the remainder of the season.

Singers Paul Simon, who together with Art Garfunkel immortalized DiMaggio in the 1960's song "Mrs. Robinson," sang the song that day in centerfield at Yankee Stadium, and DiMaggio's number 5 was shown underneath the "At Bat" sign on the stadium's scoreboards. The line from the song was bittersweet that day, but evoked memories from every generation who saw him play or even heard his name: "Where have you gone, Joe DiMaggio? Joltin' Joe has left and gone away." ◆

The American League

After the founding of the National League (NL) in 1876, many rival leagues challenged its supremacy over professional baseball in the United States, but none succeeded until the American League (AL) was born in 1899. The American League's genesis dates to a 1892 meeting in Cincinnati between Byron Bancroft (Ban) Johnson, a sportswriter for the *Commercial Gazette,* and Charles A. Comiskey, the manager of the Cincinnati Reds. Discovering a shared antipathy to the powerful National League, they set about reorganizing the minor-league Western League (WL) into a credible rival to the NL. In 1893 Johnson assumed the presidency of the league, and in 1884 Comiskey took the reins of the WL team in Sioux City, Iowa, and transferred it to St. Paul, Minnesota. That year they enlisted an important ally when a former major leaguer named Cornelius McGillicuddy, better known as Connie Mack, took over the WL Milwaukee franchise (which later became the Philadelphia Athletics).

The Western League took a great leap forward in 1899, when the coal baron Charles Somers became a major investor. Taking direct aim at the National League's monopoly on major-league status, Johnson renamed his circuit the American League in October 1899 and in 1900 took on the NL's former Cleveland franchise, which the senior circuit had shed in cutting back to eight clubs in 1900. Thus strengthened financially and organizationally, Johnson was ready to make his move, and in 1901 he declared the American League a major league, withdrawing from the association of minor league clubs.

The AL boldly fielded teams in three National League cities Boston, Chicago, and Philadelphia to round out its eight-team roster, which also featured franchises in Milwaukee, Detroit, Cleveland, Baltimore, and Washington. After St. Louis replaced Milwaukee in 1902 and New York replaced Baltimore in 1903, the American League franchise lineup remained unchanged for nearly six decades.

The new league was an immediate success, outdrawing the NL overall in 1902 and topping its attendance in the four cities where the leagues went head to head: New York, St. Louis, Chicago, and Boston. No longer able to ignore the upstart AL, the NL agreed in 1903 to recognize the AL as a major league and to participate in a three-man commission to oversee the operations of major league baseball; its members were Harry C. Pulliam, president of the NL; Ban Johnson, president of the AL; and a commissioner-at-large, August Herrmann, the owner of the Cincinnati Reds.

In 1903 the two leagues agreed to play a World Series between their respective pennant winners. In 1904, however, John McGraw, the manager of the haughty NL champion New York Giants, refused to play the American League winner, but the arrangement was formalized as a mandatory event in 1905. The AL complement of franchises held at eight until 1961, when the Los Angeles Angels and the reborn Washington Senators joined the league (the original Senators moved to Minnesota and became the Twins that year). In 1969 the AL expanded again to include the Kansas City Royals and the Seattle Pilots (who later moved to Milwaukee and became the Brewers), dividing into Eastern and Western divisions and introducing a round of playoffs between the division winners to determine the league champion. Two additional rounds of expansion brought the AL complement to 14 clubs: in 1977 the Seattle Mariners and Toronto Blue Jays joined the circuit, and the Tampa Bay Devil Rays began play in 1998. After the 1993 season both major leagues divided into three divisions Eastern, Central, and Western and included a wild card team in postseason competition, a move that created an additional round of playoffs leading up to the World Series.

The American League was slower than the National League in achieving racial integration. After the NL's Brooklyn Dodgers broke the "color barrier" by promoting Jackie Robinson to the major leagues in April 1947, the Cleveland Indians brought up Larry Doby, an African American, at the tail end of that season, but the AL did not play a full season of racially integrated ball until 1948. For the following decade the NL sought out and promoted black talent at a far brisker pace than the AL, many of whose franchises dragged their heels; the Boston Red Sox did not have a black player until 1959, by which time the NL had twice as many black players as the AL. The racial composition of the two league's has since become evenly balanced.

In 1973, alarmed by dropping popularity resulting from a paucity of offensive production, the American League approved the introduction of the designated hitter, the first radical rule change in the modern history of the sport (the National League has so far rejected the DH rule).

In 1997 the AL and NL began playing a limited schedule of interleague games during the regular season.

Donovan, Anne

NOVEMBER 1, 1961– ● BASKETBALL PLAYER

W hen three-time Olympian Anne Donovan took the basketball court, she consistently towered over the other players not only because of her height—six foot eight inches tall—but because of her extraordinary skill and dedication to the sport.

Donovan was born in Ridgewood, New Jersey. She began to attract national attention as a 15-year-old playing in the Amateur Athletic Union (AAU) in Tennessee, as the USA Basketball organization stepped up its efforts to find and groom bigger players, in an effort to counter the height of players in the Soviet Union and other countries that the United States would face in international competition. She took her basketball skills to Virginia's Old Dominion University, where she became the most celebrated player in the program's history. She won the Naismith National Player of the Year Award in 1983 and was named Kodak All-American in 1980, 1981, and 1982. Enjoying equal success in the classroom, she was named to the Collegiate Sports Information Directors GTE Academic All-American teams in 1982 and 1983 and was inducted into that organization's Academic All-American Hall of Fame in 1994.

Donovan's career at Old Dominion was nothing short of outstanding. As a freshman she led her team to a 37–1 record and an AIAW national championship in 1980. Her team finished third in the AIAW tournament in 1981, and in 1983 she led her team to the NCAA Final Four. During her four years at ODU her teams compiled a 116–20 record, and by the end of that time Donovan held nearly every school record, 25 in all. She was the Lady Monarchs' all-time leading scorer with 2,719 points and all-time leading rebounder with 1,976. Her total of 801 blocked shots still stands as an NCAA record.

Throughout the 1980s Donovan was also a major figure in international competition, playing for the United States on 11 different teams that won nine gold and two silver medals. At age 18 she was the youngest member of the 1980 Olympic team, and although the United States boycotted the Olympics that year, the Americans won the qualifying round in Bulgaria. Donovan also played on the gold-medal–winning U.S. Olympic

> *"In the same way Kareem Abdul-Jabbar changed things a lot, Anne was the first 'big girl' to really make a huge impact. She wasn't just big. She was very skilled."*
>
> Tara VanDerveer, Stanford women's basketball coach, on Anne Donovan

teams in 1984 and 1988, becoming one of just four players in history, men or women, to play on three Olympic teams. While she didn't score many points in the 1988 Olympics in Seoul, Korea, she made key contributions at critical moments in the games, enabling the United States to defend its championship by beating Yugoslavia in the gold medal game.

In 1981 she played on the World University Games team that won a silver medal. In 1983 and 1986 she was a member of the USA World Championship teams that won the silver medal (1983) and gold (1986). Donovan also played on gold-medal-winning Pan American Games teams in 1983 and 1987, and she helped lead her 1986 Goodwill Games team to a gold medal. In 1984 and 1987 she played on the R. William Jones Cup teams, winning gold in 1984. In the meantime Donovan played professionally overseas, first in Shizuoka, Japan (1983–89), then in Modena, Italy (1988–89).

In the late 1980s, with her playing days behind her, Donovan turned to coaching. She returned to Old Dominion, where she served as an assistant coach from 1989 to 1995, helping the team to four titles in the Colonial Athletic Association conference and five NCAA tournament appearances. She then took the head coaching job at East Carolina University, turning around a program that had won a total of just 10 games in the two seasons before her arrival. In her first year at East Carolina, 1995–96, she bettered that total with 11 wins; in her second year, the team won 13 games and advanced to the final game of the conference tournament for the first time since 1992. That year, 1997, she also helped coach the U.S. World Championship Qualifying team to a silver medal.

Donovan left East Carolina to accept the head coaching job with the short-lived ABL's Philadelphia Rage for the 1997–98 season. In 1996 she was appointed to the USA Basketball's Executive Committee as an athlete representative for the 1996–2000 quadrennium.

Throughout her career Donovan gave generously to the sport, participating in Women's Basketball Coaches camps and helping USA Basketball when the organization needed her. In 1995 Donovan was inducted into the Naismith Basketball Hall of Fame. Most recently, in 1999 she joined 25 other women in the inaugural class of the Women's Basketball Hall of Fame in Nashville, Tennessee. ◆

1961 Donovan is born in Ridgewood, New Jersey.

1980 Donovan leads Old Dominion, with 37–1 record, to AIAW national championship; at 18, she becomes the youngest member of U.S. Olympic team.

1983 Donovan is named Naismith National Player of the Year.

1984 Donovan plays on gold medal–winning U.S. Olympic team (also in 1988).

1995 Donovan is inducted into Naismith Basketball Hall of Fame.

Durocher, Leo

JULY 27, 1905–OCTOBER 7, 1991 ● BASEBALL PLAYER AND MANAGER

Nicknamed "The Lip," Leo Durocher parlayed a 20-year playing career as a slick-fielding infielder into one of the most successful and historically important managing careers in the annals of Major League Baseball. In a career that spanned 34 years, Durocher played with greats like Babe Ruth and Dizzy Dean and was Jackie Robinson's first manager when Robinson broke the Major League Baseball color barrier, as well as the first major league manager of the great Willie Mays. He was also the winning manager in possibly the greatest baseball game ever played.

Born in West Springfield, Massachusetts, Leo Earnest Durocher grew up in a family or railroad workers. Always a small, hot tempered boy, he was expelled from school in the ninth grade for fighting with a teacher. His scholastic career over, Durocher began working at the electric company and playing semi-pro baseball.

In 1925, Durocher's skills as a ballplayer were noticed by a Yankee scout who signed him to a contract. After two games, Durocher was sent to the minor leagues to improve his hitting. Later, despite hitting .238 and .253 in two minor league seasons, Durocher—always an excellent fielder—was brought back up to the big leagues.

At 5 foot, 10 inches and 160 pounds, Durocher always carried himself with a swagger, never taking a backward step on the field, while off the field he liked to live the life of the well-heeled, **cavorting** with movie stars and other celebrities.

cavorting: engaging in extravagant social behavior.

After two years with the Yankees—which included an on-field altercation with the pugilistic Ty Cobb; being given the nickname "All-American Out" by the legendary Babe Ruth; and being part of the 1928 world championship team— Durocher was traded to the Cincinnati Reds. After three years with the Reds, Durocher was once again traded. This time, however, he was sent to a team that fit his rough and tumble personality perfectly: the St. Louis Cardinals. Durocher's slick fielding and all-out play made him a perfect fit for a team that was known as the Gashouse Gang, a group of wildmen on the field, led by Dizzy Dean and Joe Medwick. Durocher and the Cardinals won the World Series in 1933. Yet after five years with the Cards, Durocher was once again traded, this time to the Brooklyn Dodgers, where he became player-manager in 1939.

Durocher managed the Dodgers until 1948, and in that time continued his involvement in history-making events. In 1947, Durocher was managing the Dodgers in spring training when General Manager Branch Rickey brought Robinson up to be the first African-American to play in the Majors. While many of Durocher's other players griped at the prospect of playing with Robinson, Durocher befriended him, knowing that the talented African-American second baseman would help the Dodgers win baseball games, which is all Durocher ever cared about.

Controversy found Durocher when, in 1947, he was forced to sit out the season for a suspension by commissioner Happy Chandler for reported ties to members of organized crime. After a year away from the game, Durocher switched teams, moving from the Dodgers to their bitter rivals, the New York Giants.

In the three years from 1948 to 1951, Durocher assembled the team he always wanted, and with the addition of Mays in centerfield, the Giants were a team to be reckoned with. However, in 1951, the Giants trailed the rival Dodgers by 13.5 games with 44 games left. The Giants were not to be held back though, as they won 37 of 44, forcing a three-game playoff with the Dodgers to determine who would win the pennant. With the series tied at a game apiece, and with the Dodgers leading 4–2 in the bottom of the ninth inning, Bobby Thomson's "shot heard 'round the world"—a three-run home run—won the game and the pennant for the Giants.

While the Giants would go on to lose the 1951 World Series to the New York Yankees, they would be back in the Series in 1954, and this time they swept a talented Cleveland Indians team and Durocher had his first world championship as a manager. Durocher continued managing over the next two decades, with stops with the Chicago Cubs and Houston Astros, where he finished his managing career in 1973 at the age of 68. He won 2,008 times in 3,739 games and was named Manager of the Year three times by The Sporting News. Always a fierce competitor, Durocher made many enemies in baseball, but always stayed true to the quote that is attributed to him, "Nice guys finish last," which was also the title of his autobiography. Durocher was named to the baseball Hall of Fame in 1994, three years after his death. ◆

1905 Leo Earnest Durocher is born in West Springfield, Massachusetts.

1931 Durocher starts with the St. Louis Cardinals.

1933 Durocher's Cardinals win World Series.

1939 Durocher becomes player-manager of the Brooklyn Dodgers.

1948 Durocher switches to the New York Giants.

1954 Durocher's Giants beat Cleveland Indians in World Series.

"You don't save a pitcher for tomorrow. Tomorrow it may rain."

Leo Durocher

Duval, David

NOVEMBER 9, 1971– ● GOLFER

David Duval was born in Jacksonville, Florida, on November 9, 1971. The young, rangy (6′ 0″, 180 pounds) golfer had become one of the sport's biggest stars by the late 1990s, just a few years after turning professional.

Duval showed promise at the game as a teenager. His father, Bob Duval, is also a golfer (today a professional on the senior tour), so David was exposed to the world of golf at an early age.

Duval attended Georgia Tech, and he was named Collegiate Player of the Year in 1993. That year, he also won the Dave Williams Award. Teamed with Gary Hallberg and Phil Mickelson, Duval was the only four-time, Division 1–A, first team All Americans.

With these accomplishments behind him, Duval—who wears sunglasses on the course because his eyes are very sensitive to light—decided to turn professional. Thus began one of the most amazing stories in Professional Golfers' Association (PGA) history.

The year 1995 marked Duval's first season as a pro. He had an amazing start—in fact, he set a rookie earnings record by picking up $881,436 in prize money. Duval came in second at three major matches: the AT&T Pebble Beach National Pro-Am, the Bob Hope Chrysler Classic, and the Memorial Tournament. He had eight top-10 finishes, and 14 top-25 finishes.

It was not just beginner's luck, and Duval did not go into a "sophomore slump," as so often happens in sports and other endeavors. In 1996, his second season, Duval actually improved on his own record, collecting nearly $1 million in prize money. He had two second-place finishes, and three third-place finishes.

In 1997, Duval won the last three tournaments of the season. (He was the first player since Nick Price in 1993 to achieve this.) Many fans consider this period to comprise one of the most exciting three-week periods in golf during the entire decade. His first tour title was collected at the Michelob Championship at Kingsmill, followed by the Walt Disney World/Oldsmobile Classic and then the Tour Championship. Duval finished second in official earnings with $1,885,308.

By 1998, Duval was ranked second on the PGA Tour's All-Around rankings. This was an especially impressive feat considering the high quality of the players on the Tour in recent years. With just a few seasons of professional golf behind him, Duval was already one of the dominant players on the tour.

Duval's 1998 winnings topped the PGA list. He earned a record $2,591,031 on the PGA Tour, the fastest that someone had ever reached that level in one year. He not only captured the Money title, but he also collected the scoring title, earning the **Vardon Trophy**, which is awarded to the person with the lowest stroke average for the year (69.13).

That year Duval won four tournaments: the Tucson Chrysler Classic, the Shell Houston Open, the NEC World Series of Golf, and the Michelob Championship at Kingsmill. (Duval was only the second person in history to win the Michelob tournament twice in succession; the first person to do so was Calvin Peete, in 1982–83.)

Duval had another stunning success in 1999. He shot a 59 in the final round in the final round of the Bob Hope Chrysler Classic, at La Quinta, California. This was the lowest final round score in the history of golf, tying the lowest rounds shot in the PGA by Al Geiberger (1977) and Chip Beck (1991). Duval also won four tournaments before the Masters, which takes place in April—the first time anyone had done this since Johnny Miller in 1974. Duval tied for sixth in the Masters.

By the summer of 1999, Duval was ranked the top golfer in the world (though he lost that distinction later in the year to Tiger Woods). Duval also made the U.S. team for the 1999 Ryder Cup by being second on the money list; the top 10 money winners are automatically invited to join the team, with two additional golfers chosen by the team captain. The U.S. team, captained by Ben Crenshaw, won in a dramatic final-day finish.

The young golfer's phenomenal success lies in his good all-around game. Not only can he hit the long drives consistently, but he has a good short game as well, with one of the best

1971 Duval is born in Jacksonville, Florida.

1993 Duval is named Collegiate Player of the Year.

1998 Duval is ranked number two in PGA Tour's overall rankings; earnings top the PGA list.

1999 Duval is ranked top golfer in the world; plays on winning U.S. Ryder Cup team.

Vardon Trophy: trophy given annually by the Professional Golfers Association for the player with the best scoring average over the year.

putting averages on the tour. Besides having good native athletic ability, Duval has achieved these skills by practicing diligently since he was a teenager.

For Duval, a plus of turning pro has been the interesting golfing relationship he has with his father. In 1997, David's father Bob joined the Senior PGA Tour. In his rookie year, Bob followed in his son's footsteps, finishing an impressive 28th on the tour's money list. David caddied for his father at the Transamerica tournament—and his father carried *his* clubs when David played at the 1997 Skins game.

Duval lives in Jacksonville Beach, Florida. When not playing golf, he likes to read, go fly-fishing, surf, and play baseball and other sports. ◆

Earnhardt, Dale

APRIL 29, 1951– ● RACE CAR DRIVER

No one has ever accused Dale Earnhardt of being the most polite driver on the stock-car racing circuit, but no one can deny that he is one of the best. Known as "The Intimidator" for a driving style that some celebrate as aggressive and others decry as reckless, Earnhardt has scaled the heights of his profession with an impressive winning record that includes seven prestigious NASCAR Winston Cup Series titles (the last in 1995), a record he shares with Richard Petty.

A native of North Carolina, Ralph Dale Earnhardt was born to the world of race car driving. His father, Ralph, was a sensation on NASCAR's minor league circuit in the 1950s and 1960s, driving three nights a week on tracks throughout Georgia and the Carolinas to support his five children. Beguiled by the glamour of his father's exploits on the racing circuit, young Dale found it increasingly difficult to abide his father's prolonged absences and dropped out of school in the ninth grade to pursue his own fascination with stock cars. Dale's father was not pleased, however. "It was the only thing I ever let my daddy down over," Dale later said. "He wanted me to finish [high school]; it was the only thing he ever pleaded with me to do. But I

1951 — Earnhardt is born in North Carolina.

1979 — Earnhardt wins Rookie of the Year award.

1980 — Earnhardt becomes the first sophomore driver to win the NASCAR championship, the first of seven career Winston Cup championships.

1998 — Earnhardt wins the Daytona 500.

1999 — Earnhardt wins the Winston 500.

pluck: determination and courage in the face of long odds.

was so hardheaded. For about a year and a half after that, we didn't have a close relationship."

Earnhardt scuffled for several years, working on cars and cultivating contacts. When he was 19, some friends agreed to let him begin racing their cars on short dirt tracks in the Charlotte area. He even entered many of the same events as his father, although Ralph drove in the top division while Dale was consigned to the "junker" category. Early on, he began to emulate his father's intimidating driving style and enjoyed some modest success. "Daddy had begun to help me with engine work and giving me used tires," he recalled, "and he'd talked to Mama about putting me in his car."

Then a stunning turn of fate changed the course of Dale's career. In 1973, Ralph Earnhardt collapsed and died of a heart attack while working on the carburetor of his car. Dale then inherited his father's two racing cars and his shop in Kannapolis, North Carolina. Dale recalled, "It [my father's death] left me in a situation where I had to make it on my own. I'd give up everything I got if he were still alive, but I don't think I'd be where I am if he hadn't died."

Dale endured several more years of grit before he experienced any glory. With his sights set on racing in the Grand National Division, he labored on the circuit as a welder and mechanic, surviving on a series of bank loans and waiting for the right break. In 1978, with his **pluck** and resources nearly exhausted, Earnhardt finally got a shot at Grand National racing, and then he took off: in 1979 he won the Rookie of the Year Award, and in 1980 he became the first sophomore driver to win the coveted NASCAR championship.

For an impulsive man in his late twenties, this gusher of fame and money turned out to be too much of a good thing, as Earnhardt's personal life, never an island of calm, began to spin out of control. A friend recalls, "He was the kind of guy who would wake you up at 3 A.M." Married at 17 and divorced by 19, Earnhardt remarried at 20 and was divorced again by 25. It was only after a nasty accident at Pocono in 1982 that Earnhardt began to take stock of his personal priorities. Lying in a hospital bed with a broken leg, he proposed to his current wife, Teresa Houston, who has provided the emotional anchor and business savvy that had been lacking in Earnhardt's extended adolescence.

Settling into a life of domestic tranquility, in 1988 Earnhardt bought 300 acres of woodland and has since turned it into a working farm where he raises bulls, horses, chickens, and dogs. But as much as Earnhardt began to soften some of his edge in his personal life, he has remained as relentless as ever behind the wheel, earning IROC championships in 1990 and 1995. His greatest triumph, however, came in 1998 when he finally won his first Daytona 500, the race known as "the big one." Speaking of his team's efforts in that race, Earnhardt said, "This one tops them all. It was just like Elway when he won the Super Bowl. We had that look in our eyes, and we won."

Now nearing age 50 and with career earnings of more than $31 million, Earnhardt is not ready to step aside, but he is ready to share some of the glory with his son Dale Jr., who made his debut in May 1999 in NASCAR's top series. In the Earnhardt family, the love of stock-car racing seems to run in the blood. As Dale Earnhardt told a reporter, "I love racing. It's something that's in me. It was born and bred in me by my daddy, and that's why I'm so good at it. Racing comes just like breathing to me. It's always going to be there, like my heartbeat." ◆

Earnhardt is not ready to step aside, but he is ready to share some of the glory with his son Dale Jr.

Edwards, Teresa

JULY 19,1964– ● BASKETBALL PLAYER

Teresa Edwards was born in Cairo, Georgia, on July 19, 1964. She was the oldest of four children—and the only girl. She always enjoyed playing basketball because, as she told USA Basketball, "It was the only game growing up where I could go up against the boys and beat them."

About the only thing she loved as much as basketball was her family and her hometown of Cairo, which is just outside of Atlanta. That made her choice of which school to play college basketball easy: she chose the University of Georgia. There, Edwards was her opponents' worst nightmare, winning a slew of awards and honors. She was named Freshman All-America in 1983 and Consensus All-America her junior and senior seasons. She also earned All-Southeastern Conference (SEC) honors as a sophomore, junior and senior. With Edwards leading the way, the Bulldogs compiled a 116–17 record, won three SEC titles, made the NCAA Tournament all four years, and reached the Final Four twice. Her No. 5 was retired by the University upon

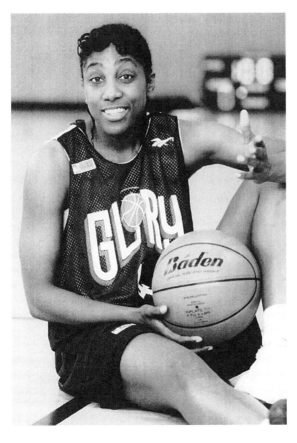

her graduation in 1986, only the third time a UGA had retired a number.

While Edwards' impact on the college game was profound, it was nothing compared to her effect on the United States national team.

Edwards acquired a taste for gold early on, helping the U.S. Olympic Festival South team win gold medals in 1981, 1982 and 1983. By 1984, at age 20, she was ready for the big time. At the 1984 Summer Olympics in Los Angeles, the 5' 11" point guard made the U.S. Women's basketball team, and became the youngest woman ever to play in the Olympics. The women's team took home the gold and, in Edwards, had found a cornerstone upon which to lay the foundation for unprecedented future success.

"T," as she became known, was a fixture on the U.S. Women's team and was a major factor in their domination of international competitions. Between 1983 and 1991, the USA women won 46 consecutive games.

Following the 1992 Olympics Edwards contemplated retirement. Had she called it a career then, Edwards would have accomplished a great deal. Over the years, she had been named USA Basketball's Female Athlete of the Year three times (1987, 1990 and 1996), and had won her share of medals. But her desire to play basketball overruled her thoughts of retirement. At 29, she made the team that represented the U.S. in the 1994 World Championships. After the team won a bronze, she again gave serious thought to retirement. After all, she had been playing overseas for the better part of nine years, including stops in Italy (1987–88), Japan (1989–93), Spain (1994) and France (1994).

But again, in 1996, at age 32, Edwards decided she wasn't through yet. She tried out for and made the 1996 Olympic team. Edwards was overcome with emotion at the press confer-

"Basketball chose me, because as a child it was the one sport in which I could outperform the boys."

Teresa Edwards in *Vanity Fair*, May 1996

ence announcing that she had made the team and would get to represent her country while playing in her home city of Atlanta.

Making the Olympic team rejuvenated her game. When Edwards took the court at the start of the 1996 Olympics, she made history as the first basketball player—man or woman—to play in four Olympiads. "T" keyed a U.S. offense that dominated the games and took home the gold medal, her third in Olympic competition. Edwards dished out a Games-high 8.0 assists per game, while adding 6.9 points on a sizzling 60.0 percent shooting from the field while pulling down 3.8 rebounds. During the Games, she set USA Olympic single-game records with 15 assists versus Australia and 3-point field goals made, with seven versus Cuba. The U.S. team was literally unbeatable, as they compiled a 60–0 overall record for the year and were named the 1996 U.S. Olympic Committee and USA Basketball Team of the Year. Later that same year, Edwards' dream of playing professionally in the United States also became reality. Edwards joined the American Basketball League (ABL) and got to play with her hometown Atlanta Glory. She dazzled, showing off her prolific scoring touch and superb all-around game. Edwards was the only player in ABL history to score over 40 points in a game, doing it four times over two years. She was named a first-team All-Star both years she played in the league and was runner up in the 1996 MVP voting. She finished her ABL career with the ABL's Philadelphia Rage in 1998.

Although she has never played in the Women's National Basketball Association (WNBA), Edwards has continued playing for the U.S. Women's National Team. She played on the 1997 World Championships squad and 1998 USA Women's National Team.

Over the years, Edwards has been a member of 18 different USA Basketball teams that have won 13 gold, one silver and three bronze medals (the 1995–96 National Team did not compete for a medal), and compiled an overall record of 145–8 for a 94.8 winning percentage. She's played in 161 games representing the United States, and has compiled some incredible statistics—1,760 points (10.9 ppg.), 693 assists, 452 rebounds and 286 steals. Edwards owns USA Olympic career records for games played (24), assists (116) and steals (56). She also is second in points (216) and third in rebounds (53).

Today, Edwards dreams of playing in her fifth Olympiad by earning a spot on the 2000 Olympic Team. She would be 36

1964 Edwards is born in Cairo, Georgia.

1983 Edwards, playing for the University of Georgia, is named Freshman All-America.

1984 At 20, Edwards is the youngest woman to play basketball in Olympics.

1987 Edwards is named USA Basketball's Female Athlete of the Year (also in 1990 and 1996).

1996 Edwards plays on the unbeaten U.S. Olympic team (60–0), becoming the first basketball player to compete in four Olympiads.

when the games in Sydney, Australia begin, but no one can deny the power of Teresa Edwards on the court. ◆

Emerson, Roy

NOVEMBER 3, 1936– ●TENNIS PLAYER

Over the next few years, Emerson perfected his game under coach Harry Hopman and developed a fast, aggressive style playing doubles.

In the late 1950s and 1960s the world of men's tennis was dominated by a fleet-footed Australian named Roy Emerson. Successor to his countryman Rod Laver as the top-ranked amateur player in the world, Emerson won 12 Grand Slam singles and 16 doubles titles during his career, for a record 28 Grand Slam championships.

Born in rural Kingsway, Australia, Emerson grew up on his father's dairy farm near Blackbutt, Queensland. In later years, he attributed his strong wrists to all the time he spent milking cows on the farm. Emerson began playing tennis on a local court, and at age 10 he started taking lessons from Norm Brimson, a local coach. The young player made rapid progress, and in 1951 his family moved from their farm to the city of Brisbane, where Emerson had more opportunities to develop his talents.

Emerson's first notable achievement was a victory over his celebrated fellow Australian, Lewis Hoad, at matches in Newport, Rhode Island, in 1954. He joined the junior squad of the Australian Davis Cup team that year and gained great experience in the competition. Over the next few years, Emerson perfected his game under coach Harry Hopman and developed a fast, aggressive style playing doubles with fellow countrymen Rod Laver and Neale Fraser.

In 1959 Emerson moved up in the Australian amateur ranks after Mal Anderson and Ashley Cooper turned professional. On the Australian Davis Cup team that year, he helped Australia win back the cup, which it had lost to the United States the year before. Besides his Davis Cup performance, Emerson won the men's doubles championships with partner Neale Fraser at Wimbledon, the U.S. Open, and the Italian championship.

Emerson played on the winning Davis Cup team again in 1960 and claimed a number two ranking among Australian players, just under Rod Laver. That same year Emerson and

Fraser successfully defended their doubles title at the U.S. Open. Emerson won his first singles Grand Slam titles in 1961, upsetting Rod Laver in both the Australian and U.S. Opens. He also teamed with Laver to win the doubles championship at the French Open, and he and Fraser won the doubles at both Wimbledon and the Italian championship.

In 1962 Emerson repeated his French doubles victory with Fraser, but lost the U.S. Open singles title to his friend and rival Laver. The Australians also successfully defended their Davis Cup title, the 11th Australian victory in 13 years. An injured rib limited Emerson's participation in the Davis Cup tournament to the doubles matches, which he and Laver won by beating Rafael Osuana and Antonio Palafox. After the Davis Cup, Laver turned professional, so Emerson became the undisputed top-ranked Australian amateur player.

Emerson started off strong in 1963, winning the singles title at the Australian Open by beating Ken Fletcher in three straight sets. However, soon after this victory, Emerson slipped into a slump, losing the U.S. National Indoor Tennis Championship and the Dixie International Tennis Championship within a week of each other. Regaining his stride, he defeated Pierre Darmon for the singles title at the French Open and teamed with Manuel Santana of Spain to win the French doubles title as well. Emerson suffered a surprising upset at Wimbledon, losing to German player Willy Bungert in the quarterfinals. He also failed to make the finals of the U.S. Open that year, losing to Frank Froehling of Florida. Emerson and his fellow Aussies also lost the Davis Cup that year to the United States, although he won his singles matches and did well in the doubles.

In 1964 Emerson won his third singles title at the Australian Open, beating Fred Stolle. Later that year he lost his French title but won his first Wimbledon singles championship as well as his second U.S. Open title. Dropped from the Davis Cup team early that year because of a dispute with the Australian Lawn Tennis Association over the financial status of amateur players, Emerson and other players were reinstated in time for the elimination rounds. The Australians went on to win back the Davis Cup from the United States.

In 1965 Emerson won his fourth singles title at the Australian Open, his second Wimbledon singles championship, and a French doubles title. He also helped Australia win its twentieth Davis Cup that year as well. During the next few years

1936	Emerson is born in Kingsway, Australia.
1959	Emerson wins the men's doubles championships at Wimbledon, the U.S. Open, and the Italian Open, with Neale Fraser.
1961	Emerson wins his first singles Grand Slam.
1964	Emerson wins his third singles title at Australian Open; wins Wimbledon. 1965 Emerson wins his fourth singles title at Australian Open, second Wimbledon singles, and French doubles.

Emerson won a number of major titles: two Australian singles titles (1966, 1967); one French singles title (1967); two Australian doubles titles (1966, 1967); a Wimbledon doubles (1971); and a U.S. doubles (1966). He also helped lead Australia to two additional Davis Cup victories in 1966 and 1967. By 1967 Emerson had played in nine straight Davis Cup tournaments, of which Australia won eight. During his Davis Cup years Emerson amassed a impressive record—22 of 24 singles wins and 13 of 15 doubles.

Emerson turned professional in 1968 and continued competing for a number of years. In 1978, as both player and coach of the Boston Lobsters in World Team Tennis, he helped lead his team to the semifinals of the league playoffs. During his professional career, Emerson won three singles titles and 30 doubles championships. Elected to the International Tennis Hall of Fame in 1982, he has continued to play occasionally on the seniors' tour. ◆

Evans, Janet

August 28, 1971– ● Swimmer

Janet Beth Evans was born to Paul and Barbara Evans on August 28, 1971, in Placentia, California. Evans would become an international swimming star through her gold-medal performances in two Olympics, and swimming fans credit her with nearly single-handedly reviving the international prestige of the United States in the sport.

Evans was able to swim by age two, and she started to compete two years later. Even as a young girl, she was an extremely focused competitive swimmer. Early on she displayed a fierce concentration and uncommon persistence in her training. The effort paid off in meet after meet. Evans' victories in local and regional swim meets gradually gave way to triumphs in national, and then international, competitions. In 1983, at age ten, she set a National Age Group record in the 200-meter freestyle, a time (2:18.07) that stood for seven years. She did well in Junior National competitions for several years, coming in in the top three in three different events in 1984. In June 1986, Evans performed adequately but not spectacularly at the World Trials. Just a month later, however, she captured two bronze medals at the Goodwill Games in Moscow, Russia (then part of the Soviet Union). And in December of that year, she took first place in three events at the U.S. Open.

In 1987, Evans' talent exploded. The teenager took first place again and again in national and international events, breaking several world records in the meantime. She was named USS Swimmer of the Year and ranked first in several National High School rankings (as a sophomore swimming for El Dorado High School). For her record-setting performance in the 1,500-meter freestyle at the Summer Nationals, Evans won the Phillips Performance Award.

By this time, perhaps due to her years of focused training, long races were clearly Evans' forte. The grueling 1,500-meter competition had emerged as her best event (though not her favorite).

In 1988, Evans did well again in National High School rankings and the USS Spring Nationals, collecting many first-places. But that year, the Olympics were foremost in her thoughts. She breezed through the Olympic Trials and was selected for the U.S. team. The Olympic Summer Games were held that summer in Seoul, South Korea. No one expected the United States swimmers to perform well against the East German women, who (like their male counterparts) had long dominated international swimming, but Evans surpassed all expectations. She set a world record in the 400-meter freestyle event, and brought home not one but three gold medals (in the 400-meter freestyle, the 800-meter freestyle, and the 400-meter individual medley).

Evans returned to her home in California a hero. To celebrate her exciting triumph in Seoul, her parents bought her a BMW with the license plate "3GOLD88." Not content to rest on her Olympic laurels, Evans kept pushing herself to excel in swimming. She loved competition, and it showed. In 1989, she took first place in many events in both national and international meets, including at the prestigious Pan Pacific Games in Tokyo, Japan. She was named the 1989 Sullivan Award winner, as the United States' top amateur athlete. That summer, she enrolled at Stanford University.

Over the next few years, Evans distinguished herself in important meets, whether swimming as an individual amateur or representing Stanford University. She was awarded the Honda-Brockerdick Cup Award, given each year to the nation's outstanding collegiate swimmer. Among other honors, she captured

1971 Janet Beth Evans is born in Placentia, California.

1987 Evans is named U.S. Swimmer of the Year; sets record in 1,500-meter freestyle at Summer Nationals.

1988 At the Olympics in Seoul, Evans sets a world record in the 400-meter freestyle and wins three gold medals.

1989 Evans takes first place at Pan Pacific Games, Tokyo; wins 1989 Sullivan Award for U.S.'s top amateur athlete.

1992 At the Olympics in Barcelona, Evans wins the gold in the 800-meter and the silver in the 400-meter.

medals and first-place times in races several NCAA Championships; at the 1990 Goodwill Games in Seattle, Washington; and at the 1991 World Championships in Perth, Australia. Also in 1991, Evans left Stanford University in order to train for the 1992 Summer Olympics.

At the 1992 Olympics, held in Barcelona, Spain, Evans did not disappoint her fans, winning the silver medal in the 400-meter freestyle event and the gold in the 800-meter freestyle. Even with two Olympics under her belt, Evans still enjoyed swimming competitively. She stayed with the sport through the 1996 Summer Olympics in Atlanta, Georgia. For those Games, Evans was chosen to serve as one of the women team's three captains (along with Angel Martino and Whitney Hedgepeth). She also received a singular honor: Evans was selected to carry the Olympic torch on one of its final legs, handing it off at the Games' opening ceremonies to boxing great Muhammad Ali, who lit the Olympic flame.

It was a very emotional moment for Evans and the world, and the swimmer got even more attention later in the Games. However, the attention was not for her swimming, which was not of medal-winning caliber in that Olympics, but for a tragic attack. As a television crew was interviewing Evans, a bomb went off in Atlanta's Olympic Park, bringing the event live to the public.

Evans retired from competitive swimming after the 1996 Olympics. In 1994, she graduated from the University of Southern California with a degree in communications, and today she remains involved in the school's swimming program. Today USC is home to the Janet Evans Invitational. Evans remains in the public's eye as an ambassador for swimming and through her multiple endorsement contracts. ◆

Evert, Chris

DECEMBER 21, 1954– ● TENNIS PLAYER

One of the most consistent competitors in the history of tennis, Chris Evert holds one of the highest win-loss records (1,309 wins and only 146 losses) of any player. She also became the first person to win more than 1,000 singles matches and 150 tournaments, and she holds a record on clay courts with a 125-match winning streak, set between 1973 and 1979. Although some considered Evert's playing style boring, she nevertheless became one of the most popular women in the sport and a favorite among both spectators and the media. Her popularity did much to increase the visibility of female players and entice more girls into the sport.

Born in Fort Lauderdale, Florida, Evert began taking tennis lessons at age six from her father, James Evert, a tennis pro and owner of Florida's largest tennis complex. Evert loved playing and was soon practicing at least two and a half hours each day after school and several hours on weekends. Through her years of practice, Evert developed great endurance, intense concentration, and unflappable poise. She also developed a power driving shot and a strong two-handed backhand that many younger players copied.

Chris Evert at the French Open.

By age 16 Evert had begun to make a name for herself, especially after she beat Australia's Margaret Smith Court in a 1970 tournament in North Carolina just shortly after Court had become only the second woman in history to win the Grand Slam—victories at Wimbledon and the U.S., French, and Australian Opens. The next year Evert won the Virginia Slims Masters tournament and became the youngest player ever chosen to play on the Wightman Cup team. During that tournament she crushed Virginia Wade, Great Britain's best female player, and helped the U.S. win the cup. Later that year, in the U.S. Open, the 16-year-old Evert exceeded all expectations and reached the semifinals before losing to Billie Jean King, the reigning star of women's tennis. Although Evert lost, she became a favorite of the spectators. The media, however, nicknamed her "Little Ice Maiden" because of her unemotional style of playing.

Evert and King faced each other again several times in 1972. At the Women's International Tennis Tournament in her hometown, Evert beat King, but later in the year she lost to

1954 — Evert is born in Fort Lauderdale, Florida.

1971 — Evert wins the Virginia Slims Masters.

1972 — Evert defeats Billie Jean King at Women's International Tennis Tournament.

1974 — Evert wins at Wimbledon; sets record with 56 consecutive wins in a year; she is ranked number one in the world (also in 1975–78, 1980, and 1981).

1975 — Evert wins first of six U.S. Opens between 1975 and 1982.

King in the quarterfinals of the Maureen Connolly Brinker tournament in Dallas, Texas. After helping the United States retain the Wightman Cup, Evert stayed in England to prepare for Wimbledon, where she advanced to the semifinals before losing to the defending champion, Evonne Goolagong of Australia. This was the start of an exciting rivalry between Evert and Goolagong that lasted several years, and one in which Evert gained a 21–12 winning edge. Later in 1972 Evert faced Goolagong again at the Bonne Belle Cup and the U.S. Clay-Court Championship, beating her rival at both tournaments. At the U.S. Open she reached the semifinals before losing to Australia's Kerry Melville.

In 1973 Evert decided to turn professional. Between then and 1979 she was practically unbeatable on clay courts, winning 125 consecutive matches and 24 tournament titles. At the French Open in 1973 Evert lost in the finals to Margaret Smith Court, but she won the next year, beating Olga Morozova for her first Grand Slam title. She also won her first singles title at Wimbledon in 1974, defeating Morozova again. Evert set a modern record in 1974 by winning 56 consecutive matches in one year.

During her career, Evert won six more French Open championships, including victories in 1975, 1985, and 1986 over rival Martina Navratilova. Evert's friendly rivalry with Navratilova, one of the most renowned in tennis history, raised the level of women's tennis to new heights and won thousands of new enthusiasts to the game. Between 1973 and 1988 the two women played 80 matches and faced each other in 14 Grand Slam finals, including the 1982 Australian Open (which Evert won). Although Evert took an early lead in their competition, Navratilova later overtook her and came out ahead, winning 43 of 37 contests. Both women finished their careers with 18 Grand Slam championships. Evert's record of 157 singles titles, more than any other tennis player—male or female—at the time, remained intact until Navratilova broke it in 1992.

In addition to her seven French Open titles, Evert won a total of six U.S. Opens between 1975 and 1982, including four consecutive wins from 1975 to 1978. Her last U.S. Open victory, in 1982, was followed by losses to her rival Navratilova in 1983 and 1984. Evert's Wimbledon victory in 1974 was followed by two more wins—a 1976 victory over Evonne Goolagong, and a 1981 title after defeating Hana Mandlikova. Evert's weakest showing was at the Australian Open, where she won only two titles, in 1982 (beating Navratilova) and 1984. Evert's record of 52 semifinal appearances in 56 Grand Slam events makes her one of the most successful Grand Slam players of all time.

First ranked number one in the world in 1974, Evert earned that ranking six more times—in 1975, 1976, 1977, 1978, 1980, and 1981. In 1976 she became the first female tennis player to earn $1 million in prize money. Evert played for the U.S. Olympic team at the 1988 Summer Olympics, but she failed to win a medal.

Evert was named female athlete of the year four times by the Associated Press (1974, 1975, 1977, and 1980). She retired from tennis in 1989 after losing in the quarterfinals of the U.S. Open to Zina Garrison. Evert later became a tennis commentator for television and was inducted into the International Tennis Hall of Fame in 1995. ◆

"This is a 16-year-old kid who's beating the best people in the world. It's beautiful."
Billie Jean King on Chris Evert, 1971

Fingers, Rollie

August 25,1946– ● Baseball Player

U ntil around 1950, the bullpen was the pitcher's purgatory, filled with unproven youngsters and declining veterans—in short, anyone who wasn't good enough to make it as a starter. Parsimonious owners who paid for good pitching didn't think they were getting their money's worth if a hurler couldn't go the full nine innings. Around World War I, two-thirds of starters pitched complete games—win or lose. That percentage slowly declined through World War II, as selected specialists like Firpo Marberry, Wilcy Moore, and Johnny Murphy gradually won respectability for the reliever's role.

After World War II, the advantages of a well-honed corps of relief specialists grew increasingly evident as a succession of late-inning firemen—most notably, Jim Constanty of the 1950 Phillies (that year's National League Most Valuable Player), Rhyne Duren of the 1957–58 Yankees, Elroy Face of the 1960 Pirates, Luis Arroyo of the 1961 Yankees, and Tug McGraw of the 1969 Mets—became indispensable to their teams' championship seasons. An assignment to the bullpen, once a stigma, is now often a ticket to superstardom.

By the 1970s the increasing vogue for relief specialists had rendered the complete game as scarce as the spotted owl, and the standout among that decade's new breed of bullpen aces was was Rollie Fingers. Fingers, whose famously mustachioed face became an autumn fixture on national television, helped lead his team, the Oakland Althetics, to three consecutive world championships from 1972 through 1974.

1946 — Fingers is born in Steubenville, Ohio.

1968 — Fingers joins the Oakland A's.

1974 — Fingers is named World Series Most Valuable Player (MVP) as the A's defeat the Los Angeles Dodgers.

1981 — With the Milwaukee Brewers, Fingers leads the league with 28 saves; wins his fourth Fireman of the Year Award, Cy Young Award, and American League MVP.

1992 — Fingers is elected to the Baseball Hall of Fame.

belied: to have given a false impression or to have actually proved something false.

Born in 1946 in Steubenville, Ohio, Fingers grew up in California, where the balmy climate allowed him to develop his baseball skills year-round under the expert tutelage of his father, George, an ex-minor leaguer in the St. Louis Cardinals farm system. The benefit of a full-time, live-in professional coach was already evident by the time Rollie entered high school in Cucamonga, California, where he excelled as both an outfielder and pitcher. As a junior college student and American Legion ballplayer, Fingers began to specialize in pitching, and his impressive mound work began to attract the attention of major league scouts, especially in 1964, when Fingers' pitching was the key to his team's victory in the National American Legion tournament.

Drafted by the Kansas City Athletics in 1965, Fingers spent his minor league career as a starter. In 1967 his promising career was threatened by every pitcher's worst nightmare: a line drive right at his face that shattered his jaw. After a slow recovery, Fingers returned to form and was called up by the A's (who had meanwhile relocated to Oakland) in 1968. For the next three seasons, Fingers languished as a spot starter for Oakland, putting up mediocre numbers that **belied** his physical talent. His main problem was his obsessive, mentally exhausting preparation. "I would plan my pitches days in advance of my start and get so wound up I couldn't sleep the night before my turn," he recalled.

Having finished only four of 35 starts, Fingers accepted the only sensible alternative—a transfer to the bullpen, where he would have only a few minutes' advance notice and thus no chance to anguish over his appearances. The shift to relief work was like a miracle cure. In 1971 Fingers notched 17 saves. In 1972 Fingers topped the league's relievers with 21 saves and 11 wins, helping Oakland to the American League West title and a playoff showdown against the Detroit Tigers, champions of the American League East. The first game of the best-of-five series was deadlocked at 1–1 in the ninth inning when the Tigers put the winning run on third with no one out. Fingers emerged from the bullpen to record the next three outs, a critical turning point in the A's playoff victory. For the first time in 40 years, the A's franchise was headed to the World Series, where they would find themselves up against the heavily favored Cincinnati Reds.

The hard-fought series went the full seven games, and Fingers pitched in six of them, stymying the formidable Reds lineup with his pinpoint control and dazzling variety of pitches, especially his nasty sinker, which tended to elicit harmless groundballs from normally potent bats. In the series he won one game, lost one, and saved two, including the climactic seventh game, in which he doused a late-inning Cincinnati rally to ensure Oakland's triumph.

Fingers enjoyed another dominating campaign in 1973, when the A's faced the New York Mets in the World Series. The A's closer again appeared in six of the seven series games and posted two crucial saves. Fingers outdid himself in 1974, helping to hoist still another pennant in Oakland and dominating the Los Angeles Dodgers in the World Series, a five-game affair in which Fingers recorded one victory and two saves. As the key to three of the four Oakland victories in that year's fall classic, Fingers received the World Series MVP award.

Although Oakland lost to the Boston Red Sox in the 1975 American League championship series and was bested by the Kansas City Royals for the division title in 1976, Fingers remained the league's premier reliever, winning 23 games and saving 44 over that two-year span. But Charley Finley, the A's volatile owner, had grown impatient with his team and began to sell, trade off, or release his biggest stars, including Reggie Jackson, Catfish Hunter, and Vida Blue. In 1977 Fingers, another big-name exile, landed with the relief-hungry San Diego Padres, whose inept starting staff gave Rollie plenty of action that year, completing only six games. Fingers saved 35 games, a career high. In 1978 he topped himself again, appearing in 78 games, saving 37 of them, and helping his teammate Gaylord Perry win the Cy Young award by saving most of his 21 victories. He also won the National League **Fireman of the Year** award.

In 1980 Fingers was traded to the St. Louis Cardinals and then, four days later, to the Milwaukee Brewers. Although the 1981 season was shortened by a players' strike, Fingers led the league with 28 saves and recorded a stunning 1.04 earned run average, a performance that earned him his fourth Fireman of the Year Award, the Cy Young Award, and the American League MVP trophy.

The Brewers were surging to a division title in 1982 when Fingers, who had already appeared in 50 games and recorded 29 saves, tore a muscle in his forearm. With their ace reliever sidelined for the rest of the season, the Brewers floundered but managed to nail down the American League championship, only to

"All [Alvin] Dark or Dick Williams or any other manager had to tell Rollie was 'Get these next two, three guys out, and everything will be fine,' and that's just what Rollie did—341 different times in his 17-year career, a major league record for saves that may never be equaled."
  Catfish Hunter on
    Rollie Fingers in
  Catfish: My Life in Baseball, 1988

Fireman of the Year: annual award given to the outstanding relief pitcher in each league of Major League Baseball, so named because relief pitchers often "save" ballgames for their teams in precarious situations and thus "put out the fire."

lose to the Cardinals in seven games in the World Series without Fingers to shore up the pitching staff.

Fingers' arm injury kept him out of the entire 1983 campaign, but he attempted a comeback in 1984, returning to form with 23 saves by July, when he suffered a herniated disk that prematurely ended his career.

Rollie Fingers's total of wins plus saves—430—is still the best in major league history. He was inducted into the Hall of Fame on August 2, 1992. ◆

Flood, Curt

JANUARY 18, 1938– ● BASEBALL PLAYER

The youngest of six children, Curt Flood was born in Houston on January 18, 1938. Before he was three, his family moved to Oakland, California, where his parents, both hospital workers, held several jobs at once to support the family. Flood excelled at baseball from early childhood, becoming a standout on American Legion teams and at McClymonds and Oakland Technical high schools. Upon graduation in 1956, he signed with the Cincinnati Reds. At the time, many facilities were still segregated and many fans were still opposed to athletic integration. Yet Flood became a star in the Carolina and South Atlantic Leagues and was called up to the Reds. After two seasons in the minors, with brief stints with the Reds in each season, he was traded to the St. Louis Cardinals for the 1958 season. He won seven consecutive Gold Glove Awards and established a reputation as one of baseball's finest defensive center fielders. In 12 seasons with St. Louis, he had a career batting average of .293 and helped the Cardinals win three National League pennants and two World Series championships (1964 and 1967).

On October 7, 1969, the Cardinals announced that Flood had been traded to the Philadelphia Phillies. In a letter to Commissioner Bowie Kuhn, Flood stated that he would not play for his new team and refused to report to Philadelphia. He brought a lawsuit against the National League, arguing that the reserve clause in his contract (and that of every major-league ball-

1938 Curtis Charles Flood is born in Houston, Texas.

1958 Flood joins the St. Louis Cardinals; wins first of seven Gold Glove awards.

1969 Flood refuses to be traded to Philadelphia; files suit against National League.

1970 Flood sits out the season and publishes autobiography.

1971 Flood signs with the Washington Senators, though it is short-lived.

player), which made a player the exclusive property of one team until released or traded, violated antitrust laws by infringing on the rights of an employee to negotiate with multiple employers in an open market.

Flood's position was widely shared by other players; in fact, the Major League Players Association voted unanimously to support his suit. After lower courts ruled against Flood, the U.S. Supreme Court held that, as established by precedent, baseball was not interstate commerce and, therefore, enjoyed special exemption from antitrust legislation. While his case was in the lower courts, Flood sat out the 1970 season, and the Phillies sent their absent star to the Washington Senators. Flood finally signed with Washington, but he played only 10 games in 1971, and by the time his case was heard in the nation's highest court

Curt Flood of the St. Louis Cardinals.

he had retired. Though Flood's challenge to the reserve system was unsuccessful, his efforts helped lay the groundwork for future gains in players' rights, including free agency and salary arbitration.

After leaving the Senators, Flood purchased a bar on the island of Majorca in Spain, which he managed until 1976, when he returned to Oakland. He found employment in the front office of the Oakland Athletics, provided radio color-commentary for the A's, and was named commissioner of Oakland's Little League. Flood later moved to Los Angeles, where he continued his work as a portrait painter and, through his participation in fantasy baseball camps, maintained his ties to baseball. He joined the old-timers' circuit, playing exhibition games in major league cities around the country. In 1987, he helped organize the Fantasy Major League Slo-Pitch Softball League. His autobiography, *The Way It Is*, written with Richard Carter, was published in 1970. ◆

Ford, Whitey

<small>OCTOBER 21, 1928– ● BASEBALL PLAYER</small>

"I don't care what the situation was, how high the stakes were—the bases could be loaded and the pennant riding on every pitch, it never bothered Whitey. He pitched his game. Cool. Crafty. Nerves of steel."

Mickey Mantle on Whitey Ford

In the storied history of the New York Yankees, one that has seen them win 25 World Championships—there may not have been a better "money" pitcher than Edward Charles "Whitey" Ford. The proof is in the record books of Major League Baseball and the New York Yankees, as Ford's name still appears first in many single-season and career categories.

Ford, who was born in New York City on October 21, 1928, originally wanted to play first base—not pitch. That's the position the 17-year-old Ford had in mind when he attended a 1946 tryout at Yankee Stadium. But the course of baseball history was forever changed when veteran scout Paul Krichell moved Ford from first base to pitcher. Ford impressed scouts enough that the Yankees offered him to a $7,000 signing bonus, outbidding the Boston Red Sox and New York Giants.

After three years of dominating the minor leagues, Ford was called up to the major leagues in October of 1950. He would become the dominant pitcher for the winningest team of the 1950s and 1960s. Ford made an immediate impact, winning nine straight decisions, including the pennant-clinching game. In the 1950 World Series, he gave a glimpse of his future domination in the Fall Classic, as he pitched the fourth game of the Series, a 5–3 victory, in New York's sweep of Philadelphia. His impressive outing—lasting eight and two-thirds innings—-in which he allowed just three runs and seven hits, would be the first of a record 10 career World Series victories.

Ford's career was put on hold by a tour of duty in the military over the next two years, but he picked up right where he' d left off when he returned to baseball in 1953. Ford went 18–6, with a 3.00 earned run average. In the World Series, he was hit hard in his first appearance, a Game Four loss to the Brooklyn Dodgers in which he pitched one inning and surrendered three runs, but came back to pitch seven strong innings in Game Six, the Series finale, won by New York, 4–3.

The crafty lefthander proceeded to win at least 11 games every year for the next 12 years, including seasons of 25 wins

(1961) and 24 wins (1963). He took home the Cy Young Award as baseball's best pitcher in 1961, even though his heroics were somewhat overshadowed by the historic home run race between Mickey Mantle and Roger Maris.

But no one could overshadow Ford's work in the post-season. Besides his performance in the 1950 World Series against Philadelphia's "Whiz Kids" and the clincher against the Dodgers, Ford pitched two of the Yankees' three wins in their seven-game series loss to Brooklyn in 1955; turned the momentum of the 1957 Series with a Game Three victory over Milwaukee; shut out Pittsburgh in Game Six of the dramatic seven-game series loss to the Pirates in 1960; and, finally, won two games to earn World Series Most Valuable Player honors in the 1961 Series sweep of Cincinnati.

Ford was given the nickname "The Chairman of the Board" by his catcher Elston Howard for the way he went out and took care of business. Ford set—and still holds—numerous World Series records, including career wins (10), strikeouts (94), and innings pitched (146). But perhaps the most impressive of Ford's marks is his streak of 32 consecutive scoreless innings in World Series play, which broke the record of 29 and 2/3 innings set by Babe Ruth.

In 1964, Ford was named the Yankees' pitcher/coach. But after battling arm problems, he retired from playing altogether in 1967. His career record of 236–106 gave him a .690 winning percentage, the highest of any pitcher in the 20th century.

Ford was elected to the baseball Hall of Fame in 1974, receiving 284 of 365 ballots cast. Fittingly, he was inducted in the same class as teammate and late-night cohort Mickey Mantle. In fact, it was their frequent late nights that inspired manager Casey Stengel to call the duo "a couple of whiskey slicks." The nickname "Slick" stuck with Ford and the two became known as the "Mick and Slick Show." Also in 1974, the Yankees retired Ford's number 16. He is the only pitcher ever to have his number retired by the Yankees.

Today, Ford is a consultant for the Yankees and works with the team in spring training, scouting future Yankee prospects to find the next great Yankee pitcher. It is doubtful, however, that he or anyone else will find the next Whitey Ford. ◆

1928 Edward Charles "Whitey" Ford is born in New York City.

1950 Ford joins the New York Yankees as pitcher; wins first of a record 10 career World Series.

1961 Ford wins World Series Most Valuable Player as the Yankees defeat Cincinnati; wins Cy Young Award as best pitcher.

1967 Ford retires with .690 winning percentage, highest among twentieth-century pitchers.

1974 Ford is inducted into the Baseball Hall of Fame.

Foreman, George

JANUARY 22, 1948– ● BOXER

Born in Marshall, Texas, George Foreman grew up in a poor Houston neighborhood, where he dropped out of school in the tenth grade, drifted into petty crime and heavy drinking, and gained a reputation as a mean street fighter. In August 1965, Foreman joined the Job Corps, where Charles "Doc" Broadus introduced him to boxing. At the 1968 Olympic Games in Mexico City Foreman won the gold medal as a heavyweight. After his victory he waved an American flag in the ring, an action which contrasted dramatically with the behavior of two other black athletes at the games, sprinters John Carlos and Tommie Smith, who had protested racial injustice by raising black-gloved fists during the playing of the national anthem.

George Foreman (left) pummels an opponent.

Foreman turned professional in 1969. He won his first 37 professional fights, and in Kingston, Jamaica, on January 22, 1973, knocked out the reigning champion Joe Frazier in two rounds to take the title. Foreman successfully defended his

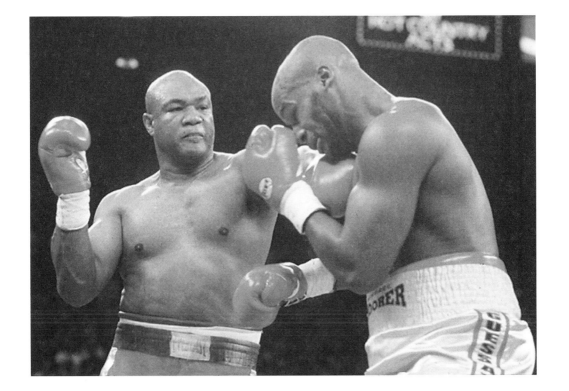

championship against Jose "King" Roman and Ken Norton, but on October 30, 1974, he lost it to Muhammad Ali in Kinshasa, Zaire. In that fight, billed as the "Rumble in the Jungle," Ali used an unorthodox "rope-a-dope" strategy, allowing Foreman to tire himself out by throwing most of the punches as Ali leaned back against the ropes and protected his head. By the eighth round, Foreman had tired significantly, and Ali was able to knock him out. Foreman won a number of fights in succeeding years, including a second match with Frazier. But he dropped a 12-round decision to Jimmy Young in San Juan, Puerto Rico, on March 17, 1977, and retired, disheartened.

After his retirement from boxing, Foreman experienced a religious conversion and became a self-ordained evangelical preacher and pastor of the Church of the Lord Jesus Christ in Houston. He also straightened out his personal life, which he described as a "total mess," including four failed marriages and a flamboyant lifestyle. In 1984 he established the George Foreman Youth and Community Center in Aldine, Tex.

In 1987, at the age of 39 and badly overweight (267 pounds, compared to 217 $^1/_2$ when he beat Frazier), Foreman returned to the ring in what was originally described as an effort to raise funds for his youth center. Many observers found it difficult to take his comeback seriously, but, after beating 24 lesser-known opponents, he gained credibility by making a good showing in a close 12-round loss to Evander Holyfield on April 19, 1991, in Atlantic City, N.J. After winning several more fights, Foreman faced Tommy Morrison in a match for the World Boxing Organization title in Las Vegas, Nevada, on June 7, 1993, but lost in a unanimous 12-round decision. After that fight, Foreman's career record stood at 73 wins (including 67 knockouts) and 4 losses. In a stunning reversal Foreman regained the heavyweight crown in 1994, fully 21 years after he first won it.

By that time, Foreman had become something of a media celebrity. His easygoing and cheerful attitude, his unique appearance (besides his girth, Foreman's shaved head made him easily recognizable), and his unlikely status as a boxer in his forties, made Foreman a favorite with many fans. He appeared on television in advertisements for a number of products, and in the fall of 1993 he briefly had his own television program on ABC, a situation comedy called "George," in which Foreman played a retired boxer who ran a youth center. In the late 1990s Foreman reaped the profits of his popular George Foreman Grill, a fat-reducing grilling machine. ◆

1949 George Edward Foreman is born in Marshall, Texas.

1968 Foreman wins the national amateur heavyweight championship; wins heavyweight gold medal at the Olympics in Mexico City.

1990 Foreman is inducted into the Olympic Hall of Fame.

1994 Foreman (temporarily) regains heavyweight title against champion Michael Moorer with a 10th-round KO.

"I had a meanness about me. I'd look at my opponent like a man who's about to shoot a deer: how is his head gonna fit on my wall as a trophy?"

George Foreman on ESPN's *Up Close Primetime*, 1997

Foyt, A. J.

JANUARY 16, 1935– ● RACE CAR DRIVER

> "I talked to the car. I talked to the good Lord and everybody that would listen that I could win and nobody would get hurt today."
>
> A.J. Foyt after winning his (record) fourth Indy 500, 1977

The first driver to win the prestigious Indianapolis 500 four times, A. J. Foyt is one of the most versatile drivers in auto racing history. Born in Houston, Texas, Anthony Joseph "A. J." Foyt, Jr. was born into auto racing. His father owned an auto mechanic's garage that specialized in race cars and was a talented midget car racer in his own right. The elder Foyt built his five-year-old son a race car that A. J. Jr. learned to drive at local tracks, and an illustrious career was born. Beginning his professional driving career at the age of 17, Foyt quickly moved up the ladder in racing circuits, and by the time he was 23 he qualified for his first Indianapolis 500 mile race. The young Foyt was in contention throughout the race until a spinout knocked him back. He was still able to finish in a respectable 16th place, a solid start to what would be one of the most successful careers ever at the "Brickyard."

Foyt quickly proved his good showing at Indianapolis was no fluke. In 1959 he won 10 United States Auto Club (USAC) races and then improved on his previous year's Indy 500 performance by finishing 10th. In 1960, he won the USAC national driving championship as the best overall performer in the season's races. In 1961, Foyt pushed through at Indianapolis. A fantastic duel with legendary driver Eddie Sachs led to a last-second victory by Foyt. With a 10-second lead and the race winding down, Foyt's fueling apparatus broke and he had to stop in the pits, allowing Sachs to take the lead. Refusing to give up, Foyt took the lead for good with only three laps to go, as Sachs made for the **pits** with tire troubles. The competition with Sachs not only led to a victory, but helped push Foyt to an Indianapolis Motor Speedway record, as he blasted around the oval track at an average of 139.13 miles per hour.

pits: area of an automobile racetrack near the course in which the cars are serviced during qualifying and during the actual race. Cars are said to go in for a "pit stop."

At age 25, the stocky six-foot Texan was on top of the USAC and Indy car world, and he was just warming up. Winning in Indy again in 1964, Foyt upped his own track record to a then-unfathomable 147.35 miles per hour. Foyt continued racing and winning in both Indy and stock cars until a 1965 accident at a stock car race in Riverside, California, left him injured and slowed his momentum.

By 1967, however, that momentum was back with a vengeance, as Foyt reclaimed his USAC championship, won his third Indy 500, and teamed with veteran U.S. racer Dan Gurney to become the first Americans to win the Twenty-Four Hours of Le Mans race in France, the premier endurance auto race in the world.

Over the next decade, Foyt only added to his reputation as one of the most talented and versatile drivers in auto racing history, competing and winning stock, midget and Indy car races. In the early 1970s, Foyt raced on the tough NASCAR circuit and proved himself up to the challenge of racing against the worlds best stock car racers, winning the Daytona 500 in 1972. Because he competed in nearly every American racing venue— from midgets to sprint cars to Indy cars; stock cars and sports cars; on tracks from quarter-mile dirt ovals to superspeedways— Foyt gained immense popularity as a racer who could win at the big races as well as at the small. He often raced in small venues to help promoters who had helped him earlier in his career. In 1977, Foyt won his record fourth Indy 500. Though it would be his last win at the Brickyard, other glories awaited him. In 1983 he was on the winning team at the Twenty-Four Hours of Daytona and in 1985 he won the Twelve Hours of Sebring, making him a winner each of the world's three major endurance races.

Foyt, who has three children with wife Lucy Zarr, including A. J. III, has had a lucrative career off the race tracks as well. He designed his own line of race cars, called Coyotes, and has owned his own successful racing teams. A recognized face on television endorsements, Foyt has helped popularize auto racing with his "everyman" approach and highly competitive nature.

While many racers might have been content with success on the Indy car circuit, A.J. Foyt proved himself a great, all-around champion by taking on all the hardest courses and toughest races in the world, emerging victorious more often than not. ◆

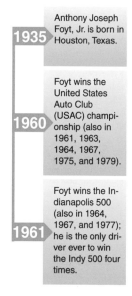

1935 ▶ Anthony Joseph Foyt, Jr. is born in Houston, Texas.

1960 ▶ Foyt wins the United States Auto Club (USAC) championship (also in 1961, 1963, 1964, 1967, 1975, and 1979).

1961 ▶ Foyt wins the Indianapolis 500 (also in 1964, 1967, and 1977); he is the only driver ever to win the Indy 500 four times.

Frazier, Joseph

JANUARY 12, 1944– ● BOXER

"Smokin'" Joe Frazier was the world heavyweight boxing champion from 1970–1973. Born in Beaufort, South Carolina, Frazier grew up in Philadelphia and began boxing at a Police Athletic League gym. After he won Golden

1944 — Joseph William Frazier is born in Beaufort, South Carolina.

1965 — Frazier knocks out Woody Goss in the first round.

1971 — It's Frazier vs. Muhammed Ali in "The Fight of the Century."

1973 — Frazier is KO'd by George Foreman.

1975 — "Thrilla in Manila": Ali KO's Frazier in the 14th round.

1976 — Frazier is KO'd (again) by Foreman.

1980 — Frazier is elected to the Boxing Hall of Fame.

"It was like death. Closest thing to dyin' that I know of."

Muhammad Ali, on fighting Frazier in the Thrilla in Manila, 1975

Gloves titles in 1962, 1963, and 1964, as well as a gold medal in the 1964 Olympics in Tokyo, Japan, a consortium of investors, incorporated as Cloverlay, Inc., sponsored Frazier's professional career.

Frazier was only five foot eleven and a half and 205 pounds, small for a heavyweight. Managed by Yancey Durham, Frazier adopted a crowded and hard-hitting style that compensated for his relative slow-footedness. Beginning with a one-round knockout of Woody Goss in August, 1965. Frazier won by knockouts his first 11 professional bouts, none of which went beyond six rounds, and he won 31 straight fights before being defeated by George foreman in 1973.

After Muhammad Ali gave up his title in 1970, Frazier won the World Heavyweight Championship, defeating Jimmy Ellis in a five-round knockout. Ali, who had been stripped of his title after the U.S. government convicted him of draft evasion (later overturned), also claimed to be the heavyweight champion because he had never retired or been defeated.

On March 8, 1971, in New York City's Madison Square Garden, Frazier defeated Ali after 15 rounds of such ferocious boxing that both men entered hospitals after its conclusion; they would later fight twice more, both times with great intensity. After the first fight with Ali, Frazier did not fight a title bout again for 10 months. He then defended his championship twice, winning both bouts, but on January 22, 1973, George Foreman knocked him out in the second round of a heavyweight title bout.

Having lost his title to Foreman, Frazier again fought Ali in a non-title bout in New York City on January 28, 1974, and lost in 12 rounds. Frazier had fights with two lesser boxers, both of whom he knocked out, then faced Ali for the heavyweight title on October 1, 1975, in the Philippines. The fight, dubbed by Ali "The Thrilla in Manila," was a hardfought contest. Ali knocked Frazier out in the 14th round.

Frazier followed the Manila bout with a second fight against Foreman on June 15, 1976, and was knocked out by Foreman early in the fight. Frazier then retired from the ring. He made a brief appearance, playing himself, in the movie *Rocky* (1976) and tried unsuccessfully to build a singing career with a group called the Knockouts. In 1981 he attempted a comeback, but was defeated by Floyd Cummings. Of his 37 career bouts, Frazier won a total of 32 fights—27 by knockouts. He then managed his son Marvis's short boxing career. In 1980 Frazier was elected to the Boxing Hall of Fame. ◆

Fu Mingxia

AUGUST 16, 1978– ● DIVER

Perhaps no one in the history of sports has had such a major impact on her sport at such a young age as diver Fu Mingxia, who is registered in the *Guinness Book of World Records* as the world's youngest Olympic champion.

As a youngster Fu paid a heavy price for her success. She was born in Wuhan, Hubei, in China, where she began diving at age eight—before she could even swim. At age nine she was taken from her home to Beijing, 600 miles away, to a diving school, where she practiced seven days a week. At that time she had problems both with her posture and with bulging knees. To

Fu Mingxia dives against the backdrop of Barcelona, Spain at the 1992 Summer Olympics.

1978 Mingxia is born in Wuhan, Hubei, China.

1990 Not yet 12, Mingxia wins Goodwill Games platform dive title.

1991 Mingxia wins the world championship.

1992 Mingxia wins Olympic gold for women's platform diving.

1994 Mingxia wins world platform and springboard championships.

1996 Mingxia wins Olympic gold medals in platform and 3-meter springboard diving.

1999 At the University Games, Mingxia wins gold medals in platform and 3-meter springboard diving.

correct these problems she was made to sit in a chair with her legs extended onto a bench while an adult would sit on her legs, forcing her to endure severe pain. During this time she was allowed to see her parents only twice a year, and when she was asked during the 1992 Barcelona Olympics in Spain what her parents did for a living, she was unable to answer.

Fu was selected to the Chinese Junior diving team in 1989 at the age of 11. She entered the record books 12 days before her twelfth birthday, when she won the 1990 Goodwill Games platform title. Then at age 12, the tiny diver—she weighed barely 90 pounds at the time—won the 1991 world championship. Her success prompted the International Amateur Swimming Federation to pass a rule requiring Olympic divers to be at least 14 years old to complete.

It looked as though Fu would be unable to participate in the 1992 Barcelona Olympics, but a further refinement in the rules admitted competitors "in their 14th year." So, just 13 years old, she climbed the 10-meter platform in Barcelona and dove into Olympic history (and onto the cover of *Time* magazine), moving ahead of her rivals with her third dive and beating her closest rival, Russian Yelena Miroshina, by nearly 50 points in the most decisive women's platform win in 60 years. Over the next four years Fu would win nearly every major international diving championship, including the world platform and springboard championships in 1994. Throughout her career Fu consistently won with dives that were more difficult than those of her competitors, which she executed with seemingly effortless ease.

Fu's training regimen for the 1994 world championships was typical of the grueling pace she and other Chinese divers maintained. She practiced six hours a day at the Sports School in Beijing, and just before the 1994 competition she practiced for two hours; she even practiced for an hour *after* receiving her gold medal. To prepare for the 1996 Olympics in Atlanta, she practiced seven hours a day, six days a week, a total of over 40 hours a week compared to at most about 24 hours a week by the top U.S. divers (largely due to NCAA restrictions on practice time). This immense dedication and attention to detail made her one of the top athletes in Chinese history while she was still in her mid-teens.

At the 1996 Olympics Fu took gold in both the platform and three-meter springboard competitions, the first woman since East Germany's Ingrid Kramer in 1960 to win both events in the same Olympics. Her win in the springboard finals was es-

The Olympics

The Olympic Games originated in ancient Greece, by most estimates as far back as 3,500 years ago. Although a number of cities hosted athletic competitions associated with pagan religious worship, it was the Olympic games, held in Olympia, Greece, every four years that became the most important. Surviving records from 776 B.C. to A.D. 217 list the names of the winners of the five-day-long competitions, which included wrestling, running, horse riding, chariot racing, and the pentathlon, along with closing ceremonies to honor the victors. The ancient Olympics came to an end in a.d. 393, when the Roman emperor Theodosius I banned them as a pagan affront to Christianity.

The modern revival of the Olympics was initiated by a Frenchman of noble descent, Baron Pierre de Coubertin, who had been fascinated with the ancient Olympics in his youth. His sociological studies as an adult convinced him that vigorous exercise and athletic competition were key components of balanced, healthy human development. After spending much of the 1880s studying and lecturing on this topic, de Coubertin first proposed a renewal of the Olympic Games in 1892, at a meeting of the Union des Sports Athlétiques in Paris. Undaunted by the lukewarm reception he received, de Coubertin pressed the idea again at an international congress on sports in Paris in 1894. Despite an apparent lack of enthusiasm for the idea among the delegates, de Coubertin succeeded in extracting a unanimous declaration of approval for a revived Olympics in 1896. De Coubertin organized an International Olympic Committee (IOC) of which he was president (a post he held until 1925) with representatives from the United States, Argentina, New Zealand, and eight European countries. They selected Athens as the site for the 1896 games, and the first Olympiad of the modern era was declared open by the King of Greece in April 1896. Despite the overall mediocrity of the athletic performances, the 1896 were a big success and emboldened the organizers to move ahead with plans for games in 1900 in Paris.

The 1900 Olympics in de Coubertin's hometown of Paris were a dismal failure, stretching out over five months of poorly organized, poorly attended events. De Coubertin hoped that the 1904 games, scheduled for Chicago, would resuscitate his flagging movement, but results were even more disastrous: the games were hastily moved to St. Louis at the eleventh hour, and few foreign athletes even made the trip.

It was the renegade Intercalated Games of 1906 still considered unofficial by the IOC that saved the languishing Olympic movement from early extinction. Organized by Greeks who hoped to hold their own international games every four years, the 1906 games were a major success and imparted fresh momentum to the Olympic movement, which mounted increasingly successful games until World War I forced cancellation of the 1916 games. The Olympic ideal of peaceful competition among nations gained renewed momentum in the wake of the barbarism of the war, and the Olympic Games thrived throughout the 1920s, adding a winter competition in 1924. When the Belgian Henri Baillet-Latour took over the presidency of the IOC in 1925, he came under increasing pressure to ease restrictions on female participation, which had persisted unofficially since 1900 but had received no formal sanction until women's swimming was introduced in

1912. In 1928 the IOC finally permitted women competitors in track and field but until 1960 prohibited them from running races longer than 200 meters.

As a highly publicized international event, the Olympic Games have inevitably served as a lightning rod for political tensions. The 1936 games in Munich, Germany, became Hitler's propaganda vehicle for Nazi theories of Aryan racial superiority. The 1940 and 1944 games were canceled because of World War II, but it wasn't long before the postwar games became an arena of the Cold War, with the spirit of international cooperation succumbing to a U.S.–Soviet race for the prestige of gold medals. The 1972 games in Munich, Germany, were rocked by a Palestinian terrorist attack that took the lives of eleven Israeli athletes, and the 1980 Moscow Games were marred by a U.S.-led boycott to protest the Soviet invasion of Afghanistan. The Soviets retaliated by boycotting the 1984 Los Angeles, ostensibly because of concern about the adequacy of security arrangements.

With the ending of the ban on professional athletes in 1981, the ever-ballooning fees for commercial TV rights, and heavy corporate sponsorship, many wonder if the Olympic spirit is drowning in a sea of commercialism. The IOC argues that without such commercial support the enormous expense of mounting the games would be prohibitive. As the modern Olympic movement enters its second century, the classical Greek ideal remains an elusive inspiration from the past and a challenge for the future.

pecially dramatic, since she entered the finals fourth after the morning's preliminary round and was China's only hope after teammate Tan Shuping belly-flopped on her third dive. Ignoring Tan's disaster and the screaming, partisan American crowd, she executed five splashless dives, the only diver to receive more than 60 points on each of her dives, and captured the gold. With three Olympic gold medals to her credit, she was only one shy of the record four held by U.S. divers Greg Louganis and Pat McCormack and only two shy of the record five medals overall.

"Like a tiny blade of grass, she stands on the 10-meter platform. Like a swallow, she circles above before slipping into the water without a sound."

From a Chinese newspaper

Citing psychological fatigue, Fu was granted permission from the Chinese government to retire from competition after the 1996 Olympics. She used her time to study economics at Qinghua University in Beijing. After a three-year layoff, though, and denying that she was pressured to do so by the government, she returned to competition in the 1999 University Games. Rested but a little rusty, she won gold medals in both the platform and three-meter springboard competitions, barely edging out her teammate, Wang Rui, in the platform dive. With her wins she gave notice that she was preparing for the 2000 Olympics in Sydney, Australia, and seemed poised to collect a fourth and record-setting fifth Olympic gold medal. ◆

Garvey, Steve

DECEMBER 2, 1948– ● BASEBALL PLAYER

For more than a decade, from the mid-1970s to the mid-1980s, Steven Patrick Garvey was one of the finest players in baseball and one of the elite first basemen of his era. While he was a Dodger, Los Angeles won four pennants and a World Series, and he also helped lift the San Diego Padres to their first pennant.

Throughout his playing career Garvey cultivated the image of a spotless All-American hero: not only smoothly competent afield but also ruggedly handsome, articulate, impeccably coiffed and attired, devoted to his family and church, generous with charities and with his fans. As one sportswriter put it, "In compulsorily hip Southern California, he was hopelessly square: -jawed, -shouldered, -dealing and -thinking." Ironically, after Garvey retired from baseball in 1988, his personal life crash-landed, generating a year's worth of toxic media coverage: a bitter divorce, paternity suits, and financial disaster. In one short year the double-edged sword of fame had sliced and diced the name of Steve Garvey. "Some people have a mid-life crisis," he said. "I had a disaster."

Garvey's unremittingly strict upbringing perhaps accounts for both his heroic rise and his tabloidesque fall. Born in Tampa, Florida, he grew up there an only child in a close-knit family that saddled the youngster with adult expectations and responsibilities. Both his parents worked—his mother in an insurance office and his father as a bus driver—so as soon as Steve returned from school each day, he had to care for his invalid grandmother, attend to housekeeping chores, and prepare dinner. His sense of

> "Some people have a mid-life crisis," Garvey said. "I had a disaster."

161

1948 Garvey is born in Tampa, Florida.

1974 Garvey bats .381 in his first World Series; voted National League's Most Valuable Player (MVP).

1981 Dodgers finally beat the Yankees; 1st Dodger championship in 18 years.

1984 Garvey leads the Padres to National League pennant with .400 batting average.; earns league MVP.

draft: the process by which individuals from high school and college are selected by the organizations and clubs of professional athletic leagues for the purposes of acquiring contract rights to individual players.

duty was enforced by stringent household discipline—"yes, ma'am," "yes, sir," and corporal punishment—that produced, in the words of one writer, "a 10-year-old going on 28." Garvey recalled, "I had more responsibility than three kids." His escape was baseball, playing imaginary games between the Dodgers and Yankees by tossing grapefruits in the air and whacking them with a bat.

Young Steve's daydreams of baseball and the Dodgers took a providential real-life turn when his father got a job driving the Dodgers' spring training bus—thus did Steve Garvey, starting at age seven, become the team's spring-training batboy for several years. Inspired by his exposure to the life of big-leaguers, the precociously serious youngster worked hard at developing his game; he flourished at Chamberlain High School, where he hit .472 his junior year and .465 his senior year, attaining all-city and all-conference honors for three consecutive years. In June of his senior year, Garvey was drafted by the Minnesota Twins but rebuffed the offer in favor of a scholarship offer from Michigan State University, where he excelled in both football and baseball.

Selected by the Los Angeles Dodgers in the June 1968 **draft,** Garvey traded the manicured lawns of academia for the dusty diamonds of the minor leagues, working away for the better part of two years before finally sticking with the Dodgers in 1971. But Garvey, playing exclusively at third base, batted a disappointing .227; 1972 saw a marked improvement to a solid if still unspectacular .269. It was not until 1973, when he was finally planted at first base for good, that Garvey really flourished, batting .304 with solid run production. Over the next eight seasons in Los Angeles, he batted from .297 to .319, drove in more than 100 runs five times, and had at least 200 hits six times. In 1974, Garvey's first trip to the World Series, Garvey was voted the National League's most valuable player. Despite Garvey's impressive .381 batting average in that Series, the Dodgers were swept by the Oakland Athletics in five games.

The Dodgers' next World Series appearance, in 1977, pitted them against the New York Yankees in a glamorous bicoastal contest that the Yankees won in six games with a memorably dominating home run spree by Reggie Jackson. The 1978 rematch between the Yankees and Dodgers again went to New York in six games, despite a heroic series performance by Garvey, who batted .389, slugged an amazing 1.222, and drove in seven runs. In the Dodgers' next trip to the World Series, in

1981, they again faced the dreaded Yankees, but this time they turned the tables, besting them in six games for the first Dodger world championship in 18 years.

After the 1982 season, when Garvey's numbers dipped to a .282 batting average and 86 runs batted in (RBI), the Dodgers traded him to the San Diego, where he enjoyed a solid season in 1983, producing a .294 batting average and 59 RBI in 100 games. In 1984 Garvey's productive regular season—.284 BA and 86 RBI—was just a prelude to his powerful performance in the league championship series, in which he led the Padres to a National League flag in five games with a .400 batting average, a .600 slugging percentage, and seven RBI, an imposing performance that earned him the MVP award for the series. The Padres and Garvey were not as successful in that year's World Series, in which they were flattened by the Detroit Tigers in five games, with Garvey batting only .200.

Garvey had another productive season in 1985—.281 BA, 81 RBI—but injury plagued him over the next two years. After the 1987 campaign, Garvey announced his retirement, ending a distinguished career that included such peaks as four Gold Glove awards and a National League record of 1,207 games played. After his personal difficulties exploded in the media the following year, Garvey endured several years of embarrassing notoriety while working briefly as a sportscaster and advertising spokesperson. He now runs the Steve Garvey Management Group, which specializes in business development and promotion. ◆

> *"Spring training is like a cat with nine lives. A baseball player has X number of lives and each spring is the birth of a new life."*
>
> Steve Garvey

Gehrig, Lou

JUNE 19, 1903–JUNE 2, 1941 ● BASEBALL PLAYER

"Today, I consider myself the luckiest man on the face of the Earth."

Baseball has had its fair share of dramatic moments in its history, but perhaps the most dramatic occurred on July 4, 1939, when a visibly weakened Lou Gehrig triumphantly strode out to a microphone set up behind home plate at Yankees Stadium. There, in front of a sold-out crowd, he proclaimed that despite having his Hall of Fame career halted by the debilitating disease amyotrophic lateral sclerosis, he had indeed lived a blessed life.

1903 Henry Louis Gehrig is born in New York City.

1926 Gehrig begins a streak of 12 consecutive seasons of batting at least .300 and driving in at least 100 runs.

1927 Gehrig wins the league's Most Valuable Player award (also in 1936).

1934 Gehrig wins the American League Triple Crown, leading league in hitting, home runs, and runs batted in.

1939 Gehrig delivers his legendary "luckiest man" retirement speech.

1941 Gehrig dies in Riverdale, N.Y., at age 37.

The most remarkable aspect of Gehrig's baseball career began rather ordinarily on June 1, 1925, when the 21-year-old rookie delivered a pinch-hit single. The Yankees manager, the legendary Miller Huggins, liked what he saw and decided the next day to substitute Gehrig in the lineup at first base for Wally Pipp, the Yankees starter who had complained of a headache.

The next time Gehrig would miss a game would be 15 seasons later on May 2, 1939. Gehrig's remarkable string of 2,130 straight contests played earned him the nickname "Iron Horse" and a permanent place in baseball immortality. His record, which most people thought was unbreakable, stood until Cal Ripken, Jr., surpassed it on September 6, 1995.

Henry Louis Gehrig was born in New York City on June 19, 1903. The only son of German immigrants, he was somewhat clumsy and plodding as a youngster, yet still managed to become a teenage sports star at New York's High School of Commerce. In 1920, Gehrig led Commerce to a dramatic victory over a Chicago high school in a national showdown at Wrigley Field with a ninth-inning grand slam home run, perhaps foreshadowing the fact that Gehrig is still the major league's all-time leader in grand slams with 23.

Gehrig attended Columbia University in New York City, where he played first base, outfield, and even pitched for Columbia's team. He also played football for a year. In 1921, Gehrig played summer league ball in Hartford, Conn., under the assumed name Henry Lewis so he could maintain his college eligibility.

In 1923, Gehrig caught the eye of a Yankees scout, who proclaimed that the collegiate standout was "the next Babe Ruth." Gehrig joined the team at the end of the spring term for a $1,500 bonus. Despite hitting for an outstanding .423 batting average in 13 games, he was sent down to the minors that summer for seasoning. The next year he hit an incredible .500 in 10 games with the Yanks, but again spent most of his time in the minors, where he batted .369.

That figure was good enough for Gehrig to stick with the parent club in 1925, but he spent most of the first two months of the season on the bench before getting his chance to crack the lineup on June 1. He, of course, was there to stay, finishing the year with a very respectable .295 average, 20 home runs, and 68 runs batted in (RBI) in 128 games.

The next season, 1926, Gehrig began two more remarkable streaks—hitting over .300 and driving in more than 100 runs for 12 straight seasons.

In 1927, playing for what is largely considered the greatest team of all time, Gehrig had perhaps his best season, hitting .373 with 47 home runs and 175 RBI and winning the league's Most Valuable Player award. He would also win the MVP in 1936. In 1934, Gehrig led the league in hitting (.363), home runs (49), and RBI (165) to win the American League Triple Crown.

Over his career, Gehrig's Yankees played in the World Series seven times. Along with Babe Ruth, the Iron Horse anchored the famed Murders' Row lineup in the late '20s, and then teamed with a young Joe DiMaggio to form the nucleus of another Yankees dynasty in the late '30s. He batted a sensational .361 overall in the Fall Classic, a full 21 points over his career regular-season average.

For all his great feats, Gehrig toiled somewhat in the shadow of the flamboyant Ruth and charismatic DiMaggio, but that never seemed to bother the somewhat reserved first baseman.

The end of Gehrig's storied career came all too suddenly. In 1938, his average slipped below .300 for the first time since 1925. By the time the 1939 campaign began, Gehrig could barely hit the ball out of the infield and his fielding range was virtually nonexistent. On April 30, Gehrig played his last major league game. Realizing that he was hurting his team with his poor play—he was hitting .143—Gehrig removed himself from the lineup before the Yanks' game on May 2 in Detroit, ending the streak and his playing career.

Gehrig continued as a nonplaying captain as his health worsened. He went to the Mayo Clinic in June where he got the bad news that he had contracted amyotrophic lateral sclerosis (ALS), a fatal and incurable hardening of the spinal cord. That diagnosis set the stage for Gehrig's dramatic speech in front of 61,808 heartbroken Yankee fans on July 4th. That oft-quoted speech was further immortalized in the 1942 biopic *Pride of the Yankees* in which Gary Cooper plays the Iron Horse.

At the time of his retirement Gehrig ranked third on the all-time home run list with 493 career home runs, behind only Ruth and Jimmie Foxx (he's currently 17th on the list). He also bowed out as the second greatest run producer in baseball history with 1,995 runs batted in, again behind Ruth. To this day he still ranks third of all time on the RBI list. Other standout statistics include a lifetime .340 average, a .632 slugging percentage, and 1,888 runs scored. His 184 RBI in 1934 still stand as an American League single-season record. In 1999, Gehrig was named to Major League Baseball's All-Century Team, picked as

"Fans, for the past two weeks you have been reading about the bad break I got. Yet today I consider myself the luckiest man on the face of the earth."

Lou Gehrig in his farewell speech, Yankee Stadium, July 4, 1939 the 34th greatest athlete of the century by ESPN, and chosen as the fifth best player of the century by *Baseball Digest*.

Gehrig continued as the Yankees captain for the rest of the 1939 season, watching from the bench as his teammates went on to win the World Series. He was elected to the Hall of Fame that year in a special election—usually candidates are not eligible until five years after they retire.

After the season he officially retired from the game he loved and was appointed by New York City Mayor Fiorello La Guardia to the Municipal Parole Commission that October. Gehrig went about his new job with the same spirit that made him one of baseball's greats, working until his conditioned further deteriorated in the spring of 1941.

He died of the disease on June 2 of that year—16 years to the day that he had stepped in for Pipp—at the age of 37 in his home in Riverdale, N.Y. ALS is now commonly referred to "Lou Gehrig's disease."

A more fitting legacy, though, is his heroic streak. As the legendary sportswriter Jim Murray said best, "He was a symbol of indestructibility—a Gibraltar in cleats." ◆

Gibson, Althea

AUGUST 25, 1927– ● TENNIS PLAYER

Althea Gibson was the first black tennis player to win the sport's major titles. Born in Silver, South Carolina, to a garage hand and a housewife, she came to New York City at age three to live with an aunt. The oldest of five children, she was a standout athlete at Public School 136 and began playing paddleball under Police Athletic League auspices on West 143rd Street in Harlem. In 1940 she was introduced to tennis by Fred Johnson, a one-armed instructor, at the courts (now named after him) on 152nd Street. She was an immediate sensation.

"Ain't that a blip, that a Harlem street rebel would go on to become a world tennis champion?"

Althea Gibson

Gibson became an honorary member of Harlem's socially prominent Cosmopolitan Tennis Club (now defunct) and won her first tournament—the American Tennis Association (ATA) junior girls title—in 1945. (The ATA is the oldest continuously operated black noncollegiate sports organization in America). Though Gibson lost in the finals of the ATA women's singles in 1946, she attracted the attention of two black physicians: Dr. Hubert Eaton of Wilmington, North Carolina, and Dr. R. Walter Johnson of Lynchburg, Virginia, who tried to advance her career.

In September 1946 Gibson entered high school in Wilmington while living with the Eatons, and she graduated in 1949. She won the ATA women's single title 10 years in a row, from 1947 to 1956. As the best black female tennis player ever, she was encouraged to enter the U.S. Lawn Tennis Association (the white governing body of tennis) events. Jackie Robinson had just completed his third year in major league baseball, and pressure was being applied on other sports to integrate. Though she was a reluctant crusader, Gibson was finally admitted to play in the USLTA Nationals at Forest Hills, New York, on August 28, 1950.

Althea Gibson demonstrates her backhand.

Alice Marble, the former USLTA singles champion, wrote a letter, published in the July 1950 issue of *American Lawn Tennis* magazine, admonishing the USLTA for its reluctance to admit Gibson when she was clearly more than qualified. Gibson's entry was then accepted at two major events in the summer of 1950 before her Forest Hills debut. She was warmly received at the Nationals, where she lost a two-day, rain-delayed match to second–seeded Louise Brough in the second round.

Gibson's breakthrough heralded more to come. The ATA began a serious junior development program to provide opportunities for promising black children. (Out of that program came Arthur Ashe, who became the first black male winner of the sport's major titles.) Sydney Llewelyn became Gibson's coach, and her rise was meteoric. Her first Grand Slam title was the French singles in Paris in 1956. Before she turned profes-

1927 Gibson is born in Silver, South Carolina.

Gibson wins the singles tournament at Wimbledon, U.S. Open; named female athlete of the year by Associated Press. **1957**

Gibson wins her second Wimbledon; she is also named U.S. national champion. **1958**

1971 Gibson is named to the National Lawn Tennis Hall of Fame.

sional, she added the Wimbledon and the U.S. singles in both 1957 and 1958, and the French women's doubles and the U.S. mixed doubles. She was a Wightman Cup team member in 1957 and 1958. After her Wimbledon victory, she was presented her trophy by Queen Elizabeth II, she danced with the queen's husband, Prince Philip, at the Wimbledon Ball, and New York City accorded her a ticker-tape parade.

The poise Gibson showed at Wimbledon and at other private clubs where USLTA-sanctioned events were played was instilled by Dr. Eaton's wife and by her time spent as an undergraduate at Florida A&M University in Tallahassee, Florida. Jake Gaither, FAMU's famed athletic director, helped secure a teaching position for her in physical education at Lincoln University in Jefferson City, Missouri. In the winter of 1955—56 the State Department asked her to tour Southeast Asia with Ham Richardson, Bob Perry, and Karol Fageros.

In 1957 Gibson won the Babe Didrickson Zaharias Trophy as Female Athlete of the Year, the first black female athlete to win the award. She also began an attempt at a career as a singer, taking voice lessons three times a week. While singing at New York City's Waldorf-Astoria Hotel for a tribute to famed songwriter W. C. Handy, she landed an appearance on the *Ed Sullivan Show* in May 1958. Moderately successful as a singer, she considered a professional tour with tennis player Jack Kramer, the American champion of the 1940s. She also became an avid golfer, encouraged by Joe Louis, the former world heavyweight champion, who was a golf enthusiast. Louis had also paid her way to her first Wimbledon championships.

The Ladies Professional Golfers Association (LPGA) was in its infancy and purses were small. But Gibson was a quick learner and was soon nearly a "scratch" player. She received tips from Ann Gregory, who had been the best black female golfer ever. Gibson, a naturally gifted athlete, could handle the pressure of professional sports. But the purses offered on the LPGA tour were too small to maintain her interest.

In 1986 New Jersey governor Tom Kean appointed Gibson to the state's athletic commission. She became a sought-after teaching professional at several private clubs in central and northern New Jersey and devoted much of her time to counseling young black players. The first black female athlete to enjoy true international fame, Gibson was elected to the International Tennis Hall of Fame in 1971. ◆

Gibson, Josh

DECEMBER 21, 1911–JANUARY 20, 1947 ● BASEBALL PLAYER

Josh Gibson was called "The Babe Ruth of the Negro Leagues" for good reason. Many of those who saw the burly catcher play the game felt that he was not only among the greatest catchers of all time, but one of the greatest home run hitter as well. While actual statistics do not exist to document the accomplishments of the Negro Leagues stars, there is no doubt that Gibson would have dominated the game had he had a chance to play in the major leagues.

Gibson was born in Buena Vista, Georgia, and moved to Pittsburgh when he was 12 years old. As a youngster, he won numerous swimming medals, and by age 16, he already stood 6'2" and weighed 220 pounds. His legendary career began in 1927 when he hooked up with the semi-pro Pittsburgh Crawfords as a backup catcher. When Pittsburgh's crosstown rival, the Homestead Grays, suffered a blow when their starting catcher got injured, Gibson switched teams and never left the lineup again. Gibson was eventually traded back to the Crawfords to join pitching sensation Satchel Paige, and the two created the greatest tandem in Negro League history. The Crawfords of the 1930s are commonly viewed as the greatest Negro League team ever assembled.

Gibson, meanwhile, set records with his bat. He won six home run crowns and hit over .400 twice during the '30s. And belting 500-foot home runs was not unusual for Gibson. While no player has ever hit a fair ball out of Yankee Stadium, Gibson's 580 foot moon shot against the Chicago American Giants came

Josh Gibson behind the plate.

The Negro Leagues

In its early years of development, seriously competitive baseball thrived mostly in an upper-class milieu of men's athletic clubs. After the Civil War, the game's mushrooming popularity led to a democratization of the playing fields, with members of all classes and races partaking of the sport that was rapidly evolving into America's athletic pastime. In this free-form atmosphere of amateur competition, both integrated and all-black teams began dotting the baseball landscape.

The first "color line" in baseball appeared on December 11, 1868, when baseball's main amateur organization, the National Association of Baseball Players, issued a ruling barring from official competitions "any club which may be composed of one or more colored persons." This edict did not, however, apply to the many professional teams and leagues that began to form in the ensuing years, which saw the formation of several integrated pro teams and the participation of all-black teams in integrated leagues. In fact, in 1884 there were two black players in the National League: the brothers Moses Fleetwood Walker and Welday Walker. But the weight of social custom soon snuffed out these promising moves toward integration, and blacks were gradually excluded from the ranks of professional baseball as well.

This segregation forced black players to form their own leagues. The first all-black professional club was the Cuban Giants, formed in 1885, one of many such teams that barnstormed independently. It was not until 1920 that the first black league, the Negro National League, was organized by Rube Foster. It was joined three years later by the Eastern Colored League, formed by Ed Bolden. Both leagues showed considerable promise in their first few years but soon succumbed to financial pressures; the Eastern Colored League folded in 1928 and the Negro National League in 1931.

Within two years a new black league was born. A new Negro National League began play in 1933, and a rival Negro American League was launched in 1937. These leagues enjoyed far greater success than their predecessors, thriving until the major leagues dropped the ban on blacks. In their heyday the Negro leagues featured some of baseball's greatest talents, among them such legendary figures as the catcher/slugger Josh Gibson and the pitcher Satchel Paige. Because statistics were not always rigorously recorded in the Negro Leagues, it is difficult to measure the scale of accomplishments of some black stars against white major leaguers. But by some reliable accounts, for example, Josh Gibson hit 84 home runs in a single season and 962 for his career. Negro League all-star squads won about half of the exhibition games they played against major league all-stars.

In 1947, when Jackie Robinson joined the Brooklyn Dodgers and became the first African American to participate in modern major league baseball, the Negro Leagues went into a rapid decline as the interest of African American fans focused on Robinson and the many other black major leaguers who followed him in quick succession. The Negro National League disbanded in 1948, followed by the Negro American League in 1960.

within two feet of the top of the stadium. Elected to the Hall of Fame in 1972, his plaque credits him with "almost 800 home runs," which would make him the all-time home run champion. And various authorities say he hit as many as 89 home runs in a season—albeit sometimes against shaky semi-pro pitching. While Gibson was not a great defensive backstop, few base runners ever tried to steal on him because of his awesome arm.

In 1940 and 1941, Gibson played south of the border to reap greater financial rewards. He starred for Vera Cruz of the Mexican League and later for the Puerto Rican Winter League, earning Most Valuable Player honors as well a batting title. Gibson was forced to abandon the Mexican League and return to the Grays in 1942 when owner Cum Posey threatened him with a lawsuit. (Gibson was under contract with the Grays and was not supposed to play with any other team.)

Gibson returned to the Grays only to lead the Negro League in batting and home runs. In 1943, Pittsburgh Pirate owner Bill Benswanger signed Gibson to a contract that would have made him the first black player in the major leagues, but Baseball Commissioner K. M. Landis vetoed the signing. The breaking of baseball's color barrier would have to wait until Jackie Robinson became the first black major leaguer in 1947.

Tragedy struck the next season when Gibson was diagnosed with a brain tumor. Despite recurring headaches, Gibson feared that surgery might leave him brain-dead and refused to let doctors operate. On January 20, 1947, only three months before Robinson was signed to the Brooklyn Dodgers, Gibson died in his sleep. Although he never had the chance to hit against major league pitching, he is remembered today as the greatest hitter the Negro Leagues ever produced. ◆

1911 Gibson is born in Buena Vista, Georgia.

1927 Gibson starts with the Negro League's Pittsburgh Crawfords as catcher (1927–29; 1932–36).

1930 Gibson joins Homestead Grays (1930–31; 1937–46).

1947 Gibson dies of a brain tumor.

1972 Gibson is inducted into the Baseball Hall of Fame.

"A homer a day will boost my pay."

Josh Gibson

Gordon, Jeff

AUGUST 4, 1971– ● RACE CAR DRIVER

Only 28 years old, Jeff Gordon has already secured his status as one the great all-time champions of stock-car racing with three NACSAR Winston Cup Series championships and 40 wins in the last four years, a record that

1971 Gordon is born in North Carolina.

1991 Gordon wins the USAC championship "dirt" title and is named stock car Rookie of the Year.

1993 Gordon is named Winston Cup Rookie of the Year.

1994 Gordon has his first major Winston Cup win at the Coca-Cola 600.

1995 Gordon wins seven races and is the second-youngest drive to win the Winston Cup title, which he also wins in 1997 and '98.

1998 Gordon ties Richard Petty's record of 13 race wins in one season.

has been matched only by legends such as Earnhardt, Petty, Yarborough, and Pearson. He is the only driver so far to have run off three consecutive seasons with at least 10 wins.

Gordon's success is a testament to the philosophy of starting early—really early. Gordon was just four years old when his stepfather, John Bickford, started molding young Jeff as a race-car driver by putting him in a bicycle motorcross. When Jeff's mother forbade this potentially dangerous activity, John shifted to Jeff a six-foot quarter-midget race car powered by a single-cylinder, 2.85-horsepower engine. He practiced relentlessly on a makeshift track that Bickford created on an abandoned fair-ground near their home in Vallejo, California. Spurred by Bickford, Jeff was soon testing his skills against other racers, entering contests nearly every weekend in all parts of the country by the time he was eight. His first championship came in 1979, when he captured the national quarter-midget crown.

Jeff's winning ways persisted as he moved up to more powerful vehicles: first a 10-horsepower go-kart and then superstock light vehicles in which the nine-year-old Jeff was handily defeating racers who were 17 and older. As Bickford recalled, "Those guys were going, 'There's no nine-year-old kid gonna run with us! Get outta here!' "

Yet by the age of 12, Jeff was already running out of adequate competition. He later said, "You get to be 12 years old, and you realize you' ve been in quarter-midgets for eight years. What's next? I was getting older, not knowing what I wanted to do next." The ever-resourceful Bickford found the answer in the sprint-car circuit in the Midwest, where several tracks, never anticipating the possibility of child entrants, had not instituted minimum age requirements. Jeff and John sank $25,000 into the building of a custom sprint car with 650 horsepower. At the age of 13, Jeff was racing on sprint tracks in Ohio, Illinois, and Indiana, registering an impressive string of victories over the next several years. He won the 1989 United States Automobile Club (USAC) Midget Rookie of the Year award.

In 1990, the 18-year-old Gordon made the move to the USAC sprint-car circuit, where he piloted open-wheel sprinters with 815 horsepower and full midget cars with 320 horsepower. But it was in the following year that Jeff's career took a great leap forward: while continuing with USAC open-wheel competition, he stepped up to the NASCAR Busch Grand

National tour, only one notch down from the top-ranked NASCAR Winston Cup circuit. Ever the prodigy, Gordon captured the USAC championship dirt title that year, becoming the youngest Silver Crown winner in the history of the series. He was also Rookie of the Year on the Busch stock car circuit, where Gordon found a clear direction for his career. As he later recalled, "The [stock] car was different from anything I was used to. It was so big and heavy. It felt very fast but very smooth. I loved it."

Gordon took the Busch circuit by storm in 1992 with a record-setting 11 poles (the top spot in the starting order earned by the car with the best qualifying time). One of his three wins that year was in Atlanta, Georgia, where Gordon's performance prompted a show of interest from Rick Hendrick, a well-known car owner on the Winston Cup circuit. Gordon signed on with Hendrick and raced for him in 1993, finishing in the top five seven times and becoming the first rookie in 30 years to win one of the 125-mile Daytona 500 qualifying races. His outstanding record that year earned $765,168 and Winston Cup Rookie of the Year honors.

Gordon's career soon zoomed into high gear. His first major Winston Cup victory came in 1994 at the Coca-Cola 600 at Charlotte, North Carolina. That triumph was eclipsed shortly thereafter by Gordon's victory at the Brickyard 400, the richest stock-car race up to that time and the first ever held at the Indianapolis Motor Speedway. In 1995 Gordon, only 24, climbed to the mountaintop, winning seven races and becoming the second-youngest man to win the Winston Cup title. Gordon captured the Winston Cup again in 1997, when he piled up an amazing 10 wins and earned the prestigious **Winston Million**. Yet he managed to surpass himself once again in 1998, winning 13 races on his way to a stunning 364-point advantage over the second place finisher in the Winston Cup final standings.

Gordon and his wife Brooke have a house on Lake Norman near Davidson, North Carolina. Reflecting on his astonishing success, he told a reporter, "I have great parents who gave me the opportunity to be a race car driver. To see the way it's all worked out, it makes my parents heroes in my mind. In Brooke, I met a person who has been wonderful for me. All of that stuff, on top of the racing, has been wonderful. I'm so happy with my life right now. I' d be crazy to say I wasn't." ◆

"A normal passenger car has about 200 horsepower. . . . We're talking 700-plus horsepower in my DuPont Monte Carlo. . . . In my car I can do 65 in first gear and 100 easily in second, and I've still got two more gears to go."

Jeff Gordon in *Sports Illustrated*, Aug. 13, 1997

Winston Million: annual NASCAR prize of $1 million awarded to a driver who finishes in the top five of any one of the five "crown jewel" NASCAR events, and subsequently wins the next "crown jewel" event.

Graf, Steffi

JUNE 14, 1969– ● TENNIS PLAYER

From the very beginning of her life, Steffi Graf was destined to become a tennis legend. Born in June 14, 1969, in the small town of Bruhl, West Germany, both her father, Peter, and her mother, Heidi, were professional tennis players who also owned a racquet club.

Growing up, Graf never really watched women's tennis. She loved only to play. When she was three years old, she began to drag out her father's racquets and ask to play. At the time, Peter Graf was a nationally-ranked player, busy giving lessons and running his tennis club with his wife. Skeptical of the satisfaction in teaching a pre-schooler to play tennis, Graf's father initially discouraged her interest in the sport. But her persistence eventually won her father over.

Steffi Graf at Wimbledon.

A few months before Graf's fourth birthday, her father sawed off one of his old racquets, gave her some simple pointers, and left her to experiment with her new-found toy. Within a few days, Graf had succeeded in destroying all of the lamps in her house. But this wasn't her last adventure with tennis at home. She later set up two chairs in the family's basement and ran a string between them. It was on this improvised court that Graf and her father began to play tennis, often for ice cream. By the time she turned five, Steffi had convinced her father that her interest in tennis was not a childish whim.

"For a long time, I believed that Steffi only wanted to play because she loved me and wanted to be with me," Peter Graf told *Tennis* magazine. "But the evidence of her talent became very strong. Unlike other children, she did not hit the ball and then look all around at other things. She was always watching the ball until it was not in play anymore."

Under her father's coaching and supervision, Graf began to compete against other young opponents. She was only six years old when she won her first junior tournament, and by age 13 she had won the German junior championship in the 18-and-under division. By the time she was 13, Graf was being tutored privately and had dropped out of school to become a professional tennis player. At the time, she was the second-youngest player to receive an international ranking. And a year later she went on to win a gold medal at the Los Angeles Summer Olympics. Improving steadily, by her 15th birthday Graf managed to beat Pam Shriver, the No. 4 player at the U.S. Open. She later told *Sports Illustrated*, "All I want to do is play good tennis and have fun."

Because she began playing tennis at such a young age, Graf had little time for anything else, making tennis her first priority. Leading the social life of a typical teenager mattered little to Graf: She didn't date much, and had few close friends at home in Bruhl. She once refused to go to a birthday party because she had to play tennis. Another time Graf went to a nightclub, but soon called her mother for a ride home, complaining of the noise. At the age of 19, Graf was beginning to realize the difficulty of forging friendships with her competitors—in part for fear of jeopardizing her tennis game. "Everyone wants to win and to get in a relationship is just so hard," Graf told *World Tennis*.

Aside from her loner existence, Graf has also had her share of public relations difficulties. Due to the heated temper of both her and her father, Graf has often acted childishly in moments that tennis officials hoped she would show more tact. In 1985, she took on Martina Navratilova in the Lynda Carter-Maybelline Classic in Fort Lauderdale, Florida. After losing the match, Graf surprised tour officials, sponsors, a national television audience, and 5,000 spectators by running off the court instead of attending the official presentation ceremonies. Local papers reported her "poor sport" behavior and ran headlines that read: "Graf Takes 2nd Place Cash, Runs."

But Graf's sometimes-difficult social ways cannot detract from the fact that she has become one of the tennis greats of her time. She was the youngest woman to win the French Open, defeating Martina Navratilova in 1987. She holds 21 Grand Slam singles titles, 106 career singles titles, and was ranked number one in the world for over 7 years. While winning all these titles

---

1969 ▸ Graf is born in Bruhl, West Germany.

1984 ▸ Graf wins the gold medal at the Olympics in Los Angeles.

1987 ▸ Defeating Martina Navratilova, Graf becomes the youngest woman to ever win the French Open; she also wins 11 tournaments, and 45 consecutive matches.

1988 ▸ Graf becomes only the fifth woman to win the Grand Slam.

1995 ▸ Graf wins Wimbledon along with the French and U.S. Opens.

1996 ▸ Graf wins the U.S. Open for the second year in a row.

"Steffi is definitely the greatest women's tennis player of all time."
Billie Jean King on Steffi Graf

has afforded her material wealth and fame, Graf is more concerned with her passion for the game. "I get enormous pleasure out of playing," she told *People* magazine. ◆

Greene, Maurice

JULY 23, 1974– ● TRACK AND FIELD ATHLETE

Sprinter Maurice Greene was born in Kansas City, Kansas, the youngest of four children. His older brother Ernest was himself a promising sprinter, running a time of 10.24 seconds in the 100-meter and making it to the semifinal round of the 1992 Olympic trials. At age eight Maurice joined the Kansas City Chargers track club, and he continued to train under the team's coach, Al Hobson, throughout his teen years and into his early twenties. Under Hobson, Greene showed that he had the potential to become a world-class sprinter. At Kansas City's Schlagle High School he dominated statewide competition, winning both the 100-meter and 200-meter state titles three times and in his senior year adding a state title in the 400-meter. During these years Greene also won numerous AAU titles.

After graduating from high school Greene stayed near home and ran for Kansas City Kansas Community College. A pulled hamstring hobbled him during the 1994 season, but he began to attract national attention in 1995 when he ran a 100-meter in 10.19 seconds and beat Olympic champion Carl Lewis with a **wind-aided** time of 9.88 at the Texas Relays. Greene had high hopes for the 1996 Olympics, but he again injured a hamstring and struggled to a seventh-place finish in the quarterfinals of the Olympic trials.

At this point in his career Greene decided he needed a change. Tearing himself away from his home in Kansas City in September 1996, he drove to Los Angeles, where he met with sprint coach John Smith and eventually found a home-away-from-home with a training club of about 20 other athletes called HS International. Smith subjected Greene to a training regimen that was **grueling** both physically and psychologically, and by the spring of 1997 Greene was convinced that his track career was a failure. Discouraged and lacking money, he consulted the newspaper want ads in search of a job—he had already worked in fast-food restaurants, at a dog-racing track, on

wind-aided: phrase attached to a finishing time in a sprint race or other track and field event when a tailwind going beyond a fixed speed assisted a competitor in achieving a particularly good time or score.

grueling: a physically punishing athletic competition or event which drives an athlete to the point of exhaustion.

a loading dock, and as a movie-theater usher. Smith, though, persuaded Greene to keep running, telling him, "This is the time to dig down and find something in yourself. You' re ready to run fast. Go out and do it, and when you see the time, act like you expected it."

Greene's journey from near despair to the top of the track world was a rapid one. Just a week later he competed in the 1997 national championships in Indianapolis, Indiana. In a preliminary round he ran a time of 9.96, carving .12 seconds off his personal best in the 100-meter. The next night, running for the national title, he scorched the field with a 9.90, making him the third fastest American in history behind Leroy Burrell (9. 85) and Carl Lewis (9.86). Less than two months later, in the 1997 world championships in Athens, Greece, he went up against Canada's Donovan Bailey, beating him with a time of 9.86 and narrowly missing Bailey's 9.84 world-record time from the 1996 Atlanta Olympics.

In Greene's mind, though—and in the mind of his training partner and rival, Trinidad and Tobago's Ato Boldon—the "real" world record in the 100 meter was 9.79. This was the time that Canadian Ben Johnson had run at the 1988 Seoul Olympics before he was stripped of his gold medal and world record when he tested positive for steroids. His time, however, became a kind of unofficial record that world-class sprinters trained to achieve. Throughout 1998 and early 1999 both Greene and Boldon boasted daily to anyone who would listen, including the press, that one of them would reach Johnson's benchmark time.

On June 16, 1999, at Olympic Stadium in Athens, Greene made good on his boast. He tore through the windless evening and matched Johnson's time of 9.79, making him the world's fastest human. In demolishing Bailey's world record, he took more time off the record in one race than any sprinter ever had since the advent of automatic timing more than three decades earlier. Then in August, at the world championships in Seville, Spain, Greene showed that his record time was no **fluke**. He won the 100-meter with a time of 9.80 seconds and added a second gold medal in the 200-meter with a time of 19.90, making him the first man since Carl Lewis in the 1984 Olympics to win the 100-200 double in a major international event.

The standard of excellence for men in the 100-meters is breaking 10 seconds. With 17 races run in under 10 seconds— more than such greats as Carl Lewis, Donovan Bailey, Leroy

1974 Greene is born in Kansas City, Kansas.

1995 Greene runs the 100-meter in 10.19; beats Carl Lewis in Texas Relays.

1997 Greene outruns Donovan Bailey at the world championships in Athens.

1999 In Athens, Greene matches Ben Johnson's 9.79 for 100 meters; in Seville, wins gold in the 100-meter and 200-meter dashes.

fluke: a stroke of luck or an unexpected and perhaps dubious result in an athletic competition when a lesser team or performer defeats a much more skilled and talented opponent.

Burrell, and Linford Christie—Maurice Greene in 1999 was on a course to become the most accomplished sub-ten-second sprinter ever and the man to beat in the 2000 Olympics in Sydney, Australia. ◆

Griffey, Ken, Jr.

NOVEMBER 21, 1969– ● BASEBALL PLAYER

With a smooth swing, spectacular defensive fielding skills, and a charismatic smile, Ken Griffey, Jr. is one of the marquee talents in Major League Baseball.

George Kenneth Griffey, Jr. was born in Donora, Pennsylvania, on Nov. 21, 1969 to Alberta and Ken Griffey, a star of the Cincinnati Reds' "Big Red Machine" of the 1970s. A superb all-around athlete, the younger Griffey played baseball and football at Cincinnati Moeller High School. He was a star tailback and wide receiver for the football team for three years and led the team to a championship as a junior.

In 1987, at age 17, Junior was the first player selected in the 1987 Major League Baseball Amateur Draft by the Seattle Mariners. He received a bonus of $160,000 from the Washington team.

Griffey wouldn't stay in the minors long. In 1989, after a superb spring training, he earned a spot on the Mariners' roster. He was the youngest player in the major leagues (19), but he proved that youth would be served, making an instant impact. He hit a double in his first major league at-bat off Oakland's Dave Stewart, and in his Kingdome debut, blasted the first pitch he saw for a home run. He finished his rookie season with a .264 batting average, 16 home runs and 64 runs batted in, and although he missed a

Ken Griffey, Jr. launches another home run.

month of the season due to a broken hand, Griffey finished third in rookie of the year balloting.

Griffey came into his own the next season, positioning himself among the league leaders in total bases, hits, triples, batting average, and slugging percentage. He became the second-youngest player in history and the first Seattle Mariner to start in the All-Star Game. Later that season he and Ken, Sr. became the first father-son combo to play in the same lineup, and on Sept. 14 of that season, the Griffeys hit back-to-back home runs. Junior capped off the season by becoming the second-youngest player to win a Gold Glove.

Making the All-Star Game and winning Gold Glove would become annual occurrences, as Griffey has not missed an All-Star Game since he came into the league. He has won eight Gold Glove awards and is a perennial candidate.

Griffey has always been one of the top vote-getters. He has led the American League in ballots received seven times, and five times he's led all of baseball, including 1994, when he set the major league record, receiving 6,079,688 votes. Griffey has also put on amazing shows at the All-Star Game Home Run Derby, which he won in 1999 for the third time.

As Griffey matured, he became the leader of the Mariners. He displayed amazing power, hitting 42, 39, 38, and a league-leading 40 homers from 1992–1995. He drove in at least 100 runs three of those four years.

In 1993 Griffey rewrote the Seattle record books, setting new marks for home runs (45), runs scored (113), total bases (359), intentional walks (25) and slugging percentage (.617). He also tied a major league record by hitting at least one home run in eight straight games. Griffey continued to excel on defense, establishing a new American League record for outfielders with his 542nd consecutive errorless chance.

The next season Griffey finished second only to Chicago's Frank Thomas in the Most Valuable Player balloting after leading the league in homers (40), driving in 90 runs (seventh in the league), batting .323 (eighth). Griffey also ranked among the leaders in home run-ratio (1:10.8 at-bats), intentional walks (19) and total bases (292), runs (94), slugging percentage (.674), extra-base hits (68), and hits (140).

As good as his numbers were, Griffey was frustrated by the Mariners' lack of team success. That changed in 1995, when they won the American League Western Division. Although Griffey missed 90 games due to a broken wrist, his strong lead-

1969 Griffey is born in Donora, Pennsylvania.

1990 Ken Griffey Sr. and Ken Griffey Jr. of Seattle become first father and son to play on the same major league team.

1993 Griffey sets Mariners' records for home runs, runs scored, and total bases.

1996 Griffey sets Seattle franchise records with 49 homers and 140 runs batted in.

2000 Griffey traded to Cincinnati Reds.

ership upon his return, combined with Randy Johnson's pitching, led to a Mariners surge that saw them catch the California Angels in the final days of the season, then win a one-game playoff against them. The Mariners then came from two games down to win the best-of-five Divisional Series against the New York Yankees. Griffey capped off the Mariners' series-winning rally in the 11th inning of Game Five by scoring all the way from first base on a double by Edgar Martinez. The Mariners weren't beaten until the American League Championship Series, which they lost to the Cleveland Indians in six games.

Griffey again rewrote the Seattle record books in 1996, setting franchise records with 49 home runs (third in the American League) and 140 RBI (fifth in the American League). He did this despite missing 20 games (June 20-July 13) with a broken bone in his wrist.

The year 1997 was another banner season for Griffey and the Mariners. Seattle won the West with a 90–72 record, but lost to Baltimore in the divisional playoffs. Griffey belted 56 home runs and drove in 147 runs. Included in those 56 home runs was career homer No. 250, which came off Toronto's Roger Clemens. Griffey became the fourth-youngest player ever to reach that mark, and the 13th player ever to win unanimous MVP selection.

Griffey almost matched his 1997 numbers the following season as he blasted 56 home runs and drove in 146 runs. He was chosen to play in his ninth consecutive All-Star Game and won the **Home Run Derby** competition there. Griffey became only the third player to hit 50 home runs in consecutive seasons (joining Babe Ruth, 1920–21, 1927–28) and Mark McGwire (1996–98) and became the only major leaguer with three 140+ RBI seasons since 1963.

Home Run Derby: event in which baseball players engage in a home run–hitting contest; annual event at the Major League Baseball All Star festivities in which players swing at pitches thrown by a batting practice coach to determine who can hit the most home runs.

Griffey ended 1999 in typical fashion, hitting 48 homers, driving in 134 runs, and leading the major leagues in votes for the All-Star Game. He also was voted to the All-Century Team. At the start of the 2000 season, Griffey was traded to the Cincinnati Reds, the team he grew up with. Griffey's swing has made him the favorite among current players to pass Hank Aaron as the all-time home run king and in April 2000, he became the youngest player ever to hit 400 home runs.

Griffey's million-dollar smile, which adorns everything from billboards for the All-Star Café (Griffey is a partner) to cereal boxes, has made him one of baseball's most marketable players. He is also one of the best players in the history of the game. ◆

Labor Unrest

Over the past quarter century, all four major professional sports leagues in the United States Major League Baseball, the National Football League (NFL), the National Basketball Association (NBA), and the National Hockey League (NHL) have endured major work stoppages. Each major sports labor drama has had its unique twists and turns, but they all seem to draw on the same basic plot outline: increasingly militant players' unions on one side and increasingly assertive owners on the other in pitched battles over the division of vast TV-and fan-generated revenues.

With the strongest union of the big four leagues, baseball has, not coincidentally, the longest and most acrimonious labor history: eight work stoppages since 1972. The 1981 strike was the first to take a major chunk out of a season; it began on June 12 and ended on August 9 and forced Major League Baseball to concoct a widely derided split-season format to settle the division races that year. The 1994 baseball strike was the longest and most bitter labor dispute in modern American sports history. At the prodding of Chicago White Sox owner Jerry Reisndorf (also the owner of the NBA's Chicago Bulls), the owners pressed for a salary cap, claiming that escalating salaries were bringing many franchises to the brink of financial ruin.

The Major League Baseball Players' Association, led by the labor lawyer Donald Fehr, disputed the owners' figures and argued that the free market should determine players' compensation. After prolonged negotiations failed to produce a new basic agreement, the players walked out on August 11, 1994. In contrast to previous strikes, in which management folded fairly quickly in the face of player intransigence, this time the owners stood firm, a task made easier by the lack of a strong commissioner who might have exerted pressure for a settlement (the owners had fired Fay Vincent as commissioner in 1992 and did not replace him, preferring the temporary, owner-friendly stewardship of Milwaukee Brewers owner Bud Selig). The World Series fell victim to the strike, the first cancellation of the fall classic since its official launching in 1905. The stalemate persisted until the following spring, when the teams opened spring training camps with replacement players. The union held firm, however, and on March 31, after a U.S. District Court judge issued an unfair labor-practice injunction against Major League Baseball, the owners relented and agreed to proceed with the season under the pre-existing rules. Ballpark attendance and TV ratings dipped sharply after the strike and recovered only gradually.

The NFL's first major labor dispute arose in 1982, when no games were played during the players' 57-day walkout. With the NFL's basic agreement set to expire on August 27, 1987, the players' unsuccessfully pressed for the right to unrestricted free agency at the end of their contracts. When the owners rebuffed this demand, the players struck on September 22, 1987. The owners canceled the following week's games but then resumed play with replacement players. The union's solidarity began to crack, and many striking players began to offer to return to their teams. When the league turned them away, the players filed a complaint with the National Labor Relations Board (the NLRB), which ordered the owners to accept the returning players and pay them some $25 million in lost wages for that weekend. The NFL then completed its slightly shortened (15 games) and compromised (three weeks of farcical replacement-player games) season. The football players' union has yet to recover from that debacle.

The NBA's 1998–99 season was nearly scuttled when the owners imposed a lockout on the players in July 1, 1998, over a dispute with the players' union on how to divide the NBA's revenues of roughly $2 billion. The impasse lasted throughout the fall and into January, when it seemed that cancellation of the season was imminent. Just 29 hours before the owners' self-imposed deadline for canceling the season, the Players Association executive director, Billy Hunter, and the NBA commissioner, David Stern, came out of an all-night bargaining session with a deal that called for both a new ceiling and minimum for players' salaries. The NBA then played out a shortened campaign with little apparent loss of fan interest. Hockey was hit by its first players' strike on April 1, 1992, just four days before the scheduled end of the season. With the owners claiming annual losses of $9 million and the players claiming owner profits of $24 million, the union walked out at a critical juncture, just before the start of the lucrative postseason playoffs. Nevertheless, the NHL's president, John Ziegler, managed to extract an agreement that some regarded as a victory for management: although the players won the right to license their own photographs, a $100,000 salary minimum, and a larger slice of playoff, insurance, and pension funds, the owners minimized the players' free agent rights, imposed a longer season, and limited the agreement to two years.

After talks on a new basic NHL agreement stalled in the summer of 1994, the owners feared that the hockey players would strike during the season. Despite a no-strike pledge from the players, the owners locked the players out on October 1, 1994, the scheduled opening date of the season. As the sides edged closer to the unprecedented loss of an entire professional sports season, they finally came to terms on a six-year contract on January 13, 1995. The owners achieved most of their objectives except a payroll tax to limit salaries and a team salary cap. The strike-shortened season (48 games as opposed to the normal 84) was welcomed by the hockey-starved fans: eight teams sold out their home games, and eleven other teams filled 90 percent of their seats.

Griffith, Yolanda

MARCH 1, 1970– ● BASKETBALL PLAYER

Yolanda Griffith, who was born in Chicago, got her education in tough, physical play in pickup basketball games with her brothers on the city's south side. She first captured the attention of basketball fans when she was a *Parade* All-American and won All-State honors while she was at Illinois' Carver Area High School.

In 1988 Griffith won a scholarship to the University of Iowa as a Proposition 48 athlete, meaning that she couldn't play until she proved herself in the classroom. She never played at Iowa, however, because during her first semester there she became pregnant. So Griffith instead honed her skills at Palm Beach Junior College in Florida. During the 1989–90 season she compiled some impressive numbers: over 28 points per game, nearly 20 rebounds per game, and a sparkling 72.7 shooting percentage from the field. While still at Palm Beach she was also named National Junior College Athletic Association All-Region and All-State in 1991.

Griffith continued her education at Florida Atlantic University, where she played during the 1993–94 season, averaging 22 points and 14 rebounds per game en route to being named a Kodak Division II All-American and WBCA Player of the Year. In the meantime Griffith played on the 1990 U.S. Olympic Festival North team, and while she averaged only 7 points per game, she was the festival's second-leading rebounder, averaging 8.8 rebounds per game. Griffith's only other participation in international competition for the United States to date has been as a member of the U.S. National Team that finished 2–3 against Australia in the Goldmark Cup.

In 1993 Griffith faced the dilemma that many women basketball players faced prior to the late 1990s: There was no women's professional basketball league in the United States. She still wanted to play and develop her game—she had yet to play in the highest levels of competition—so, like many of her contemporaries, she took her game to Europe. From 1993 to 1997 she played professionally in Germany, in her final season leading the European League in scoring (24.7 points per game) and rebounding (16 per game). It was this "double-double" capacity (double figures in scoring and rebounding) that attracted the attention of a new U.S. women's basketball league, the ABL.

Griffith was the number one pick of the 1997 ABL expansion draft, selected by the Long Beach StingRays. During the 1998 season she showed U.S. fans what Europe had known for several years: that Yolanda Griffith was a top-notch player. At 6′3″ and 175 pounds, she demonstrated a potent combination of scoring, rebounding, and defense at her forward position. She led Long Beach and was fourth in the ABL in scoring with an 18.8 average. She also led the ABL in steals, was the league's second-best shot blocker, and was third in the league in field goal percentage. Along the way Griffith was a starter in the ABL All-Star Game and led the StingRays to the ABL Finals, recording 10 double-doubles in the ABL playoffs. For her efforts she was named first team all-ABL, was the ABL's Defensive

1970 Griffith is born in Chicago, Illinois.

1993 Griffith is named WBCA player of the year; Kodak Div. II All-American.

1998 As the number one draft pick, Griffith goes to the Long Beach StingRays; she leads the ABL in steals and is named league defensive player of the year.

1999 Griffith is named to the Women's National Team to play in 2000 Olympics in Sydney.

Player of the Year, and came in second to Matalie Williams in the ABL's Most Valuable Player voting.

When asked what she considered her greatest achievement, Griffith cited her year with Long Beach and the team's surprising success. In the abbreviated 1999 season, before the ABL folded, she carried another expansion team, the Chicago Condors, where she ranked fifth in the league in scoring (17.2 points per game), first in rebounding (12.3 per game), second in steals, and second in blocked shots.

When the Women's National Basketball Association (WNBA) was formed, Griffith was assured of a spot. The only question mark was where. That question was answered when the Sacramento Monarchs made her their top pick, the number two pick overall in the 1999 draft. Commenting on her selection, Monarchs general manager Jerry Reynolds said, "We believe she is the most versatile big player in women's professional basketball. She has the ability to play both the **power forward** and center positions and is still athletic enough to defend small forwards."

power forward: position in basketball usually occupied by a player much taller than a guard, yet shorter than a center; specializes in rebounding and physical play with the ability to score.

The Monarchs' selection proved to be a good one. During the 1999 season Griffith was twice named WNBA Player of the Week and had 10 points and 5 rebounds in the 1999 WNBA All-Star game. She helped her team to the third best record in the Western Conference, showing the same balanced game she always had: a league-leading 11.3 rebounds per game, a second-best 18.8 points per game, and a third-best 1.9 blocked shots per game. She was named to the All-WNBA first team, and crowned her season when she was named the 1999 Newcomer of the Year, 1999 Defensive Player of the Year (edging Sheryl Swoopes of the Houston Comets by a single vote), and 1999 WNBA Most Valuable Player—all this despite suffering a serious knee injury late in the season. Also in 1999 Griffith was named by USA Basketball to the 1999–2000 Women's National Team that will compete in the Olympics in Sydney, Australia in 2000. ◆

Griffith-Joyner, Florence

DECEMBER 21, 1959–SEPTEMBER 21, 1998 ● TRACK AND FIELD ATHLETE

Florence Griffith was born in Los Angeles, the seventh of 11 children of an electronics technician and a garment worker. When she was four, her parents separated and she moved with her mother and siblings to the Jordan Downs housing project in the Watts section of Los Angeles. Griffith began running at age seven in competitions sponsored by the Jesse Owens National Youth Games for underprivileged youth and won races at ages 14 and 15. She became a member of the track team at Jordan High School, where she set two school records before graduating in 1978.

In 1979 Griffith enrolled at California State University at Northridge, where she met assistant track coach Bob Kersee. However, she was forced to drop out of college the next year due to lack of funds. With the help of Kersee, who had moved to the University of California at Los Angeles (UCLA), Griffith won an athletic scholarship to UCLA and returned to college in 1981. Griffith competed on the track team, and in 1982 she won the NCAA championships in the 200 meters. In 1983 she won the NCAA championships in the 400 meters and graduated from UCLA with a major in psychology. In the 1984 Olympics in Los Angeles, she finished second to fellow American Valerie Brisco-Hooks in the 200 meters.

After the Olympics Griffith worked as a customer-service representative for a bank during the day and as a beautician at night. In early 1987, however, she decided to train full-time for the 1988 Olympics. In October 1987 she married Al Joyner, brother of athlete Jackie Joyner-Kersee.

After strong showings in the world championships and the U.S. trials, Griffith-Joyner was a favorite for the 1988 Olympics in Seoul, Korea. Flo-Jo, as she was dubbed by the media, did not disappoint, winning three gold medals and one silver medal. Griffith-Joyner set an Olympic record in the 100 meters and a world record in the 200 meters. She ran the third leg for the American winning team in the 4 100-meter relay and the anchor leg for the American silver-medal winners in the 4 400-meter relay. Griffith-Joyner's outstanding performance and

1959 Florence Delorez Griffith is born in Los Angeles.

1984 Griffith-Joyner wins the Olympic silver medal.

1988 Griffith-Joyner wins one silver and three gold Olympic medals.

1993 Griffith-Joyner co-chairs the President's Council on Physical Fitness and Sports.

1998 Griffith-Joyner dies unexpectedly at age 38.

striking appearance (including long, extravagantly decorated fingernails and brightly colored one-legged running outfits) earned her worldwide media attention. She won the 1988 Jesse Owens Award and the 1988 Sullivan Award, given annually to the best amateur athlete.

Griffith-Joyner settled comfortably into post-Olympic life with numerous endorsements and projects, including designing her own sportswear line and a brief acting stint on the television soap opera *Santa Barbara* (1992). In 1993 President Bill Clinton named her cochairwoman of the President's Council on Physical Fitness and Sports.

Griffith-Joyner died suddenly in September 1998 at the age of 38. An autopsy revealed that she suffocated during an epileptic seizure caused by a congenital blood flow abnormality. ◆

Gwynn, Tony

May 9, 1960– ● Baseball Player

Tony Gwynn has never been one for change. Born May 9, 1960 in Los Angeles, California, the smooth-swinging San Diego Padres outfielder still calls Southern California his home. Gwynn, the oldest of three brothers (including Chris, who played in the major leagues for 10 years) attended Polytechnic High School in Long Beach, then went to college at San Diego State. There, he played both baseball and basketball. As a **point guard** for the Aztecs, he set the school career record for assists, a record that still stands. In 1981, he was selected to the All-Western Athletic Conference. Gwynn was later drafted in the 10th round by the NBA's San Diego Clippers in the NBA draft.

point guard: position in basketball usually occupied by one of the shorter players on a team, who has the best ability to dribble the basketball up the court on offense, organize offensive plays on the court, and distribute the basketball to teammates most frequently.

Unfortunately for the Clippers, that same day Gwynn was drafted in the third round by the San Diego Padres of the National League. For Gwynn, who had also been voted All-Western Athletic Conference in baseball—the only player in WAC history to be named all-conference in two sports the same year—it was no contest. He was going to play baseball.

Gwynn entered the minor leagues swinging. He earned most valuable player honors in the rookie league, after hitting .331 with Walla Walla of the Rookie Northwest League.

Gwynn finished his rookie season by hitting .462 over the final three weeks after being promoted to Double A.

In 1982 Gwynn started in Triple A, and after hitting at a solid .328 clip, he got a call up to the major leagues. He went 2 for 4 in his first game, then went on to hit in a team-high 15 consecutive games, before suffering a broken wrist that cost him three weeks of action. Gwynn came back, and hit .348 over the month of September. Another broken wrist slowed him at the beginning of 1983, but he finished with a flourish, including a career-high 25-game hitting streak, which set the stage for 1984, Gwynn's breakthrough year.

While the Padres were on their way to their first World Series in franchise history, Gwynn was on his way to his first batting title. He hit a league-leading .351 and led the majors in hits (213) and multi-hit games (69). He also was chosen to start in the All-Star Game, the first of 15 straight appearances in the mid-summer classic (a streak that still stands) and finished third in the most valuable player voting. In the post-season, Gwynn hit a scorching .368 against the Chicago Cubs in the National League Championship Series (NLCS) and hit .316 overall. But in the World Series, the powerful Detroit Tigers defeated Gwynn and the Padres four games to one.

That would be the last time Gwynn would see postseason play for 14 years, but he was just getting started at winning batting titles and frustrating major league pitchers.

The master of consistency, Gwynn stayed around the 200-hit mark each of the next three years, getting 197, 211 and 218 hits. In 1987, his 218 hits led the league, as did his .370 batting average. That batting title was Gwynn's second and would mark the start of a three-year run (1987 through 1989) in which he would win the **Silver Slugger Award** for the National League's highest batting average.

As the 1990s began, Gwynn, a four-time batting champion, continued to take the slow and steady route. He may not have won a batting title between 1990 and 1993, but Gwynn never dipped below the .300 mark and he still was one of baseball's toughest batters for a pitcher to strike out. In fact, in 1993 he hit a remarkable .358.

In 1994, at age 33, Gwynn made a run at history. No major league hitter had finished with a season batting average of .400 since Boston's Ted Williams—considered by many to be the greatest hitter ever—hit .406 in 1941. But Gwynn took his best

1960 Gwynn is born in Los Angeles, California.

1984 Gwynn leads the major league in batting average (.351), hits, and multihit games.

1987 Gwynn leads the league in hits and batting average; wins Silver Slugger award (also in 1988 and 1989).

1994 Gwynn's .394 batting average comes closest to matching Ted Williams's .400+ records.

Silver Slugger Award: annual award given in the American and National Leagues of Major League Baseball; the award is given to the player at each position (third base, second base, etc.) who has the highest batting average of all players who play that position.

shot. With his signature smooth swing and ability to hit the ball to all fields, Gwynn hit a blazing .475 (19 for 40) in August and .433 (26 for 60) over the final 15 games, but came up just short, hitting .394. Through the 1999 season no one has hit .400 in a season since 1941, but Gwynn's .394 remains the closest to the mark. Though he didn't catch Ted Williams, no other hitters caught him and he took home his fifth batting title. His 165 hits were enough to lead the league in that category, also for the fifth time.

Following the magical 1994 season, Gwynn hit as consistently as ever. He would win batting titles the next three years, hitting no lower than .353, to give him eight for his career, tying him with Hall of Famer Honus Wagner for second, behind only Ty Cobb, who won 12 batting titles. One of the most rewarding seasons of Gwynn's career occurred in 1998. Despite having what some considered an off year—he "only" hit .321, which is still better than most major league players—Gwynn and the Padres won the National League West, then beat the Houston Astros in the Divisional Playoffs and shocked the Atlanta Braves in the NLCS to reach the World Series. In the World Series, however, San Diego was swept by the nearly unstoppable New York Yankees.

The Padres had a down season in 1999, as much of their roster was replaced in a move to help the team cut costs. Gwynn, however, remained his reliable self at the top of the Padres order. He hit a solid .338, with 139 hits. Though San Diego fans had little to cheer about that year, Gwynn was, as usual, a source of optimism, as he again chased history. This time, however, the goal was well within his reach. He started the season only 72 hits away from the magical 3,000 hits plateau. Gwynn would get number 3,000 in the first inning of an August 6 game in Montreal.

stratospheric: descriptive term signifying outstanding statistical production in particular athletic endeavors.

While so much is made of Gwynn's prolific hitting and his **stratospheric** batting averages, he has been as unforgettable and noteworthy as a class individual and a giving role model. Tony and his wife, Alicia (they have a teenage son, Anthony II, and a daughter, Anisha Nicole) have established the Tony and Alicia Gwynn Foundation, which assists many worthy causes in the San Diego area.

Perhaps the most amazing thing about Tony Gwynn is that in an age where few ball players stay with one team for any length of time, Gwynn has chosen to stay in San Diego his entire 18 years. After all, change isn't Tony Gwynn's style. ◆

Hamm, Mia

MARCH 17, 1972– ● SOCCER PLAYER

If you were widely considered the world's best woman soccer player, and had appeared in a Gatorade commercial with Michael Jordan, *and* had seen your name on *People* magazine's 1997 list of the world's 50 most beautiful people, you might have reason to get a swelled head. But not Mia Hamm. Best player? "I'm no better than anyone else out there," Hamm says. Most beautiful? "It's obvious that I'm not," she says, viewing her selection as more of a joke than an accolade. "I'm not this perfect person." Maybe not perfect, but by any reasonable measure, she is extraordinary. In the words of U.S. national coach Tony DiCicco, "So she's uncomfortable with the label Best Woman Soccer Player in the World. But when she's on her game, I would agree with that label."

Hamm has been on her game since the age of 14, when she was already dominating the competition as a high school All-American. She has since compiled the most goals of any American female player—111 in 179 appearances—and was named U.S. soccer's Female Athlete of the Year for an unprecedented five consecutive years (1994–98). Beguilingly shy, earnest, and modest off the field, she is a guided missile of determination between the lines. As DiCicco observed, "On the field, she would cut your heart out. She can let everything out on the field. It's her dark side, out there."

Perhaps this ferocity comes of being the fourth of six children, always feeling the need to shout to get a share of attention. "I was never very good at expressing myself," Hamm told a reporter. "I was this really emotional kid—still am—and I would get attention by screaming and yelling." Hamm's mother, a for-

> *"I'm just a soccer player. That's pretty much all I know."*
>
> Mia Hamm in *Sports Illustrated*

Mia Hamm celebrates a U.S. victory.

mer ballerina, tried to interest the five-year-old Mia in ballet, but she was instinctively drawn to the soccer field, at first joining in with her brothers and sisters. "When I was a kid," she recalled, " I'd quit a lot of games because I hated losing so much. I thought if I'd quit before the game was over then I really didn't lose." But her siblings taught her self-discipline and persistence, refusing to let her play unless she stuck it out to the end.

The next step was pee-wee teams on which she was often the only girl player and always by far the best. Soccer was an ideal way for Mia to cope with constant uprooting during her childhood, part of her father's Air Force position—as the family made its way through Alabama, California, Texas, Virginia, and Italy, Hamm found that her soccer prowess provided a quick and easy path to popularity in strange towns. "You moved to a new base and had new friends as soon as you joined a team," she recalled.

By the age of 14 she so far outclassed her high school competition in Texas that her coach in Waco, John Cossaboon, called Anson Dorrance, the head coach of the women's soccer team at the University of North Carolina, insisting that he fly to Texas to behold this pony-tailed force of nature. Flooded with such calls, Dorrance was skeptical, but he made the trip. He recalled, "I didn't want to know who the player was. I wanted her to emerge from the game. John's team kicked off, and the girl who received made a pass to her right, and I saw this young kid accelerate like she was shot out of a cannon. Without seeing her touch the ball, I ran around saying, 'Is that Mia Hamm?'"

Hamm's progress to the front ranks of international soccer was sure and swift. At age 15 she became the youngest member in the history of the U.S. National Women's Team and then accepted a scholarship to join Dorrance's North Carolina squad, which won the national championship in each of her four years there. A three-time collegiate All-American, she set conference career marks in goals (103), assists (72), and points (278).

At the age of 19, Hamm was the youngest woman on the victorious 1991 U.S. Women's World Cup Team, for which she started five of six games and scored a pair of goals. She was voted the most valuable player (MVP) of the 1994 Chiquita Cup by soccer fans and named the MVP of of the Women's World Cup in Sweden in 1995, scoring three goals on long-range free kicks (including a critical tying goal against Norway in the final). As a member of the U.S. squad at the 1996 Olympics, she sprained her ankle in the first round but played in every game of America's charge to the gold medal; and she played a key role on the U.S. team that captured the 1999 Women's World Cup.

The chief test of her character in recent years came off the field. At 16, her older brother Garrett, also a gifted athlete, was diagnosed with aplastic anemia, caused by the blood's deficiency in producing healthy **platelets.** By restricting his physical activities, Garrett, an adopted child, was able to lead a reasonably normal life, marrying and fathering a son. But by his late twenties the condition worsened, evolving into myelodysplasia, an impairment of red-blood cell production. In 1997 he was told that without a bone-marrow transplant, he had only months to live. But finding a suitable donor was complicated by Garrett's American-Thai heritage. Despite the Hamms' success in locating his biological father and obtaining a marrow donation, Garrett was so weakened that he succumbed to a fungal infection and died at the age of 28. Mia was devastated by his loss. She said, "I'd give up all this in a heartbeat to have him back, just to give him one more day or one more week," she said. "But

1972 — Hamm is born in Selma, Alabama.

1991 — At 19, Hamm is the youngest woman on U.S. Women's World Cup team, which won the world championship.

1994 — Hamm is named U.S. soccer's Female Athlete of the Year for first of an unprecedented five consecutive seasons.

1995 — Hamm is named Most Valuable Player of the Women's World Cup in Sweden.

platelets: small, flattened bodies of blood.

I know that Garrett wouldn't want that." Mia has since formed a foundation and organized an annual all-star soccer game to raise funds for research into bone marrow disease.

Hamm and her husband of five years, Christian Corey, a marine pilot-in-training, reside near Washington, D.C. ◆

Henderson, Rickey

DECEMBER 25, 1958– ● BASEBALL PLAYER

1958 Henderson is born in Chicago.

1979 In Henderson's first (partial) season with Oakland A's, he steals 33 bases in 89 games.

1980 Henderson, in his first full season, steals 100 bases, breaking Ty Cobb's record.

1981 Henderson wins the Gold Glove award.

1991 Henderson becomes the all-time stolen base leader.

Rickey Henderson was born in Chicago, but when his father left two months later, the family moved to Arkansas and then settled in Oakland, California. Henderson was a star running back at Oakland Technical High School and was vigorously recruited to play football by a number of colleges. Despite the promise of a football scholarship in a top college program, Henderson chose to sign with the hometown Oakland Athletics, who selected him in the fourth round of the 1976 baseball draft.

After two and a half seasons in the minor leagues, Henderson was brought up to the majors during the 1979 season and in only 89 games stole 33 bases. The following year, in his first full season, Henderson became an overnight superstar by stealing 100 bases, thereby breaking Ty Cobb's 65-year-old American League record of 96 thefts. In 1982, after the strike-shortened season of 1981, Henderson set his sights on Lou Brock's major-league record of 118 stolen bases and easily surpassed it with 130.

Besides his record-breaking accomplishments on the base paths, Henderson quickly established himself as one of the greatest players of the modern era. His .450-plus on-base percentage, coupled with his base-running abilities, makes him the best leadoff hitter of all time. Henderson has hit over .300 in several seasons and also hits for considerable power, a rarity among leadoff men. Henderson twice hit more than 20 home runs in a season, and holds a career record for the most home runs hit when leading off a game. On defense, Henderson has excelled as one of the game's finest left fielders and in 1981 was awarded a Gold Glove.

In 1984 Henderson was traded to the New York Yankees for six players, and stayed with the Yankees until 1989, when he was traded back to the Athletics, where he remained until late summer 1993, when he was traded to the Toronto Blue Jays.

In 1991 Henderson became the all-time stolen base leader when he broke Lou Brock's mark of 938 career steals. He began the 2000 season as a member of the New York Mets. ◆

Hingis, Martina

SEPTEMBER 30, 1980– ● TENNIS PLAYER

Martina Hingis, a record-breaking tennis champion, was born to become a tennis great on September 30, 1980 in Kosice, Czechoslovakia (now Slovakia). Named for Martina Navratilova, another tennis legend, both her parents' lives revolved around tennis. Her father, Karol Hingis, was a tennis coach and is currently a tennis club administrator, and her mother, Melanie Molitor, was a tennis player.

Hingis's parents divorced when she was young, and she moved to Trubbach, Switzerland with her mother, who had married Swiss computer salesman Andrew Zogg (they later divored in 1996). Even at this early stage of life, Hingis was being groomed for a career in tennis. Her mother has always been her coach. Hingis received her first lesson at age two, after she had just learned to walk. She told *Vogue* magazine that she started playing on a real court when she was only three years old.

But Hingis, unlike other child prodigies, has never seemed uncomfortable with her early success. She told GQ magazine that her natural gift for the sport is her mother. But it is her utter devotion to tennis that has carried her to the top of today's tennis world.

Before turning professional at age 14, Hingis played in her first tournament for children when she was just four (though she was defeated). But by age nine, she knew her talent would enable her to compete and a year later she was winning national and international tournaments. Hingis also held a number of European junior championships and won a Junior U.S. Open and Junior Wimbledon. After turning pro, she became at age 15 the youngest player ever to win a Wimbledon event, when she and Helen Sukova took the doubles crown in 1996.

Though Hingis had left public school in order to keep her competitive schedule, she did enroll in a private school de-

> *"So many players want to hunt me and beat me because I haven't lost for a very long time. I still think I have nothing to lose when I step on the court."*
> Martina Hingis

1980 Hingis is born in Kosice, Czechoslovakia.

1996 At 15, Hingis becomes the youngest player to win at Wimbledon (doubles, with Helen Sukova).

1997 Hingis wins the Australian Open, becoming the youngest player in 100 years to win one of the four Grand Slam tournaments.

1998 Hingis wins the Australian Open again, making her the youngest player in 100 years to win a Grand Slam tourney two years in a row.

signed for aspiring athletes. Her mother encouraged her to ride horses, ski, swim and enjoy other sports. But Hingis's first love was tennis, and in keeping with her age, she often showed a lot of emotion on the court, pouting and slamming her racket down in anger.

However, unlike other teens, Hingis had a signed contract with the American Agency International Management Group (IMG) and landed endorsement deals for Yonex rackets, Opel Automobiles and Sergio Tacchini in excess of $10 million.

In 1997, Hingis won the Australian Open, making her the youngest player in more than 100 years to win a Grand Slam title. (The Grand Slam consists of the Australian Open, French Open, U.S. Open, and Wimbledon tournaments.) She also took center stage at the Australian Open doubles in 1997. Hingis was ranked number one that year, making her the youngest player in the century to reach that mark. She then became the youngest player of the century to win the singles event at Wimbledon.

In the beginning of 1998, Hingis continued with her winning streak, becoming the youngest player in over 100 years to win two consecutive Grand Slam singles titles at the Australian Open, where she also won the doubles title. She did hit one bump in the road when, later that year, she lost her number-one ranking to Lindsay Davenport in October. But Hingis vowed to win it back and began forging ahead with a win at the Chase Championships in November.

Hingis is currently ranked number one in the world. When she is not playing in tournaments, she lives in Trubbach, where she plays wit her German Shepherd, Zorro. She also has a home in the Czech Republic so that she can spend time with her father.

After her 17th birthday, Hingis revamped her image. She decided to lose a few pounds and dyed her hair a deep black. She later appeared on the cover of GQ magazine in June of 1998 and began dating Spanish tennis pro Julian Alonso.

While she's not headed to college in the near future, Hingis speaks four languages and keeps a tutor on the road to make sure she keeps her academics in check. However, she recently told *Seventeen* magazine that her experiences as a young professional athlete have given her a different perspective on learning. "Traveling and meeting all kinds of people has been an incredible education," she said. ◆

Hogan, Ben

August 13, 1912–July 25, 1997 ● Golfer

William Benjamin Hogan was born in Texas on August 13, 1912. The boy who would become one of golf's most respected and influential players had a difficult childhood. His father (variously identified as either a mechanic or a blacksmith in Dublin, Texas) committed suicide when Ben was just nine years old. According to some reports, Ben was present in the room when his father killed himself.

With three children in the family, Ben's mother had trouble making ends meet, and Ben worked wherever he could in order to contribute to the family's income. Among his "odd jobs" were selling newspapers and caddying at a nearby golf course. Caddying for golfers sparked an interest in playing the game.

Compact in size (around 135 pounds and 5' 7" or 5' 8"), Hogan was an excellent athlete, and he found that he had a special talent for golf. At age 19, Hogan was working as a bank clerk, and he decided to give that up to become a professional golfer. It was 1931—one of the hardest years of the Great Depression. Making a living as a golfer was not easy during that trying economic period, but Hogan persevered, despite going broke several times during the 1930s. He had a will of iron and a fierce determination to succeed.

Hogan knew that to excel as a professional, he would need top-notch skills in the sport. He practiced constantly. He was a perfectionist, and he would spend hours working on his swing and his form. He would practice until his hands bled. He developed very powerful wrists and forearms. (Today, golf historians credit him with "inventing" the notion of using regular, disciplined practice to improve one's game.) Before a tournament, Hogan would arrive days ahead of time in order to analyze and memorize the characteristics of the particular golf course. Later on, this habit would earn him the nickname "The Hawk."

Hogan won his first tournament in 1938. By 1940, he had become the leading money earner on the U.S. Professional Golfers' Association (PGA) Tour. But even as his career was on the upswing, war clouds were brewing in Europe.

From 1940 to 1945, Hogan served in the U.S. Army. Once World War II was over, Hogan returned to the world of golf. He

> Before a tournament, Hogan would arrive days ahead of time in order to analyze and memorize the characteristics of the particular golf course.

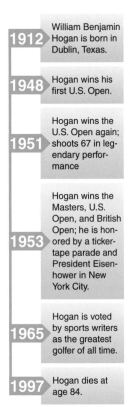

1912 William Benjamin Hogan is born in Dublin, Texas.

1948 Hogan wins his first U.S. Open.

1951 Hogan wins the U.S. Open again; shoots 67 in legendary performance

1953 Hogan wins the Masters, U.S. Open, and British Open; he is honored by a ticker-tape parade and President Eisenhower in New York City.

1965 Hogan is voted by sports writers as the greatest golfer of all time.

1997 Hogan dies at age 84.

won his first major tournament in 1946, and he debuted in the international Ryder Cup (playing, of course, on the U.S. team) the following year. In 1948, he won his first U.S. Open. But in 1949, Hogan was involved in a terrible car accident: a bus hit his car, and he was almost killed. Hogan and his wife survived, but his legs and pelvis were broken, and he developed severe blood clots. Doctors doubted that he would walk again—much less play golf.

But Hogan's fierce will would prove the doctors wrong. In a year, Hogan was back on the fairways. He walked with a limp and for the rest of his life was often in great pain, but he continued to compete, and to win. In recognition of this formidable achievement, the Ben Hogan Award is given each year to a golfer who has overcome injury to compete again.

In 1951, Hogan triumphed at the U.S. Open at Oakland Hills in Birmingham, Michigan. He had won the tournament twice before, but his performance here was legendary. In the final round he shot an amazing 67, on a course that was designed to make it very difficult for anyone to break 70. Many people consider this the greatest round of golf ever played.

The year 1953 was a spectacular one for Hogan, and the apex of his career. He won the Masters, the U.S. Open, and the British Open that year. When he returned to the United States from playing in the legendary British tournament, he was honored by a ticker-tape parade in New York. President Dwight D. Eisenhower led the welcoming committee.

Some parade-goers may have been disappointed when they saw Hogan in the flesh, because he was not a very outgoing individual. In fact, he was quite taciturn, with what some would term a bland personality. He was totally focused on the game when he played, and paid virtually no attention to the gallery. He did not laugh and joke, or even smile. His no-nonsense silence on the course became as legendary as the trademark white hat he wore. Thus, he was respected rather than liked, and he inspired such nicknames as "The Iceman."

Hogan's intensely focused and determined approach to playing golf resulted in 63 tour victories, and he was one of just a handful of players to have won all four Grand Slam titles. Hogan won the British Open and the U.S. PGA Championship and took the Masters and the U.S. Open Tournaments four times each. He served as either player or captain on four Ryder Cup teams.

These figures are all the more impressive when one realizes that after his car accident, Hogan limited the number of competitions he entered. Because of the constant pain, he never played in more than half a dozen or so tournaments per year. He marshaled all his energies and skill for those few tournaments, however, and the results speak for themselves.

Hogan played professionally well into the 1960s, and he devoted much time to starting a company that manufactured golf clubs (it still exists today). In 1965, a group of American sports writers voted him Greatest Golfer of All Time. The man with the winningest swing died on July 25, 1997, at age 84. ◆

> *"You'll never get anywhere fooling around those golf courses."*
> Clara Hogan to her son Ben, at 16

Holdsclaw, Chamique

July 9, 1977– ● Basketball Player

In an era where female athletics has steadily grown in stature and prominence, each sport has had its own breakout star. In women's basketball, that star is Chamique Holdsclaw. Born in Astoria, a neighborhood in New York City, Holdsclaw found her gift in basketball as a pre-teen on the hardcourts of Queens. By the time she enrolled in Christ the King High School, her all-around game could match the boys she played with regularly.

At Christ the King, Holdsclaw was the leading scorer and rebounder for a team that went 106–4 in her four years, winning a remarkable four state championships and one national title. Overall, Holdsclaw's statistics showed her amazing versatility on the court as she averaged 22.5 points, 16.7 rebounds, 3.2 blocked shots and 2.4 steals per game.

With her amazing play came a host of individual awards for Holdsclaw: She was the New York high school Class A most valuable player for three consecutive years (1993–1995); a USA Today All-American for three years; and the Rawlings/WBCA Player of the Year in 199. She won the 1995 Naismith Award from Atlanta's Tip-Off Club; was named New York City's Player of the Year for three consecutive years (the first player male or female to win that honor); and she was chosen the 1995 Player of the Year by the Columbus, Ohio, Touchdown Club.

1977 — Holdsclaw is born in Astoria (Queens), New York City.

1995 — Holdsclaw leads Tennessee to three consecutive NCAA championships.

1998 — Holdsclaw graduates as the all-time leading scorer in Southeastern Conference and is a four-time All-America starter.

1999 — Holdsclaw joins the Washington Mystics and quadruples the team's wins from the previous season; she is named a WNBA all-star and Rookie of the Year.

Chamique Holdsclaw during a college game.

Holdsclaw also showed her academic side by doing a solid job in the classroom and writing a bi-weekly diary for USA Today during her junior season. She wrote a similar piece for the New York Daily News her senior year. Following an all-out recruiting blitz by colleges all over the nation, Holdsclaw chose the University of Tennessee her home for the next four years. A political science major, Holdsclaw's time as a Volunteer served as a primer on how to break records and win championships. That began during her freshman year, when she she started every game and led in points (16.2 ppg) and rebounds (9.1 rpg) en route to a national championship. Holdsclaw was named a Kodak All-American and is the first Lady Vol freshman to receive that honor.

After winning another national title in her sophomore season, Holdsclaw led the Lady Vols her junior season in an amazing campaign that saw Tennessee go a perfect 39–0 and record their third consecutive national championship.

Despite rumors that Holdsclaw would turn pro and join the fledgling Women's National Basketball Association (WNBA), she stayed in school to get her degree and try to bring Tennessee their fourth consecutive title. Unfortunately this was not to be, as Holdsclaw ended the season with a loss for the first time in her basketball career, as the Lady Vols lost in the NCAA tournament. Still, Holdsclaw ended her collegiate career as a four-time All-American. She won three national titles, averaging 20.2 points and 9 rebounds, and was a two-time winner of the Naismith Award as national player of the year.

For Holdsclaw, however, the dream was just getting better. Already recognized as possibly the best female basketball player of all-time, she was named the number one overall pick in the WNBA draft by the Washington Mystics.

The Mystics were coming off of a miserable 3–27 season in their first year of existence, but with Holdsclaw now in the lineup, they finished the 1999 season at 12–20 and won six of their last nine games. Holdsclaw also continued to pile up individual accolades, averaging 16.9 points and 7.9 rebounds per game. She was also named an all-star and Rookie of the Year to cap an incredible first campaign. As an added bonus, Holdsclaw was chosen as one of the players to represent the United States in the 2000 Olympics in Sydney, Australia, and she always plays on any American women's basketball team that plays internationally. Holdsclaw is often called the "female Michael Jordan" for her slashing style of play and ability to dominate a game with her all-around play. She also wears the same number as Jordan —23. But it is Holdsclaw's positive demeanor and humble attitude that continue to make her even more of a fan favorite. Now, as the boys she used to play basketball with on the streets watch her play, the rest of the world can enjoy her amazing ability as well. ◆

> *"We've had a lot of All-Americas and Olympians here. But there is only one Chamique."*
> Pat Summitt, University of Tennessee coach, on Chamique Holdsclaw

Holmes, Larry

NOVEMBER 3, 1949– ● BOXER

Larry Holmes, the seventh of 12 children born to share-cropper-steelworker John Holmes and his wife Flossie, was born in Cuthbert, Georgia, but grew up in Easton, Pennsylvania. Holmes dropped out of school after the seventh grade and worked in a car wash to help support the family, which was otherwise dependent upon his mother's income from welfare.

Holmes began his professional career on March 21, 1973, with a fourth-round win over Rodell Dupree. On June 9, 1978, he won the World Boxing Council heavyweight title from Ken Norton. The six-foot three-inch, 215-pound champion did not lose a match until Michael Spinks defeated him in September 1985. During this stretch he defeated Earnie Shavers, Leon spinks, Gerry Cooney, and an over-the-hill Muhammad Ali, among other opponents. Because of his lack of a spectacular knockout punch, however, the long-reigning champion never gained the respect and recognition that boxing fans showed other titleholders, such as Muhammad Ali and Mike Tyson.

1949 Holmes is born in Cuthbert, Georgia.

1978 Holmes beats Ken Norton to win the World Boxing Council heavyweight title.

1985 In his first loss since Norton in 1978, Holmes loses to Michael Spinks.

1986 Holmes retires after losing a re-match with Spinks.

After losing a second decision to Spinks in a rematch in 1986, Holmes retired. He tried to come back in February 1988, but was knocked out in four rounds by a much younger Mike Tyson. In 1992 he came out of retirement for a second time. He won several matches against unheralded rivals and then lost to the heavyweight champion Evander Holyfield. The following year Holmes continued his comeback campaign by defeating a string of unknown fighters at a casino in Mississippi.

In 1987 Holmes, who has amassed a career record of 54–4, was named the sixth greatest heavyweight of all time by *Ring Magazine* . He has also successfully built a real estate and investment firm in Easton, Pennsylvania. ◆

Holyfield, Evander

OCTOBER 19, 1962– ● BOXER

E vander Holyfield was born in Atmore, Alabama, but his family moved to Atlanta soon after his birth. He began boxing at age nine. Holyfield continued to box as an amateur through his adolescence, and in 1983 he defeated Ricky Womack for the National Sports Festival light heavyweight boxing title. Holyfield qualified for the 1984 U.S. Olympic boxing team as a light heavyweight and won the bronze medal at the Los Angeles Games.

In November 1984 Holyfield turned professional. He won his first five professional bouts as a light heavyweight, and in 1985 he moved up one weight class to the 190-pound cruiserweight level. Holyfield won his next six cruiserweight fights by knockout. In 1986 he captured the World Boxing Association (WBA) and International Boxing Federation (IBF) cruiserweight titles with a 15-round split decision over Dwight Muhammad Qawi.

After successfully defending his titles, Holyfield unified the cruiserweight championship in 1988 with an eight-round technical knockout of Carlos DeLeon, the World Boxing Council (WBC) champion.

Holyfield then moved up to the heavyweight class and, despite being smaller and lighter than his opponents, won his next three bouts by knockout, including a tenth-round technical knockout of former heavyweight champion Michael Dokes.

On October 25, 1990, Holyfield easily knocked out a poorly trained Buster Douglas to capture the undisputed heavyweight

> *"There should be a place in the heavyweight pantheon for a champion who travels without an entourage, for a man who truly cares about others."*
>
> Steve Wulf on Evander Holyfield, *Time*, 1996

Evander Holyfield, former heavyweight champion.

championship. He successfully defended his new title three times, with decisions over George foreman and Larry holmes and a knockout of Bert Cooper. But in 1992 Holyfield lost his title by unanimous decision to the much larger Riddick bowe in a 12-round fight marked by toe-to-toe ferocity. Immediately after the loss to Bowe, Holyfield announced his retirement.

Holyfield, like many boxers, didn't stay retired for long, and he returned to the ring in June 1993, when he won by decision over Alex Stewart. He then accepted a rematch with Bowe in what came to be one of the strangest events in boxing history. The November title fight was stopped during the seventh round when a man flying a paraglider landed on the ring's ropes. During the fight Holyfield's hit-and-run strategy paid off, and he recaptured the heavyweight title with a majority decision.

In May 1994 Holyfield lost the championship to Michael Moorer in a 12-round decision. One month later Holyfield announced his retirement again, this time after a medical examination revealed two potentially life-threatening disorders in his heart. But idleness did not sit well with the former champ, and he even resorted to a "miracle cure" with an evangelist before

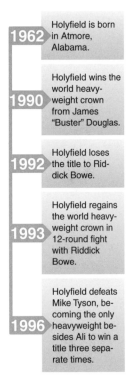

1962 Holyfield is born in Atmore, Alabama.

1990 Holyfield wins the world heavyweight crown from James "Buster" Douglas.

1992 Holyfield loses the title to Riddick Bowe.

1993 Holyfield regains the world heavyweight crown in 12-round fight with Riddick Bowe.

1996 Holyfield defeats Mike Tyson, becoming the only heavyweight besides Ali to win a title three separate times.

deciding to reenter the ring. He made a victorious comeback in a 10-round decision against Ray Mercer on May 20, 1995.

His quest to reclaim the title suffered a setback on November 4, 1995, when he was stopped in the eighth round by Riddick Bowe. Once again defying calls for his retirement, he took on Bobby Czyz on May 10, 1996 and won in a fifth-round TKO, thereby earning a shot at Mike Tyson's WBA heavyweight title.

The heavily promoted match took place on November 9, 1996, and Holyfield outlasted Tyson and scored an eleventh round knockout to regain the WBA crown. In their rematch on June 28, 1996, Tyson, either losing his wits or deciding to disrupt what seemed like a lost cause, took a bite out of Holyfield's ear in the third round. Tyson was disqualified immediately and eventually suspended from boxing in Nevada for a year.

Holyfield's next challenge came from Michael Moorer on November 8, 1997. Holyfield stopped him after eight rounds to win the IBF heavyweight championship. He followed up with a 12-round unanimous decision over Vaughn Bean on September 19, 1998.

But Lennox Lewis, a truly formidable challenger, was waiting in the wings. On March 13, 1999, Lewis faced Holyfied at New York City's Madison Square Garden. In an epic see-saw battle that most observers viewed as a victory for Lewis, Holyfield retained his title when the judges ruled the fight a draw, prompting suspicions of improper manipulation of the decision by the notoriously shady promoter Don King, who denied the charges.

The two fighters met in a rematch on November 13, 1999. This time Holyfield lost a 12-round decision to Lewis. After the fight Holyfield made no formal announcement about his future in boxing. ◆

Hornsby, Rogers

APRIL 27, 1896–JANUARY 5, 1963 ● BASEBALL PLAYER

Rogers Hornsby was short-tempered and argumentative. He had a yen for the racetrack and a distaste for his managers. He even refused to read books or go to the movies for fear it would hurt his eyesight. Despite these shortcomings, Hornsby is considered by many to be the greatest right-handed hitter that ever lived.

Hornsby was a scrawny 19-year-old shortstop when he first reached the major leagues in 1915. A native of tiny Winters, Texas, Hornsby was discovered by the St. Louis Cardinals while playing in the Texas League, where he was a solid hitter, but his rookie season was unspectacular: he hit just .246 and struggled defensively in a late season trial. He earned a regular job with the Cardinals the following year, alternating at all four infield positions and showing promise with the bat. Over the next three years, Hornsby kept his average above .300 in spite of the pitching-heavy league. His biggest problem was defense; he was too error-prone to play shortstop and he spent the ensuing years at all the field positions except pitcher and catcher.

Hornsby's breakout year came in 1920. "The Rajah," as he was called, moved to second base full time and the positional stability seemed to cause his bat to explode. He led the league with a .370 average in the first of a six-year tear in which his batting average would exceed .400. He topped it all off with a .424 mark in 1924, which is the highest single season batting average in the twentieth century. Unlike Ty Cobb, to whom he was compared as the top hitters of their day, Hornsby could hit the long ball. He belted 301 career home runs and won the Triple Crown in both 1922 and 1925. In 1926, upon being named player-manager, he led the Cardinals to their first World Championship, in a stunning upset over Babe Ruth and the Yankees. Just weeks after his triumph, he was dealt to the New York Giants for future Hall of Famer Frankie Frisch. When he left the Cardinals, Hornsby sold all his stock in the team and settled for $120,000—nearly triple his initial investment.

The Rajah spent the latter half of his playing career as a journeyman. Because of his volcanic temper and his strict, perfectionist approach, he enraged managers and teammates alike. After a brief tenure on the Giants, he joined the Braves and then the Cubs, with whom he won a most valuable player award thanks to a .380 average and 39 homers in 1929. Despite his torrid hitting, he was left off the playoff roster in 1932 when the Cubs won the pennant. Hornsby finished his career with the Browns—he retired just 70 hits shy of 3,000—and then managed for 15 years in the minor leagues. He ended his career as a Mets scout in the early 1960s.

Hornsby was never more than an average defensive player, and as he aged, his defensive abilities only grew worse. And his hot temper drew comparisons to legendary misanthrope Ty Cobb, although in truth, he was not so much a flawed character as a maniacal competitor. And his competitive streak paid off:

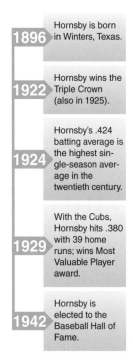

1896 Hornsby is born in Winters, Texas.

1922 Hornsby wins the Triple Crown (also in 1925).

1924 Hornsby's .424 batting average is the highest single-season average in the twentieth century.

1929 With the Cubs, Hornsby hits .380 with 39 home runs; wins Most Valuable Player award.

1942 Hornsby is elected to the Baseball Hall of Fame.

"People ask me what I do in winter when there's no baseball. I'll tell you what I do. I stare out the window and wait for spring."

Rogers Hornsby

his .359 average is surpassed only by Cobb; his two Triple Crowns are equaled only by Ted Williams; and his six year tear from 1920 to 1925 remains an unparalleled hitting streak that includes the amazing .424 mark over a single season. While he never received due press because of his fierce attitude, Hornsby was elected to the Hall of Fame in 1942. He died in Chicago in 1963 at the age of 67. ◆

Hunter, Jim "Catfish"

APRIL 8, 1946–SEPTEMBER 9, 1999 ● BASEBALL PLAYER

sharecropping: system in which a tenant farmer is provided with credit, seed, tools, housing, etc., farms land, and shares in the proceeds with the landowner.

James Augustus Hunter was born in Hertford, North Carolina, on April 8, 1946. He was the fourth of eight children in Abbott and Millie Hunter's poor **sharecropping** family. The young Jim Hunter enjoyed hunting, fishing, and playing baseball with his brothers. His pitching skill, which included uncanny control and a blazing fastball, attracted major league baseball scouts to see his high school games, in which he was 26–2 including five no-hitters. But during his senior year, Hunter's brother accidentally shot him while duck hunting, blowing off a toe, and lodging 30 shotgun pellets in his foot. It looked like his pitching career was over, and the scouts stopped coming.

Although part of his foot was paralyzed, Hunter proved he could still pitch, relying on pinpoint control to compensate for his lost speed. Only Kansas City Athletics scout Clyde Klutz showed interest though, convincing owner Charlie Finley to sign Hunter to a contract with a $75,000 bonus in June, 1964. The colorful Finley, who loved nicknames, wanted to know if Hunter had one. He didn't. Finley asked Hunter if he had any interests. Hunter's brother volunteered that Jim liked fishing, and added that Jim liked to eat catfish when he was younger. That was enough for Finley, who concocted a tale about how a six-year-old Jim Hunter had run away from home and gone fishing. When his parents found him that night, he had caught two catfish and was reeling in a third. Hunter agreed to go along with the false story, thinking the nickname "Catfish" would never stick. It did.

bonus babies: term used for outstanding draftees of professional athletic teams who are paid handsome sums of money for signing a contract.

In Hunter's first professional season, a rule regarding players signed to big bonuses, or **"bonus babies,"** as they were called, forced Finley to keep Hunter on the A's 1965 roster or risk losing him to another team. Before long Hunter was a starting pitcher for the A's, one of the few major league players who skipped the minor leagues. He made the All-Star team in 1966 and 1967 as the best player on a lackluster Kansas City team. Due to poor attendance, Finley moved the A's to Oakland, California prior to the 1968 season. On May 8, 1968, Hunter pitched the first regular season perfect game by an American League pitcher since 1922, retiring all 27 Minnesota Twins batters he faced in a row to accomplish one of baseball's rarest feats.

Finley spent the next several years putting together a talented roster of players. The maverick owner encouraged his team to go against many of baseball's traditional mores. Many of his players had long hair and mustaches. The team wore **garish** green and gold uniforms, and white shoes instead of the traditional black. They were a cocky, brawling group. Several A's were involved in fights with each other, but most were united in their dislike of Finley, who could be abrasive, insensitive and frugal. Despite the commotion surrounding the A's, they won the American League pennant every year from 1971 through 1974, winning World Series titles in 1972, 1973, and 1974.

In 1971, Hunter became a 20-game winner for the first time, finishing 21–11, with a 2.96 earned run average (ERA). It was his first of five straight 20-win seasons. In 1972, he improved to 21–7, and in 1973, he continued to dominate with a 21–5 record. In 1974, his league-leading 25–12 record and 2.49 ERA won him the Cy Young Award, given to the league's best pitcher. It was his last season in Oakland, and it would be the A's last league championship until 1988.

Hunter's contract had called for Finley to pay half of his $100,000 salary to a life-insurance fund, and when Finley reneged for most of the 1974 season—either by refusal or oversight—Hunter decided to challenge his contract. At the time, baseball contracts had a "reserve clause" that bound a player to a team forever, unless he was traded. If a player could not come to terms with the team that owned his rights, he did not have the right to negotiate with other teams as a "free agent." But when Hunter's contract was declared void by an arbiter because Finley had reneged, Hunter became a free agent, and a bidding war, previously unseen, ensued. Owners from 15 major league clubs sent representatives to North Carolina. Six major league owners showed up in person to try to woo the game's best pitcher. On New Year's Eve 1974, New York Yankees' owner

1946 Hunter is born in Hertford, North Carolina.

1968 Hunter pitches the first regular season perfect game in American League since 1922, retiring all 27 Minnesota Twins; Oakland wins 4–0.

1971 Hunter has the first of five straight 20-win seasons.

1974 Hunter wins the Cy Young Award.

1987 Hunter is elected to the Baseball Hall of Fame.

garish: excessively vivid and bright coloring.

George Steinbrenner prevailed, and Hunter signed a five-year contract worth $3.75 million, an unheard-of sum at the time.

The big contract did not spoil the humble Hunter. The Steinbrenner-owned Yankees were as colorful as the A's had been. The team became known as "the Bronx Zoo," a pun based on where they played, the autocratic owner, a pugnacious manager, and several outlandish players. Hunter, with his rural, common-sense approach, was a calming influence in the turbulent Yankees clubhouse. After a 23-win season for the Yankees in 1975, he helped the Yankees win the 1976 American League pennant, their first in 12 years, with a 17–5 record. By then he was experiencing arm trouble, which would later prove the end his career after the 1979 season at the young age of 33.

But Hunter pitched a few more seasons before his retirement. In 1977 he won nine games, helping the Yankees to their first of two consecutive World Series titles. In March, 1978 Hunter was diagnosed as having diabetes, but still won 12 games, as well as the final game of the 1978 World Series. He ended his career with a 224–166 record, a 3.26 ERA and five World Series championship rings.

After retirement, Hunter went back to farming in North Carolina. In 1987, in his third year of eligibility, he was elected to baseball's Hall of Fame. In September of 1998, Hunter was diagnosed with Amyotrophic Lateral Sclerosis (ALS), also know as Lou Gehrig's disease because it claimed the life of the Yankee legend Gehrig in 1941. ALS attacks nerves in the spinal cord and brain, causing progressive muscle paralysis, and eventually, death. Hunter succumbed to the disease on September 9, 1999. ◆

Inkster, Juli

JUNE 24, 1960– ● GOLFER

Ask any golf fan from California to name a star close to home on the women's professional circuit and the name likely to come up is Juli Inkster. Inkster was born in Santa Cruz, California, as Juli Simpson, and she remained a California resident all her life, settling in Los Altos, where she plays out of the Los Altos Country Club (and where her husband, Brian, is the club pro). Golf fans knew that she was a future star in 1979, when she was named a collegiate All-American at San Jose State University, an honor she went on to repeat over the next three years.

Inkster's amateur career in the early 1980s was one of extraordinary accomplishment. She won the U.S. Women's Amateur title in 1980, 1981, and 1982, becoming the first and only golfer, male or female, to win three consecutive U.S. Amateur titles. In 1981 she won the California Amateur title, was named the state's Amateur of the Year, and was *Golf Digest*'s number one-ranked am-

The Ladies Professional Golf Association (LPGA)

Now a half century old, The Ladies Professional Golf Association (LPGA) is America's oldest professional sports organization for women. It roots extend back to the 1930s, when professional golf tours and exhibitions by popular women golfers such as Babe Didrikson and Joyce Wethered began to point to the commerical promise of a professional women's tour. Under the leadership of the professional golfer Hope Seignious, the Women's Professional Golf Association (WPGA) was formed in 1944. The group foundered until it received financial backing of Wilson Sporting Goods in 1948, when the WPGA launched an aggressive promotional campaign directed by Fred Corcoran, Didrikson's manager.

Despite the WPGA's progress in heightening the public profile of women's golf, its leading pros grew restive under the tight reins of Seignious's leadership, and many withdrew in disaffection, leading to the demise of the WPGA in 1949. Plans were already underway, however, to form an alternative group, and in May of that year a meeting was convened by several women competing in the Eastern Open in Essex, New Jersey. They proposed the launching of a new organization for women pro golfers under the leadership of Corcoran, then in the employ of Wilson. He proposed the name Ladies Professional Golf Association, and the new group was on its way.

Officially chartered in 1950, the LPGA included most of leading women golfers of the day, including Babe Zaharias, Patty Berg (the group's first president), and Louise Suggs, along with rising stars such as Betsy Rawls, Marilynn Smith, and Peggy Kirk (Bell). In its inaugural season the LPGA sponsored eleven events awarding a total of $50,000 in prize money (purses). Within only two years the schedule had nearly doubled to 21 tournaments, and by the end of the decade, spurred by the dominant Mickey Wright, the LPGA was sponsoring 26 matches worth $200,000 in purses. By 1966 that sum had more than doubled to $509,500, spread over 37 matches.

Despite the rise of a new generation of stars such as Carol Mann, Sandra Haynie, Judy Rankin, Jane Blalock, and Donna Caponi, the tour sagged in the late 1970s, perhaps in part because of the unremitting dominance of Kathy Whitworth; by 1971 the tour had retrenched to 21 events. To counter this decline, the LPGA named Bud Erickson as the group's first executive director. Under his stewardship the tour rebounded dramatically, offering an aggregate purse of $1,471,000 by 1973.

The league suffered another setback with a bruising, protracted legal battle with Jane Blalock over charges that she had cheated; a hefty out-of-court settlement left the LPGA cash-shy and hungry for new leadership, which it found in Ray Volpe, the group's first commissioner. A former NHL executive, Volpe deployed his marketing savvy to boost the tour's purses to $6.4 million by 1982. Expanded television coverage financed much of the increase, along with the advent of the LPGA's first made-for-TV superstar, Nancy Lopez, in the late 1970s.

The numbers for the women's tour have been rising into the stratosphere ever since: an annual purse of $10 million by 1986, with television coverage of 18 of its 36 tournaments, and a 1999 LPGA tour schedule that included 43 events, with total purses in excess of $36.6 million.

ateur, a feat she repeated in 1982, when she was named Bay Area Athlete of the Year and won the Broderick Award. She was also a member of the U.S. Curtis Cup team in 1982 and played on the 1980 and 1982 World Cup teams.

By 1983 Inkster was ready to turn professional, and she enjoyed almost immediate success. In just her fifth outing she won the SAFECO Classic, prompting *Golf Digest* to name her Rookie of the Year in 1983. In 1984 the LPGA followed suit by naming her Rookie of the Year after she became the first rookie ever to win two major championships in one season—the Nabisco Dinah Shore tournament and the du Maurier Ltd. Classic.

Perhaps her most successful year was 1986, when she won an incredible four titles: the Women's Kemper Open, the McDonald's LPGA Championship, the Lady Keystone Open (defending her 1985 title), and the Atlantic City Classic. That year she also posted her career-low round of 64, which she would later match in the 1998 Standard Register PING. During the 1980s Inkster won several tournaments twice, including the SAFECO Classic (repeating in 1988), the Nabisco Dinah Shore (repeating in 1989), the Crestar Classic (1988 and 1989), and the Atlantic City Classic (repeating in 1988). She almost rejoined the winner's circle of a major tournament in 1988, when she led the U.S. Women's Open after 36 holes but faltered in the final round to finish seventh. The sting of this disappointment, though, was eased by her 12 top-10 finishes in 1988.

In the early 1990s Inkster's priorities shifted slightly with the birth of her two daughters: Hayley in 1990 and Cori in 1994. Although juggling a busy personal life with that of a professional athlete, she continued to enjoy some success—she won the LPGA Bay State Classic in 1991 and the JAL Big Apple Classic in 1992—but major tournament wins eluded her. In 1992, for example, she was in two major championship playoffs, but she lost the Nabisco Dinah Shore to Dottie Pepper on the first extra hole and to Patty Sheehan at the U.S. Women's Open, despite leading by two strokes with two holes to play—a loss that she described later as "devastating."

By 1997, though, Inkster's career was back in gear when she won the Samsung World Championship of Women's Golf—her 16th career victory—in a sudden-death playoff. That year she also posted 10 top-10 finishes and a career-best scoring average of 70.64, helping her career earnings pass the $3 million mark.

1960 Inkster is born in Santa Cruz, California.

1980 Inkster wins the U.S. Amateur title (also in 1981 and 1982).

1984 Inkster is named LPGA Rookie of the Year.

1986 Inkster wins four championships.

1998 Inkster wins her second Samsung World Championship of Women's Golf, her 17th career title.

1999 Inkster wins the U.S. Women's Open at 16 under par; she also wins the McDonald's LPGA and Safeway Classic championships.

"When I first started teaching her five years ago, she didn't have much confidence and didn't think she could win again. To see how hard she has worked on her ball-striking and her putting and to see her play such flawless golf is un-believable."

Mike McGetrick, Inkster's swing coach, after the 1999 U.S. Women's Open

In 1998 she defended her Samsung title to win her 17th career title and recorded seven top-five finishes, shot her first tournament hole-in-one (in the third round of Lifetime's AFLAC Tournament of Champions), and was a member of the victorious U.S. Solheim Cup Team (on which she also played in 1992).

The momentum Inkster gathered in 1997 and 1998 culminated in 1999, when she captured three major tournaments. In June she erased the memory of her 1992 U.S. Women's Open loss by recording a 16-under-par 272 to win the Open championship in dramatic fashion. Inkster struggled in the early holes of the final round, and with just three holes to play she was in a three-way tie for the lead. But she eagled the 16th hole, hit an eight iron tee-shot to within three feet of the hole to birdie 17, and sunk a 25-foot birdie putt on the 18th. Later that month she won the McDonald's LPGA championship, and then in September, she won the Safeway Classic. Validating a two-decade-long career as one of the world's top golfers, she joined just 14 other golfers that year in the LPGA Hall of Fame. ◆

Jackson, "Shoeless" Joe

JULY 16, 1889–DECEMBER 5, 1951 ● BASEBALL PLAYER

One of the greatest hitters in baseball's history is also one of its most controversial. "Shoeless" Joe Jackson batted over .300 the 10 last seasons he played in the major leagues, but as a member of the 1919 Chicago White Sox, Jackson was one of eight players accused of losing games on purpose in exchange for money, which resulted in his lifetime banishment from baseball. Today, over 80 years since that series, the ban is still in place and Jackson, who died in 1951, has yet to be enshrined along with baseball's other all-time greats in the Hall of Fame.

Joseph Jefferson Jackson was born on July 16, 1889, just outside Greenville, South Carolina. He spent his youth working in the mills of the area, where his only escape from the drudgery of the factory was playing baseball. Jackson began playing semipro ball and **barnstorming** with mill teams as a teenager and soon caught the eye of major league scouts.

It was during this time that Jackson acquired his colorful nickname. Legend has it that one day Jackson's cleats were bothering him, so he decided to play the rest of a game barefoot. In his first at bat after taking off his shoes, Jackson hit a triple and the nickname stuck.

In 1908, Jackson signed with the Philadelphia Athletics, but after playing infrequently over two seasons he returned home. The outfielder returned to the major leagues again in 1910 with the Cleveland Indians and in 1911, his first full season in the majors, he promptly hit .408, the fourth highest single-season average in American League history. Even with

> *"Say it ain't so, Joe."*
>
> A young boy, to Jackson after the Black Sox scandal of 1920, possibly **apocryphal**

apocryphal: description of quoted statements that are of questionable authenticity, and/or wrongfully attributed.

1889   Jackson is born near Greenville, South Carolina.

1915   Jackson joins the Chicago White Sox.

1917   The White Sox win the American League pennant (again in 1919).

1919   In the infamous "Black Sox Scandal" Jackson and 7 others are barred from baseball for life.

1951   Jackson dies.

that lofty average, Jackson finished second in the batting race to the great Ty Cobb. In fact, the next two seasons Jackson hit a robust .395 and .373 only to lose out in the batting race to his rival Cobb both times.

Despite Jackson's batting heroics, Cleveland was miserable on the field, so midway through the 1915 season the team traded Jackson to the Chicago White Sox. Jackson helped lead the Sox to the American League Pennant in 1917 and again in 1919.

That later year, the Sox were heavy favorites to defeat the Cincinnati Reds in the World Series. Despite Jackson hitting .375 with 12 hits and six runs batted in, the Reds prevailed five games to three.

The next season, whispers began to surface that the White Sox had lost the Series on purpose in exchange for money from gamblers who'd bet against them. A Chicago grand jury was convened to investigate the claim. During the testimony, Jackson, who could neither read nor write, admitted to accepting $5,000 from one of his crooked teammates, but as his statistics and excellent play in the field showed, he did nothing to throw the games. Still, by accepting the money, Jackson was considered as guilty as his other teammates. Baseball commissioner Kennesaw Mountain Landis immediately barred Jackson, who was hitting .382 at the time, and seven other Sox from baseball for what became known as the "Black Sox Scandal."

Although a jury later acquitted all eight White Sox players—their confessions mysteriously had disappeared—Landis never reinstated any of the shamed players. Jackson "retired" with an astounding .356 batting average, which today is still the third-highest lifetime mark in major league history. His involvement in the scandal was a crushing blow to baseball's innocence and spawned the famous phrase, "Say it isn't so, Shoeless Joe."

Jackson later sued the White Sox owner, Charles Comiskey for lost wages and was awarded over $16,000 until a judge overturned the decision and sent Jackson to jail for perjury. Jackson's stay in prison was brief and he and Comiskey later came to a significantly smaller financial settlement.

His baseball career over at the age of 32, Jackson returned to his native South Carolina and continued to play in semi-pro leagues, where he was understandably a box-office draw. He also was involved with several businesses and ran a liquor store.

In 1951, the city of Cleveland decided to open a sports Hall of Fame. Though his name wasn't even on the ballot, Jackson was the fourth-highest vote-getter in the initial election of inductees. The story piqued Ed Sullivan's curiosity, who booked Jackson for his popular TV show. However, on December 5, the day before Jackson was scheduled to appear on the show, he suffered a fatal heart attack. He was 62 years old.

In death Jackson's legend has continued to grow. The critically-acclaimed 1988 movie *Eight Men Out* told the story of the Black Sox scandal. The next year, the movie *Field of Dreams* starring Kevin Costner added a mystical quality to Jackson's plight. Costner played as an Iowa farmer who hears a mysterious voice that instructs him to build a baseball diamond in his cornfield. Once completed, the magical field allows Shoeless Joe and his teammates to play baseball again in a heartwarming story of redemption.

Today there is a growing movement supporting Jackson's reinstatement and election to the Hall of Fame. Baseball greats Ted Williams and Bob Feller have voiced their support for Jackson. In 1999, a baseball tournament was played on the actual Field of Dreams in Dyersville, Iowa, to further promote awareness of Jackson's story. ◆

> *" 'I loved the game,' Shoeless Joe went on. 'I'd have played for food money. I'd have played free and worked for food. It was the game, the parks, the smells, the sounds.' "*
>
> W. P. Kinsella, *Shoeless Joe*, 1983

Jackson, Reggie

MAY 18, 1946– ● BASEBALL PLAYER

To even casual baseball fans, the nickname "Mr. October" means Reggie Jackson, the flashy slugger who seemed to thrive in the national spotlight of the World Series—he was the only player in baseball history to win two World Series Most Valuable Player (MVP) awards and is the holder of the lifetime record for World Series slugging percentage (.755).

His renowned power is equally evident in his regular-season lifetime totals: 593 home runs, but also 2,597 strikeouts, an all-time high. But that was Jackson's all-or-nothing style of hitting—each swing a high-stakes bet, not just on home runs, but on home runs that would inspire awe, wonder . . . and ticket sales: "Taters [baseball slang for home runs]," Jackson once said.

Reggie Jackson hits one of his record three home runs in one World Series game in 1977.

"After Jackie Robinson, the most important black in baseball history is Reggie Jackson. I really mean that."

Reggie Jackson

"That's where the money is." And Jackson hauled in gaudy sums of it (for his era), especially in the last decade of a 21-year major league career (1967 to 1987) during which the copiously muscled and notoriously self-appreciative slugger streaked to an enduring if troubled superstardom, playing on 10 division title winners, six pennant winners, and five world champions.

Reginald Martinez Jackson was born on May 18, 1946, to a Latin father and African-American mother in Wyncote, Pennsylvania, a suburb of Philadelphia. After Reggie's parents divorced when he was young, three of the six children joined his mother in Baltimore, while Reggie and two siblings moved in with his father in Cheltenham, Pennsylvania, where Mr. Martinez set up a dry-cleaning and tailoring shop. Reggie's father had been a semipro baseball player and supported his son's athletic ambitions in Cheltenham High School, where Reggie starred in basketball, football, and baseball, pitching three no-hitters and batting .550 in his senior year.

Although Jackson received numerous offers for football scholarships, he chose a combined baseball/football program at Arizona State, long known as the nation's finest college baseball program, the last amateur stop for many of the top major league stars of the past quarter century. ASU's ballpark was soon swarming with major league scouts lured by word of Jackson's prodigious blasts.

Following his sophomore year, Jackson, passed up by the New York Mets, was snapped up by the Oakland Athletics, then under the new ownership of the innovative, mercurial Charley Finley. Jackson signed for a $95,000 bonus and moved on to Lewiston, Idaho, in the Northwest League, where he so dominated the competition that after only 12 games he was promoted to Modesto in the California League, where he batted .299 and jolted an amazing 21 homers in only 56 games.

After putting up more solid numbers over most of 1967 playing on the Birmingham, Alabama, club of the Southern League (.293, 17 homers, 17 triples, 232 total bases), he was called up to the big club at the tail end of the season and floundered, hitting only .178 with one home run in 35 games.

Jackson's began his first full season with the Oakland A's in 1968, an auspicious time for the franchise as Finley began to assemble the core talent—Jackson, Rollie Fingers, Sal Bando, Bert Campaneris, Gene Tenace, Vida Blue, Catfish Hunter— that would soon make Oakland the dominant team of the early seventies. Jackson made an impressive full-season debut that year, hitting .250 with 29 home runs but striking out an eye-popping 171 times, the most of his career and the highest total in baseball history to that time.

In 1969, Jackson slugged his way into the big time, reaching the 40 home-run mark by August 1 and fueling speculation that he might break Roger Maris's single-season mark of 61. But Jackson crumpled under the late-season pressure, hitting only seven more and ending the season with 47 home runs, 118 runs batted in (RBI), and a league-leading slugging percentage of .608. Jackson's power surge helped lift the A's to a second-place finish in the American League Western Division. The A's were runner-ups again in 1970, when Jackson slumped to a disappointing season: .237, 23 homers, and 66 RBI.

Jackson returned to Oakland in 1971 with renewed confidence and discipline, and his power numbers returned, as the A's dominated the American League West, coasting to their first division title with 101 wins, only to bow to the Baltimore Orioles in the American League playoffs. The personal highlight of Jackson's solid 1971 season (.277, 32 homers, and 80 RBI) occurred at the All-Star Game in Detroit, at which Jack-

1946 Reginald Martinez Jackson in Wyncote, Pennsylvania.

1968 Jackson has his first full season with Oakland A's.

1969 Jackson hits 47 home runs, 118 runs batted in.

1973 A's win Series over Mets; Jackson wins both World Series and American League Most Valuable Player (MVP) awards.

1977 With the New York Yankees, Jackson sets World Series home run records and wins his second Series MVP.

1993 Jackson is elected to the Baseball Hall of Fame.

The World Series

The World Series is baseball's showcase, a best-of-seven showdown between the champions of the American and National leagues. The name "World Series" is, perhaps, something of a misnomer, since only professional franchises from the United States and Canada are eligible to participate. It can at least be said that the series determines the North American baseball championship and, given the superior level of competition in the major leagues, most likely the world championship as well.

Although the modern World Series began in 1903, baseball's tradition of postseason championship play extends back to the 1880s, when there were various regional and local championship series after the close of the regular professional season: In 1882 Cleveland beat Cincinnati for the Ohio championship, and in 1883 Philadelphia and New York held city championship series. Informally organized, these series had no formal league sponsorship or standardized formats.

The earliest "world" series was a two-game set in 1882 between the champions of the National League (NL) and the fledgling American Association (AA), in which each club shut out the other. But the leagues viewed these as exhibition games since the NL did not formally recognize the legitimacy of the AA. A proposed championship series for 1883 was canceled, but in 1884, the pennant winners in each league the NL's Providence Grays and the AA's Metropolitan Club squared off in a three-game set, the winner of which, the Grays, was declared "champion of the world."

From 1885 to 1890 the NL and AA champions met in postseason championship series in varying formats extending from six to fifteen games. But the burgeoning World Series ended with the collapse of the AA after the 1891 season, causing a one-year hiatus in postseason play. In 1892 the NL expanded from eight to twelve teams, taking in four former AA clubs, and played a split season, with the winner of the first half playing the winner of the second half in a postseason series for the world championship. Boston topped Cleveland in that 1892 "World Series," but the split-season format proved unpopular and was scrapped the following season.

In 1894 a new postseason format arose when William C. Temple announced the awarding of a trophy the Temple Cup to the winner of a postseason series between the first-and second-place clubs of the NL. This best-of-seven series served as the world championship competition for four years but failed to attract sufficient fan interest to persist beyond 1897.

The next semblance of a World Series occurred in 1900, when the fans of the runner-up Pittsburgh Pirates pressed for a championship series against the pennant-winning Brooklyn Superbas, who handily disposed of the Pirates with only one loss in the best-of-five series.

When the rival American League declared itself a major league in 1901, a genuine World Series again became a possibility. Once the NL overcame its resistance to the new circuit and forged an agreement with the AL in 1903, the two league champions Pittsburgh (NL) and Boston (AL) met in a best-of-nine series that was a popular and financial success. When manager John McGraw of the haughty New York Giants, the NL champions in 1904, refused to play Boston in a series that year, the howls of fan and press protest led to the formal institutionalization of the World Series in 1905. The World Series has adopted a best-of-seven format in very year except 1919–1921, when it reverted briefly to best-of-nine.

The drama and excitement of World Series play have enlivened every American October since then, with the exception of 1994, the year of the prolonged players' strike that torpedoed that year's Series. The New York Yankees are the twentieth century's undisputed leaders in World Series competition, having won 25 fall classics through 1999. The second-highest Series victory total (nine) belongs to the St. Louis Cardinals.

son launched a right field blast off a light tower at Tiger Stadium to lead the American League to its first All-Star victory in nine years.

In 1972 the Athletics came into their own, capturing their first of three consecutive world championships. Although he missed that year's World Series because of a pulled hamstring muscle, Jackson played a key role in the pennant drive, batting .265 with 25 homers and 75 RBI. His contribution was even more decisive in 1973, when he batted .293 and led the league in home runs (32) and RBI (117). He went on to bat .310 and drive in six runs in that year's World Series victory over the New York Mets, earning the World Series Most Valuable Player (MVP) award. In November he received the American League MVP award as well.

In 1974 Jackson and the A's extended their winning ways (during the season Jackson batted .289 with 29 homers and 93 RBI), capturing their third straight world title in a five-game romp over the Los Angeles Dodgers in that year's World Series. After that campaign, however, the eccentric Finley began to dismantle his championship club, trading or selling off his increasingly pricey stable of talent. He dealt Jackson to the Baltimore Orioles, where he spent the 1976 season patiently awaiting his shot at free agency and the big-money, big-market spotlight awaiting him with George Steinbrenner's New York Yankees.

After the 1976 campaign, Jackson did indeed pick up Steinbrenner's pen and inked a then-record $3 million, five-year deal with the Yankees, making them the heavy favorites to dominate the league in 1977. Jackson's arrogance and insecurity came quickly into play as he arrived at spring training camp and announced himself "the straw that stirs the drink," **denigrating** Thurman Munson, the Yankees' team leader, and generally

denigrating: insulting and belittling.

The Bombers recovered their momentum in 1980, however, as Jackson powered them to a division title with a league-leading 41 home runs, a .300 batting average, and 111 RBI.

alienating his teammates, the fans, and reporters. After a rocky start for both Jackson and the Yankees, piloted by volatile manager Billy Martin, the Bronx Bombers righted themselves (Jackson's season totals were .286, 32 homers, and 110 RBI), although not without a near-fistfight between Martin and Jackson in the Yankee dugout in Boston in June. The Yankees pressed on to a pennant and six-game victory against the Los Angeles Dodgers in the World Series, which Jackson dominated, setting records with five home runs for the series and four straight through two games, climaxing the streak with three shots in three pitches in the decisive sixth game in Yankee Stadium, a performance that earned him his second World Series MVP award.

In 1978 the Yankees recovered from a 14-game deficit in July, jettisoning Martin as manager in midseason and surging past the Boston Red Sox in a dramatic one-game playoff for their second straight pennant. Jackson again led the way with a strong season (.274, 27, 97) as the Yanks recaptured the world title, again beating the Dodgers in six games. Although Jackson's numbers were robust in 1979 (.297, 29, 89), the Yankees fell out of the division chase early that season, reeling from the impact of Thurman Munson's midseason death in a plane crash. The Bombers recovered their momentum in 1980, however, as Jackson powered them to a division title with a league-leading 41 home runs, a .300 batting average, and 111 RBI. The Yankees failed to make the series, however, losing to the Kansas City Royals in the American League Championship Series.

The Yankees returned to the World Series in the strike-shortened season of 1981, losing to the Dodgers in six games, but Jackson's disappointing numbers that year (.237, 15, 54) led George Steinbrenner to let Jackson go at the end of his contract, a move the Yankee owner later regretted as "my biggest mistake." Jackson rebounded in 1982 with the California Angels, leading the league with 39 round-trippers and batting in 101 runs on the way to a division title. Jackson remained with the Angels through 1985, but his numbers continued to decline. He returned to the Oakland A's in 1987 and then retired at the end of that season.

Reggie Jackson was elected to the Baseball Hall of Fame in 1993. Since his retirement from play, he has remained busy with a broad array of business interests and served as a part-time coach and baseball advisor to George Steinbrenner. His baseball legacy—two parts awesome talent to one part preening, temperamental star—is distilled in the short-lived Reggie Bar, a fulfillment, however fleeting, of Jackson's prediction that if he ever played in New York, "they'd name a candy bar after me." Hearing the remark, one sportswriter responded, "When you unwrapped it, it told you how good it was." ◆

Jarrett, Dale

NOVEMBER 26, 1956– ● RACE CAR DRIVER

Normally, finishing behind four other drivers in a NASCAR race is no cause for celebration. But it was a joyous occasion for Dale Jarrett at the Homestead Miami Speedway on November 14, 1999, when his fifth-place finish in the Pennzoil 400 gave him a clinching total of 5,087 points in NASCAR's annual $2 million Winston Cup competition. "Fantastic!" Jarrett yelled after emerging from his No. 88 Ford. "I've just got to thank God for the talent on this race team and putting me here with such great people."

Needing only a ninth-place finish in the race to capture his first Winston Cup, Jarrett said that as he entered the final 10 laps, "I was just thinking about not hitting anything." Dale's father, Ned, a former champion stock-car racer who is now a racing commentator for CBS and ESPN, won two NASCAR series championships, making them the second father-son combination (along with Lee and Richard Petty) to win NASCAR/ Grand National titles. "I give my dad a lot of credit and thanks for everything that's happened in my career," Jarrett said after the race. Through the Pennzoil 400 Jarrett's championship 1999 season included five victories and four each of second-, third-, and fourth-place finishes. Over one 19-race span he finished in the top five 17 times.

Until 1996 Jarrett was just another struggling stock-car driver, best known as the son of a celebrated father. But that season he formed a new team and sped to the front ranks of the NASCAR circuit, beginning with a victory in the prestigious Daytona 500, the first race of the season. His subsequent victory in the daunting Coca-Cola 600, the circuit's longest race, gave him a shot at the Winston Million, a million-dollar prize for any driver who finishes first in three of NASCAR's four top competitions. Although that prize eluded Jarrett, he went on to post victories in the Brickyard 400, the Busch Clash (an elite race at

> *"My faith is what has gotten me to this point. It's gotten me through not only some difficult times, but helped me make some very important decisions in my life."*
>
> Dale Jarrett

1956 — Jarrett is born in North Carolina.

1993 — Jarrett wins the Daytona 500.

1996 — Jarrett wins the Daytona 500, the Coca-Cola 600, the Brickyard 400, the Busch Clash, and the GM Goodwrench 400.

1997 — Jarrett wins seven races; finishes second in Winston Cup points; and is named Driver of the Year by National Motorsports Press Association.

1999 — Jarrett wins five races and claims his first Winston Cup championship.

the Daytona International Speedway for the year's top-rated racers), and the GM Goodwrench 400, placing him third in that year's Winston Cup competition and bringing his season's winnings to $2.2 million.

Jarrett sustained his momentum in 1997, winning seven races—the Prime Star 500 (Atlanta), the Transouth Financial 400 (Darlington), the Pennsylvania 500 (Pocono), Goody's Headache Powders 500 (Bristol), the Miller 400 (Richmond), the UAW GM Quality 500 (Charlotte), and the Dura Lube 500 (Phoenix)—and finishing second in Winston Cup points. He also won the 1997 National Motorsports Press Association Driver of the Year award. Jarrett fell off slightly in 1998 but still had an impressive season with three victories, 19 top-five finishes, and a third-place ranking in the Winston Cup competition.

Jarrett gravitated to stock-car racing because it was an exciting career that could keep him close to his family. A multisport athlete in high school in Conover, North Carolina, he made his racing debut in 1977 in the Limited Sportsman Division at the Hickory Motor Speedway, a track once managed by his father. Jarrett's first Winston Cup race was in 1984, when he started 24th and finished 14th in a race in Martinsville, Virginia. He drove in a few more Winston Cup races in 1984 and 1986 but did not become a full-time participant in the circuit until 1987. His first victory did not come until his 129th race, in 1991.

Jarrett's first early breakthrough was his 1993 victory at the Daytona 500, which Ned Jarrett called as an announcer on network television, shouting "Can you believe it?" as his son streaked across the finish line. The victory was hard won, coming only after Jarrett was able to pass Dale Earnhardt. On his first attempt Jarrett almost touched Earnhardt's car at 210 mph and nearly lost control after he slid 30 feet across the track. Jarrett pulled alongside Earnhardt again as they approached the last lap and this time succeeded in passing him and streaking to victory.

Jarrett had only one win each in 1994 and 1995, however, so he switched teams at the end of 1995, joining Robert Yates racing, a move that propelled him toward his banner season of 1996. Jarrett has been in the front ranks of stock-car drivers ever since.

Jarrett makes his home with his wife Kelley and their four children in Hickory, North Carolina, where he relaxes by playing golf and racquetball. ◆

Jenner, Bruce

OCTOBER 28, 1949– ● TRACK AND FIELD ATHLETE

The second of four children, William Bruce Jenner was born in Mount Kisco, New York, on October 28, 1949. His father, William, was a descendant of the famous English doctor Edward Jenner, who discovered the virus that causes smallpox.

The Jenner family moved to a lakefront home in Newton, Connecticut, when Bruce was a child. It was there that he began to show interest in many sports, including waterskiing. Jenner would later write that athletics boosted his self-confidence: "As a young child, I had to overcome the challenge of being dyslexic. I would sit in class terrified that the teacher would call on me to read aloud. . . . My total lack of self-confidence gave me the determination to be the very best at something. For me, it was athletics."

By the time Jenner reached high school, his promise as an athlete was beginning to materialize. He went on to earn letters in football, basketball, and track, and he was an all-state high jump and pole vault champion. He also excelled as a waterskier, winning the East Coast waterskiing championship for the first time in 1966 when he was just 16 years old, later repeating in 1969 and 1971.

Jenner hoped that his athletic performance would lead to attractive scholarship offers from major colleges and universities. Yet despite his accomplishments, the offers never came. The best offer he received was a $250-a-year football scholarship from Graceland College, a small school in Lamoni, Iowa, connected with the Reorganized Church of Jesus Christ of Latter-day Saints. Jenner accepted and in 1969 left his

A victorious Bruce Jenner at the 1976 Olympics.

home on the East Coast for the Midwest and the religious college's strict moral standards.

Jenner's goal of playing football was shattered during his freshman year when he injured his knee. He played basketball, though, and the college's track coach, recognizing his athletic versatility, encouraged him to compete in the decathlon at the Drake University Relays, a prestigious collegiate track event held annually in Des Moines, Iowa. Jenner finished sixth in the Drake Relays, compiling 6,991 points, a school record. He had found his niche, and over the next few years he dedicated himself to year-round training for the decathlon, a grueling, two-day, 10-event competition that demands from athletes not only skill but speed, strength, endurance, and versatility.

In 1972 Jenner arrived at the Olympic trials in Eugene, Oregon, as a complete unknown in a field of 22 athletes. After the first seven events he was in seventh place, a respectable showing but not good enough to win a spot on the Olympic team and a ticket to Munich, Germany. Jenner's best events, however, would always be the later ones, and after a strong showing in the pole vault, the javelin throw, and the 1,500-meter race, he had clawed his way to the third spot on the Olympic team. He competed in the 1972 Olympics, his first time up against the best decathletes in the world, and came in tenth with 7,772 points. That year, Nikolai Avilov from the Soviet Union won with a world record 8,454 points. Jenner was disappointed, but he vowed to win the decathlon in the 1976 Olympics in Montreal, Canada.

The decathlon is unique among track-and-field events because it requires the athlete to train, day in and day out all year, to become a champion not just in one or two events but in ten. Jenner's strategy for winning in Montreal was to train not just with other decathletes, who tend to be good in a range of events, but to train with the very best athletes in each event. To this end, in 1973 he moved to San Jose, California, where many top U.S. athletes lived and trained. Despite being slowed by a back injury and then a broken foot, between 1973 and 1976 he entered 13 decathlons and won 12 of them, including the 1974 and 1976 National AAU Outdoor Championships and the 1975 Pan-American Games. His only loss came at the 1975 National AAU meet, where he lost his concentration on the pole vault and failed to complete the event. After amassing 8,524 points in a meet against the Soviet Union and Poland the next year, he was the odds-on favorite to win in Montreal.

Jenner's plan was to stay as close as possible to his archrival, Avilov, during the first day of competition and rely on his strong second-day events to overtake Avilov and win. His plan, though, turned out to be unnecessary. In the first day of competition he scored personal bests in four out of the five events, and after the third event of the second day he had already clinched the gold medal. He could have coasted, but he showed the determination that marked his career, and in the final event, the punishing 1,500-meter race, he ran his fastest time ever. When it was over he had amassed 8,618 points, a new world and Olympic record.

After the 1976 Olympics Jenner virtually retired from competition. His all-American good looks and winning personality enabled him to go on to a successful career as a sports commentator, a product endorser (his picture was on the Wheaties cereal box), author, motivational speaker, and businessman. He also starred in television programs and movies. In 1976 he won the Sullivan Award for outstanding amateur athlete, and in 1986 Jenner was inducted into the U.S. Olympic Hall of Fame. ◆

> *"The most challenging aspect of the decathlon is not the events themselves, but how you train to become the best 100-meter runner you are on the same day that you're the best 1,500-meter runner."*
>
> Bruce Jenner

Johnson, John "Jack"

MARCH 31, 1878–JUNE 10, 1946 ● BOXER

The third of six surviving children, Jack Johnson was born in Galveston, Texas, to Henry Johnson, a laborer and ex-slave, and Tiny Johnson. He attended school for about five years, then worked as a stevedore, janitor, and cotton picker. He gained his initial fighting experience in battle royals, brutal competitions in which a group of African-American boys engaged in no-holds-barred brawls, with a few coins going to the last fighter standing. He turned professional in 1897. In his early years Johnson mainly fought other African-American men. His first big win was a sixth-round decision on January 17, 1902, over Frank Childs, one of the best black heavyweights of the day. The six-foot, 200-pound Johnson developed into a powerful defensive boxer who emphasized quickness, rhythm, style, and grace.

In 1903, Johnson defeated Denver Ed Martin in a 20-round decision, thus capturing the championship of the unofficial Ne-

1878 John Arthur Johnson is born in Galveston, Texas.

1908 Johnson knocks out Tommy Burns in the 14th round in a bout in Australia, becoming the first African American world heavyweight champion.

1910 Johnson defeats former champ James J. Jeffries after 15 rounds; race riots break out.

1915 Johnson loses his title to Jess Willard.

promoters: individuals or a group of people who assume the financial responsibilities for boxing matches (and other athletic events), including contracting the opponents, renting the site, and collecting the box office proceeds.

gro heavyweight division, which was created by West coast sportswriters to compensate for the prohibition on blacks fighting for the real crown. Johnson, who was then the de facto leading heavyweight challenger, sought a contest with champion Jim Jeffries but was rebuffed because of the color line. Racial barriers largely limited Johnson's opponents to black fighters like Joe Jeanette, whom he fought 10 times. Johnson's first big fight against a white contender was in 1905, against Marvin Hart, which he lost by the referee's decision, despite having demonstrated his superior talent and ring mastery. Hart became champion three months later, knocking out Jack Root to win Jeffries's vacated title. Johnson's bid to get a title fight improved in 1906, when he hired Sam Fitzpatrick as his manager. Fitzpatrick knew the major **promoters** and could arrange fights that Johnson could not when he managed himself. Johnson enhanced his reputation with victories in Australia, a second-round knockout of 44-year-old ex-champion Bob Fitzsimmons in Philadelphia, and two wins in England.

In 1908 Canadian Tommy Burns became champion, and Johnson stalked him to Australia, looking for a title bout. Promoter Hugh McIntosh signed Burns to a match in Sydney on December 26 for a $30,000 guarantee with $5,000 for Johnson. Burns was knocked down in the first round by Johnson, who thereafter verbally and physically punished Burns until the police stopped the fight in the 14th round. White reaction was extremely negative, and a search began for a "white hope" who would regain the title to restore to whites their sense of superiority and to punish Johnson's arrogant public behavior. A proud, willful man, Johnson recklessly violated the taboos against the "proper place" for blacks, most notoriously in his relationships with white women. Though much of the black middle class viewed his lifestyle with some disquiet, he became a great hero to lower-class African Americans through his flouting of conventional social standards and his seeming lack of fear of white disapproval.

Johnson defended his title five times in 1909, most memorably against middleweight champion Stanley Ketchell, a tenacious 160-pound fighter. Johnson toyed with Ketchell for several rounds, rarely attacking. Ketchell struck the champion behind the ear in the twelfth round with a roundhouse right, knocking him to the canvas. An irate Johnson arose, caught the attacking challenger with a right uppercut, and knocked him out. Johnson's only defense in 1910 was against Jim Jeffries, who was encouraged to come out of retirement by an offer of a $101,000 guarantee, split 3:1 for the winner, plus profits from film rights. When moral reformers refused to allow the match to be held in San Francisco, it was moved to Reno, Nevada. The former champion, well past his prime, was overmatched. Johnson taunted and humiliated him, ending the fight with a 15th-round knockout. Fears that a Johnson victory would unleash racial hostilities were quickly realized as gangs of whites randomly attacked blacks in cities across the country.

In 1910, Johnson settled in Chicago, where he enjoyed a fast lifestyle; he toured with vaudeville shows, drove racing cars, and in 1912 opened a shortlived nightclub, the Cafe de Champion. Johnson defended his title once during the two years following the Jeffries fight, beating "Fireman" Jim Flynn in nine rounds in a filmed fight in Las Vegas, New Mexico. Subsequently, in response to anti-Johnson and antiboxing sentiment and concern about films showing a black man pummeling a white, the federal government banned the interstate transport of fight films.

In 1911, Johnson married white divorcee Etta Terry Duryea, but their life was turbulent and she committed suicide a year later. Johnson later married two other white women. His well-publicized love life caused much talk of expanding state antimiscegenation statutes. More important, the federal government pursued Johnson for violation of the Mann Act (1910), the so-called "white slavery act," which forbade the transportation of women across state lines for "immoral purposes." The law was seldom enforced, but the federal government chose to prosecute Johnson, even though he was not involved in procuring. Johnson was guilty only of **flaunting** his relationships with white women. He was convicted and sentenced to one year in the penitentiary, but fled the country to Europe through Canada. He spent several troubled years abroad, defending his title twice in Paris and once in Buenos Aires, and struggled to earn a living.

In 1915 a match was arranged with Jess Willard (6′ 6″ and 250 pounds) in Havana. By then Johnson was old for a boxer and had not trained adequately for the fight; he tired and was knocked out in the 26th round. The result was gleefully received in the United States, and thereafter no African American was given a chance to fight for the heavyweight title until Joe Louis. Johnson had hoped to make a deal with the government to reduce his penalty, and four years later claimed that he threw the fight. Most boxing experts now discount Johnson's

"[N]ever in the wildest moments of my boyhood imagination did I vision myself the champion fighter of the world, and the first man of my race ever to attain that distinction."

Jack Johnson in his autobiography, *Jack Johnson—In the Ring—and Out* (1927)

flaunting: making a flashy or ostentatious display of wealth, success, or good fortune.

claim and believe it was an honest fight. Johnson returned to the United States in 1920 and served a year in Leavenworth Penitentiary in Kansas. He subsequently fought a few bouts, gave exhibitions, trained and managed fighters, appeared on stage, and lectured. His autobiography, *Jack Johnson: In the Ring and Out,* appeared in 1927; a new edition was published, with additional material, in 1969. Johnson died in 1946 when he drove his car off the road in North Carolina.

Johnson's life was memorialized by Howard Sackler's play *The Great White Hope* (1969), which was made into a motion picture in 1971. Johnson finished with a record of 78 wins (including 45 by knockout), 8 defeats, 12 draws, and 14 no-decisions in 112 bouts. He was elected to the Boxing Hall of Fame in 1954. In 1987 *Ring* magazine rated him the second greatest heavyweight of all time, behind Muhammad Ali. ◆

Johnson, Michael

SEPTEMBER 13, 1967– ● TRACK AND FIELD ATHLETE

> *"I saw a blue blur go by, whoosh, and thought, 'There goes first.'"*
>
> Ato Boldon of Trinidad, on Michael Johnson in the 200-meter dash, 1996 Olympics

Without a doubt, Michael Johnson is considered one of the most revolutionary performers in the history of track and field. In both the 200-meter and the 400-meter events, where he currently holds world records, the previous standard was the longest-standing in the sport. Yet it's more the nature of his events that truly amaze insiders: The 200-meter is an out-and-out sprint to the wire, while the 400-meter has always been viewed as more of a middle distance event—and each requires vastly different talents and training methods. Johnson is the first and only athlete ever to be so accomplished in both events and the first runner in history to win Olympic gold medals in both. "I always wanted to bring the two events together in a way that nobody has ever done," says Johnson. "This sums up what my career is about."

Johnson was born on September 13, 1967, in Dallas, Texas. Already an outstanding athlete at Skyline High School in Dallas, Johnson truly started to blossom to world class level at Baylor University under coach Clyde Hart. Johnson also gives Hart a lion's share of the credit for running such a unique combination of events. "Coach Hart developed a training program for me to overcome the leg problems I used to have all the time,"

Michael Johnson celebrates another victory.

Johnson says. "Among other things, he had me run in lots of sprint relays. They gave me the speed work I needed and the relay 400's gave me the strength work. I got a good base while working on my speed at the same time."

Johnson's first international breakthrough came in July 1990, in Edinborough, Scotland. He outraced a field of 200-meter athletes that included defending Olympic champion Joe DeLoach in a sparkling 19.85 seconds. He began to run the 400-meter competitively toward the end of the 1990 season, mainly to break the boredom of running one 200-meter after another. Soon, however, running the longer event became far more than just a diversion; Johnson immediately ran four consecutive sub-45 second 400's, defeating world record holder Butch Reynolds in the process. Johnson went on to become national and Goodwill Games champion in the 200-meter in 1990, then produced the greatest consecutive seasons ever for a sprinter in 1990–91 by convincingly winning the 200-meter at the 1991 World Championships in Tokyo, Japan. Johnson was the first athlete ever ranked No.1 in the world in both the 200- and 400-meter

The Olympic Bombing of 1996

The 1996 Olympic Games in Atlanta, Georgia, marked the centennial of the modern games and were eagerly anticipated as a glittering display of America's peerless sportsmanship, showmanship, and technology. Olympic officials and law-enforcement authorities, aware of the prominence of the United States as a target for terrorist groups, mounted the largest internal peacetime security operation in U.S. history to ensure that violence would not mar the world's most august athletic event.

After the first week of competition, all these elaborate precautions were blown sky high. Early in the morning of July 27, the police received an anonymous phone call warning them that a bomb was set to go off within minutes near the main Olympic sites. Shortly thereafter, a security guard named Richard Jewell alerted the police to the presence of a suspicious-looking knapsack leaning against a television tower in Centennial Olympic Park, the main tourist area. Eighteen minutes after the call, as police were clearing out the park, a primitive bomb inside the pack went off in a deafening blast that shook the main plaza, sending thousands of visitors into a panic. One person died from the impact of the blast, and a photographer running to cover the event died of a heart attack at the scene.

This was the first violent incident at the Olympics since the attack by Palestinian terrorists at the 1972 games in Munich, Germany, which resulted in the deaths of eleven Israeli athletes. The Atlanta explosion occurred only a few days after the mid-air explosion of TWA flight 800, a Paris-bound 747 out of New York that many at the time believed had been a terrorist target. Police and FBI investigators focused on domestic rather foreign suspects, however, and their first target was Richard Jewell, the man who had first alerted police to the presence of the knapsack. After months of intense questioning, the FBI finally cleared Jewell of any suspicion. Jewell subsequently sued the police, the FBI, and the media for the months of anguish he endured.

Despite a reward of $500,000, no other leads ever developed in the Olympic bombing, which remains an unsolved crime.

races. Johnson also became the first runner in history to go under 21 seconds in the 200-meter and under 44 seconds in the 400-meter at the same meet.

After cruising through the 1992 Olympic trials—he won the 200-meter in a meet record 19.79 seconds—Johnson contracted food poisoning at the Barcelona Games and, severely weakened physically, failed to make the finals. Still, he was a member of the gold medal winning 400-meter relay team. Also, at the USA championships in 1993, Johnson fairly crushed both Reynolds and Olympic Champion Quincy Watts with a time of 43.74 seconds, the fastest 400-meter ever run on American soil. He then won the 400-meter in Stuttgart, Germany at the World Championships in 43.55 and added another gold medal in the relay. Johnson maintained his momentum with a great 1994, winning every single one of his 400-meter races and receiving the prestigious Jesse Owens Award. He was ranked No.1 in the world in both the 200-meter and 400-meter at the end of the year. Amazingly, 1995 was even better for Johnson; he was a double gold medalist at the World Championships at Goteborg, Sweden—the first man to ever accomplish that amazing feat in both 200-meter and 400-meter events.

But Johnson still wasn't finished. He topped all previous accomplishments at the 1996 Olympic Games in Atlanta, Georgia, by winning the 200-meter in an astonishing world record in 19.32. (Johnson broke the previous record of 19.79 at the Olympic trials with a time of 19.66.) Three days later, in a feat of unprecedented endurance he won the 400-meter in an Olympic record 43.49.

Johnson defended his world championship title in 1997, winning easily in Athens with a time of 44.12 seconds. However, he was injured in the much-hyped "World's Fastest Human" race against Canadian sprinter Donovan Bailey and missed the rest of the season.

Still suffering from continuous hamstring problems, Johnson went undefeated (with the exception of a third-place finish Oslo, Norway) in 1998. He won a gold at the Goodwill Games and anchored a world record-setting 400-meter relay. And his injuries were finally eased when a creative massage therapist found an imbalance in his hips.

In 1999, Johnson finally broke the 11-year-old world record for the 400-meter, running a remarkable 43.18 at the World Championships at Seville, Spain. He intends to try for double gold medals once again at the 2000 Olympic Games in Sydney, Australia. ◆

1967 Johnson is born in Dallas, Texas.

1994 Johnson wins prestigious Jesse Owens award and is named number one in the world in the 200-meter and 400-meter events.

1995 Johnson wins two gold medals at World Championships in Goteburg, Sweden.

1996 Johnson becomes the first man in Olympic history to win both the 200-meter and 400-meter dashes.

1999 In Seville, Spain, Johnson breaks the 11-year-old world record for the 400-meter.

Johnson, Walter

NOVEMBER 6, 1887–DECEMBER 10, 1946 ● BASEBALL PLAYER

Walter Johnson was nicknamed the "Big Train," because early in the 20th century when he pitched, trains were the epitome of size and speed. At 6′ 1″ and 200 pounds, Johnson was a large man for his day. The blazing sidearmed fastball he threw in "buggy whip" fashion made him one of the most dominant pitchers ever. During a 21-year

career, Johnson won 417 games—the most in the 20th century. His 2.17 earned run average (ERA) is seventh best all-time, and his 110 shutouts has never been matched. His list of achievements is replete with superlatives: for seven consecutive seasons, pitching for a habitually poor Washington Senators team, Johnson won at least 25 games. He led the American League in victories and ERA six times, and completed a remarkable 531 of his 666 career starts. Johnson led the American League in strikeouts 12 times, including eight years in a row. His 3,509 career strikeouts ranks seventh best of all-time, and was accomplished at a time when batters struck out less than 2/3 the rate they do today.

Johnson was born on November 6, 1887 in Humboldt, Kansas, to Swedish immigrant farmers. He developed his mighty physique working in his father's wheat field. In 1907, the 19-year-old Johnson was working in Idaho digging postholes for the Weiser Telephone Company, and pitching for the company's baseball team. Legend has it that a traveling salesman (and Washington Senators fan) continually sent letters to Washington manager Joe Cantillon with details of Johnson's pitching feats. "He throws the ball so fast it's like a little white bullet going down to the catcher," the salesman wrote. In the days before formal scouting, it was quite common for big league teams to get exaggerated reports of phenoms, so the letters were ignored.

That summer, though, the Senators were interested in an outfielder named Clyde Milan, and they dispatched injured catcher Cliff Blankenship to go out west to scout him. While there, Blankenship was told he might as well check out the kid in Idaho the salesman had been writing about. Blankenship sent back favorable reports about Milan, who went on to a 15-year career with the Senators, but his real find was Johnson and his blazing fastball. Blankenship signed him on the spot for a $100 bonus and $350 a month.

Johnson made his debut on August 2, 1907, going 5–9 and 14–14 in his first two seasons for the miserable Senators, one of the major league's worst teams. In 1908, he showed flashes of brilliance by not allowing a run against the New York Highlanders (later the Yankees) in three consecutive games played in four days, allowing just 12 in the games. Three days later he beat the Philadelphia Athletics two days in a row, giving him five wins in eight days. Despite such occasional heroics, Johnson struggled. In 1909, he was the league's second-best strikeout artist, but lost 25 games for the awful Senators, who finished 56 games out of first place.

In 1910, Johnson's career turned around. He turned the previous year's 25 losses into 25 wins, going 25–17 and completing 38 of his 42 starts. His career high 313 strikeouts won him the first of his 12 strikeout titles. It began a string of 10 consecutive years in which Johnson won at least 20 games, but even with his talent, the Senators only mustered a seventh place finish in 1910.

After a 25–13 record in 1911 for another seventh place Senators' team, Johnson compiled the most dominant back-to-back pitching seasons ever, going 33–12 with a 1.39 ERA in 1912, and 36–7 with a 1.14 ERA in 1913. The Senators challenged for the pennant both years, finishing second. In 1913, Johnson established a consecutive scoreless inning record of 56 innings, since broken, and won 16 consecutive games. He was voted the American League's Most Valuable Player (MVP).

While Johnson continued to top 20 wins in each of the next six seasons, the Senators didn't challenge for the pennant again during the next decade. A new rival major league, The Federal League, tried to lure Johnson after the 1914 season, in which he went 28–18 with a 1.27 ERA. The Senators met the $25,000 a year offer, more than doubling his salary, and Johnson went on to spent the rest of his playing career with Washington. He went 118–76 the next five seasons, but slipped to 8–10 in 1920. His ERA jumped to 3.13. The decline continued the next three seasons, when his ERA was 3.51 in 1921, 2.99 in 1922 and 3.48 in 1923. His record those three years was a mortal 49–42.

It looked like Johnson's career was winding down, when in 1924—at age 36—he led the league with 23 wins, against only 7 defeats, and gained his fifth ERA title with a 2.72 mark. He won his second MVP award, and the Senators won the first pennant in their history, capped by Johnson's relief appearance in the final deciding game of the World Series, a 12-inning, 4–3 Senators' victory. Johnson took the Senators to a second American League pennant in 1925, going 20–7, but lost the deciding seventh game of the World Series against Pittsburgh, after having won games one and four by allowing just one run. After a 15–16 season in 1926, Johnson broke his leg in 1927's spring training. He returned from the injury and finished the season 5–6. He retired at age 40 following the season, with a career 417–279 record and 2.17 ERA.

Johnson came back as the Senators manager in 1929, and the team won more than 90 games in three of his four seasons at

"He's got a gun concealed on his person. You can't tell me he throws them balls with his arm."

Ring Lardner, on Johnson's fastball

Johnson took the Senators to a second American League pennant in 1925, going 20–7.

the helm. He managed again for the Cleveland Indians from the middle of 1933 until the summer of 1935. When the first election for Baseball's Hall of Fame was held in 1936, Johnson joined Ty Cobb, Babe Ruth, Honus Wagner and Christy Mathewson as a charter member. Johnson died from a brain tumor on December 10, 1946, in Washington D.C. ◆

Jones, Bobby

MARCH 17, 1902–DECEMBER 18, 1971 ● GOLFER

When Robert Tyre Jones II was born in Atlanta, Georgia, he had sports in his genes. His father, an attorney, was also a skilled amateur baseball player, and his mother was an accomplished amateur golfer. Bobby was a sickly child, though, and in an effort to build him up physically,

his parents bought a summer house near the fairways of Atlanta's East Lake Country Club. There Bobby watched as the club pro taught his students, and soon, using sawed-off clubs, he was mimicking the pro's swing. He quickly improved as a golfer, and at age 11 he shot an 80 on the East Lake course. At age 13 he began to enter amateur tournaments, beginning a 15-year amateur career—Jones never turned pro—as a golf prodigy and, in the 1920s, joining such fabled characters as Babe Ruth, Bill Tilden, and Jack Dempsey as mythic figures in America's Golden Age of Sports.

Jones's first success came in the Roebuck Invitational Tournament, when he beat the top amateur players in the South as a 13-year-old. At age 14 he qualified for the U.S. Amateur Championship, shooting a 74 in the first qualifying round to lead the field, though he lost in the third round. Between 1916 and 1922, however, Jones's early promise as a golfer seemed to fade. During these years he played in 11 national and international tournaments but failed to record a victory, primarily because he had problems with his temper. Famed sports writer Grantland Rice described him as "a short, rotund kid, with the face of an angel and the temper of a timber wolf." Jones himself later said, "To me, golf was just a game to beat someone. I didn't know that someone was me."

Finally, in 1923 Jones conquered his temper and began to realize his early potential, winning the U.S. Open at the Inwood Country Club in New York. With three holes left Jones looked like the winner, but he finished the round with two bogeys and a double bogey, opening the door for Bobby Cruickshank to tie him and force an 18-hole playoff round. On the par-four 18th hole, Jones hit his tee shot into loose dirt at the edge of the rough 190 yards from the green. If he went for the green, he faced the real possibility of landing in the water and losing the tournament. He grabbed his two iron and drilled his shot over the water to within eight feet of the pin. Two putts later, he had his first win in a major tournament.

During the 1920s Jones pursued interests other than golf, and in fact played only three months out of the year. He was an excellent student and earned degrees in mechanical engineering from Georgia Tech and literature from Harvard. After studying law at Emory University in Atlanta, he passed the **bar examinations** in 1928. It seems incredible that with all these demands on his time, plus a growing family, he was able to dominate the world of golf, but between 1923 and 1930 he won 13 major tournaments, a record that would stand for 40 years. He repeated as U.S. Open champion in 1926, 1929, and 1930. In 1926 he became the first amateur in 29 years to win the British Open, and he repeated as British Open champion in 1927 and 1930. In 1930 he won the British Amateur (considered a major tournament at the time). He won the U.S. Amateur (again, considered a major tournament at the time) in 1924, 1925, 1927, and 1928, and when he repeated in 1930, he completed the Grand Slam—the only golfer ever to win the four recognized major tournaments in the same year. In the process he became a major celebrity; at the U.S. Amateur, he needed seven Marine bodyguards to protect him from adoring fans.

While many of Jones's wins came easy, many provided high drama. He led the 1929 U.S. Open, for example, by six strokes with six holes left. But after a series of disastrous holes he

"Jones is the greatest golfer who ever lived and probably ever will live. That's my goal. Bobby Jones. It's the only goal."
Jack Nicklaus, on Bobby Jones, 1960

bar examination: exhaustive test given to recent graduates of law school who attempt to pass in order to gain license to practice law in the individual state administering the exam.

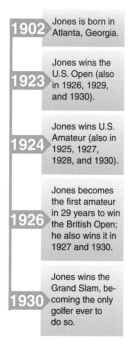

1902 — Jones is born in Atlanta, Georgia.

1923 — Jones wins the U.S. Open (also in 1926, 1929, and 1930).

1924 — Jones wins U.S. Amateur (also in 1925, 1927, 1928, and 1930).

1926 — Jones becomes the first amateur in 29 years to win the British Open; he also wins it in 1927 and 1930.

1930 — Jones wins the Grand Slam, becoming the only golfer ever to do so.

needed a 12-foot putt on the 18th hole to tie Al Espinosa and force a playoff. He stroked the putt, and after hesitating at the lip of the cup, the ball dropped in. Late in the 1930 U.S. Open, he appeared to have the tournament locked up, but he double-bogeyed the 71st hole and needed a 40-foot birdie putt on the final hole to win. His putter, nicknamed "Calamity Jane," didn't let him down, and he sank the putt to win. Ironically, the golfer who struggled with his temper early in his career was at his best when the pressure was on.

With the Grand Slam behind him and an ailing back, Jones felt that he had nothing left to accomplish on the golf course, so he retired from competition and practiced law. He left behind another legacy, though. In 1930 he joined with Alister Mackenzie to design the Augusta National Golf Course near Atlanta, and with the help of Clifford Roberts established The Masters Tournament, one of the major golf tournaments today. He served as an officer during World War II and later became active in politics. He was elected to the PGA Hall of Fame in 1940 and to the PGA/World Golf Hall of Fame in 1974. In 1958 he became the first American since Benjamin Franklin to receive the Freedom of the City Award from St. Andrews in Scotland, home of the leading golf club in the world.

In 1948 Jones contracted syringomyelia, a crippling disease of the spinal cord. The former athlete spent the last years of his life in a wheelchair and died from the effects of the disease in 1971. ◆

Jones, Marion

OCTOBER 12, 1975– ● TRACK AND FIELD ATHLETE

Marion Jones may share the initials of a few other great athletes—basketball great Michael Jordan and fellow track star Michael Johnson—but she certainly isn't in anyone's shadow. Already considered the Florence Griffith-Joyner or Jackie Joyner-Kersee for the next millennium, Jones is the dominant figures in women's track and field after just three short years of international competition.

Born on October 12, 1975, in Los Angeles, Jones first attended Rio Mesa High school in Oxnard, California, then transferred to Thousand Oaks High School for her senior year. It was apparent early on that she was a brilliantly gifted athlete. In 1992, as a high school junior, she finished fourth in the 200-meter at the U.S. Olympic trials (running the event in an American Junior record 22.58 seconds), earning a trip to Barcelona as a member of the U.S. relay team. But in a surprising move, Jones felt she was too young for the Olympics and declined the invitation. With that she put the world on notice that she possessed not only strong athletic skills but also strong convictions.

Jones went on to finish her high school career in outstanding form. She won both the 100- and 200-meter sprints at the California State Championship from 1990–93. In 1992, she won both events at the USA Juniors as well, and she added

a long jump victory in 1993. In the process, Jones also set five national prep records in the 200-meter and she currently holds four world records in the 15- and 16-year-old age group.

In addition to her skills on the track, Jones is also a talented basketball player. She scored 22.8 points per game as a high school senior and was named California Dvision I Player of the Year. To no one's surprise, she was named USA High School Athlete of the Year two years in a row, in 1991 and 1992.

Following her high school graduation, Jones enrolled at the University of North Carolina at Chapel Hill, where she immediately helped the Tar Heels win the women's NCAA basketball title in her freshman season. In 1996, however, Jones broke a bone in her foot while preparing for the World University Games, and she was forced to sit out the entire season as a result. After the injury Jones gave up basketball in order to devote herself to what she says was her first love: track and field.

Jones's new focus would pay off. Though she was fairly unknown in the track and field arena, Jones burst on to the scene in 1997, easily winning the 100-meter (in a sizzling 10.83 sec-

1975 Jones is born in Los Angeles, California.

1997 Jones wins the 100-meter and 400-meter relay gold medals at World Championships in Athens.

1998 Jones wins triple gold at the USA Championships and the 100-meter and 200-meter at the Goodwill Games.

1999 Jones wins 100-meter gold at the World Championships in Seville, Spain.

onds) as well as the 400-meter relay gold at the 1997 World Championships in Athens, Greece.

The following season, Jones went undefeated in every competition until her last one of the year (where Heike Dreischler of Germany bested her long jump for the World Cup gold medal). But that was Jones's only loss: she won an incredible 35 of 36 competitions. She also won three golds at the USA Championships and both the 100-meter (with a time of 10.90) and the 200-meter (in 21.80 seconds) at the Goodwill Games. She also doubled in the Grand Prix Final and in the World Cup, where her time of 10.65 seconds in the 100-meter was a personal record. For her efforts Jones was named Athlete of the Year by *Track and Fields News* (unanimously) and International Amateur Athletics Female Athlete of the Year.

Jones arrived in Seville, Spain, for the 1999 World Championships looking to win four gold medals, but after suffering a season-ending back injury during the semifinals of the 200-meter race, she was forced to "settle" for just one gold medal, in the 100-meter. She also took home a bronze medal in the long jump competition. Now fully recovered from her back injury, Jones is looking forward to attempting to win an unprecedented five gold medals (100-meter, 200-meter, long jump, 400-meter relay, and 800-meter relay) in the 2000 Olympic Games in Sydney, Australia. "There is no doubt in my mind that Marion can win all five events," says world champion sprinter Michael Johnson. "She certainly has the talent." ◆

Joyner-Kersee, Jacqueline

MARCH 3, 1962– ● TRACK AND FIELD ATHLETE

Born and raised in East St. Louis, Illinois, Jacqueline Joyner entered her first track and field competition at age nine. Five years later, she won the first four Amateur Athletic Union Junior Pentathlon championships. At Lincoln High School, she received All-American selections in basketball and track. Joyner graduated in the top 10 percent of her high school class and accepted a basketball scholarship to the University of California at Los Angeles (UCLA). A four-year starter for the Lady Bruins basketball team, she continued her track and field career, winning the National Collegiate Athletic

Association (NCAA) heptathlon title in 1982 and 1983. After winning the heptathlon at the 1984 U.S. Olympic Trials, Joyner won a silver medal at the Olympic Games in Los Angeles.

In 1986 Joyner married her coach, Bob Kersee. Later that year, at the Goodwill Games in Moscow, she set a world record in the heptathlon when she led all competitors with 7,148 points. Breaking the old mark by 200 points, Joyner-Kersee became the first American woman since 1936 to establish a multievent world record. That same year, she broke her own world record at the U.S. Olympic Sports Festival in Houston and won the Sullivan Memorial Trophy, awarded to America's top amateur athlete. At the 1987 World Track and Field Championships in Rome, Joyner-Kersee won the gold medal in both the long jump and heptathlon competitions and became the first woman to win gold medals in multisport and individual events at the same Olympic-level competition. She repeated this feat at the 1988 Olympics in Seoul, winning the long jump with an Olympic record leap of 24′ 3 1/2″ and the heptathlon with a new world record of 7,291 points.

Joyner-Kersee continued to dominate the heptathlon into the 1990s; she won at the 1990 Goodwill Games, the 1992 Olympics in Barcelona (where she also earned a bronze medal in the long jump), the 1993 World Championships, and, once again, at the Goodwill Games in 1994. At the 1994 USA/Mobil Outdoor Track and Field Championships, she won gold medals in the long jump and the 100-meter hurdles. Eager to provide inspiration and support for young people and women interested in athletics, she established the Jackie Joyner-Kersee Community Foundation in her home town of East St. Louis. In 1992 she was named Amateur Sports Woman of the Year by the Women's Sports Foundation.

Joyner-Kersee qualified for the 1996 Olympic team at age 34. She won a bronze medal in the individual long jump, but was forced to withdraw from the heptathlon after pulling a muscle. In 1997 Joyner-Kersee published her autobiography, *A Kind of Grace: The Autobiography of the World's Greatest Female Athlete.* ◆

1962 Joyner is born in East St. Louis, Illinois.

1987 Joyner-Kersee wins the heptathlon at the Pan American Games.

1988 Joyner-Kersee wins Olympic heptathlon gold at Seoul; sets world record of 7,291 points.

1992 Joyner-Kersee wins Olympic heptathlon gold at Barcelona.

1999 Joyner-Kersee is named Greatest Female Athlete of the Twentieth Century by *Sports Illustrated.*

"She's the greatest multi-event athlete ever, man or woman."

Bruce Jenner

Kaline, Al

DECEMBER 19, 1934– ● BASEBALL PLAYER

He never won a Most Valuable Player award. He never led the league in home runs or runs batted in. He won only one batting title in 22 seasons. But it didn't matter: Al Kaline is considered by many to be the steadiest, most consistent player of his generation.

Kaline was born in Baltimore on December 19, 1934. He played baseball well enough with his high school team that upon his graduation day, he signed with the Detroit Tigers. Amazingly, it took Kaline just one week in the minor leagues before he had convinced Detroit to take a chance on the youngster. He was activated when starting outfielder Steve Souchock broke his wrist, and only a few days into his starting role, Kaline threw runners out at second, third, and home in successive innings against the White Sox. At the age of just 19, Kaline started 135 games for a mediocre fifth-place ball club, and while scouts knew he was a terrific defensive player, they were surely unprepared for his offensive contributions. Although he struggled at times with the bat, Kaline managed a respectable .276 in his rookie campaign.

In his second season, the 20-year-old right fielder became the youngest man to lead the league in batting average (.340) and hits (200). Kaline led the Tigers to their first winning season in five years and finished second only to Yankees catcher Yogi Berra in MVP voting. He started the All-Star Game in the first of 16 All-Star appearances and was the youngest player to

"I don't deserve such a salary. I didn't have a good enough season last year. This ball club has been so fair and decent to me that I'd prefer to have you give it to me when I rate it."

Kaline, in a letter to Jim Campbell, Tiger's general manager, when offered the club's first $100,000 contract, 1971

appear in the Summer classic until 19-year old Mets pitcher Dwight Gooden appeared in 1984.

Kaline's consistency over the years made him one of the most popular players of his era and earned him the nickname "Mr. Tiger." He had 100 or more hits an amazing 18 times; hit 20 or more home runs nine times; hit .300 or better eight times; and was named *The Sporting News* Player of the Year twice. Both a power and a contact hitter, he nonetheless never struck out more than 75 times in a single season. He was also a stellar defensive right fielder, showing great range, an extremely dependable glove and a cannon arm, as his 10 Gold Glove Awards and his 242-game errorless streak in 1971–72 can attest. And he never left Detroit, making him one of the most beloved Tigers of all time.

Kaline was the hero of his only World Series appearance, against the St. Louis Cardinals in 1968, the "Year of the Pitcher." Down three games to one, the Tigers came back in Game Five when Kaline singled in the tying and go-ahead runs. In Game Six, he singled twice in the 10-run third inning as the Tigers trounced the Cards 13–1. He wound up leading the World Champions with a .379 batting average and eight runs batted in for the series. The victory was all the more sweet for Kaline, who earlier in the season had found himself on the disabled list for the first time in his career (Oakland Athletics pitcher Lew Krausse broke Kaline's arm with a wild pitch).

In 1974, Kaline needed 139 hits to reach 3,000 and became a full-time designated hitter, a switch some baseball traditionalists were none too happy about. Many felt that the outfielder was taking advantage of the DH rule—despite his deteriorating skills—solely in order to reach the 3,000 hit plateau. Indeed he did reach the milestone, retiring with 3,007 hits along with 399 home runs. Kaline's uniform number 6 was taken out of circulation by the Detroit Tigers when he was elected to the Hall of Fame in 1980. ◆

1934 Kaline is born in Baltimore, Maryland.

1968 Kaline leads the Tigers to a World Series victory with a .379 batting average.

1974 Kaline retires with 3,007 hits, 399 home runs.

1980 Kaline is inducted into the Baseball Hall of Fame.

King, Betsy

Aᴜɢᴜsᴛ 13, 1955– ● Gᴏʟꜰᴇʀ

Betsy King is well known not only for her success as a professional golfer—as of 1998 she ranked number one in career earnings with over $6 million—but for her humanitarian efforts throughout the 1990s.

Born in Reading, Pennsylvania, King first tasted success on the golf course in 1972, when she was a semifinalist in the USGA Junior Girls Championship. She took her skills to Furman University in South Carolina, where her team won the National Collegiate Championship in 1976, the same year she posted the low amateur score at the U.S. Women's Open. Combining success on the course with excellence in the classroom (she majored in physical education), she was named Furman's Athlete of the Year and Woman Scholar Athlete of the Year in 1977.

King joined the professional tour in 1977. Her career exemplified the value of persistence, for she did not win an event for seven years. She finally broke through with her first career tournament win in the 1984 Women's Kemper Open. With that win she began a six-year run of 20 tournament titles, making her the winningest professional golfer between 1984 and 1989.

In 1984 she went on to win the Freedom Orlando Classic and the Columbia Savings Classic, along the way earning *Golf Digest*'s Most Improved Player award and recognition as Rolex Player of the Year. In 1985 she won the Samaritan Turquoise Classic and the Rail Charity Classic, posting in the latter a career-low round of 63 (a feat she later tied in the 1990 JAL Big Apple Classic). In 1986 she won the Henredon Classic and defended her Rail Charity Classic title. In 1987 she captured the Tucson Open, the McDonald's Championship, and the Atlantic City Classic, but the highlight of that year was winning the Nabisco Dinah Shore after sinking a bunker shot on the 70th hole to put her into a sudden-death playoff against Patty Sheehan. She also won the Vare Trophy with an average round score of 71.14.

In 1988 King won the Women's Kemper Open, the Cellular One-Ping Golf Championship, and repeated as the Rail Charity Classic winner. With 1989 wins in the Jamaica Classic, the

King was named Furman's Athlete of the Year and Woman Scholar Athlete of the Year in 1977.

1955 King is born in Reading, Pennsylvania.

1987 King wins the Tucson Open and the Nabisco Dinah Shore title.

1989 King becomes the first player in LPGA history to pass $500,000 and $600,000 in single-season earnings; she is named LPGA Rolex Player of the Year.

1990 King wins U.S. Open and the Nabisco Dinah Shore title.

1995 King is the first player in LPGA history to pass $5 million in career earnings.

Women's Kemper Open, the USX Golf Classic, the McDonald's Championship, the Nestle World Championship, and the U.S. Women's Open, King became the first player in Ladies Professional Golf Association (LPGA) history to surpass both the $500,000 and $600,000 mark in single-season earnings. That year she shot 33 rounds in the 60s and had 20 top-10 finishes (out of 25 tournament starts).

The awards piled up in 1989: King repeated as the LPGA's Rolex Player of the Year award (an award she would capture for the third time in 1993), won the Founders Cup and *Golf Digest*'s Mickey Wright Award, and was named *Golf World*'s Player of the Year and the Golf Writers Association of America Female Player of the Year.

King's enormous success continued in the 1990s. She repeated as U.S. Women's Open champion and won back her Nabisco Dinah Shore title in 1990, as well as winning the JAL Big Apple Classic, recording 13 top-10 finishes during the year (and two holes-in-one). In 1991 she won the LPGA Corning Classic and defended her JAL Big Apple Classic title. In 1992 she totaled 14 top-10 finishes, including wins in the Phar-Mor tournament, the Mazda Japan Classic, and the Mazda LPGA Championship—an event in which she became the first player in LPGA history to record four rounds in the 60s in a major tournament (68–66–67–66). In 1993 King totaled 15 top-10 finishes, including five times as runner-up (one a sudden-death loss to Brandie Burton in the du Maurier Ltd. Classic) and a win in the Toray Japan Queens Cup. That year King also captured her second Vare Trophy.

Although she recorded 11 top-10 finishes in 1994, it marked the first time in a decade that she was without a win. But in 1995 King erased the relative disappointments of 1994 when she recorded her thirtieth tournament win at the ShopRite LPGA Classic, earning her membership in the LPGA Hall of Fame. That year, too, she became the first player in LPGA history to cross the $5 million mark in career earnings. In 1997 she earned her 31st career victory, repeating as Nabisco Dinah Shore winner and joining Amy Alcott as the only two players ever to have won the same major championship three times. King was also a member of the 1990, 1992, 1994, 1996, and 1998 Solheim Cup teams.

As if the rigors of the professional tour were not enough, King is also a noteworthy humanitarian. In 1987 she won the Samaritan Award, which acknowledges humanitarian and charitable efforts by a player. She was active in the LPGA

Christian Fellowship, and organized Habitat for Humanity house-building projects in Phoenix, Arizona, in 1993 and in Charlotte, North Carolina, in 1995. After the 1993 and 1994 seasons she joined a group of players working with an orphan relief organization in Romania. ◆

King, Billie Jean

NOVEMBER 22, 1943– ● TENNIS PLAYER

One of the most celebrated tennis players in history, Billie Jean King established herself as a trailblazer who is famous the world over for spearheading the women's movement in tennis and for her life-long struggle for equality in women's tennis.

Billie Jean Moffit was born on November 22, 1943, in Long Beach, California. In her early years, she was an exceptional softball player, yet she realized that there was no future for a woman in softball. Her parents introduced her to the world of tennis, the game that would change her life and the lives of many others.

Billie Jean later married Larry King on September 9, 1965, adding the famous component to her name, a title that would almost become appropriate in the years to follow. By the time she was only 34, King had already won 20 Wimbledon titles, six of them in singles competition, won the US Open four times, won the French Open, and the Australian Open. She had ranked in the Top 10 a total of 17 years. In her overall career she has won 71 singles titles, including 12 Grand Slam singles titles.

Aside from her victories on the court, King has helped women to triumph. In 1973, she won a "Battle of the Sexes" match, defeating Bobby

1943 King is born in Long Beach, California.

1966 King wins Wimbledon (also in 1967, 1968, 1972, 1973, and 1975).

1967 King wins the U.S. Open (also in 1971, 1972, and 1974).

1973 King beats Bobby Riggs in the "Battle of Sexes."

1997 King publishes her autobiography, *Billie Jean.*

1999 King is ranked third on *Sports Illustrated's* list of the 100 Greatest Female Athletes of the Twentieth Century.

Riggs in a national television event at Houston's Astrodome that still holds the record for most people to attend a single tennis match with 30,472 fans eagerly watching. Riggs had been baiting King for years, saying that she should stay home, barefoot and pregnant. But she proved him wrong and became the first female athlete to win over $100,000 in prize money in a single season.

She also spoke out for women and their right to earn comparable money in tennis and other sports. Her consistent lobbying has literally "paid" off breaking down many of the discriminating barriers for women in the world of sports. "We still have a long, long way to go," King said recently about the improvements in women's sports. "We need sponsors who believe in women's tennis to understand there's a vision, that they'll really get a bang for their buck."

But while she was winning battles for women, another storm was brewing. After divorcing her husband in the late 1980s, she kept "King" in her name, but knew she hadn't told her fans the whole truth. Late in her career King came out reluctantly, disclosing her homosexuality to little enthusiasm from crowds and sponsors and causing her to lose millions of dollars. "I felt lonely a lot," she says of those pivotal years. "It wasn't easy being always out front."

King decided to try her hand at coaching and in 1974 became the first woman to coach a professional team with men when serving as player/coach for the Philadelphia Freedom of World Team Tennis.

In 1990, Life magazine named King one of the "100 Most Important Americans of the 20th Century." And in 1994, she ranked No. 5 on the *Sports Illustrated* "Top 40 Athletes" list in the "40th Year Anniversary" issue for significantly altering or elevating sports in the last four decades.

Now, at the age of 56, King continues to share her strength by promoting tournaments and tennis exhibitions, as well as serving on the board of directors for the Elton John AIDS Foundation, the National AIDS Fund the Women's Sports Foundation and her own group (The Billie Jean King Foundation). She also does tennis commentary for HBO and is the captain of the US Fed Cup team.

In a recent interview, King talked about her commitments to young athletes. "I want to inspire young tennis players . . . to gain the qualities that they need to meet all of life's challenges head-on," says the tennis superstar. And she's certainly pre-

"A champion is afraid of losing. Everyone else is afraid of winning."

Billie Jean King

pared for the future. "I'm getting happier every year," she recently told Women's Sports and Fitness. "I'm not totally there yet, but at least I'm going in the right direction." ◆

Korbut, Olga

MAY 16, 1956– ● GYMNAST

Olga Valentinova Korbut was born in Hrodna, Belarus, on May 16, in either 1955 or 1956 (sources vary). At that time, Belarus was called Belarussia, a satellite of the Soviet Union. The youngest of four daughters born to Valentin, an engineer, and Valentina, a cook, Korbut showed exceptional athletic ability while in elementary school. One of her sisters, Ludmilla, was an accomplished gymnast, having earned the coveted title "Master of Sport." Her example helped Korbut to focus her talent on gymnastics.

Olga Korbut on the balance beam.

1956 Korbut is born in Hrodna, Belarus (in former USSR).

1971 Korbut wins the Master of Sports title after Soviet national championships.

1972 Korbut wins Olympic gold in floor exercises and balance beam at Munich while the USSR wins team event gold; Korbut is the youngest gymnast ever to be named Honored Master of Sport by USSR.

1991 Korbut emigrates to the United States and settles in Atlanta.

In that era, the Soviet Union placed a premium on identifying potential stand-out athletes at an early age. The government would then provide them with the intensive training and other resources necessary to help them excel, and triumph, in competitive international athletics. The system produced many world-class gymnasts.

Olga Korbut became a beneficiary of this training system at age eight. She tried out for a place in a highly prestigious "sports school," run by Renald Kynsh, and was eventually accepted.

The relationship between Kynsh and the young gymnast was strained from the start. Kynsh was a quiet man who found it hard to discipline the headstrong and exuberant Korbut. Yet she flourished in the demanding environment of the school. She learned quickly and worked hard.

After several years, Kynsh took over as Korbut's personal coach. He urged her to be daring, to incorporate more innovative moves and elements into her gymnastics. Though the two argued fiercely, Korbut excelled at the sport. In 1967 and 1968, she won important junior championships, competing against some of the Soviet Union's best young gymnasts.

When she was 14, Korbut was given special permission to compete in senior gymnastic competitions. Usually one had to be at least 16 to participate in those competitions, but after seeing Korbut perform, the head coach of the Soviet women's gymnastics team interceded on her behalf. Korbut thus participated in her first national Soviet championship in 1969. She did not receive any medals there, placing fifth. However, she unveiled several spectacular new moves at the competition: the Korbut Salto, a backward aerial somersault on the balance beam; and the Korbut Flip, a backflip to a catch on the uneven bars.

In 1970, Korbut came in eighth in the Soviet national championships. The Soviet team took her along as a reserve gymnast to the world championships that year. There, Korbut impressed the judges but failed to rack up high marks.

Fighting an ankle injury and illness, Korbut was out of competition for most of 1971. However, she managed to come in fourth at the 1971 Soviet national championships. In that year, Korbut was granted the "Master of Sports" title.

The 1972 Munich Olympics were looming, and Korbut was busy in preparation. She trained relentlessly. She unveiled another new move, the Korbut flic-flac, on the balance beam, at the Riga Cup. Around this time she also graduated from secondary school, one of her biggest goals.

The Soviet Union Cup competition would determine who would be on the women's gymnastics team for the Munich Olympics. There was a startling upset: Korbut defeated Ludmilla Tourischeva, the favorite to win, and captured the cup. That gave Korbut the right to be captain of the team, but she left that honor to Tourischeva.

From the start of the Olympics gymnastics competition, Korbut was in the limelight. She did well in the compulsories but really caught fire in the team optionals, winning the hearts of the audience with her charm as well as her athleticism. Korbut performed respectably in the vault, but with her routine on the uneven bars, the world knew it had a new sports star. Her routine included the Korbut Flip and ended with a back somersault in the layout position. Korbut landed with a huge smile. In her final event that evening, she performed a back Salto on the balance beam, with a front Salto **dismount**—another eye-opener.

The next competition was for the Individual All-Around title. Korbut did well on the vault and the floor exercise, but she faltered on the uneven bars. Upon dismounting, she ran to the sidelines and cried. Audiences around the world were moved by her disappointment, but the judges were not: Korbut was out of the running for a medal in the All-Around.

The competition for individual medals—the pinnacle of the Olympics gymnastics events—was held the following day. Korbut regained her equilibrium and triumphed, winning the gold medals in the balance beam and the floor exercise. But she came in second, winning the silver medal, for her performance on the uneven bars. (When the judges released their score of 9.8, the audience thought it should be higher. The crowd protested so vigorously that the competition was delayed for 25 minutes.)

Korbut's emotional athleticism, so different from the grim, all-business appearances of other Soviet gymnasts, won her millions of fans. The gold medalist was a sensation around the world. In the Soviet Union, she was named "Honoured Master of Sport" in gymnastics, the youngest person so honored. Korbut's exhibition tours with the Soviet gymnastics team in Europe and the United States were sold out.

Over the next several years, Korbut traveled the world, appearing in such international venues as the World University Games of 1973 and Expo '74. Her relationship with trainer Renald Knysh, however, was in trouble, and she began working with other coaches. (Later she would accuse him of having ex-

"I didn't care what the judges thought. I performed for the people."
Olga Korbut

dismount: in gymnastics, the dismount is the move gymnasts make to end their routine by leaving the apparatus they are on, such as the balance beam, uneven bars, rings, and others.

Korbut was
named captain
of the Soviet
women's gym-
nastics team for
the Montreal
Olympics of
1976.

ploited her sexually, a charge he fiercely denied.) Injuries, which had slowed her down occasionally in the past, plagued her in 1975 and 1976.

Korbut was named captain of the Soviet women's gymnastics team for the Montreal Olympics of 1976, but her performance was far overshadowed by that of Romanian dynamo Nadia Comanechi. Korbut won only a single individual medal, a silver on the balance beam.

In 1977, still in her early twenties, Korbut retired from gymnastics competition. She graduated from college and began teaching gymnastics, and she married Leonid Borkevitch in 1978. The following year, Korbut gave birth to a son, Richard. She still occasionally performed in gymnastics exhibitions, but she also indulged other interests, becoming a nationally ranked equestrienne in the Soviet Union as well as a gymnastics television commentator. After the nuclear disaster at Chernobyl, Korbut used her celebrity to help raise money for the victims. In 1991, Korbut and her family emigrated to the United States, settling in Atlanta, Georgia. ◆

Koufax, Sandy

DECEMBER 30, 1935– ● BASEBALL PLAYER

Though his baseball career lasted a relatively short 12 seasons, in his prime Sandy Koufax is considered the most dominant left-handed pitcher the game has ever seen.

Koufax was born Sanford Braun on December 30, 1935, in Brooklyn. He took the name of his stepfather, Irving Koufax, when he was three. As a youth Koufax played a variety of sports in the Jewish community centers where he spent his time, excelling most in basketball.

Koufax was a good enough basketball player that he attended the University of Cincinnati on a basketball scholarship, with plans to become an architect. After averaging 9.7 points for the freshman basketball team, Koufax decided to tryout for the varsity baseball team. A 6′ 2″, 215-pound weak-hitting first baseman in high school, Koufax, who was blessed with enormous hands and long fingers, transformed himself into a spectacular pitcher, striking out 51 batters in just 32 innings.

His mound exploits attracted the attention of a scout from his hometown Brooklyn Dodgers, and at the age of 19, Koufax made it into major league baseball. His $14,000 signing bonus reflected both his potential on the mound and at the box office, where it was thought the young, attractive player would be a big draw.

Though he showed amazing potential, keeping batters off-balance with a blazing fastball and darting curveball, Koufax was plagued by control troubles. Because of the rules of baseball at the time, Koufax could not be sent back to the minor leagues, forcing him to learn to pitch at the major league level. Not unexpectedly for a player with such little experience, the first six seasons of his career were downright ordinary. Entering the 1961 season, Koufax had 36 career wins against 40 losses and had allowed 405 walks in 691 $2/3$rd innings pitched. With his career at a crossroads in the spring of 1961—the Dodgers, who had moved to Los Angeles in 1958, had cut his salary following an 8–13 season—Koufax luckily heeded the advice of a teammate. Backup catcher Norm Sherry told the young pitcher to just concentrate on getting every pitch over the plate and to forget trying to "break the sound barrier" with his fast pitches. Suddenly everything clicked for the young hurler.

That season, Koufax led the league in strikeouts with 269 and was named to his first All-Star team. In 1962, Koufax's team moved into spacious Dodger Stadium, and Koufax really began to flourish, posting a 2.54 earned run average, notching 14 wins, and making another All-Star appearance before missing the final three-and-a-half months of the season with a circulation problem. But that season also marked the beginning of one of the most-dominant five-year pitching performances in Major League history. From 1962 to 1966, Koufax racked up an astounding 111–34 win-loss record (a .766 winning percentage), with a miniscule 2.02 earned-run average (ERA).

In 1963, Koufax was close to unstoppable, leading the National League with 25 wins (against just five losses), a stunning 1.88 ERA, and 366 strikeouts. That performance not only earned Koufax the pitcher's Triple Crown (the league's leading player in wins, ERA, and strikeouts), but both the National League's Most Valuable Player award and the Cy Young Award,

1935 Koufax is born as Sanford Braun in Brooklyn, New York.

1955 Koufax signs with the Brooklyn Dodgers at age 19.

1961 Koufax leads the National League in strikeouts and is named to the All-Star team.

1963 Koufax wins pitcher's Triple Crown (again in 1966), National League Most Valuable Player, and the Cy Young Award (again in 1965 and 1966).

1965 Koufax pitches a perfect game against the Chicago Cubs; for the season, he sets a record with 382 strike-outs

1966 Koufax retires at age 30.

1972 At 36, Koufax is the youngest player elected to the Baseball Hall of Fame.

"A guy who throws what he intends to throw—that's the definition of a good pitcher."

Sandy Koufax

Yom Kippur: the holiest day of the Jewish year, it is observed with fasting and prayer.

given to the outstanding pitcher in the major leagues (today it is given to the best pitcher in each league).

Over the next three seasons, Koufax lead the league in ERA each year, while twice leading the National League in strike-outs, wins, innings pitched, and complete games. He also pitched three no-hitters, including a perfect game in 1965. (For his career, Koufax pitched four total no-hitters, a record at the time.) Koufax was awarded the Cy Young again in 1965 and 1966 for his heroics on the mound, which included again cap-turing the Triple Crown of pitching in each season. In 1965, Koufax set a record for strikeouts with 382, which was later bro-ken by Nolan Ryan by only one strikeout.

Koufax, a deeply principled man, is often best remembered for refusing to pitch in Game 1 of the 1965 World Series, which fell on **Yom Kippur**, the holiest day in the Jewish year. His teammates, however, respected and supported his convictions, especially after he led the team to the title by shutting out the Minnesota Twins in both Game 5 and 7. Overall, appearing in eight games over four Fall Classics, Koufax posted a 0.95 ERA.

While diving for a ball late in the 1964 season, Koufax fell on his left elbow, aggravating the arthritis that was developing in that crucial joint. Despite his strong statistics over the next three seasons, the pain in his elbow just kept getting worse. Af-ter winning his third Cy Young with a 27–9 record and 1.73 ERA in 1966, the pain in his arm had become too much to bear, and Koufax sought the advice of doctors, who told him that he might lose the use of his arm if he kept playing.

In November of 1966, the 30-year-old lefty stunned the baseball world by announcing his retirement. With a lifetime winning percentage of .655, Koufax easily gained entry into the Baseball Hall of Fame in 1972. At the age of 36, he was the youngest player ever to be enshrined in Cooperstown.

In 1999, Koufax was honored again when he was selected as the starting left-handed pitcher on baseball's All-Century Team. ESPN chose the hurler as the 42nd best North American ath-lete of the century and *Baseball Digest* picked him as the 18th best baseball player of the last 100 years. As Pittsburgh Pirates Hall-of-Famer Willie Stargell once said, "Hitting against Sandy Koufax is like drinking coffee with a fork." ◆

Krone, Julie

JULY 24, 1963– ● JOCKEY

A fter Julie Krone had galloped to victory at the Belmont Stakes in 1993, a reporter asked her how it felt to be the first woman to win a Triple Crown race. She responded, "I don't think that the question should be genderized." Indeed, Krone's career accomplishments as a jockey leave most of her male competitors in the dust. The only woman ever to break into the front ranks of horse racing, Krone amassed 3,543 career victories and climbed to 16th on the all-time earnings list before a string of injuries forced her to retire in April 1999.

Thanks to Krone's talent and drive, women jockeys are now a common sight at America's race tracks. But before 1968,

Julie Krone rode to over 3,500 victories during her career.

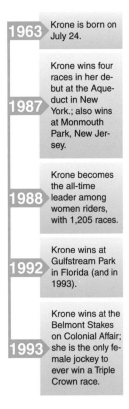

1963 Krone is born on July 24.

1987 Krone wins four races in her debut at the Aqueduct in New York.; also wins at Monmouth Park, New Jersey.

1988 Krone becomes the all-time leader among women riders, with 1,205 races.

1992 Krone wins at Gulfstream Park in Florida (and in 1993).

1993 Krone wins at the Belmont Stakes on Colonial Affair; she is the only female jockey to ever win a Triple Crown race.

women were barred from horse racing, and it was only with Krone's debut more than a decade later that male dominance of the field was significantly challenged. Julieann Louise Krone was literally born to her destiny as a pioneer woman jockey. She grew up on a spacious farm near Eau Claire, Michigan, where her mother, a horse enthusiast, instilled a love of horses and riding in Julie from the age of two: When Mrs. Krone put her daughter on a horse that began to trot away, with the aplomb of a future champion Julie grabbed the reins and turned the horse back. It wasn't long before young Julie was an accomplished equestrian, garnering prizes at various Michigan horse shows, including a first-place finish at a major show when she was only 12.

With her diminutive stature (at her adult peak she was four feet, ten and a half inches tall and weighed 100 pounds) and passion for horses, Julie knew that racing was in her future, especially after she spent a summer spent as a morning workout rider at Churchill Downs, home of the Kentucky Derby. The following fall, when she was only 16, she began entering races near her Michigan home, and she was hooked. Within a few weeks she had dropped out of high school and set out for her grandparents' Florida home, near the Tampa Bay Downs track, to attempt to earn her first chance at a professional race. On January 30, 1980, she got her shot, and a little over a month later she had her first win. She quickly racked up nine more victories, attracting the attention of an agent who steered her to the prestigious Pimlico track in Baltimore, the home of the Preakness.

Her initial successes notwithstanding, at first Krone found very few takers for her services as she made her way around the eastern circuit trying to prove her mettle. By 1982 her record was impressive enough to break down the racing community's clubby resistance to a woman jockey: 155 victories and purses worth $1 million at Atlantic City alone in one year, earning her top honors at that track. On the brink of stardom, Krone was caught smoking marijuana and was suspended from racing for two months. More determined than ever to capitalize on her opportunities in the face of this setback, Krone came roaring back to another title at the Atlantic City track in 1983. A nasty spill, however, resulted in a broken back, but the determined Krone she was back in the saddle four months later.

Krone began to branch out from Atlantic City to several other New Jersey tracks, and a long string of successes led her, in 1987, to a shot at New York's prestigious Aqueduct, where she rode to four victories in her debut. Krone was now approaching the upper echelons of the nation's jockeys: her 324 victories in 1987 made her the nation's sixth-winningest jockey, and in 1988 she became the all-time leader among women riders with 1,205 races.

The next few years brought her still closer to the top: she won the annual title at Monmouth Park in 1989, but in November of that year she was thrown from her mount and suffered a severe fracture of her left arm. The indefatigable Krone again rebounded quickly, though, placing among the top 10 jockeys of 1990.

Despite all her success, Krone was unable to crack a Triple Crown race until 1991, when she became the first woman to ride in the Belmont Stakes. That race was the scene of one of her greatest triumphs when, in 1993, she guided Colonial Affair to a first-place finish and became the first woman to win a Triple Crown race. Shortly thereafter, however, her career almost came to a tragically early end. On August 30, 1993, Krone was in the middle of a pack during a race at Saratoga when her horse buckled and threw her to the track. Her right ankle was nearly destroyed—the repair required two plates and 14 screws—and she suffered severe lacerations of an already-injured elbow and a cardiac **contusion**. Her physician commented, "This is not a typical athletic injury. It is more like what you see in a car or plane accident."

But Krone refused to let the injury end her career. In only nine months she was racing again, but her performance never rose to her previous levels. Nevertheless, she stubbornly persisted in the face of pain. "It's a passion for riding race horses and being in the winner circle," she said. "I can't emphasize enough that now I know how dangerous it is. I'm willing to make that trade-off."

Only five months later Krone paid the price of her passion again. In 1995 in a race at Gulfstream Park, a spill caused hand injuries so severe that Krone's confidence finally buckled, and this time she needed a psychiatrist to help her find her way back to the track. Although she eventually returned to racing, her bodily and psychic injuries had taken their toll. She just wasn't the same Julie Krone. On Sunday, April 18, 1999, she rode in her last professional race at Lone Star Park in Grand Prairie, Texas, ending an 18-year career in which she attained a unique distinction for a woman athlete: competing head-on against men and emerging as one of the best in her sport. ◆

"I don't want to the be the best female jockey in the world; I want to be the best jockey."
Julie Krone

contusion: a bruise or other injury to the skin that does not involve a cut.

LaMotta, Jake

JULY 10, 1921– ● BOXER

The Academy Award winning 1980 film *Raging Bull* is considered by many to be the best movie of all time. Based on a 1970 book of the same name, it tells the life story of Jake LaMotta, a pugnacious, stubborn middleweight boxing champion in the 1940s and 1950s whose life outside the ring was marred by association with street thugs and organized crime figures. His career in the ring is remembered for his violent fury. His rage was coupled with a granite chin that allowed him to absorb flurries of punches, making him virtually unstoppable in the ring.

Giacobe (Jake) LaMotta was born on July 10, 1921, in the Bronx, New York. He began boxing at an early age when his father made him fight other neighborhood kids to entertain the local adults who threw coins. It helped to pay the poor LaMotta family's rent. The tough streets of the Bronx did nothing to put the young LaMotta on a straight and narrow path, and after hundreds of street fights and several run-ins with the law, he was sent to reform school, where he further developed his fighting skills. In 1941, at the age of 19, LaMotta turned pro. In those days, professional boxing was a crooked, savage world, controlled by organized crime figures.

LaMotta's unrelenting style, in which he lowered his head and plowed forward, throwing punch after punch, earned him the nickname "the Bronx Bull." In his first year as a professional, he won 14 of his first 15 fights, three by knockout, with one draw. Fighting mostly out of his native New York, LaMotta

"Raging Bull" Jake LaMotta.

continued to work his way up in the rankings over the next year.

LaMotta is best remembered for his six fights with Sugar Ray Robinson, considered by many to be the best middleweight of all time. The fights contrasted two dissimilar styles, with LaMotta the ultimate brawler, a boxer with a street fighter's mentality, and the smooth Robinson, renowned for his speed and grace in the ring. They met for the first time in New York on October 2, 1942. LaMotta had compiled a record of 25 wins, 4 losses and 2 draws to that point. Robinson, was undefeated, and remained so, winning a 10-round decision.

LaMotta continued fighting top-ranked opponents over the next several months, winning five bouts, three by knockout, before meeting Robinson again four months later. In 41 pro fights, and 80 amateur bouts, Robinson had never lost, but in Detroit on February 5, 1943, LaMotta, with his crouched style, face and fists forward, became the first man to beat the "invincible" Robinson, taking a 10-round decision. The two met again three weeks later in Detroit again, and this time Robinson controlled the fight, except for a seventh round LaMotta blow which left him dazed. Robinson recovered and won by decision.

LaMotta won most of his bouts between 1943 and 1947, bringing his record to 61 wins, 10 losses and 3 draws at the end of 1946. Seventeen of his wins had been by knockout. He continued to fight a slew of top-ranked opponents, in weight classes ranging from welterweight to light heavyweight. His nemesis continued to be Robinson, whom he fought twice in 1945, losing a 10-round decision in New York on February 23, and a 12-rounder in Chicago on September 26.

Despite LaMotta's world ranking in 1947, the underworld figures that controlled boxing refused to give him a shot at the middleweight title unless he agreed to take a dive against a fighter named Billy Fox. Fight fixing, although illegal, was fairly common in those days. Using threats or coercion, hoodlums got fighters to lose on purpose, and knowing the fight's outcome in advance, they bet on his opponent. LaMotta desperately wanted a shot at the middleweight title. He had a wife and children and feared getting older without ever getting his chance at a title and a big payday. He put his pride aside and agreed to the fix. To that point, he had never lost by knockout, but on November 14, 1947, with a promise of a title shot, LaMotta went down on purpose in the fourth round against Fox.

Even so, it took another year and a half before LaMotta got a title shot, and he had to pay money under the table to get it. Despite the shady circumstances, he made the most of his chance with a technical knockout of middleweight champion Marcel Cerdan on June 16, 1949, in Detroit. The two never met for a rematch because Cerdan tragically died in a plane crash soon after. In 1950, LaMotta successfully defended his title against Tiberio Mitri and Laurent Dauthuille. LaMotta was losing the September 13, 1950, bout with Dauthuille, who had beaten him the year before, but he staged a miraculous 15th round knockout to retain his title. The bout was voted *Ring Magazine*'s fight of the year.

LaMotta's reign as middleweight champion came to an end on February 14, 1951, in Chicago Stadium, against his dreaded foe Ray Robinson. It is one of boxing's most famous fights. Determined not to lose, a bloodied and battered LaMotta absorbed a tremendous beating, refusing to fall. The referee stopped the fight in the 13th round, and Sugar Ray Robinson took over as middleweight champion. But the fight was testament to LaMotta's incredible will. He lost his title, but salvaged a personal victory by staying on his feet.

LaMotta fought through 1952, was inactive in 1953, and retired after three fights in 1954. His final record in 106 bouts, was 83 wins, 19 losses and 4 draws, with 30 knockouts. He was inducted into the International Boxing Hall of Fame in 1990. In 1998, tragedy struck LaMotta twice: first, his son Jake LaMotta, Jr. died from cancer; then, just seven months later, son Joe LaMotta was one of 229 people killed in a Swissair plane crash off Nova Scotia, Canada. LaMotta, who also has four daughters, lives in New York City, where he occasionally does stand-up comedy. ◆

1921 Giacobe "Jake" LaMotta is born in the Bronx, New York City.

1942 LaMotta loses his first match against Sugar Ray Robinson.

1943 LaMotta beats the "invincible" Robinson in the tenth round.

1949 LaMotta regains the middleweight title with a TKO of Marcel Cerdan.

1950 LaMotta retains his title with a fifteenth round knockout of Laurent Dauthuille.

1951 LaMotta loses final match against Robinson.

1990 LaMotta is inducted into the International Boxing Hall of Fame.

Lasorda, Tommy

SEPTEMBER 22, 1927– ● BASEBALL PLAYER AND MANAGER

One of the most colorful and recognizable figures in the history of baseball, Tommy Lasorda spent 47 years with the Brooklyn and Los Angeles Dodgers, including 20 seasons as the team's highly successful manager.

Born in Norristown, Pennsylvania, outside of Philadelphia, Lasorda spent many years in the Dodgers' farm system as a left-handed relief pitcher. After a brief and unsuccessful stint in the major leagues, Lasorda decided he might be better suited to coaching. He managed for a number of years in the Dodgers' minor league system, slowly working his way up until he became the protégé of Dodgers' legendary manager Walter Alston. When Alston retired following the 1976 season, Lasorda was named manager and turned in a stellar debut season, leading the Dodgers to the National League pennant behind a 98–64 record. Although the Yankees trounced the Dodgers in six games, thanks to Reggie Jackson's heroics, Lasorda brought the Dodgers back to the Series the following year—an unprecedented feat for a young manager. The Dodgers lost to the Yankees again in 1978, but Lasorda got his first World Series victory in 1981 when the Dodgers upset the Yankees in six games. It was the club's first world championship since 1965.

Lasorda was an advocate of good pitching and defense, and the Dodger teams of the 1980s always competed for the National League's Western Division title. Assembling a pitching staff that included the pudgy lefthander Fernando Valenzuela, the bullish righty Orel Hershiser and the seasoned veteran Bob Welch, Lasorda turned in winning seasons year after year and steered the focal point of the game to the mound and away from the bat.

Lasorda led the Dodgers to their second title in 1988, as they beat the New York Mets in seven games for the pennant and then swept the powerful Oakland Athletics. With great pitching by Hershiser, who set the consecutive scoreless innings record earlier that year, and Kirk Gibson's memorable Game One homer—when he limped around the bases barely able to walk—the Dodgers victory was as dramatic as they come. Lasorda was named Manager of the Year for his leadership and

1927 Lasorda is born in Norristown, Pennsylvania.

1976 Lasorda leads the Dodgers to a National League pennant.

1977 Lasorda's Dodgers return to the World Series, but lose to the New York Yankees.

1981 Lasorda's Dodgers beat the Yankees in the World Series, their first championship since 1965.

1988 The Dodgers sweep the Oakland A's in the World Series; Lasorda is named Manager of the Year.

1997 Lasorda is elected to the Baseball Hall of Fame.

Gibson and Hershiser were named Most Valuable Player and Cy Young Award winners, respectively.

Lasorda managed the Dodgers until 1996, when a heart attack led to his retirement. He left baseball as only the fourth manager to guide the same team for 20 seasons. During his long tenure, Lasorda won 1,600 ball games, eight division titles, four pennants, and two World Series. He also managed four All Star Games and is currently the Dodgers' Front Office Vice President. Beloved in Los Angeles and known throughout America as the national spokesman for SlimFast, Lasorda was elected to the Baseball Hall of Fame in 1997. ◆

> *"You can plant two thousand rows of corn with the fertilizer Lasorda spreads around."*
>
> Joe Garagiola

Laver, Rod

AUGUST 9, 1938– ● TENNIS PLAYER

Rod Laver was born in the town of Queensland, Australia, on August 9, 1938. The redhead began hitting balls on a nearby court at an early age. His father soon recognized his talent and took him to a tennis clinic run by the late Harry Hopman, a renowned tennis coach at the time. Hopman called his young student "the Rocket," a nickname that would follow Laver throughout his career.

During his youth, Laver was known for his sharp forehand, which was considered much more essential than his backhand. But his first coach, Charlie Hollis, eventually helped him to become of the first left-handed players to roll his backhand, making it a more important part of his tennis game. With his 5'8" build, Laver was one of the shortest tennis players in the history of the game, but that didn't stop him from becoming a physical powerhouse.

When he was only 17, Laver appeared at England's highest tennis championship, Wimbledon, for the first time. But Italian champion Orlando Sirola won with a significant lead over Laver. Three years later Laver reached the finals for the first time, but lost again—this time to Alex Olmedo.

Laver decided that he would not be discouraged by these losses. In 1961, he was ready to take charge of his game. His intensely competitive nature on the court was helping him win matches, and he managed to cinch Wimbledon just before his

> *"When he is in a tough spot, Laver doesn't in any way retreat. He gets bolder and bolder and uses his wide range of shots without fear. He has sheer bravery and a beautiful sense of play."*
>
> C. M. Jones on Rod Laver

1938 Laver is born in Queensland, Australia.

1960 Laver wins Australian Open (again in 1962 and 1969).

1961 Laver wins Wimbledon (and again in 1962, 1968, and 1969).

1962 While still ranked as an amateur, Laver wins the Grand Slam and the U.S. Open.

1969 Laver wins wins the Grand Slam which now includes the U.S. Open.

23rd birthday. He followed up this amazing feat in 1962 by winning the Grand Slam—which at the time consisted of Wimbledon, the French Open, and the Australian Open; the U.S. Open was considered an amateur competition—the highest achievement in tennis.

Unfortunately, the rules of amateur vs. professional tennis at that time prevented Laver from returning to the courts until 1968. But he came back with a bang, winning the U.S. Open—now considered a professional Grand Slam event—at the age of 30. The following year he went on to become the only man to win Grand Slam tennis with the inclusion of the U.S. Open as one of the four competitions. A tireless leader, Laver also led Australia to defeat the United States 5–0 in the Davis Cup in 1973. Out of his 50 singles games played at Wimbledon, Laver was able to win 43, a record that would make him a legend in his own time.

After retiring from competitive tennis in 1977, the married father of one decided he would try his hand at coaching. Though he had become the first tennis player to earn over a million dollars in prize money, what mattered to Laver was that he continued to teach passion for the game that he loved. ◆

LeMond, Greg

JUNE, 26 1961– ● BICYCLIST

> *"The most important decision I ever made in my career was to live my life in sports as honestly and ethically as possible."*
>
> Greg LeMond

Before Greg LeMond, only one American had ever attempted bicycling's most prestigious race, the Tour de France. In fact, no American had ever won a major European cycling race. LeMond put America on the cycling map, dominating the sport in the 1980s, including three Tour de France wins. His last Tour de France victory, in 1990, came after an improbable comeback from a hunting accident that nearly killed him.

Greg LeMond was born on June 26, 1961, in Lakewood, California. Before his tenth birthday, his family settled down near Reno, Nevada, where LeMond's first love was skiing. He took up biking as an offseason activity, and fell in love with the sport. At 14, he entered his first club race on his ten-speed bike, and beat the older, more experienced riders, most of whom rode professional bikes. He quickly ascended to the top of the local race circuit, winning the first 11 events he entered.

In 1977, LeMond was racing on the junior circuit, but some events gave permission for him to compete with the older, more physically developed seniors. His first senior race was the three-day Tour of Fresno in central California, which included members of the powerful Exxon racing team led by John Howard, considered America's best cyclist in the 1970s. LeMond finished second to Howard, only 10 seconds behind after the race's three stages. Later that year, LeMond won the junior national championship. In 1979, he won the junior world championships in Buenos Aires, Argentina, but he was still unknown in the elite European racing circles. That changed in the spring of 1980, when the United States National Team went to Europe for a six-week trip. In the Circuit de la Sarthe, one of the few European races open to both professionals and amateurs, the unknown 18-year-old American won. No American had ever won a major stage race in the history of cycling, and LeMond was also the youngest rider of any nationality to have won a major pro-am cycling event. The next year he began his pro career, racing for Renault, the team that boasted cycling's most dominant rider, Bernard Hinault.

LeMond's first major title came at the 1983 World Championships in Zurich, Switzerland, where he also won the Pernod Trophy given to the year's best cyclist. The next year, he became only the second American to ever attempt the Tour de France, which was established in 1903. Stage races like the Tour de France are demanding tests of conditioning that take several weeks, covering thousands of miles over mountainous terrain. The Tour de France is known for its grueling stages in the Alps, where exhausted riders climb stretches that rise 3,000 feet or more in only a few miles. LeMond finished third in the 1984 Tour de France, proving himself a climber capable of leaving tired opponents behind in the mountains.

Prior to the 1985 racing season, LeMond joined the La Vie Claire team to ride with his old teammate Hinault, who had left Renault. Heading into the Tour de France, Hinault, the team captain, assured LeMond the team would ride without a preordained leader. Most of a team's members, known as "domestiques," ride for the benefit of a leader, breaking the wind and chasing down opponents so the leader can conserve his energy. Despite their pact, the team owner wanted Hinault to win his

1961 LeMond is born in Lakewood, California.

1979 LeMond wins the junior world championships in Buenos Aires, Argentina.

1980 LeMond wins Circuit de la Sarthe at age 18.

1983 LeMond wins the world championships in Zurich, Switzerland, and is awarded the Pernod Trophy as the year's best cyclist.

1986 LeMond is the first non-European winner of the Tour de France (he also wins in 1989 and 1990).

"Wonderful, it just feels wonderful. I was nervous, but everything went perfect today."
Greg LeMond after becoming the first non-European ever to win the Tour de France, 1986

appendectomy: a surgical procedure in which a person's appendix is removed. The appendix is a small tube attached to the large intestine that has no known medical use; a person can live without an appendix with no complications.

mitochondrial myopathy: a form of muscular dystrophy, usually diagnosed in children, that makes the body unable to use oxygen rapidly enough to provide sufficient energy for athletic (or even everyday) activities. The cause of the disease is unknown.

fifth Tour de France, and even though LeMond led the race by several minutes, a coach duped him into slowing down so Hinault could catch up. Hinault went on to win, and LeMond finished second. When it was over, Hinault promised an upset LeMond he would help him win the race the next year, but when the time came Hinault abandoned his promise and intended to win the 1986 Tour de France. He fought LeMond the whole way, but LeMond prevailed, and became the first non-European ever to win the race. At the age of 25, LeMond was the number one cyclist in the world, and the powerful Dutch team PDM signed him to a two-year contract.

LeMond's place on top of the cycling world ended disastrously a few months later, when in April, 1987, his brother-in-law accidentally shot him at close range while turkey hunting. LeMond suffered a collapsed lung, lost a kidney, and suffered damage to his liver, diaphragm and intestine. He was left with 37 shotgun pellets in his body, including two in the lining of his heart. He was lucky to be alive. In the months that followed, his body consumed most of its muscle in its efforts to survive, and his cycling career was presumed over. An emergency **appendectomy** four months later set him back even farther, but LeMond was determined to come back. His first try, in 1988, was abandoned when he was forced to have surgery for tendonitis in his leg.

Before the start of the 1989 season, LeMond signed with the unheralded Belgium-based team, ADR. With a weaker team supporting him, expectations were minimal. In his early season races, riders LeMond had once dominated outdistanced him with relative ease. He was diagnosed with anemia, an iron deficiency, and began taking iron injections. Little attention was paid to him as the 1989 Tour de France began. He just hoped to finish in the top 20 at the end of the 23-day, 2,025 mile race. LeMond shocked everyone with an exciting come-from-behind victory, taking the race by only seven seconds. He capped his improbable comeback with a September, 1989, win at the world championships in Chambery, France, to become only the fourth cyclist to win the world championship and Tour de France in the same year. LeMond won the Tour de France again in 1990, but then began a slow demise due to a rare muscle disorder called **mitochondrial myopathy** that led to his retirement in 1994. The disease may be a result of the shotgun pellets still lodged in his body. Despite these setbacks, LeMond still competes as car racer, and he has his own line of racing bicycles. ◆

Lendl, Ivan

MARCH 7, 1960– ● TENNIS PLAYER

Ivan Lendl was born in the industrial town of Ostrava, Czechoslovakia, on March 7, 1960. Despite a difficult childhood in which the communist government of Czechoslovakia attempted to assert its power, Lendl went on to become one of the most respected players in the tennis world.

Like many other professional tennis players, Lendl got his first racket at a young age—he was six—and spent every spare minute playing against a wall or on a tennis court. However, since his parents were involved in professional tennis, they began to put enormous pressure on the young Lendl to succeed.

By the time he was nine, Lendl was traveling to tournaments in other towns. He usually went by himself because his parents' jobs prevented them from joining him.

As a teenager, he was already a national champion, but he was also skinny and shy. The boys called him Nit, the Czech word for thread. He wasn't particularly interested in dating, and his parents discouraged him from any activities that would take away his focus on tennis. This consistently controlling attitude was something that Lendl would have to surpass in order to become confident in his own desires and ability to play the sport.

In addition to being an outstanding tennis player, Lendl was extremely bright. He eventually learned six languages, including English. And while his teachers often permitted him to skip classes so that he could practice his tennis, he still studied a lot and did extremely well on tests and papers.

Over his 17-year professional career—in which he ranked in the top three for 10 years and finished four years at the top spot—Lendl worked hard to conquer the nerves that undermined him in four Grand Slam finals between 1981 and 1983.

It was Lendl's first Grand Slam title that showed him that he could excel beyond his expectations. However, he also started to notice just how sensitive his back had become. If in his prime he was known as a merciless player who was also in fantastic physical shape, he soon became handicapped by his injuries.

In December of 1994, at the age of 34, Lendl announced his retirement from competitive tennis. After extensive therapy for back problems he realized that he couldn't take the stress anymore and that it was time to ease the pace.

> *"If you want comedy or tantrums don't look at me."* Ivan Lendl to a reporter, referring to comments that he was aloof and tight-lipped

1960 Lendl is born in Ostrava, Czechoslovakia.

1985 Lendl wins the U.S. Open (and in 1986 and 1987).

1986 Lendl wins the French Open (and in 1987).

1989 Lendl wins the Australian Open (and in 1990).

He currently lives on an estate in Goshen, Connecticut that he shares with his wife and four daughters. The family also has many German shepherds.

While Lendl has acknowledged in interviews that he misses professional tennis, he has taken up a number of sports, such as golf, in which he can participate without straining himself. He told the New York Times, "I played golf in the championship at one of the clubs out here [in Connecticut] and the same intensity was there. I was even nervous about it."

These days, Lendl's attachment to tennis mainly comes in the form of owning and running a tennis facility in Westchester County, New York. He sometimes spends time coaching young athletes there when he has the chance. ◆

Lenzi, Mark

JULY 4, 1968– ● DIVER

Olympic springboard diver Mark Lenzi was born in Huntsville, Alabama, on July 4, 1968. As a teenager living in Virginia, Lenzi became interested in competitive diving after watching Greg Louganis's gold-medal–winning performances at the 1984 Summer Olympic Games. Lenzi eventually joined a team in Washington, D.C. The compact, 5'5" young man had always liked diving, but with the structure and drive of a team behind him, it was immediately clear that he had a special talent for the sport. He had a clean and daring style, and could complete the more difficult dives. Lenzi attended a meet only three weeks after starting with the team—and was offered five full scholarships from different universities.

In 1986, Lenzi accepted a scholarship offer from Indiana University. There, training under coach Hobie Billingsly, Lenzi studied the physics and mechanics of diving, and he learned how to be "mentally tough." The unusual approach to the sport paid off. While at Indiana University, Lenzi dove competitively around the United States and the world, gaining valuable competition experience and earning significant collegiate athletic titles and awards.

Among other honors, in 1989 Lenzi was named the Ultra Swim College Coaches Diver of the Year. The following year, he won the Miles S. Barton Award and the L. G. Balfour

Award. In both 1989 and 1990, he was named Big Ten Diver of the Year as well as the National Collegiate Athletic Association (NCAA) Diver of the Year. Lenzi set records in the Big Ten one-meter springboard (586.03 points), the Big Ten three-meter springboard (614.61 points), and the NCAA one-meter springboard events (604.86 points). Throughout college, Lenzi was a varsity letterman.

Lenzi graduated from Indiana University with a degree in General Studies, and began setting his sights on a lofty goal: the Olympics. He focused on the three-meter springboard event, and everything he did was calculated to make the Olympic team and go for the gold.

He succeeded. At the 1992 Summer Games, held in Barcelona, Spain, Lenzi won the gold medal in the three-meter springboard event.

With that accomplishment, Lenzi was thrust into the world spotlight. For months he was in demand to appear on television talk shows. He thought his life was going to change; that he would become rich and always be famous. Then—nothing. After a few months of saturation, the public and the media were no longer interested in him. Lenzi fell into what he calls "post-Olympics blues," something that he contends happens to too many Olympians, as they are first put onto a pedestal and then forgotten.

Lenzi stopped diving in 1993 and went into a long depression, gaining 35 pounds in the process and feeling like he'd hit rock-bottom. Finally, he pulled himself together and started training again. He began to focus on the future and to prepare for the 1996 Olympics.

However, Lenzi's diving at the 1996 Games, held in Atlanta, Georgia, was less spectacular than during the 1992 Olympics, a disappointment that bothers him to this day. He had trained seriously for only six months before the Games, and he was not in the best of health. He had been suffering from the flu, and he had torn the rotator cuff in his shoulder. Lenzi won the bronze medal in the three-meter springboard event, but says that he dove terribly.

Lenzi earned a second college degree at Indiana in 1997, this time in telecommunications with a minor in history. In 1998, he became a diving coach at DePauw University in Greencastle, Indiana. There he is able to help other divers perfect their techniques, utilizing Billingsly and Lenzi's "Olympian physics" approach to the sport. Lenzi contends that raw talent and prac-

1968 Lenzi is born in Huntsville, Alabama.

1989 Lenzi is named the Big 10 Conference Diver of the Year and NCAA Diver of the Year (both also in 1990).

1992 Lenzi wins the Olympic gold medal in the 3-meter springboard.

tice are the only important aspects of diving. If people understand the physics involved in a dive—the physical forces at work on the body—he says, they can become very competent divers. While he is gaining valuable coaching experience, Lenzi is also training for the 2000 Summer Olympics (to be held in Sydney, Australia), hoping to improve upon his 1996 Olympic showing.

Lenzi is also working on a graduate degree and cultivates many interests besides diving. He loves outdoor sports and is an amateur physicist, astronomer, and meteorologist. He also holds a private pilot's license.

During his diving career to date, Lenzi has been World Champion twice and U.S. National Champion eight times. In 1991, he was the Pan Am Games gold medalist. He has collected 18 international titles and was the first person to complete a front $4^1/_2$ somersault in competition. He is the world record holder for the most points ever scored on the three-meter (764) and one-meter springboard (659 points) ◆

Leonard, Ray "Sugar Ray"

MAY 17, 1956– ● BOXER

> *"My ambition is not to be just a good fighter. I want to be great, something special."*
>
> Sugar Ray Leonard

Named after the musician Ray Charles, Ray Leonard was born in Wilmington, North Carolina, and spent his childhood in Palmer Park, Maryland, just outside Washington, D.C. Leonard took his nickname from "Sugar Ray" robinson, the former middleweight champion. By the time he was 20 years old, Leonard had completed one of the most successful amateur boxing careers in modern history. During a tour of Moscow in 1974 with the U.S. National Boxing Team, judges awarded the decision to Leonard's Soviet opponent, who then spontaneously turned around, marched across the canvas, and handed the award to Leonard. Leonard's 145 5 amateur record culminated with his winning the light-welterweight gold medal at the Montreal Olympics in 1976. His lightning-quick punches and charismatic style made Leonard an instant television and crowd favorite.

The following year Leonard turned professional. With Janks Morton as coach and Mike Trainor as promoter, Leonard rose rapidly in the professional ranks by defeating such top-rank fighters as Rafael Rodriguez, Floyd Mayweather, Armando Muniz, and Adolfo Viruet. In 1979, Leonard won both the North American Boxing Federation and World Boxing Council's welterweight championships by knocking out Pete Ranzany and Wilfred Benitez.

Leonard's two most famous fights as a welterweight were in 1980. In June, he lost his WBC crown by decision to Roberto Duran in Montreal. In November, he won it back in New Orleans, in what came to be called the "no mas" (no more) fight, a reference to Duran's cryptic announcement to Leonard when he abruptly quit in the middle of the eighth round for no apparent reason. A year later, Leonard took on Tommy Hearns, the undefeated welterweight champion of the World Boxing Association, and knocked him out in 14 rounds, thereby be-came the undisputed welterweight champion. Leonard was named "Sportsman of the Year" by *Sports Illustrated* in 1981.

After a three-year retirement due to an eye injury sustained in 1984, Leonard returned to the ring in 1987 as a middle-weight, dethroning Marvin Hagler as WBC champion in a controversial 12-round split decision in Las Vegas. The victory over Hagler increased his career earnings to $53 million. In 1988, Leonard knocked out Canadian Don Lalonde, the WBC light heavyweight champion, which earned him both the WBC light heavyweight and super middleweight titles, making him the first boxer ever to win at least a share of titles in five different weight classes. His 37 professional bouts over 14 years included 35 wins, 25 by knockout. Since his retirement in 1991, Leonard has worked as a commentator on boxing broadcasts and has appeared in several television commercials. ◆

Leslie, Lisa

<small>JULY 7, 1972– ● BASKETBALL PLAYER</small>

Lisa, who took
after her mother,
was already
about six feet
tall by the time
she was 12.

Basketball player Lisa Leslie was born on July 7, 1972, to Christine and Walter Leslie. The family lived in Compton, California, outside of Los Angeles. When Lisa was about four years old, her parents split up, and Lisa and her older sister Dionne lived with their mother, Christine. Christine worked as a mail carrier for several years, then bought a tractor-trailer and became a trucker. She made much more money, but the lifestyle was hard on the family. During the school year she was sometimes on the road for weeks at a time, so she hired a live-in housekeeper to take care of the children. During the summers, Lisa and Dionne—and, later, Christine's youngest daughter, Tiffany—would travel around the country with her, sleeping in a narrow compartment behind the cab of the truck.

Lisa, who took after her mother, was already about six feet tall by the time she was 12. As she and her sisters grew, they could no longer fit easily in the bunk in the truck, and their summer activities began to demand more of their time. Eventually they moved in with Christine's sister and her children in nearby Carson, which allowed them to live a more "normal" life.

At Whaley Junior High School, Lisa was asked to join the eighth grade basketball team. Lisa loved being a part of a team, but she soon realized that she needed more than height to play good basketball. She was surprised at how good the players on the team were. The coach started working with her, and as Lisa's level of play and understanding of the game improved, it became apparent that she was exceptionally talented. At the end of the basketball season, Lisa began playing with her cousin Craig Simpson.

When she finished her homework after school, Lisa and her cousins would go to the gym. Craig encouraged Lisa her to improve her overall physical fitness, expand her basketball skills, and learn more about the fundamentals of the game. She played in many pick-up games with boys, a challenge that elevated her level of play.

While attending Morningside High School in Inglewood, California, Leslie joined the Morningside Lady Monarchs. Coach Frank Scott had her play center. By the end of her first year with the team, Leslie was one of the best on the team, and basketball coaches around Southern California began to take notice. By her senior year, Leslie was 6'5" tall and considered the best player in Los Angeles. She was unstoppable on the court—in one memorable game, she racked up 101 points in the first half, and the other team's coach refused to let his players return from halftime to finish the game. In 1990, USA Today named her Player of the Year. The Lady Monarchs were rated among the top 10 girls' basketball teams in the United States.

Leslie also became famous for something not many female basketball players can do: dunk the ball by jumping above the rim. The flashy move earned her the nickname "Dunkin'."

Playing basketball was not the only thing in which Leslie excelled. She maintained a 3.5 average in high school, and in 1989 earned the Dial Award, given to the top scholar-athlete in the United States. Leslie enrolled in honors courses and participated in numerous school activities. She played on the volleyball and track teams and was elected president of the class in her sophomore, junior, and senior years.

Leslie was inundated with offers of basketball scholarships from colleges across the country and eventually chose the nearby University of Southern California. Despite her high grades in high school, however, Leslie found that her education in the somewhat disadvantaged urban schools in Los Angeles had its limitations. She scored 680 on her SATs—not good enough to be admitted to USC, which required at least a 700 score out of the possible 1600. She studied hard and brought the score up to 750. Keeping up with the demanding academic demands of USC would take up more of her time and effort than she had imagined.

During her years playing for the USC Lady Trojans, Leslie continued her winning ways. Among other honors, she was named National Collegiate Athletic Association (NCAA) Freshman of the Year. During the following summer, she played on the U.S. team at the World University Games. Each year at USC (1990 to 1994), she was named First-Team All Pacific 10 Conference, and in 1994 she won the title College Player of the Year.

After graduating from USC, Leslie played on the World Championship Team, easily qualifying with her size, strength, and agility. The squad competed in Australia in June 1994 but was edged out by superior teams; Brazil won the championship. Leslie was disappointed but had gained valuable international

1972 Leslie is born near Los Angeles.

1989 Leslie wins the Dial Award as the top scholar-athlete in the United States.

1990 Leslie is named (high school) Player of the Year by USA Today; she is also named NCAA Freshman of the Year.

1994 Leslie is named College Player of the Year.

1996 At the Olympics, Leslie scores most points in a final game (29); U.S. wins gold.

1997 Leslie joins the WNBA's Los Angeles Sparks; named top center, First-Team All-Star.

1999 Leslie is named USA Basketball Female Athlete of the Year; and Most Valuable Player of the WNBA's All-Star game.

experience, and she played for a season with an Italian professional basketball league.

In 1995, Leslie joined Team USA and began training for the 1996 Summer Olympic Games, held in Atlanta, Georgia. During the Olympics, she played her best and helped Team USA to win the final game for the gold, 111 to 87. Leslie was the high scorer, racking up 29 points.

Leslie toured for a time with Team USA, and, signed by the Wilhelmina Agency, did some modeling work. In 1997, she joined the Women's National Basketball Association (WNBA), playing for the Los Angeles Sparks. By 1997, she was the WNBA's top center and was named a First-Team All-Star. In 1998, she was honored as the 1999 USA Basketball Female Athlete of the Year, In 1999, she was named Most Valuable Player (MVP) of the WNBA All-Star Game. Today Leslie still revels in the challenge of professional basketball and is recognized as one of the world's best and most influential players. ◆

Lewis, Carl

JULY 1, 1961– ● TRACK AND FIELD

Born in Birmingham, Alabama, track star Frederick Carlton ("Carl") Lewis was raised in the Philadelphia suburb of Willingboro, New Jersey. Although he played Little League baseball, Lewis did not particularly excel at sports, unlike his brothers and sisters. In fact, as a child, Lewis remained physically undeveloped. His parents, though, were both high school track coaches, and Lewis ran with them in a track club. By the age of 10 was showing some ability as a long jumper, and when he began to grow physically in high school, his speed and jumping ability turned him into a track star. In his junior year he improved his long jump distance to 25 feet 9 inches, and when he graduated in 1979 he was the New Jersey Long Jumper of the Year and was regarded as one of the top high school track athletes in the country. That year he won his first long jump medals, a bronze at the Pan American Games and a silver in the U.S. Nationals.

Several colleges heavily recruited Lewis; he chose the University of Houston, where Coach Tom Tellez helped him to develop a long-jumping technique called the double-hitch kick.

This technique enabled Lewis to dominate collegiate competition in 1980 and 1981. In 1980 he won both the indoor and outdoor NCAA long jump and, with his sister Carol, was picked to represent the United States in the Olympics. Unfortunately, the United States boycotted the Olympic Games in Moscow that year to protest the former Soviet Union's invasion of Afghanistan.

In 1981 Lewis successfully defended both of his NCAA gold medals and added two more—the 100-meter dash in the outdoor championships and the 55-meter dash in the indoors. That year, too, Lewis won gold medals in the long jump and the 100-meter dash at the U.S. Nationals. For his efforts he was named winner of the 1981 Sullivan Award, which is presented annually by the Amateur Athletic Union (AAU) to the nation's top amateur athlete.

Carl Lewis at the 1992 Olympics.

With these wins Lewis began a string of gold-medal–winning and record-setting performances that lasted until 1996; to him, winning a silver or a bronze medal must have seemed like a crushing disappointment. He won the USA/Mobil Indoor Championships long jump title in 1982 and 1983, adding a gold in the 55-meter dash in 1983. In the 1982 U.S. Nationals he won the gold in the long jump and 100-meter. And in the first World Track and Field Championships in Helsinki, Finland, in 1983, he won gold in the long jump and the 100-meter dash and was a part of the winning 400-meter relay team. Returning to the U.S. Nationals in 1983, he won gold in the 100-meter and 200-meter dashes and the long jump.

All of this was a warm-up for his first Olympic competition in 1984. That year in Los Angeles, Lewis reached perhaps the pinnacle of his success when he joined Al Kraenzlein (1900) and the legendary Jesse Owens as the only Americans to win four track and field gold medals in one Olympics, winning the same events Owens did in 1936: the long jump, the 100-meter

1961 Lewis is born in Birmingham, Alabama.

1984 Lewis wins four Olympic gold medals in the same events as Jesse Owens, his track hero.

1985 Lewis is elected to the U.S. Olympic Hall of Fame well before his eventual retirement.

1988 At Seoul, Lewis becomes the first person to win consecutive Olympic long-jump medals.

1992 At Barcelona, Lewis wins two more gold medals (long jump and 400-meter relay).

1996 In Atlanta, Lewis wins his ninth Olympic gold medal and fourth consecutive long-jump title.

dash, the 200-meter dash (setting an Olympic record with a time of 19.80 seconds), and anchoring the 400-meter relay (setting world and Olympics records with a time of 37.83 seconds).

Between the 1984 and 1988 Olympics, Lewis continued to win medals in major U.S. and international competitions. In 1984 he won the gold medal in the long jump in the USA/Mobil Indoor Championships. In the 1986 Goodwill Games he took bronze in the 100-meter dash and gold in the 400-meter relay. He enjoyed another big year in 1987: In the World Championships he won silver in the 100-meter and gold in the 400-meter relay and the long jump; in the Pan American Games he won gold in the 400-meter relay and long jump; and in the U.S. Nationals he won silver in the 100-meter dash and gold in the 200-meter and long jump.

Lewis was elected to the U.S. Olympic Hall of Fame in 1985, but he wasn't anywhere near done as an Olympian. In the 1988 Olympics in Seoul, South Korea, Lewis became the first athlete to win consecutive Olympic long jump gold medals. He was also awarded the gold medal in the 100-meter dash when Canadian Ben Johnson, who had won the event, was later disqualified after testing positive for anabolic steroids. That year Lewis also won the silver medal in the 200-meter dash.

After continuing to win either gold or silver medals in the Goodwill Games (1990) and the World Championships (1991), Lewis competed in the 1992 Olympic Games in Barcelona, Spain. That year he added two more gold medals when he won his third consecutive long jump title and anchored the world-record-setting 400-meter relay team. Incredibly, he won his ninth Olympic gold medal and a fourth consecutive long jump title in the 1996 games in Atlanta.

Throughout his career Lewis was a figure of some controversy. In the 1984 Los Angeles Olympics, he was criticized for waving a large American flag during his 100-meter victory lap and for passing up opportunities to break Bob Beamon's long jump record. Some observers accused him of being a showoff, and he repeatedly had to deny charges that he used performance-enhancing drugs. What is undeniable, though, is that for over a decade, Lewis rewrote the track and field world record book, including the indoor record in the long jump in 1981, 1982, and 1984 (adding an even foot to bring the record to 28 feet 10 1/4 inches); the outdoor record in the long jump (28 feet 3 inches) in 1982; an outdoor record at 200 meters (19.75) in 1983; the indoor record at 60 yards in 1983 (6.02); the sea-level record for 100 meters (9.96) in 1983; the record for 100 meters (9.86) in 1991; and a record 37.40 in the 400-meter relay in 1992.

In 1990 Lewis published his autobiography, *Inside Track: My Professional Life in Amateur Track and Field*. He retired from competition in 1997. ◆

Lieberman-Cline, Nancy

JULY 1, 1958– ● BASKETBALL PLAYER

Guard Nancy Lieberman-Cline, nicknamed "Lady Magic" for her passing prowess, is one of the most accomplished women in basketball history. Born Nancy Lieberman on July 1, 1958, she is a three-time All-America. She became the first woman to play in a men's professional basketball league, and she played in the inaugural season of the Women's National Basketball Association (WNBA).

By the time she was fifteen, Lieberman-Cline was already one of the top female basketball players in the United States. That year, she was named to the U.S. National Team. Two years later, she earned a slot on the U.S. Women's Olympic Basketball Team, which competed at the 1976 Summer Olympic Games, held in Montreal, Canada. The U.S. team won the silver medal.

Lieberman-Cline was a member of the Junior National Team in 1977, and she played on several World Championship teams, winning a gold medal in 1979. As a member of several Pan Am Games teams, she won the gold in 1975 and the silver in 1979.

Lieberman-Cline studied at Old Dominion University in Virginia, and the tall (5′10″) athlete found her niche on Old Dominion's power-

1976 At 17, Lieberman-Cline plays on silver medal winning U.S. Olympic basketball team.

1978 At Old Dominion University, Lieberman-Cline wins the Kodak All-America award (and wins again in 1979 and 1980).

1979 Lieberman-Cline wins the Broderick Cup and Wade Trophy (both also in 1980).

1981 Lieberman-Cline becomes personal trainer to tennis star Martina Navratilova.

1986 Lieberman-Cline joins the United States Basketball League, becoming the first woman to play in a men's professional league.

1996 Lieberman-Cline is inducted into the Naismith Memorial Basketball Hall of Fame.

ful women's basketball team. She received many honors during her collegiate career, including three Kodak All-America awards (1978 through 1980). Lieberman-Cline was named All-America three times (1978 through 1980) and Old Dominion University Outstanding Female Athlete of the Year from 1977 through 1980. She was the recipient of the Broderick Cup in 1979 and 1980. She won two Wade Trophies (1979 and 1980), the only athlete to do so. In the 134 games that she played during her college career, Lieberman-Cline accumulated 2,430 points, 1,167 rebounds, 983 assists, and more than 700 steals.

After college, Lieberman-Cline planned to play on the 1980 U.S. Olympic Team. However, the team was unable to participate in the 1980 Summer Games, because they were held in Moscow, Russia then part of the Soviet Union. President Jimmy Carter had called for a U.S. boycott of the Moscow Olympics to protest the Soviet Union's invasion of Afghanistan. Lieberman-Cline was in agreement with this decision, though it was a huge disappointment to her and, of course, to all the other U.S. Olympic athletes on a personal level.

Lieberman-Cline decided to become a professional, and she joined the first of four pro leagues of her career to date. She was the top draft pick for the Dallas Diamonds, of the Women's Professional Basketball League (WPBL). She was first in the Diamonds in scoring and led the team to the 1981 championship series.

After the 1980–1981 basketball season, Lieberman-Cline decided on a change of pace, becoming personal trainer to Martina Navratilova. She served as trainer to the superstar tennis player for three years, then was eager to return to professional basketball. She rejoined the Dallas Diamonds, which by then were part of the Women's American Basketball Association (WABA). During the Diamonds' short season in 1984, Lieberman-Cline distinguished herself as the top scorer, and she led the Diamonds to another league championship victory.

In 1986, Lieberman-Cline decided to do something really unusual: She joined the U.S. Basketball League (USBL), thus becoming the first woman ever to play in a men's professional league. She played in the USBL for two years. During that time, Nancy met player Tim Cline, and the couple married a year later.

Lieberman-Cline eventually joined her fourth professional league, the Women's National Basketball Association (WNBA). But while she is never far from the court, playing occasionally for such teams as the Mercury Sparks, Lieberman-Cline has greatly expanded her professional roles over the past decade and a half. She owns a sports marketing company called Events Marketing and writes occasional columns for USA Today, the Dallas Morning News, and other publications. She has become very well known as a television sports commentator, covering such events as the Olympics and various National Collegiate Athletic Association (NCAA) games.

Lieberman-Cline is also deeply involved in several charities, including the Special Olympics, Girl Scouts, and Juvenile Diabetes. She is very concerned about issues affecting women and children. (She and Tim Cline have a son, Timothy Jr., or TJ.) She has written two books, one, her autobiography, entitled *Lady Magic: The Nancy Lieberman-Cline Story*. With ESPN/ABC commentator Robin Roberts, she co-authored *Basketball for Women: Becoming a Complete Player*.

In May 1996, Lieberman-Cline was inducted into the Naismith Memorial Basketball Hall of Fame. During the 1996–1997 season, she was a member of Athletes in Action, a squad of former college greats that scrimmages with the nation's top college teams. In 1998, Lieberman-Cline was named the head coach and general manager of the Detroit Shock, a WNBA team. ◆

> *"She was the beginning of the scoring point guard, the flashy point guard, who could drive and dish and post you up."*
>
> Cheryl Miller on Nancy Lieberman-Cline

Liston, Charles "Sonny"

MAY 8, 1932–DECEMBER 30, 1970 ● BOXER

Sonny Liston was the 10th of 11 children of Helen (Baskin) Liston and impoverished Arkansas cotton farmer Tobe Liston, who already had 14 offspring by his first wife. Sonny moved with his mother to St. Louis in 1945; there the illiterate youth became a juvenile delinquent, and later an armed robber. He was convicted in 1950 of robbing a gas station and served 19 months in prison. A prison priest directed him into boxing, and in 1953 he won the national Golden Gloves championship. Liston turned professional, achieving a 14 1 record, but assaulted a policeman and returned to prison in 1956. After his release, he won his next 19 bouts, becoming number-one contender in 1960. He won the championship from Floyd Patterson on September 25, 1962, with a first-round knockout. However, the New York State Boxing

> *"Floyd Patterson can't beat Sonny at anything but a spelling bee. Liston could probably knock him out via smoke signals, and Floyd will probably get woozy if Liston just drove past his house in Scarsdale."*
>
> Jim Murray, *Los Angeles Times*, 1963

1932 Charles "Sonny" Liston is born in St. Francis County, Arkansas.

1962 Liston KO's Floyd Patterson; wins world heavyweight title.

1964 Liston loses his title to Cassius Clay (later known as Muhammad Ali).

Commission refused to license him because of reputed underworld connections. His aura of invincibility was strengthened by a first-round knockout in a rematch with Patterson in July 1963.

Liston had an awesome physical presence, delivered a crushing left hook, and had a remarkable ability to take punches. He fought Cassius Clay, a rank underdog, on February 25, 1964, losing on a TKO when unable to answer the bell for the seventh round because of a shoulder injury. The rematch on May 25, 1965, was equally shocking as Clay (who by then had changed his name to Muhammad Ali) gained a first-round knockout (1:52) with a phantom right. Most experts felt that Ali had landed a blow on a physically and mentally washed-up Liston. Liston had a career record of 50 4 (with 39 knockouts). He died in 1970, six months after his last fight. ◆

Lobo, Rebecca

OCTOBER 6, 1973– ● BASKETBALL PLAYER

Rebecca Lobo could be the girl next door. Well, provided the girl next door was a two-time All-America basketball player, who set a state high school record for most career points, didn't lose a basketball game for the better part of three years, jogged with the President of the United States, appeared on David Letterman, and co-authored a book with her mother at the age of 21. So, while Lobo might look like the average girl next door, her athletic accomplishments make her anything but average.

> *"The athlete is not the one who decides whether or not they're a role model. It's the young kid out there who's watching you, and you respect that responsibility."*
>
> Rebecca Lobo

Rebecca Rose Lobo was born on Oct. 6, 1973, in Hartford, Connecticut, the youngest of three children to mother, RuthAnn and father, Dennis. Her brother Jason is six years older, while her sister Rachel is two years older.

Growing up, the three Lobo kids were always in competition, in every sport imaginable. Rebecca grew especially fond of basketball, constantly practicing her shooting at the hoop in the family's backyard, which had originally been put up for Jason.

Her competitive nature paid off when she got to high school. Rebecca completely outclassed the opposition as a center for the Southwick-Tolland Regional High School basketball team. She got off to a great start, scoring 32 points in her first game. Her best game as a high school player saw her tally 62 points, and she finished her four-year career with 2,710 points, the most for a high school player in Massachusetts history—male or female.

She was class salutatorian at Southwick High and received scholarship offers from more than 100 colleges. Lobo chose to stay close to home, however, attending the University of Connecticut. The UConn women's program would never be the same.

Lobo picked up at UConn where she left off at Southwick. Her first season she averaged 14.3 points and 7.9 rebounds per game and was named the 1992 Big East Conference Rookie of the Year. The next year Lobo was named to the All-Big East first team, as she averaged 16.7 points and 11.2 rebounds.

Lobo's junior year saw continued success for her as well as the Huskies, but was tempered by tragedy close to home. It was during that season that her mother RuthAnn was diagnosed with breast cancer. Rebecca responded to the pressure by continuing to excel on the court and in the classroom, earning Kodak First-Team All-America honors, while simultaneously offering solid support to her mom. Their battle with and eventual triumph over RuthAnn's affliction were chronicled in a best-selling book the pair co-authored that was called *The Home Team*.

Rebecca Lobo of the New York Liberty.

Rebecca came back for her senior season as determined as ever and led the Huskies on a march to history. The 1994–95 Huskies put together one of college basketball's most remarkable seasons, finishing 35–0 and winning the national championship. For Lobo, it capped off a superb career at UConn.

During the Lobo era, the Huskies compiled a 106–25 record (an .809 winning percentage), won the Big East championship in 1994 and 1995, and reached the NCAA Tournament all four years, culminating in the school's first national championship. She left Connecticut as the school's all-time leader in rebounds

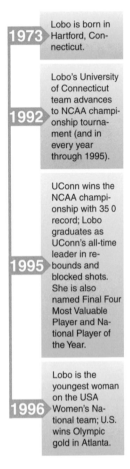

1973 Lobo is born in Hartford, Connecticut.

1992 Lobo's University of Connecticut team advances to NCAA championship tournament (and in every year through 1995).

1995 UConn wins the NCAA championship with 35 0 record; Lobo graduates as UConn's all-time leader in rebounds and blocked shots. She is also named Final Four Most Valuable Player and National Player of the Year.

1996 Lobo is the youngest woman on the USA Women's National team; U.S. wins Olympic gold in Atlanta.

and blocked shots, was second in points and games played, and fourth in field goal percentage. Her senior season she was named a Kodak First-Team All-America for the second straight season, was named the most valuable player of the Final Four, and topped it off by being honored as the consensus national Player of the Year.

The 35–0 season also began a remarkable streak that saw Lobo be a part of 102 straight wins on the basketball court. After graduating from UConn with a degree in political science, she became the youngest woman ever to play on the U.S. women's national team. That team won 56 straight games in pre-Olympic and Olympic competition, earning the gold medal at the 1996 Summer Olympics in Atlanta. Lobo had been part of 91 straight wins when she left the team after the Olympics.

Following the Olympics, both of the women's professional leagues—the American Basketball League (ABL) and the Women's National Basketball Association (WNBA)—actively recruited Lobo. She chose the WNBA and was assigned to the New York Liberty. Lobo immediately became one of the new league's star attractions and one of its most popular players. In her initial season, Lobo started all 28 games and averaged 12.4 points and 7.3 rebounds per game. The Liberty finished with a 17–11 record and made it to the inaugural WNBA championship game before losing to the Houston Comets .

In her second season, Lobo again played in all 30 games and led the Liberty in field-goal percentage (.484, sixth in the WNBA), rebounds (6.9 per game, sixth in the league), and blocked shots (1.10 per game, sixth in the league).

Her third season, however, was a nightmare, as Lobo tore the anterior cruciate ligament in her left knee in the first minute of the first game of the season. The injury caused her to miss the entire season, which saw the Liberty again reach the championship round of the playoffs before losing to Houston again. Despite the injury, fans proved just how popular she was when they still voted her onto the starting team in the WNBA's first All-Star Game.

Lobo's popularity was apparent long before last season. Her charismatic personality impressed the likes of President Bill Clinton, with whom she went jogging while on a visit to the White House; late-night talk show host David Letterman, who invited her to be a guest on his show; and the ESPN sports cable channel, which hired her as a color analyst for their coverage of the NCAA women's basketball tournament.

Lobo, a fitness fanatic who works out at least four hours a day, is expected to make a full recovery from her injury and return to the Liberty to try and win that elusive WNBA championship. ◆

Lopez, Nancy

JANUARY 6, 1957– ● GOLFER

A leader in the world of women's golf since the late 1970s, Nancy Lopez also has been a crowd favorite because of her winning smile and her unpretentious manner. While raising three daughters and a stepson, she has managed to win almost every major women's tournament, and was the first golfer (male or female) to exceed $1 million in earnings.

Born in Torrance, California, to Domingo Lopez and Marina Griego, Nancy Lopez and her older sister, Delma, spent their childhood in Roswell, New Mexico, where their father owned an automobile repair shop. Her parents introduced her to golf when she was only about eight. After realizing she had natural talent, they shifted money in their household budget to pay for her golf expenses. Her father became her first (and, throughout her career, only) coach.

Lopez quickly gained attention when she won the New Mexico Women's Amateur Tournament at the age of 12. She won the U.S. Girls' Junior title twice while in high school (1972 and 1974), and was awarded an athletic scholarship to the University of Tulsa. But during her sophomore year, after struggling to balance her studies and her golf game, Lopez decided to leave college and turned professional.

Lopez's first full season on the professional circuit in 1978 was remarkable. After placing second in the first three tournaments she entered, Lopez won five consecutive LPGA (Ladies Professional Golf Association) tournaments, including the coveted LPGA title. She was named LPGA Rookie of the Year and Player of the Year.

In 1978 Lopez also met and married Tim Melton, a sportscaster, but the marriage quickly collapsed. In 1982 she married baseball player Ray Knight; they have three daughters and a son from Ray's previous marriage. Although Lopez returned to the golf circuit as soon as possible after each child was born, she has always said that her family comes first.

> *"Golf is a difficult game, but it's a little easier if you trust your instincts. It's too hard a game to try to play like somebody else."*
>
> Nancy Lopez in
> *The Quotable Golfer*

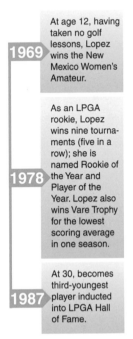

At age 12, having taken no golf lessons, Lopez wins the New Mexico Women's Amateur.

1969

As an LPGA rookie, Lopez wins nine tournaments (five in a row); she is named Rookie of the Year and Player of the Year. Lopez also wins Vare Trophy for the lowest scoring average in one season.

1978

At 30, becomes third-youngest player inducted into LPGA Hall of Fame.

1987

Lopez went on to become the LPGA Player of the Year three more times after her rookie season (1979, 1985, and 1988). In 1983 she became the first golfer to earn more than $1 million during her career. Lopez was named to the LPGA Hall of Fame in 1987, the year in which she became eligible by winning the required 35 career titles; she was the youngest woman ever elected.

In the mid-1990s Lopez's career faltered; she won no tournaments between 1994 and 1996, and began to gain weight. As she jokingly told Golf World in March 1998, "I was basically a fat little mom." Lopez began a rigorous exercise and diet program; it worked, and her career was revived. In 1997 she almost won the one title that had eluded her throughout her career: the U.S. Women's Open. Lopez finished all four rounds in the 60s (a tournament record), but she lost to Alison Nicholas by a single stroke, finishing second in the tournament for the fourth time. Ironically, Nicholas had considered withdrawing from the tournament, but Lopez persuaded her to play.

Lopez lives with her husband and children in Albany, Georgia, where she is active in numerous charities and markets her own line of golf equipment. She has written two books: *The Education of a Woman Golfer* (1979) and *Nancy Lopez's The Complete Golfer* (1987). ◆

Louganis, Greg

JANUARY 29, 1960– ● DIVER

World-class high diver Gregory Efthimios Louganis was born on January 29, 1960, in San Diego, California. His birth parents—his mother of Swedish background, his father Samoan—were young, unmarried high school students, and they put the infant up for adoption. When Greg was nine months old, he was adopted by Peter and Frances Louganis.

Louganis was brought up in El Cajon, a suburb of San Diego. He was an athletic child with many interests. Although he enjoyed dance, acrobatics, and gymnastics, he decided to concentrate on diving when problems with his knees limited his participation in those other sports. At age 11, Louganis scored a perfect 10 in the Amateur Athletic Union Junior

Olympics. He worked hard over the next few years to build up his diving skills and endurance, competing often and training hour after hour.

Louganis prepared carefully for the 1976 Montreal Summer Olympics. For nine months he lived at the home of his trainer at the time, Dr. Sammy Lee, and Lee's wife Roz. Lee was himself a two-time Olympic gold medalist, and he knew the amount of work that would be required to be competitive in the Games. He told Louganis that he would need to train every day if he wanted to win gold medals on both the springboard and platform.

Their strategy succeeded. Louganis, then age 16, won the silver medal in the platform event. At the Pan American Games in 1979, Louganis won gold medals in both the springboard and platform events. His chances to triumph at the 1980 Summer Olympics in Moscow looked very good. However, Louganis was unable to compete there when the United States boycotted the event due to the Soviet Union's invasion of Afghanistan.

Greg Louganis.

Like the other American athletes whose Olympic dreams were sidelined in 1980, Louganis was very disappointed, but he continued to practice and compete. His efforts paid off at the 1982 World Aquatic Championships, where he was the first diver ever to be granted a 10—a perfect score—from all of the judges. His excellence was recognized the following year when he set three-meter springboard records.

Louganis's competitors and sports fans around the world knew by now that he was an especially gifted diver. His technical precision and ballet-like grace—and good looks—made his dives seem like an art form. As the 1984 Summer Olympics approached, the modest, shy young man was under terrific pressure to perform well.

The 1984 Summer Games were held in Los Angeles, California, and Louganis was up to the challenge. Poised and focused,

Olympic Diving

The origins of modern Olympic diving lay less with swimming than with the revival of gymnastics in Germany and Sweden in the seventeenth century. In the summertime, gymnasts would move their equipment to beaches and practice their acrobatics over water, often to the delight of admiring spectators. Their sport evolved into what became known as "fancy diving," the name it carried to the 1904 Olympics although there was nothing fancy about it. Divers took off straight from a forward position, and the goal in that first Olympic diving competition was simply to plunge in from a 10-meter platform and swim underwater for as long as possible.

In the years following the 1904 Olympics, diving as we know it began to take shape. Springboard diving was added in 1908, but both the springboard and platform competitions remained men's events until 1912, when women's platform diving was introduced, and 1920, when the women's springboard event was added. In the 1920s divers began to develop many of the techniques that have since turned diving into a glamour event, including the pike and the tuck, both of which made twists and multiple somersaults possible.

The Germans and the Swedes dominated Olympic diving until 1920. That year, though, U.S. divers won three out of four gold medals and went on to dominate Olympic diving until the 1990s, winning 46 out of 75 gold medals. Notable names in U.S. Olympic diving competition include Pat McCormick, who won the women's springboard and platform titles in 1952 and 1956, and Greg Louganis, who repeated McCormick's feat in 1984 and 1988. In the 1990s Chinese divers began to wrest superiority from the United States, winning three out of four gold medals in 1996. Diving fans throughout the world looked forward to the addition of synchronized diving in the 2000 Olympics in Sydney, Australia.

Diving is judged by a panel of seven judges, who score the diver on such elements as approach, take-off, execution, and entry into the water. Each diver performs a series of dives and is awarded up to ten points based not only on execution but on the dive's degree of difficulty.

he took home gold medals in the three-meter springboard and the ten-meter platform events. It was the first time a diver had won both in more than half a century. With his victories, Louganis had established himself as the premier diver in the world—perhaps the greatest of all time, as many people believed. But in case anyone thought he had had an advantage because the Soviet Union and some Eastern European countries boycotted the 1984 Summer Games, he dashed any doubts in the 1988 Olympics in Seoul, South Korea. He again took home double gold in the same events he had won in 1984. It was the only time a male diver won both events in successive Olympics.

The stunning win was all the more amazing because during one of his dives in the springboard competition, Louganis miscalculated on his launch off the board and cracked his head against it. The live image flashed across the globe on television as Louganis curled up and hit the water. The world gave a collective sigh of relief when he emerged from the pool unharmed except for a gash on the head, which required several stitches. The next day, Louganis completed his dives and won the event.

After the 1988 Games, Louganis retired. The Olympian extraordinaire had won 47 national championships and 13 world championships.

Louganis still dives to keep in shape, and because he enjoys it. He has become an actor, primarily on the stage, and a dog breeder. The diver with the invincible spirit gives generously of his time for many causes, lending his celebrity to inform the public about such causes as drug and alcohol rehabilitation, organizations for the dyslexic, and gay rights.

In his well-received, best-selling 1995 autobiography, *Breaking the Surface*, Louganis spoke openly of his tough teenage years, during which he struggled with racial prejudice, dyslexia, depression, and several suicide attempts. Louganis also revealed that he had been infected with the HIV virus for many years; he quickly became a leading activist in the fight against AIDS. ◆

> *"I didn't realize I was that close to the board. When I hit it, it was kind of a shock. But I think my pride was hurt more than anything else."*
> Greg Louganis, after hitting his head while performing a reverse somersault pike, 1988 Olympics

Louis, Joe

MAY 13, 1914 APRIL 12, 1981 ● BOXER

Joe Louis Barrow was born to a sharecropping couple in Chambers County, Alabama, the seventh of eight children. Louis's father, Munroe Barrow, was placed in a mental institution when Louis was two, apparently unable to cope with the strain of the dirt farming life. (It has been suggested by a few observers that Louis's mental and emotional problems in later life may have resulted from congenital causes rather than blows in the prize ring.) Louis's father died in Searcy State Hospital for the Colored Insane nearly 20 years later, never having learned that his son had become a famous athlete.

Lillie Barrow, Louis's mother, remarried a widower with a large family of his own named Pat Brooks who, in 1920, moved the family to Mt. Sinai, Alabama. In 1926 Brooks migrated north to Detroit to work for the Ford Motor Company. The family, like many other African-American families of this period of the

Heavyweight champ Joe Louis.

Great Migration, followed suit soon after, settling in Detroit's burgeoning black ghetto.

At the time of the move to Detroit, Louis was 12 years old. He was big for his age, but because of his inadequate education in the South and his lack of interest in and affinity for school, he was placed in a lower grade than his age would have dictated. Consequently, he continued to be an indifferent student and eventually went to work when his stepfather was laid off by Ford at the beginning of the depression.

Like many poor, unskilled, undereducated, ethnic urban boys of the period, Louis drifted into boxing largely as an opportunity to make money and to release his aggression in an organized, socially acceptable way. Although his stepfather was opposed to his entry into athletics, his mother supported and encouraged him.

Competing as a light heavyweight, Louis started his amateur career in 1932 but lost badly in his first fight and did not return to the ring until the following year. Following this brief hiatus, however, Louis quickly rose to prominence in boxing and African-American or "race" circles. By 1933 he compiled an amateur record of 50 wins, 43 by knockout, and only 4 losses. In 1934, shortly after winning the light heavyweight championship of the Amateur Athletic Union, Louis turned professional and moved up to the heavyweight division. His managers were two black numbers runners, John Roxborough and Julian Black. Louis's trainer was a white man, the former lightweight fighter Jack Blackburn.

Thanks to generous coverage by the black press, Louis was already a familiar figure in the black neighborhoods of northern cities by 1934. At a time when color bars prohibited blacks from competing with whites in every major professional sport other than boxing, Louis became a symbol of black aspirations in white America. Through the prime of his career, Louis's fights were major social events for African Americans, and spontaneous celebrations would erupt in urban ghettos after his victories.

At the start of his professional career, Louis faced a number of obstacles in trying to obtain the heavyweight title. First, under a "gentlemen's agreement," no black fighter had been permitted to fight for that title since Jack Johnson, the first black heavyweight champion. Johnson lost the title in Havana, Cuba, to Jess Willard in 1915. Second, Louis had an entirely black support and management team, making it difficult for him to break into the big market for the fight game in New York City and to get a crack at the name fighters against whom he had to compete if he were to make a name for himself.

Louis's managers overcame the first problem by making sure that Louis did not in any way act like or remind his white audience or white sportswriters of Johnson, who scandalized white public opinion with his marriages to white women and other breaches of prevailing racial mores. Louis was not permitted to be seen in the company of white women, never gloated over his opponents, was quiet and respectful, and generally was made to project an image of cleanliness and high moral character. The second problem was solved when Mike Jacobs, a fight promoter in New York City, decided to take on Madison Square Garden's monopoly on boxing with his 20th Century Sporting Club and formed a partnership with Louis's managers to promote him with the intention of guiding him to the championship.

Louis, 6′1″, with a fighting weight around 200 pounds, soon amassed a glittering record. Starting in his first professional bout, a first-round knockout of Jack Kracken on July 4, 1934, to his winning the heavyweight title, in an eighth-round knockout of Jim Braddock on June 22, 1937, Louis recorded a record of 30 wins, 25 by knockout, and 1 loss. The most memorable of his fights during this period included the easy knockouts of former heavyweight champions Max Baer and Primo Carnera in 1935. Louis's one loss during this period was critically important in his career and in American cultural history. On June 19, 1936, the German Max Schmeling knocked out Louis, then a world-class challenger to the heavyweight crown, in 12 rounds, giving the highly touted black fighter his first severe beating as a professional. This loss greatly reduced Louis's standing with white sportswriters, who had previously built him up almost to the point of invincibility. (The writers had given him a string of **alliterative** nicknames, including the "Tan Tornado" and the

> "*Joe Louis was my inspiration. I idolized him. He wrote the book on boxing the way he stood, the way he blocked shots was beautiful. I just give lip service to being the greatest. He was the greatest.*"
> Muhammad Ali on Joe Louis

alliterative: when two or more words or syllables in a sentence or phrase start with the same initial letter. For example, "Mickey Mantle mashed a monster moonshot," is alliterative.

1914 Joseph Louis Barrow is born in Chambers County Alabama.

1936 Louis's suffers his first pro defeat by Max Schmeling, a German heavyweight.

1937 Louis KO's James Jack Braddock; wins heavyweight championship.

1938 Louis comes back with first-round KO against Schmeling.

1942 Louis enlists in the United States Army.

1949 Louis retires (temporarily).

1951 After being KO'd by Rocky Marciano, Louis retires for good.

1981 Louis dies in Las Vegas at age 66; he is buried at Arlington National Cemetery at the request of President Reagan

"Dark Destroyer," but it was the "Brown Bomber" that stuck.) However, Louis's loss was also a watershed as it marked a slow change on the part of white sportswriters, who began to stop patronizing him.

The loss also set up a rematch with Schmeling on June 22, 1938, after Louis had become champion by defeating Braddock the previous year. The second bout with Schmeling was to become one of the most important fights in American history. It was not Louis's first fight with political overtones. He had fought the Italian heavyweight Primo Carnera (beating him easily) as Italy was beginning its invasion of Ethiopia, and both fighters became emblems of their respective ethnicities; Louis, oddly enough, became both a nationalistic hero for blacks while being a kind of crossover hero for non-Italian, antifascist whites. By 1938, Hitler was rapidly taking over Europe and Nazism had clearly become a threat to both the United States and the world generally. Schmeling was seen as the symbol of Nazism, an identification against which he did not fight very hard.

Under the scrutiny of both their countries and most of the rest of the world, Louis knocked out Schmeling in two minutes of the first round.

Following the second Schmeling bout, Louis embarked on a remarkable string of title defenses, winning 17 fights over four years, 15 by knockout. Because of the general lack of talent in the heavyweight division at the time and the ease of Louis's victories, his opponents were popularly referred to as "The Bum of the Month Club." The only serious challenge came from Billy Conn in 1941, who outboxed the champion for 12 rounds before succumbing to Louis's knockout punch in the 13th.

Louis was drafted into World War II on January 12, 1942, but remained active as a boxer, continuing to fight professionally during the war. He contributed his earnings to both the Army and the Navy Relief Funds. While this was a wise move politically, it was disastrous for Louis financially. (In fact, even before he joined the service, he contributed the purse from his Buddy Baer fight on January 9, 1942, to the Navy Relief Fund.)

"We're going to do our part, and we will win," Louis intoned at a Navy Relief Society dinner on March 10, 1942, "because we are on God's side." This moment, perhaps more than any other in Louis's career, signaled the complete transformation of the image of the man in the mind of the white public. Louis rose from being the sullen, uneasy "colored boy" from black Detroit who was considered in 1935 the **wunderkind** of boxing, to become in seven years, the mature, patriotic American who could speak both to and for his country. Louis could now not simply address his audience but command it. He could, as one pundit put it, "name the war." Louis's phrase, "We're on God's side," became one of the most famous phrases in American oratory during World War II.

After the war, Louis's abilities as a fighter diminished as his earnings evaporated in a mist of high living and alleged tax evasion. After winning a rematch against Jersey Joe Walcott on June 25, 1948—only the second black fighter against whom Louis defended his title, indicating how much of a presence white fighters were in the sport well into the twentieth century—on the heels of winning an earlier controversial match on December 5, 1947, that most observers felt he had lost, Louis retired from the ring in 1949. At that time he made a deal with the unsavory Jim Norris and the International Boxing Club, which resulted in the removal of an old, sick Mike Jacobs from the professional boxing scene. Louis's deal with Norris created an entity called Joe Louis Enterprises that would sign up all the leading contenders for the heavyweight championship and have them exclusively promoted by Norris's International Boxing Club. Louis received $150,000 and became a stockholder in the IBC. He was paid $15,000 annually to promote boxing generally and the IBC bout specifically. In effect, Louis sold his title to a gangster-controlled outfit that wanted and eventually obtained for a period in the 1950s virtual control over both the management and promotion of all notable professional fighters in the United States.

By 1950, however, an aged Louis, reflexes shot and legs gimpy, was forced back into the ring because of money problems. He lost to Ezzard Charles in a 15-round decision on September 27. On October 26, 1951, his career ended for good when he was knocked out in eight rounds by the up-and-coming Rocky Marciano.

In 66 professional bouts, Louis lost only three times (twice in the last two years of his career) and knocked out 49 of his opponents. He was elected to the Boxing Hall of Fame in 1954. He died of a heart attack at his home in Las Vegas on April 12, 1981. ◆

wunderkind: German in origin, a wunderkind is a very talented athlete who has succeeded at his or her sport at a very young age. Also applies to non-sporting activities.

By 1950, however, an aged Louis, reflexes shot and legs gimpy, was forced back into the ring because of money problems.

Lukas, D. Wayne

SEPTEMBER 2, 1935– ● HORSE TRAINER

W idely considered the most successful trainer in the past quarter century of horse racing, D. Wayne Lukas was voted into the racing Hall of Fame by a landslide in 1999, his first year of eligibility. The overwhelming vote was well-deserved in recognition of his spectacular record of successes: winner of three Kentucky Derbies, four Preakness Stakes, and three Belmonts; thirteen Breeders' Cups winners; nineteen Eclipse Award Champions; 3,712 total races won; 13 years as the country's top-earning trainer; the first trainer to reach career earnings of $100 million (in 1990), with some $200 million for his career; and a single-year earnings record of $17.8 million in 1998.

Darrell Wayne Lukas was born on September 2, 1935, in the agricultural town of Antigo, Wisconsin. His love for horses dates back to his earliest childhood on his family's dairy farm. During his boyhood, he was devoted to hauling his pony to local fairgrounds to participate in races. As his mother told a reporter, "He could be with a horse for five minutes and have him following him around. He seemed to speak their language." At these fairground races, young Lukas learned the down home techniques of preparing horses for races.

breaking horses: taking young and/or wild horses and training them so that they accept wearing a saddle and being ridden.

Lukas turned his knowledge to profitable use by **breaking** and selling horses in partnership with a friend. When he went off to college at the University of Wisconsin, he took his business instincts and devotion to horses with him. As he later told a reporter, "Every weekend I'm throwing my saddle into my pickup, getting on my blue jeans and heading down the road. I was always working, always hustling, always trying to hit the sales."

But horses weren't the sole preoccupation of the restlessly ambitious Lukas, who also dreamed of becoming a college basketball coach. After graduating from college he taught and coached basketball for two years in Blair, Wisconsin, and then went back to the University of Wisconsin to pursue graduate studies and to work as the assistant basketball coach for the freshman squad. After completing his graduate studies, Lukas became the head basketball coach at Logan High School in LaCrosse, Wisconsin. A strict disciplinarian, he demanded not only the utmost concentration on the court, but also a high level of decorum off of it—he outfitted the team in matching sport coats and ties on trips and hired hostesses from a local Holiday Inn to coach team members in table manners.

All the while Lukas kept one foot in the horse business, still training and selling and trading as he began to specialize in quarter horses (horses that run quarter-mile races). Juggling all his responsibilities resulted in a punishing schedule: rising at four in the morning, he would make the hour's drive to supervise the morning training of his horses, then he would dash back to school just in time to teach his classes. After the basketball season was over, he often made a second evening trip to visit the horses.

In 1967, unable to sustain this double life, Lukas quit teaching after six years to make a full-time commitment to training quarter horses. Within three years he became a major presence in quarter-horse racing. In 1970 he already had more wins than any other trainer in the field, and by 1975 he had more than 150 victories, twice the previous record.

Having conquered the quarter-horse world, Lukas was ready to take the step up to the even higher-stakes world of thoroughbred racing, where he progressed with equal speed, chalking up his first major win after only a year in the field. Lukas's rapid rise and unorthodox training methods caused some of the old-school thoroughbred trainers to resent him; they accused him of racing his horses excessively and running slightly injured horses in those states that allowed the administering of pain medication. Lukas's response was, "When they're hot, they're hot. You better run 'em. Tomorrow they might be dead." Some of his critics also found (and continue to find) fault with what they regard as an almost military approach to his work. As one reporter put it, "His rivals are put off because he has grooms manicure the grounds around his stable, because he insists the bridles and the buckets and the blankets be stacked just so. They make fun of the creases in his jeans, and the starch in his manner."

With an improbable run of winners and a booming business in yearling sales during the 1980s, Lukas's wealth mushroomed, and he wasn't shy about brandishing the flashy signs of his success: a Rolls Royce, Armani suits, and increasingly influential friends and clients. The following decade was less kind to Lukas, however. When Calumet Farm, one of his leading clients, went bankrupt in 1991, it cost Lukas roughly $3.1 million. Even worse things were in store in 1993. When the horse Union City broke a foreleg in the Preakness Stakes that year and had to be

1935 Lukas is born in Antigo, Wisconsin.

1967 Lukas commits to the full-time training of quarter horses.

1975 Lukas surpasses 150 victories, double the previous record.

1990 Lukas's earnings pass $100 million.

1991 Lukas's Calumet Farm goes bankrupt.

1993 Lukas's horse Union City breaks foreleg at Preakness Stakes.

1999 Lukas is voted into the horseracing Hall of Fame.

destroyed, Lukas was subjected to a hailstorm of criticism for having run an apparently injured horse. The episode plunged Lukas into a deep despair that required the intervention of close friends.

In December of 1993, Lukas's son Jeff, his closest personal and business associate, was nearly killed while trying to calm a horse that had been sparked into a panic. As Lukas recalled, "I was on the phone in my office, and I leaned forward to look out and saw Jeff standing there, waving his arms." The horse continued charging at Jeff. "Jeff went straight up in the air and upside down," Lukas told a reporter. "When he hit, he landed on his head, and the sound was like a gunshot." Jeff eventually emerged from a deep coma but remained in the hospital for several months and still must undergo physical therapy. While still active in his father's business, his duties have shifted to administrative matters, leaving more of the training responsibilities to the elder Lukas.

In the wake of these reverses, Lukas has begun slowly to rebuild his shrunken empire. In 1998 he married his fourth wife, Laura Pinelli, a horse trainer who is 23 years his junior. He is training more than 150 horses at three major tracks: Santa Anita, Churchill Downs, and Belmont. Notwithstanding his unparalleled successes, he is still intent on achieving his only major unfulfilled career goal: winning all three Triple Crown races in one year. ◆

Mack, Connie

DECEMBER 22, 1862–FEBRUARY 8, 1956 ● BASEBALL MANAGER

In baseball's rich mythos of heroes and rogues, Connie Mack stands out as the sport's grand patriarch. His tenure of 50 consecutive years as manager of the Philadelphia Athletics is a baseball record that seems as unbreakable as Joe Dimaggio's 56-game hitting streak. But Connie Mack was notable for far more than mere longevity. Called by one writer "the master builder of baseball teams," Mack pioneered so many aspects of modern strategy, player development, and team building that to recount his career is to trace the history of modern baseball itself.

He was born Cornelius Alexander McGillicuddy on December 22, 1862, in East Brookfield, Massachusetts. Although by some reports he adopted the foreshortened "Mack" to oblige headline writers, he once said, "Except when we voted, our people always called themselves Mack." The young Connie began to play baseball while working in a shoe factory to support his mother after his father's death. His catching skills attracted notice, and in 1884 he signed on with his first professional club, Meridien of the Connecticut State League; he moved on to Hartford of the North East Connecticut State league the following season.

With a growing a reputation as a canny and skilled backstop who was a weak hitter, Mack ascended to the Washington Nationals in September 1886 and clinched the starting catching job with a strong performance down the stretch run. After three solid seasons in Washington, Mack signed with Buffalo of the new Players League, which folded after only one season. In 1891

> *"You're born with two strikes against you, so don't take a third one on your own."*
>
> Connie Mack's advice to players

he joined the Pittsburgh club, where he spent his final six seasons as a player. Known as the "Pirates" for its aggressive raids on other teams' players, Pittsburgh made a strong but unsuccessful run at the pennant in 1893. Their success that year was due in no small measure to Mack's skill behind the plate. Playing before the invention of shin guards and with only a primitive mitt, mask, and chest protector, the frequently battered Mack enhanced his defensive skills with subtle tricks, such as "accidentally" interfering with batters' swings with his mitt and generating an artificial foul-tip sound to deceive the umpire into calling out batters who had not actually made contact with the ball.

When the Pirates faltered badly in 1894, Mack was named the team's player-manager. One of his first innovations was to freeze the supply of baseballs before the game to thwart the opponent's offense (cold baseballs didn't travel as well as warm ones). Despite leading the Pirates to winning marks in 1895 and 1896, Mack was fired by a meddlesome owner. In 1897 he moved on to the manager's post of the Milwaukee club of the Western League, which in 1900 evolved into the present-day American League. When the Athletics debuted as the American League club in Philadelphia, Mack joined them as part-owner and manager.

Breaking baseball's managerial mold of the gruff, foul-mouthed dictator, Mack inspired loyalty with his gentleness and patience. His on-field eccentricities became beloved trademarks: flouting the baseball tradition of the uniformed manager, the elegantly tall and lanky Mack always called the shots from the dugout in a freshly pressed suit and tie. He was also well-known for directing his fielders' positioning by waving a scorecard.

Blending a gentlemanly style with unrivaled baseball knowledge, he quickly assembled a winning team, capturing the American League pennant for Philadelphia in 1902 with the help of an impressive pitching staff headed by Rube Waddell, Chief Bender, and Eddie Plank. The National League, the snooty "senior circuit," had not yet recognized the upstart American League, so it was not until 1905, when Philadelphia next finished first, that Mack managed his first World Series, losing to John McGraw's formidable New York Giants four games to one.

After that loss Mack set about the first of his many famous rebuilding efforts, shedding some expensive older talent like Waddell and nurturing "hungry" young players like Eddie Collins and Frank "Home Run" Baker. With his renowned "$100,000" infield of Collins, Baker, Jack Barry, and Stuffy McInnis, Mack led the Athletics to world championships in 1910, 1911, and 1913, and an A.L. crown in 1914, when the A's lost the World Series to the "miracle" Boston Braves.

Despite the Athletics' winning ways, the franchise faced mounting economic pressures: attendance dipped markedly in 1914, the short-lived Federal League lured Plank and Bender away with fat contracts, and the onset of World War I clouded the prospects for baseball as a whole. Mack responded by selling the team's high-priced veterans, and in 1915 the team plummeted to last place, performing poorly for the next seven years.

By the early 1920s Mack gradually began to piece together another winner, adding future superstars such as Lefty Grove, Al Simmons, and Jimmie Foxx (all members of the Hall of Fame) to a solid **nucleus**. By 1927 the Athletics were second only to the powerhouse New York Yankees. After another second-place finish in 1928, the A's sailed to an easy pennant and world championship in 1929, beating the Chicago Cubs in the World Series in five games. Mack's famous tactical move in that contest was his choice of Harold Ehmke, regarded by many as a has-been, to pitch the opener at Chicago's Wrigley Field. Mack thought that with a largely white-shirted crowd, Ehmke's sidearm motion would baffle the Cub batters, and he was right: Ehmke not only cruised to an impressive 3–1 victory, but he also struck out 14 batters, setting a World Series mark that stood until 1952. After the Series that year, Mack was honored as one of Philadelphia's greatest citizens when he received the Edward W. Bok Award.

In 1930 the Athletics won still another pennant and defeated the St. Louis Cardinals in the World Series. A.L. champs again in 1931, the Athletics lost to the Cardinals in that year's World Series. After respectable second-place showings in 1932 and 1933, Mack was obliged to face the financial consequences of maintaining baseball's highest payroll during an unyielding economic Depression that caused sagging attendance, and he once again sold off his best players. In 1935 the Athletics were back in last place, where they remained for nine of the following 12 years.

Connie Mack never managed another pennant winner. After another last-place finish in 1950, the 85-year-old Mack retired as manager but retained his majority financial interest in

"Any minute, any day, some players may break a long-standing record. That's one of the fascinations about the game—the unexpected surprises."

Connie Mack on baseball

nucleus: In scientific terms, the nucleus is the center of an atom, which is the tiny piece of matter that all things in the universe are made of. In sports terms, the nucleus of a team is the group of players who are most important to that team's success.

the club. Interviewed when he was 79, he declared, "My greatest thrill was starting Howard Ehmke as surprise pitcher against the Cubs in the first game of the 1929 World Series. My biggest disappointment was the 1914 team that lost four in a row to the Braves in the World Series."

Connie Mack's bust at the Baseball Hall of Fame bears the title "Mr. Baseball." He died at the age of 93 on February 8, 1956. ◆

Maddux, Greg

APRIL 14, 1966– ● BASEBALL PLAYER

Gregory Alan Maddux was born in San Angelo, Texas. His baseball career began in earnest at Valley High School in Las Vegas, Nevada, where he was an All-State baseball player during his junior and senior years. In the second round of the 1984 free-agent draft, the Chicago Cubs signed Maddux right out of high school. He played for the Cubs' Triple A affiliate in Iowa until the Cubs called him up near the end of the 1986 season—at age 20, the youngest Cubs' player in nearly two decades. Maddux finished that season with a 2–4 record and a 5.52 earned run average. During the 1987 season the young pitcher continued to pay his dues. He started the year back at Iowa but was soon promoted to the Cubs' starting rotation. He struggled to a 6–14 record and a 5.61 earned run average (ERA), losing his last six decisions.

Given this inauspicious start, few baseball fans might have predicted that Maddux would develop into one of the most dominating right-handed pitchers to ever play the game. In an era when many pitchers unleashed fastballs approaching—and even topping—100 miles an hour, Maddux's 85-mile-an-hour fastball seemed average at best. Moreover, to many baseball fans, he didn't "look" like a world-class athlete. Many observers quipped that when he took the mound, the bespectacled Maddux looked more like an accountant than a Cy Young Award–winning pitcher. However, looks were deceiving. Starting with the 1988 season, Maddux showed that what he lacked in brawn and power he made up for with determination, detailed knowledge of the hitters he faced, and an array of pitches that he could deliver with seemingly laserlike accuracy.

That year Maddux was 15–3 going into the All-Star break; during June he was 5–0 with a 2.22 ERA. He finished his breakthrough season with an 18–8 mark and a 3.18 ERA. He continued to improve in 1989, when he won 19 games—second in the National League—and lowered his ERA to 2.95. His performance on the mound dimmed slightly in 1990, when he compiled a 15–15 record and a 3.46 ERA, including an eight-game losing streak, but that year he showed his talent in the field by winning the first of seven consecutive Gold Glove Awards. In 1991, posting a 15–11 record, he showed his amazing accuracy by striking out 198 batters while walking just 66 in his league leading 263 innings on the mound.

Maddux's last year with the Cubs was 1992. That year he posted a 20–11 record with a 2.18 ERA and won the first of four straight Cy Young awards as the best pitcher in the National League. Once again he led the league in innings pitched with 268 and, amazingly, he gave up just seven home runs. As a free agent at the end of the season, Maddux signed with the Atlanta Braves, who were in the process of building the most dominating pitching staff in the major leagues. In 1993, his first year with the Braves, Maddux repeated as the Cy Young winner while compiling a 20–10 record—a win-loss record that might have been better had his teammates managed to score more than a total of 15 runs in the 10 losses.

In 1994 Maddux became the first pitcher ever to win three straight Cy Young awards. That year he went 16–6 with a major-league-leading 1.56 ERA, the third best ERA in the majors since 1919, and gave up just four home runs and 31 walks all season. In 1995 Maddux continued to baffle opposing hitters, whose batting average against him was a meager .197. On his way to a record fourth straight Cy Young Award he compiled a 19–2 record with a 1.63 ERA and an incredible 23 walks in 209 innings. Throughout the late 1990s his statistics continued to

1966 Maddux is born in San Angelo, Texas.

1986 Maddux joins the Chicago Cubs at age 20.

1990 Maddux wins the first of seven consecutive Gold Glove awards.

1992 Maddux wins the first of four straight Cy Young awards; signs with the Atlanta Braves.

be impressive. In 1996 he went 15–11 with a 2.72 ERA while winning his seventh consecutive Gold Glove Award. In 1997 he went 19–4 while lowering his ERA to 2.20, and in 1998 he compiled an 18–9 record with a 2.22 ERA. Although his ERA in 1999 jumped to 3.57 and he failed to record a shutout for the first time since 1987, Maddux still managed to post a 19–9 record. Throughout his career, he ranked at or near the top of the major leagues in games started (432), complete games (93), wins (221), and innings pitched (3,068)—all while striking out 2,160, yielding just 157 home runs and 691 walks, and compiling a composite 2.81 ERA.

Maddux and his wife, Kathy, head up the Maddux Foundation, which is involved in several charitable activities, including donating Braves tickets to nonprofit organizations. In his spare time Maddux enjoys playing golf and Nintendo. ◆

Man o' War

MARCH 29, 1917–NOVEMBER 1, 1947 ● THOROUGHBRED RACEHORSE

Near midnight on March 29, 1917, the mare Mahubah gave birth to a colt at Major August Belmont's Nursery Stud Farm near Lexington, Kentucky. The youngster was chestnut in color, with a star on his forehead and a narrow stripe leading from the right of the star down the center of his nose. The next morning, the Nursery Stud daybook recorded that the foal, named Man o' War, had a height of 42 inches, a girth of 33 inches.

Normally, Major Belmont would have been there, but he was in New York, where he was in charge of securing and training horses for the U.S. military, then engaged in World War I. But though he could not be present at the foaling, Belmont had played a critical part in the birth: He was the one who had decided to breed Mahubah with the fiery stud Fair Play, guessing that this pairing would make for some "hot" blood. Maybe this would be a real runner.

Indeed he was. Man o' War would become what many people in the racing world consider the greatest racehorse of the twentieth century, if not of all time.

Deeply involved in the war effort, Belmont decided to sell 21 of the Nursery Stud's yearlings. Thus, Mahubah's colt was sold to Samuel Riddle of Glen Riddle Farms in Pennsylvania, at an auction in August 1918. Riddle had initially been reluctant to bid, but he was urged to make the investment by his wife and by his trainer, Louis Feustel. At one time Feustel had worked for Belmont, and he knew that Nursery Stud's yearlings were top-notch. Thus pressured, Riddle bid, and Man o' War fetched a price of $5,000, nearly five times the average price for yearlings at the auction.

The chestnut colt proved hard to break. True to his heritage, he was spirited and lively, and he resisted being controlled. But he was nonetheless a favorite at the training grounds at Havre de Grace and Pimlico. For a time he was called "Red," after Feustel's titian-haired brother; then he was called "Big Red," as he grew to be more than 16 hands high.

The trainer had to be patient with Mahubah's headstrong colt, but eventually Man o' War was deemed ready to start in a race. He won handily at his first competition at Belmont Park, on June 19, 1919, running five furlongs in just 59 seconds.

Between then and October 1920, Man o' War won all of the races in which he was entered, including the Preakness Stakes, the Belmont Stakes, the Stuyvesant Handicap, the Dwyer Stakes, the Travers Stakes, the Kenilworth Park Gold Cup, and the Jockey Club Stakes (now the Gold Cup). Though he did not race in the Kentucky Derby (along with the Preakness Stakes and the Belmont Stakes, one of U.S. racing's Triple Crown), Man o' War's list of accomplishments was legion. He set many time records by a breathtaking margin, and he triumphed in all sorts of track conditions and distances. His American record for the $1\frac{1}{2}$ mile Jockey Club Stakes would hold for 17 years.

Man o' War was an exceptionally strong thoroughbred, often giving huge weight concessions to his competitors. In one race, the horse carrying the next highest weight ran with 32 pounds less than Man o' War. Wrote racing historian Joe Palmer: "He did not beat, he merely annihilated. He did not run to world records, he galloped to them." Man o' War's superiority was noticed by bettors. He was odds-on favorite in all 21 of his races. If before there had been doubt before about which was the greatest racehorse of the young century, there was no longer any question. Man o' War was exceptional, head and shoulders—so to speak—above the competition. He dominated horseracing like no other equine competitor had ever done.

After Man o' War's astonishing winning streak at 20 of his 21 races in just two seasons (1919–1920), Samuel Riddle, his

1917 Man o' War is born near Lexington, Kentucky.

1919 Man o' War wins his first race, at Belmont.

1920 Man o' War retires after winning 20 of 21 races.

1947 Man o' War dies at age 30; is mourned worldwide.

owner, decided to retire the thoroughbred to stud. By then, Man o' War was a legend in his own time, and Riddle was offered $1 million for him. But he declined to sell the champion. Man o' War proceeded to serve 23 years at stud, producing 64 stakes winners, including War Admiral—a Triple Crown and horse of the year winner. The fillies that he sired **foaled** 124 stakes winners.

foaled: gave birth to, in horse terms. Young horses are known as foals.

Riddle's exceptional thoroughbred was not just a great stud horse; he was also a celebrity. It is estimated that after his retirement, between $1^1/_2$ million and 3 million people went to visit Man o' War in Riddle's farms in Lexington, Kentucky. He was known throughout the world, and people traveled great distances just for a glimpse of him.

Man o' War died on November 1, 1947, at age 30. His death was announced throughout the world, and his funeral was a somber occasion attended by many mourners. He was buried in the Kentucky Horse Park in Lexington, Kentucky. The gravesite, crowned by a sculpture of the great thoroughbred, is an attraction to thousands who come to pay tribute. ◆

Mantle, Mickey

OCTOBER 20, 1931–AUGUST 13, 1995 ● BASEBALL PLAYER

Everything about Mickey Mantle seemed to bespeak a mythic baseball destiny: the wondrous speed and power, to be sure, but also the granite jaw and blond, boyish handsomeness, the tree-stump forearms, the accidental discovery by the legendary Yankees—even the alliterative gallantry of his name. And Mantle even lived out a mythic fate: the great ballplayer was tragically felled by the blows of ill-fortune (chronic injury) and the flaws of his character (alcoholism). One of the two or three great baseball heroes of the postwar era, he paced the Yankee juggernaut to an astounding 14 pennants in 16 seasons with 536 regular-season home runs (a career record for a switch hitter) and a record 18 in the World Series.

Mickey Charles Mantle was born in Spavinaw, Oklahoma, on October 20, 1931. His father, Mutt, an ardent baseball fan, named him after Detroit Tigers catcher Mickey Cochrane and began his son's baseball lessons as soon as he could walk, teach-

Mickey Mantle, Sr. and
son Mickey Jr.

ing him early on the switch-hitting that later helped to propel
him to the Hall of Fame.

When Mantle was four, the family moved to Commerce,
Oklahoma, where the family struggled on Mutt's meager wages
as a zinc miner. It was while assisting his father in the mines as
a "screen ape," smashing large rocks into small stones with a
sledgehammer, that young Mantle developed such awesome
strength in his wrists, arms, shoulders, and forearms.

Mantle excelled in all sports growing up but almost had his
playing days cut short from when he was kicked in the shin
while playing high school football; the wound developed into
osteomyelitis, a chronic bone disease. While the doctors considered amputation, they administered massive doses of a then-
new drug, penicillin, that blocked the spread of the disease but
left him with the first of many disabilities that would haunt him
throughout his career. Exempted from military service because
of his leg injury, Mantle signed on with a local semipro baseball
team, the Baxter Springs Whiz Kids. In 1948 Yankee scout Tom
Greenwade came to see Mantle's teammate, the third baseman

1931 Mantle is born in Spavinaw, Oklahoma.

1951 Mantle starts with the New York Yankees at age 19.

1955 Mantle leads the American League in home runs with 37.

1956 Mantle wins the American League Triple Crown and the Most Valuable Player award.

1995 Mantle dies at age 63.

1999 Mantle is posthumously named to baseball's All-Century Team.

Billy Johnson, but he soon forgot about Johnson as he watched the 16-year-old Mantle jolt two prodigious homers, one from each side of the plate. Unable to sign Mantle because of his age, Greenwade made the Mantles promise to wait for his return upon Mantle's graduation from high school. A year later, with diploma in hand, Mantle took Greenwade's pen and signed with the Yankees for $1,500.

Mantle spent his first minor league season, 1949, playing class D ball in Independence, Kansas, hitting a promising .313 but making an alarming 47 errors in 89 games at shortstop. In 1950 he was promoted to C ball at Joplin, Missouri, where his 55 errors in 137 games were overshadowed by a whopping .383 batting average.

Promoted to the Yankees at the start of the 1951 season, the shy 19-year-old from Oklahoma was so awestruck that he found himself unable to speak to his teammate and hero, Joe DiMaggio. As his teammate Whitey Ford recalled, "He was a real country boy, all shy and embarrassed. He arrived with a straw suitcase and two pairs of slacks and one blue sports jacket that probably cost about eight dollars." Cowed by the magnitude of New York and Yankeedom, Mantle faltered at first, striking out so often that manager Casey Stengel returned him to the minors for further seasoning. But in less than two months he was back to stay, moving to right field (it was DiMaggio's last campaign in center) and ready to make his mark in baseball history.

In the World Series that year, Mantle pulled up short to avoid an outfield collision with DiMaggio, caught his heel in a drain pipe, and collapsed as though he'd been shot. Surgery was required to repair the resulting torn ligaments in his knee, the first of many baseball injuries that shadowed his career.

In 1952 Mantle batted .311 with 23 homers and made his first All-Star team as the Yankees captured their fourth straight championship. In 1953, when the Yankees again won a record fifth consecutive World Series, Mantle hit a 565-foot blast in Washington's Griffith Stadium. Fans begin to take notice of the young center fielder who, as Stengel said of him, "has more speed than any slugger and more slug than any speedster—and nobody has ever had more of both of them together."

Mantle led the American League in home runs for the first time in 1955 with 37 clouts, but the Brooklyn Dodgers finally edged out the Yankees in seven games in that year's World Series. It was in 1956, however, that Mantle's gifts finally reached full flower: "The Mick" captured the American League Triple

Crown that season with 52 home runs, 130 runs batted in (RBI) and a .353 batting average (he also led the league in home run percentage, runs scored, and slugging percentage). Unfortunately, Mantle's off-field exploits were also peaking—his nighttime carousing with teammates Whitey Ford and Billy Martin set him on a path of alcoholism that shortened his playing career and his life.

But for the time being Mantle was young enough to slough off the toll of his dissipations, and he remained the terror of American League pitchers for years to come. He won his second straight Most Valuable Player (MVP) award in 1957, beating out Ted Williams of Boston by 24 votes. The Yankees lost the World Series to the Milwaukee Braves that year, but recaptured the world title in 1958, when Mantle turned in a solid if less spectacular season, leading the league in homers again.

The Yankees and Mantle both had an "off" year in 1959, when the Yankees dropped to third place. The Bombers rebounded in 1960, when they acquired Roger Maris to bolster an already potent attack. Although Maris captured the MVP that year, Mantle led the American League in homers. The Yankees dropped the Series to the Pirates in seven games despite trouncing them in nearly every statistical category.

In 1961 Mantle and Maris held the nation spellbound with a season-long assault on Babe Ruth's longstanding season mark of 60 home runs. Two weeks before the end of the season, Mantle developed an abscessed hip that took him out of the running, and it was left to the less-popular Maris to surge past the Babe with 61 homers (Mantle ended up with 54), a record that stood until Mark McGwire demolished it with 70 homers in 1998. The 1961 Yankees, widely considered one of baseball's greatest teams, steamrolled the Reds in the World Series that year, even though Mantle saw only limited action.

A relatively healthy Mantle paced the Yankees to another American League pennant in 1962, winning his third and last Most Valuable Player award with a .321 batting average and spurring the Bombers to a seven-game victory over the San Francisco Giants in that year's World Series. The Yankees won pennants again in 1963 and 1964, losing to the Dodgers and Cardinals, respectively, in those World Series. Those were Mantle's last two productive seasons in baseball; he clouted his 18th career World Series homer in 1964, a record that still stands.

Over his final four seasons, from 1965 to 1968, the cumulative ravages of injury and alcoholism finally exacted a terrible

"No man in the history of baseball had as much power as Mickey Mantle. No man. When you're talking about Mickey Mantle, it's an altogether different level. Separates the men from the boys."

Billy Martin

price, and The Mick hobbled toward retirement at the beginning of the 1969 season. He ended his playing days with 536 home runs (eighth on the all-time list), a .298 career batting average, and 1,509 RBI.

Mantle spent his retirement years as a genial if directionless sports celebrity, playing in golf tournaments and appearing at autograph and memorabilia shows. Elected to the Baseball Hall of Fame in 1974, he never really found a secure path in his post-baseball years as he ebbed ever deeper into an alcoholic haze, neglecting his family and suffering recurrent bouts of ill health that culminated in the tremors and memory loss that drove him to seek help at the Betty Ford Clinic in 1994. He said at the time, 'For all those years I lived the life of somebody I didn't know. A cartoon character. From now on Mickey Mantle is going to be a real person. I still can't remember much of the last 10 years . . . but I'm looking forward to the memories I'll have in the next ten."

posthumously: an event that occurs after a person's death. For example, when baseball player Roberto Clemente was killed in a plane crash, he was honored posthumously for all the charity work he did while he was alive.

But his effort at self-reformation came too late. He developed cancer of the liver in 1995 and required a transplant. A little more than a month after the operation, on August 13, 1995, Mickey Mantle died at the age of 63. At Mantle's funeral sports broadcaster Bob Costas said, "He was a presence in our lives—a fragile hero to whom we had an emotional attachment so strong and lasting that it defied logic."

Mickey Mantle was **posthumously** named to baseball's All-Century Team in 1999. ◆

Marciano, Rocky

SEPTEMBER 1, 1923–AUGUST 31, 1969 ● BOXER

Born Rocco Marchegiano in Brockton, Massachusetts, Rocky Marciano was the only heavyweight boxing champion to retire undefeated. At 5' 10" and 185-pounds, Marciano, nicknamed the "Brockton Blockbuster," was one of the smallest heavyweight champions of all time, and was often smaller and slower than most of his opponents; however, he was able to make use of his most prominent assets to always come through the victor. Those assets were a powerful punch using either hand, a rock-solid chin and, most importantly, a will to win that surpassed any fighter of his generation.

Growing up during the Great Depression, Marciano worked several different jobs to help support his family, including at a shoe factory with his father, Pierino. During World War II, when Marciano was just 20 years old, he was drafted into the U.S. Army and sent overseas to England. He had just been transferred back to the United States to prepare for combat duty in Japan when, in 1945, the United States dropped two atomic bombs on Japan and ended the war.

Marciano had taken up boxing during his stint in the military, representing his unit in amateur contests. By the time he returned to Massachusetts, Marciano had boxing in his blood. After a short and successful amateur career that saw him win the New England Golden Gloves title, Marciano turned professional and knocked out Lee Epperson in three rounds on March 17, 1947, in his pro debut. In 1950, Marciano made his first mark on the world boxing scene, when he beat another undefeated contender, Roland LaStarza, in a hard-fought 10-round decision.

One year later, Marciano fought an important, yet heartbreaking, match against his boyhood hero, former heavyweight champion Joe Louis. The 37-year-old Louis was on the comeback trail, but was no match for the powerful fists of Marciano, who knocked the "Brown Bomber" back into retirement with a devastating seventh round knockout.

The victory over a fighter of Louis's caliber thrust Marciano into the national spotlight and into a title fight against 38-year-old champion Jersey Joe Walcott. Walcott was a crafty fighter who had been plying his trade for nearly two decades, and his experience showed as he knocked Marciano down in the first round and built up a sizable lead on the scorecards over the first 12 rounds. However, in the 13th round, Marciano landed what many boxing experts still consider the perfect punch—a right cross that traveled perhaps six inches and landed squarely on the chin of Walcott. Marciano had every bit of his considerable power and leverage into the shot, and Walcott slumped to the canvas, unconscious. Marciano, the man who'd been told that he was too short and slow to be a good fighter, was the heavyweight champion of the world.

Marciano defended his title six times, against the best opposition of his day. He gave Walcott a rematch, but Jersey Joe fared no better the second time around, as Marciano put him down for the count in the first round. Former heavyweight champion Ezzard Charles gave Marciano two memorable fights,

1923 Rocky Marciano is born as Rocco Marchegiano in Brockton, Massachusetts.

1951 In a seventh-round KO, Marciano knocks Joe Louis back into retirement.

1955 Marciano wins his last fight, KO'ing light-heavyweight champ Archie "the Ol' Mongoose" Moore in the seventh round.

1956 Marciano retires undefeated.

but Marciano's will to win carried him through, especially in their second fight, during which the "Brockton Blockbuster" had to survive a severely cut nose to win the fight.

Marciano's final fight was against light-heavyweight champion Archie Moore, another crafty fighter. Moore knocked Marciano down in the first round, just as Walcott had done, but Marciano pulled himself up and knocked Moore down three times to win his final fight via a ninth round stoppage.

Marciano retired shortly after the fight with Moore, and did something so very few boxers are able to do—he stayed retired, finishing his career with a record of 49–0 with 43 knockouts. His record stands unparalleled in boxing annals—no other fighter, including greats such as Muhammad Ali, Joe Louis, or Evander Holyfield, has ever retired as undefeated heavyweight champion.

Tragically, just one day before his 46th birthday, on August 31, 1969, Marciano died in a plane crash in Iowa. However, the "Brockton Blockbuster's" memory lives on in all that saw his tenacity in the ring, or admired his efforts as the only undefeated champion in boxing history. ◆

Maris, Roger

SEPTEMBER 10, 1934–DECEMBER 14, 1985 ● BASEBALL PLAYER

Roger Maris (whose family name of Maras was legally changed in 1955) was the son of Rudolph Maris, Sr., a railroad mechanics supervisor, and Anne Corrine Sturbitz, a housewife. His family moved from Minnesota to Grand Forks, North Dakota, before settling in Fargo, North Dakota, when Maris was in junior high school. Roger and Rudy, his older brother and only sibling, participated in all sports, encouraged by their father, a former semiprofessional hockey and baseball player.

Direct and uncomplicated, but sensitive, Maris revealed his superior athletic ability while playing for Bishop Shanley High School. He also displayed a stubborn streak that came out when he believed he had been ill-treated. In 1951 he established a national high school football record with four kickoff returns for touchdowns in one game. He also starred in basketball and track and was the most valuable player on the state champion American Legion baseball team in 1950.

Maris graduated from high school in 1952. A solidly built young man who would fill out to six feet and about 200 pounds at maturity, he was widely recruited to play college football; after visiting the University of Oklahoma, Maris realized he could not endure classroom confinement and returned home. But the multitalented Maris had also attracted the attention of professional baseball. Given the opportunity to try out by the Cleveland Indians organization, Maris impressed Cleveland's general manager Hank Greenberg. He was offered $5,000 to join the organization, with the promise of $10,000 more when he made the parent club.

An outfielder, Maris progressed steadily through the Cleveland organization, but he also developed a reputation for defiance, for example, by demanding to play with hometown Fargo (of the Class C Northern League) in 1953 and by walking off the field when he felt unjustly treated by his manager with Reading (Class A Eastern League) in 1955. Playing for Indianapolis (Class AAA American Association) in 1956, he starred in the minor league Little World Series. That same year Maris married Patricia Anne Cavell, his high school sweetheart.

His minor league apprenticeship over, Maris played with the Cleveland Indians in 1957. He was having a good rookie year when he suffered broken ribs trying to break up a double play; he never regained his momentum that season. He would incur many injuries through aggressive play, adversely affecting his career. In June 1958, after a poor start in his sophomore season, Maris was traded to the Kansas City Athletics. Playing regularly before supportive fans in a relaxed atmosphere, he started well in 1959 but an emergency appendectomy and several prolonged slumps ruined a potentially great season.

During the 1959 season, Maris voiced his desire to remain with the Athletics, but on December 11, 1959, he was traded to the New York Yankees. Although disappointed at the trade, Maris quickly provided the caliber of play desperately sought by the Yankees management. His all-out playing style and quiet, solid demeanor fit in well with his teammates and the image-conscious Yankees organization. He helped the team win the American League pennant in 1960 by batting .283, hitting 39 home runs (one fewer than league-leading teammate Mickey Mantle), leading the league in runs batted in (112) and slugging percentage (.581), and winning the Most Valuable Player award.

1934 Maris is born in Hibbing, Minnesota.

1960 Playing for the New York Yankees, Maris leads the league in runs batted in and slugging percentage; he is voted Most Valuable Player (MVP) of the American League.

1961 Maris wins the race with teammate Mickey Mantle and breaks Babe Ruth's single season home run record; he is also voted MVP for the second year in a row.

1966 Maris is traded to the St. Louis Cardinals.

1967 The Cardinals win the World Series.

1968 Maris retires after the Cardinals lose the World Series to the Detroit Tigers.

> *"As a ballplayer, I would be delighted to do it again. As an individual, I doubt if I could possibly go through it again."*
> Roger Maris on his 61 home runs in the 1961 season

Maris had a reasonable relationship with the press in 1960, but he was never at ease with aggressive reporters, and his terse responses to their questions were often misconstrued as rudeness. Meanwhile, Mantle, who held similar sentiments and who had been vilified during his disappointing 1959 season, was slowly regaining fan support and reaching an amicable accommodation he had never previously enjoyed with baseball writers.

By August 1960, Maris was hitting home runs at a rate that threatened Babe Ruth's mark of 60, established in 1927. Questioned at that time regarding the chances of breaking Ruth's record, Maris diplomatically answered that neither he nor anyone else would ever accomplish that feat. Rib injuries shortly nullified whatever chance Maris had that year. But in 1961, both Maris and Mantle would capture the nation's attention as they each hit home runs at a record-breaking pace for much of the season. Ordered by Yankee management to concentrate on home runs, Maris hit 15 in June. By month's end, he had hit 27 and Mantle 25, and the nation's sportswriters started to treat their challenge to Ruth's record seriously. On July 17, Baseball Commissioner Ford C. Frick, concerned that the newly expanded 162-game American League playing schedule might taint Ruth's record, ruled that a new home-run record would only be recognized if it was achieved within the first 154 games.

The home-run challenge brought out hordes of reporters wherever the Yankees played. Inundated with often simplistic, repetitive questions, badgered for interviews, and besieged by autograph-seekers, Maris withdrew deeper within himself to preserve his privacy. The self-perpetuating nature of the media furor led to inevitable inaccuracies, distortions, and misinterpretations of Maris's words. And Maris, **taciturn** by nature, harmed his own cause; his curt replies, once published, tended to suggest a surly, abrasive personality. Some writers attempted to play up the story of a feud between Maris and Mantle; in reality, the two men got along well and even shared an apartment that summer with teammate Bob Cerv.

taciturn: silent, not talkative by nature.

Mantle kept pace with Maris for much of the season, but a hip abscess in September sidelined him and left Maris alone in the full glare of the media spotlight. Yankee officials did nothing to shield their player from media onslaughts as he neared the record. The pressure became almost intolerable for Maris; at one point, he suffered hair loss caused by nervous strain. He failed to equal Ruth's total in 154 games, but on October 1, 1961, the final game of the season, while facing Boston Red Sox pitcher Tracy Stallard at Yankee Stadium, Maris hit the record-breaking 61st home run. He went into the record book but his accomplishment was besmirched by an asterisk next to the number 61, keyed to a footnote announcing that Ruth's record for a 154-game season was still valid.

Maris was named Most Valuable Player for the second time in his career and received a plethora of other awards, but his phenomenal season had become a kind of curse. From the start of spring training in 1962, his problems with the press multiplied. Certain reporters portrayed him as a moody, surly complainer. Also in 1962, Maris became a target for fan abuse. Although he had an excellent season, finishing with 33 home runs and 100 runs batted in, and making a key fielding play that was instrumental in the team's World Series victory (over the San Francisco Giants), he was treated as if he was a failure because he did not match or surpass his 1961 totals. This problem of impossible expectations would blight the rest of his career.

Maris suffered from a variety of injuries that limited his playing time and productivity in 1963, but he finished strong in the final month of the 1964 season as the Yankees rallied to win their fifth consecutive American League championship. It would be his last statistically productive year. In 1965, Maris suffered a serious hand injury. X-rays by several doctors failed to reveal any broken bones, but Maris claimed he was in considerable pain and unable to properly grip the bat. Under pressure from team management to play, and doubted by his teammates, baseball writers, and fans as a malingerer, Maris felt betrayed. The severity of his injury was finally discovered months later. He underwent surgery, but he never regained full strength in his right hand and lost partial feeling in several fingers. The incident further strained his already damaged relationship with team management.

After a dispiriting, injury-plagued season in 1966, during which he informed team management of his intention to retire, Maris was traded to the St. Louis Cardinals on December 8, 1966. He decided to postpone retirement and played for two more years. No longer able to hit for power, he contributed to the team's success with his professionalism, experience, and work ethic. In St. Louis, Maris found an appreciative management, respectful teammates, and supportive fans. Careful observers recognized that Maris was a complete player, doing the little things that help win games. In the 1967 World Series, his .385 batting average and seven runs batted in played a major

For his heroics in 1961, Maris was named Most Valuable Player for the second time in his career and received a plethora of other awards.

role in the Cardinals victory over the Red Sox. Maris retired after the 1968 World Series (the Cardinals lost to the Detroit Tigers) to operate an Anheuser-Busch beer distributorship with his brother in Gainesville, Florida.

In 12 seasons he batted .260 with 275 home runs. For several years, Maris kept his distance from baseball, occasionally participating in Old Timers Games, but resolutely declining all invitations tendered by the New York Yankees. Gradually, his attitude softened. On April 12, 1978, he appeared with Mantle at the Yankees home opener, where he received a warm fan reception. On July 21, 1984, his uniform, number 9, was officially retired in ceremonies at Yankee Stadium.

Maris was diagnosed with lymphoma in 1983. After a brief remission his illness returned in 1985, and Maris died on December 14 that year at age 51. ◆

Martin, Christy

JUNE 12, 1968– ● BOXER

As women in this century have gained credibility in nearly every sphere of athletics, boxing has long remained the elusive final frontier. With the rise of Christy Martin, the premier woman boxer in the United States, female fisticuffs have moved from sideshow to the big time, as women's bouts have become commonplace undercards for male boxing matches.

Very few professional women fighters were encouraged to nurse pugilistic ambitions as young girls, so, like most of them, Martin came to the sport as a young adult. The daughter of a coal miner who died of black lung disease—she bills herself as "The Coal Miner's Daughter"—Martin grew up as Christy Salter in the mining town of Mullens, West Virginia, where she showed early athletic promise as a Little League catcher and an all-state high school basketball star. A basketball scholarship took her to Concord College in Athens, Georgia, where a fateful dare lured Martin into entering a local "toughwoman" boxing match. The college freshman surprised herself by winning the match and $1000. Buoyed by the sense of power and challenge, Martin was hooked. She won the contest each of the next two years, pocketing another $1000 for each victory. She now knew that boxing was her professional destination. All she needed was the proper vehicle to get her there.

Enter Jim Martin. Despite some early success, Christy plodded in obscurity for her first three years in the ring. Boxing in the lightweight division, she won her first bout on October 1, 1987, a three-round decision over Sue McNamara. From then until the end of 1990, Martin compiled an impressive record but little renown or cash. In 1991, while she was working as a substitute teacher in West Virginia, a promoter told her about a trainer named Jim Martin who could kick-start her career. She set out for Jim Martin's gym in Bristol, Tennessee, determined to prove her mettle as a prospective fighter. At first Jim was wary of handling a woman client and, in a misguided attempt at chivalry, he even planned to have a sparring partner break her ribs to discourage her. But Christy's talent and determination won him over, and he became, in rapid succession, Christy's trainer, manager, and, later that year, husband. "It was love at first sight," Martin said later, "after Jim got over being upset about me being in his gym."

The newlyweds moved to Orlando to accept a businessman's offer to set them up in a gym. When the man **reneged** on his offer, Christy's parents lent them the money to set up a gym that Jim now runs. Under Jim's management Christy's wins piled up over the next two years, leading to her big break. In 1993, the controversial big-time boxing promoter Don King saw Christy in a club match with the Texas policewoman Melinda Robinson and was wowed by Christy's powerful ring presence. In October of that year she signed a contract with King, and her career took off. She appeared often as the undercard at heavily promoted King events, and her name recognition and income began to soar.

The first breakthrough to a mass audience for Martin—and women's boxing—came on March 16, 1996, when she appeared in an undercard against Deirdre Gogarty before more than a million pay-per-view television subscribers to the Mike Tyson-Frank Bruno bout in Las Vegas, Nevada. Martin's driving, unrelenting attack and technical mastery carried to her to a six-round decision over Gogarty, and many journalists deemed their matchup a better display of boxing skill than the men's main event later that night. Her fame mushrooming, Martin drew a paycheck of $150,000 for her technical knockout of Andrea DeShong on June 27, 1997.

Martin's reign as the queen of the ring went unchallenged until December 18, 1998, in a bout with Sumya Anani at the War Memorial Auditorium in Fort Lauderdale, Florida. Anani inflicted a bloody nose on Martin in the first round and

1968 Martin is born in West Virginia.

1993 Martin signs a contract with promoter Don King.

1997 Martin earns a technical knockout against Andrea DeShong.

1998 Martin suffers her first loss in a decade, to Sumya Anani.

reneged: went back on one's word; made an offer and then canceled or backed out on that offer for no good reason.

knocked her down in the third. Martin recovered slightly in the middle rounds, but Anani's persistent blows were taking their toll. After the final round, Martin's nose was bloodied and her eyes were swollen, whereas Anani was unscathed. The decision went to Anani, and Martin suffered her first loss in nearly a decade.

A battered Martin told a post-fight press conference, "She's a good fighter, but it was a head butt that cut me earlier. And when she knocked me down, it was with elbows and arms and wasn't a clean shot." She tearfully raised the possibility of retiring unless she could face Lucia Rijker, her long-time rival.

But not everyone in the women's boxing community mourned Martin's temporary dethronement. Many had accused King of artificially inflating Martin's reputation by pitting her against **incompetent** challengers. "She hasn't fought anyone who is anyone," said rival boxing promoter Diane Fisher. "There would have been plenty of talent for Christy Martin if she'd wanted it." Some suspect that a series of contract disputes with King led the crafty impresario to lead her into a trap against the scrappy Anani; according to one published report, King negotiated a deal to represent Anani during her match with Martin.

incompetent: inadequate for the situation that is at hand; lacking talent or knowledge.

Martin recovered her footing over her next two bouts: On April 24, 1999, she knocked out Jovett Jackson less than a minute into the first round, and on October 2, 1999, Martin bested Daniella Somers of Belgium with a fifth-round technical knockout. Despite widespread talk of a showdown between Martin and Lucia Rijker, the bout has yet to materialize.

With an imposing record of 38–2–2 (including 30 knock-outs), Martin can justly claim to have lifted women's boxing to a level of popular and commercial success that seemed inconceivable when she first entered the ring. ◆

Mathias, Bob

November 17, 1930– ● Track and Field Athlete

Robert Bruce Mathias's storybook athletic career began in the small farming town of Tulare, California, where he was the second of four children. As a child Mathias displayed the all-around athletic ability that would eventually lead to two Olympic gold medals, despite suffering from anemia, a blood disorder. He overcame his early frailty through sports, as a 12-year-old managing a high jump of five feet six inches in the backyard track he had built for himself.

By the time Mathias reached high school a steady diet of good food, iron supplements, and sports was paying off. He had overcome the effects of his anemia, and when he graduated he was no longer a gangly kid but a handsome, strapping athlete. He was one of California's outstanding athletes in football and basketball, and he showed enormous versatility in track and field, winning 40 first-place finishes, setting 21 high school records, and in 1947 winning the California Interscholastic Federation discus and shot put

Bob Mathias throws the discus.

championships. The first person to spot his Olympic potential was his high school track coach, Virgil Jackson, who persuaded him to enter the decathlon—a grueling ten-event competition that demands speed, agility, skill, and endurance—at the Pacific Coast games. Mathias quickly trained for the event and amazed everyone by winning his first-ever decathlon. With financial help from his hometown he traveled to the Olympic trials in New Jersey, where he won a spot on the Olympic track and field team—the youngest U.S. Olympic track team member ever.

In 1948 Mathias, still just 17 years old, arrived from his small California town to the world stage in Wembley, England, to compete in the decathlon against 34 other athletes. After the first day of the two-day competition, and battling miserable weather that required him to huddle under a blanket between events, Mathias led in the shot put and high jump but was third overall. On the second day, though, a strong discus throw put him into the lead, and when the final event, the punishing 1,500-meter race, was over, Mathias had done what seemed im-

"A winner never quits; a quitter never wins."
Bob Mathias

1930 Mathias is born in Tulare, California.

1948 At 17, Mathias wins Olympic gold in track and field; he also wins the Sullivan award as the outstanding amateur athlete in the United States.

1952 Mathias sets a world record in the decathlon at the AAU Championships; he also wins his second Olympic gold, with a record total of points.

1974 Mathias is named to the National Track and Field Hall of Fame.

1980 Mathias is named to the U.S. Olympic Hall of Fame.

possible: he had become the youngest man in the history of the modern Olympics to win a gold medal in track and field. His incredible win earned him the James E. Sullivan Memorial Award for outstanding amateur athlete that year.

After the 1948 Olympics Mathias continued to compete in decathlons, winning gold or finishing first in the National Amateur Athletic Union (AAU) Championships (1948, 1949, 1950, and 1952), the Southern Pacific AAU (1948), and the Swiss Championships (1950). He enrolled in Stanford University in California, where he also played fullback on the football team, once scoring a 96-yard touchdown and playing in the Rose Bowl on New Year's Day in 1952. That year he set a world record in the decathlon in the AAU Championships, so as the 1952 Olympics in Helsinki, Finland, approached, he was clearly the man to beat.

Despite a leg injury he suffered during the competition, Mathias capped his career by easily defending his gold medal, winning five of the ten events and totaling 7,887 points, a new world and Olympic record. In 1952 the Associated Press named him Male Athlete of the Year and the Hall of the Athlete Foundation named him Athlete of the Year. Other awards would follow: In 1974 he was elected to the National Track and Field Hall of Fame, in 1975 he won the Pierre de Coubertin International Fair Play Trophy, and in 1980 he was named to the U.S. Olympic Hall of Fame. Bob Mathias had won every decathlon he entered, in the minds of many supplanting Jim Thorpe, winner of the 1912 Olympic decathlon and pentathlon, as the greatest all-around athlete in history. His unprecedented performance, combined with his all-American good looks and sense of fair play, helped bring glamour to the decathlon. He owed his success not only to hard work and determination but to his ability to relax, leading one competitor to remark that between events he looked like he was sleeping.

Mathias continued his high level of achievement after his days as an athlete came to a close. He earned his degree from Stanford in 1953. He was an officer in the Marine Corps, a television and movie actor (he starred in a movie about his own life, *The Bob Mathias Story*), and director of his own boys' camp. He later became a four-term member of the U.S. House of Representatives. After Congress he was named director first of the Olympic Training Center, then of the National Fitness Foundation. He later served as president of the American Kids Sports Association. ◆

Mays, Willie

MAY 6, 1931– ● BASEBALL PLAYER

The son of steel-mill worker William Mays and Ann Mays, Willie Mays was born in Westfield, Alabama. After his parents divorced soon after his birth, Mays was raised by an aunt in Fairfield, Alabama. At Fairfield Industrial High School, Mays starred in basketball, football, and baseball.

At the age of 17, began his professional career, joining the Birmingham Black Barons of the Negro National League. During three seasons with the Black Barons, he played 130 games in the outfield and compiled a batting average of .263. In 1950, he started the season with the Black Barons, but was soon signed by the New York Giants. Mays played on the Giants' minor league teams until early in the 1951 season, when he joined the major league club. Mays was voted the National League Rookie of the Year, and acquired the nickname "the 'Say Hey' Kid" when he forgot a Giants' teammate's name in 1951 and used the phrase.

In 1952 and 1953 Mays served in the U.S. Army, but he returned to baseball in 1954 to play one of his best seasons ever. He led the National League with a .345 batting average and had 41 home runs and 110 runs batted in. Mays led the Giants to the 1954 National League pennant and world championship. In the first game of the World Series with the Cleveland Indians at the Polo Grounds in New York City, Mays made one of the most famous catches in baseball history: With his back to home plate, he ran down Vic Wertz's 440-foot drive to center field, wheeled around, and fired a perfect throw to the infield, thus preventing the Indians from scoring. Mays was named the National League's Most Valuable Player for 1954. He won the award a second time in 1965.

Willie Mays most famous catch.

1931 Mays is born in Westfield, Alabama.

1951 Mays joins the New York Giants and wins Rookie of the Year honors.

1954 Mays leads the Giants to the World Series championship; he is voted Most Valuable Player (and again in 1965).

1957 Mays wins the first of twelve consecutive Gold Glove awards.

1979 Mays is inducted into the Baseball Hall of Fame.

Mays is often considered the most complete ballplayer of the postwar era, if not of all time. He excelled in every aspect of the game. He hit over .300 in 10 seasons. His total of 660 career home runs is the third best to date. He was one of the game's great baserunners and a superlative fielder. (His fielding earned him 12 consecutive Gold Gloves, from 1957 to 1968). Mays played in every All-Star game from 1954 to 1973 and in four World Series (in 1951 and 1954 with the New York Giants; in 1962 with the San Francisco Giants; and in 1973 with the New York Mets).

Because of his formidable abilities, and because of racism, Mays was also the target of an inordinate number of "bean balls"—pitches thrown at the batter's head. However, Mays was one of the first black superstars to receive widespread adulation from white fans. In the 1960s, Mays was among the many black athletes who were criticized for not publicly supporting the civil rights movement. As on most controversial issues, Mays projected a naive innocence when confronted about his political silence. "I don't picket in the streets of Birmingham," he said. "I'm not mad at the people who do. Maybe they shouldn't be mad at the people who don't."

Mays played with the Giants (the team moved to San Francisco in 1958) until 1972, when he was traded to the New York Mets. The following year he retired as a player but was retained by the Mets as a part-time coach. Mays was inducted into the National Baseball Hall of Fame in 1979. Three months later, he was ordered by Major League Baseball Commissioner Bowie Kuhn to choose between his job with the Mets and fulfilling a public relations contract with the Bally's Casino Hotel. Mays, along with Mickey Mantle, chose the latter and was banned from any affiliation with professional baseball. In 1985, the new Commissioner, Peter Ueberroth, lifted the ban. ◆

McCray, Nikki

DECEMBER 17, 1971– ● BASKETBALL PLAYER

Basketball guard Nikki McCray was born in Colliersville, Tennessee, on December 17, 1971. The oldest of four daughters, McCray first became known in the town not for her athletic ability but for her beautiful singing voice. In her early teens, however, Nikki tried basketball and was immediately hooked. A natural athlete who trains hard at her sport, she has since become one of the biggest names in women's professional basketball. McCray's participation has helped to increase the exposure of and regard for the sport.

On the varsity team in high school in Colliersville, McCray's skills as a guard made her stand out, both in Tennessee and across the United States. The national publications *Parade Magazine* and *USA Today* gave her All American honors.

Not surprisingly, the University of Tennesse offered her a scholarship to play with the university women's basketball team, the Lady Vols. It was a dream come true for McCray, but that dream was almost sidelined when she tore a ligament in her knee in her first season playing for the team. Forced to sit out the entire basketball season, McCray focused on recovering from the injury. The physical rehabilitation worked not only to rebuild her knee but also made her bigger and stronger. (She stands 5'11" and weighs about 158 pounds.) By the end of her four years with the Lady Vols, Tennessee had won 122 games and lost only 11 when "Nik-Nik" (as McCray is nicknamed) was playing. She won four SEC Championships and made four trips to the National Collegiate Athletic Association (NCAA) Tournament with the Lady Vols. In 1994 and 1995, she was named Southeastern Conference (SEC) Player of the Year.

In 1995, McCray graduated from the University of Tennessee with a degree in sports marketing and education. Her days with the Lady Vols were over, but not her basketball career. Her immediate goal was to make the U.S. Olympic women's basketball team.

She succeeded, and though it was a worthwhile experience, it was not an altogether pleasant one. McCray was clearly a superb basketball player, but her game was not without its flaws. Though she was fast, she was not always controlled in her handling of the ball. Finally, in one game on the Olympic team in which McCray was not playing well, the hard-driving coach Tara VanDerveer told the other players to stop passing the ball to McCray. It was humiliating for the young player, but it also galvanized her to improve her skills, and her teammates' defense of her to the coach created an invaluable camaraderie among them all. At the 1996 Summer Olympic Games in Atlanta, Georgia, Team USA brought home the gold medal.

After the Olympics, McCray signed up with the Columbus Quest, an American Basketball League (ABL) team. She was

1971 McCray is born in Colliersville, Tennessee.

1994 McCray is voted the Southeastern Conference Player of the Year (also in 1995).

1997 McCray is voted Most Valuable Player in the American Basketball League.

1998 McCray joins the WNBA for the Washington Mystics; she leads the team in scoring.

McCray soon felt it was time for a change, and in January 1998, she joined the Washington Mystics, a new team of the Women's National Basketball Association (WNBA).

one of the youngest players on the team, but her experience with Team USA had sharpened both her skills and her self-confidence. She soon was considered a star of the Quest, helping the team to earn the 1997 First Team ABL All Star designation. That year, McCraw was named the ABL's Most Valuable Player.

McCray soon felt it was time for a change, and in January 1998, she joined the Washington Mystics, a new team of the Women's National Basketball Association (WNBA). It was a good move for her (the ABL later folded), and the statistics proved it. In 1998, she led the Mystics in scoring (averaging 17.7 points per game—ranking fourth in the WNBA). She was also first in three-point percentages (.315, ranking 11th in the WNBA) and in assists (3.1 average per game, a ranking of 11th). In 1998, McCray also ranked second among the Mystics players in three-pointers (23, ranking 18th). This was a particular triumph for her, as in earlier years this skill had been one of her weaknesses. She came in third on steals (1.48 steals per game, 16th in WNBA rank). The year 1998 was a good one for McCray in another way: She played for the U.S. National Team at the FIBA Women's World Championship, held in Germany. In 1999, McCray's exceptional record continued, and she was voted a starter for the East team for the inaugural WNBA All-Star Game. McCray has a full life outside of basketball. Married to college sweetheart Thomas Penson, she has sung the National Anthem at various sporting events. She has been involved in the Boys and Girls Club throughout her career, and she looks forward to starting a foundation of her own or working in sports marketing when she retires from pro basketball. ◆

McEnroe, John

FEBRUARY 16, 1959– ● TENNIS PLAYER

A tennis champion who, in his epic battles with Bjorn Borg and Jimmy Connors, brought unparalleled popularity to his sport, John Patrick McEnroe Jr. was as well known for his temper tantrums and court antics as he was for his dominant play throughout the 1980s.

Although always referred to as a New Yorker, John McEnroe was born in Wiesbaden, Germany, where his father served in the United States Air Force. The first of three McEnroe boys, the family moved to the Queens borough of New York City when John was four months old.

A talented all-around athlete and driven student, McEnroe began playing tennis at age eight. While attending the famous Trinity School in Manhattan, McEnroe played football and soccer, but it was on the tennis courts where he really thrived, winning several junior singles and doubles titles.

While attending Stanford University in California in 1977, McEnroe made a big splash while still in his teens by winning the French Open mixed doubles title and reaching the singles semifinals at Wimbledon.

All this took place while McEnroe was still an amateur—in 1978 he won the NCAA singles title during an All-American freshman year at Stanford. With the challenges of college competition waning and the professional game beckoning, McEnroe gave up his college eligibility and turned pro in late 1978.

It didn't take McEnroe long to make a huge impact on the professional game, as his slick, left-handed style of play and combination of power and finesse proved effective on any court he played. In his own state, at the hard courts of the U.S. Open in Flushing, N.Y., McEnroe won three consecutive singles championships, in 1979, 1980 and 1981.

His victory over Borg in 1980 at Flushing is often considered one of the greatest men's tennis matches of all time. Both men had amazing ups and downs throughout the match, before McEnroe finally prevailed in a five-set masterpiece, 7–6, 6–1, 6–7, 5–7, 6–4.

On the grass courts of Wimbledon in 1981, McEnroe trounced his rival Borg in four sets, ending Borg's five-year reign, and becoming the youngest top-ranked player in the history of men's tennis.

McEnroe held tennis' top spot for four years, winning another Wimbledon singles title in 1983 and completing an amazing 1984 campaign that saw him win both Wimbledon and U.S. Open singles titles.

But McEnroe's greatness as an athlete was often overshadowed by his fiery on-court demeanor and explosive temper. Many sports broadcasts began with highlights of a McEnroe verbal assault of an umpire. Nicknamed "The Brat," McEnroe quickly became the kind of player that drew all types of fans, some who want to see him win, some who want to see him lose. Often the latter were left disappointed, however, since McEnroe's losses in the early 1980s were few and far between.

1959 McEnroe is born in Wiesbaden, Germany at a United States Air Force base.

1979 McEnroe wins his first U.S. Open (and wins in 1980, 1981, and 1984).

1981 McEnroe defeats Bjorn Borg at Wimbledon, becoming the youngest top-ranked player in the history of men's tennis.

1984 McEnroe wins Wimbledon and the U.S. Open.

Aside from the singles field, McEnroe was arguably the best men's doubles player of all time. With partner Peter Fleming, John won four Wimbledon titles and three U.S. Open titles, and dozens of other titles. He's also teamed, with equal success, with Mark Woodforde, his brother Patrick McEnroe, and Michael Stich.

McEnroe holds 77 career singles titles, including seven Grand Slams and 74 doubles titles, including eight Grand Slams. Another of his great accomplishments was his play and coaching of the U.S. Davis Cup teams. McEnroe holds the U.S record for Davis Cup wins with 54 (39 singles and 15 doubles) in the international battle of nations.

McEnroe never officially retired from tennis, but now works primarily as a network television commentator for the major networks at most important tennis tournaments. He also plays in certain senior events where he is able to play his old rivals Connors and Borg. McEnroe is captain of the 2000 U.S. Davis Cup team.

McEnroe was married to actress Tatum O'Neal from 1986 to 1994. He remarried in 1997, to singer Patty Smyth. A father of four children—Kevin, Sean, Emily, and Anna—McEnroe often gives to children's causes.

McEnroe continues to speak his mind, yet he has mellowed considerably. He has broadened his artistic side, playing the guitar and having opened the John McEnroe Gallery in New York City, which features many respected works of art. ◆

McGraw, John

APRIL 7, 1883–FEBRUARY 25, 1934 ● BASEBALL PLAYER AND MANAGER

John McGraw was born in Truxton, New York, in 1883. At the age of 12, he lost his mother, two sisters and two brothers to a diphtheria epidemic, and was sent to live with relatives. Despite this tragic start, the young McGraw excelled at baseball. By the age of 16, having made a name for himself on the local Truxton team, McGraw was earning $2 a game playing for a team in East Homer, five miles away. In 1890 he signed a $40-a-month contract to play for Olean, New York, of the New York and Pennsylvania League, and was converted from a pitcher to a third baseman. The following August the National League's Baltimore Orioles signed him to a major league contract.

McGraw emerged as a fiery, tough ballplayer with a shameful mean streak, who easily made enemies among umpires, opposing players, and managers. When the umpire wasn't looking, his tactics included grabbing an opponent's belt to slow him down as he rounded third base. Other times, McGraw stood deliberately in a runner's way in the base path. Or, when taking throws at third base, he would purposely step on the runner's feet. He was described as vicious, willing to maim a player or umpire if it helped his team.

At just 5′ 7″ and 155 pounds, the left-handed hitting McGraw was nicknamed "Mugsy." He was a star player for 16 seasons, batting .321 or better nine straight years, and .334 for his career. Twice he led the league in runs and walks. He stole 436 career bases, and his .466 career on base percentage ranks third on baseball's all-time list behind Ted Williams and Babe Ruth. McGraw's skill included an uncanny knack for fouling off balls until he got the perfect pitch to hit. Well after the height of his career, in the spring of 1930, an aging McGraw purposely fouled off 26 straight pitches during an at-bat. When he couldn't get on base by hitting the ball, McGraw wasn't afraid to lean over the plate and get hit by a pitch in order to be awarded first base.

Baseball was still a relatively young game in the late 1800s, and McGraw and teammate Wee Willie Keeler perfected a staple of today's game, the **hit-and-run**, in which a base runner takes off during a pitcher's delivery, and the batter swings. If the batter hits the ball, it allows the runner to advance an extra base. That style of "inside baseball" became an Oriole trademark, helping them capture three straight National League pennants from 1894 to 1896. They played with a brash style and swagger that was attributed in large part to McGraw. In 1899 he became player-manager, but a year later, the Orioles franchise was dropped by the National League, and McGraw was sold along with two other players for $15,000 to the St. Louis Cardinals. McGraw did not want to play for the Cardinals, and reported late. He appeared in 99 games, batting .344.

In 1901, McGraw took over as player-manager of a new Baltimore franchise in the young American League. He repeatedly clashed with the team's owner and league president, Ban Johnson, who did not approve of McGraw's run-ins with umpires. After being suspended indefinitely in July of 1902, McGraw moved back to the National League, becoming manager of the New York Giants. Thus began a 31-year tenure, in which he

1883 McGraw is born in Truxton, New York.

1901 McGraw becomes player-manager of the Baltimore Orioles.

1902 McGraw becomes manager of the New York Giants, a position he holds for 31 years.

1905 Under McGraw's leadership, the Giants win the World Series (and win in 1921 and 1922).

1937 McGraw is elected to the Baseball Hall of Fame.

hit-and-run: in baseball, the hit-and-run play involves the batter at the plate and any baserunners who are on base at the time. The play occurs when, as the opposing pitcher makes his pitch to the batter, the baserunner(s) take off running before the ball reaches the batter, who then hits the ball (if he can) to advance the runner(s) even further.

compiled a 2,583–1,790 record, managing the Giants to 10 National League Pennants and three World Series championships.

McGraw was a revolutionary manager. In addition to his hit-and-run, he popularized the use of the bunt to advance runners. He was the first manager to hire a player for the sole purpose of pinch hitting, and was one of the first to utilize pitchers solely as relievers. He managed his teams like a field general, always ready with the right tactic to counter an opposing manager's move. His nickname became "Little Napoleon" because of his size and iron-fisted managerial style, similar to the diminutive French general.

Immediately upon taking over the last place Giants, McGraw began building a dynasty. In 1904, New York captured the National League Pennant with a franchise-best 106–47 record. Because of his lingering feud with Johnson, and his belief that the American League was inferior, McGraw refused to let his team meet the American League champion Boston Pilgrims in what would have been the second World Series. It was the only year, until the strike-ended 1994 season, that a World Series was not played.

The following year, the Giants repeated as league champions, and won the World Series four games to one after McGraw agreed to play the Philadelphia Athletics. McGraw's star pitcher, Christy Mathewson, won three games by shutout. Mathewson was a genteel college graduate in an era when baseball was dominated by ruffians. McGraw's greatest asset was his ability to assess raw talent, and one of his methods was to sign college players, who he found more willing to be coached. New York won pennants again in 1911, 1912, 1913 and 1917, but lost the World Series each year. McGraw's fiercely combative temperament was demonstrated in a June 1917 incident which led to a fistfight with umpire Bill Byron during a game. McGraw was fined $500, the biggest fine in baseball history to that point, and was suspended for 16 days. Angry, he charged that the league president was out to get the Giants. McGraw only narrowly escaped banishment from baseball when he apologized, but not before paying another $1,000 in fines. From 1921 to 1924, McGraw became the first manager—and the only one to date—to win four consecutive league titles. His Giants won back-to-back World Series crowns over the cross-town rival Yankees in 1921 and 1922.

McGraw's health was in decline his last few years, and he resigned as Giants' manager on June 3, 1932. His overall man-

Abner Doubleday

Ask nearly any baseball fan who "invented" the game of baseball and the answer is likely to be "Abner Doubleday—of course everybody knows that." Baseball, though, is a game surrounded by legend and nostalgia. In the popular imagination, Doubleday's name has become so entwined with the early history of baseball that it may never be possible to convince the game's fans that this "fact" is probably not true.

Doubleday's name would survive in the history books even without baseball. Born in Ballston Spa, New York, in 1819, Doubleday came from a family that was prominent in civic and military affairs. He entered the West Point military academy, graduating in 1842, and over the next two decades he rose to the rank of general. Doubleday actually fired the first Union gun in defense of Fort Sumter when it was attacked by the Confederates at the start of the Civil War. He later led troops at Chancellorsville, and at Gettysburg, where he led the I Corps of the Third Division, a statue stands to honor him. Doubleday died in 1893.

In 1907 his friend, one A. G. Mills, headed up a commission that reported that Doubleday had invented baseball in Cooperstown, New York, in the 1830s. It's been speculated that the commission wanted to enhance the stature of baseball by associating it with the name of a prominent war hero. Many historians, too, are skeptical. They point out that similar games with bases existed long before Doubleday's time, including a French game called prison ball. In 1834 a book called "Base, Goal, or Ball," describing an English game called rounders that is very much like baseball, was published in the United States. In fact, the true "father of baseball" was probably Alexander J. Cartwright, who in 1845 set down many of the baseball rules that are still in effect today. Sadly, though, Cartwright's name is lost in the mists of time while Doubleday's survives as that of the inventor of the great American pastime.

agerial record was 2,783–1,948. Only Connie Mack, with 3,731 wins has more victories as a big league manager. McGraw died from cancer on February 25, 1934, and was elected to Baseball's Hall of Fame in 1937. ◆

McGwire, Mark

OCTOBER 1, 1963– ● BASEBALL PLAYER

On August 25, 1986, Mark McGwire, a third baseman with the Oakland Athletics, strode to the plate to face Walt Terrell, a pitcher for the Detroit Tigers. The Athletics had called up the burly rookie from the minor leagues just days before, and he responded by powering his first major league

Mark McGwire hits one of his record-setting 70 home runs in 1998.

home run over the fence. By the time he hit his 522nd home run near the end of the 1999 season, he had long established himself as one of the most dominating power hitters in baseball during the 1990s.

Born in Pomona, California, McGwire showed early promise as a long ball hitter. When he was just 11 years old, he hit 13 home runs for his Little League team in nearby Claremont, California, a record that stood for two decades. Ironically, though, he began his career as a pitcher—first in high school, then, after turning down an offer from the Montreal Expos when he graduated in 1981, at the University of Southern California. It was at the plate, though, that McGwire shined: During three years at USC he compiled a career slugging percentage of .718, and in his final season, 1984, he hit 32 home runs, a Pac-10 Conference record that still stands. That year he began to make the transition from pitching to playing the infield, first as a third baseman, later at first base.

McGwire was selected in the first round of the free-agent draft by the Oakland Athletics in 1984. He spent the 1985 season with their single A farm team in Modesto, where he was named the California League's Rookie of the Year. During his 1986 minor league season, first at Huntsville (AA), then at Tacoma (AAA), his statistics were impressive: a .311 batting average, 148 hits, 23 home runs, and 112 runs batted in. In August he was called up to the major leagues by Oakland, and during the remainder of the 1986 season he played in 18 games, hitting three home runs and batting .189 in 53 at bats.

In 1987, though, "Big Mac" showed that he was ready to face big-league pitching. During his first full season in the major leagues he led the American League with 49 home runs, and his .618 slugging percentage was highest in the major leagues. That year he was selected to the American League All-Star team and finished sixth in the league's Most Valuable Player voting. He was unanimously picked as baseball's Rookie of the Year.

In the years that followed, the home runs kept coming. In 1988, despite back stiffness that took him out of the lineup late in the season, McGwire finished with 32 home runs. A herniated disk hobbled him at the start of the 1989 season, yet his 33 home runs that year ranked him third in the American League. With 39 homers in the 1990 season, he became the first player ever to hit more than 30 in each of his first four full seasons. His numbers might have been even more impressive had opposing pitchers not "pitched around" him: That year, he led the major leagues with 110 walks, a pattern that continued throughout his career.

McGwire's 1991 season was a disappointing one. He ended his streak of 30-plus homers with just 22. Worse, his batting average was a career low .201. He rebounded, though, in 1992, finishing the season as runner-up in the home run race with 42 and leading the league with a home run in every 11.1 plate appearances.

McGwire began the 1993 season on a roll. In the first 25 games he had 28 hits—15 for extra bases—nine home runs, and a .726 slugging percentage. On May 14, though, he went on the disabled list, and in September he underwent surgery to repair an injury to his left heel. Injuries continued to slow him during the 1994 season, when he played in only 47 games.

McGwire had to rebound again, and with the 1995 season he began a display of raw power that may never be equaled. That year he hit 39 home runs in just 317 at bats, breaking Babe Ruth's major league record with one homer for every 8.1 at bats. In 1996 he led the major leagues with 52 home runs. He began the 1997 season with 34 homers for Oakland, then, after he was

1963 McGwire is born in Pomona, California.

1984 At the University of Southern California, McGwire sets a Pacific 10 Conference record for home runs.

1990 McGwire, a member of the Oakland Athletics, becomes the major leaguer to hit more than 30 homers in first four seasons.

1995 McGwire hits 39 homers in 317 at-bats, breaking a Babe Ruth record.

1996 McGwire leads the major leagues with 52 home runs.

1997 McGwire is traded to the St. Louis Cardinals.

1998 McGwire breaks Roger Maris's record, ending the season with 70 home runs.

1999 McGwire hits 65 homers and becomes the only player in major league history to hit 50 or more homers in 4 straight seasons.

"You go to the ballpark to see somebody hit a home run or somebody throw a ball at close to 100 miles an hour. That was the exciting thing when I was a kid, and I think it still is."

Mark McGwire

traded to the St. Louis Cardinals in July, he added another 24, giving him a major-league-leading 58.

As the 1998 season began, and McGwire homered in each of the first four games, baseball fans were wondering if McGwire could possibly break Roger Maris's single-season home run record (61), a mark that had stood for nearly four decades. Throughout the summer McGwire engaged in a titanic struggle with the Chicago Cubs' Sammy Sosa for the home run title. McGwire had 27 through May, 37 through June, 45 through July, and 55 through August—all records. Sosa kept pace, though, and sometimes even pulled ahead. Then, in the final days of the season, with the nation watching, McGwire unleashed a display of brute power to end the season with an incredible 70 homers, although in the minds of some observers, his record was tainted when he admitted that he took performance-enhancing substances, even though the drugs were legal.

As if to prove that 1998 was no fluke, he totaled 65 homers in 1999, becoming the only player in history to hit 50 or more home runs in four consecutive seasons. The three longest home runs ever hit (since they've been measured), and the longest home runs in six ballparks, have all come off the bat of Mark McGwire.

McGwire is admired not just for his baseball talents. He showed the highest level of sportsmanship during his season-long duel with Sosa. He donates $1 million a year to his foundation to help abused children, and he regularly takes part in charity events such as celebrity golf tournaments. Always a gentleman, he was even named "Most Mannered Person of the Year" for 1998 by the National League of Junior Cotillions; and a section of Interstate 70 near St. Louis is named in his honor. ◆

Miller, Cheryl

January 3, 1964– ● Basketball Player

Born in Riverside, Calif., the third of five children (a younger brother, Reggie Miller, would go on to become a star player in the National Basketball Association),

Cheryl Miller gained recognition for her superb play on her hometown Polytechnic High School women's basketball team. While at Polytechnic, she scored a record 105 points in one game, and was named to the Parade All-American Team four years in a row, the only person ever recognized in this way.

A 6′3″ forward, Miller is considered by many to be the most dominant female basketball player of all time. She played college basketball for the University of Southern California (USC; 1982 1986), leading her team to two National Collegiate Athletic Association (NCAA) championships. She was named an All-American four times, NCAA Player of the Year three times, and Most Valuable Player of the NCAA play-offs twice. She graduated in 1986 with a degree in communications.

Miller was the highest scorer on the U.S. Women's gold-medal-winning basketball team at the 1984 Summer Olympics held in Los Angeles. In the summer of 1986 she played for the gold medal U.S. team in the World Championships, as well as for the U.S. team in the Goodwill Games in Moscow. That year she was drafted in the first round by the California Stars of the National Women's Basketball Association (NWBA), but the league dissolved later in the year. Miller joined ABC Sports as a television broadcaster in January 1988, and reported on the Winter Olympic Games held in Calgary, Alberta. However, a knee injury kept her from the 1988 Summer Olympic team.

On September 3, 1993, Miller became the coach of the USC women's basketball team. During her rookie coaching season, her team won the Pac 10 Conference championship, and reached the NCAA tournament quarterfinals. In acknowledgment of this feat, the Black Coaches Association named Miller one of the Coaches of the Year in 1994. ◆

Cheryl Miller (right) at the 1984 Olympics.

"Cheryl was the best player this game has ever had."

Leon Barmore, Louisiana Tech coach, on Cheryl Miller

Miller, Shannon

MARCH 10, 1977– ● GYMNAST

"In our family it's understood that you do schoolwork first and then other things. Shannon is an achiever."

Ron Miller, Shannon Miller's father

Curiously, "Shannon" has never become the type of household name in the world of gymnastics as "Olga," "Nadia" or "Mary Lou" has. But it probably should have. Shannon Miller is one of the most decorated American gymnasts of all time, male or female, earning seven Olympic medals and nine World Championship medals throughout her career. Miller is also the only American ever to win consecutive World Championship All-Around titles (only three female gymnasts have accomplished that particular feat in the sport's history) and her second place finish at the 1992 Olympics in Barcelona, Spain, was the highest ever for an American gymnast in a nonboycotted Games. Her amazing tally of five medals in Barcelona (two silver, three bronze) was the most medals won by a USA athlete in any sport as well.

Yet Miller's exceptional career began in a rather mundane fashion. Born in Rolla, Missouri, Miller was four months old when her family moved to Oklahoma City; when Miller was a toddler the family finally settled in Edmond, Oklahoma. There Miller was raised by her mother, a banker, and her father, a university professor, along with older sister Tessa and younger brother Troy. "I had no special inclination or anything for gymnastics. I started to go to the gym when I was about five years old only because Tessa was going," says Miller. "She was two years older than me. And, like every little girl who is that age, I just wanted to do whatever my older sister was doing."

Though gymnastics was "just a recreational, fun thing at first," Miller's parents were worried that she was taking the sport too seriously. "My Mom, especially, thought that I might be getting involved it too intensely for my own good," Miller recalls. "But my Dad said, 'just let her grow out of it.'"

And, Shannon, of course, never did.

Instead, as she was getting better and better, she transferred to Steve Nunno's Dynamo Gymnastics Gym at the age of eight. "This was a gym that took things much more seriously than my old one did," Miller recalled. "Steve had elite athletes, national contenders, all over the place. And, though at first I wasn't up there with them at all in my ability, their very presence presented me with a greater challenge daily. And I'm a person who really enjoys a challenge."

Miller also proved to be a person who was loyal. Unlike most gymnasts who change coaches almost regularly, Miller remained with Nunno throughout her entire career. "Steve taught me so much, and not just about my routines," she says. "In particular, the one thing Steve taught me that I'll always be grateful for is how to deal with frustration."

At age 11, in her first-ever international competition, Shannon provided a glimpse of her future potential by finishing second in the All-Around competition, and third on the uneven bars, in the junior Pan American Games in Ponce, Puerto Rico. "By then I knew this was my calling," the always serious Miller says. "So I was practicing eight hours a day, six or seven days a week." Miller earned first international victory in the 1990 Catania Cup in Italy. She finished first in the All-Around, the vault, the balance beam, and the floor exercise.

By this time Miller was a mature gymnast, and as a result of her determination, success followed. In the 1991 World Championships she became the only U.S. woman to qualify for all four individual event finals a first for an American. Her performance propelled the U.S. women's team to win their first-ever medal, a silver. Finishing sixth in the All-Around, Miller also captured a silver medal in the uneven bars.

Still, practically lost among all the great Russian and Romanian female gymnasts, no one thought much of Miller's Olympic chances the next year in Barcelona, Spain. So when she lost the All-Around gold medal to the Unified Team's Tatyana Gutsu by a mere 0.12 points, it was a serious shocker. "I was just coming off elbow surgery," says Miller. "And everyone in the U.S. was promoting Kim Zmeskal's chances anyway. So I had nothing to lose. So, instead of being frustrated by losing the gold medal by so little, I was just so happy and proud of everything I accomplished."

After winning consecutive World Championship gold medals in the All Around in 1993 and again in 1994, Shannon absorbed her first loss in over two years at the 1994 Goodwill Games. But she rebounded in time for the 1996 Olympic Games in Atlanta, Georgia, helping the American women to their first-ever team gold. Miller finished eighth in the All-Around but won her first individual Olympic gold in her favorite event, the balance beam.

1977 ▸ Miller is born in Rolla, Missouri.

1992 ▸ Miller wins the Olympic silver medal in the balance beam, and all-around events.

1993 ▸ Miller wins the gold medal in the Championships of the USA competition.

1996 ▸ Miller wins the Olympic gold medal for the balance beam; the USA team wins the gold.

"Doing your best is more important than being the best."
Shannon Miller

After taking a year and a half off from gymnastics, and getting married to Chris Phillips, a physician, Shannon is now back in training. She will be a producer of the gymnastics competition for NBC in the 2000 Olympics in Sydney, Australia, and remains involved in the sport behind the scenes. ◆

Moody, Helen Wills

OCTOBER 5, 1905–JANUARY 1, 1998 ● TENNIS PLAYER

Helen Wills Moody is truly a legend in women's tennis. The daughter of a surgeon, she was born Helen Wills in 1905 and raised in Centerville, California. The Wills family was well-off, and although Helen grew up in high society, she never actually took a tennis lesson. She learned the game by watching tennis players at the Berkeley Tennis Club.

As a teenager, Moody favored playing with her father's heavy racket. She continued to use heavy rackets, which accounted for a powerful shot unique among the women players of her time. One year after she started playing at age 14, Moody won the first of her two girls' national titles. She also competed regularly in junior tournaments at Golden Gate Park and the California Tennis Club. A plaque is dedicated to her at the Golden Gate Park clubhouse, and the Helen Wills Invitational for junior players is a fixture at the park each summer.

In 1923, at 17, Moody won the U.S. women's singles championship, becoming the youngest champion at that time. She won the Olympic gold medal in Paris in 1924, the last time tennis was a medal sport before it returned at the 1988 Games in Seoul, Korea. But she had other interests as well. She received a degree in fine arts from the University of California and painted throughout her life, maintaining studios in San Francisco and Carmel. She was chosen as the model for Mexican artist Diego Rivera's two-story mural "Riches of California," commissioned for $2,500 in 1930 and later unveiled at the San Francisco Stock Exchange.

In addition to the eight Wimbledon championships she won between 1927 and 1938, Moody also captured seven U.S. and four French titles. After losing to Kitty Godfree in the 1924 Wimbledon final on her first appearance, Moody remained unbeaten in 50 singles matches at the All England Club. She did

1905 Moody is born in Berkeley, California.

1923 At age 17, Moody wins the U.S. Women's Open (and again in 1924, 1925, 1927–1929, and 1931).

1924 In Paris, Moody wins the Olympic gold in women's singles.

1927 Moody wins the first of eight Wimbledon victories (through 1938).

1928 Moody wins the first of four French Opens (also in 1929, 1930, and 1932).

1959 Moody is inducted into the International Tennis Hall of Fame.

not believe in displays of emotion and was known for being very well groomed, with not a hair out of place. Beneath her white visor her expression was so impassive that in 1929 Life magazine printed a couplet that led to her famous nickname: "Little Poker Face."

Due to Moody's standoffish public appearance, tennis fans often favored her competitors. Helen Jacobs, a gregarious Californian, and Suzanne Lenglen, known for her glamorous ways, were more appealing to the masses. Moody met Lenglen only once, in 1926, at tournament in Cannes, France, in which Lenglen was the winner.

However, Moody's ability to keep her emotions hidden gave her an advantage during many of her games, largely because of the genteel approach to tennis at that time. Her strong will, combined with enormously powerful strokes, helped Moody attain a winning record that few have matched. According to Jack Kramer, a former Wimbledon champion, "She had quite a forehand, a powerful shot. She couldn't serve for aces, but she mixed it up. She never missed." She was later named Associated Press' female athlete of the year in 1935 and inducted into the International Tennis Hall of Fame in 1959.

Helen Wills Moody.

Moody did have some admirers outside of the tennis community. Many of her fans were the Los Angeles actors of the '30s and '40s, for whom tennis was a pastime. When Charlie Chaplin was asked to name the most beautiful thing he had ever seen, he responded: "The movement of Helen Wills playing tennis."

Moody divorced her first husband, Frederick Moody, in 1937 and two years later married Irish polo player Aiden Roark, one of the best players of his generation. However, by 1977 she had become a recluse at her home in Carmel, California. She didn't repond to any unwanted phone calls and often pretended to be her own Spanish maid. She had stopped playing tennis at

82 and many of those who knew her felt that she never found anything to replace it. While her low profile and reluctance to leave home caused tennis great Alice Marble to call her "the Greta Garbo of tennis," she did remain outspoken in her admiration for Chris Evert and her displeasure with Jimmy Connors for the way he behaved. She was also happy to see Pete Sampras come along because he reminded her of her generation of tennis players.

Moody was the author of three books, including her autobiography, *15–30: The Story of a Tennis Player*, published in 1937. In the 1920s she wrote a tennis instruction book and a mystery, *Death Serves an Ace*.

She donated all of her trophies and tennis memorabilia to the University of California at Berkeley, her alma mater, before dying at Carmel Convalescent Hospital on New Year's Day in 1998. She was 92. ◆

> *"Moody was all muscle . . . brute strength. She'd blow you off the court with her power. . . . I don't think any tennis player ever got as many hard first serves in as Helen did."*
>
> Elizabeth Ryan on Helen Wills Moody

Moses, Edwin

AUGUST 31, 1955– ● TRACK AND FIELD ATHLETE

Born and raised in Dayton, Ohio, Edwin Moses began running hurdles at Dayton Fairview High School. An excellent student, Moses accepted an academic scholarship at Morehouse College in Atlanta after he failed to secure a college athletic scholarship. In his junior year at Morehouse, he began to compete in the 400-meter hurdles and qualified for the United States Olympic Team. Moses was the first hurdler to perfect a 13-step approach between each hurdle (most runners required 14 or 15 steps). At the 1976 Montreal Summer Olympics, he won the 400-meter hurdles in the world-record time of 47.64 seconds. Following the Olympics, Moses returned to Morehouse to finish his degree in aerospace engineering. He graduated in 1978.

> *"It just happens that my slow is faster than most athletes' fast. People either think that I'm a freak or that the other guys aren't any good."*
>
> Edwin Moses

Beginning in 1977, Moses won 122 consecutive races, establishing a record for the most consecutive victories in track and field competition. In 1983, he set a new world record in the 400-meter hurdles (47.02 second) and won the Sullivan award, given to the top amateur athlete in the United States. The following year, he won his second Olympic gold medal at the Los Angeles Games and was named Sportsman of the Year by both the U.S. Olympic Committee and *Sports Illustrated*. In 1985, Moses was elected to the U.S. Olympic Hall of Fame. He retired from competition in 1988 and subsequently served as chairman of substance abuse committees for the Athletic Congress and the United States Olympic Committee. Moses was one of several track and football stars who joined the United States Olympic bobsled program in the early 1990s. A brakeman for the top two-man sled for the United States, he won a bronze medal at a 1990 World Cup event in Winterberg, Germany. Moses attempted to return to track and field competition for the 1992 Summer Games in Barcelona, but was hampered by injuries and did not qualify. He maintains his ties to the United States Olympic movement, however, through his involvement with the U.S. Olympic Committee's Athletes' Advisory Council. ◆

> *"Any individual sport is basically a gladiator sport. Back in the old days only one guy would walk out of the arena. In track, it's basically the same thing."*
>
> Edwin Moses

Musial, Stan

NOVEMBER 21, 1920– ● BASEBALL PLAYER

Born Stanley Frank Musial in Donora, Pennsylvania, Stan "the Man" Musial was one of the most prolific hitters in Major League Baseball history. Named to the Baseball Hall of Fame in 1969, at the time of his retirement Musial held 17 Major League, 29 National League, and nine All-Star game records.

Musial grew up in a mining and steel town during the Great Depression years. His father wanted him to go to college, and Stan so excelled at high school basketball that it appeared he would be offered a scholarship at the University of Pittsburgh as a basketball player. However, Stan's first love was baseball and, as a hard throwing left handed pitcher, he decided instead to sign a minor league contract, leaving his father's dreams of college behind. After having marginal success his first two seasons in the minor leagues, Musial was 18–5 in the Florida State League in 1940 when his pitching career was ended: he fell on his left arm during one of his moonlighting stints as an outfielder, and it went numb. The injury proved to be a blessing in disguise, however, as Musial joined the St. Louis Cardinals minor league system as an outfielder and began a rapid ascent to the major leagues. By 1941 he was there, where he hit .426 in 12 games during the stretch run of a pennant race.

> *"How good was Stan Musial? He was good enough to take your breath away."*
>
> Vin Scully, 1989

For Musial, it was the beginning of an unbelievable career as an outfielder and first baseman. Hitting from a unique, crouched stance, he would uncoil at the pitch, the result generally being a hard-hit ball to any part of the field. He was one of the hardest hitters to strike out in baseball, having struck out only 696 times in nearly 11,000 at-bats.

In 1943, in only his second full year in the major leagues, Musial showed just how special a hitter he was: At the age of 22, he hit .357 and led the league in hits, doubles and triples as the Cardinals won the National League Pennant and he was named Most Valuable Player.

Aside from the 1945 season, when he served in the Navy during World War II, no one put up more consistently superlative statistics than Musial. And as he matured physically, his home run statistics began to climb as well.

In 1947, Musial had his best season at the plate, hitting .376 with 39 home runs and 131 runs batted in, missing the National League Triple Crown (leading in home runs, batting average, and runs batted in) by only one home run. He also led the league in hits (230), doubles (46), triples (18), runs scored (135), and slugging percentage (.702). His best day at the plate was May 2, 1954, when he hit five home runs in a doubleheader, a record that still stands today. Overall, the statistics Musial put up in his 22-year career (all with the Cardinals) are staggering.

Musial led the National League in total bases and slugging percentage six times; won seven batting titles; was named Most Valuable Player in 1943, 1946, and 1948; and was named to the National League All-Star team 24 times. He helped lead the Cardinals to World Series championships in 1942, 1944, and 1946.

The Sporting News named Musial Major League Player of the Year in 1946 and 1951 and Sportsman of the Decade for the years between 1946 and 1956. *Sports Illustrated* named him Sportsman of the Year in 1957. During the one year (1967) that Musial served as General Manager for the Cardinals, they won the World Series. Remaining with the Cardinals, Musial was also given national honors, being named Director of the National Council on Physical Fitness by President Lyndon Johnson.

In more recent years, Musial has worked with the University of Missouri-St. Louis, helping with many fund-raising efforts. On the university's twentieth anniversary, they awarded Musial an Honorary Doctor of Laws Degree. ◆

Navratilova, Martina

OCTOBER 18, 1956– ● TENNIS PLAYER

Some would say that the name Martina Navratilova is synonymous with the most powerful woman in tennis. In the 1980s, she ruled over the courts like a queen on a throne. But her journey took many years of ups and downs before she became the champion that she is today.

Born Martina Subertova on October 18, 1956, in Prague, Czechoslovakia, Martina grew up in an athletic family. Her grandmother had been a tennis champion who at her peak was ranked number two in Czechoslovakia. Martina's mother, Jane Subertova, was a top skier who gave lessons for a living. Her father was a ski patrolman. When they married, they moved to a ski lodge called Martinovka, which means Martin's place. Martina was named after the cozy lodge.

When Martina was three, her parents' marriage broke up. She moved with her mother to a one-bedroom home overlooking a tennis court. She soon learned to ski and play many sports, such as hockey and

1956 Navratilova is born in Prague, Czechoslovakia.

1978 Navratilova wins Wimbledon (and in 1979, 1982–1987, and 1990).

1983 Navratilova wins the Australian Open, the U.S. Open, and Wimbledon.

1984 Navratilova wins the French Open, the U.S. Open, and Wimbledon.

1990 At age 33, Navratilova wins her ninth Wimbledon, breaking the record she had shared with Helen Wills Moody.

soccer. Her mother eventually married a man named Mirek Navratil, who taught tennis lessons. In Czechoslovakia, wives (and daughters) add the ending "ova" to their husband's last name, so Martina Subertova became Martina Navratilova.

By the time she was six, Navratilova was eager to play tennis with her parents. At first, she chose to only hit the ball against a wall. But she soon learned from her stepfather how to play. From the beginning Navratilova preferred the attacking style of Billie Jean King to the conservative, baseline game taught by her stepfather.

She became devoted to her tennis game and when winter came, she went with her stepfather to Prague, 16 miles away, to try out with George Parma, a former tennis champion who was now a coach with the Czech Tennis Federation. Parma recognized her talent immediately and soon Navratilova was taking the train to Prague once a week for lessons.

At age 12, she had already traveled to other cities and even West Germany to play tournaments. This was significant at a time when the Soviet Union controlled Eastern Europe and made travel between countries unusual and extremely difficult. When she was 16, Navratilova was finally able to go to the United States, for a two-month trip. She quickly became very fond of American culture, especially the food. She was known to stuff herself with everything from hamburgers and French fries to pancakes.

While the American players and fans were beginning to take a liking to her daring, aggressive style, her emotions were often unstable and prevented her from truly taking charge and beating more disciplined players such as Chris Evert.

Navratilova was able to return to America when she was 18 years old, and she promptly became the tenth ranked female tennis player in the world. She was also named rookie of the year. Most of her winnings went to the Czech Tennis Federation to help other young players, but Navratilova saved enough of her prize money to buy her parents a car so they could travel throughout Eastern Europe to see her play.

In 1975, Navratilova showed the world how powerful she had become. She beat top players such as Virginia Wage and reached the finals of the French, Italian, and Australian Opens. She soon teamed up to play doubles with Chris Evert and together they won four tournaments in 1975, including the French Open.

But Navratilova's success created a difficult situation. The Czech government was worried that she might want to become an American citizen. If she decided to give up her Czech citizenship and become an American, she could never go back to the country where she was born. But in the end, Navratilova decided that the American lifestyle was too good to give up. She soon moved into a friend's house in Beverly Hills, California, and began the process of gaining her American citizenship.

For the first time in her life, Navratilova was in control of her own life. With no one telling her what to do, she spent large amounts of money on furs, cars, and jewelry. She also began eating extraordinary amounts of food at one sitting, such as entire pizzas and gallons of ice cream. Her activities were taking a toll on her tennis game.

Luckily Navratilova recognized her own destructive behavior, and after two years of hard work, she learned to overcome it. She improved so much that she won the 1978 French Open and beat Evert in the Wimbledon finals.

Off the court, the openly gay Navratilova fell in love with famous author Rita Mae Brown. Brown encouraged in Navratilova a love of culture, and soon she was visiting museums and plays instead of spending all of her time on the court.

In 1979, Navratilova's family decided to move to the United States. But the visit did not last long. They decided that they were more comfortable in Czechoslovakia and soon returned home. Navratilova bought them a big house, but the political climate at the time meant that she could not visit her parents in the new house.

By 1980, Navratilova's ranking had slipped to number three. She knew that she could improve if she worked out more often. She began practicing tennis for three hours each day as well as running sprints, lifting weights, and doing all sorts of drills and exercises. She hired a **nutritionist** to keep her healthy and in top physical condition. She eventually improved so much that she won 90 of her 93 matches in 1982, winning 15 out of 18 tournaments and reclaiming the number-one ranking from Evert. Navratilova was so dominant that she became the first female player to earn over $6 million in a single year.

Navratilova's hard work and mental alertness had turned her into the best player of the 1980s. In 1991, at the age of 35, she matched Chris Evert's career record of 157 tournament championships, giving her the most wins of any female tennis player ever. She now holds the all-time record in singles play (beating Helen Wills Moody) with nine Wimbledon championships, including a record six in a row.

> *"Martina revolutionized the game by her superb athleticism and aggressiveness, not to mention her outspokenness and her candor."*
>
> Chris Evert on Martina Navratilova

nutritionist: a scientist or other professional who specializes in the study of food and it's effects on the human body.

Today, Navratilova serves as a tennis commentator/broadcaster for HBO. Though she never attended college, she was awarded an honorary degree from George Washington University in Washington, DC in 1996. She continues her intense involvement with women's tennis by participating on the board of the Women's Tennis Association and has also authored a number of books about her playing experiences. ◆

Nelson, Byron

FEBRUARY 4, 1912– ● GOLFER

> *"When we arrived at a course Byron would quietly find out what was the course record and who held it. If it was held by the local pro or amateur, he'd never try to break it. He knew that record meant more to them than it would to him. That's a perfect example of the kind of man he is."*
>
> Ken Venturi, a protégé of Byron Nelson

Byron Nelson, possibly the most consistent golfer of all time, was born and raised in Fort Worth, Texas. The Nelson family lived near Fort Worth's Glen Garden Club, and when Byron was in his early teens, he began caddying at the club's golf course. At age 14, Nelson and his friend, future pro golfer Ben Hogan, tied for the club's caddy championship. Before long, Nelson learned to play the game, and when he was 16 he tasted his first success, winning the Glen Garden Club junior title. That year he left school to work, but in his free time he practiced his golf game.

A harbinger of things to come for Nelson came in 1930, when, at age 18, he won the Southwest Amateur title. Two years later, in 1932, he turned professional, but the next five years were frustrating ones. During his first year on the pro tour, when the nation was in the depths of the Great Depression, he won just $12.50, although he did tie for third in the Texarkana Open. He persisted, though, supplementing his income by serving as the club pro at the Texarkana Country Club (earning $60 a month) and teaching golf at country clubs in New Jersey and Pennsylvania. In 1935 he won the New Jersey Open, and his winnings of $2,700 enabled him to continue golfing. During these years he identified a problem with a hook in his swing and was able to correct it. His performance improved, and in the years that followed he developed into perhaps the steadiest performer in men's professional golf.

In 1937 Nelson's hard work began to pay off when he won his first major tournament, The Masters, largely on the strength of his putting. That year, to confirm his arrival, he also was named to the U.S. Ryder Cup team. His peak year was 1939, when he won the U.S. Open, the Western Open (never leaving the fairway once in 72 holes), and the North-South Open; came in second in the PGA Championship; won the Vardon trophy for low scoring average; and returned to the Ryder Cup team. The following year, 1940, he won the Texas Open and the PGA Championship.

During World War II Nelson was exempt from military service because of a blood-clotting disorder. This allowed him to continue to play while many of his competitors were off fighting the war. In 1941 and 1942 he won the All-American Open, a title he regained in 1944 and 1945. He won the Greensboro Open in 1941 and 1945, regained his Masters title in 1942, won the Canadian Open in 1945, and won the Los Angeles Open in 1945 and 1946. In 1945 he also repeated as winner of the PGA Championship. Throughout the war years Nelson also played in many exhibitions for the Red Cross and the United Service Organization. In 1944 he won 22 events, posted a scoring average of 69.67, and earned a record $37,900 (payable in War Bonds). In 1945 he recorded an accomplishment that may never be topped: he won a record 18 tournaments (out of 30 he entered) and, between March 8 and August 4 of that year, won a record 11 in a row. No golfer since then has won more than five in a row. Also, in 1944 and 1945 he finished in the money—the top ten—113 consecutive times, and throughout the 1940s he finished in the money 133 times. These accomplishments led the Associated Press to name Nelson as the Male Athlete of the Year in 1944 and 1945.

By the end of the war Nelson was enduring severe back pain and was growing uncomfortable with being the center of attention, so he began to think about retiring. He made the decision after his caddy accidentally kicked his ball in the 1946 U.S. Open, costing Nelson the championship. He returned to Texas to become a rancher, managing an 800-acre cattle ranch near Roanoke. He didn't leave golf behind entirely, though. He served as a golfing commentator for ABC, coached such notable golfers as Tom Watson, and, as a player, joined the Ryder Cup team in 1947 and won the Texas PGA Championship in 1948, the Bing Crosby Invitational in 1951, and the French Open in 1955. He was also non-playing captain of the 1965 Ryder Cup team. In 1953 he was elected to the PGA Hall of Fame, and in 1974 he was elected to the PGA/World Golf Hall of Fame. By the time his career ended, Nelson had won 49 PGA tournaments. And his consistent, powerful swing—pulling the

1912 Nelson is born in Fort Worth, Texas.

1937 Nelson wins the Masters and is named to the U.S. Ryder Cup team.

1939 Nelson wins the U.S. Open, the Western Open, and the North-South Open; he also finishes second in the PGA Championship.

1940 Nelson wins the Texas Open and the PGA Championship.

1942 Nelson wins the Masters.

1953 Nelson is elected to the PGA Hall of Fame.

1974 Nelson is inducted into the PGA/World Golf Hall of Fame.

club rather than pushing it into the ball on the downswing—would influence the way future golfers played the game.

In 1993 Nelson published his autobiography, *How I Played the Game*. ◆

Nicklaus, Jack

JANUARY 21, 1940– ● GOLFER

Fellow golfer Johnny Miller probably best summarized the golfing career of Jack Nicklaus, the "Golden Bear," when he said, "When he plays well, he wins. When he plays badly, he finishes second. When he plays terrible, he finishes third." Given that Nicklaus has an incredible 100 career tournament victories to his credit, Miller's exaggeration seems only a slight one.

Nicklaus was born in Columbus, Ohio, the son of a prominent pharmacist who took up golf after his doctor advised him to walk each day to strengthen his leg after an injury. Young Jack caddied for him, but offered a glimpse of things to come when, at age ten, he shot a nine-hole 51 his first time on the course as a player. He took a golf class from the club pro at the Scioto Country Club in Columbus, and at age 13 he shot a 69 on the 7,000-plus-yard course, already demonstrating his power. At age 13 he won the Ohio State Junior championship, and throughout his high school years he won a number of other junior championships—all in addition to playing football, baseball, and basketball. In 1957, at age 17, he qualified for the U.S. Open, although he missed the cut after the first two rounds.

Nicklaus attended Ohio State University, initially wanting to fol-

Jack Nicklaus clinches the 1986 Masters.

low in his father's footsteps and become a pharmacist (though he never took his degree, a fact that he always regretted). During his college years he won the U.S. Amateur Championship twice, in 1959 and 1961, and was runner-up to legend Arnold Palmer in the 1960 U.S. Open. His Ohio State team also won the NCAA championship in 1961. In light of this success he decided to turn pro in 1961, beginning a three-decade-long career as arguably the best golfer in history. In his first 17 tournaments in 1962 he finished in the top 10 eight times, with five second- or third-place finishes. In his 18th tournament that year, the U.S. Open, he defeated Arnold Palmer to win the first of his 18 major pro tournament titles and to join Palmer and Gary Player in what came to be called the Modern Triumvirate of golf.

A recital of Nicklaus's accomplishments seems endless. First there are the major championship wins. He won the U.S. Open four times (1967, 1972, and 1980, in addition to his win in 1962). He holds a record six wins in the Masters (1963, 1965, 1966, 1972, 1975, and 1986; in the 1986 Masters he shot a 65 in the final round, at age 46 becoming the oldest player ever to win the tournament). He won PGA Championships five times, in 1963, 1971, 1973, 1975, and 1980. And he won the British Open in 1966, 1970, and 1978.

Then there are the countless other wins: five times in the Tournament of Champions between 1963 and 1977; five times as a World Cup team member between 1963 and 1973; six times in the Australian Open between 1964 and 1978; six times as a member of the U.S. Ryder Cup team between 1969 and 1981; and one or more wins in a variety of tournaments, including the Phoenix Open, the Memphis Open, the Westchester Classic, the Western Open, the Byron Nelson Classic, and many others. Nicklaus also won the World Series of Golf five times between 1962 and 1976, and placed second six times.

In 1990 Nicklaus joined the Senior Tour, and the wins just kept on coming, 10 in all during the 1990s. He won two of the first four tournaments he entered in 1990, and in the 1991 U.S. Senior Open he shot a 65 in an 18-hole playoff with Chi Chi Rodriguez, calling that round one of the greatest of his career. He repeated as U.S. Senior Open champion in 1993.

Wins are one way to tell the story of Nicklaus's success, but statistics also tell the story: 100 career tournament wins, including 71 official PGA wins, 10 Senior events, and 19 unofficial or international events; 58 second places (19 in major tourna-

1940	Nicklaus is born in Columbus, Ohio.
1959	Nicklaus wins the U.S. amateur championship (and also in 1961).
1962	Nicklaus defeats Arnold Palmer in the U.S. Open.
1963	Nicklaus wins the Masters (also in 1965, 1966, 1972, 1975, and 1986) and PGA Championship (also in 1971, 1973, 1975, and 1980).
1966	Nicklaus wins the British Open (also in 1970 and 1978).
1967	Nicklaus is named PGA Player of the Year (first of five times).
1990	Nicklaus joins the Senior Tour.

Professional Golfers' Association of America (PGA)

Professional golfers in Britain organized a national association in 1901, but it was not until 1916 that their American counterparts followed suit. The Professional Golfers' Association of America (PGA) owes its existence largely to the efforts of one man, Robert White, a Scotsman who came to the United States in 1894 and worked as a golf pro at various clubs. Seeking to popularize the game and to promote high standards of play, the PGA was launched in 1916 with White as president and Herbert Strong as first secretary. Rodman Wanamaker was an early benefactor of the PGA, donating the cup that is awarded to the winner of the PGA championship.

The PGA grew slowly in its first years; it had only about a hundred members when White retired in 1920. The group took off during the prosperity of the 1920s and has grown into one of the most powerful professional sports associations in the world, with a membership of 23,000. From its offices in New York City it oversees a schedule of some 40 tournaments a year. It even has its own golf course in Port Lucie, Florida.

The PGA's history has not been free of controversy. Throughout the 1960s the tournament players began to feel that they lacked an adequate voice on the executive committee and in overall policy. The long-simmering dispute boiled over in 1968, when a group of star players broke away from the PGA and formed American Professional Golfers Inc. The rebels whose ranks included champions such as Frank Beard, Billy Caspar, Gardner Dickinson, Dourg Ford, Don January, Jack Nicklaus, and Dan Sikes began to organize their own tournament schedule. By December 1968 the two sides reached an agreement that created a tournament players division within the PGA, and the breakaway group disbanded.

When the PGA was formed in 1916, it immediately launched an annual tournament, which was based on match play until 1958, when the format changed to what is now the standard for all major tournaments, four rounds of 18 holes each, scored by strokes. The first PGA championship was held in 1916 in Siwanoy, New York, and was won by Jim Barnes. The 1999 title went to Tiger Woods, who collected a $630,000 prize.

ments) and 36 thirds (nine in major tournaments); number one in scoring average eight times between 1964 and 1976, and runner-up six times; top money winner eight times between 1964 and 1976, and runner-up four times, with a total of over $8 million in career earnings (over $5.6 million, plus $2.4 million as a Senior). Nicklaus can even boast 17 career holes-in-one.

A third way to tell the Nicklaus story is through awards. He was named PGA player of the year five times between 1967 and 1976. Sports Illustrated named him Athlete of the Decade for the 1970s. Twice he has been named Golfer of the Century, first by *GOLF Magazine* in 1988, then by *Golf Monthly* in 1996. His success as a golf-course designer, his major professional interest in the late 1980s and 1990s (his company, Golden Bear Inc., has designed and built golf courses all over the world.), led *Golf World* to name him Golf Course Architect of the Year in 1993. Nicholas has also written several books about golf. All this from a man who at first wasn't sure he wanted to be a pro golfer.

Nicklaus is respected not only for his golfing prowess but for his family involvement as well. He is the father of five children, and his desire to be an active, involved parent caused him to limit his tournament appearances to no more than 20 events, even during his peak years, leading Chi Chi Rodriguez to quip, "Jack Nicklaus is a legend in his spare time." ◆

Norman, Greg

FEBRUARY 10, 1955– ● GOLFER

Movie-star handsome, gracious in both victory and defeat, Greg Norman is one of the most popular and charismatic figures on the pro golf tour. His powerful frame, generating a swing that was measured at a remarkable 130 miles per hour, propels some of the most prodigious drives in the game (his longest measured shot was 483 yards).

In contrast to the many great athletes who seem to have begun training in their cribs, Norman was a very late starter who didn't begin taking golf seriously until the age of 16. Born in the mining town of Mount Isa in Queensland, Australia, Norman was a thin boy who sought to develop his physique by working out with weights and participating in rough-and-tumble team sports. At school he excelled in rugby, football, cricket, squash, track, and Australian rules football. He was also an avid swimmer and surfer.

It was not until midway through his 16th year that Norman, after caddying for his mother (a three-handicap golfer) began to play around with her clubs on the practice tee. He found that he could effortlessly hit enormous drives, and he soon began to take the game seriously, spending hours at the practice tee. At first he concentrated on distance rather than accuracy, a strategy recommended by his first coach, Charlie Earp of Brisbane's Royal Queensland Gold Club. Once satisfied with his distance, which routinely exceeded 300 yards, Norman began to rein in his power to achieve greater directional control.

Shortly after graduating from high school, Norman became an apprentice pro under Charlie Earp at Royal Queensland,

Greg Norman is one of the most popular and charismatic figures on the pro golf tour.

1955 Norman is born in Mount Isa, Queensland, Australia.

1980 Norman wins the Australian Open.

1981 Norman wins the Australian Masters (also in 1983, 1984, and 1987).

1986 Norman wins the British Open and the Kemper Open.

1993 Norman wins the U.S. Open and the British Open.

antic: zany, good-natured, playfully funny.

where he augmented his meager salary by playing $100 rounds against wealthy members. Lacking the money to pay if he lost, in these matches Norman cultivated the unflappable temperament that later served him so well on the pro tour.

After routing the competition in local amateur tournaments, Norman made the move to the Australian professional tour in 1976. It was still a period of learning and adjustment for Norman, who progressed steadily, winning one tournament for each of his first five years on the tour. His first significant victory was the Australian Open in 1980, which was followed by wins in the Australian Masters in 1981, 1983, 1984, and 1987; the Queensland Open in 1983; the Victoria Open in 1984; and the New South Wales Open in 1983 and 1986. On the international tour he also captured the European Martini in 1977, 1979, and 1981; the Hong Kong Open in 1979 and 1980; the French and Scandinavian opens in 1980; and the Dunlop Masters in 1981. He also led the European Order of Merit tour in 1982.

Norman's first big splash in the United States was his fourth-place finish at the 1981 Masters. In 1983 he played in nine PGA tournaments and did well enough to qualify for the PGA tour in 1984, when he won the Kemper Open and, nearly, the U.S. Open as well—in the latter he tied Fuzzy Zoeller at the end of regulation play but dropped the playoff by a disheartening eight strokes. Nevertheless, his **antic** charm in defeat—waving a white towel and joking with Zoeller— earned him the high regard of the public and his fellow pros. Reflecting on that episode, Norman recalled, "I may have been burning inside, but I don't understand why so many players get keyed up about the bounces a golf ball takes." Later that year Norman topped his boyhood idol Jack Nicklaus in the Canadian Open, was runner-up in the Western Open, and made the top 10 in the Georgia-Pacific Atlanta Classic on the way to becoming the sixth-ranked earner on the 1984 tour.

Norman had no victories on the PGA tour in 1985, but he earned prize money in 12 of his 16 contests. The victories began to pile up in 1986, however, including the Panasonic Las Vegas Invitational, his second Kemper, and his first major tournament, the British Open. He entered the final round leading the three other majors that year (the U.S. Open, the Masters, and the PGA) but in each case was undone by a disappointing final round.

Norman slumped again in 1987, failing to win a single PGA event, although he still ranked seventh in earnings that year with $535,450. Since then Norman has remained among the most competitive of golfers on the U.S. and international tours, regularly finishing among the leaders in yearly earnings. In 1993 he added two more PGA major crowns to his collection, finishing first in both the U.S. Open and the British Open.

Despite his impressive earnings, Norman is known for runs of bad luck: for example, Norman was on the threshold of victory at the 1986 PGA tournament when Bob Tway sunk a shot from a sand trap on the 72nd hole to eke out a win with what Tway himself described as a once-in-a-lifetime shot. Norman has lost three other important tournaments to opponents who holed off-the-green shots on the last hole—including the 1987 Masters. Still a fierce competitor on the tour, Norman missed most of the 1998 tour with a shoulder injury but rebounded nicely in 1999, finishing third in the Masters and carding six rounds in the sixties on his way to earnings of $577,018.

Known as the "Great White Shark," both for his Nordic platinum mane and his one-time fondness for shooting sharks from his boat, Norman attributes his success to his aggressive style of play, which has both admirers and detractors among his competitors. Jack Nicklaus observed, "His biggest fault, if he has one, is that he is so aggressive with his game that he can't tone it down at the end when he might need to." Others have noted the advantages of Norman's **predatory** instincts on the course. Nick Price said of him, "He's like a leopard hunting. . . . He plays for what he is, an outspoken Australian. It's what people expect. And he's fearless."

But Norman's game thrives on more than just his primal hunger for victory. On his property he maintains practice greens where he spends hours each day on diligent drills, honing his stroke to razor sharpness. With endorsement contracts that bring his annual income to an estimated $10 million, Norman can now afford to ease his travel schedule and spend more time with his family. But with over a dozen tournaments under his belt in 1999, the Great White Shark shows no signs of retreating to calmer waters. ◆

> *"You create your own luck by the way you play. There is no such luck as bad luck."*
> Greg Norman

predatory: literally, intending to injure or harm another creature identified as your prey. In sports, it means having the instincts to defeat your opponent when you have them down, to finish them off.

Oerter, Al

AUGUST 19, 1936– ● TRACK AND FIELD ATHLETE

Whether growing up on the tough streets of Lower Manhattan in the 1940s, or struggling mightily as a high-school sprinter a few years later on Long Island, even Al Oerter himself had no way of knowing that one day he would be acknowledged as the greatest clutch performer of all time in athletic competition.

Oerter was born in Astoria, Queens, and lived in New York City until the age 12. His father, a plumbing contractor, and mother, who worked in film distribution for Paramount Pictures, always encouraged his athletic endeavors , but Oerter did not even get near a discus until he was a high school sophomore—despite an unbelievable throwing arm in baseball and football.

"I was always interested in track—but as a sprinter or a miler," Oerter said. "And, really, I was not very good at either. Then one day an errant discus accidentally fell near me as I was running on the track. Thing is, when I threw it back it went twice as far as the real discus guy's toss. I think he's still chasing it. From then on, I was in love. I was a discus thrower for life."

Though in only his second year of throwing he had already broken the New York State High School record, Oerter decided to go to the University of Kansas on a full academic scholarship. There, coached by Hall of Famer Bill Easton, Oerter first set a national freshman collegiate record then, as a 19-year-old sophomore, made the 1956 Olympic team in a huge upset over far more seasoned throwers.

> "I was in love. I was a discus thrower for life."

345

1936 Oerter is born in Astoria (Queens), New York City.

Oerter wins the Olympic gold medal in the discus throw at Melbourne, Australia.
1956 Oerter also wins a gold medal and sets a record at the Tokyo Olympics in the discus competition.

Oerter wins his fourth Olympic
1968 gold medal in a row at Mexico City.

Of course, at the Melbourne, Australia, Olympics, he was an even bigger underdog; no one paid any attention to the unknown Oerter. Italy's Adolfo Consolini and U.S. World Record holder, Fortune Gordien (194 feet, 6 inches), were the overwhelming favorites. But when Oerter's turn came in the first round, he felt incomprehensibly keyed up and inspired. He let loose with what was by far the best throw of his career (184–11), psyching out his opposition in the process. No one's throw came within five feet of Oerter for the rest of the competition. On the victory platform, Oerter finally realized that he actually won. His knees buckled and he almost fell as the enormity of his achievement slowly dawned upon him.

In the ensuing years, however, Oerter had plenty of time and opportunity to get used to the feeling; he won the next three Olympic golds, the four titles in a row in the same event a record that has only been equaled by Carl Lewis (in the long jump) since. (And some believe that Lewis was helped by the Communist-block boycott that kept some of his major opponents out of competition in 1984.)

If possible, Oerter's unparalleled achievement is made even more amazing by the fact that in not one of his four winning Olympic Games was he the reigning world record holder—or even the favorite. (Oerter did set four World Records between Olympc Games, including the first throw ever over 200 feet.) He managed to win as an underdog every time, remaining totally relaxed in the face of the great athletic pressure of the Olympic Games.

"I had an ability to just enjoy myself at the Olympics," Oerter says. "I knew that for four years, each and every day, I worked hard and did everything possible to be at my very best on that one special day for the Olympic discus throw. So, secure in that knowledge I just relaxed and enjoyed." Others, far more highly regarded than Oerter, routinely battled their nerves.

Besides more highly favored throwers, Oerter had to overcome a plethora of other trials as well in order to win four gold medals in a row. In 1957 he suffered serious injuries in a near-fatal car crash—but luckily he recovered in time for the Rome Olympics in 1960. World Record holder Rink Bubka led the competition until the last round at 190–4, with Oerter second at 189–1. Bubka then told Oerter that he seemed to be carrying his left arm too low as he spun. Oerter thanked his rival for the advice—then went on to throw 194–2 on his last attempt to beat Bubka to the gold.

In the 1964 Olympics in Tokyo, Oerter had to face world record-holder Ludvik Danek of Czechoslovakia (who won 45 straight competitions) while suffering from a chronic cervical disc injury that caused him to wear a neck harness. Oerter also had torn cartilage in his lower ribs. Doubled over in intense pain, Oerter nonetheless won on his fifth throw once again while setting a new Olympic record (200–1).

In Mexico City in 1968, the 32-year old Oerter was considered the underdog once again, this time to fellow American L. Jay Silvester, who held the world standard at 224–5. The discus final, however, was delayed an hour by rain, upsetting the already-nervous Silvester, who was considered unbeatable at the time. In the third round, Oerter—then in third place—uncorked a lifetime best 212–6. The throw upset Silvestri—who fouled on his last three throws—along with the rest of the world's best throwers. Al Oerter had his fourth gold medal in a row.

But Oerter did not stop there. Though he retired and did not take part in the 1972 and 1976 Olympics, he came back to try out for the 1980 team. Unfortunately, the U.S. athletes could not go to Moscow to compete due to the anti-Soviet boycott. Still, at the age of 43, Oerter finished fourth in the U.S. Trials, just missing the team. "Still, I threw my best results between the ages of 39–45, including my personal best 227–11," he later said. "And I'll always remain extremely proud of that."

Oerter is retired from sports and living in Fort Myers Beach, Florida, with his wife Cathy Carroll, a world-class long jumper in her own right. He coaches young athletes and is much in demand as a motivational speaker. ◆

> *"Given any other environment, I would have stopped. But these were the Olympic games, and you die for them."*
>
> Al Oerter, on a record-breaking discus throw, despite torn cartilage in his rib cage, at the 1964 Olympics in Tokyo (quoted by Bud Greenspan in *Parade*)

Otto, Kristin

FEBRUARY 7, 1966– ● SWIMMER

Kristin Otto was born in Leipzig, East Germany (now part of the reunited Germany), on February 7, 1966. She was a natural athlete in a nation that placed high value on excellence in sports. She thus thrilled swimming fans in East Germany, and around the world, when she won six gold medals—four of them individual—at the Summer Olympic Games in Seoul, South Korea, in 1988. Her exceptional all-around performance at the Games also won her the Paek Sang crown for the Most Valuable Athlete.

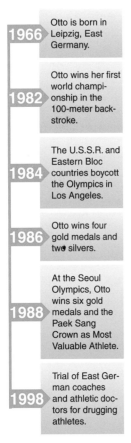

At an early age, Otto was recognized in East Germany as being a potential star swimmer. She was entered into the East German government's rigorous and unforgiving athlete development program, which excelled at producing world-class athletes in numerous sports. The government's gamble on Otto paid off handsomely. In 1982, at age 16, the hard-working teenager won her first World Championship, in the 100-meter backstroke. Otto was focused and determined, and her prospects for triumph at the 1984 Summer Olympic Games, to be held in Los Angeles, California, seemed assured.

But international politics intervened. Under order of President Jimmy Carter, the United States had boycotted the Games held in Moscow, Russia (then part of the Soviet Union) in 1980. The Soviet Union and some of its "satellite" countries, including East Germany, retaliated by boycotting the Los Angeles Olympics in 1984. Thus Otto was prevented from participating in that competition. Olympic glory for all the hard years of training would have to be postponed until the next Games, in 1988.

The year 1984 was deeply disappointing for Otto in another way: An injury threatened to derail her athletic career entirely. She cracked a vertebra and had to spend nine months in a neck brace. She finally was able to return to swimming in 1985, and she quickly built up her strength and stamina, training relentlessly. She persevered at competition and was gradually rewarded with wins in various regional and international swimming meets. In 1986, Otto won four gold medals (in the 100 meter freestyle, 200 meter medley, and two relays) and two silvers.

Otto's Olympic moment finally arrived in Seoul in 1988, when she was 22 years old. The young woman was at the top of her form. She consistently out-paced the competition, capturing the individual gold medals for the 50-meter freestyle, the 100-meter freestyle, the 100-meter backstroke, and the 100-meter butterfly. She also won team gold medals for her participation in the 4 × 100 meter freestyle and the 4 × 200 medley relays. Her brilliant performance brought her not only the six gold medals but public adoration.

After the Olympics, Otto retired from swimming and became a television commentator for the German press. The collapse of the East German Communist government and the reunification of Germany resulted in some staggering news for the swimming world: It was revealed that for two decades the East German government had systematically drugged its athletes with performance-enhancing drugs. There are allegations that no swimmer was exempt, coerced through the threat of severe punishment if not compliant, and tempted by financial rewards when compliant. It is also alleged that some of the athletes who were given the illegal, performance-enhancing drugs did not know that the substances they were given were not allowed by international athletic organizations such as the International Olympics Committee.

As a result of the revelations of institutionalized illegal drugging in East Germany, Otto's record has come into question—fairly or unfairly—as have the records of all East German swimmers, and, indeed, all East German athletes. The innuendos and allegations have been personally and professionally damaging. At a recent World Championships in Perth, Australia, it had been planned that Otto would be honored as a past Olympian. (She attended as a reporter.) In light of the ongoing drugging revelations and scandal in the world-class swimming world, however, the plan was abandoned. ◆

> *"Competing in the Olympics is the highest point one can achieve as an athlete. Gold makes me happier than a world record."*
> Kristin Otto

Owens, James "Jesse"

SEPTEMBER 12, 1913–MARCH 31, 1980 ● TRACK AND FIELD ATHLETE

Born in 1913, the tenth surviving child of sharecroppers Henry and Emma Owens, in Oakville, Alabama, Jesse Owens moved with his family to Cleveland, Ohio, for better economic and educational opportunities in the early 1920s. His athletic ability was first noticed by a junior high school teacher of physical education, Charles Riley, who coached him to break several interscholastic records and even to make a bold but futile attempt to win a place on the U.S. Olympic team. In 1933 Owens matriculated at Ohio State University on a work-study arrangement and immediately began setting Big Ten records. In Ann Arbor, Michigan, on May 25, 1935, he set new world records in the 220-yard sprint, the 220-yard hurdles, and the long jump and tied the world record in the 100-yard dash.

In the racially segregated sports world of 1936, Owens and Joe Louis were the most visible African-American athletes. In late June, however, Louis lost to German boxer Max Schmeling, making Owens's Olympic feats all the more dramatic. At

> *"An unrivaled athletic triumph, but more than that, a triumph for all humanity."*
> President George Bush on Jesse Owens' victories in Berlin, upon awarding the Congressional Medal of Honor (posthumously)

Jesse Owens long jumps for Ohio State University.

Berlin in early August 1936, he stole the Olympic show with gold-medal, record-making performances in the 100 meters, 200 meters, long jump, and relays. All this occurred against a backdrop of Nazi pageantry and Adolf Hitler's daily presence and in an international scene of tension and fear. Out of that dramatic moment came one of the most enduring of all sports myths: Hitler's supposed "snub" in refusing to shake Owens's hand after the victories. (Morally satisfying but untrue, the yarn was largely created by American sportswriters.)

Owens was flooded with business and entertainment offers in the wake of the Berlin games, but he quickly found most of them were bogus. Republican presidential candidate Alf Landon paid him to stump for black votes in the autumn of 1936. After that futile effort, Owens bounced from one demeaning and low-paying job to another, including races against horses. He went bankrupt in a dry-cleaning business. By 1940, with a wife and three daughters to support (he had married Ruth Solomon in 1935), Owens returned to Ohio State to complete the degree he had abandoned in 1936. However, his grades were too low and his educational background too thin for him to graduate. For most of World War II, Owens supervised the black labor force at Ford Motor Company in Detroit.

In the era of the cold war, Owens became a fervent American patriot, hailing the United States as the land of opportunity. Working out of Chicago, he frequently addressed interracial school and civic groups, linking patriotism and athletics. In 1955 the U.S. State Department sent him to conduct athletic clinics, make speeches, and grant interviews as means of winning friends for America in India, Malaysia, and the Philippines.

In 1956 President Dwight D. Eisenhower sent him to the Melbourne Olympics as one of the president's personal goodwill ambassadors. Refusing to join the civil rights movement, Owens became so politically conservative that angry young blacks denounced him as an "Uncle Tom" on the occasion of the famous black-power salutes by Olympic athletes Tommie Smith and John Carlos at Mexico City in 1968. Before he died of lung cancer in 1980, however, Owens received two of the nation's highest awards: the Medal of Freedom Award in 1976, for his "inspirational" life, and the Living Legends Award in 1979, for his "dedicated but modest" example of greatness. ◆

1913 Owens is born in Oakville, Alabama.

1935 Owens sets new world records in sprint races, hurdles, and the long jump on a single day as a member of the Ohio State University track team.

1936 Owens wins Olympic gold medals in the 100-meter and 200-meter dashes, long jump, and relays.

1980 Owens dies on March 31 in Tucson, Arizona.

Paige, Leroy Robert "Satchel"

JULY 7, 1906–JUNE 8, 1982 ● BASEBALL PLAYER

By far the best known of those who played baseball in the relative obscurity of the Negro Leagues, pitcher and coach Satchel Paige became a legendary figure from Canada to the Caribbean basin. Born in a shotgun house (a railroad flat) in Mobile, Alabama, to John Paige, a gardener, and Lulu Paige, a washerwoman, he combined athletic prowess and exceptional durability with a flair for showmanship. In 1971, the Baseball Hall of Fame made Paige—Negro League ball incarnate—its first-ever selection from the (by then defunct) institution.

Paige gained his nickname as a boy by carrying satchels from the Mobile train station. Sent to the Mount Meigs, Alabama, reform school at age 12 for stealing a few toy rings from a store, he developed as a pitcher during his five years there. After joining the semipro Mobile Tigers in 1924, he pitched for a number of Negro League, white independent, and Caribbean teams until he joined the Cleveland Indians as a 42-year-old rookie in 1948. The first African-American pitcher in the American League, Paige achieved a 6-1 record that helped the Indians to the league pennant. His first three starts drew over 200,000 fans.

But it was in the Negro Leagues and Caribbean winter ball that Paige attained his status as independent baseball's premier attraction. During the 1920s and 1930s, he starred for the Birmingham Black Barons and the Pittsburgh Crawfords, where he teamed up with catcher Josh Gibson to form what was possibly baseball's greatest all-time battery. Between 1939 and 1947, Paige anchored the strong Kansas Monarchs staff, winning

"I never threw an illegal pitch. The trouble is, once in a while I toss one that ain't never been seen by this generation."

Satchel Paige

1906 Leroy Robert "Satchel" Paige is born in Mobile, Alabama.

1924 Paige joins the semi-professional Negro League Mobile Tigers.

1948 Paige joins the Cleveland Indians, a major league rookie at 42.

1952 Paige makes the American League all-star team.

1971 Paige is the first Negro League player elected to the Baseball Hall of Fame.

three of the Monarchs' four victories over the Homestead Grays in the 1942 Negro League World Series. Developing a reputation as a contract jumper, he led Ciudad Trujillo to the 1937 summer championship of the Dominican Republic and later pitched in Mexico, Cuba, and Venezuela.

Playing before an estimated 10 million fans in the United States, Canada, and the Caribbean, the "have arm—will pitch" Paige, according to his own estimates, threw 55 no-hitters and won over 2,000 of the 2,500 games in which he pitched.

The 6′3 1/2″, 180-pound Paige dazzled fans with his overpowering fastball (called the "bee ball"—you could hear it buzz, but you couldn't see it), his hesitation pitch, and unerring control. Stories of him intentionally walking the bases full of barnstorming white all-stars, telling his fielders to sit down, and then striking out the side became part of a shared black mythology. "I just could pitch!" he said in 1981. "The Master just gave me an arm. . . . You couldn't hardly beat me. . . . I wouldn't get tired 'cause I practiced every day. I had the suit on every day, pretty near 365 days out of the year."

Probably the most widely seen player ever (in person), Paige was a regular at the East-West Classic (the Negro League all-star game), and also appeared on the 1952 American League all-star squad. His 28 wins and 31 losses, 476 innings pitched, 3.29 earned run average in the majors represented only the penultimate chapter of a professional pitching career that spanned five decades.

Paige ended his working life as he began it, on the bus of a barnstorming black club, appearing for the Indianapolis Clowns in 1967. In 1971, after the Hall of Fame belatedly began to induct Negro Leaguers, he led the way. As his Pittsburgh Crawfords teammate Jimmie Crutchfield put it, when Paige appeared on the field "it was like the sun coming out from behind a cloud." ◆

Palmer, Arnold

SEPTEMBER 10, 1929– ● GOLFER

Arnold Palmer is one of the few athletes worthy of the much-overused label of "legend." From the late 1950s through the mid 1960s, as television began to transform the face of American sports, it was mainly through Palmer's mushrooming popularity that golf found its way out of the narrow precincts of the private country club and into the cultural mainstream. Voted the Athlete of the Decade for the 1960s in an Associated Press poll, he was a key factor in a sea change that transformed golf from the pastime of a moneyed elite into one of the most popular leisure activities in the United States.

Like many great athletes, Arnold Palmer was a child prodigy in his sport, seemingly born to his calling. His father, Milfred J. Palmer, was the golf pro and superintendent at the Latrobe Country Club in Latrobe,

Golf legend Arnold Palmer.

Pennsylvania, from 1921 until he died in 1976. When Arnold was only four years old, his father handed him his first set of clubs, cut down from a regulation set for the toddler. Within a few years Palmer was beating players many years his senior. His caddying, which he began at age 11, kept him busy observing and thinking about the game even when he wasn't practicing.

By the time he entered high school, Palmer was the dominant golfer in western Pennsylvania, winning five West Penn Amateur Championships and a host of other regional and national junior tournaments. At Wake Forest College he quickly established himself as one of the nation's most promising young golfers. In 1950, his senior year, just when Palmer's ascent into golf's elite seemed imminent, Palmer's classmate and best friend, Bud Worsham (the younger brother of Lew Worsham, the U.S. Open winner in 1947), was killed in a car crash. Paralyzed with grief, Palmer dropped out of college and the golf scene and signed on with the Coast Guard for three years.

After his discharge from the service, Palmer returned to Wake Forest briefly, and he soon began taking golf seriously again. He moved to Cleveland to accept a job as a salesman, and while there he won two consecutive Ohio Amateur championships. The turning point in Palmer's golf career came in 1954, when he won the U.S. National Championship. Several months later he joined the pro tour.

1929 Palmer is born in Latrobe, Pennsylvania.

1955 Palmer wins the Canadian Open.

1958 Palmer enjoys a breakthrough win at the Masters (and wins in 1960, 1962, and 1964).

1960 Palmer wins the U.S. Open and the Masters; he is named *Sports Illustrated* Sportsman of the Year and receives the Hickok Athlete of the Year award.

1961 Palmer wins the British Open (also in 1962).

1981 Palmer wins the PGA Seniors Championship.

1982 Palmer wins the U.S. Senior Open.

Palmer's progress on the tour was at first steady but unspectacular. His first professional tournament victory was the Canadian Open in 1955. Palmer enjoyed modest success over the next few years, winning two tournaments in 1956 and four in 1957. But his breakthrough was his victory in the 1958 Masters, one of golf's "big four" tournaments. From that point through 1964 he was the dominant figure on the professional tour, with three additional Masters titles (1960, 1962, and 1964), two British Open titles (1961 and 1962), and a dramatic come-from-behind victory in the U.S. Open in 1960. Palmer has finished second three times in the PGA, the only major golf title he has failed to win.

Although Palmer never won any of the majors after 1964, his performance from 1960 to 1964 was so dominant that it permanently secured his stature as one of golf's all-time greats. In that five-year span Palmer won 29 titles and earned $400,000 in prize money at a time when tournament purses were a small fraction of today's lavish sums, even when adjusted for inflation. He was the top money earner in three of those years and on two occasions represented the United States in the Ryder Cup match, leading the U.S. team to victory in 1963. In 1960 he was honored with both the prestigious Hickok Athlete of the Year Award and *Sports Illustrated*'s Sportsman of the Year trophy.

As impressive as Palmer's record was in these years, his persona and gritty playing style loomed even larger in his magic touch with the public. In contrast to the laconic reserve of the traditional golf champion, Palmer, medium of height and stocky of build, trudged earnestly down the fairway, hair mussed, smiling and waving, occasionally getting a light from onlookers. His swing was the kind of high-effort slash that the weekend duffers in the TV audience could easily identify with. In short, he was the ideal persona for the democratization of golf in the TV age. As the sportscaster Vin Scully put it, "In a sport that was high society, he made it High Noon." His soaring popularity spawned ever-larger gallery crowds, "Arnie's Army" as the media's dubbed the huge and adoring throngs that hung on his every stroke and gesture through 72 holes of play.

Palmer's celebrity also helped to boost the pro golf's purses, which rocketed from $820,360 in 1957 to $3,704,445 in 1966. After Palmer won his last major, the 1964 Masters, Palmer's nine-year career earnings were a record $506,494. It took him only another four years to double that total to become the first million-dollar golfer.

As Palmer's short game began to betray him in the late 1960s, taking him out of contention in the major tournaments, his talent for the business game was just beginning to mature. For many years he was the sporting world's most sought-after pitchman, with his yearly endorsement fees approaching $15 million by the early 1990s. His business empire has expanded to include myriad ventures in golf course design, construction, and development. Palmer stays on top of his demanding schedule by piloting his own Lear jet to his appointments around the country.

Although he has shifted much of his energy to building and designing golf courses, he has not given up playing on them. Palmer won the first event he entered on the Senior Tour, the PGA Seniors Championship, in 1981. In 1982 he became the first former U.S. Open Champion to win the U.S. Senior Open. But although undeniably impressive, his career record of 60 wins—fourth on the all-time list—is not the key to his elevation to near-mythic stature among his fellow golfers and the public. It is his common touch, his years as golf's first heroic tribune of the common man, that has etched his name in the history of twentieth-century sports. ◆

"In a sport that was high society, he made it 'High Noon.'"

Vin Scully on Arnold Palmer

Patterson, Floyd

JANUARY 4, 1935– ● BOXER

The second youngest heavyweight champion in boxing history, Floyd Patterson was born in 1935 in Waco, North Carolina, one of 11 children of Thomas and Anabelle Patterson, and grew up in the slums of Brooklyn. A wayward youth, he attended Wiltwyck School, a correctional institute (1945 1947), where he learned to read and box. He was taken up by Cus D'Amato, who observed his quick hands and punching power. He twice won the Golden Gloves and took the gold medal in the middleweight division at the 1952 Olympics. He then turned pro, and quickly became a contender for the heavyweight crown vacated by Rocky Marciano. On November 30, 1956, he KO'd 43-year-old light-heavyweight champion Archie Moore for the title.

Patterson seemed too gentle a person for his chosen career; once he helped retrieve an opponent's mouthpiece. After at-

"Fear was absolutely necessary. Without it I would have been scared to death."

Floyd Patterson

1935 Patterson is born in Waco, North Carolina.

1952 Patterson wins the Olympic gold medal in middleweight boxing.

1956 Patterson KO's Archie Moore, winning the light-heavyweight title.

1972 Patterson retires with a 55 8 1 record.

taining the title, he defeated four nondescript challengers until matched with Ingemar Johansson on June 26, 1959. Patterson was knocked down seven times in the third round and lost in an upset. He went into seclusion, returning to the ring one year later to knock out Johansson in the fifth, becoming the first heavyweight titlist to regain the crown. On September 25, 1962, he fought the awesome Sonny Liston, who knocked out Patterson in the first round, a defeat that caused him to sneak out of Chicago in disguise. Their rematch in 1963 ended with the same result. Patterson retired in 1972, finishing with a record of 55-8-1.

Patterson has served as head of the New York State Athletic Commission, and in 1985 was appointed director of Off-Track Betting. He was elected to the Boxing Hall of Fame in 1977 and the Olympic Hall of Fame in 1987. ◆

Pelé (Edson Arantes do Nascimento)

OCTOBER 23, 1940– ● SOCCER PLAYER

> *"Pelé doesn't have a nation, race, religion or color. People all over the world love Pelé. Edson is a man like other men. Edson is going to die someday. But Pelé doesn't die. Pelé is immortal."*
>
> Pelé, referring to his birth name, Edson Arantes do Nascimento

Born in Dico (now Tres Coracoes), Minas Gerais, Brazil, Pelé grew up mainly in Bauru, Sao Paulo, where, inspired by the soccer skills of his father, Joao Ramos do Nascimento (Dondinho), he excelled at versions of street soccer, or *peladas*, thus acquiring his future nickname. He played his first professional game with the Santos Football Club on September 7, 1956. The following year he became a member of the Brazilian national team, and in 1958 scored six goals in helping Brazil win its first World Cup. Although Brazil retained its title in 1962, Pelé was hurt and contributed little. In 1966 injuries kept Brazil from reaching the second round, but in his last World Cup (Mexico, 1970) Pelé led a creative team to permanent possession of the Jules Rimet Trophy. Scoring some 1,300 career goals, Pelé also played on clubs that won state and national championships, the Copa Libertadores de America, and the world interclub competition. His style was often more impressive than his numbers.

In 1974 Pelé retired from the Santos club, then surprised the world by joining the New York Cosmos (1975–77) of the fledgling North American Soccer League. Despite the league's eventual demise, Pelé gained popularity in the United States and inspired a younger generation to try his sport. After leaving competition, Pelé worked in films, music, public relations, journalism, and volunteer coaching. He also coauthored a mystery novel and several pieces about his life and soccer. Through an emotional divorce, temporary economic setbacks, and criticism for failing to denounce Brazil's military regimes, Pelé retained his outward optimism and charm. A unique talent who epitomized the culture and aspirations of his countrymen, "the king" remains for most the world's best soccer player ever and a national hero.

In 1994 the president of Brazil, Fernando Henrique Cardoso, named Pelé special minister of sports, a newly created Cabinet-level post. As minister, Pelé worked to root out corruption in soccer management and to boost wages and improve working conditions for professional players. Disillusioned with politics, Pelé left his post in 1998 and returned to the Santos club to train young soccer players. ◆

Soccer legend Pelé.

Perrot, Kim

JANUARY 18, 1967–AUGUST 19, 1999 ● BASKETBALL PLAYER

Anyone who has seen even part of the newsreel of Lou Gehrig's farewell speech at Yankee Stadium in 1939 understands the poignancy of an athlete dying young. So beloved was Kim Perrot by her teammates and fans, so sudden and swift the unfolding of her bout with cancer—less than four months from diagnosis to her death—that her brief but valiant struggle to survive impacted not only members and fans of the WNBA but also the wider community. "Her fight off the court against cancer was heroic and brave," said Houston's

1967 ▸ Perrot is born in Lafayette, Louisiana.

1989 ▸ Perrot is the top collegiate scorer in the nation; she graduates with 26 school records.

1990 ▸ Perrot begins professional play abroad.

1997 ▸ Perrot joins the Houston Comets.

1999 ▸ Perrot dies from cancer at age 32.

mayor, Lee Brown. "Although she lost her battle, she leaves the legacy of a winner."

Pluck and determination were nothing new to Kim Perrot, who, at just five feet five inches, needed liberal quantities of both in cutting an unlikely swath to stardom in women's professional basketball. Born in Lafayette, Louisiana, Perrot excelled in high school basketball and accepted a scholarship to Southwestern Louisiana, where the play of the diminutive Perrot soon towered over that of her teammates and opponents. In her four years there, Perrot notched six of USL's top seven game scoring marks. In all, she established 26 school records, including the all-time marks for scoring (2,157 career, 19.6 per game), assists (254), and steals (421). Her 58-point performance against Southeastern Louisiana is the second-highest single-game total in NCAA history. In her senior year she was the nation's top scorer, averaging 30 points per game and exceeding 40 points six times.

When Perrot graduated, there was no professional women's basketball league in the United States, so she shopped her talents abroad. Her international professional career took her all over Europe and even to the Middle East: she played for Vasby in Sweden (1990–91), Bramen Wuppertal in Germany (1991–92), Maccabbi Tel Aviv in Israel (1994–95), and Racing Strasbourg in France (1996–97).

With the formation of the WNBA in 1997, Perrot returned to the United States to try out for the new women's professional league. Competing in an open tryout against dozens of larger players, Perrot impressed the Houston Comets' coach, Van Chancellor, with her scrappy, aggressive style, and she was chosen as a developmental player in the spring of 1997. On June 19, 1997, she was placed on Houston's active roster.

In Houston's first two seasons, Perrot, a point guard, played in the shadows of Houston's "big three"—Cynthia Cooper, Sheryl Swoopes, and Tina Thompson—but she was still a key to Houston's relentless attack, which produced league championships in those first two years. As *The New York Times* put it, "By the end of the WNBA's first season, Perrot was in charge of the league's best team." After Houston seized its second consecutive WNBA crown in 1998, Chancellor said of Perrot, "The big three are going to get all of the publicity, but poor old Kim is always there. I told her 'Kim, just get me one rebound.' And she got me three among all of those giants. That's coaching right there. That's listening. I didn't ask for but one."

Perrot's **indefatigable** drive and spirit registered impressively in the statistics: in 1997 she led the Comets in steals (2.46 per game, third in the WNBA), was second on the team in assists (3.1 per game), and was third in three-point shots made (28) and attempted (99). Her numbers in 1998 were equally impressive: she led the Comets in assists (4.7 per game, sixth in the WNBA) and steals (2.8 per game), and was the fourth-ranked Comet in number and percentage of three-point shots made (29 and .269, respectively).

After the 1998 season, Perrot was beset with headaches. Medical tests revealed a lung cancer that had already spread to her brain. After knowledge of her grave illness became public, Perrot told a television interviewer, "I have the will to win. I won't accept anything less than winning. With this type of illness I'm facing now, I take the same approach. I won't be defeated. I just feel confident this is just a challenge, just a trial for me. . . . I work really well under pressure."

Perrot then submitted to a trying series of treatments: brain surgery, radiation, and, finally, alternative therapy in Mexico rather than the highly toxic **chemotherapy** prescribed by her physicians. While battling for her life, she gave nearly 100 motivational speeches, mostly at schools. She also continued to write her column, "Yo!" for the *Houston Chronicle*'s teen supplement, in which she wrote, "It's such an exciting time to be a female athlete in the U.S.A. I encourage you young women to follow your dreams. It will take a lot of hard work and determination, but there are no limits on what you can do."

She accepted her second championship ring during a Comets home game on June 22, 1999, when she said, "Who would have thought Kim Perrot would be a two-time WNBA champion? When no one else believed in me, my teammates and the fans stuck with me."

Kim Perrot died on August 19, 1999, at the age of 32. ◆

indefatigable: untiring; unflagging; unable to be beaten down, no matter how bad a situation seems.

chemotherapy: a common medical treatment, most often for cancer, that involves administering closely regulated doses of powerful drugs designed to kill cancer cells.

Petty, Richard

JULY 2, 1937– ● RACE CAR DRIVER

Before there was Dale Earnhart, Dale Jarrett or Jeff Gordon, there was Richard Petty in his familiar blue and red No. 43.

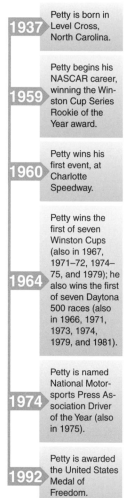

1937 Petty is born in Level Cross, North Carolina.

1959 Petty begins his NASCAR career, winning the Winston Cup Series Rookie of the Year award.

1960 Petty wins his first event, at Charlotte Speedway.

1964 Petty wins the first of seven Winston Cups (also in 1967, 1971–72, 1974–75, and 1979); he also wins the first of seven Daytona 500 races (also in 1966, 1971, 1973, 1974, 1979, and 1981).

1974 Petty is named National Motorsports Press Association Driver of the Year (also in 1975).

1992 Petty is awarded the United States Medal of Freedom.

Known simply as "The King," Richard Petty helped take stock car racing from dirt tracks in North Carolina to new speedways throughout the country and onto the front pages of sports pages throughout the nation. With his ultra-competitive driving style, Petty was a major cog in the engine that helped make stock car racing a television staple and one of the most popular sports in the nation today.

Born in Level Cross, North Carolina, Petty came from a family of auto racing and car enthusiasts. His father, the late Lee Petty, won three Grand National titles (now known as the prestigious Winston Cup). While Petty's brother Maurice went on to a career working on engines, Richard, who originally dreamed of being chief mechanic for his father's cars, followed in his father's footsteps and in 1958 drove in his first event. The following year he was voted Winston Cup Series Rookie of the Year, and in 1960, Petty won his first event at the Charlotte Speedway. It was a win that showed he was ready to live up to all his promise as a great driver; drivers Petty came in ahead of included racing legend Junior Johnson, and his own father, Lee.

That first win was a sign of things to come. Over the next 32 years, Petty won 199 more races on the NASCAR Winston Cup circuit, for a record 200 victories. And the record is likely to stand in the foreseeable future: the next closest driver, the retired David Pearson, has 105. Petty's last victory was at the 1984 Firecracker 400 in Daytona, a track that has become synonymous with the Petty name as seven of "The King's" 200 wins came at the Daytona 500.

With his trademark cowboy hat, mustache and sunglasses, Richard Petty became the signature star of the National Association of Stock Car Auto Racing (NASCAR). But for Petty, his substance has always outshined his considerable style, as vehicles have always been in his blood. From the time he was five years old, when his uncle let him drive a 1938 Ford truck through the fields to help workers baling hay, controlling a vehicle has never been a problem for Petty.

In his racing career, The King amassed records and honors that may never be approached: seven Winston Cup championships; seven Daytona 500 wins; 27 wins in one season (1967), including 10 wins in a row; and National Motorsports Press Association (NMPA) Driver of the Year in 1974 and 1975. Petty ran 1,185 total races and had 713 top 10 finishes. He also became the sport's first million-dollar driver in 1971; his career winnings total nearly $8 million. Petty was also popular with racing fans: He was voted the "Most Popular Winston Cup Series Driver" nine times in the 1960s and 1970s. He was inducted into North Carolina Athletic Hall of Fame in 1977, and into the International Motorsports Hall of Fame in 1997. Perhaps the greatest testament to his popularity, Petty received the Medal of Freedom—the highest U.S. civilian award—in 1992.

Married to Lynda Owens Petty, and with four children and nine grandchildren, Petty still resides in North Carolina, where his family has lived for more than 200 years. Though he retired from driving in 1992, he has not wandered too far from the NASCAR circuit. He now owns Petty Enterprises, which is responsible for two Winston Cup teams, and a NASCAR Craftsman Truck Series race truck. In addition, the Petty name continues to make NASCAR headlines, as Richard's son Kyle has been a highly competitive driver for many years, and now, one of Richard's nine grandchildren, Adam Petty, is attempting to make his presence felt as a driver as well. ◆

"We do this for four and a half hours, no time-outs, no substitutes. You use your physical ability, you use your mental ability, and if something happens they come out and scrape you off the wall."

Richard Petty on racing, 1992

Reese, Harold "Pee Wee"

JULY 23, 1918–AUGUST 14, 1999 ● BASEBALL PLAYER

The captain and shortstop on the great "Boys of Summer" Brooklyn Dodger teams of the 1940s and 1950s, Pee Wee Reese was the heart and soul of perhaps the most beloved team in the history of baseball.

Born Harold Henry Reese in Ekron, Kentucky, just outside of Louisville, Reese earned his nickname as a kid because of his expertise at shooting a game of marbles called "pee wee." His baseball career began in 1938 when he signed with the last place Louisville Colonels, a minor league affiliate of the Red Sox. By the following year, Reese had completely turned the Colonels around and led them to a pennant, leading the league in triples and stolen bases. At age 19, Reese was already getting noticed by big league scouts. Red Sox boss Tom Yawkey, in particular, took a liking to the hustling shortstop, and pegged him as the heir to Joe Cronin, the Boston Hall of Fame shortstop. Cronin, however, apparently averse to the idea of being replaced by a rookie, returned from a scouting trip to Louisville with a negative evaluation of Reese. Since Cronin was a beloved fixture in Boston, Yawkey found himself in a corner and unwisely sold Reese to the Dodgers for $75,000. Cronin would only play through 1944, finishing his illustrious career with a couple of poor seasons, and many feel that the sale of Reese is one of the worst trades in the history of the game.

Reese's major league career, however, got off to a slow start. His rookie year was plagued by injuries as he broke a bone in his heel in May and later that season was hit by a ball thrown by Reds pitcher Jake Mooty. The following season, Reese hit a pathetic .229 and led the league with 47 errors. While the

> Pee Wee Reese was the heart and soul of perhaps the most beloved team in the history of baseball.

Dodgers made it to the World Series that year against the Yankees, Reese hit only .200 and made three errors in the Yankee sweep. But by 1942 he'd made a comeback: he was named to the All-Star team for the first of 10 consecutive years and led National League shortstops in putouts and assists.

Reese was drafted during World War II, and he played on the same Navy team as Yankee star shortstop Phil Rizzuto. As a testament to Reese's leadership and fielding ability, their manager, Bill Dickey, played Rizzuto at third and Reese at short. Reese returned to the Dodgers in 1946. "The Little Colonel," as he was sometimes called, made his most important show of leadership in 1947. He welcomed rookie Jackie Robinson, the first black player in baseball, with a friendly hug. The whole team rallied behind Robinson, and Reese enjoyed his finest offensive season.

Reese would lead the league in walks in 1947, in runs scored in 1949, and in stolen bases in 1952, always compensating his lack of power for the scrappy intangibles that win ball games. As captain of the team, he always paid a visit to the mound when a pitcher was in trouble. And while he was only a career .269 hitter, Reese was an expert base thief and bunter, and often relied on both skills to move runners into scoring position.

While Reese led the Dodgers to seven pennants in his 16 seasons, no season was more magical than the Dodgers lone championship season of 1955. Reese was 37 years old, and his statistics were dwarfed by teammates Duke Snider, Gil Hodges and Roy Campanella, who won the Most Valuable Player (MVP) award. Reese still managed to score 99 runs while hitting .282. The Dodgers beat the Braves by 13 1/2 games to the pennant, but when the Yankees took the first two games of the Series, the Dodgers seemed to be in trouble again. Reese drove in two runs in a Game Three Dodger victory and led the turnaround that produced Brooklyn's first World Series win ever. Reese was also instrumental in Game Seven, when Reese lead off the top of the sixth inning with a single and scored to give the Dodgers a 2–0 lead. In the bottom of the sixth, Reese's double play stifled the last Yankee threat.

Reese moved to third base in 1957 as newcomer Charlie Neal moved to short, and the following season, the Dodgers moved to Los Angeles. The 39-year old Reese played a few games for Los Angeles, but he soon after retired to become a coach. After leaving baseball, Reese returned to Louisville, where he had an executive role with Hillerich and Bradsby, manufacturers of the Louisville Slugger bat. ◆

Women's Professional Baseball

Sporadic and fleeting efforts to organize professional women's baseball teams date back to the late nineteenth century, but the only such undertaking that became a major success was the All-American Girls Professional Baseball League (AAGPBL), which lasted from 1943 to 1954.

This first and only sustained women's pro baseball league was the creation of Philip K. Wrigley, chewing gum magnate and owner of the Chicago Cubs. Because World War II had siphoned off so much of the best major league talent into the armed forces, by late 1942 Wrigley saw commercial possibilities in an all-women's pro league. Scouring the country's schools and colleges for the top female talent, Wrigley's organizers recruited enough personnel to begin play in 1943 with four teams: the Rockford (Illinois) Peaches, the South Bend (Indiana) Blue Sox, the Racine (Wisconsin) Belles, and the Kenosha (Wisconsin) Belles, which played a 108-game schedule before a season total of 176,000 fans. After the 1944 season, when Wrigley was satisfied that major league baseball would survive the war, he sold the league to Arthur Meyerhoff, a Chicago advertising executive whose promotional talents helped the fledgling league to a spirited start in its first few years.

The AAGPBL's athletes were serious competitors who played a serious brand of ball under the managing guidance of some of baseball's top retired stars such as Bill Wambsganss, Max Carey, Jimmie Foxx, and Dave Bancroft. In 1943 the league was playing modified fast-pitch softball with variations to speed up the game: runners were allowed to lead and steal, and the diamond was larger than a regulation softball field but smaller than a standard baseball configuration. As the league grew in popularity, the rules were further modified to enhance the pace and appeal of the game: the size of the ball gradually shrank and its liveliness gradually increased to standard baseball specifications; the pitcher's mound was moved back from 40 feet in 1943 to 50 feet in 1949 to 55 feet in 1950 and finally to 60 feet in 1954. In 1948 the league allowed overhand pitching, which, along with the livelier ball, boosted offensive statistics in the circuit's last seven years.

In the AAGPGL's first decade, attendance rose steadily to a peak of 910,00 in 1948. Thereafter the league went into a steady decline because of postwar social pressures for women to return to domestic life; the resurgence of the major leagues, abetted by the advent of televised games; the increasing availability of other forms of entertainment with growing prosperity; and the lack of a farm system in which to develop new talent. The league folded after the 1954 season. After languishing in obscurity for decades, the legacy of the AAGBL attracted renewed interest in the 1980s when a group of the league's alumnae campaigned for inclusion in the National Baseball Hall of Fame. A splash of newspaper and magazine articles caught the attention of Hollywood, and the 1992 feature film *A League of Their Own* evoked the glory days of the AAGBL.

Retton, Mary Lou

JANUARY 25, 1968– ● GYMNAST

Mary Lou Retton was born on January 24, 1968, in Fairmont, West Virginia. She began studying dance and acrobatics at age four and started training in gymnastics a year later.

Mary Lou was clearly a talented athlete, but she might not have excelled as she did, becoming one of women gymnast's greatest stars, had she not watched the 1976 Summer Olympics Games in Montreal, Canada. The young girl was mesmerized by the performance of Romanian gymnast Nadia Comaneci. Wishing to follow in the footsteps of her hero, in 1982 Retton moved to study with Comaneci's flamboyant coach Bela Karolyi at the United States Gymnastics Center in Houston, Texas.

Retton's talent blossomed under Karolyi's exuberant but demanding regimen. She trained relentlessly, realizing that she would become an Olympic champion only by persistent hard

Mary Lou Retton competes during the 1984 Olympics.

work and risk-taking. As her skills increased, she began participating in more and more prestigious gymnastics meets, gaining
valuable competitive experience as well as multiple titles and
awards.

During the early 1980s, Retton entered a variety of major
American and international competitions during the early
1980s. She did well, building an international reputation as a
fine gymnast as well as filling her trophy case with mementos of
her successes. Retton became the first American to win the title for Combined Events at Japan's Chunichi Cup in 1983. Also
in that year, she won the first American Cup of her career. She
would win two more, in 1984 and 1985.

In 1984, Retton entered the U.S. national gymnastics
championships and performed spectacularly. She won first place
in the floor exercise, the vault, and in combined events.

After that triumph, Retton focused on preparations for the
1984 Olympic Summer Games, to be held in Los Angeles, California. She and coach Karolyi had formed a superb partnership,
and he helped her to develop a style that perfectly suited her
compact, muscular frame and powerful athleticism. Even at her
young age, Retton was like a ball of fire in competition. At the
time, most women gymnasts favored an esthetic, ballet-like approach to the sport. But Retton's dynamic style emphasized
speed, precision, and sheer power. Her approach helped to
transform women's gymnastics into a compelling, dramatic
sport that was followed by millions of fans.

At the U.S. Olympic trials, which determine who will be
named to the U.S. women's gymnastics team sent to the
Olympics, Retton did more than perform well; she excelled.
Retton placed first overall and locked up a spot on the 1984
U.S. Olympic Team. Her high scores in the trials were a portent
of things to come in the Olympics itself. At the Games, Retton
won five medals: bronze medals in the floor exercise and uneven
bars; silver in the vault and team competition; and gold in the
all-around. She was the first American to capture gold for the
women's all-around gymnastics event. In fact, she was the first
American woman ever to win an Olympic gold medal in gymnastics, period.

Retton's bubbly personality and explosive gymnastics style
endeared her to sports fans watching the Olympics around the
world, and she became a star of the Games, her every move
documented by media crews. But she particularly won the
hearts of Olympics-watchers for her vaults during the competi-

1968 ▸ Retton is born in Fairmont, West Virginia.

1982 ▸ Retton moves to Houston to study with Bela Karolyi.

1983 ▸ Retton is the first American to win combined events at Japan's Chunichi Cup; she also wins the American Cup (also in 1984 and 1985).

1984 ▸ At the Olympics, Retton is the first American woman to win a gold medal in gymnastics; she is named *Sports Illustrated* Sportswoman of the Year.

1985 ▸ Retton is elected to the U.S. Olympic Hall of Fame.

tion for the all-around medals. In that event, Retton did well but trailed a Romanian gymnast, Ecaterina Szabo, by 0.05 points going into the final rotation of the event. Retton needed a perfect 10 on her vault in order to win the gold medal.

Under this enormous pressure, Retton decided to perform a very difficult vault—a twisting layout back somersault. Her execution was perfect, and the judges awarded the vault a 10. The gold was hers, and the crowd went wild. Exhilarated, Retton repeated the flawless vault for the audience, good-naturedly proving to any potential nay-sayers that that perfect score was no fluke.

Retton also won the All-Around title at the 1984 U.S. National Championships, and *Sports Illustrated* magazine named her sportswoman of 1984. Soon after the Olympics, Retton's photograph was featured on the cover of the Wheaties cereal box—an important honor for any athlete, and the first such distinction for a woman. Retton was inducted into the U.S. Olympic Hall of Fame in 1985 and retired from competitive gymnastics in 1986.

After her triumph at the 1984 Summer Olympics, Retton became a favorite of the media. She participated in product endorsements and began public speaking. Audiences found her warm and down-to-earth, and she averaged 40 to 50 speaking engagements per year as well as serving as commentator in television sports.

Retton attended college at Tuskegee Institute and married former University of Texas quarterback Shannon Kelly. They have two daughters, Shayla and McKenna, and hope for more. She once joked, "If we keep being blessed with children, we may have an entire team for the 2012 Olympic Games." In order to spend more time with her family, she has cut down the number of speaking engagements but continues to enjoy her role as sports commentator. ◆

Rickey, Branch

DECEMBER 20, 1881–DECEMBER 9, 1965 ● BASEBALL EXECUTIVE

Branch Rickey is best known as the baseball executive who broke baseball's "color barrier" by signing Jackie Robinson, who in 1947 became the first black major league player. At the time, public facilities in many American cities were segregated, as were the armed forces. Blacks were still being lynched in parts of the country. Rickey's move to integrate baseball was one of the most significant events in the United States' social history.

Rickey was a larger-than-life personality, with bushy eyebrows and big jowls, who wore wire-rimmed glasses and bow ties and smoked enormous cigars. He had a penchant for using big words, which he used to obscure facts when it benefited him. His thriftiness was legendary. Cardinals' Hall of Fame player Enos Slaughter once said that Rickey would go to the vault to get change for a nickel. Eddie Stanky described a contract negotiation with the long-winded Rickey by saying, "I got a million dollars worth of advice and a very small increase." Before integrating baseball, Rickey was responsible for several baseball innovations, including the creation of the first "farm system," a network of minor league teams used to develop baseball players for the St. Louis Cardinals in the 1920s and 1930s. In the 1940s, he converted an old military base in Vero Beach, Florida into "Dodgertown," a state-of-the-art spring training complex, where he introduced the first "Iron Mike" mechanical pitching machine.

Rickey was born on December 20, 1881, in Stockdale, Ohio, and was raised on a rural farm in a strict Methodist family. He paid his way through Ohio Wesleyan College by coaching and playing semipro baseball and football. He promised his mother he would not play, work, or travel on the Sabbath, and throughout his career as a player, manager, and executive, his teams always played Sundays without him there.

In the summer of 1903, the 21-year-old Rickey was coaching baseball for Ohio Wesleyan when he witnessed the injustices of "Jim Crow" laws that discriminated against blacks. Charles Thomas, a black first baseman, was refused admission to a South Bend, Indiana, hotel on a trip to play Notre Dame. Rickey persuaded the hotel manager to allow Thomas to share his room. According to Rickey, when they got to the room, Thomas began rubbing his hands together and cried out, "Black skin! Oh, if only I could make it white." Rickey said the incident was the genesis of a vow he made to break major league baseball's color barrier.

Rickey began a professional career as a baseball player in 1903, and was good enough to merit a short stint in the major leagues. When an injured arm ended his career, he began taking

"As a matter of fact I do not deserve any recognition from anybody on the [Jackie] Robinson thing. It is a terrible commentary on all of us that a part of us should not concede equal rights to everybody to earn a living."
Branch Rickey to
Frank Stanton,
1949

law classes at the University of Michigan, and in 1911 he became the school's baseball coach. After getting his law degree, he took a job scouting for the St. Louis Browns, and in 1913, became a full-time Browns' employee, soon rising to general manager. In the final weeks of 1913, he took over as manager, a position he held through the 1915 season.

In 1917, Rickey moved across town to become president of the bankrupt St. Louis Cardinals. It was the beginning of a 25-year relationship in which he served as manager from 1919 to 1925, after which he became the club's business manager. The destitute Cardinals could not afford to compete with other clubs to purchase top players from the independent minor league teams that survived by selling their best players. By necessity, Rickey revolutionized the game by buying semi-pro and minor league teams, and stocking them with young talented players. It was baseball's first "farm system." Rickey hired a network of scouts, and organized tryout camps to find undiscovered players he could sign for little money. When he was done, the Cardinals farm system included 33 teams, and the players it developed allowed the Cardinals to compete with richer teams in larger cities. Rickey's skill at bringing in undiscovered talent brought several Cardinals pennants in the 1920s and 1930s.

In 1942, Rickey moved to the Brooklyn Dodgers as president and general manager, and bought 25 percent of the team. Although the major leagues had no written policy excluding blacks, Commissioner Kenesaw Landis had long enforced baseball's unstated segregation policy. When Landis died in 1944, Rickey sensed the timing was right to tap the Negro Leagues, where hundreds of talented African Americans played in relative obscurity.

On October 23, 1945, Rickey signed Jackie Robinson, his chosen man to break baseball's color barrier. Robinson, a 26-year-old shortstop for the Negro Leagues' Kansas City Monarchs, had been an Army officer and a four-sport star at UCLA. He was a man of great pride, but in him Rickey sensed someone capable of turning the other cheek to the racial slurs, insults, and threats that would accompany his pioneering role. In their first meeting, Rickey warned Robinson about the abuses he would have to endure without retaliation. An angry Robinson asked, "Do you want a player afraid to fight back?" Rickey replied, "I want a player with the guts not to fight back." Robinson met Rickey's challenge, fighting the bigotry he faced with base hits and stolen bases instead of fists.

When he joined the Dodgers in 1947, Robinson became an immediate star. It gave Rickey a jump on the rest of baseball in signing talented blacks, such as Don Newcombe, Roy Campanella, Joe Black, and Junior Gilliam. As a result, from 1947 to 1956 the Dodgers won seven pennants in 10 years.

The 1950 season was Rickey's last with the Dodgers. Before retiring, he spent several years as the general manager and board chairman of the Pittsburgh Pirates. His last venture was a proposed new baseball league in 1960, a response to Major League baseball's repeated refusal to expand. The idea for the new league, called the Continental League, was abandoned when baseball initiated an expansion program that began with three new teams in 1962. Rickey died in 1965, shortly before his 84th birthday, and was inducted into Baseball's Hall of Fame in 1967. ◆

Riggs, Bobby

FEBRUARY 25, 1918–OCTOBER 25, 1995 ● TENNIS PLAYER

Bobby Riggs was born in Los Angeles, California, where he began playing tennis when he was 12 years old. Tennis instructor Esther Bartosh saw him hitting some balls around, recognized his potential, and began giving him lessons. Riggs made rapid progress, and in 1934, when he was just 16, he beat Frank Shields, who had been a finalist at Wimbledon. Two years later he was the fourth-ranking player in the United States on the strength of his first major tournament wins, the U.S. clay court singles championship (which he would go on to repeat in 1937 and 1938), and the U.S. clay court doubles, which he won with Wayne Sabin. In 1937 and 1938 he moved up to second, behind tennis legend Don Budge.

Riggs's peak year as an amateur was 1939, when, at the age of 21, he was the top-ranked tennis player in the world. That year he won the Wimbledon singles, doubles, and mixed doubles titles and the first of his three U.S. Open singles titles. The following year Riggs lost his U.S. singles title to Don McNeill but gained it back in 1941, beating Frank Kovaks. Other major amateur titles included the U.S. mixed doubles, U.S. indoor singles, U.S. indoor doubles (with Elwood Cooke), and U.S. indoor mixed doubles (with Pauline Betz), all in 1940. Riggs also

"He was undoubtedly the cagiest player of all time and was a superb 'gamesman' as well. . . . [H]e was speedy, enormously talented and, more than any other player, exemplified the champion's 'will to win.' . . . [He was] never out of the match until the last point was over."

Julius D. Heldman
on Bobby Riggs

1918 — Riggs is born in Los Angeles, California.

1938 — Riggs plays on the U.S. Davis Cup team (also in 1939).

1939 — As an amateur, Riggs wins Wimbledon, as well as the first of three U.S. Opens; he is ranked first in the world.

1967 — Riggs is named to the U.S. Tennis Hall of Fame.

1973 — Riggs challenges Billie Jean King to a "Battle of Sexes" match and loses.

played on the U.S. Davis Cup team in 1938 and 1939, compiling a 2–2 record.

Riggs turned pro in 1941, and during much of the 1940s he carried on a spirited professional rivalry with Don Budge. He first played against Budge for the U.S. pro singles title in 1942, but lost. They didn't meet again until 1946, when Riggs defeated Budge for the pro singles title. The two went on tour and frequently played against each other, with Riggs taking 23 matches to Budge's 21. They met again in the pro finals in 1947, when Riggs successfully defended his title in five long sets. In 1948 Riggs lost the title to Jack Kramer, whom he had beaten the year before in Kramer's pro debut before 15,000 fans at New York City's Madison Square Garden. He gained it back in 1949, again beating Don Budge. The rivalry between Riggs and Budge, though, didn't extend to their doubles partnership; the two teamed up to win the U.S. doubles titles in 1942 and 1947.

Riggs was never known as a power player, unlike bigger and stronger rivals such as Budge and Kramer. Instead he relied on craftiness and his defensive ability, often baffling the power hitters with his forehand and backhand drop shots and a defensive lob that he was able to mask and whose length he masterfully controlled. When he won, he won with intelligence and court sense; when he lost, his tenacity and calm forced his opponents to a fourth and often fifth set.

Following his 1949 singles championship, Riggs began to withdraw from competition and tried his hand in the early 1950s as a tennis promoter. Although he played in some senior tournaments and was named to the U.S. Tennis Hall of Fame in 1967, he faded into virtual obscurity until social currents, particularly the women's liberation movement, brought him back to the public eye in 1973. That year he challenged women's tennis great Billie Jean King to a $100,000 winner-take-all "Battle of the Sexes Match." The event became a national spectacle. Riggs practiced for the match wearing a "men's liberation" T-shirt and publicly declared, "If I am to be a chauvinist pig, I want to be the number one pig." King's colleague, Rosie Casals, responded by calling Riggs "an old man who walks like a duck, can't see, can't hear, and besides, he's an idiot."

Thirty thousand people turned out at the Houston Astrodome to see the match, while an estimated 50 million watched on television. A circus atmosphere surrounded the event. Riggs made a grand entrance in a chariot pulled by women, while King entered on a red-velvet-covered litter carried by toga-clad football players from the University of Houston. Although Riggs was favored, King soundly defeated him in three sets, wearing him down with long rallies while he tried to counter with spins, lobs, and drop shots. Some fans called the match "the libber versus the lobber." King bore Riggs no animosity, though—the two had been friends for 25 years—and she noted later that her match with Riggs had done much to advance women's tennis as a money and spectator sport. Riggs was a good sport about the loss and later quipped, "Billie and I did wonders for women's tennis. They owe me a piece of their checks." Unfortunately, many tennis fans know Riggs's name not for his genuine athletic achievements in the late 1930s and 1940s but for the theatrical sideshow of 1973.

In 1994 Bobby Riggs established the Bobby Riggs Tennis Museum Foundation to promote awareness of prostate cancer, the disease that claimed his life 1995 in Leucadia, California. ◆

> *"I paid Billie Jean $100,000. But my payoff lasted five years. I made a million and a half."*
>
> Bobby Riggs on the 1973 "Battle of the Sexes" match with Billie Jean King, which he organized and she won

Ripken, Cal, Jr.

AUGUST 24, 1960– ● BASEBALL PLAYER

Despite his two Most Valuable Player awards and being named the starting shortstop on Major League Baseball's All-Century Team, Cal Ripken Jr. will forever be remembered for doing the most mundane of tasks—simply showing up for work. Of course, Ripken wasn't just your average clock-puncher. He played in a staggering 2,632 consecutive games, shattering Lou Gehrig's legendary record—a mark many experts deemed unbreakable—by 502 games.

Calvin Edward Ripken Jr. was born on August 24, 1960 in Harve De Grace, Maryland. Ripken grew up surrounded by baseball. His dad, Cal Sr., was a career baseball man who began priming his son for a major league career at a young age. With Ripken's dad managing in the Baltimore Orioles minor league system, Cal was a frequent visitor on the field and in the locker room, and he befriended many players. Ripken enjoyed an outstanding high school career and was chosen in the second round of the 1978 amateur draft by the Orioles. The junior Ripken quickly progressed in the minors and was called up to the parent club, where his father was now a coach, on August 8, 1981. He got his first hit nine days later.

Ripken began the next season as the Orioles' starting third baseman, but he struggled early on. On May 29, Ripken sat out the second game of a doubleheader—it would be the last game he missed until September 20, 1998. Ripken's swing eventually came around and he ended the year batting .264 with 23 home runs and 93 runs batted in, good enough to win American League Rookie of the Year honors. Late in the season Ripken shifted to shortstop in what was deemed a stop-gap measure. He would stay at the position, defying expectations that a 6–4 player could excel there, until moving back to third in 1997.

In 1983, Ripken made the first of a record 17-straight All-Star starts (through 1999) and helped lead the Orioles to a World Series victory with an outstanding year. He batted .318 with 47 doubles, 27 home runs, 102 RBI and a league-leading 211 hits, and also led American League shortstops in assists for the first time (he would do it six more times). For his efforts Ripken was voted the American League's Most Valuable Player.

Through the '80s, Ripken continued to excel at both the plate and in the field as he methodically began to build his streak.

In 1986, Cal Sr. was named the manager of the Orioles, making Ripken just the third son ever to be managed by his father. On July 11, a fourth son—and the second Ripken—joined that elite fraternity when Ripken's younger brother Billy joined the club. On September 14, Ripken left a game early, ending a streak of 8,243 consecutive innings played, which is believed to be a record (by contrast Gehrig only played every inning of every game one season). In 1988, Cal Sr. was fired six games into the season, but he remained as a coach until the 1993 season. He passed away on March 25, 1999. Billy Ripken was released by the team in 1993.

To begin the next decade, Ripken played in his 1300th straight game on June 22, 1990, putting him second on the all-time list, behind only Gehrig. But with Ripken having just an average year, the whispers began that it was time for him to take a day off. The next season, Ripken silenced his critics by re-bounding with another MVP year, becoming only the third player ever to win the award in a year that his team finished with a losing record. He hit .322 with 34 home runs and won his first Gold Glove award, given for outstanding fielding.

As the record game approached, any time Ripken would be-gin to slump the whispers that he should sit out a game or two would start again. A lesser player would have bristled at the crit-icism, but Ripken just continued to play. Perhaps Johnny Oates, the Orioles' manager in the mid-'90s put it best when he said, "If the good Lord wants Cal to have a day off, He'll let it rain."

Leading up to the record-breaking game in 1995, Ripken admitted that he was growing nervous and uncomfortable with all the hoopla. The night of September 6, 1995, game 2,131 of the streak, was one of the more anticipated contests in baseball history. President Bill Clinton was in attendance as Ripken took the field that evening and to add to the dramatics of the event, Ripken cracked a home run in the fourth to put the Ori-oles ahead 3–1. When the game became official after five-and-a-half innings, the crowd erupted and play was halted for 22 minutes as Ripken entered the stands to hug his family and then took a spontaneous victory lap around the field. After the game, New York Yankees great Joe DiMaggio, a teammate of Gehrig's, assured Ripken and the sold-out crowd that "Lou Gehrig is looking down and giving his approval."

Beyond setting the record, the game and the streak were widely credited with restoring America's love affair with the na-tional pastime, a relationship that had suffered grievous wounds following a labor stoppage that forced the cancellation of the World Series the season before. Ripken himself touched on this theme when he said in a postgame speech, "I know if Lou Gehrig is looking down tonight, he isn't concerned about some-one playing one more consecutive game than he did. Instead, he is viewing tonight as just another example of what is good and right about the great American game."

In fitting fashion, the streak ended not with an injury or a benching. On September 20, 1998, Ripken simply told his man-ager 30 minutes before the game that he would like to sit that

1960 Ripken is born in Havre de Grace, Maryland.

1982 Ripken, playing for the Baltimore Orioles, is named American League Rookie of the Year.

1983 Ripken is the American League's Most Valuable Player (MVP).

1990 Ripken wins a second MVP; wins his first Gold Glove award.

1995 Ripken breaks Lou Gherig's record of 2,131 consecutive games played.

night. The crowd at the Orioles last home game of the year was shocked when Ryan Minor trotted out to third to start the game. Ironically, the season after the streak ended, Ripken had to be placed on the disabled list twice for an ailing back. Even though he no longer plays every day, Ripken remains one of baseball's most cherished players. As the new century was beginning, Ripken was closing in on two **milestones**: 400 home runs (he had 398 through 1999) and 3,000 hits (2,991 through 1999). When and if he ever decides to retire, Ripken is a favorite for election to the Hall of Fame. ◆

milestone: a significant event in a person's life, or in this case, sports career. These are often tied to statistical achievements in sports—hitting 500 home runs, winning 300 games, and so on.

Rizzotti, Jennifer

MAY 15,1974– ● BASKETBALL PLAYER

Basketball guard Jennifer Rizzotti was born in Connecticut on May 15, 1974. As a youngster she lived in Japan for four years, where her father was working. The family had the opportunity to travel all over Asia.

Jennifer was an athletic child who discovered a special affinity for the game of basketball, which her father taught her how to play in their backyard. In an era of extremely tall players, Rizzotti's mastery of the game might seem surprising, as she is only 5′6″, rather short by modern basketball standards. But she is fast and aggressive, and can handle the ball well.

Rizzotti attended the University of Connecticut at Storrs. The UConn women's basketball team was loaded with talent in the 1990s, contributing substantially to the growing popularity of women's basketball, both within the state and nationally. Rizzotti's outstanding work as a guard helped the UConn team become one of the greatest in the United States. With UConn, Rizzotti went to the Final Four during both her junior and senior seasons, and to the National Collegiate Athletic Association (NCAA) Championship in 1995 (for the 1994–1995 season). The UConn women won the Championship—which Rizzotti describes as her favorite basketball moment. Rizzotti averaged 11.4 points during her college basketball career and racked up 637 assists and 349 steals.

Rizzotti considered learning, not basketball, to be her top priority in college. Her philosophy was reflected by her consis-

1974 Rizzotti is born in Connecticut.

1992 Rizzotti begins her collegiate career at the University of Connecticut.

1995 UConn wins the NCAA championship (1994–95 season).

1996 Rizzotti is named AP Player of the Year for the 1995 96 season; wins Naismith Award.

tently high grades. She was named an Academic All-American while at the university.

Rizzotti was drafted profession- ally after college. She had decided that if she were not drafted, she would have worked as a coach or gone on to graduate school, studying biology. But she was quickly snapped up by the New England Blizzard, part of the American Basketball League (ABL).

Rizzotti played three seasons for the Blizzard, staying with the team until the ABL folded after the 1998–1999 sea- son. During her tenure, she was de- servedly showered with accolades. For her work during the 1995–1996 season, she was named Associated Press (AP) Player of the Year for the 1995–1996. She was also a Francis Pemeroy Naismith Award winner. She was honored by Kodak, United Press International (UPI), and the United States Basketball Women's Association (USBWA) as an All-American. She also won the award for Big East Player of the Year.

Rizzoti scores for UConn.

In the 1997–1998 season, Rizzotti's spectacular game was re- warded by winning a slot on the ABL All-Star Team. During the 1998–1999 season, she played in another ABL All-Star game.

When the American Basketball League came to an end, ABL talent was spread throughout the Women's National Bas- ketball League (WNBL). Competition was fierce to be chosen for the WNBL—a situation that boded well for overall play in the league. Houston Comets coach Van Chancellor noted that "There's a great talent level improvement in the league." Riz- zotti was selected to play guard for the Comets—the two-time defending WNBA champion team. She helped take the guard place vacated by Kim Perrot, who was battling cancer (sadly, Perrot died later in 1999).

Rizzotti has had some adjustments to make in her transition from the ABL's New England Blizzard to the WNBA's Houston

Comets. She has not been on the floor during games as much, but she feels confident that her time will come. Meanwhile, she observes that her participation in the team, whether in practice or in games, helps the group overall.

Rizzotti has worn the number 21 since her college days. She enjoys reading and playing golf, and spends as much time as possible with her family and friends. During 1999 she planned her wedding to Bill Sullivan, whom she met while attending UConn. The event promised to be a "family affair," with former UConn teammates Rebecca Lobo, Colleen Healy, Jamell Elliott, and Missy Rose slated to be in the Rizzotti-Sullivan wedding party. ◆

Robinson, Jackie

JANUARY 31, 1919–OCTOBER 24, 1972 ● BASEBALL PLAYER

> "He bore the burden of a pioneer and the weight made him stronger. If one can be certain of anything in baseball, it is that we shall not look upon his like again."
>
> Roger Kahn, *The Boys of Summer*, 1971, on Jackie Robinson

Born in Cairo, Georgia, the youngest of five children of sharecrop farmers Jerry and Mallie Robinson, Jackie Robinson was raised in Pasadena, California, where the Robinson family confronted American racism. White neighbors tried to drive the family out of their home; segregation reigned in public and private facilities. Nevertheless, Robinson became an outstanding athlete at Pasadena Junior College, before transferring to U.C.L.A. in 1940, where he won renown as the "Jim Thorpe of his race," the nation's finest all-around athlete. Robinson was an All-American football player, leading scorer in basketball, and record-setting broad jumper, in addition to his baseball exploits.

Drafted into the Army in the spring of 1942, Robinson embarked on a stormy military career. Denied access to Officers' Candidate School, Robinson protested to heavyweight champion Joe Louis, who intervened with officials in Washington on Robinson's behalf. Once commissioned, Robinson fought for improved conditions for blacks at Camp Riley, Kansas, leading to his transfer to Fort Hood, Texas. At Fort Hood, Robinson was court-martialed and acquitted for refusing to move to the back of a bus. Robinson's Army career demonstrated the proud, combative personality that would characterize his postwar life.

After his discharge from the Army in 1944, Robinson signed to play with the Kansas City Monarchs of the Negro

American League. After several months of discontent in the league, Robinson was approached by Branch Rickey of the Brooklyn Dodgers, who offered him the opportunity to become the first black player in major league baseball since the 1890s. Robinson gladly accepted the opportunity and responsibility of this pioneering role in "baseball's great experiment."

In 1946 Robinson joined the Montreal Royals of the International League, the top farm club in the Dodger system. Following a spectacular debut in which he stroked four hits including a three-run home run, Robinson proceeded to lead the league with a .349 batting average. An immediate fan favorite, Robinson enabled the Royals to set new attendance records while winning the International League and Little World Series championships. Robinson's imminent promotion to the Dodgers in 1947 triggered an unsuccessful petition drive on the part of southern players to keep him off the team. In the early months of the season, beanballs, death threats, and rumors of a strike by opposing players swirled about Robinson. Through it all, Robinson paraded his excellence. An electrifying fielder and baserunner as well as an outstanding hitter, Robinson captured the imagination of both black and white Americans. He batted .297 and won the Rookie of the Year Award (since renamed the Jackie Robinson Award in his honor) en route to leading the Dodgers to the pennant.

Over the next decade Robinson emerged as one of the most dominant players and foremost gate attractions in the history of the major leagues. In 1949 he batted .342 and won the National League Most Valuable Player Award. During his 10 years with the Dodgers the team won six pennants and one World Championship. Upon his retirement in 1956 Robinson had compiled a .311 lifetime batting average. He was elected to the Baseball Hall of Fame on the first ballot in 1961.

Jackie Robinson, pioneer.

"Many people resented my impatience and honesty, but I never cared about acceptance as much as I cared about respect."

Jackie Robinson

1919 Robinson is born in Cairo, Georgia.

1941 Robinson plays professional football with the Los Angeles Bulldogs in the Pacific Coast League.

1947 Robinson plays his first major league game with the Dodgers and is named Rookie of the Year.

1949 Robinson is named the National League's Most Valuable Player.

1956 Robinson retires with a lifetime batting average of .311.

1961 Robinson is elected to the Baseball Hall of Fame.

1972 Robinson publishes his autobiography; dies at age 53.

1997 The baseball season is dedicated to Robinson on the 50th anniversary of his major league debut.

But Robinson's significance transcended his achievements on the baseball diamond. He became a leading symbol and spokesperson of the postwar integration crusade, both within baseball and in broader society. During his early years in Montreal and Brooklyn, Robinson had adhered to his promise to Branch Rickey to "turn the other cheek" and avoid controversies. After establishing himself in the major leagues, however, Robinson's more combative and outspoken personality reasserted itself. Robinson repeatedly pressed for baseball to desegregate more rapidly and to remove discriminatory barriers in Florida training camps and cities like St. Louis and Cincinnati. He also demanded opportunities for black players to become coaches, managers, and front office personnel. Baseball officials and many sportswriters branded Robinson an ingrate as controversies marked his career.

Upon retirement Robinson remained in the public eye. He continued to voice his opinions as speaker, newspaper columnist, and fundraiser for the NAACP. A believer in "black capitalism" through which blacks could "become producers, manufacturers, developers and creators of businesses, providers of jobs," Robinson engaged in many successful business ventures in the black community. He became an executive in the Chock Full O' Nuts restaurant chain and later helped develop Harlem's Freedom National Bank and the Jackie Robinson Construction Company. Robinson also became active in Republican Party politics, supporting Richard Nixon in 1960, and working closely with New York Gov. Nelson Rockefeller, who appointed him Special Assistant for Community Affairs in 1966. These activities brought criticism from young black militants in the late 1960s. Ironically, at this same time Robinson had also parted ways with the NAACP, criticizing its failure to include "younger, more progressive voices."

By the late 1960s Robinson had become "bitterly disillusioned" with both baseball and American society. He refused to attend baseball events in protest of the failure to hire blacks in nonplaying capacities. In his 1972 autobiography, *I Never Had It Made*, he attacked the nation's waning commitment to racial equality. Later that year the commemoration of his major league debut led him to lift his boycott of baseball games. "I'd like to live to see a black manager," he told a nationwide television audience at the World Series on October 15, 1972. Nine days later he died of a heart attack. ◆

Robinson, Sugar Ray

MAY 3, 1921–APRIL 12, 1989 ● BOXER

Sugar Ray Robinson was born in 1921 to Marie and Walker Smith in Detroit. In 1933 Robinson moved with his mother to Harlem, where he attended DeWitt Clinton High School. Representing the Salem Athletic Club, he began boxing, using the identification card of a Ray Robinson. He won the New York Golden Gloves in 1939 and 1940 and turned professional late in 1940. A reporter described his technique as "sweet as sugar." Robinson won his first 40 fights (26 knock-outs) until Jake LaMotta beat him on a decision in 1943. He served as a private during World War II, mainly appearing in boxing exhibitions on tour with his idol, Joe Louis. Robinson demanded fair treatment for blacks in the military, refusing to appear at one show until blacks were allowed into the audience,

Sugar Ray Robinson batters Carmen Basilio.

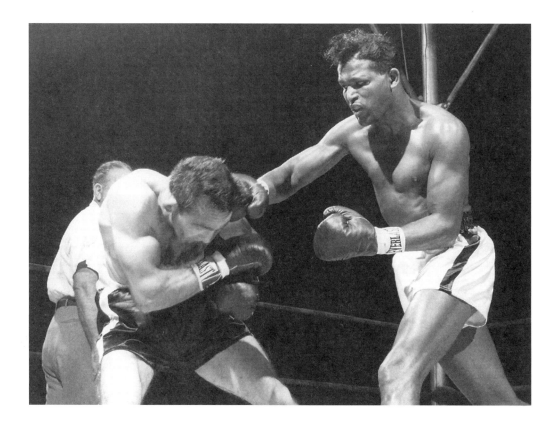

1921 — Sugar Ray Robinson is born as Walker Smith Jr. in Detroit, Michigan.

1940 — Robinson wins the Golden Gloves featherweight title at age 20.

1946 — Robinson wins the welterweight title against Tommy Bell.

1951 — Robinson beats Jake LaMotta in the "St. Valentine's Day Massacre."

1989 — Robinson dies on April 12 in Culver City, California, at age 67.

"Someone once said there was a comparison between Sugar Ray Leonard and Sugar Ray Robinson. Believe me, there's no comparison. Sugar Ray Robinson was the greatest."

Sugar Ray Leonard on Robinson

and getting into a fight with a military policeman who had threatened Louis for using a phone in a whites-only area.

Robinson won the vacant welterweight (147 pounds) championship on December 20, 1946, in a 15-round decision over Tommy Bell. In Robinson's first defense, Jimmy Doyle suffered fatal brain injuries in an eighth-round knockout. When questioned if he had intended to get Doyle into trouble, Robinson responded, "Mister, it's my business to get him in trouble." He moved up to the middleweight division (160 pounds), besting champion Jake LaMotta in the 1951 "St. Valentine's Day Massacre," which got its name from the punishment LaMotta took until the fight was stopped in the 13th round. Robinson lost the title on a decision five months later to Randy Turpin in London, making his record 128-1-2. Two months later he regained the title from Turpin with a dramatic tenth-round knockout in New York as he bled heavily from a cut above his left eye. In 1952 he fought Joey Maxim for the light heavyweight championship at Yankee Stadium. Though far ahead on points, Robinson collapsed after the 13th round in 100-degree heat.

Robinson retired from the ring in 1953 and worked two years as a tap dancer. He returned to boxing in 1955 and in his seventh bout regained the middleweight crown with a second-round knockout of Bobo Olson on December 9, 1955. He lost the title on January 2, 1956, to Gene Fullmer, regaining it in a rematch four months later, knocking Fullmer unconscious in the fifth. Carmen Basilio dethroned Robinson on September 23 but lost the rematch on March 25, 1958, by decision. Robinson held the middleweight title until defeated by Paul Pender on January 22, 1960. Robinson lost the rematch and two other title bouts, and he retired in 1965. He held the middleweight championship a record five times.

Robinson was renowned for his flashy living. He owned a nightclub, Sugar Ray's, and other Harlem properties and on tours took a large entourage, including a valet and barber. He appeared in television and films. Once he was well established, he acted as his own manager and was regarded as a tough negotiator. An IRS tax dispute led to a ruling that allowed income averaging. However, Robinson went through $4 million so fast he had to continue boxing well past his prime. In 1969 he moved to Los Angeles, where he established the Sugar Ray Robinson Youth Foundation for inner city youth. He lived there with his second wife, Millie Bruce, until he died of

Alzheimer's disease and diabetes in 1989. Robinson had a record of 174 (with 109 KO's) 19-6-2. Renowned for his superb footwork, hand speed, and leverage, he was so powerful that he could knock out an opponent when moving backwards. He was elected to the Boxing Hall of Fame in 1967. ◆

Rose, Pete

APRIL 14, 1941– ● BASEBALL PLAYER

"Charlie Hustle" was Pete Rose's nickname, evoking the countless line drives streaking off his quick bat, the hat flying off as he motored around the bases, the chunky legs sprinting eagerly to first base on walks, the heedless head-first slides as he charged hungrily for the extra base. In an age of the soft-spoken, briefcase-toting player-as-financier, he was a throwback to the hard-nosed, rough-hewn firebrands of an earlier era. And in 24 major league seasons he

Pete Rose, baseball's "Charlie Hustle."

put up the numbers to match the attitude: 4,256 hits, the most in baseball history; most games played (3,562), most at-bats (14,053), most singles (3,315), and most singles with at least 200 hits (10). The 16-time All-Star was named baseball's Player of the Decade (1970–1979) by the Sporting News and played on three world champions: the 1975 and 1976 Reds and the 1980 Phillies.

Notwithstanding these enormous successes, Pete Rose's legacy will remain one of personal failure: his exclusion from baseball and the Hall of Fame because of well-documented charges—still publicly denied by Rose—that he bet on baseball games, including games in which he played and managed for the Cincinnati Reds in the late 1980s.

Rose was born in Cincinnati, Ohio, the third of four children. His

1941 Rose is born in Cincinnati, Ohio.

1963 Rose joins the Reds; he is named National League Rookie of the Year.

1970 The Reds reach the World Series (and again in 1972, 1975, and 1976) and win in 1975 and 1976.

1973 Rose bats .338; he is voted Most Valuable Player.

1978 Rose signs as a free agent with the Philadelphia Phillies.

1985 Rose surpasses Ty Cobb as the all-time leader in base hits.

1989 Rose is banned from baseball for gambling offenses.

1990 Rose is convicted of tax evasion and sentenced to five months in prison and a $50,000 fine.

father, Harry, played semipro baseball and football and prodded young Pete toward athletic endeavors. Rose later recalled, "He wanted me to share his love of sports, and I did. One time Mom sent him to the store to buy a pair of shoes for my sister. Instead, he came back with a pair of boxing gloves for me." Harry trained Pete to become a switch hitter. A scrawny high schooler of 140 pounds, Pete seemed more talented in football than baseball, but he was fortunate enough to have an uncle, Buddy Bloebaum, who scouted for the Cincinnati Reds and was willing to give his nephew a shot at the major leagues.

In 1960, Rose's first season in the minor leagues, he led the league in errors but batted a respectable .277 and showed promise with his hustle and speed. He was eventually moved to second base, and after an off-season of bulking up with weights (he would eventually be listed at 5′11″ and 200 pounds), he put up big-league numbers the following season. In 1963 Rose was called up to the Reds and made the most of the opportunity: he batted .273 and was named the National League Rookie of the Year.

Rose's flashy debut proved to be no fluke. In 1965 Rose achieved notable firsts that would become trademarks of his career: 200 hits (ten times) and a .300 average (he hit at least .300 14 times after that). Despite his limited power and mediocre defensive skills, Rose's uncanny instincts, unrelenting hustle, and sharp observations of opposing players allowed him to make the most of a modest physical endowment. He once said, "I don't mind lazy players, as long as they're on the other side."

Rose's take-no-prisoners style of play extended even to the All-Star Game, an exhibition that normally elicits an earnest if relaxed approach from many participants. Rounding third with the winning run in the tenth inning of the 1970 game at Cincinnati, Rose crashed into American League catcher Ray Fosse, dislocating Fosse's shoulder and ending his promising career. In the 1973 National League playoffs Rose's on-field dustup with diminutive Ken Harrelson of the New York Mets sparked an all-out brawl between the clubs and earned him the enduring enmity of New York fans.

By the early 1970s, with the addition of stars such as Joe Morgan, Johnny Bench, George Foster, and Ken Griffey, Sr., the Cincinnati club had evolved into the "Big Red Machine" that appeared in four World Series (1970, 1972, 1975, and 1976) and won two consecutive world titles (1975 and 1976). An integral part of this juggernaut, Rose won a Most Valuable

Player award in 1973 when he stroked 230 hits and batted .338 to win his third battng title.

In December 1978, Rose, a free agent, was signed by the Philadelphia Phillies to the richest contract in the history of the game to that time (though it would barely merit notice by 1999's lavish standards): $3.2 million for four years. He did not disappoint the fans in Philly: He passed the 3,000-hit mark on May 5 of 1979.

Rose's tenure at Philadelphia was productive, leading to another world championship ring in 1980. A free agent again in 1984, Rose signed with the Montreal Expos. Later that season he got his 4,000th hit and began to close in on Ty Cobb's lifetime major league record of 4,191.

Having returned to Cincinnati in August 1984 as a player-manager, Rose was poised to break the record before his hometown loyalists in 1985. Tied with Cobb, Rose faced Eric Show of San Diego before a sellout crowd of 42,237. He ripped a single to left-center, and the game was halted as Pete Rose, Jr., ran onto the field to embrace his father, baseball's new all-time hit leader. After a seven-minute ovation, a tearful Rose addressed the throng: "I was doing all right until I looked up and started thinking about my father. I saw him up there. Right behind him was Ty Cobb."

Although Rose retired as a player after the 1986 season, he stayed on as manager of the Reds. During the late eighties he reportedly bet heavily on sports and had fallen heavily into debt to bookies and the IRS. The commissioner's office launched an investigation of Rose's gambling; the resulting report by the attorney John Dowd, issued in August 1989, concluded that Rose had bet on more than 50 Reds games in 1987 alone, often for daily sums exceeding $10,000. Commissioner A. Bartlett Giamatti permanently banned Rose from organized baseball, although Rose was allowed to apply for reinstatement after one year. The measure, which renders him ineligible for election to the Hall of Fame, has thus far been upheld by the current commissioner, Bud Selig, despite a measure of fan sympathy for Rose, whose problems did not end there. In 1990 he was found guilty of federal tax evasion and served five months in jail and three months in a halfway house.

Now a radio sports talk-show host and familiar face on autograph-for-money shows and on the Home Shopping Network, Rose enjoyed an unexpected honor when Commissioner Selig allowed him to stand on the platform with other all-time

"I'd go through hell in a gasoline suit to play baseball."

Pete Rose

The National League

The National League was not the original professional baseball league in the United States, but it was the first to establish the sport on a firm and enduring footing. Its predecessor, the National Association of Baseball Players, was founded in 1871 but after five years finally collapsed under the cumulative weight of scheduling problems, player desertion, contract breaches, game throwing, and surly player conduct.

Professional baseball was reborn in 1876, thanks largely to the efforts of William A. Hubert, a Chicago businessman and owner of the Chicago White Stockings (later the Cubs) and Albert Spalding, a former Boston pitcher and future sporting-goods baron. On February 2, 1876, the two men huddled in a New York hotel room with representatives of pro teams from St. Louis, Cincinnati, and Louisville. Intent on appealing to a broad middle-class public and avoiding the chaos and ill-repute of the National Association, Hubert and Spalding proposed the following regulations for the new league: no gambling or alcohol sales at games; no games on Sunday; each club must represent a city of at least 75,000 people; all teams must complete a full 70-game schedule, meeting each opponent ten times, five at home and five away; each club must pay an entry fee of $100 and submit yearly dues; and the team with the best record at the end of the season would receive a pennant worth at least $100. The representatives agreed, and the National League was born.

In the new league's opening contest on April 22, 1876, Boston defeated Philadelphia 6–5. The league's inaugural season was largely a success, despite the expulsion of the New York and Philadelphia franchises for refusing to complete their schedules and the firing of four Louisiville players for gambling. Baseball boomed along with the economy of the 1880s, and the National League became the nation's leading baseball organization despite competition from 18 other professional leagues. Its only serious rival during this decade was the American Association, dubbed "the beer league" because so many of its owners owned breweries and because it allowed the sale of beer at its games. From 1884 through 1890, the pennant winner from the National League met the champion of the American Association in a World Championship series.

The most serious threat to the National League came from its own players, who bristled at the league's strict bans on drinking, its salary caps, arbitrary fines, and, most important, the reserve clause in contracts, which forbade the players from selling their services to the highest bidder on an open market. The players finally rebelled en masse, and in 1890 eighty percent of them bolted to form the new Players' League. With three baseball organizations competing for the public's dollars, the 1890 season was a dismal one for all of them. With its superior resources and management skills, the National League was the last one left standing: the Players League dissolved after one season, and the stumbling American Association folded after a disastrous 1891 season, after which the National League absorbed its franchises in Baltimore, St. Louis, Washington, and Louisville.

Now with 12 teams and a monopoly on serious professional baseball, the National League entered a stable but stagnant decade, hobbled by the lack of a postseason championship series and a depressed economy. It again faced a serious rival in 1900 when Ban Johnson's Western league renamed itself the American League and began to raid National League teams of its players. The two leagues signed a peace pact in 1903, agreeing to respect each other's reserve clauses, setting up a three-man commission to oversee their operations, and playing a World Series in 1903 that became an official annual competition in 1905.

The National League stabilized at eight franchises in 1900 and did not expand until 1962, when it added the New York Mets and the Houston Colt .45s (later the Astros). In 1969 the NL added two more franchises, the San Diego Padres and the Montreal Expos; divided the league into Eastern and Western divisions; and introduced a round of playoffs between the division winners to determine the league champion. There have been two more rounds of expansion in the past decade, with the Colorado Rockies and Florida Marlins joining the league in 1993 and the Arizona Diamondbacks in 1998, bringing the NL total to 16 clubs. After the 1993 season both major leagues divided into three divisions Eastern, Central, and Western and included a wild card team in postseason competition, a move that created an additional round of playoffs leading up to the World Series.

The National League's Brooklyn Dodgers was the first team to break the "color line" in major league baseball when it promoted Jackie Robinson to the big club in 1947. During the 1950s and 1960s the National League remained far more hospitable to black and Latino talent: by 1959 it had twice as many blacks as the American League. Since then both leagues have had offered equal opportunity to players of all backgrounds.

In 1997 the American League and National League launched a limited schedule of interleague play during the regular season.

greats at the 1999 World Series to accept his place on baseball's All-Century Team, to which he was voted by the fans. After the ceremony, Rose, still basking in the fans' sustained ovation, was subjected to persistent, withering questioning on national television by NBC's Jim Gray—an episode that elicited a storm of protest against Gray and a gale of renewed fan and media sympathy for Rose, who persists in denying the heavily documented charges in the Dowd report. Selig, however, seems unmoved. After the incident he told reporters, "In life, you have to do what you think is right—as Bart [Giamatti] did, as other commissioners did. . . . You can't be governed by what you think a number of people feel." ◆

Rudolph, Wilma

JUNE 23, 1940–NOVEMBER 12, 1994 ● TRACK AND FIELD ATHLETE

Wilma Glodean Rudolph was born in St. Bethlehem, Tennessee, but shortly afterwards she and her large family—she was one of 22 children, including stepbrothers and stepsisters—moved to Clarksville, Tennessee, where she grew up.

Rudolph overcame staggering odds to become a track star and Olympic champion. She was a small, sickly child who suffered from polio as well as bouts of pneumonia and scarlet fever that left her left leg paralyzed. She received therapy, much of it with the help of her older brothers and sisters, and by the age of eight she was able to walk with a brace, then with the aid of a specially built shoe. Her condition continued to improve, and

by age 11 she didn't need the shoe anymore, allowing her to pursue her first love, basketball, which she learned playing in the family's backyard. At age 13 she tried out for the high school basketball team and quickly became a star, earning All-State honors all four years and averaging over 30 points a game in her sophomore and junior years.

The first person to recognize Rudolph's track potential was Ed Temple, coach of the women's track team at Tennessee Agricultural and Industrial State University in Nashville. Temple watched Rudolph play basketball and, seeing her tremendous speed, convinced her high school coach to form a track team. Rudolph was state champion in the 50-, 75-, and 100-yard events for three years running and never lost a race. During the summers she worked out with Temple's Tigerbelle Track Club in Nashville, and when she was just 16 years old she teamed with three other members of the club in the Melbourne, Australia, Olympics to win a bronze medal in the 4x100-meter relay.

From 1957 to 1961 Rudolph attended Tennessee State University, where she was a track star, though once again she was sidelined by health problems. She missed the 1958 season because of an illness, and in 1959 she pulled a leg muscle in a meet with the Soviet Union. Then early in 1960, with the Olympics fast approaching, she had her tonsils removed. She overcame these setbacks, though, and joined the U.S. Olympic track team in Rome.

The 1960 Rome Olympics were the pinnacle of Rudolph's success as a sprinter. In the 100-meter dash she tied the world record of 11.3 seconds in the semifinal race and won the final heat by three yards. In the next event, the 200-meter dash, she won with a time of 24.0 seconds. In the 4x100-meter semifinal, she and her teammates set a world record of 44.4 seconds. In the final race Rudolph took the baton at her anchor position, came from behind, and won by three-tenths of a second. She was the first American woman to win both sprint gold medals and the first to win three gold medals at the same Olympics. Soon she was dubbed the World's Fastest Woman.

Rudolph also won a total of 14 gold medals at the National Amateur Athletic Union Championships. At the AAU Outdoor Championships she won gold in the 4x100-meter relay (1956, 1959, 1960, 1962), the 100-meter dash (1959, 1960, 1961, 1962), and, in 1960, the 200-meter dash in a world-record time of 22.9 seconds. At the AAU Indoor Championships she won gold in the 50-yard dash (1959 and 1960), the 100-yard dash (1960 and 1961), and the 220-yard dash (1960). In 1961 she competed in the all-male Millrose Games in New York City, winning the 60-yard dash and tying her own world-record time of 6.9 seconds. United Press International named Rudolph Athlete of the Year in 1960, and the Associated Press named her Female Athlete of the Year for 1960–61. In 1961 she won the James E. Sullivan Award for outstanding amateur athlete, the only woman in 31 years to win the award. In 1974 she was elected to the National Track and Field Hall of Fame and the Black Athletes Hall of Fame, and in 1983 she entered the U.S. Olympic Hall of Fame.

After her retirement as a runner, Rudolph remained active. She was an assistant director of the Youth Foundation in Chicago, which developed girls' track and field teams. She created the Wilma Rudolph Foundation in Indianapolis, Indiana,

1940 Rudolph is born in St. Bethlehem, Tennessee.

1960 Rudolph wins Olympic gold in the 100-meter and 200-meter dashes and 4 x 100 relay; she is named Female Athlete of the Year by the Associated Press.

1961 Rudolph sets a world record for 100 meters; wins Sullivan Award as the top amateur athlete in the U.S.

1974 Rudolph is inducted into the National Track and Field Hall of Fame.

1980 Rudolph is inducted into the International Women's Sports Hall of Fame.

to encourage underprivileged children academically and athletically. She also served as a goodwill ambassador to French West Africa and coached briefly at DePauw University in Indiana. Her 1977 autobiography, *Wilma*, was made into a movie, and she wrote *Wilma Rudolph on Track* for children in 1980. She was the mother of four children.

Wilma Rudolph died in Brentwood, Tennessee, in 1994 of brain cancer. ◆

Ruth, George Herman "Babe"

FEBRUARY 6, 1895–AUGUST 16, 1949 ● BASEBALL PLAYER

Before Michael Jordan and Muhammad Ali, there was Babe Ruth. No other American athlete has so thoroughly dominated every aspect of their sport or attained such near-mythic heights of mass adulation. Arguments will rage over the title "Athlete of the Century," but in any credible ranking, the Babe's name will appear among the top three.

To take the full measure of Babe Ruth's staggering achievement, imagine that Ken Griffey, Jr., before passing a decade as the American League's most feared slugger, had already spent several seasons as its best pitcher—indeed, had already set a record for consecutive scoreless innings pitched in the World Series. Further imagine that in his last couple of seasons playing primarily as a pitcher, he had led the league in home runs. Finally, imagine that after converting to the outfield, he set a new single-season home run record by hitting 14 percent of the league's home runs for the season, as the Babe did when he swatted 60 in 1927—except that now that 14 percent would translate into 300 home runs in one season. That, in a nutshell, is the superhuman legacy of Babe Ruth.

Ruth's heroic stature grew out of a hardscrabble childhood that rivals any imagined by Dickens. He was born George Herman Erhardt (no one is quite sure where the Ruth came from) on February 6, 1895, to a poor family. Recalling his childhood, Ruth said, "My folks lived in Baltimore, and my father worked in the [waterfront] district, where I was raised. We were very poor. And there were times when we never knew where the next meal was coming from. But I never minded. I was no worse off than the other kids with whom I played and fought."

By the age of seven his resume of petty theft was long enough to land him in a reformatory, St. Mary's Industrial School, where one of the teachers, Brother Gilbert, took a special interest in the robust but unruly youngster and encouraged him to channel his aggressive energies into sports. The young Ruth quickly established himself as a standout athlete. He recalled, "Even as a kid I was big for my years, and because of my size I used to get most any job I liked on the team. . . . It was all the same to me. All I wanted was to play. I didn't care much where."

Ruth had developed into an exceptional baseball talent by the age of 18, leading Brother Gilbert to contact Jack Dunn, the manager of the Baltimore Orioles (then a minor league franchise) about his **phenom**. After watching the kid throw for a few minutes, Dunn hastily signed him for $600—an entire season's salary—and became his legal guardian. When Ruth entered the Orioles clubhouse in 1914, a coach exclaimed, "Well, here's Jack's newest babe now!" He remained the "Babe" for the rest of his life.

Soon after Ruth tossed an exhibition shutout against Connie Mack's formidable major league Philadelphia Athletics, Dunn sold him to the major league Boston Red Sox. Sent to the Boston's Providence farm club for seasoning, Ruth went 22–9 in 46 starting appearances and earned a spot on the big club in 1915, when he won 18 games. He notched 23 victories in 1918, when he also hurled the longest complete game in the history of the World Series—14 innings—to beat the Dodgers 2–1. Because of his awesome power at the plate, the Babe was playing mostly in the outfield by 1918, although he still pitched often enough to register records of 13–7 in 1918 and 9–5 in 1919, leading the league in home runs both years! He ended up as baseball's only lifetime .300 hitter to have amassed more than 1,000 innings on the mound.

"There's no question about it, Babe Ruth was the greatest instinctive baseball player who ever lived."

Coach Leo Durocher

phenom: in sports, a young player who shows incredible talent and the potential to be a superstar.

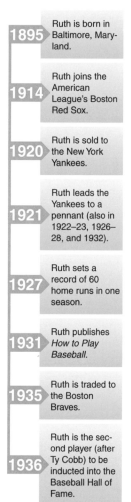

In December of 1919, Red Sox owner Harry Frazee made a decision that still haunts Red Sox fans. Frazee, a theatrical producer deep in debt, decided to fund his Broadway production of the musical *No No Nanette* by selling his star pitcher-outfielder to the New York Yankees. Frazee's folly has come to be known to Red Sox fans as "The Curse of the Bambino": Ever since then, the Yankees have been a baseball powerhouse while the last Red Sox world title came in 1918.

Ruth's impact on the Yankees was immediate: now hitting in the cozy confines of the Polo Grounds, he launched 54 home runs in his first year with New York, shattering his own previous record by 25 (the rest of the American League hit a combined 315 home runs that year). His slugging percentage that year was a Herculean .847, a mark that has been approached only once since—by Ruth himself, the following season, when he slugged .846.

Cheerful and robust—someone once described his face as a smiling catcher's mitt—Ruth whose outsized accomplishments on the field and Rabelasian appetites off of it seemed the perfect expression of the rambunctious roaring twenties, when Ruth became America's first undisputed national sports celebrity—in fact, the most famous American of that era. After smashing all previous home run records and leading the Yankees to a string of pennants by 1927, Ruth was earning $80,000 (about $1 million in 1999 dollars), more than the president of the United States; when asked if he thought this proper, Ruth reportedly replied, "Well, I had a better year than he did."

Ruth carried a fair share of his youthful delinquency into adulthood. His Yankee manager, Miller Huggins, found his so unruly that he suspended him for a portion of the 1921 campaign. As tales of his drinking and gambling made the rounds of the city, even New York State Senator Jimmy Walker (later a carousing mayor of New York) publicly exhorted the Babe to make himself a role model for the all the worshipful "dirty-faced kids in the streets." Although the Babe's prodigal lusts remained unchecked, he arranged many well-publicized visits to children's hospitals, which included famous but unverified incidents of home runs promised to sick children one day and fulfilled the next.

His legendary slugging prowess had led the Yankees to construct a vast new baseball cathedral in 1923—Yankee Stadium—to contain the throngs who longed to see the Babe swat a prodigious blast or peg a perfect throw from deep in right field to nab a heedless base runner. In that maiden season in "The House that Ruth Built," the Bambino hit .393, leading the Yankees to their third straight AL flag and their first of 25 world championships.

Ruth remained the centerpiece of the Yankees throughout the 1920s, leading his team to six pennants and three World Series in that decade alone. Although a livelier ball had been introduced in 1920 to stimulate offensive production, it was still an era dominated by great pitching, singles, and stolen bases, and Ruth was the league's only legitimate home run threat. With the exceptions of 1922 and 1925, Ruth led the American League in home runs every season from 1919 through 1931. But he was also a deceptively quick man—he stole 17 bases in 1923.

By 1927, Ruth had been joined by a wealth of talent that included Hall of Famers Lou Gehrig, Bob Meusel, and Bill Dickey. "Murderers' Row," as they were called, won 110 ball games and swept the Pirates in four games in the 1927 World Series. Ruth's 60 home runs that year was a record that remained unbroken for 34 years, while also topping the total amassed by any other entire team in the league that year. Even the mighty Philadelphia A's could only muster 56 home runs that season.

Ruth finished his playing career in 1935. The Yankees' owner, Jacob Ruppert, offered Ruth the opportunity to manage the Yankees' top farm club. An insulted Ruth instead signed with the Boston Braves for his final three seasons. He enjoyed a final moment of greatness on May 25, 1935, when he belted three home runs, including one ball out of Forbes Field, against the Pirates. A few weeks later, Ruth retired with numbers unmatched for years. His 714 home runs have since been topped by Hank Aaron's 755, but his .342 career average remains ninth on the all-time list, and nobody has approached his mammoth .690 career slugging percentage.

On the inaugural ballot for the Hall of Fame in 1936, the Bambino became one of the first six inductees. Ruth served one year as the first-base coach for the Brooklyn Dodgers in 1938, but it remained one of his great disappointments that he was never offered a managerial position. As one baseball executive put it, "He cannot even control his own life. How is he going to control a baseball team?"

After several years of relaxed retirement devoted mostly to golf and work with disadvantaged children, Ruth developed throat cancer in 1948. Knowing the end was near, he made a dramatic appearance at Yankee Stadium. With his his voice re-

> *"He made home run hitting look easy. . . . There was no violence in the stroke. He put everything into it, but he never looked like he was extending himself."*
>
> Shirley Povich,
> *Washington Post,*
> on Babe Ruth

duced to a faint, hoarse whisper and his once-strapping frame withered to a bent reed, he leaned over the microphone using a baseball bat as a crutch to thank his fans and "the only real sport, I think, baseball."

Two months later, on August 16, 1948, the world learned that Babe Ruth had succumbed to cancer. For two days, as his body lay in state at the entrance to Yankee Stadium, countless thousands of fans streamed past for a last good-bye to the man who transcended a sport to become an icon of twentieth-century American life. ◆

Ryan, Nolan

JANUARY 31, 1947– ● BASEBALL PLAYER

"You don't face Ryan without your rest. He's the only guy I go against that makes me go to bed before midnight."

Reggie Jackson on Nolan Ryan

Few baseball players have ever single-handedly dominated a single statistic the way flame-throwing Nolan Ryan made the strikeout his very own. In 1983, Ryan passed Walter Johnson to become baseball's all-time strikeout king. Ryan then when on to add to his seemingly insurmountable total for over a decade, finally retiring in 1994 with 5,714 strikeouts, a staggering 1,578 more than second-place Steve Carlton.

Lynn Nolan Ryan was born on January 31, 1947, in Refugio, Texas. The son of a rancher, Ryan grew up outside Alvin, Texas, hurling baseballs against the side of a barn with incredible power. In high school, he developed a following for his blazing fastball. In one game he hit the first batter in the arm and broke the batter's arm. The next batter he hit in the head, splitting his helmet. The third batter begged his coach not to make him face the wild right-hander.

His senior year, Ryan attracted the attention of a New York Mets scout and the fledgling franchise selected the Texan in the eighth round of the 1965 amateur draft. Ryan's early career mirrors that of another acclaimed pitcher, Sandy Koufax. Like the Dodger great, Ryan struggled early in his career; showing great promise, but having control problems. And again like Koufax, once Ryan was able to master his blazing fastball, he dominated. In fact, Ryan would go on to break several of Koufax's pitching records.

While hurlers Tom Seaver and Jerry Koosman were garnering the headlines for leading the Mets to the 1969 World Series championship, Ryan bounced between the rotation and the bullpen. He did pick up a win in the playoffs and a save in the World Series, the only time in his 28-year career he played in the Fall Classic. In four full seasons with the Mets from 1968 to 1971, Ryan won 29 games and lost 38. After the 1971 season, the Mets gave up Ryan and his 100 mile per hour fastball, shipping him out West to the California (now Anaheim) Angels in exchange for Jim Fregosi.

Ryan blossomed in the Southern California sun, averaging over 20 wins and leading the American League in strikeouts each of his first three seasons with the Angels. In 1973, he set a major-league record with 383 strikeouts, besting Koufax's single-season total by one. After eight spectacular seasons with the Angels—in which he led the league in strikeouts seven times, pitched four no-hitters to tie Koufax's record, won 138 games, and made four All-Star teams—Ryan became a **free agent** in 1979. Longing to return to his native Texas, Ryan signed with the Houston Astros, becoming baseball's first $1 million-per-year player.

Ryan pitched for nine seasons with the Astros, racking up strikeouts, wins and no-hitters along the way. On Independence Day 1980, Ryan recorded his 3,000th strikeout. Three seasons later, on April 27, 1983, he set the new major league record for strikeouts with 3,508 by whiffing Montreal Expo Brad Mills. On September 26, 1981, Ryan pitched his fifth no-hitter, setting a new record.

Despite having won back-to-back strikeout titles in 1987 and 1988, Ryan was again granted free agency after the '88 season. At the age of 41, Ryan didn't want to leave his beloved Texas, so he signed with the Texas Rangers, for what many thought was a final season.

In 1989, Ryan quickly established that he was no dinosaur and captured the hearts of the home-state fans by recording his first 300-plus strikeout season since 1977, leading the majors with 301, and by tallying his highest win total, 16, since 1982.

Strikeout king Nolan Ryan.

free agent: a professional athlete whose current contract has expired, making him or her free to negotiate and sign with any other professional team.

1947 ▸ Ryan is born in Refugio, Texas.

1971 ▸ The New York Mets trade Ryan to the California Angels.

1973 ▸ Ryan sets a major league record for strikeouts.

1979 ▸ Ryan signs with the Houston Astros.

1980 ▸ Ryan throws his 3,000th strikeout.

1989 ▸ Ryan has the first 300-plus strikeout season since 1977.

1999 ▸ Ryan enters the Baseball Hall of Fame and is named to the All-Century Team.

Ryan continued to flourish and add to the legend of the Ryan Express by recording his sixth no-hitter in 1990 and his seventh in 1991. On July 31, 1990, he recorded his 300th career victory.

After developing arm troubles in 1993, Ryan finally decided to hang up his cleats. He left the game with 5,714 strikeouts, 324 wins (tied for 12th overall), and over 50 major league records including his unbreakable strikeout and no-hitters totals.

After retiring, Ryan stayed true to his Texas roots, retreating to his Texas ranch and settling into his role as another in a long line of Texas folk heroes. Today he owns several ranches and helps run the Nolan Ryan Center, where there is a collection of memorabilia from his storied career. In 1999, Ryan entered baseball's Hall of Fame in his first year of eligibility, garnering the second highest vote percentage of all time (just .01 percent behind Tom Seaver's record 98.8 percent).

That same year Ryan was voted as the starting right-handed pitcher on Major League Baseball's All-Century Team and was selected as the 27th best player of the century by *Baseball Digest*.

No player who ever had to face Ryan's fearsome fastball will ever forget the terrifying experience. As Hall of Fame slugger Reggie Jackson explained: "Nolan Ryan is the only guy who put fear in me. Not because he could get me out, but because he could kill me." ◆

Sales, Nykesha

MAY 10, 1976– ● BASKETBALL PLAYER

B asketball guard/forward Nykesha Sales, nicknamed "Cool Keesh," was born on May 10, 1976, in Hartford, Connecticut. From a young age, it was clear that Nykesha had great athletic talent. As she grew (she now stands six feet tall and 160 pounds), basketball seemed a natural choice. But it was more than her height that would dictate her focus in that direction. She simply loved the game, and she worked hard to improve her endurance and agility on the court.

In high school in Connecticut, her skill in handling the ball and moving around the basketball court made her well-known in basketball circles. For the 1993–1994 season, *USA Today* named her the National High School Player of the Year. Sales averaged 36.2 points per game and 12.3 rebounds per game as a senior. She was asked to be a member of the 1993 U.S. Olympic Festival East Team and the All-Tournament Team.

Sales chose to attend the University of Connecticut at Storrs (UConn). Her home-state university just happens to have one of the best collegiate women's basketball team in the United States, and during her years there, Sales helped it to stay that way. UConn achieved a win in the National Collegiate Athletic Association (NCAA) tournament championship in 1995, and made it to the Final Four in 1996. Sales herself was voted Big East Conference Rookie of the Year for the 1994–1995 season.

For the 1996–1997 season, Sales was named a Kodak All-American. In 1997–1998, the Associated Press (AP) voted her All-American. She played in both the 1996–1997 and 1997–1998 All-Big East First Teams, and was named Big East Defensive Player of the Year for her senior season (1997–1998).

> Sales was voted Big East Conference Rookie of the Year for the 1994–1995 season.

1976 Sales is born in Hartford, Connecticut.

1995 Sales, playing for the University of Connecticut, is named Big East Conference Rookie of the Year (1994–95 season).

1997 Sales is named Kodak All-American (1996–97); sets a UConn record for most points in a game.

1998 Sales is named an Associated Press All-American; she is also named Big East Defensive Player of the Year (1997–98).

1999 Sales makes her WNBA debut with the Orlando Miracle.

Today Sales still holds UConn records for career points (2,178) and steals (447). She set UConn's record for most points in a single game, 46, against Stanford University in December 1997. She ranks sixth in NCAA Division I in career steals. Besides her obvious athletic prowess, Sales also excelled in her studies. Her superb grades earned her a spot on the Big East Academic All-Star Team in 1995–1996 and Sales obtained her college degree with a major in business.

Sales was the leading scorer of the 1997 USA Basketball World University Games Team, which won the gold medal. She also collected gold medals in two out of three outings as a member for the Jones Cup National Team.

During her last month as a member of the UConn team, Sales was sidelined by a serious injury—a ruptured Achilles tendon. The problem persisted for the next year, keeping her out of what would have been her rookie professional season with the Women's National Basketball Association (WNBA) in 1998.

After undergoing surgery and rehabilitation, Sales played in Brazil with the WNBA's post-season touring squad. She was then ready to play with her WNBA team, the brand-new Orlando Miracle. She was the first player assigned to the team.

The Miracle had a superb inaugural season, and Sales contributed substantially to the team's success. In her WNBA debut on June 10, 1999, against the well-regarded Houston Comets, she posted 13 points, six rebounds, and three steals. Later that month, in Orlando's thrilling 68–66 win over the Comets, she scored 23 points and five steals, and added four rebounds and four assists.

Also in June, Sales achieved a game-high—and her professional career-high—of 29 points, three steals, and five assists in an 88–86 win over the Los Angeles Sparks. She posted a team-high of 20 points, four rebounds, five assists, and three steals in an 80–76 win against the Phoenix Mercury. The WNBA took notice that Sales was back on top, fully recovered from her injury, and she was named to the East team for the first WNBA All-Star Game, played on July 14.

Sales is a great favorite among young basketball fans. She devotes time to sharing her knowledge and encouraging them. On the website for the Orlando Miracle, she regularly conducts "online chats" in which she answers fans' questions and provides inspiration for budding athletes. She will not reveal one thing, however: her pre-game ritual.

Sales's favorite sports figures are Gary Payton, Michael Jordan, and Grant Hill and considers winning the last game of the 1994–1995 season—which happened to be the NCAA Championship Game for UConn—her most memorable basketball moment. ◆

Sampras, Pete

AUGUST 12, 1971– ● TENNIS PLAYER

P ete Sampras was born in Washington, D.C., to Greek immigrant parents who never watched him play tennis because it made them too nervous. He began playing by hitting balls against the wall in his basement with an old wooden racquet. After the family moved to Rancho Palos Verdes in California, he began to show promise as a tennis player when his parents took him to a nearby park with his sister Stella (herself an accomplished player who later would win an NCAA doubles title and coach tennis at UCLA). People would watch him play and were impressed by the six-year-old's ability to run down balls and hit fluid ground strokes.

In 1979 Sampras began taking lessons at the Jack Kramer Tennis Club near the family's home, and his game quickly developed. His tennis hero was Rod Laver, and he often watched tapes of Laver's play and tried to model his game after the Australian's. Sampras entered his first junior tournament when he was nine, and over the next several years he competed primarily in tournaments for older children. While most of the time he lost against his bigger and older opponents, he was developing the powerful serve and the precise ground strokes that would later make him the top tennis player in the world. In fact, he won only one junior tournament, the International Grass Court doubles in 1987, the year he changed his backhand from the two-handed style to one-handed.

Despite relatively few tournament wins, Sampras turned pro in 1988. Over the next two years he beat some of the best players on the tour, but he didn't record his first tournament win until 1990. That year he stormed onto the world tennis stage with four wins, beginning with the U.S. Pro Indoor tournament in Philadelphia. Then, still just 19 years old, he became the

> *"For whatever I do the rest of my career, I'll always be a U.S. Open champion."*
>
> Pete Sampras on accepting his U.S. Open trophy, 1990

Pete Sampras
demonstrates his
backhand shot.

youngest player ever to win the U.S. Open. Entering the tournament as a number 12 seed, he knocked off three-time champion Ivan Lendl in the quarterfinal, four-time champion John McEnroe in the semifinal, and Andre Agassi in the final—recording a total of 100 aces during the tournament. After winning the Grand Slam Cup later that year, Sampras ended 1990 as the fifth-ranking tennis player in the world.

Sampras continued to make progress in 1991 and 1992. He won the ATP Tour World Championship both of those years and the U.S. Hard Courts Championship in 1991; he was a U.S. Open finalist in 1992; and he played on the victorious 1992 U.S. Davis Cup team. His play, however, was marked by some inconsistency, as he often seemed to lose concentration on the court. He rarely showed emotion, and some fans—used to the flamboyant personalities of players like Jimmy Conners and John McEnroe—thought he was robotic and uninteresting, even boring.

But starting in 1993 Sampras left no doubt that he was destined to become one of the great tennis players in history. That year he won both Wimbledon and the U.S. Open, recorded over 1,000 aces during the season, and became the number one ranked player in the world, a position he would hold for a record six consecutive years. When he won the 1994 Australian Open, he became the first player in 25 years to win three Grand Slam events in a row. He successfully defended his Wimbledon title in 1994, and when he beat Boris Becker at Wimbledon in 1995, he joined Fred Perry and Bjorn Borg as the only men in 80 years to win three straight titles there. That year, too, he regained his U.S. Open title and accounted for all three U.S. wins in the Davis Cup team's victory over Russia.

In 1996 the wins kept coming. He successfully defended his U.S. Open title against fellow American Michael Chang, and throughout the year he appeared in nine finals, winning eight. In 1997 he took two Grand Slam events, beating Spain's Carlos Moya in straight sets in the Australian Open and Cedric Pioline in straight sets in the Wimbledon final. In 1998 he tied Bjorn Borg's record by winning his fifth Wimbledon title in a grueling five-set, two-tie-breaker match against Goran Ivanisevic, tying Rod Laver and Bjorn Borg with 11 Grand Slam titles and closing in on Roy Emerson's record of 12 titles. In early 1999 Sampras postponed the inevitable by pulling out of the Australian Open to get some rest and recover from injuries. But on July 4 of that year he tied Emerson's record, winning his twelfth Grand Slam title when he beat Andre Agassi in straight sets at Wimbledon, becoming the first man in the open era to win Wimbledon six times. That year Sampras was in the news when he decided late to join the Davis Cup team but gracefully insisted on playing only doubles in deference to teammates who had been with the team all year.

Despite his enormous success—over 56 career singles titles and $22 million in earnings—one title eluded Sampras. Never a strong clay court competitor, he often made an early exist from the clay at the French Open, although in 1996 he made it to the final. ◆

1971	Sampras is born in Washington, D.C.
1988	Sampras turns professional.
1990	Sampras, at 19, becomes the youngest player to ever win the U.S. Open; he also wins the Grand Slam Cup and is ranked fifth in the world.
1993	Sampras wins Wimbledon and the U.S. Open.
1994	Sampras wins the Australian Open and Wimbledon.
1995	Sampras becomes only the third man in 80 years to win three Wimbledon tournaments in a row.

Scully, Vin

NOVEMBER 29, 1927– ● BROADCASTER

When Vin Scully sat down at the microphone for opening day of the 1999 baseball season, it was the start of his fiftieth consecutive season as a play-by-

play announcer for the Dodgers—first in Brooklyn, where he joined the legendary Red Barber in 1950, and later in Los Angeles, the club's home since 1958. But Scully's achievements extend well beyond the local franchise: his five decades of broadcasting excellence have brought his voice to hundreds of millions of listeners across the nation on radio and TV broadcasts of the World Series, the All-Star Game, NFL football, and championship golf. Often celebrated as baseball's "poet laureate," Scully brings to his broadcasts a uniquely musical, unmistakable cadence and an almost literary fluency that have influenced and inspired an entire generation of sportscasters. Dick Enberg has said, "At times I'll be listening to him and I'll think, Oh, I wish I could call upon that expression the way he does. He paints the picture more beautifully than anyone who's ever called a baseball game."

Broadcasting was in Scully's blood as far back as he can remember. Born in 1927 in the Bronx, Scully grew up in the Washington Heights section of New York City, where he daydreamed of broadcasting glory. "I was about eight years old, and we had an old radio on four legs with crossed bars between the legs," Scully said, "and I would come home to listen to a football game—there weren't other sports on—and I would get a pillow and I would crawl under the radio, so that the loudspeaker and the roar of the crowd would wash all over me, and I would just get goose bumps like you can't believe. And I knew that of all the things in this world that I wanted, I wanted to be that fella saying, whatever, home run or touchdown. It just really got to me."

A standout baseball player at Fordham prep, Scully accepted a baseball scholarship to Fordham University. After a year's tour of duty in the Navy, Scully returned to Fordham, where he forsook baseball in his final year in order to take a job at a local radio station. After graduating in 1949, he landed a radio job at WTOP, the CBS station in Washington, D.C., and caught the notice of a CBS executive, who recommended him to Red Barber, then the head announcer for the Brooklyn Dodgers and the director of sports at CBS. Barber asked Scully to go to Boston to do the play-by-play of a football game between Boston University and the University of Maryland. Scully, thrilled by his first network opportunity, rushed to Boston only to find that no announcing booth has been set aside for him, so he went up to the roof, coatless and gloveless and trailing a mike cord, and delivered a first-rate description of the game.

Barber was so impressed by Scully's command in the face of adversity that he ended up offering him the number-three spot in the Dodgers' announcing rotation. "We just needed somebody to sort of take an inning here and there and just do little things. As I put it, carry our briefcases if necessary," Barber recalled. "Scully was a very apt young man. And he took right over. He made the most of his opportunity."

Scully has always acknowledged his huge debt to Barber's mentoring. "Red never taught me how to broadcast, he never taught me baseball, or anything like that," Scully recalled. "What he did teach me was, among other things, an attitude— get there early and do your homework and bear down. Use the crowd." Scully learned these lessons well, never coasting, always meticulously preparing; typically, he spends about two hours in his hotel or at home poring over notes and statistics before a broadcast and arrives at the park three hours in advance to study the game notes and talk with players and coaches.

After Red Barber left the Dodgers and moved to the Yankees in the mid-1950s, Scully became the Dodgers' chief announcer. Just as Scully's star began to rise in New York, the Dodgers announced that they were moving from Brooklyn to Los Angeles for the start of the 1958 season. Scully recalled, "My first feeling was of tremendous relief when [Walter O'Malley, the Dodgers' owner] told me I was in his plans to go to Los Angeles. But I was saddened because being a New Yorker, everything I had and loved in the world was back there."

Scully took to Los Angeles with surprising ease, marrying Joan Crawford (not the actress Joan Crawford) his first season there. The uprooted Dodgers took a bit longer to adjust, but not by much. They fell to seventh place their first season in Los Angeles, but in 1959 they surged all the way back to the top, beating the Milwaukee Braves in a thrilling playoff before topping the Chicago White Sox in six games in the World Series.

Los Angeles quickly fell in love with the Dodgers and with Scully, whose voice permeated the always-clogged freeways of the city's car culture during the baseball season. As transistor radios proliferated in the late 1950s and early '60s, Scully's words **cascaded** through the tiers of Dodger Stadium, audible even to the players on the bench in quiet moments.

Scully's engaging tones frequently made their way to the national airwaves as well, accompanying the Dodgers on their trips to the fall classic when NBC still used hometown announcers through the mid-1970s. Scully later worked as the regular voice

"It's a mere moment in a man's life between an All-Star game and an Old-Timer's game."

Vin Scully

cascaded: poured or rushed, as if in a waterfall. In this context, the announcer's words filled every part of the stadium.

of NBC's baseball telecasts from 1983 through 1989, including the Major League Baseball Game of the Week, three World Series, and four All-Star Games. When NBC lost the national baseball contract after the 1989 season, Scully did the CBS national radio broadcasts of the World Series from 1990 through 1997. In all, he has called 25 World Series and 12 All-Star games.

In his half century on the air, Scully has described some of baseball's most dramatic, memorable scenes: Don Larsen's perfect game in the 1956 World Series; Johnny Podres's shutout of the Yankees in the seventh game of the 1955 World Series, which gave Brooklyn its first world championship; Hank Aaron's record-breaking 715th career home run; and Kirk Gibson's dramatic game-winning home run off Oakland's Dennis Eckersley in the opening game of the 1988 World Series.

Scully's awards and honors are legion: he has received the country's Outstanding Sportscaster award 22 times from the national Sportscasters and Sportswriters Association; he was awarded the Lifetime Achievement Sports Emmy Award from the National Academy of Television Arts and Sciences in 1996 for his "distinguished and outstanding" work; he had his star placed on the Hollywood Walk of Fame in 1982; and in 1982 was inducted into the broadcasters' wing of the National Baseball Hall of Fame (the Ford C. Frick award). Scully even made his Hollywood movie debut this year, playing himself in *For Love of the Game*, a Universal Pictures release about an aging ballplayer (played by Kevin Costner) flirting with a perfect game at Yankee Stadium. As he approaches his 72nd birthday, Vin Scully remains at the top of his game, with no intention of stepping down anytime soon. ◆

Seattle Slew

1974– ● THOROUGHBRED RACEHORSE

The great racehorse Seattle Slew was born in Kentucky in 1974. Bred by Ben Castleman, the brown colt had an excellent pedigree: he was born of mare My Charmer (born in 1969) and sire Bold Reasoning (1968).

Dr. James Hill, a veterinarian, recommended the young thoroughbred to Mickey Taylor, who bought Seattle Slew for only $17,500 as a gift for his wife, Karen. Dr. Hill and his wife, Sally, shared in the purchase.

Seattle Slew was trained by Billy Turner in the state of Maryland. There the gangly colt was affectionately nicknamed "Baby Huey," after a particularly clumsy cartoon character.

Seattle Slew soon proved to be not so clumsy after all—he won his first two starts, in New York in 1976. He was then entered in the esteemed Champagne Stakes. In that race, Seattle Slew started fast and won by nearly 10 lengths, clocking the fastest mile ever run by a two-year-old. He was now awarded the title of "Champion."

In 1977, after a winter off, Seattle Slew was entered in a Hialeah seven-furlong allowance race. He won again by another breathtaking margin: nine lengths. Next, in the Flamingo Stakes—the first major race for sophomores—Slew triumphed again. This time he won by a smaller margin, however. The jockey, Jean Cruget, purposely slowed the horse down in order to save him for more important races. He did the same at the horse's next outing, the Wood Memorial at Aqueduct, which Seattle Slew nonetheless won easily.

By now everyone knew about Seattle Slew. He was odds-on favorite among bettors to win the Kentucky Derby, one of the most prestigious events in all of racing. But Seattle Slew was not at his best at this first of the Triple Crown races (the other two being the Preakness and the Belmont Stakes). He left the gate off balance and fell behind the other horses. This was the first time that Seattle Slew had not shot to the front of the field right out of the gate. However, he regained his composure and shouldered his way through the field. By the mile post, Seattle Slew was in front. He won the Derby by a comfortable one length.

In his next two outings, the Preakness and Belmont Stakes, Seattle Slew had much better starts. He won handily, even turning in the second-fastest time in Preakness history.

The three-year-old colt was now a member of an exclusive club: one of only 10 horses to win all three Triple Crown events in the same year. He was also the first undefeated colt ever to do so. At the end of the year, Seattle Slew was honored as Leading Three-Year-Old and Horse Of The Year.

The year 1977 was not all good for Slew, however. Against trainer Billy Turner's advice, the horse's owners decided to send him to race in California's Swaps Stakes, in Hollywood Park. It was a mistake. Seattle Slew was tired from the travel and his work in the Triple Crown, and he came in fourth—his first de-

1974 Seattle Slew is born in Kentucky.

1977 Seattle Slew is the first undefeated colt ever to win a Triple Crown; he is also named Thoroughbred Horse of the Year.

1978 Seattle Slew wins at Aqueduct and Saratoga.

feat. At that point, the owners replaced Turner with trainer Doug Peterson.

Seattle Slew did not race again that year. He developed a virus that not only put a stop to his racing but also threatened his life. Fortunately, he recovered, and eventually he was put back into training.

By May 1978, Seattle Slew was well enough to compete again. He won that month in a seven-furlong Aqueduct allowance race, but was not entered again until August, in Saratoga. He won at that race, another seven-furlong allowance event, but he took second place at a subsequent Paterson Handicap race at The Meadowlands.

Seattle Slew's next race was a big event: the nine-furlong Marlboro Cup. It was the first-ever meeting of two Triple Crown winners—Seattle Slew and Affirmed. Seattle Slew won by three lengths. Two weeks later the durable champion also triumphed at the Woodward Stakes at Belmont. In his next race, the Jockey Club Gold Cup, Seattle Slew crossed the line with Exceller, but the latter was judged to be the winner.

Just one more race was in the cards for Seattle Slew: the Stuyvesant Handicap at Aqueduct. He carried 134 pounds but still won, seemingly without much effort. It was a noble end to the great horse's racing career. He had started 17 times and won 14 of those races, earning $1.2 million.

Slew was retired and put out to stud at Spendthrift Farm. His value was set at a record-setting $12 million. His offspring include Slew o' Gold, Landaluce, A.P. Indy, Tsunami Slew, Slewpy, and many others.

In time Seattle Slew was moved to Three Chimneys Farm in Midway, Kentucky, where he will live to the end of his days. Now in his mid-twenties, the great champion is saddled up and exercised every day. ◆

Seaver, Tom

NOVEMBER 17, 1944– ● BASEBALL PLAYER

Tom Seaver was one of the authentic "franchise" pitchers in baseball history: It was chiefly by dint of his nearly invincible mound presence that the Mets catapulted from baseball's perennial lovable losers—still languishing near the cellar in 1968—to a stunning world championship in 1969.

George Thomas Seaver was born on November 17, 1944, in Fresno, California. His father was a successful amateur golfer who owned a raisin-packing business. A standout in baseball and basketball in high school, Seaver served six months in the Marines and then spent six months packing fruit for his father before enrolling at Fresno City College. After a year he was lured to the University of Southern California to pitch for the superb Trojan squad.

Seaver quickly emerged as one of the hottest pitching prospects on the college baseball circuit and was drafted by the Los Angeles Dodgers in 1965, but he refused to sign. The following year the Atlanta Braves drafted Seaver, and after the start of the college season, Seaver signed—a violation of the draft rules that prevailed then. Signing a pro contract also cost him his college eligibility. The commissioner of Major League Baseball, William Eckert, ruled that there would be a drawing for Seaver's rights. Three teams—the Indians, Phillies, and Mets—vied for Seaver's services, and the Mets won the draw.

Seaver spent the 1966 season in the minors polishing his skills. In his 1967 major league debut he displayed the command and mettle of a veteran star, notching 16 victories, a 2.76 earned run average (ERA), and winning the National League Rookie of the Year award. That season also marked the first of Seaver's eight appearances in the All-Star Game.

In 1969 Seaver pitched the traditionally hapless Mets all the way to the a World Series championship on the strength of a 25–7 record and 2.21 ERA—overpowering numbers that earned Seaver the first of his three Cy Young Awards. In the Mets' startling five-game upset of the powerhouse Baltimore Orioles in the World Series, Seaver pitched the Mets to a ten-inning 2–1 victory in game four. Seaver was also named *Sports Illustrated*'s Sportsman of the Year for his role in inspiring the Mets to overcome the Chicago Cubs' nine-and-a-half game lead in mid-August to charge to their improbable world title.

Although the Mets faltered in 1970, Seaver did not, highlighting another imposing season on April 22, 1970, when he fanned the last 10 Padres to face him to set a new single-game record of 19 strikeouts (since surpassed by Roger Clemens's mark of 20). In his second Cy Young season, 1973, Seaver again pitched the Mets to the World Series, where they ended up losing to the Oakland A's in seven games. Seaver won his third Cy

1944 Seaver is born in Fresno, California.

1967 Seaver is named National League Rookie of the Year.

1969 Seaver drives the New York Mets to a World Series victory; he also wins the first of three Cy Young awards and is named *Sports Illustrated* Sportsman of the Year.

1992 Seaver is inducted into the Baseball Hall of Fame.

"Blind people come to the park just to listen to him pitch."
Reggie Jackson on Tom Seaver

Young in 1975. In his decade with the Mets, Seaver won at least 20 games three times—in 1971, 1972, and 1975—and led the National League in strikeouts five times and in ERA three times.

In 1977 Seaver again logged more than 20 victories, but not all of them were for the Mets. Halfway through their dismal 1977 season, the Mets' management decided to unload Seaver's expensive contract as the first step in an effort to rebuild with fresh talent; despite an outcry from the fans and the media, Seaver was traded to the Cincinnati Reds, breaking the hearts of their fans. Seaver immediately won over the Reds faithful and went on to win 21 games that season. In 1978 he pitched a no-hitter, and the next year he helped the Reds to a division championship in 1979 by going 16–6.

Age and arm troubles began to limit Seaver's effectiveness in the early 1980s. By Seaver's standards, 1980 was a disappointing if not respectable campaign in which he posted a 10–8 won-lost record and a 3.64 ERA. Although he rebounded to a 14–2 mark in the strike-shortened season of 1981, he struggled in 1982, when he posted the only losing record of his career (5–13) and an ERA (5.50), nearly two runs higher than any previous year; the Reds released him after that season. In 1983 Seaver resigned with the Mets, hoping to recapture the magic of '69 and '73. Despite a solid effort, he posted a disappointing 9–14 record that year, and in 1984 he moved on again, signing with the Chicago White Sox.

In the twilight of his career, Seaver pitched solidly for three more seasons, with Chicago and the Boston Red Sox, before retiring in 1986. In 1985 he joined the select fraternity of pitchers with 300 wins after defeating the New York Yankees in the city where he was still a beloved figure.

He retired after the 1986 season with 311 wins, tied for 16th on the all-time list. He ranks fourth in career strikeouts, with 3,640, and seventh in career shutouts, with 61. Perhaps most impressive is his sterling career ERA of 2.85.

Despite playing half his career outside of Queens, Seaver will always be considered a Met. In fact, he still dominates the club's record book with 395 starts, 171 complete games, 198 victories, 3,045 innings pitched, a 2.57 ERA, 2,541 strikeouts, and 44 shutouts. In 1999, Seaver rejoined the Mets yet again, working as an announcer and in the club's front office.

Seaver was elected to the Hall of Fame in 1992, the first year he was eligible. He was named on 98.9 percent of the ballots, the highest percentage for any player in the hall's history. ◆

Secretariat

MARCH 30, 1970–OCTOBER 4, 1989 ● THOROUGHBRED RACEHORSE

Secretariat may have been the greatest thoroughbred to ever live, certainly the most dominant since Man O'War a half century earlier. In 1973, he captured the imagination of the entire world when he made a shambles of horse racing's Triple Crown, winning all three of the prestigious races (the Kentucky Derby, the Preakness Stakes and the Belmont Stakes) in astounding fashion. At the height of the Vietnam War and Watergate, Secretariat was a much-needed American hero. With a beautiful chestnut coat that earned him the nickname "Big Red" and a distinctive white star on his forehead, his combination of style, power, and grace earned him so much popularity that at the height of his fame he appeared simultaneously on the covers of *Time*, *Newsweek*, and *Sports Illustrated*.

Coincidentally, one of the winningest horses in history, was gotten on a bet—a losing bet. In 1969, horse owner Helen

Legendary race horse Secretariat.

1970 Secretariat is born at Meadow Stud in Doswell, Virginia.

1973 Secretariat wins first the Triple Crown since 1948; he is named Horse of the Year and is featured on the covers of *Time, Newsweek,* and *Sports Illustrated.*

1989 Secretariat dies at Claiborne Farm in Paris, Kentucky.

"Penny" Tweedy lost a coin toss for the right to choose the first foal of a thoroughbred named Bold Ruler. Each year, Tweedy's Meadow Stable sent two mares to Ogden Phipps' Claiborne Farm to be bred with Bold Ruler, the greatest sire at the time. Tweedy and Phipps flipped a coin every other year to determine who would get first choice of the offspring, with the loser getting first choice the following year. Phipps won the coin toss in 1969. Tweedy had to wait a year to pick first, and she chose Secretariat, the son of Somethingroyal and Bold Ruler, born on March 30, 1970. Secretariat turned out to be the greatest consolation prize in horse racing history.

In 1972, the year before winning the Triple Crown, Secretariat, trained by Lucien Laurin, became just the third two-year-old ever to be voted Horse of the Year. In his debut on July 4, 1972, Secretariat finished fourth. It was the only time he would ever finished worse than third. As a two-year-old, he won seven of eight races, finishing second once when a victory was taken away for bumping another horse.

Heading into his third year, in a shrewd but risky deal, a breeding syndicate bought the right to assume his ownership at the end of his racing days. The price was a then record $6.08 million. The purchase looked brilliant when Secretariat easily beat the field in his first two starts of the year. But in his final tune-up for the Kentucky Derby, he finished third in the Wood Memorial, behind Angle Light and Sham, a colt considered to be Secretariat's main rival for the Triple Crown. Many questioned Secretariat's stamina with the 1-1/4 mile Kentucky Derby only 2 weeks away.

Secretariat's legendary 1973 Triple Crown began at the Kentucky Derby in Churchill Downs. Jockey Ron Turcotte had won the Derby the year before with Riva Ridge, Secretariat's stablemate. Even though Secretariat entered the race with doubts hanging over him, he was favored to win. The 13-horse race was expected to be a duel between Secretariat and Sham. After breaking near the back of the pack, Secretariat started to catch up on the first turn, passing horse after horse. He pulled away from Sham for a 2-1/2-length victory, clocked at 1:59-2/5. It was the first and only sub two-minute time in the history of the Derby.

Two weeks later, Secretariat won the Preakness Stakes, going from last to first as the field of six horses came down the backstretch. Again, Secretariat bested Sham by 2-1/4-lengths for the victory. Due to a malfunctioning automatic clock, the official time was recorded by a hand timer at 1:54-^{2}/5, two-fifths of a second off the track record. Several independent clockers thought his time had been even better, including two from the Daily Racing Form who timed him at a would-be record 1:53-^{2}/5.

In the last leg of the 1973 Triple Crown, the Belmont Stakes, only four other horses dared to challenge Secretariat, even though the previous seven horses to have won the Kentucky Derby and Preakness had failed in the brutal 1-^{1}/2 mile long Belmont. Secretariat was more than up for the challenge, turning in the greatest performance in racing history. Secretariat and Sham both went for an early lead, and the first six furlongs were clocked in 1:09-^{4}/5, a time guaranteed to wear out most horses. The two horses were by themselves on the backstretch, when Secretariat made the biggest moves ever seen in a Triple Crown race. Sham could not sustain the pace, dropping back to last.

Meanwhile, Secretariat, with no competition other than himself, seemed to pick up steam as the frenzied crowd cheered him on. In a famous call, track announcer Chick Anderson yelled, "Secretariat is alone. He is moving like a tremendous machine! He's going to be the Triple Crown winner. Unbelievable! An amazing performance. He's 25 lengths in front!" Secretariat won the race by 31-^{1}/2 lengths, an all-time record. His time, 2:24, knocked more than two-and-a-half seconds off the track record. The record is considered unbreakable.

Secretariat came along at a time when horse racing was in the doldrums. It had been more than two decades since Citation had last won the Triple Crown. But despite his propensity for beating unreal expectations in big races, Secretariat may have captured people's imaginations because he showed many human characteristics. He didn't always win. In 21 career starts over a short 16-month career, Secretariat lost five times, reminding people that even the greatest athletes are not invincible.

He raced six more times, winning four and finishing second twice. He won his last race by 6 ^{1}/2 lengths on October 28, 1973, and was retired to Claiborne Farms in Paris, Kentucky, where he sired several future champions including 1986 Horse of the Year Lady's Secret, and Risen Star, who won the 1988 Preakness and Belmont Stakes. Secretariat's life ended tragically when, suffering from laminitis, a painful hoof disease, he was given a lethal injection on October 4, 1989. An autopsy following his death revealed a heart that weighed 22 pounds, almost three times bigger than that of an average horse. ◆

> *"He looked like a Rolls-Royce in a field of Volkswagens."*
> Chick Lang, former general manager, Pimlico, on Secretariat

Racing's Triple Crown

Now associated with American baseball and horse racing, the phrase "Triple Crown" was coined in Great Britain, where it originally designated a rugby team that defeated all of its opponents in a season. In later British usage this honorific was bestowed on the winner of England's three major horse races: the Two Thousand Guineas, the Derby, and the St. Leger. It was not until 1930 that the American sportswriter Charles Hatton used "Triple Crown" to describe Gallant Fox's sweep of the Kentucky Derby, the Preakness Stakes, and the Belmont Stakes. The phrase has since become a standard label for that series of three races or for the winning of all three by a single horse.

The distinction was unofficial until 1987, when the three events organized the Triple Crown Challenge, an award of $5 million to any horse that sweeps the three races and a premium of $1 million to the horse with the best record in the absence of a sweep. This official Triple Crown bounty was offered only until 1993, however. Official or unofficial, the prize has been an elusive one: only 25 horses have taken the first two races, and only 11 of them have completed the sweep: Sir Barton was the first, in 1919, and Affirmed was the last, in 1978.

The three Triple Crown races for throroughbreds are the Kentucky Derby (held on the first Saturday of May), the Preakness Stakes (the third Saturday of May), and the Belmont Stakes (the second Saturday of June). The oldest of the races is the Belmont Stakes, first run in 1867 at Jerome Park. It moved to Morris Park in 1890 and to Belmont Park in 1905. Named after the American Jockey Club's first president, August Belmont, the race is 1.5 miles, the longest of the Triple Crown contests.

The Preakness Stakes was first run in 1873, at the Pimlico Race Course in Baltimore, where it still resides. The race is named for the horse who won the first race at Pimlico on its opening day in 1870. Although its distance has varied over the years, the Preakness Stakes course now measures 1 3/16 miles. The winner of the race receives the Woodlawn Vase, an ornate trophy designed by Tiffany & Co. in 1860.

The youngest of the Triple Crown races, the Kentucky Derby, has become the most prestigious. Its home is in Louisville, Kentucky, at the legendary track Churchill Downs, whose designer, Meriwether Lewis Clark, Jr., established the Kentucky Derby in 1875 to rival England's renowned Epsom Derby. Initially a contest of only regional interest, the Kentucky Derby began to attract national participation and attention after 1902, when Colonel Matt J. Winn became head of the track. By 1920 the Derby had become America's most famous race, the climax of a week's worth of splashy festivities in Louisville. Each year the 1 1/4-mile race attracts a crowd of 100,000 and a huge national television audience.

Seles, Monica

DECEMBER 2, 1973– ● TENNIS PLAYER

Had her father not been a newspaper cartoonist, Monica Seles may never have grunted her way to the top of women's tennis.

Seles was born in Novi Sad, Yugoslavia, where her father gave her a tennis racquet when she was six years old. After a few weeks, though, she lost interest, and it was not until her older brother, Zoltan, won the Yugoslav junior championship two years later that Seles showed renewed interest in the game. To keep her interested in the sport, her cartoonist father drew her favorite cartoon characters—Tom and Jerry—on her tennis balls. He also put stuffed animals on the tennis court, giving her something to aim at.

Seles improved rapidly, winning the Yugoslav 12-and-under championship in 1983 when she was just nine years old. Two years later, in 1985, Seles was named Yugoslavian Sportswoman of the Year on the strength of her 1984 win in the European 12-and-under tournament. That year marked a turning point when she competed in a 12-and-under tournament in Miami, Florida. There she caught the eye of famed tennis coach Nick Bollettieri, who offered her a full scholarship to his tennis academy in Bradenton, Florida. Her family, always supportive of her career, pulled up stakes and moved to Florida, where Monica practiced six hours a day. During this time she developed her unique style of play: Because she hit both forehands and backhands two-handed, she had to move quickly to catch up to wide shots. To avoid being worn down in long rallies, she tried to pass her opponents by hit-

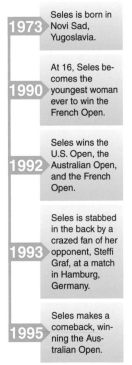

1973 Seles is born in Novi Sad, Yugoslavia.

1990 At 16, Seles becomes the youngest woman ever to win the French Open.

1992 Seles wins the U.S. Open, the Australian Open, and the French Open.

1993 Seles is stabbed in the back by a crazed fan of her opponent, Steffi Graf, at a match in Hamburg, Germany.

1995 Seles makes a comeback, winning the Australian Open.

ting the ball extremely hard, giving rise to her trademark grunt every time she hit the ball.

During these years Seles stayed out of the public eye, quietly developing her game largely in private. In 1989 she turned pro and served notice that she was a player to be reckoned with when she beat Chris Evert in the final of the Virginia Slims tournament, the youngest player ever to reach the final of that event. In Grand Slam events that year she reached the semifinals of the French Open and the fourth round at both Wimbledon and the U.S. Open. At the end of 1989 she was the sixth-ranked tennis player in the world.

Seles's breakthrough year was 1990. Despite struggling early in the year because of her physical growth—and despite tension between her family and Bollettieri, causing her to leave the academy—Seles won the Lipton International Players Championship. That year she went on to win the U.S. Hard Court Championship, the Italian Open, and the Virginia Slims Championship. Most importantly, she also captured her first Grand Slam event, beating Steffi Graf in the final of the French Open.

Seles opened 1991 with wins at the French and Australian Opens, making her the number one ranked player in the world. Many observers thought that she might win all four Grand Slam titles that year, but just before Wimbledon she mysteriously withdrew, later citing shin splints and a stress fracture in her left leg. She recovered from her injuries, though, and won her third Grand Slam title that year when she beat Martina Navratilova 7–6, 6–1 in the U.S. Open. In 1992 she held her number one ranking by winning the French Open (making her the first woman to win three straight French Open titles since Hilde Sperling in 1935–37), the Australian Open, and the U.S. Open—her seventh Grand Slam title. But once again a fourth Grand Slam title in one year eluded her when Steffi Graf beat her in the final at Wimbledon.

Seles started 1993 by successfully defending her Australian Open title, but she was plagued by injuries. In April of that year she returned to tournament play, but during a tournament in Germany on April 30, she was stabbed at courtside by a spectator, a disturbed fan of Steffi Graf. Her physical wound quickly healed, but the psychological scars were harder to overcome, and she didn't compete during the rest of 1993 and all of 1994—the year she became a naturalized U.S. citizen. When she came back in 1995 she won her first event, the Canadian

Open, and in her second event she reached the final of the U.S. Open.

Although Seles continued to enjoy success in the late 1990s, her game never quite returned to the level it was before she was assaulted. In 1996 she won her first grass court title at Eastbourne, England, and she won her fourth Australian Open, defeating Anke Huber in the final. In 1997 she won the Acura Classic and the du Maurier Open, and in 1998 she won the Princess Cup and successfully defended her du Maurier Open title. In 1999 she took a 33–0 record into the semifinals of the Australian Open before losing to Martina Hingis. Her win in the 1999 Bausch & Lomb Championships gave her a total of 43 career titles.

Seles also became something of a popular culture icon. She threw herself into American life, going to Broadway plays, learning to play the guitar and shoot pool, standing on the sidelines of a New York Giants football game, appearing on the MTV Video Music Awards at Radio City Music Hall, and modeling for such magazines as *Vogue*, *Seventeen*, and *Elle*. Though she was all business on the court, she smiled and often giggled her way through interviews and press briefings. She once said, "Everything about life is funny. If you can't laugh at life, then why are you living?" ◆

"Fourteen years ago when we signed on, I don't think we really thought that what we would be reporting on a daily basis about sports would be so far removed so often from the final score."

Bob Ley, on ESPN's *SportsCenter*, after the stabbing of Monica Seles, 1993

Shoemaker, Willie

AUGUST 19, 1931– ● JOCKEY

The legendary jockey Willie Shoemaker is the Hank Aaron of horse racing—like Aaron's career mark of 755 homers, Shoemaker's lifetime record of 8,833 victories is a summit few seem likely to scale. This lofty total, which encompasses 1,009 stakes races, 11 Triple Crown wins, and 10 national money titles, has generated about $10 million for Shoemaker, his cut of $123 million in purses he has earned.

William Lee Shoemaker was born in Fabens, Texas, on August 19, 1931. His parents divorced while he was still a young boy, and at age 10 he moved with his father, Bebe, to El Monte, California, where Shoemaker was a standout high school wrestler and boxer despite his small stature (he was 4 feet, 11 inches and 96 pounds in his adult prime). He dropped out of school at 15

and, desperate for work, took a job at a nearby thoroughbred ranch, where, in the intervals of cleaning stables, he absorbed the lore of horses and followed racing on radio broadcasts.

By the age of 16, Shoemaker had decided to turn his bantam frame to his advantage by becoming a jockey. After Shoemaker worked for a few months exercising horses at Santa Ana racetrack, George Reeves, a trainer, recognized his talent and in short order Shoemaker had an agent, his first professional ride (March 19, 1949), and his first victory (just a month later). Later in life, Shoemaker recalled, "She was a chestnut filly, and you bet I remember her. I think I got about 10 dollars." By the year's end, Shoemaker had amassed 219 victories, a stunning total for a rookie—only the veteran Gordon Gilsson rode more winners that year. In his second year on the circuit, Shoemaker's victory total rose to 388, which tied him for first in 1950. In 1951 he galloped to purses worth $1,329, 890, tops for the year. In 1953, only his fifth year as a pro, his 485 victories set a new record that endured for two decades.

Shoemaker's first Kentucky Derby crown came on May 1, 1955, atop Swaps, bringing him to the peak of personal achievement. Only two years later, however, the Kentucky Derby became the stage for his greatest professional embarrassment. Riding Gallant Man, he led comfortably in the stretch but misjudged the location of the finish line, stood up too soon, and allowed Iron Liege to pass him before the wire. Churchill Downs punished Shoemaker with a 15-day suspension. Shoemaker was defended by another great jockey, Eddie Arcaro, who said, "They changed the finish line that year. They lengthened the stretch by a 16th of a mile. After the race they did what they should have done 50 years before. They put lines on the fence to show the finish." A month later, Shoemaker at least partially redeemed himself by scoring his first Belmont Stakes win, again atop Gallant Man.

In fact, Arcaro, although Shoemaker's main rival, was also his close friend and mentor, and helped Willie overcome his chronic reticence and shyness. Shoemaker said, "Before I met Eddie, I wondered what he would be like. I guess I was awed by him. But he was so friendly and easy to know that he made me feel comfortable. The greatest thing he did was to ease me out. I may not have shown it, but I was very tense. Then he gave me confidence in the things I was doing."

Over the next seven years, Shoemaker was unstoppable, becoming racing's biggest earner by far with a string of high-stakes titles that included the Kentucky Derby in 1959; the Preakness in 1963 and 1967; and the Belmont stakes in 1957, 1959, and 1962 (he added a fourth Belmont Stakes crown in 1975). By 1964, Shoemaker had become the leading money winner of all time; by 1965, he had been atop the annual money pile for seven consecutive years.

By the late 1960s, injury began to throttle the Shoemaker express. A spill from a horse broke his leg in 1968, and in 1969 another mishap caused a ruptured bladder and a broken pelvis. Although he mounted a comeback with some important victories in 1970, the pace of his successes slowed considerably from then on. Some highlights included his victory in the Arlington Million, the first million-dollar race; and the 1986 Kentucky Derby, in which he rode the long shot (18 to 1) horse Ferdinand to a first-place finish.

But by 1988 the glory days were over. Shoemaker was reduced to waiting for rides in jockey rooms around Southern California, mostly in vain. Contemplating retirement, Shoemaker decided to take one last grandiose victory lap, touring major and minor tracks around the world for nine months and garnering $1 million in fees. His last official win came on January 20, 1990, and his last race on February 3, 1990, at Santa Anita—mount number 40,352. He finished fourth that night.

Not long after Shoemaker retired from racing and began working as a trainer, he suffered a near-fatal driving accident in which his Ford Bronco veered from the road and tumbled down a steep embankment. Shoemaker suffered total paralysis below the neck. His misfortunes multiplied when his third wife, Cindy, divorced him in 1994. Yet Shoemaker never succumbed to despair. He said, "I never gave up. A few times I didn't think I was going to make it. But I never quit." He resumed his work as a trainer, finally retiring in 1997, having compiled an impressive record of victories in that field as well. ◆

> *"I've always believed that anybody with a little ability, a little guts and the desire to apply himself can make it."*
> Willie Shoemaker

Smith, Katie

JUNE 4, 1974– ● BASKETBALL PLAYER

Katie Smith, a guard for the Minnesota Lynx of the Women's National Basketball Association (WNBA), has weathered recurring frustrations and, more recently,

1974 Smith is born in Logan, Ohio.

1993 Smith is named National Freshman of the Year following her first season for Ohio State University.

1996 Smith is named Big 10 Conference Player of the Year.

1997 Smith joins the Columbus Quest (ABL); the team wins the championship.

1998 The Quest wins its second league championship.

1999 Smith signs with the Minnesota Lynx of the WNBA.

a potentially career-ending injury to emerge as one of the leading stars of professional women's basketball.

Growing up in Logan, Ohio, a small rural town about 100 miles from Columbus, Katie showed exceptional physical grace and at the age of four was already taking tap and ballet lessons. But her competitive spirit needed a more direct challenge, and in the fifth grade Katie became the first girl to play in the local all-boys' basketball league. She knew she had found her calling. It wasn't long before her tap shoes and tutus began gathering dust in the closet while she wore out countless pairs of hightops on the fast track to basketball stardom.

Progressing rapidly through elementary-school leagues and junior-high competition, Smith arrived at Logan High as one of the best young players in the state, and in her senior year she paced the Logan squad to the state finals in Columbus, where Smith faced her first major frustration in a tough loss in the championship game.

But that scene of disappointment shortly became the arena of her proudest achievements. Relishing the chance to study and play at a first-rate university near her home, Smith enrolled at Ohio State University in Columbus. "I wanted to be close to home, " Smith said. "I wanted to give back and let the people close to me enjoy what I was doing. It came down between Stanford and Ohio State. If I went out to Stanford, they would never have gotten to see me play."

The local fans were amply rewarded by her decision. Smith was the National Freshman of the Year in 1993, when the Ohio State Buckeyes won the Big Ten title and steamrolled to the finals of the NCAA Women's Championship, where they encountered a Texas Tech team led by the formidable Sheryl Swoopes. Still smarting from Logan's defeat a year earlier, Smith went on a 28-point rampage, an imposing performance that bested all previous championship records. But Swoopes was a juggernaut in that game, scoring a record-breaking 47 points, enough to nudge Tech ahead by the final buzzer, 84–82.

Smith had fallen short of another summit, but her frustration only fueled her drive. During her college years Ohio State won 70.2 percent of its games and advanced to another NCAA tournament in 1996. Smith compiled some imposing individual accomplishments as well: her 2,437 career points were an Ohio state record (male or female); she was twice named an All-American, was the 1996 Big Ten Conference player of the year, and in 1996 was named the GTE co-Academic All-American of the year. She was also a member of the WBCA College All-Star Team in 1996.

By the end of her junior year, Smith, well established as one of the country's leading college players, was offered a tryout for the 1995 U.S. national women's team. That summer she traveled to Colorado Springs to compete for a coveted spot and a near guarantee of joining the 1996 Olympic squad. Despite a strong showing at the camp, she fell short of the first team and was named an alternate. Once again, she got close enough to glimpse the mountaintop—but no closer.

Shut out of the 1996 Olympics and reluctant to travel abroad to pursue professional opportunities, Smith's post-college plans began to focus on following her father into dentistry until word came of the formation of the American Basketball League, the first professional women's league in the United States in 16 years. In the league's inaugural season of 1997 Smith played for the Columbus Quest, made the league All-Star team, and led the Quest to the league's best record, 31–9. Once again the mountaintop of a championship loomed tantalizingly near, but the Quest nearly faltered against the Richmond Rage in the best-of-five championship series. The teams were tied at two games apiece as the series moved back to Columbus for the climactic fifth game. Nothing could deter Smith this time. The Quest leaped to a quick lead that they never relinquished, with Smith streaking the length of the court with key rebounds and shots.

"I've been pretty much a runner-up my whole career," said Smith. "In high school I was runner-up at state. In college I was runner-up. Finally we got over the hump and won. It is great; we not only win games, but we get along and really are friends. It was well worth waiting for to win the championship the way we did."

After a lifetime of dealing with frustration, Smith grew accustomed to the taste of victory, helping the Quest to another league championship in 1998. But another challenge was lurking. In November 1998, during a practice with the Quest, she suffered a devastating knee injury, tearing not only her anterior cruciate ligament, but also her medial lateral ligament, causing a deep bone bruise. During her protracted and demanding rehabilitation program, the ABL folded, but the fully recovered Smith was then signed by the WNBA's Minnesota Lynx; now a bit slower, perhaps, but still a key element of her team's attack. "When I play on my right leg, there's pain when you stop, and sometimes that catches you off-guard," she said. "It's just the lit-

> In 1997 Smith played for the Columbus Quest, made the league All-Star team, and led the Quest to the league's best record, 31–9.

tle things that are kind of annoying at times. For the most part, it's getting confidence back . . . and having those muscles keep getting stronger."

Smith, at age 25, is well on her way to another trek toward the basketball mountaintop. And her application to dental school is still nestled safely in the closet, next to her ballet slippers and tap shoes. ◆

Snead, Sam

MAY 27, 1912– ● GOLFER

Before Sam Snead joined the Professional Golfers Association (PGA) tour in the late 1930s, the conventional wisdom had it that long hitters couldn't shoot straight. With his classically fluid, dynamic swing, Snead defied the conventional wisdom and helped to launch the era of the power game in golf. Along the way he became one of the sport's all-time greats, amassing a record 81 PGA tour victories, a mark that seems relatively safe, though the emergence of Tiger Woods may change that. A colorful character known for his folksy charm—"sassy, spunky, and hillbilly homespun," as one writer put it—Snead became one of golf's most popular figures.

Samuel Jackson Snead emerged into sports history from the wooded hills of Hot Springs, Virginia, where he grew up the youngest of six children in a family of poor farmers. A tough, resourceful, and adventurous boy who went shoeless all summer, he roamed the hills playing hide-and-seek and trapping game for spending money. At the age of seven, Sam began caddying at the Cascades Gold Course, just down the road from the family farm. One of the master golf hustlers as an adult, Snead nurtured his betting skills early, playing pitch and putt with the other caddies for two cents a hole. Enamored with the game but too poor to afford equipment, he fashioned clubs out of mable branches, used rocks for golf balls, and buried his mother's tomato cans outside to create his own putting green.

In his school years the athletically gifted Snead excelled in a variety of sports—track, football, and basketball (he was the team's leading scorer)—but when a back injury ended his dreams of football stardom, Snead focused his energies on golf. After two years of cleaning and repairing clubs for 20 dollars a month at the Cascades, Snead was finally able to afford his own set, which he used to begin polishing his game. When Snead finished third at a Cascades tournament in 1936, his booming drives led to a position as an assistant at the prestigious Greenbrier Club in nearby Sulphur Springs, West Virginia, where, years later, Snead became the head pro (and is still the emeritus pro). With the promise of 45 dollars a month and a 50 percent cut of his fees from golf lessons, Snead was now a professional golfer.

Setting his sights on the pro tour, Snead began cutting his teeth on local tournaments, winning the West Virginia Open and the West Virginia PGA in 1936. The latter victory resulted in a $500 endorsement deal with Dunlop, a windfall that enabled Snead to head for the West Coast to try his luck on the PGA tour. He earned $600 for his sixth-place finish in his first tournament, the Los Angeles Open, but charged from behind to win his second effort, the Oakland Open ($1,200). He went on to pocket another $1000 dollars for winning the Bing Crosby Pro-Am that year before coming back east for his first shot at the U.S. Open, where he finished second, foreshadowing a trend. The U.S. Open is the only major title that has eluded Snead, who finished second there four times from 1937 to 1949.

The colorful, jaunty Snead soon became a gallery favorite on the tour, sporting a trademark palmetto hat and tossing off racy stories and nuggets of country wisdom between his cannonlike drives—"Daniel Boone with a driver" was how one writer described him. In the 1930s and 1940s the gallery was not roped off as it is today, and spectators would crowd right up to the tee. "They gave you just enough room to swing," Snead told a reporter "Then you'd hit it, and they'd race ahead to see where it had gone, sometimes knocking the club right out of your hands. . . . Some guys on tour would shake like a leaf in front of

1912 Snead is born in Hot Springs, Virginia.

1936 Snead wins the Bing Crosby Pro-Am.

1937 Snead wins five tournaments; finishes second at the U.S. Open.

1942 Snead wins the PGA (also in 1949 and 1951).

1946 Snead wins the British Open.

1949 Snead is named Player of the Year.

a crowd. But because of basketball, where the fans were screaming and yelling all the time, I was used to it."

Snead's poise helped him accumulate an impressive record that fully justified his bravado. In 1937 he won five tournaments, notching at least two for each of the following nine seasons. He didn't win his first major until 1942, when he captured the PGA, a feat he repeated in 1949 and 1951. In 1946, a sponsorship deal obliged a reluctant Snead to travel to St. Andrews in Scotland to play in his first British Open. Snead collected $600 for winning the tournament but figured that his expenses for the trip came to $2,000. When a British reporter asked him if he would return to defend his title, Snead retorted, "Are you kidding?"

After winning six tournaments, two of them majors, in 1949, Snead was voted the Player of the Year. The following year he piled up 11 victories and led the tour with $35,758 in earnings—but Ben Hogan, staging a comeback after a near-fatal car automobile accient, won the U.S. Open and was named Player of the Year in 1950. The slight still rankles Snead, who said, "They could have given him a six-foot-high trophy that said 'Great Comeback.' "

During the 1950s Snead began to lose confidence in his putting and experimented with various approaches, including croquet-style and side saddle. But he never lost his overall touch, remaining competitive far longer than his peers. He became the oldest golfer to win a PGA event when he won the 1965 Greater Greensboro Open. In his last season on the PGA tour, 1979, he became the only golfer in history to shoot his age by carding rounds of 67 and 66 in the Quad Cities open. Snead was also instrumental in founding the Senior Tour and was a major contributor to the U.S. Ryder Cup team, playing on seven squads and serving as captain for three.

Snead never practiced as diligently as many other pros, but he always claimed that his elegant swing never needed constant fine-tuning off the tee. He once said, "Everyone who knows me knows I love music. I used my music to help me maintain my swing's rhythm. For me, waltz time, or 3/4 time, was perfect for the correct golf swing tempo. I used to whistle a lot on the course, and I feel it kept my timing and rhythm in sync."

With advancing age, Snead has been spending less time on the golf course and more time hunting and fishing. When he does play, it's still strictly business. "People today, doctors and lawyers, want to play for twosies and fivesies," Snead told a reporter in 1994. "Cheapest I'll play for is a $25 Nassau. Any less than that, I'd rather sit home and watch the squirrels. Must be the economy. I only got 12 games between April and October." ◆

Snider, Edwin "Duke"

SEPTEMBER 19, 1926– ● BASEBALL PLAYER

Overshadowed by New York's other Hall of Fame center fielders, Mickey Mantle and Willie Mays, Edwin Donald Snider nonetheless hit more home runs in the 1950's than any other major leaguer and led the Brooklyn Dodgers to their only World Championship in 1955.

Snider was born and raised in Los Angeles and first reached the major leagues as a 20-year old in 1947. Snider chose the Dodgers because of his admiration for Brooklyn stars Pee Wee Reese and Pistol Pete Reiser. Snider was a reserve outfielder during his first two seasons, but Dodger general manager Branch Rickey took a liking to the handsome Californian. He instructed coach George Sisler, a Hall of Famer, to work him in the batting cage for three hours a day—but not to hit. Sisler had the Duke call each pitch a ball or strike, and ultimately, Snider learned the strike zone perfectly.

After Reiser went down with a career-ending injury in 1949, Snider became the Dodgers regular center fielder and cleanup hitter. He helped the Dodgers clinch the pennant on the last day of the season by driving in the winning run. But his World Series debut was a disaster, and the Yankees swept the Dodgers in five games. Snider redeemed himself in the 1952 Series with ten hits, four of them home runs, to tie the mark shared by Babe Ruth and Lou Gehrig. The Dodgers, however, lost that series to the Yankees in seven games. Snider exploded the following season, hitting .336 with 42 home runs—the first of five successive 40-homer seasons, tying the major league record held by Pittsburgh's Ralph Kiner. Unfortunately, the Dodgers lost to the Yankees again in the World Series.

The Brooklyn Dodgers did win the 1955 World Series— their only crown—and Snider joined Hall of Famers Pee Wee Reese, Jackie Robinson and Roy Campanella as the nucleus of the famed "Boys of Summer" lineup. Snider led the league in

1926 Edwin Donald "Duke" Snider is born in Los Angeles, California.

1947 Snider joins the Brooklyn Dodgers at age 20.

1952 Snider gets ten hits and four home runs in the World Series, matching Babe Ruth and Lou Gehrig's records.

1955 The Dodgers win the World Series; Snider is the only player to twice hit four homers in the fall classic.

1959 Snider leads the Dodgers (now in Los Angeles) to the World Series; he sets a National League record for home runs in the Series.

runs batted in and runs scored, while also hitting 42 home runs. He added four more homers in the World Series, becoming the only player to hit four home runs in the Series twice.

When the Brooklyn Dodgers moved to Los Angeles in 1958, Snider continued to play well, but was slowed by injuries over the next few seasons. While he led the L.A. Dodgers to a 1959 title, hitting a home run against the Chicago White Sox to set the National League record for career World Series home runs (11), that would be his last Series. A number of nagging physical problems would force the Duke into a pinch-hitting role, and he spent his last few seasons on the expansion New York Mets before hanging up his spikes. Snider retired with a .295 batting average and 407 home runs — the eighth highest total at the time of his retirement, and now 28th on the all time list.

After his playing career, Snider managed several Dodger farm teams and scouted for the Dodgers and, later, the San Diego Padres. He also spent time as a broadcaster for those teams as well as for the Montreal Expos. He was elected to the Hall of Fame in 1980, and remains one of the most popular players on one of the most beloved teams ever. ◆

Sorenstam, Annika

OCTOBER 9, 1970– ● GOLFER

Annika Sorentam is just now reaching the prime of what is already one of the most successful careers in women's professional golf. Only she and Nancy Lopez have enjoyed the distinction of receiving the Rolex Player of the Year Award and Vare Trophy (1995) only one year after having received the Rolex Rookie of the Year Award.

Growing up in Sweden, Sorenstam dreamed of greatness on the tennis court rather than the golf course. By the age of five, she was already entering tennis tournaments, but after a surge of promise in her childhood, her prospects faded in her teens. But Sorenstam had already begun playing golf, to which she had been introduced at age 12 along with her younger sister Charlotta, who is also a successful golf pro on the European tour. Initially Sorenstam's main attraction to golf was that it allowed her to practice for as long as she liked without having to depend on a partner. She did indeed put in endless hours on the course and on the practice tee, refining every aspect of her game. In 1988 she watched a telecast of her countrywoman Liselotte Neumann winning the U.S. Open, and it inspired her to believe that she could do the same. "It was a delayed telecast, but I remember staying up all night to watch it," Sorenstam said. "I did think, 'Yeah, that could be me someday.' "

While playing at an amateur tournament in Japan, Sorenstam attracted the notice of a golfer from the University of Arizona, who suggested that her coach have a talk with Sorenstam about joining their program. The following year Sorenstam enrolled at the University of Arizona, where she made important strides despite her discomfort with the regimented style of coaching there. As she told a reporter, "The Swedish system is different. The philosophy is that people are like plants. Some need space, some grow close together. You need to find your way."

Annika Sorenstam.

Before and during her years at the University of Arizona, Sorenstam began attracting notice as an amateur competitor. A member of the Swedish National Team from 1987–1992, she was the World Amateur champion in 1992, took second place at the 1992 U.S. Women's Amateur tournament, and was the runner-up amateur at the U.S. Women's Open that year. She also captured seven titles in collegiate tournaments while at Arizona, collecting a daunting array of trophies in the process: she was named the 1991 College Player of the Year, NCAA champion of 1991, PAC-10 champion in 1991, and NCAA All-American twice, in 1991 and 1992.

After graduation, Sorenstam participated in both the European and LPGA pro tours, rapidly distinguishing herself in both. In 1993 she was the Rookie of the European tour, and earned the same distinction on the LPGA tour in 1994. In only five seasons of LPGA competition, Sorenstam has racked up a

1970 Sorenstam is born in Stockholm, Sweden.

1992 Sorenstam is named world amateur champion.

1994 Sorenstam is named LPGA Rookie of the Year.

1995 Sorenstam wins the U.S. Women's Open (also in 1996); she is named LPGA Player of the Year.

stunning 17 tournament victories, including two majors: successive U.S. Women's Open titles (1995 and 1996).

With her Open win in 1996, she topped the $1 million mark in career earnings. In 1996 she also won her second consecutive Vare Trophy, awarded to the tour player with the lowest average score for the year. In 1997, after finishing among the top three money earners for the third straight season, she received the Rolex Player of the year Award for the second time in three years. The following year Sorenstam won her third Player of the Year award in four years and again was the Vare Trophy winner, the first to average under 70 for the season.

Enormous success has not bred complacency in Sorenstam, who still practices several hours per day on all aspects of her game. "I have lots of weaknesses," she told a reporter, mentioning her short game and long irons as particular areas of concern. Not that these supposed flaws have noticeably hampered her winning ways, of course. A fellow pro, Jill Briles-Hinton, said, "When I'm struggling with my swing, I watch Annika." ◆

Sosa, Sammy

NOVEMBER 12, 1968– ● BASEBALL PLAYER

Sammy Sosa was born on November 12, 1968, in San Pedro de Macoris in the Dominican Republic, 45 miles east of Santo Domingo, the capital. Sosa, his four brothers, and two sisters grew up in an impoverished family that lived in a two-room unit of an abandoned public hospital. When he was seven his father died, which meant that Sosa had to become a breadwinner for his family. On the streets he sold oranges for 10 cents and shined shoes for 25 cents.

As a boy Sosa and his equally poor friends played baseball using tree branches as bats and milk cartons shaped as gloves. With the encouragement of his older brother Luis, Sosa began playing organized baseball in 1983, at the age of 14. Major League scouts soon began showing an interest in him. In 1984 he signed with the Philadelphia Phillies, but the contract was nullified because Sosa was under 16. The following year Sosa received $3,500 to sign with the Texas Rangers.

From 1986 through 1988 Sosa rose meteorically through the Rangers' minor league system. In 1989, at age 20, he played

25 games in the major leagues before Texas traded him to the Chicago White Sox, who on March 1992 traded him across town to the Chicago Cubs. From 1989 through 1992 his record was mediocre at best. Although possessed of considerable raw talent, the right-handed batter swung wildly at bad pitches, hitting for low averages and striking out many times. In addition, his outfield play was careless.

Beginning in 1993 Sosa's play improved considerably. That year he joined the select 30-30 club, hitting 33 home runs and stealing 36 bases; two years later he repeated the feat and was elected to the National League All-Star team. In 1996 Sosa hit 40 home runs. He hit 37 home runs and had 119 runs batted in during 1997. Yet he was still an undisciplined hitter, striking out 174 times and hitting just .246; he also remained an undistinguished fielder. But in mid-1997 the Cub organization showed their faith in Sosa's promise, signing him to a four-year, $42.5 million contract extension; many in the baseball world were shocked at the disproportion between Sosa's accomplishments and the size of the contract.

But in the 1998 season Sosa more than earned his keep. Finally becoming a mature player, he learned the finer points of fielding, such as hitting the cutoff man consistently. At the plate, he chose his pitches more carefully and hit outside pitches to the opposite field. Most dramatically, his improved skills enabled him to participate in one of the most thrilling events in sports history: his race with St. Louis Cardinal first baseman Mark McGwire to equal and exceed Roger Maris's record 61 home runs for a season, set in 1961.

On May 23 Sosa had just 9 homers, 15 behind McGwire, But Sosa got into the home-run race by hitting 20 homers in June, an all-time record for one month. On August 19 Sosa hit his 48th homer to go ahead of his rival for the first of only two times. McGwire broke Maris's record with his 62nd round tripper on September 8. Five days later Sosa tied McGwire with his 61st and 62nd home runs. On September 25 Sosa slugged his 66th to surpass his opponent, but that was his last homer, while McGwire reached the 70-home-run mark.

Yet in the balloting for the National League's Most Valuable Player, Sosa easily won with 30 of the 32 first-place votes, the other two going to McGwire. One reason is that Sosa led his Cubs to a spot in the postseason playoffs, while McGwire's Cardinals were well out of the running. Another is that Sosa had the better overall hitting record, batting .308, leading the major

1968 Sosa is born in San Pedro de Macoris, Dominican Republic.

1995 Sosa is named to the National League All-Star team as a member of the Chicago Cubs.

1997 Sosa signs a four-year, $42.5-million contract extension.

1998 Sosa carries on a home-run race with Mark McGwire; he passes Roger Maris's record and ends the season with 66 homers.

1999 Sosa sits beside the First Lady at State of the Union address for his humanitarian efforts.

leagues with 158 runs batted in (RBI), and scoring a National League-leading 134 runs.

During and after the 1998 season Sosa was celebrated not only in the United States and the Dominican Republic but throughout the world, and not only because of his hitting feats. An ebullient baseball enthusiast with a ready smile, Sosa was also a charming, modest, and eminently likeable man. In addition, he was a humanitarian, contributing heavily to Dominican charities and arranging for the dispatch of relief supplies to his native country after it was hit by a hurricane in the fall of 1998.

After the 1998 season Sosa received a ticker-tape parade in New York City. Invited in January 1999 to attend the State of the Union address in an honored seat near First Lady Hillary Clinton, he received a rousing ovation from Congress after being introduced by President Bill Clinton during the address. ◆

Spinks, Michael

JULY 13, 1956– ● BOXER

Born in St. Louis, Missouri, and raised in one of the city's housing projects, Michael Spinks took up boxing as a youth in emulation of his brother, Leon, and as a method of self-defense in the tough neighborhood where the Spinks family lived. Spinks started boxing as a teenager. His amateur career was crowned by success at the 1976 Olympic Games in Montreal, where he won the middleweight gold medal (and Leon won the heavyweight gold). After Montreal, Spinks turned professional, but his career was stalled by poor management and promotion, and by Spinks's overinvolvement in his brother's boxing career.

Spinks remained in relative obscurity until he decided to act as his own manager. Moving up to the light-heavyweight class, he put himself in contention for the title. He became famous for a powerful righthanded overhand punch that was labeled "the Spinks Jinx." Spinks won a 12-round fight against Eddie Mustafa Muhammad on July 18, 1981, securing the World Boxing Association (WBA) championship, and won recognition as champion from the World Boxing Council (WBC) after defeating the WBC champion, Dwight Muham-

1956 Spinks is born in St. Louis, Missouri.

1976 Spinks wins the middleweight gold medal at the Montreal Olympics.

1981 Spinks wins the World Boxing Association championship.

1985 Spinks defeats Larry Holmes (again in 1986 rematch).

1988 Spinks ends his career after he is KO'd by Mike Tyson.

mad Qawi, in 1983. Spinks remained undefeated in 31 fights as a light-heavyweight.

In 1986 Spinks abandoned his light-heavyweight title to fight in the stronger and more lucrative heavyweight class. In 1985, fighting as a heavyweight, Spinks won a disputed world title by defeating Larry Holmes. In 1986 he beat Holmes again in a rematch, and knocked out contender Gerry Cooney in 1987. Spinks's career came to a lucrative, if embarrassing, end in July of 1988 in Atlantic City when Mike Tyson knocked him out after just 90 seconds. Spinks retired with a $13 million share of the purse. Since his retirement from the ring, Spinks has worked in New York as a promoter of fights with the Butch Lewis organization. ◆

Spitz, Mark

FEBRUARY 10, 1950– ● SWIMMER

Born in Modesto, California, on February 10, 1950, Mark Andrew Spitz seemed destined from childhood to become a world-class swimmer. Even as a boy, he exhibited grace and speed in the water. By the time he was ten, Mark had won 17 national titles.

His winning streak continued through his teens, and the sports world was put on notice that a new swimming star was on the scene. Spitz became particularly well known for his excellence at 100-meter and 200-meter freestyle and butterfly events. He broke the 400-meter world record three times. In 1966, he came within 0.4 second of the 1,500-meters world record. In 1967, Spitz set world records in the 400-meter freestyle event and in the 100-meter and 200-meter butterfly events.

Spitz trained for several years at California's Santa Clara Swim Club, which has produced many excellent American swimmers, and he attended Indiana University in Bloomington. While at Indiana, he served as captain of the school's intercollegiate swimming team and collected four national and two college championships. In 1971, Spitz was named America's Outstanding Amateur Athlete, winning the Sullivan Award. He graduated from college in 1972, the same year that he attended his second Olympics.

> *"I'm trying to do the best I can. I'm not concerned about tomorrow, but with what goes on today."*
> Mark Spitz

Mark Spitz at the 1972 Olympics.

Spitz's first Olympic experience was in 1968, at the Summer Games held in Mexico City. Always very self-confident, Spitz created controversy by boasting that he would win six gold medals there. In fact, he won "only" two, in freestyle team relays (the 4 × 100 meter and the 4 × 200 meter) rather than in individual events. He also captured the bronze medal in the freestyle 100-meter race, and the silver in the 100-meter butterfly. Put off by his arrogant prediction, however, people focused on what he had not achieved rather than what he had.

In his next Olympics, in Munich, Germany, in 1972, Spitz was more careful in what he said to the press, letting his performance speak for itself. It did, loudly. Spitz won gold medals and set world records in all four of the individual men's swimming events that he entered: the 100-meter and 200-meter freestyle, and the butterfly events for the same distances. Spitz added three more gold medals to his collection as a member of victorious U.S. men's teams (in the 400-meter and 800-meter freestyle relays, and in the 400-meter medley relay); the teams' times also set world records.

Sports fans were thrilled. This was the first time an athlete had won seven gold medals in a single Olympics. Spitz was now

The Olympic Massacre of 1972

The 1972 Olympic Games in Munich offered the German people an opportunity to heal the wounds inflicted by the 1936 Olympics in Munich, which Adolf Hitler exploited as a showcase for the supposed racial superiority of his prized "Aryan" athletes. But these games, dedicated to a renewed spirit of brotherhood and reconciliation, quickly descended into a nightmare of hatred and violence.

Early in the morning on September 5, 1972, eight Palestinian terrorists pierced the security perimeter of the Olympic village and stormed into the dormitory housing the Israeli athletes. The attackers immediately killed two Israelis and seized another nine as hostages. During a nerve-shattering standoff with the German police, the Palestinians issued a series of demands, including the release of some 200 Palestinians prisoners in Israel and immunity for themselves. Having elicited no guarantees, the terrorists proceeded to the airport, where German sharpshooters killed three Palestinians but also triggered a shootout that resulted in the deaths of all nine Israeli athletes and one German policemen.

In the ensuing international outcry of indignation and grief, the athletic competitions seemed to pale in significance, and there were widespread calls for a cancellation of the rest of the games. But the International Olympic Committee (IOC), under the leadership of Avery Brundage, deferred to the wishes of the Israeli government and decreed that the games would go forward after a 34-hour suspension and a memorial service in the main stadium. Brundage declared that the peaceful spirit of the Olympics must not be annulled by "a handful of terrorists." Although the games did resume, a number of athletes ignored Brundage's call and departed after the memorial service, citing concerns for their safety.

Other political controversies hounded the benighted 1972 Olympic Games. Under the threat of a boycott by 27 African nations, the IOC, which had already banned South Africa from the games because of its apartheid policies, sent home the 30-athlete delegation that had already arrived from Rhodesia, another African white-supremacist regime.

a star recognized around the world. Just hours after his final victory, however, he was flown back to the United States. Spitz is Jewish, and a group of terrorists murdered a group of Jewish athletes from Israel within the Olympic Compound in Munich. Officials feared for Spitz's life.

Spitz returned home safely and began planning his postOlympics life. He posed for a poster wearing only his brief swimming trunks and all seven medals, which earned him thousands of dollars. It also made him a professional in the eyes of the International Olympics Committee; thus, until restrictions were softened in later years, Spitz was unable to participate in the next Olympic Games.

Spitz retired as a swimmer after the 1972 Olympics, but the public did not want to let him go. That year he was named World Athlete of the Year, and he was in heavy demand for per-

1950   Spitz is born in Modesto, California.

1968   Spitz wins two gold medals, a silver, and a bronze.

1971   Spitz wins the Sullivan Award, given to America's most outstanding amateur athlete.

1972   Spitz breaks seven world records and wins seven gold medals; he becomes the first athlete to win seven gold medals in an Olympiad.

sonal appearances and speeches. For a time he even tried acting, but he gave it up when he realized it was not his forte.

Eventually, Spitz decided to become an orthodontist. He spent several years earning his degree and began practicing. However, the competitor and athlete inherent in Spitz were not compatible with dentistry, and he opted to look at other avenues in life. In 1976, Spitz became a commentator for ABC Sports and gradually built up a reputation as a motivational speaker.

In 1983, Spitz was inducted into the U.S. Olympic Hall of Fame. In later years he would try again for the Olympics but would be shut out by younger swimmers. He could be comforted, however, by his amazing 32 world and 38 American swimming records—and, of course, all of the Olympic medals he won in earlier years.

Over the years Spitz has become seriously involved in competitive yachting, and he is an "ambassador" for the sport of swimming, believing that it builds character as well as physical strength. Spitz and his wife Suzey, whom he married in 1970, live in California and have two children, Matt and Justin. ◆

Staley, Dawn

MAY 4, 1970– ● BASKETBALL PLAYER

There is a mural of Dawn Staley that decorates the side of a building at the corner of 8th and Market streets in Philadelphia. It stands seven stories high and serves as a reminder of the success attained by the neighborhood native. Staley has served as the same kind of inspiration to teammates at the University of Virginia, USA Women's Basketball, the ABL's Philadelphia Rage and the WNBA's Charlotte Sting.

Born in Philadelphia, Pennsylvania, on May 4, 1970, Staley learned early on about how tough life can be. One of five children, she attended high school at nearby Dobbins Tech. She stayed out of trouble by playing basketball with the boys on the neighborhood playgrounds, where she practiced the moves she saw her hero, 76ers point guard Maurice Cheeks, making.

Staley later took her own moves and winning attitude to the University of Virginia. The energetic point guard never averaged less than 14.5 points per game in any of her four years, while averaging 5.6 assists and 3.5 steals per game. Under Staley's leadership, UVA compiled a 110–21 record (an .839 winning percentage), two Atlantic Coast Conference (ACC) regular season titles, three ACC Tournament Titles, four NCAA Tournament appearances and three Final Four appearances (1990–92).

Staley earned ACC Rookie of the Year honors in 1989, and was named Conference Player of the Year in 1991 and 1992. She also earned Kodak All-America honors in 1990, 1991 and 1992, was National Player of the Year in 1991 and 1992.

She still holds the NCAA career record for steals with 454 and the ACC career record for assists with 729. Virginia later showed its admiration for Staley by retiring her jersey number 24, only the third time a Virginia basketball player has been so honored.

Staley's pursuit of playing professionally after college led her to teams in Italy, France, Brazil and Spain, before she finally came back to the United States to play in the newly-formed American Basketball League (ABL).

While it took Staley until 1997 to play professional ball in the United States, the 5'8", 125-pound point guard was still representing the United States as part of the women's national team. She starred for the U.S. in the 1994 Goodwill Games, setting a tournament record for assists in with 23. Staley led the attack for the gold-medal–winning women's team at the 1996 Olympics in Atlanta, dishing out 28 assists in the eight games—many of the dazzling variety—and made nine steals.

Playing in the ABL proved to be doubly sweet for Staley, as not only was she playing professionally in her home country, but she also was playing in her home city, with the Philadelphia Rage. She rose to the occasion, averaging 14.0 ppg, 7.2 apg and 3.5 rpg in 1996–97 and 1997–98 for the Rage and twice played in the ABL All-Star Game.

As amazing as her play has been her ability to come back from two major knee operations, the kind of adversity that might have caused someone with less resolve to give up. But Staley's pro career was just getting started, and was about to get even better.

On August 31, 1998, Staley signed with the WNBA. She was selected by the Charlotte Sting as the ninth overall pick. She continues to wow the opposition with her masterful passing (the no-look is her specialty) and high-intensity play.

Staley averaged 11.5 ppg and 5.5 apg (third in the league), while helping the Sting reach the 1999 Eastern Conference fi-

1970 Staley is born in Philadelphia, Pennsylvania.

1989 Staley is named Atlantic Coast Conference Rookie of the Year.

1991 Staley is named Conference Player of the Year and National Player of the Year (both again in 1992).

1996 Staley is a member of the gold medal winning U.S. Olympic team.

1997 Staley joins the Philadelphia Rage (ABL); participates in the All-Star game.

1998 Staley signs with the Charlotte Sting (WNBA); she wins the WNBA Sportsmanship Award.

nals and earned the 1999 WNBA Sportsmanship Award. She continued her consistent play in the post-season, averaging 11.5 ppg, 1.9 rpg and 5.5 apg in four 1999 WNBA playoff games.

Staley also is continuing her excellence on the international level. She keyed the USA Women's gold medal effort at the 1998 World Championships, where she set a USA all-time World Championship record with 52 assists and tied the single-game assist record with 12 in the '98 gold medal game versus Russia.

A relentless competitor and a perfectionist—she wears a rubber band on her wrist and snaps it every time she commits a turnover—Staley now has her sights set on another gold medal. This time she's shooting for the 2000 Olympics in Sydney, Australia.

While she continues to look ahead, Staley hasn't forgotten to look back, remembering where she came from. She actively works with Philadelphia's inner city youth through the Dawn Staley Foundation. In 1999 she received the 1999 WNBA Entrepreneurial Spirit Award in recognition of her work with the Foundation.

Of course, the greatest recognition is on display at the corner of 8th and Market streets in the City of Brotherly Love, where figuratively and literally, this giant of a player stands seven stories high. ◆

Starbird, Kate

July 30, 1975– ● Basketball Player

Catherine Evelyn "Kate" Starbird was born in West Point, New York, on July 30, 1975, where both of her parents were born—her family's history of military service at the U.S. Military Academy goes back four generations. One of five children, Kate's interest in hoops came relatively late for a pro: she didn't start playing in earnest until the age of 14, when her family moved to the state of Washington and "the Washington weather made the gym my favorite place to be."

Like most of her colleagues in this generation of professional women basketball players, Kate Starbird was forced to dribble and shoot through a minefield of male taunts in the pickup games of her youth. Through her father, a retired colonel, she gained access to the gym at Fort Lewis, near her hometown of

Tacoma, Washington, where she braved the ridicule of the mostly male players and worked hard at developing her game, concentrating on perfecting her famously unlovely but deadly accurate set shot.

She not only had to endure the derision of her male peers but also the skepticism of her father, well into her college years. "My dad always told me, 'Basketball isn't going to put one piece of bread on your plate.' Now he's become this superfan," Starbird wryly recalled. It was a lonely quest, mostly devoid of women role models. "I probably didn't see more than five or 10 women's basketball games when I was younger," she said. "Every once in a while, if my mom would see one on TV, she'd tape it for me. That was it." She admired the flashy moves of the NBA players, but she never sought to emulate them, appreciating the extent of the difference between their game and hers. "I can look at some of the moves," she recalled," and I can do some of them. It's just that they're not nearly as interesting to watch me do them."

As she progressed through high school, Starbird learned to appreciate women's basketball's greater emphasis on team play rather than individual heroics, even though she was clearly the best player on her squad at Lakes High School in Lakewood, Washington. In fact, she was the best in state history, setting the all-time Washington State high school career scoring record (boys and girls).

Starbird accepted a scholarship offer from Stanford, eager to play under the school's revered women's basketball coach Tara VanDerveer. Although still reliant on her **ungainly**, old-fashioned set shot (Stanford assistant coach Amy Tucker called it "the ugliest thing I'd ever seen"), Starbird broadened her attack at Stanford, developing and refining a dazzling repertoire of ball-control techniques—dribbling and passing behind her back and through her legs—that have reminded some observers of Magic Johnson at his peak. She mastered all this with a cracked kneecap that went undiagnosed until she got to Stanford, where she overcame it with a rigorous program of physical therapy and weights.

Starbird's fierce dedication paid off in one of Stanford's most distinguished basketball careers: in her four years there, the Cardinals won three consecutive Pac-10 Conference titles and appeared in four straight NCAA tournaments. Her individual accomplishments form a long and imposing list: 1997 Naismith National Player of the Year and two-time Kodak All-American

1975 Starbird is born in West Point, New York.

1996 Starbird is named Kodak All-American (also in 1996–97).

1997 Starbird graduates as Stanford's all-time leading scorer; she is named Naismith National Player of the Year.

1999 Starbird joins the Sacramento Monarchs of the WNBA.

ungainly: awkward or clumsy in appearance. lacking grace or smoothness.

(1995–96, 1996–97); 1996–97 Player of the Year by the WBCA, RCA, and *The Sporting News* and Pac-10 Player of the Year; AP All-American in 1997; Stanford's all-time leading scorer, with 2,215 points.

With exquisite timing, Starbird's record-smashing college career ended just as two new women's basketball leagues were forming, the ABL and the WNBA. Picked fourth by the Seattle Reign of the ABL, she enjoyed two outstanding seasons there before the league folded in January 1999. She was then selected by the WNBA's Sacramento Monarchs in the third round (number 26 overall) of the WNBA draft, for whom she enjoyed a moderately successful season in 1999. ◆

Steding, Katy

DECEMBER 11, 1967– ● BASKETBALL PLAYER

Katy Steding is one of the pioneers of the current wave of professional women's basketball in the United States. Her professional debut in 1996 with the Portland Power of the American Basketball League (ABL)—the now-defunct league she helped to found—capped a distinguished career that included a national championship at Stanford in 1990 and an Olympic gold medal in 1996.

Like many outstanding athletes, Steding showed both exceptional physical talent and fierce dedication at a young age. Soon after Katy's birth in Portland, Oregon, on December 11, 1967, her parents separated, and her mother raised Katy and her older sister, Julie, in Lake Oswego, a suburb of Portland. By the third grade Katy was already in love with basketball and, along with two of her friends, joined the local Youth Basketball Association league, where she already towered over most of the boys. Inspired when the local NBA franchise, the Portland Trailblazers, won the pro championship in 1977, the fifth-grade Katy Stedman announced her ambition to become a professional basketball player, a goal she pursued singlemindedly through elementary-school leagues and her junior high school team.

Already measuring five feet 11 inches by the time she made the high school team in her freshman year, Steding became a starter by midseason and after that played in every game for Lake Oswego until her graduation. By high school she had also

> Like many outstanding athletes, Steding showed both exceptional physical talent and fierce dedication at a young age.

become the starting center, setting school records for scoring and rebounding, and made the all-state first team in her sophomore, junior, and senior years—all while excelling as a volleyball player as well.

Steding's high school basketball stardom brought the inevitable stream of lavish college scholarship offers, but the one that caught her eye came from Tara VanDerveer, the renowned head coach of Stanford's women's basketball team. Wowed by Stanford's outstanding academic reputation, its ambitious basketball program, and its proximity to her home, Steding signed a letter of intent to attend Stanford.

Before taking that step, however, Steding capped her record-setting pace at Lake Oswego by passing the career 3,000 point mark early in her senior year and being named Oregon Class 3A Girls Basketbal Player of the Year. Steding's only disappointment was seeing her team lose to St. Mary's Academy in the state semifinals.

At Stanford, the challenge of playing with and against much taller and more capable players did not daunt Steding, whose shooting and rebounding skills won her a starting spot as a power forward midway through her freshman year. She faced her first major hurdle in her sophomore year, when a bigger, stronger freshman pushed her out of her starting slot. Determined to master a skill that would place her back in the starting five, Steding put in countless hours of practice on the just-introduced three-point shot, even remaining at Stanford that summer to polish her perimeter shooting.

Although Steding's sophomore numbers suffered as she reinvented her game, her detour paid off in a vast overall improvement. The Stanford team as a whole was progressing, too: at the beginning of Steding's first year, Stanford was not a serious national force in women's basketball; a year later, Stanford was ranked 19th in the nation; in Steding's junior year (1988–89), the Cardinal had progressed to the final eight of the NCAA tournament but bowed to Louisiana Tech in the regional final.

Steding's senior year was the pinnacle of achievement for her and her team: Stanford emerged as stronger than ever, going 30–1 during the regular season and surging through the NCAA tournament to face Auburn in the finals for the national championship. Before 16,000 fans and a national television audience, Steding sank six of her 15 three-point attempts, and Stanford hung on to win a tense contest, 88–81.

1967 Steding is born in Portland, Oregon.

1986 Steding begins college basketball at Stanford University.

1989 Stanford wins the NCAA championship.

1991 Steding leads the U.S. team to a championship at the World University Games.

1996 Steding helps to launch the ABL.

acclimated: to become used to a new situation; to adapt to new living arrangements or a new environment.

The glory of a national championship to crown her college career could not fill the emptiness that now faced Steding: In 1990 there was no professional women's basketball league in the United States, so Steding set her sights on foreign leagues. The most attractive offer came from the Bank of Japan's franchise, the Golden Eagles, so Steding packed her Japanese phrase book and headed for a new career. Just as she was becoming **acclimated** to her new surroundings and beginning to enjoy some success, she suffered every athlete's nightmare: an awkward pushoff for a layoff tore the anterior cruciate ligament (ACL) in Steding's right knee, ending her season and forcing her return to Stanford's medical center for corrective surgery.

Steding now faced months of demanding, tedious rehabilitation, with no guarantee that she could return to basketball. After months of a rigorous weight and track regimen, she was ready to return to the Golden Eagles, for whom she starred for the following three years.

In the intervals of her seasons in Japan, Steding pursued other dreams. In July 1991, she helped to lead the U.S. national team to a championship at the World University Games in Sheffield, England, and in 1992 she tried out for the U.S. Olympic team, falling just shy of making the team. Although bitterly disappointed, she returned to Japan for a third starring year with the Golden Eagles. After that season, however, the Japanese league banned foreign players, and Steding was looking for work again.

brooding: to dwell on something and view it in a negative manner, to ponder gloomily.

Steding's next stop was Madrid, where she toured with a Spanish professional team before tearing her left ACL. Back in Oregon, **brooding** about her prospects during another extended rehab stint after still another operation, she toyed with giving up basketball. But providentially, she received a call from her Stanford coach, Tara VanDerveer, now the head coach of the 1996 U.S. Olympic team, who implored Steding to start training for the team. "Just remember that we need you," VanDerveer reminded her.

Steding seized the opportunity and ran with it. In January 1995 Steding began a punishing training routine, putting in an average of five hours per day on weights and running. It all paid off in May 1995, when she won a spot on the 1996 Olympic team, which galloped through the opposition to a 111–87 trouncing of Brazil in the finale, earning the coveted gold medal that had eluded the U.S. women's team four years earlier.

Buoyed by the prestige of an Olympic victory, U.S. women's basketball was ready to go professional, and Katy Stedman joined several of her Olympic teammates in planning, organizing, and launching the all-women's American Basketball League in the fall of 1996 [the rival Women's National Basketball Association (WNBA) began play the following summer]. Stedman was the chief attraction for her hometown ABL franchise, the Portland Power, but the long preceding year of Olympic training and play had taken its toll, and Stedman's play was disappointing. By the 1997–98 season, she had been relegated to bench duty. With the demise of the ABL in January 1999, Steding did not to make herself available to the WNBA draft, choosing instead to concentrate on community relations work for Portland's prospective WNBA franchise (yet to be named), which will begin play in the 2000 season if it meets the league minimum for season-ticket deposits. ◆

Stengel, Charles "Casey"

JULY 30, 1890–SEPTEMBER 29, 1975 ● BASEBALL PLAYER AND MANAGER

I n addition to his remarkable skills as a manager, baseball great Casey Stengel is considered to be one of the most beloved personalities in the history of the baseball.

Charles Dillon Stengel was born on July 30, 1890. He started playing semi-professional baseball when he was still in high school. In 1910, Stengel joined the Class C affiliate of the Brooklyn Dodgers, and less than three years later, he was in the major leagues. Stengel was a quick and scrappy left-handed hitter, and the Brooklyn fans immediately took a liking to him, bestowing the nickname Casey in reference to his hometown of Kansas City.

But Stengel almost didn't make it to the big leagues at all. He spent the winter after his first two minor league seasons studying dentistry at Western Dental College in Kansas City. Although he was a good student, he was known throughout the school as a prankster. He even once stuck a cigar in a corpse's mouth during anatomy class. Stengel abandoned his studies when he was called up to Montgomery, his last minor league stop, but he refused to abandon his clowning around. During

> In 1910, Stengel joined the Class C affiliate of the Brooklyn Dodgers, and less than three years later, he was in the major leagues.

1890	Charles Dillon "Casey" Stengel is born Kansas City, Missouri.
1910	Stengel enters professional baseball.
1925	Stengel begins managing minor league teams.
1949	Stengel becomes manager of New York Yankees, leading the team to ten pennants and seven championships.
1961	Stengel publishes his autobiography.
1962	Stengel manages the New York Mets (through 1965).
1966	Stengel is elected to the Baseball Hall of Fame.

"Managing is getting paid for home runs someone else hits."

Casey Stengel

one game at Montgomery, he noticed a manhole in right field, and while nobody was watching, he pried off the cover and hid. When a batter hit a fly ball to right, he popped out and caught the ball to a stadium full of laughter.

Stengel was finally called up to the Dodgers in July of 1912, and managed to bring his trademark clowning to a new arena. While a hazing ritual prevented rookies from taking batting practice, Stengel decided to hand out business cards as an introduction and requested that he be allowed to take his swings. In January 1918, he was traded to the Pirates. In his first game back in Brooklyn, the home fans booed him, but Stengel, always aiming to please, pulled another prank. He somehow caught a young sparrow and hid the bird under his baseball cap. When he came to bat and the fans started hissing, he doffed his cap and the bird flew out. Aside from being one of the more famous baseball stories, it perfectly characterized the witty and outrageous Casey Stengel.

Stengel's playing career was winding down by the early 1920's, and although his two home runs in the 1923 World Series helped beat the powerful Yankees, he retired with a mediocre .284 batting average. He left the major leagues in 1925 to become player-manager and club president for Worcester of the Eastern League, a minor league affiliate of the Dodgers. Stengel managed there until 1934, when he returned to New York manage a paltry Dodger team. But even Stengel couldn't do anything with the lackluster ball club, and after three losing seasons, he was fired. He moved on to unsuccessfully helm a terrible Boston Braves team for the next six seasons, but still couldn't turn them into a winning team. He was fired again in 1943.

After a few years of managing minor league teams such as the Oakland Oaks and the Class AAA Milwaukee Brewers, Stengel got his big break. George Weiss, an old buddy of his from his days at Worcester, had become the general manager of the Yankees and, in a bold move, Weiss hired his friend Stengel. New York fans were shocked and the press was rough on Stengel, calling him a clown and a fool. But Stengel quieted his critics when he proceeded to win ten pennants and seven World Series in the following 12 years, including an unprecedented five straight titles in his first five seasons on the job. It still stands as the greatest run by any manager in baseball history.

Stengel also kept having a good time. Managing in an effortless style, he once smuggled firecrackers into Comiskey

Park. When Clete Boyer hit a home run, Stengel lit the fireworks off on the dugout steps and danced a jig. But when the Yankees lost the World Series to the Pirates in 1960, on Bill Mazeroski's famous home run, the 70-year old Stengel was forced into retirement. "They paid me off and told me my services are not desired any longer," he told the press. "I'll never make the mistake of being 70 again."

Stengel wrapped up his managing career with the expansion New York Mets in 1962, the worst team in baseball history. The Mets won 40 games against 120 losses, and played bizarre, often horrendous, baseball. But despite their failures, Casey and the "Amazin' Mets," as they were called, were a tremendous success off the field. Nobody seemed to mind if the 70-something Stengel would doze off for an inning — he was already a beloved fixture in New York. ◆

> *"I was not successful as a ball player, as it was a game of skill.*
> Casey Stengel

Stewart, Payne

JANUARY 30, 1957–OCTOBER 25,1999 ● GOLFER

Throughout the 1990s Payne Stewart may not have been the top golfer on the professional tour, but he was without doubt the most recognizable. When he stepped onto the course wearing his trademark knickers and tam-o'-shanter cap, he looked to his legions of fans as though he had just emerged from the mists of Scotland, where the game of golf originated.

William Payne Stewart was born in Springfield, Missouri. He graduated from Southern Methodist University in 1979, the same year he joined the professional tour. Throughout the 1980s he enjoyed modest success. He won his first Professisonal Golfers Association (PGA) tournament, the Quad Cities Open, in 1982 and went on to win the Magnolia Classic (1982), the Walt Disney World Golf Classic (1983), the Hertz Bay Hill Classic (1987), and the MCI Heritage Golf Classic (1989). In the meantime he also won international tournaments in Indonesia, India, and Australia, and later he would win international tournaments in Holland and Morocco.

It wasn't until 1989, though, that he won his first major tournament. In that year's PGA Championship he entered the final round trailing Mike Reid by six strokes but rose to the

> *"Knickers are good for my golf game. They're cooler in hot weather because the air circulates in them and they're warmer in cold weather because they trap the body heat."*
> Payne Stewart in *The Quotable Golfer*

1957 Stewart is born in Springfield, Missouri.

1987 Stewart is a member of the U.S. Ryder Cup team (also in 1989, 1991, 1993, and 1999).

1989 Stewart wins the PGA championship.

1991 Stewart wins the U.S. Open.

1999 Stewart wins the U.S. Open with record-making putt and plays in the Ryder Cup; later that year he dies in a crash involving his private jet.

challenge by shooting a 67 in the final round to capture the title, with Reid, Andy Bean, and Curtis Strange just one stroke behind. With 11 top-ten finishes, including three second places and two third places, 1989 was his best year on the tour. In 1990 he followed up his PGA Championship win by successfully defending his MCI Heritage title and winning the GTE Byron Nelson Classic.

When Stewart won his next major tournament, the 1991 U.S. Open (in an 18-hole playoff against Scott Simpson), he seemed destined to emerge as one of golf's greats. Unfortunately, though, he hit a major slump, and over the next eight years he won only one tournament, the 1995 Shell Houston Open (erasing a seven-stroke deficit to force a playoff against Scott Hoch, which he won on the first hole). His fans began to say that despite his overall success—by the end of 1998 he was seventh on the all-time money list with career earnings of nearly $10 million—he couldn't win the big tournaments

In 1998 he began to set the stage for a comeback. That year he played in 19 events, finishing in the top 10 six times. He had the lowest round, 65, in that year's Players Championship; he led after each of the first three rounds of the U.S. Open (losing in the final round by just one stroke to Lee Janzen), along the way tying a record with six consecutive birdies over two days; and he shot 64, 69, and 65 in the first three rounds of the Greater Vancouver Open (though despite a respectable 70 in the final round he lost by three strokes to Brandel Chamblee). And in spite of two rounds of 67 in the Michelob Championship, he finished fourth. Stewart couldn't quite break through with a win, but he often played brilliantly and seemed poised to silence his critics.

And silence them he did in the 1999 U.S. Open. In a dramatic finish, Stewart showed that he could still win a major tournament. On the final hole at Pinehurst in North Carolina, he calmly sank a 15-foot putt—the longest putt ever to decide a U.S. Open on the final hole in its 99-year history—to beat Phil Mickelson by one stroke. The win earned him a spot on the 1999 U.S. Ryder Cup team, which he had played on in 1987, 1989, 1991, and 1993. To many observers, his vocal, fervent presence provided the team with the emotional lift it needed to record an incredible come-from-behind victory.

Stewart began 1999 with two goals: to win a major tournament and to return to the Ryder Cup team. He accomplished those goals, leading Ryder Cup captain Ben Crenshaw to remark that Stewart was "in the prime of his career" and that he was "a proven gamer." In all he had won 18 tournaments, including three majors. His success in 1999—he also won the AT&T Pebble Beach National Pro-Am—made his untimely death that year especially poignant.

On October 25 he boarded a private jet in Florida bound for the Tour Championship in Houston, Texas. Experts think that when the plane's occupants lost consciousness because of a loss of cabin pressure, the plane went off course and flew uncontrolled for hours until it ran out of fuel and crashed in South Dakota, killing the 42-year-old Stewart and the members of his party. Stewart was memorialized by his peers in a moving tribute prior to the start of the Tour Championship in Houston. ◆

Swoopes, Sheryl

MARCH 25, 1971– ● BASKETBALL PLAYER

Even though basketball had become the world's most popular indoor sport in the mid 1990s, only men could compete as professionals in the United States. However, that changed dramatically in 1997, when the Board of Governors of the National Basketball Association (NBA) approved the Women's National Basketball Association (WNBA). Already a basketball legend, Sheryl Swoopes became one of the first two women the WNBA signed on.

Sheryl Denise Swoopes was born March 25, 1971, in Brownfield, Texas. She grew up with her mother, Louise, and three brothers. Swoopes played basketball with her brothers, and scoring against her 6′ 4″ brother taught Swoopes that she could take on any female. Swoopes grew to six feet and played high school basketball. She became an All-State and All-American high school player, a remarkable beginning, as more American high schools compete in basketball than any other sport.

College basketball teams recruited Swoopes, including the University of Texas in Austin, which was 400 miles from Brownfield. Impressed with that institution's reputation, she did not consider any other colleges. However, Swoopes became overwhelmed by homesickness and returned home after four days, dropping her full scholarship. She enrolled at nearby

> *"It didn't matter how good I was. It was always, 'You're a girl. You can't play with the guys.' It's always been motivation for me."*
>
> Sheryl Swoopes

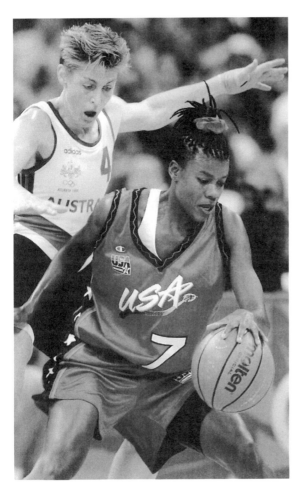

Cheryl Swoopes of Team USA.

South Plains Junior College. Again Swoopes earned a national honor, becoming the National Junior College Player of the Year after her second season.

In 1991 Swoopes started at Texas Tech University in Lubbock, close to home. With her help, Texas Tech's Lady Raiders won two consecutive Southwest Conference titles. Swoopes delighted her coach and fans with her charisma and team spirit. She averaged 27 points per game to lead her team to a 31–3 record. In a final game against the University of Texas at Austin, Swoopes scored an amazing 53 points.

In the NCAA tournament of 1993, Texas Tech won the championship in a final game against Ohio State University. Not only was the game a cliff-hanger with a final score of 84 to 82, Swoopes wowed the basketball world with an outstanding personal performance. She scored 47 points, breaking the record for most points scored in an NCAA final game, men's or women's. The record was previously held by Bill Walton, who had gone on to become a top-ranked NBA player.

Swoopes's big win brought her national attention and a number of awards. She was named Sportswoman of the Year by the Women's Sports Foundation and companies sought her endorsement for sports products. Eager to move up in the basketball world, she faced the hard reality of women's basketball: There were no professional women's teams in the United States. A man with her outstanding record would have entered the NBA draft, the process by which the NBA obtains new players from among former college players.

Swoopes's only option for professional play was an overseas team. In 1993 she played for an Italian professional women's league, but she only lasted 10 games before returning home. She finished her college degree and volunteered as a coach.

Swoopes then played for the undefeated USA Basketball Women's National Team, playing around the world in preparation for the 1996 Summer Olympic Games. Swoopes earned a $50,000 salary as well as income from the first Nike shoe named for a woman, the Air Swoopes. She helped the USA Women's Olympic Team win the gold medal at the 1996 Summer Games in Atlanta.

In 1996 and 1997 Swoopes helped make basketball history. On April 24, 1996, the NBA Board of Governors approved the Women's National Basketball Association (WNBA), and on October 23, 1996, the first players, Sheryl Swoopes and Rebecca Lobo, were signed on. Eight cities were soon selected to be homes to the WNBA's charter teams.

The inaugural WNBA season began on June 21, 1997. In that same month, Swoopes and her husband, Eric Jackson, had their first child, a son they named Jordan, after her hero, basketball star Michael Jordan. Within six weeks of the birth, Swoopes was on the court with the Houston Comets. Commentators and players alike were amazed at her quick postpartum comeback. Swoopes told the press, "It's very important to me to show [young girls] that it is very possible to be able to manage being a mom and an athlete at the same time."

The Comets won the 1997 WNBA championship. In September 1998 the Comets repeated their victory, beating the Phoenix Mercury in an 80 to 71 final game. Swoopes told reporters, "I'm just really excited that I had the opportunity to come back and be a part of this wonderful organization. I want to say thank you, Houston, and I look forward to doing it again." ◆

1971 Swoopes is born in Brownfield, Texas.

1992 Swoopes leads Texas Tech to an NCAA Division I championship (1992–93 season); she scores an NCAA record 47 points in a championship game over Ohio State.

1993 Swoopes is named National Player of the Year by Sports Illustrated and USA Today.

1996 Swoopes plays on the gold medal winning U.S. Olympic team.

Thompson, Tina

FEBRUARY 10, 1975– ● BASKETBALL PLAYER

For a young girl with a passion for basketball, winning the lottery can seem more likely than getting "game" on a playground court dominated by boys. But those long odds never stopped the young Tina Thompson, now a forward for the WNBA champion Houston Comets. Weathering snickering and ridicule from the boys who dominated the basketball courts of her youth, Tina Thompson held her ground, proved her mettle, and became a star in the game she loved.

Thompson, a Los Angeles native, began her **ascent** to basketball fame innocently enough, stubbornly following her older brother Tommy and his friends on their trips to the local recreation center. When they barred her from the indoor court, she just wedged her way into games on the outdoor courts. "A lot of the boys there didn't like the fact that a girl was playing basketball, 'their' sport. They were actually rather cruel," Thompson recalled. "At the rec center, they'd toss the basketball around outside of the gym. This was something very serious for them. There were some points where they didn't let some of the guys play with them, so a girl was someone they definitely didn't want."

But her perseverance on the outdoor courts paid off: by the time she entered the sixth grade, Thompson—already five feet, 11 inches—had mastered a surefire outside shot that soon gained her admission into the exclusive indoor courts of the rec center. "I was probably one of the tallest people in my class," said Tina. "I'd be in the back row for pictures and stuff."

ascent: an upward climb, either literally, as in climbing a mountain slope, or figuratively, as in moving upward in a social situation.

1975 — Thompson is born in Los Angeles, California.

1994 — The University of Southern California offers Thompson a scholarship; she is named Pac-10 Freshman of the Year.

1995 — Thompson is named to the USA World University Games team.

1998 — Thompson helps the Houston Comets to a WNBA championship.

As she neared high-school age, Thompson, paired with her father or brother, became a local legend on the playgrounds, easily beating all challengers. It took a while to win over the more stubborn skeptics, though, according to Thompson's father: "Every time we showed up to challenge someone, there'd be some talking. One time a guy said, 'Aw, you brought your daughter—and she's a girl!' I said the same thing. I always said, 'Hey, man—she's got game. You won't be talking that mess after we play. In about 30 minutes, you'll be wishing she was on your side, not mine."

"We'd win one game and they'd say, 'That was luck!' Then we'd win the second one, and they wouldn't have much to say. Then, in the third game, they'd go to some really hard checking and bumping. Tina always got knocked around pretty good, but she could dish it out, too. Those tough games, that's when she really made her game."

Thompson's hardscrabble playground apprenticeship served her well at Morningside High School, where she was named the 1993 California AAA Player of the Year and led the team with career totals of 1,500 points and 1,000 rebounds. She was also a top volleyball player, but obsession with the hoop cost her a spot on the team. As Thompson put it, "I was so involved with basketball that I had a problem with shooting the volleyball. That ruined the balls; they would hit the rims and mess up the leather. My coach would warn me, but I continued to do it and do it and do it, and finally she said, 'You know what? Basketball's for you. Volleyball isn't.'"

Following high school, Thompson accepted a scholarship offer from USC, where the six-foot-two-inch freshman rapidly refined her game under the tutelage of her coach, Cheryl Miller (now the head coad of the Phoenix Mercury), and her teammate Lisa Leslie, then a senior (and now a star for the Los Angeles Sparks). Thompson was the 1994 Pacfic 10 Conference Freshman of the year, was named to the 1994 Freshman All-American Team by Basketball Times, and set a USC freshman record for rebounds with an average of 10.5 per game in 1994. Fondly recalling Miller's firm guidance, Thompson said, "She never let me say 'no,' or that I couldn't do something."

In fact, it seemed as though there was very little that Thompson could not do. She ended her college career as the Pac 10's third-highest all-time scorer and its second-best career rebounder. In Thompson's four seasons there, USC won 67.5 percent of its games, played in three NCAA tournaments, and advanced to one Final Eight.

During and after her USC years, Thompson found time to contribute her talents to the USA Basketball program as well: she was a member of the 1995 USA World University Games Team that won the silver medal; earned All-Tournament honors at the 1997 USA Basketball Women's Inernational Invitational Tournament; and was a member of the 1999 USA Basketball Women's Winter European Tour.

Even with this imposing hoop resume, Thomspon nearly forsook the basketball court for the court of law. With an excellent record as a sociology major, Thompson had started sending away for law school applications during her senior year at USC when the formation of the WNBA was announced. As the new league's first draft pick, Thompson followed her heart to the Houston Comets, where she became a key factor in Houston's drive to the 1998 WNBA championship. She still plans to study law, but only after she has fulfilled her goals as a professional basketball player.

It may have taken a sterling college career and a WNBA crown to do it, but now, even by the merciless standards of L.A.'s toughest playgrounds, Tina Thompson has definitely earned the right to play with the best of them. ◆

Thomspon nearly forsook the basketball court for the court of law.

Thorpe, Jim

MAY 28,1888–MARCH 28, 1953 ● FOOTBALL, BASEBALL, TRACK AND FIELD
ATHLETE

As one of the world's greatest athletes, Jim Thorpe had an athletic versatility that was virtually unmatched in his time. During his career he became an outstanding college and professional football player, a professional baseball player, and an Olympic gold medal winner in two of track's most grueling competitions: the pentathlon and the decathlon. In 1950, American sportswriters voted him the greatest male athlete of the first half of the twentieth century.

James Francis Thorpe was born near Prague, Oklahoma, to a farming family on May 28, 1888. His father, Hiram P. Thorpe, was half Irish and half Sac and Fox Indian. His mother, Charlotte Vieux (a name Anglicized to View) was of French American and Potawatomi Indian descent. Thorpe had a twin brother named Charlie, who died when the boys were nine years old.

As a youth, Thorpe attended the Sac and Fox reservation boarding school near Tecumseh, Oklahoma, and the Haskell

Jim Thorpe, perhaps the best athlete ever.

Institute in Lawrence, Kansas. After his mother died in 1900, Thorpe stayed out of school for four years, mostly working on the family ranch. Then in 1904, at his father's urging, he enrolled at Carlisle Indian Industrial School, a trade school in Pennsylvania, and began studying tailoring. His father died that same year, leaving Thorpe with a profound sense of loneliness.

Thorpe plunged himself into athletics at Carlisle, excelling at almost every sport he tried. Stories say that Coach Glenn S. "Pop" Warner recruited him to the school track team in 1907 after he outdid the varsity high jumpers at practice by clearing a 5-foot 9-inch high jump bar in street clothes. Thorpe went on to become a track star at Carlisle and broke many school records. He later played halfback on the varsity football team, on which he proved to be a powerful runner and an accurate kicker. His punts were said to be so high and long that he could run across the field to catch them as they came down. Thorpe was also an effective blocker and tackler. His outstanding performance in football led his small school to the national collegiate championship and national fame in 1912 and won him all-American honors in 1911 and 1912.

In 1912, Thorpe competed in the Summer Olympic Games in Stockholm, Sweden, where he represented the United States in the high jump, long jump, pentathlon, and decathlon. The pentathlon consisted of five events: the running broad jump, the discus throw, the javelin throw, the 200-meter run, and the 1500-meter run. The decathlon was made up of 10 events: the running broad jump, shot put, high jump, discus throw, pole vault, javelin throw, 100-meter dash, 400-meter run, 110-meter high hurdles, and the 1500-meter run. Thorpe took first place in both the pentathlon and the decathlon, a feat never before accomplished, and set a world record in the decathlon. At the presentation of his trophies and gold medals, King Gustav of Sweden pronounced Thorpe the "greatest athlete in the world." It was the proudest moment of Thorpe's life.

The young athlete's pride was soon shattered when in early 1913 the Worcester Telegram, a Massachusetts newspaper, reported that Thorpe had played minor-league baseball in the summers of 1909 and 1910. The Amateur Athletic Union (AAU) investigated the story, charged Thorpe with "professionalism," and ordered him to return all his medals and trophies. Despite widespread public condemnation of the action, his name was wiped from the record books, and Ferdinand Bie of Norway and Hugo Weislander of Sweden, who had taken second place in the pentathlon and the decathlon respectively, became the new gold medal winners of the events. The incident left Thorpe humiliated and heartbroken.

Thorpe left Carlisle in 1913 and followed the path of many college athletic stars by becoming a professional athlete. Baseball offered the most opportunity at the time, so in 1913, he accepted what was the best rookie contract of the day: a $6,000 salary and a $5,000 signing bonus for playing with baseball's best team, the New York Giants. Thorpe played professional baseball as an outfielder until 1919 on three different teams. In 1915, he also began playing professional football, his favorite sport, beginning with the Canton Bulldogs. Over the duration of his football career, Thorpe played for seven different teams and attracted large crowds to the game. In 1920, he became the first president of the American Professional Football Association, now known as the National Football League (NFL). In 1929, Thorpe announced his retirement from sports.

After leaving professional sports, life was difficult for Thorpe. He held a number of low-paying jobs and he toured and lectured about his life, the benefits of athletics, and the Indian

1888 Thorpe is born near Prague, Oklahoma.

1912 At the Olympics in Stockholm, Thorpe wins the pentathlon and the decathlon.

1913 Thorpe is compelled to return his medals; he signs with the New York Giants.

1920 Thorpe co-founds the American Professional Football Association (now the NFL) and is named the organization's first president.

1932 Thorpe co-authors *Jim Thorpe's History of the Olympics*.

1953 Thorpe dies at age 64 in Lomita, California.

1982 Thorpe's gold medals are restored by the International Olympic Committee.

people and culture. He also spent some time working in tribal politics and aided in the war effort during World War II by working at a plant in Michigan that produced military vehicles and by serving on an ammunition ship for the U.S. Merchant Marines.

Beginning in the late 1940's, there was a resurgence of public interest in Thorpe, and he began to receive an increasing number of offers to make public appearances and work with young athletes. In 1945, he married his third wife, Patricia Askew. His first two marriages, through which he had fathered eight children, had ended in divorce.

In 1951, the year after Thorpe was pronounced the greatest male athlete by the nation's sportswriters, Warner Brothers released a film about him called "Jim Thorpe—All American", starring Burt Lancaster. Stories about Thorpe filled the press, and when news broke that the great athlete had no money to pay for lip cancer surgery, concerned fans rallied to the cause and raised several thousand dollars to pay his expenses.

Thorpe died of a heart attack in his trailer home in Lomita, California, on March 28, 1953, but his fame has lived on. He has been inducted into a number of halls of fame, including the Professional Football Hall of Fame in Canton, Ohio, and the Track and Field Hall of Fame. In 1972, after a long campaign by his family and many others to restore Thorpe's reputation, the AAU finally restored Thorpe's 1912 amateur status. Then in 1982, 70 years after Thorpe's historic Olympic performances, the International Olympic Committee voted to give copies of Thorpe's Olympic gold medals to his family and to reinstate Thorpe's name in the record books, where he is listed as co-winner with Bie and Wieslander. ◆

Tilden, Bill

FEBRUARY 10, 1893–JUNE 5, 1953 ● TENNIS PLAYER

With a cannonball serve, a powerful forehand and backhand, and a dazzling assortment of lobs, chops, slices, and half volleys, Bill Tilden dominated the game of tennis in the 1920s.

Born in Philadelphia, Pennsylvania, William Tatem Tilden II was one of five children, three of whom had died in a diphtheria epidemic in 1884. His surviving brother, Herbert, tried to teach young Bill to play tennis, but with little success. He was educated at home by private tutors, but when his mother became ill in 1908, he was sent to Germantown Academy. He later attended the University of Pennsylvania but dropped out after his mother died in 1911. He returned to the university a year later, but when his father and Herbert both died in 1915, he left school permanently and decided to make a career of tennis.

Tilden's earliest success on the court came as a doubles player; he and Mary K. Browne won the U.S. National Championship mixed doubles in 1913 and 1914, and he made it to the U.S. National mixed doubles final with F. A. Ballin in 1916, 1917, and 1919. He also played men's doubles, with Vincent Richards winning the U.S. National Championship in 1918 and playing in the finals in 1919. He and Richards also teamed up to win the U.S. Indoor Championship in 1919 and 1920. Playing singles, he was a U.S. National Championship finalist in 1918 and 1919 and won the U.S. Clay Court Championship in 1918.

Tilden's breakthrough year was 1920. That summer, after losing the first set, he crushed the reigning Wimbledon champion, Australia's Gerald Patterson, becoming the first American ever to win the Wimbledon singles titles. Later that summer he wrested the U.S. National Championship title from the number one ranked U.S. player, Bill Johnston. With these wins Tilden began a decade-long dominance of tennis that has never been matched. He repeated his U.S. National Championship six consecutive times from 1921 to 1926 and again in 1929. He successfully defended his Wimbledon singles title in 1921. Beginning in 1922 he won six consecutive U.S. Clay Court Championships. He played on the U.S. Davis Cup team from 1920 to 1930, leading the U.S. to victories seven consecutive years (1920–1926). He was also a dominant doubles player, winning the U.S. National Championship doubles four more times (1921, 1922, 1923, 1927), the mixed doubles a fourth time (1924), and the U.S. Indoor doubles twice more (1926, 1929). Between 1920 and 1925 he was the number one ranked player in the world, and until 1929 he remained the number one ranked player in the United States—despite a severe knee injury in 1926. He capped his amateur career in 1930 by again winning the Wimbledon singles title at age 37. Throughout his amateur career, Tilden played in 192 tournaments, winning

1893 William Tatem Tilden II is born in Philadelphia, Pennsylvania.

1918 Tilden wins the U.S. Clay Court Championship.

1920 Tilden becomes the first American to win singles at Wimbledon; he takes the U.S. national championship and is the top-ranked player in the world (through 1925).

1922 Tilden wins his second U.S. Clay Court Championship (and again in 1923–27).

1931 Tilden turns professional; he wins U.S. Pro Championship.

1949 Tilden is named AP Tennis Athlete of the First Half-Century.

1953 Tilden dies in Hollywood, California.

138, placing second in 28, and compiling an astounding 907–62 match record.

Tilden's final years as an amateur were marked by controversy. He was removed from the 1928 Davis Cup team that competed for the first time in France because he had been paid for writing press accounts of Wimbledon that year, violating the rule against amateurs receiving payment in connection with their sport. He was later reinstated when both France and the U.S. ambassador to France protested; he went on to win a thrilling match against France's René Lacoste, who had won their previous four meetings—the only Davis Cup match the U.S. team won that year. However, the same charge relating to his writing of the press accounts led to his suspension from the 1928 U.S. National Championship.

When Tilden began his pro career in 1931, he was a major celebrity; 13,000 fans turned out at New York City's Madison Square Garden for his pro debut. That year he won the U.S. Pro Championship, repeating in 1935 and winning the Pro Championship doubles title in 1932. His final victories came in the Professional World Doubles Tournament, which he won five consecutive years between 1934 and 1938. Throughout the 1930s and well into the 1940s he barnstormed the country on the professional tennis tour, often driving all night and playing just a few hours after his arrival. After World War II he helped organize the Professional Tennis Players Association. In 1949 the Associated Press named him tennis athlete of the first half-century, and in 1959 he was named to the Lawn Tennis Hall of Fame.

personification: the representation of a thing or a concept by a person who is very closely associated with that thing or concept. A famous athlete is so involved in his or her sport that he or she becomes a physical representation of that sport.

Late in his career Tilden remained the **personification** of tennis, and he continued to attract huge crowds, playing well enough in his late forties and early fifties to reach the late rounds in pro tournaments. He was tall, lean, and graceful, and he had a dominating personality that made him the center of attention (and often left him open to charges of arrogance). Among his friends were other celebrities, including Hollywood actors and politicians, and he spent his money lavishly on travel and entertainment. His tennis career brought him fame and wealth, but he was a poor businessman and made a series of bad investments. Compounding his financial problems was a conviction on morals charges involving a minor (Tilden was a homosexual), and he emerged from prison after several months in poor health and broken in spirit. In 1953 he was found dead in his Hollywood apartment, his bags packed for a trip to Cleveland to play in the U.S. Pro Championships. ◆

Tyson, Mike

JUNE 30, 1966– ● BOXER

Born in Brooklyn, New York, Michael Gerard "Mike" Tyson was raised in a crime-ridden neighborhood and became a young street tough, committing muggings and other crimes. At the age of 13, he was sent to the Tryon School, a juvenile detention facility in Johnstown, New York. There he met Cus D'Amato, an experienced boxing trainer who recognized Tyson's potential as a fighter. D'Amato took Tyson under his wing, becoming both his coach and his legal guardian.

After winning the 1984 Golden Gloves amateur heavyweight championship. Tyson had his first professional fight in Albany, New York, on March 5, 1985. By the end of the year, he had defeated 15 opponents, not one of whom lasted more than four rounds. On November 22, 1986, in Las Vegas, Nevada, Tyson won the World Boxing Council heavyweight title from Trevor Berbick with a technical knockout in the second round—becoming the youngest heavyweight champion in history. Tyson captured the World Boxing Association championship by beating James "Bonecrusher" Smith in Las Vegas on March 7, 1987, and on August 1 of that year defeated Tony Tucker in Las Vegas to gain the International Boxing Federation (IBF) title. One of Tyson's most impressive efforts came in Atlantic City, New Jersey, on June 27, 1988, when he knocked out the former IBF champion Michael Spinks in 91 seconds of the first round.

1966 Tyson is born in Brooklyn, New York.

1986 Tyson becomes the youngest world heavyweight champ in boxing history.

1987 Tyson wins the World Boxing Association heavyweight title.

1989 Tyson is awarded an honorary Doctorate of Humane Letters.

1992 Tyson is convicted of rape and sentenced to prison.

1996 Tyson loses to Evander Holyfield in an eleventh round technical knockout (TKO).

1997 Tyson bites a chunk from Holyfield's ear during a fight; he is fined $3 million and his license is revoked.

At 5′11″ and with a fighting weight of 212 to 221 pounds, "Iron Mike" Tyson was known as a devastating puncher. His seeming invincibility made him a favorite of many sports fans. In 1989 he was awarded an honorary Doctorate of Humane Letters by Central State University in Wilberforce, Ohio. In six years as a professional boxer, Tyson amassed some $60 million dollars, including more than $20 million from the Spinks fight alone.

Even as Tyson won respect for his accomplishments in the ring, controversy surrounded his personal life, especially after D'Amato died in 1985. After D'Amato's death, his associates Jim Jacobs and Bill Cayton became Tyson's managers, but after Jacobs died in 1988, Tyson split with Cayton in a dispute over the management of his financial affairs. That same year, the controversial Don King became Tyson's promoter. Also in 1988, Tyson married actress Robin Givens. After months of a stormy and well-publicized conflict, including allegations that he had beaten her, the couple divorced. Before the year ended, Tyson was arrested after engaging in a late-night brawl with boxer Mitch Green in a Harlem clothing store.

In Tokyo, Japan, on February 11, 1990, an out-of-shape Tyson lost the championship in a stunning tenth-round knockout by the unheralded Buster Douglass. Before he had a chance to regain the title in an anticipated match with Evander Holyfield (who had subsequently taken the championship from Douglass), Tyson's career was interrupted by his arrest for the July 1991 rape of Desiree Washington, an 18-year-old contestant in the Miss Black America pageant in Indianapolis. Even after his conviction on February 10, 1992, Tyson asserted his innocence, contending that Washington had voluntarily consented to sexual relations with him.

While serving a six-year sentence at the Indiana Youth Center in Plainfield, Tyson maintained his physical condition in the hope of resuming his boxing career after an early release from prison. He also began to read widely but failed a high school equivalency examination in March 1994. Tyson announced that he had adopted Islam in 1994, declaring his affection for Minister Louis Farrakhan, leader of the nation of islam. Upon Tyson's release from prison in 1995, a parade was planned in New York City to celebrate his return, but strong opposition emerged within the black community, and the parade was canceled. He announced his return to the ring shortly thereafter, and made his long-anticipated comeback on August

Don King

Boxing promoter Don King burst on the scene in the mid-1970s and soon became a cultural phenomenon. With his booming laugh, brash manner, eccentric vocabulary, and trademark hairstyle which one writer described as looking "as if he's being blasted by hot air from some hellish pit below his feet" King was the constant butt of jokes by late-night talk show comedians and the subject of countless articles about the state of professional boxing.

Who is Don King? The answer depends on who's telling the story. To his supporters, the story goes something like this: King pulled himself up from the ghettos of Cleveland, Ohio, to live his version of the American Dream by becoming the world's most successful boxing promoter, with more than 500 world-championship fights to his credit. In 1974 he became almost a household name after sponsoring the famous "Rumble in the Jungle" fight between Muhammad Ali and George Foreman in Zaire, Africa. For this fight he promised each boxer more than $5 million, an unheard-of amount at the time. His fights between Mike Tyson and Evander Holyfield shattered records for television audiences, and the second Tyson–Holyfield fight grossed a record $14 million in gate receipts. King's supporters also assert that he has unstintingly given back much of his wealth to a variety of charitable and community organizations.

Not everyone, though, is a Don King supporter. To his opponents King is a crook and a con man, a latter-day P. T. Barnum more adept at the arts of publicity and self-promotion than professional sport. King's critics allege that he was a criminal before he became involved in boxing and that during his career, King has rigged fights, cheated virtually every boxer he's dealt with, maintained ties to the Mafia, shown no regard for the health of his boxers, and in general has had a corrupting influence on boxing.

Whichever version of the story is true, the undeniable fact is that Don King turned pro boxing into a marquee sport. His name has become synonymous with American boxing, for better or worse.

19, 1995, at the MGM Grand in Las Vegas, stopping his opponent, Peter McNeeley, after only one minute of the first round. In Tyson's next bout, on December 16, 1995, he was nearly as quick in disposing of Buster Mathis, who hit the canvas to stay at 2:32 of the third round.

Tyson's impressive comeback earned him another shot at the world title—at least the WBC version of it—against Frank Bruno on March 16, 1996, at the MGM Grand. Tyson was no less invincible that night, knocking out Bruno 50 seconds into the third round. He captured the WBA title shortly thereafter when he knocked out Bruce Seldon at the 1:49 mark of the first round on September 24, 1996, at the MGM Grand. A court order awarded the WBC title to Lenox Lewis, however, and Tyson was forced to surrender that title on September 7, 1996.

Tyson's biggest test of this period was Evander Holyfield's challenge to his WBA crown. On November 9, 1996, Tyson entered the ring against Holyfield, who outlasted Tyson and knocked him out in the 11th round, handing Iron Mike the second loss of his professional career. The eagerly anticipated rematch took place on June 28, 1997, and Tyson, perhaps sensing Holyfield's superiority, seemingly snapped in the ring and took a bite out of Holyfield's ear. The bout was halted immediately, and the title remained Holyfield's. At first unrepentant, Tyson sought to mollify an enraged public and boxing establishment by expressing contrition before a hearing of the Nevada State Athletic Commission. But it was too little, too late, and the commission revoked his license and fined him $3 million.

After the minimum one-year waiting period, Tyson applied for reinstatement on July 29, 1998, and after two hearings the commission renewed his boxing license on October 19, 1998. Although seemingly securely launched on the comeback trail, the volatile former champ kicked one motorist and puched out another, both much older and smaller than he, after a minor three-car collision in Maryland on August 31, 1998. After pleading no contest the following December, he was sentenced to two years in jail and was fined $5,000. In the meantime, Tyson resumed his ring career in January 1999, knocking out Francis Botha in the fifth round. He entered jail in February 1999 and was paroled 108 days later.

Tyson's first bout after leaving jail was a first-round trouncing of Orlin Norris on October 23, 1999. On December 9, 1999, Tyson announced plans to make his European debut in a bout in Manchester, England, against British heavyweight champion Julius Francis on January 29, 2000. ◆

Unser, Al, Jr.

APRIL 19, 1962– ● RACE CAR DRIVER

Al Unser Jr.'s racing heritage extends back four generations to the turn of the century, when his great-grand-
father Louis began work as a mechanic on those
newfangled machines known as motor cars. Louis begat Jerry, an
auto racer and movie stunt driver, who begat Al and Bobby,
both Indy 500 winners, who begat Al Jr., himself a great racing
champion and winner of the Indianapolis 500 in 1992 and
1994.

Al Unser Jr. ("Little Al") started racing at six years of age on
motorized minibikes. At age nine he moved up to go-karts under the patient tutelage of his champion father. Al Sr. said, "I
wanted him to race. When we started in go-karts, it was me
pushing it. I think I got more of a charge out of it than he did.
We used to go out every weekend and run the karts. That's how
we started."

Al Jr. drove a small dirt-track racer in his first professional
race at the age of 16. He recalled, "Racing sprint cars on the dirt
taught me to hustle the race car and run wheel to wheel." Upon
graduating from high school, he became a full-time sprint-car
racer and enjoyed considerable early success on that circuit, im-
pelled more by personal ambition and pride than by financial
need. A friend commented, "Probably Al Jr. had everything he
ever wanted. At some point, though, he had to buckle down
and say, 'Okay, I want to be a race-car driver and I'm going to
work hard to do that.' And he did."

Unser soon graduated from sprint cars to Super Vees—racers with Volkswagen motors—and in 1981 he set six track

records on the way to winning the Super Vee championship and the Sports Car Club of America (SCAA) Rookie of the Year award. In 1982 he won the Super Vee crown again and made his Indy Car debut in the Championship Auto Racing Teams (CART) series. The following year he won the Pike's Peak race in record time, thus extending a six-decade tradition of Unser family victories in that race.

In 1983 Al Jr. competed in his first Indianapolis 500—the most prestigious of all auto races—racing against his father, already a two-time Indy 500 winner. His father told him, "This is not a magical place. It's just another race track, and if you treat it like that, you'll be all right." Al Jr. finished a respectable tenth, becoming the youngest driver ever to exceed 200 mph at the Indy 500. A year later he won his first race on the Indy circuit at the Portland International Raceway.

During the 1985 season Al Jr. and Al Sr. were locked in a tense battle for the national championship, and Sr. barely nosed out Jr. in the points total, 151 to 150. Al Jr. wryly observed, "My father taught me everything I know about racing, but he hasn't taught me everything he knows."

In 1986 Al Jr. took three out of four races in the International Race of Champions (IROC) series (in which all drivers race the same cars so that there is no variation in the result but driving skill), becoming the youngest man in history to capture that title. The fourth race was won by Al Sr., who had won the 1985 IROC crown.

Al Jr. enjoyed a banner year in 1990, setting a CART record with four straight Indy-car victories (Toronto, Michigan, Denver, and Vancouver) and capturing the championship, making the Unsers the first father-son champions. Al Jr. said, "Winning the championship means we accomplished the goal we set at the beginning of the season. It means all the hard work and all the dedication, desire, and sacrifice that it takes to win the title is worth it."

Al Jr. reached the pinnacle of professional racing in 1992: his first win at the Indianapolis 500, but by a hair's breadth—the margin of victory was .043 seconds. Despite his Indy 500 glory, the span of 1991–1993 was a disappointing one for Al Jr., who won only one race in each of those years. Unser thought he needed a change of sponsorship, and in 1993 he signed to race in 1994 with Team Penske, the organization that had helped Al Sr. to victory at the Indy 500 in 1987 and to IndyCar championships in 1983 and 1995. Al Jr.'s turnabout in 1994 was immediate and dramatic: he won eight out of 16 races that year, including his second Indy 500, captured the PPG national Indy Car title, and was honored with the ABC Wide World of Sports Athlete of the Year award.

In 1995 Al enjoyed another superb season, winning four out of 17 races, including seven podium finishes, and ranking second in the CARTpoints standings. But since then his fortunes have taken another downturn. Without a single victory in 1999 and none since that 1995 season, in August 1999 Unser announced that in the 2000 season he would be leaving Team Penske. Unser commented, "Roger [Penske] and Marlboro Team Penske and I have had great success over the past few years. What can I say? He gave me my second Indy 500 win and my second CART series championship."

In 1999 Unser was also beset by a series of personal crises: his 12-year-old daughter, Cody, was diagnosed with a rare spinal condition that paralyzed her below the chest, and Al Jr. and his wife Shelley announced their impending divorce.

Still uncertain about his direction for 2000—he is considering either remaining in CART or moving to the rival Indy Racing League—the 37-year-old Unser will try to build on an already enviable record of accomplishment: two CART championships, two Indianaplis 500 wins, 31 Champ car victories (among active drivers second only to Michael Andretti), and a record $18.6 million in PPG Cup earnings. ◆

1962	Unser, Jr. born in Albuquerque, New Mexico.
1986	Unser wins three out of four races at the International Race of Champions.
1990	Unser wins four straight Indy-car victories.
1992	Unser wins the Indianapolis 500 (and again in 1994).
1994	Unser is named ABC "Wide World of Sports" Athlete of the Year.

Unser, Al, Sr.

MAY 29, 1939– ● RACE CAR DRIVER

Al Unser, Sr., one of the most successful race-car drivers in history, is heir to a family tradition of automotive competition that is almost as old as motorcars themselves. Louis Unser, the grandfather of Al Sr. and his brother Bobby (also a racing champion), was an auto mechanic in Colorado Springs, Colorado, early in this century. All three of Louis's sons—Louis Jr., Jerry, and Joe—were pioneer auto racers, earning renown in the 1920s with the first automotive scaling of Pike's Peak in Colorado—even though the road stopped three quarters of the way to the top! Soon after they also won the first race to the top of the mountain, since all the other drivers dropped out.

Al Unser, Sr. celebrates his victory in the Indianapolis 500.

Jerry Unser built and raced cars in the intervals of working as an airplane pilot and Hollywood stunt driver. In 1936 the family settled in Albuquerque, New Mexico, where Jerry started a gas station and car service center. His four sons—Jerry Jr., Louie, Bobby, and Al—began racing Model A Fords as children—Bobby was racing his on dirt roads by the age of eight. By their mid-teens they were all driving race cars in competitions in Colorado, Arizona, and New Mexico. Jerry Jr. was the first to win big, capturing the United States Auto Club (USAC) stock-car crown in 1957 and becoming the first in the family to compete in the Indianapolis 500, in 1959. Even though his promising career was cut short by a fatal accident later that year, first Bobby and then Al were undeterred in their ambitions to become champion drivers.

Al Sr. entered and won his first race at the age of 17, in a stock car his father and brother had built. He and Bobby earned the scorn and wary respect of the older drivers they regularly trounced. Bobby recalled, "Grownups don't like kids to outrun them, so I started racing with Al. He and I would take turns who was going to win each race. . . . If anyone gave us trouble after the race, we'd fight them."

For seven years Al competed in supermodified stock cars on weekends and then raced almost exclusively in midget cars in 1964, the year he earned his first major victory by capturing the Pike's Peak race in record time. His win broke a six-race winning streak by Bobby and launched an intense but always manageable family rivalry. As Bobby recalled, "It would get tense between me and Al about who would win, but it never stayed. We were able to separate business and family—we never really got in a fight. We never let it come down to anything other than racing."

In 1965 Al got his first shot at racing's crown jewel, the Indianapolis 500, a race he eventually won four times, one of only four drivers to do so. He later said, "When I was a kid, every year when the Indianapolis was run, I was glued to the radio, and I said that someday I would go there." Driving an A. J. Foyt-owned car, he finished ninth despite having started in the last row. The next year a more experienced Unser was in third place when an accident took him out of the race. In 1967, he moved up another notch, finishing second behind A. J. Foyt. Bobby's victory in the 1968 Indy further whetted Al's appetite for victory; in 1971 his five victories earned him the pole position at the Indianapolis 500, an advantage he parlayed into his first Indy 500 victory, earning a winner's share of $250,000 (more than $1 million in 1999 dollars) in that race's first million-dollar purse.

Al utterly dominated the circuit that year, winning 10 of 18 races, the USAC national championship, the dirt-track championship, and the Triple Crown of racing (all three 500-mile contests: the Indy, Ontario, and Pocono). As one observer said at the time, "When it came to those long races like the 500s, Al Sr. was going to be there."

At the 1971 Indy 500 Unser started in the third position and faced stiff competition from three McLaren M-16s, which featured an advanced spoiler-wing design. Undaunted, Al managed to maneuver his way to a second straight Indy victory, only the fourth driver to ever achieve that feat. Although he had to settle for a second-place Indy finish in 1972, the following year he again won the dirt-track championship.

Unser then suffered a long dry spell, with no major victories in the next four seasons. He rebounded with victories in the International Race of Champions series in 1977 and again in 1978, the year he also beat Tom Sneva to capture his third Indy 500. Unser won his second national championship in 1983 and his

1939 Unser, Sr. is born in Albuquerque, New Mexico.

1967 At the Indianapolis 500, Unser finishes second behind A. J. Foyt.

1970 Unser wins the Indianapolis 500 and the Triple Crown; he also takes the USAC national championship.

1971 Unser wins the Indy 500 (and again in 1978 and 1987).

1983 Unser wins his second national championship (his third in 1985).

1991 Unser is inducted into the International Motor Sports Hall of Fame.

third in 1985, when he raced to 11 top-ten finishes in 14 races to edge out his son, Al Jr., by one point in the competition for the CART/PPG Cup Championship. Al commented, "It's the same way I treated my brother Bobby when we were racing together. But that feeling was a lot easier to handle than this one."

In the spring of 1987, Al was having trouble finding a car in which to enter the Indianapolis 500. Eventually Roger Penske's team offered him a Ford that had been used at auto shows. Despite Unser's unfamiliarity with the car, he managed to qualify for the twentieth position. Unser got off to a slow start and then stalled out while emerging from the pit stop, but then he surged steadily forward until he found himself in a dead heat with Roberto Guerrero in the final laps. When Guerrero lost ground because of an overheated, slipping **clutch**, Unser streaked past him and captured his fourth Indy by a mere four and a half seconds. Unser said, "The Speedway has been good to me, you know."

In 1994, after failing to qualify for the Indy 500, Al Unser announced his retirement. He now invests in race-car driving teams and enjoys time with his second wife and his daughter at the family lodge in Chama, New Mexico. A man of few words but many accomplishments, Unser can look back on one of the great records in the history of auto racing: four Indy 500 wins and three consecutive years of victories on paved ovals, road courses, and dirt tracks in a single season (1968–1970). In 1991 he was inducted into the International Motor Sports Hall of Fame of America. ◆

clutch: in motor vehicles with a manual transmission (as opposed to an automatic transmission), the clutch is the mechanism that allows the driver to shift from one gear to the next.

Van Dyken, Amy

FEBRUARY 15, 1973– ● SWIMMER

Born on February 15, 1973, and reared in Englewood, Colorado, swimmer Amy Van Dyken became a sensation after her stunning performance at the Summer Olympic Games in Atlanta, Georgia, in 1996. Though she had not been identified before the Games as being a standout of the U.S. Women's Team, Van Dyken won four gold medals.

Her "whatever it takes to get the job done" attitude has served as a model for young athletes who must overcome adversity in order to excel in their chosen sports. In recognition of those who have to struggle especially hard to achieve their goals, she dedicated her fourth Olympic gold medal to "all the nerds out there."

Van Dyken was not an early prodigy in swimming. In fact, on her high school swim team, several of Van Dyken's teammates refused to swim with her in relays because, she was, as she says, "so bad." She was bigger than the typical swimmer (today she stands close to six feet and weighs about 160 pounds). Van Dyken faced the additional hurdle of **asthma**, which causes breathing problems and has limited her to approximately 65 percent of normal lung capacity. She once said that when she was growing up, people would tell her, "Oh, Amy, you can't do that." She proved them wrong. (In an interview, she once said that she got a bit of a kick out of running into those old unsportsmanlike teammates at a mall and saying, "So, I'm swimming in five events at the Olympics. What are you up to?") She took up swimming after a doctor advised that it would help her asthma.

asthma: a disease that causes a constriction in the lungs, which makes it very difficult to breath and often causes coughing and shortness of breath. It can range from very mild to severe cases that can be fatal.

1973 Van Dyken is born in Englewood, Colorado.

1994 Van Dyken is named NCAA Female Swimmer of the Year.

1996 Van Dyken wins four Olympic gold medals (including two for the relay team); she is named AP Female Athlete of the Year.

By the end of high school, Van Dyken's swimming had improved so much that she was viewed as a potential star swimmer at the National Collegiate Athletics Association (NCAA) level. She enrolled in the University of Arizona but had a string of disappointing performances at meets; she simply was not swimming well. In addition, Van Dyken was forced to quit training for the entire summer of 1993 due to a severe case of mononucleosis. The long summer break reminded her of how much she enjoyed the sport, and she returned to it, renewed and enthusiastic, as her health returned.

In 1994, Van Dyken decided to transfer to Colorado State University, in Colorado Springs. There she joined the U.S. National Resident Team. That year, Van Dyken was named the female NCAA Swimmer of the Year (she had been rated fourth in NCAA rankings in 1992 and third in 1993). In 1995, Van Dyken won two important meet events, in the 50-meter freestyle and the 100-meter butterfly.

Somewhere along the way, Van Dyken developed her distinctive pre-race routine. Calculated to psyche out the other swimmers, Van Dyken snarls and spits, paces around, and glares at her opponents. She considers her start the weakest part of her race and uses this ritual to give herself an edge.

At the 1996 Olympics, her pre-race routine would paid off handsomely. However, initially it seemed she would disappear from medal standing without a splash. In her first race, the 100-meter freestyle, she came in fourth and then collapsed onto the pool deck with leg cramps and breathing difficulties. (The NBC television cameras recorded the scene for all to see, which embarrassed Van Dyken.) But she recovered and went on to win four gold medals. Two were for individual events—the 50-meter freestyle and the 100-meter butterfly. She also helped to power the U.S. relay teams to victory in the 4 × 100-meter freestyle relay and the 4 × 100-meter medley relay. She swam the fastest split in the freestyle relay (53.9 seconds).

Van Dyken has a good sense of humor, and it served her well when dealing with the press at the Olympics. One journalist called her "the interview of the year." The Associated Press voted her Female Athlete of the Year.

Not surprisingly, that year brought Van Dyken many other honors and accolades. She was featured on the cover of the Wheaties cereal box and was named Swimmer of the Year by U.S. Swimming. She also collected the Phillips Performance Award for the Most Outstanding Race of the Year, for her swim in the Olympics' 50-meter freestyle, when she posted an American-record-setting time (24.87 seconds). Van Dyken was named the U.S. Olympic Committee Sports Woman of the Year and the ESPN-ESPY Female Athlete of the Year. ARETE bestowed its Courage in Sports Award on Van Dyken, and she was given the title of Sports Woman of the Year by the Women's Sports Foundation, among other honors.

Van Dyken lives in Lone Tree, Colorado, and still trains with the Resident Team at Colorado State, her alma mater. She has continued to swim competitively in both national and international events. She is a six-time All-Star team member and a six-time National A team member (both since 1994). She ranked among the top three women swimmers in the world from 1994 to 1998.

In June 1998, Van Dyken faced the possible end of her career when she had to have shoulder surgery. With her usual grit and determination, however, she came back from the injury to swim, and win, competitively.

Van Dyken is involved with many activities other than swimming. She enjoys hiking, volleyball, and basketball. She is also well known for her work with children and with the deaf. She knows American Sign Language and works with Make-A-Wish and the United Way. Besides serving as an ambassador for the sport of swimming, she hopes one day to work with the deaf. ◆

"If you could bust inside Amy's head in the moments before the race, it might be frightening what you would find."
John Mattos, Amy Van Dyken's coach at Colorado State

Wagner, John Peter "Honus"

FEBRUARY 24, 1874–DECEMBER 6, 1955 ● BASEBALL PLAYER

John Peter "Honus" Wagner was the National League's greatest player during what is known as baseball's Deadball Era, when pitchers dominated the game and home runs were still rare and precious things.

Bow-legged and stocky, with a bulbous nose and, as legend has it, arms that hung to his knees, Wagner hardly looked like a professional athlete. Born John Peter Wagner to a German middle class household in little Chartiers, Pennsylvania, he was called "Johannes" by his parents, and later "Honus" by his classmates who mispronounced his German nickname. In spite of his **gangly** appearance, Wagner reached the major leagues in 1897 as an outfielder with the Louisville Sluggers and played three seasons until the city was dropped from the league following the 1899 campaign. Team owner Barney Dreyfuss bought a franchise in Pittsburgh the following year and took Wagner with him. In 1900, manager Fred Clarke moved him to shortstop in an effort to utilize his long arms. He answered by leading the league with a .381 batting average — the first of a record 17 consecutive seasons of hitting .300 or better.

Wagner was dubbed "The Flying Dutchman" by turn-of-the-century **muckrakers** who incorrectly identified him as having Dutch ancestry. One such journalist wrote that Wagner "looked like a loop rolling down the baselines." And throughout his career, Wagner put up with the taunts of opposing fans, who tried to unnerve the Dutchman with personal remarks. But Wagner never lost his cool. With a calm, collected demeanor, he steadily dominated the National League, recording eight

gangly: loose-limbed and awkward in appearance, often characterized by long arms and legs and a skinny body.

muckrakers: members of the media who try to stir up trouble by digging up facts or stories from people's backgrounds. Most often used in reference to journalists who cover politics.

batting titles, leading the league in steals on five occasions, and playing sterling defense thanks to his gangly arms and legs which actually allowed him to cover more space.

Wagner was the antithesis of his hot-headed American League counterpart, Ty Cobb—while Cobb never won fans for being a nice guy, Wagner was the consummate gentleman. He was strictly against gambling and corruption in baseball, and refused to participate in the sale of his card in chewing tobacco packs. To this day, only a handful of Wagner's baseball cards exist — all of which are worth thousands of dollars and are considered the most valuable cards on the market.

Wagner's only encounter with Cobb came during the 1909 World Series when the Pirates met the Tigers. Wagner steadily out-performed Cobb, hitting over 100 points higher for the series in spite of Cobb's constant personal insults. As legend has it, Cobb singled and informed Wagner he was going to steal second. "Get ready, Dutchman," he yelled across the diamond. "I sharpened my spikes just for you!" On the next pitch, Cobb broke for second and Wagner artfully avoided Cobb's spikes while tagging him out across his face. It was a rare moment of humiliation for Cobb, but Wagner remained expressionless, having silenced his archrival.

The Dutchman also led the Pirates to pennants in 1901, 1902 and 1903, and according to baseball historians, had there been a Most Valuable Player (MVP) award at that time, Wagner almost certainly would have won on six occasions. Still a good player at 42, Wagner closed out his career in 1917 to coach baseball at Carnegie Tech in Pittsburgh and operate a sporting goods store with fellow Pirate Pie Traynor.

Hard times hit Wagner during the Great Depression and in 1933, new Pirates owner Bill Benswanger made Wagner a coach—a position he held for 19 years. Wagner boosted attendance and often took infield practice before games to the joy of fans and players alike, who would gaze at the living legend in silent wonder.

Wagner was elected to the Hall of Fame in the inaugural class of 1936. He was, without a doubt, the most popular player of the Deadball Era, and his slick fielding and tremendous speed set the standard against which all shortstops are judged. He retired with a lifetime .327 batting average, and his 3,430 hits are sixth all-time. Wagner is also sixth on the career doubles list, third in triples, and ninth in stolen bases. Put simply, Honus Wagner is the greatest shortstop to play the game. ◆

Williams, Serena

SEPTEMBER 26, 1981– ● TENNIS PLAYER

Born in Saginaw, Michigan, Serena Williams was raised 12 miles south of Los Angeles in Compton, California, the youngest of five girls. It's virtually impossible to discuss her career as a tennis player without referring to her family. For one thing, her older sister Venus is a top player on the women's tennis tour, and their brief careers have been intertwined not just on court but off court as well. The two have vowed to become the number one and number two ranked players in the world, and although Venus has enjoyed more success, many tennis observers consider Serena to have more potential. Despite their occasional rivalry, the two sisters remain close; they are each other's biggest fans, they constantly refer to one another in interviews, they live and practice together, and together Serena and her sister have become one of the world's most formidable doubles teams.

To many observers, their father Richard Williams represents the stereotype of the overinvolved "stage parent." He's loud, assertive, opinionated, and not at all shy when it comes to bragging about his daughters. Two weeks before the 1999 U.S. Open he brashly predicted that his daughters would meet in the final of that event. (He was almost right.) He once claimed that Steffi Graf, not one of his daughters, was his favorite tennis player, and he once asked Martina Hingis, his daughters' biggest nemesis, to autograph his arm. While he has drawn criticism, he and his wife, Oracene, must have done something right. Among their older children, one is in medicine, another is in law, and a third is a college student, while Serena and her sister are among the most level-headed, articulate, and (as they are fond of noting) well-educated players on the tour.

Williams's introduction to tennis came at the hands of her father, who was determined to mold her into a tennis champion so that she could escape the "drug-infested ghetto" of Compton. At his urging, she avoided the junior tour in favor of practice, practice, and more practice. When she was just four years old, her father took her to a neighborhood court daily and taught her to play, noting, "I also taught [her] to hit the ground if we heard gunshots." Serena attracted attention not only because of

Williams's introduction to tennis came at the hands of her father, who was determined to mold her into a tennis champion so that she could escape the "drug-infested ghetto" of Compton.

her enormous talent but also because, as an African American with beaded hair from a poor community who learned the game not at a country club but on a run-down city court, she emerged from a background that historically might have excluded her from tennis.

Williams turned pro in 1997, and she quickly served notice that she was on her way. In just her second Women's Tennis Association (WTA) event and only the fifth pro tournament in her career she beat two top-ten players in Chicago, number seven Mary Pierce in the second round and number four Monica Seles in the quarterfinals. At the time she was ranked number 304, making her the lowest ranked player ever to defeat two top-ten players in the same tournament. Her ranking jumped to 102.

In 1998 she continued to climb in the rankings while knocking off major competitors. In the WTA Tour event in Sydney, Australia, she beat number two Lindsay Davenport to advance to the semifinals. In the Lipton Championships she beat three top-30 players—Irina Spirlea (ten), Patty Schnyder (17), and Barbara Paulus (26)—and although she lost the final in a third-set tie-break, she had two match points on number one ranked Martina Hingis. That year Williams played in her first Grand Slam event, the Australian Open, losing to her sister Venus in the second round. In all, she compiled a 29–11 record in her 1998 matches and earned over $300,000 in prize money.

In 1999 Williams began to prove that she had the ability to make a run at becoming the top women's tennis player. That year she captured five titles, and she won her first WTA event, the Open Gaz de France, by beating Amelie Mauresmo in the final. The next week she won the Evert Cup, beating Lindsay Davenport in the second round, Mary Pierce in the quarterfinals, and Steffi Graf in the final. In the Lipton Championships she beat Monica Seles in the fourth round, Amanda Coetzer in the quarterfinals, and Martina Hingis in the semifinals, but her streak was stopped when she lost to Venus in the final—the first all-sisters tennis final in 115 years. Williams got back on track by winning the Acura Classic, beating Arantxa Sanchez-Vicario and Martina Hingis along the way. She also won the Grand Slam Cup that year.

Williams's crowning achievement of 1999, though, came at the U.S. Open. Venus and Serena were in different brackets, and as the tournament progressed, it looked as though their father's prediction of an all-Williams final might come true. But when

---

Venus lost to Martina Hingis in the semifinals, the hopes of the Williams family rode on Serena's shoulders. She took the first set easily, 6–3, but blew two match points in the second set, setting up a tie-breaker. She hadn't lost a tie-breaker all year. She won the tie-breaker 7–4, becoming the first African-American since Arthur Ashe in 1975 and the first African-American woman since Althea Gibson in 1958 to win a Grand Slam title. She also teamed up with Venus to win the doubles title. ◆

Williams, Ted

AUGUST 30, 1918– ● BASEBALL PLAYER

I n a storybook ending to one of the most famed careers in baseball history, Ted Williams hit a home run in his last time at bat. The man they called "The Splendid Splinter,"

1918 Williams is born in San Diego, California.

1939 Williams makes his major-league debut; leads league in runs batted in.

1940 Williams makes the first of 17 All-Star teams.

1942 Williams wins the Triple Crown (again in 1947).

1946 Boston wins the American League pennant, and Williams the Most Valuable Player (again in 1949).

1958 Williams leads the league in hitting.

1960 Williams hits a homer in his final at-bat and retires.

who may have been the best pure-hitter the game has ever seen, walked off the field at Fenway Park for the last time in high style. The last player to hit over .400 in a season (.406 in 1941), Williams attained a record that today's best players are still far from attaining.

Williams was born in San Diego, California, on August 30, 1918. He made his major league debut on April 20, 1939, and his impact was immediate. He hit .327 and led the league with 145 runs batted in. Though just a rookie, Williams finished fourth in the Most Valuable Player (MVP) voting behind baseball legends Joe DiMaggio, Jimmie Foxx and Bob Feller. Red Sox fans knew they had a special player in left field.

Williams would not disappoint his faithful fans. In 1940 he made his first of 17 All-Star teams. The following year brought a season that, in any other year, would surely have netted Williams an MVP award: he had six hits in a doubleheader in Philadelphia on the last day of the season, topping the major leagues with a .406 average. He also led the league with his 135 runs, 37 homers, 145 walks, a .551 on-base percentage and a .735 slugging percentage. Despite these numbers, Williams' MVP trophy would have to wait as the great Joe DiMaggio won it that year, largely due to his 56-game hitting streak—a feat just as amazing as Williams' .406 batting average. The following year Williams again looked like a favorite for the MVP award. He won the Triple Crown (top batting average, home runs and runs batted in) as he bested both the American and National Leagues that year. He also led in runs, walks, on-base percentage and slugging. But this time he lost the MVP trophy to the Yankees' Joe Gordon by 21 votes. Gordon batted 34 points less, had 53 fewer runs, 34 fewer runs batted in, and 18 fewer home runs—not to mention he led the league in strikeouts and errors. Red Sox fans were outraged at the media, who comprised the voting group. Williams would have to wait four years to make another run at winning his first MVP award. World War II had begun, and Williams became a U. S. Navy pilot. When he finally returned to baseball in 1946, he wasted no time in continuing his quest to be the best, and this time, his team was right there with him. In 1946, Boston won the American League pennant, and Williams finally was named MVP. Williams lost out on a World Series ring however, losing to Stan Musial and the St. Louis Cardinals in seven games.

An old rivalry was renewed in 1947 when DiMaggio beat out Williams—who again won the Triple Crown—by one vote for MVP. Oddly, Williams was completely left off of a Boston sportwriter's ballot, which may have accounted for his loss to DiMaggio. Williams and the Boston press had a contentious relationship, and this probably cost him the MVP honor in the final analysis.

In 1949, Williams would not be denied his second MVP award, but he did miss his third Triple Crown by .0002 batting percentage points. His Red Sox also missed the pennant by just one game to the Yankees.

Although Williams had missed almost two full seasons due to military service and a broken collarbone, he was named Player of the Decade for the 1940's by *The Sporting News*. On April 30, 1952 the Red Sox held "Ted Williams Day" to honor him before he left for the Korean War. He promptly hit a game-winning, two-run home run in his final at-bat.

Upon his return to baseball, Williams was once again considered for the MVP award, but this time it went to the Yankees' Mickey Mantle. Though Williams led the league with a .388 average and had 38 homers, Mantle had more hits, runs, walks, and his Yankees made it to the World Series. Williams last led the American League in hitting in 1958, and in 1960 he had his final at-bat, putting a cap on a career that would lead him to the Hall of Fame in 1966.

Williams finished his career sixth all-time in batting average (.344); 11th all-time in home runs; second only to Babe Ruth in walks (2,019), first in on-base percentage (.483) and second in slugging percentage (.634).

In 1969, Williams became the manager of the hapless Washington Senators. He improved their record by 21 wins in his first season, but the team steadily declined after that. After the franchise's first season in Texas in 1972, Williams' managerial career came to an end.

Williams was named to the All-Century team in 1999 and continues to inspire and encourage the best hitters in the game today. His most famous quote is one that will live forever in baseball legend, and exemplifies the dream of everyone who ever picks up a bat: "I wanted to be the greatest hitter who ever lived. A man has to have goals—for a day, for a lifetime—and that was mine; to have people say, 'There goes Ted Williams, the greatest hitter who ever lived.'" ◆

"[Ted Williams was] absolutely the best hitter I ever saw. I never felt the comparisons between us were fair. It was either Ted, or it was me. But I realize now that it was flattering, because what people were saying was that at that time we were the best."

Joe DiMaggio on Ted Williams

Williams, Venus

JUNE 17, 1980– ● TENNIS PLAYER

W omen have held a key place in the sport of tennis ever since the first amateur world championships for women took place in Wimbledon, England, in 1884. Following in these footsteps, but bringing a bold new energy to the "country-club sport," 17-year-old Venus Williams made her Wimbledon debut in 1997. With long, nimble limbs and beaded braids flashing, Williams created a sensation on the courts.

Venus Ebone Starr Williams was born June 17, 1980, in Los Angeles, the fourth of five daughters of Richard and Oracene (Price) Williams. Michigan-born Oracene practiced nursing, and Richard, son of a Louisiana sharecropper, headed a security business. By the time Venus was five, Richard had her on the courts in their Compton neighborhood hitting tennis balls. All the daughters played tennis, but Richard concentrated on Venus and Serena, her younger sister.

Venus Williams.

Venus began competing in 1989. By the age of 10 she had won numerous titles on the Southern California junior tennis circuit and soon became the number one player in her age group in California. Serena also competed, and the girls soon tasted minor celebrity.

In 1991, accepting scholarships for Venus and Serena at the tennis academy of coach Rick Macci, the family relocated to Florida, eventually purchasing a home in Palm Beach Gardens. Richard then made an unusual move by withdrawing the girls from junior competitions. Instead they practiced six hours a day, six days a week. The Williamses also home schooled the sisters.

In October 1994 Venus emerged on the professional circuit, playing a tournament in Oakland, California. Although the 14-year-old had not competed in three years, she beat the 59th ranked woman in the world and also gave a close game to Arantxa Sanchez-Vicario, the No. 2 player. Puzzled by Richard Williams's change of mind, observers guessed that new rules from the World Tennis Association lay behind it. After 1994, 14-year-olds would no longer be allowed to enter the pros. Also, women under 18 entering the pros after 1995 would be limited to a certain number of tournaments. After Oakland, though, Venus did not compete again until August 1995.

In the spring of 1997 Venus made her debut at the French Open, and a month later she debuted at Wimbledon. She did not do well, but the world had seen her talent. That summer, Venus performed better at the U.S. Open, advancing from 66th to 25th in the rankings in one day. Williams became the first African-American female to appear in the finals of the U.S. Open since Althea Gibson won the title in 1958. Martina Hingis beat Williams; however, Williams created more of a stir than any other player. She defeated 8th-seeded Anke Huber in the third round and toppled No. 11, the Romanian Irina Spirlea, in a tight semifinal round. In that match, an incident occurred in which Williams and Spirlea appeared deliberately to bump into each other. Afterwards, Richard Williams proclaimed Spirlea a racist, though he later retracted his accusation. At 1998's U.S. Open, Venus, 18, made it to the semifinals and by autumn she was ranked No. 5 in the world.

At 6′ 2″ and 168 pounds, Venus powers a serve that has reached 125 mph, equal to the standing women's record. Richard Williams often boasted that someday Venus and Serena would go head-to-head for first place. The sisters played each other for the first time at the Australian Open in January 1998. Venus won. Off court, the girls are best friends and close to their family. As practicing Jehovah's Witnesses, Serena and Venus visit door-to-door to discuss the Bible. While they abstain from alcohol, tobacco, and premarital sex, the sisters are famous for skintight tennis dresses and beaded braids. They have been called cocky, and Venus has displayed emotional outbursts on court. However, both Venus and Serena are considered well spoken and intelligent by the press as well as many enthusiastic fans. *The New York Times* once quoted Venus as saying, "I never thought anyone was better than me. Once you do that, you lose." ◆

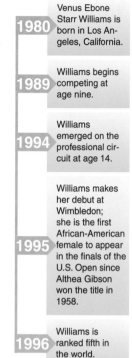

1980 Venus Ebone Starr Williams is born in Los Angeles, California.

1989 Williams begins competing at age nine.

1994 Williams emerged on the professional circuit at age 14.

1995 Williams makes her debut at Wimbledon; she is the first African-American female to appear in the finals of the U.S. Open since Althea Gibson won the title in 1958.

1996 Williams is ranked fifth in the world.

Woods, Eldrick "Tiger"

DECEMBER 30, 1973– ● GOLFER

Eldrick "Tiger" Woods is the most acclaimed golfer of African-American ancestry to compete on the Professional Golfers' Association (PGA) tour. His enormous success is attributable to his great talent and personal appeal, especially among young people. Woods's greatest achievement thus far is his 1997 victory in the prestigious Masters Tournament by a record margin of 12 strokes. He was the youngest Masters champion in history.

Born and raised in Cypress, California, Woods became interested in golf at a young age. At 2 he putted against Bob Hope on the Mike Douglas Show. By 17 he had won three U.S. Junior Amateur Championships (1991–1993). His come-from-behind victory at the 1996 U.S. Amateur Championship capped an impressive amateur career including the NCAA title and three successive U.S. Amateur victories.

Woods turned professional in August 1996, hoping to earn enough money in eight tournaments ($150,000) to qualify for the 1997 PGA Tour. He stunned the golf world by winning the Las Vegas Invitational and the Disney/Oldsmobile Classic, earning $790,594 and finishing 25th on the money list. He was the PGA Tour's 1996 Rookie of the Year.

Woods won five tournaments in 1997, including his Master's victory. He finished 1997 with a record $2,066,833—a PGA Tour record for single season earnings—and was selected 1997 Player of the Year by the PGA Tour, PGA of America, and Golf Writers Association of America. In 1998, Tiger Woods won two tournaments, finishing the year ranked number one in the world.

The following year, 1999, proved to be another extraordinary year for

Golf's Four Majors

The Professional Golfers' Association of America (PGA) sponsors dozens of tournaments each year. In 1999 the organization sponsored or cosponsored some 40 tournaments with lavish "purses," or prizes. Four of these tournaments the U.S. Open, the PGA, the Masters, and the British Open stand out as the "majors," in which only the very best golfers compete for the highest purses before the largest national television audiences.

The most venerable of the big four is the British Open, which dates back to 1860. The idea of an open championship was first broached in a meeting at the Prestwick Golf Club in Ayshire, but the first official tournament did not take place until 1860, a three-round match with eight entrants, all professionals, on a 12-hole course. The winner was Willie Park with a score of 174. Several amateurs entered over the next few years, but the tournament remained a local event until Tommy Morris's three successive wins (1868–70) attracted wider notice.

After a year's hiatus the Open resumed in 1872 and began the tradition of awarding the Championship Cup. From then until 1890 the tournament was played at Prestwick, St. Andrews, and Musselburgh. Over the years the tournament traveled to an ever-wider array of links throughout the British Isles. As the popularity of the tournament grew, the organizers required that, aside from a few specially selected exceptions, all entrants must play two qualifying rounds. Entry money was charged for the first time in 1891, and gate money was charged for the first time in 1926. The prize money has rocketed from a five-pound winner's share in 1863 to $493,500, the sum pocketed by 1999's winner, Scotland's Paul Lawrie.

The U.S. Open is America's oldest golf tournament. Its sponsor is America's main amateur golfing organization, the United States Golf Association (USGA). The first U.S. Open was held in Newport, Rhode Island, in 1895, shortly after the formation of the USGA. The winner that year was Horace Rawlins, a 19-year-old Irishman, who scored 173 for the 36-hole match. The U.S. Open expanded to 72 holes in 1898, eight rounds at the nine-hole links at the Myopia Hunt Club in Hamilton, Massachusetts. The original purse in 1895 was $335, with a $150 winner's share. The figures for the 1999 Open champion, Payne Stewart, were $3.5 million and $625,000, respectively.

The Masters Tournament, known as "the championship of champions," is held annually at the Augusta National Club in Augusta, Georgia. Designed by Bobby Jones and the golf course architect Dr. Alister Mackenzie, the beautiful but challenging course opened in 1931 and played host to the first Masters in 1934. Only invitees and past winners of major tournaments were allowed to compete hence the name the Masters. The first winner was Horton Smith, with a score of 285. The 1999 winner, Jose Maria Olazabal, received a check for $725,000.

When the PGA was formed in 1916, it immediately launched an annual tournament, which was based on match play until 1958, when the PGA Championship format changed to four rounds of 18 holes, each scored by strokes. The first PGA Championship was held in 1916 in Siwanoy, New York, and was won by Jim Barnes. The 1999 title went to Tiger Woods, who collected a $630,000 prize.

1973 Woods is born in Cypress, California.

1991 At 17, Woods wins the first of three U.S. Junior Amateur Championships (also in 1992 and 1993).

1997 Woods turns professional; he is named the PGA Tour's Rookie of the Year. Woods wins five tournaments, including the Masters; he finishes the year ranked first in the world.

1999 Woods wins eight tournaments, becoming the eleventh man to win eight or more times in a season on the PGA tour.

the young golfer. After modifying his swing and improving his physical conditioning, Woods improved his game dramatically. He won eight tournaments in 1999, becoming just the 11th player to win eight or more times in a season on the PGA Tour. He won the PGA Championship in August as well as the last four tournaments of the year—including the Tour Championship—bringing his 1999 earnings to a record $6,616,585. Woods received many honors in 1999, including the Vardon Trophy, awarded to the PGA Tour professional with the lowest adjusted scoring average; the PGA and PGA Tour Player of the year awards; and the Associated Press Male Athlete of the Year, an honor he had also received in 1997. Woods was also a proud member of the victorious 1999 Ryder Cup Team.

In the year 2000, Woods picked up right where he left off in 1999. He began the season by winning the Mercedes Championship, his fifth straight win over two years. In his next tournament, he added to his already sizable legend when he came from seven shots back of the leader with just seven shots to play to win the AT & T Pebble Beach Pro-Am. It was a remarkable victory, and it tied the modern record for most consecutive tournaments won.

The Tiger Woods Foundation, chaired by Tiger's father, Earl Woods, conducts junior golf exhibitions and clinics in inner cities and offers scholarships and grants in order to encourage young people of varying ethnic and economic backgrounds. ◆

Young, Denton "Cy"

MARCH 29, 1867–NOVEMBER 4, 1955 ● BASEBALL PLAYER

Cy Young is the winningest pitcher in major league history, as well as the most durable. His record numbers of 511 wins, 313 losses and 815 starts set standards that will likely never be surpassed.

Born Denton True Young in Gilmore, Ohio, just two years after the Civil War ended, Young became a star for Canton of the Tri-State League, a small semi-pro league, in the late 1880s. He earned the nickname "Cyclone" due to the velocity of his pitches. Often, his pre-game pitches splintered the fence he used as a backstop, intimidating the opposing team and ushering chants of "Cy!" from the home team crowd. In 1890, at age 23, Young signed with the Cleveland Spiders and threw a three-hitter in his big-league debut. The following season he became a star, winning 27 ball games, the first of nine straight seasons of 20 or more wins. Throughout the 1890s, Young proved extremely durable; while he led the league in wins only once, he threw over 400 innings five times and never less than 333. He normally threw both ends of a doubleheader, a practice that has long since been abandoned for fear of ruining a pitcher's arm.

In 1901, Young joined the Boston Pilgrims of the new American League and established himself as that league's top pitcher. As baseball developed in the new century, and the role of pitching and defense became essential to a successful team, Young changed the game with his workhorse approach. He pitched over 300 innings every year until 1908, winning 20 or more six times. His 44 consecutive scoreless innings—23 of them hitless as well—from April 25 to May 5, 1904, was a

1867 Denton True "Cy" Young is born in Gilmore, Ohio.

1890 Young signs with the Cleveland Spiders.

1901 Young joins the Boston Pilgrims.

1903 Young leads the Pilgrims to victory in the first World Series.

1937 Young is elected to the Baseball Hall of Fame.

1955 Young dies in Newcomerstown, Ohio.

1955 The Cy Young Award is established.

record that stood for 64 years until Don Drysdale broke it in 1968.

Young was also a pioneer of the complete game, finishing what he'd started a record 749 times. "I never had a sore arm and I pitched every third day," he once told a journalist. In fact, he once pitched every other day for a stretch of 18 days in 1903. As legend has it, Young would request only 12 warm-up pitches before a game.

Young led the Boston Pilgrims to the championship in the first World Series in 1903, thanks to a 26–16 record. And at age 41, he showed no sign of wear and tear, going 21–11 with a 1.26 ERA for the 1908 Pilgrims. He returned to Cleveland in 1909, but soon thereafter lost his effectiveness. He retired in 1911.

Elected to the Hall of Fame in 1937—the second class to join Cooperstown—Young holds a bevy of records that almost certainly will never be broken. As the game has changed over the years, pitching is no longer the dominant force it was in the so-called Deadball Era. Since pitchers no longer throw the innings that Young compiled, his wins, losses, complete games and innings records seem untouchable. In addition, Young is third on the all-time shutouts list and 14th in strikeouts.

Young died in Newcomerstown, Ohio, on November 4, 1955. He was immortalized the following year with the establishment of the Cy Young Award, given annually to the best pitcher in each league. Don Newcombe of the Brooklyn Dodgers was the first recipient of the Cy Young Award in 1956. ◆

Article Sources

The following authors contributed the new articles for **Macmillan Profiles:**
Athletes and Coaches of Summer:

Gabe Geltzer
William Kaufman
Tom Kertes
Mitchell Lavnick
Lisa Clyde Nielsen
Patricia Ohlenroth
Richard O'Malley
Michael O'Neal
Karen Pasternack
William K. Wolfrum

The following articles were adapted from the *Encyclopedia of African-American Culture and History*, edited by Jack Salzman, David Lionel Smith, and Cornel West, and published by Macmillan Library Reference in 1996:

Aaron, Henry
Ali, Muhammad
Armstrong, Henry
Ashe, Arthur
Ashford, Evelyn
Campanella, Roy
Flood, Curt
Foreman, George
Frazier, Joe
Henderson, Rickey
Holmes, Larry
Holyfield, Evander
Johnson, Jack
Leonard, Sugar Ray
Liston, Sonny
Louis, Joe
Mays, Willie

Moses, Edwin
Owens, Jesse
Paige, Satchel
Patterson, Floyd
Robinson, Jackie
Robinson, Sugar Ray
Spinks, Michael
Tyson, Mike

The following articles were adapted from **Macmillan Profiles:** *Black Women in America,* published by Macmillan Library Reference in 1999:

Gibson, Althea
Griffith-Joyner, Florence
Joyner-Kersee, Jackie
Miller, Cheryl
Swoopes, Sheryl

The following articles were adapted from **Macmillan Profiles:** *Latino Americans,* published by Macmillan Library Reference in 1999:

Clemente, Roberto
de la Hoya, Oscar
Lopez, Nancy
Pelé
Sosa, Sammy

The following articles were adapted from *The Scribner Encyclopedia of American Lives,* edited by Kenneth T. Jackson and published by Charles Scribner's Sons in 1998:

Dempsey, Jack (written by Bruce J. Evensen)
Maris, Roger (written by Edward J. Tassinari)

Photo Credits

Photographs appearing in *Athletes and Coaches of Summer* are from the following sources:

Hank Aaron (page 1): AP/Wide World

Andre Agassi (page 3): AP/Wide World

Muhammad Ali (page 10): AP/Wide World

Mario Andretti (page 18): AP/Wide World

Eddie Arcaro (page 21): AP/Wide World

Lance Armstrong (page 24): Archive Photos, Inc.

Arthur Ashe (page 27): AP/Wide World

Evelyn Ashford (page 28): AP/Wide World

Jennifer Azzi (page 31): Archive Photos, Inc.

Yogi Berra (page 44): AP/Wide World

Ruthie Bolton-Holifield (page 52): AP/Wide World

Bjorn Borg (page 57): AP/Wide World

Don Budge (page 62): Corbis

Roy Campanella (page 65): AP/Wide World

Harry Caray (page 69): Corbis

Roberto Clemente (page 77): National Archives and Records
   Administration

Ty Cobb (page 78): Archive Photos, Inc.

Nadia Comaneci (page 83): AP/Wide World

Maureen Connolly (page 90): Corbis

Jimmy Connors (page 92): AP/Wide World

Cynthia Cooper (page 95): AP/Wide World

Oscar de la Hoya (page 108): AP/Wide World

David Duval (page 128): AP/Wide World

Dale Earnhardt (page 131): Gale Group

Teresa Edwards (page 134): AP/Wide World

Chris Evert (page 141): AP/Wide World

Curt Flood (page 149): Archive Photos, Inc.

George Foreman (page 152): AP/Wide World

Fu Mingxia (page 157): AP/Wide World

Althea Gibson (page 167): AP/Wide World

Josh Gibson (page 169): AP/Wide World

Steffi Graf (page 174): AP/Wide World

Ken Griffey, Jr. (page 178): AP/Wide World

Florence Griffith-Joyner (page 185): Archive Photos, Inc.

Mia Hamm (page 190): AP/Wide World

Chamique Holdsclaw (page 198): AP/Wide World

Evander Holyfield (page 201): AP/Wide World

Juli Inkster (page 207): AP/Wide World

Reggie Jackson (page 214): AP/Wide World

Bruce Jenner (page 221): AP/Wide World

Michael Johnson (page 227): Archive Photos, Inc.

Bobby Jones (page 232): AP/Wide World

Marion Jones (page 235): Archive Photos, Inc.

Al Kaline (page 240): AP/Wide World

Billie Jean King (page 243): AP/Wide World

Olga Korbut (page 245): Archive Photos, Inc.

Julie Krone (page 251): AP/Wide World

Jake LaMotta (page 256): AP/Wide World

Ray Leonard (page 267): AP/Wide World

Carl Lewis (page 271): AP/Wide World

Nancy Lieberman-Cline (page 273): AP/Wide World

Rebecca Lobo (page 277): AP/Wide World

Greg Louganis (page 281): AP/Wide World

Joe Louis (page 284): AP/Wide World

Greg Maddux (page 294): AP/Wide World

Mickey Mantle (page 299): Library of Congress

Bob Mathias (page 311): AP/Wide World

Willie Mays (page 313): AP/Wide World

Mark McGwire (page 322): AP/Wide World

Cheryl Miller (page 325): AP/Wide World

Helen Wills Moody (page 329): Archive Photos, Inc.

Martina Navratilova (page 333): AP/Wide World

Jack Nicklaus (page 338): AP/Wide World

Jesse Owens (page 350): AP/Wide World

Arnold Palmer (page 355): Library of Congress

Pelé (page 359): AP/Wide World

Mary Lou Retton (page 368): Archive Photos, Inc.

Cal Ripken, Jr. (page 376): Archive Photos, Inc.

Jennifer Rizzotti (page 379): AP/Wide World

Jackie Robinson (page 381): AP/Wide World

Sugar Ray Robinson (page 383): AP/Wide World

Pete Rose (page 385): Archive Photos, Inc.

Wilma Rudolph (page 390): AP/Wide World

Babe Ruth (page 392): Library of Congress

Nolan Ryan (page 397): Archive Photos, Inc.

Pete Sampras (page 402): AP/Wide World

Secretariat (page 411): AP/Wide World

Monica Seles (page 415): AP/Wide World

Sam Snead (page 422): AP/Wide World

Annika Sorenstam (page 427): Archive Photos, Inc.

Mark Spitz (page 432): AP/Wide World

Sheryl Swoopes (page 446): AP/Wide World

Jim Thorpe (page 452): Library of Congress

Mike Tyson (page 457): AP/Wide World

Al Unser, Sr. (page 464): Corbis

Venus Williams (page 478): AP/Wide World

Tiger Woods (page 480): AP/Wide World

Additional Resources

GENERAL SOURCES

BOOKS

Arnold, Peter, ed. *The Pictorial History of Boxing.* Gallery Books, 1988.

Collins, Douglas, ed. *Olympic Dreams: 100 Years of Excellence.* St. Martin's Press, 1996.

Dewey, Donald, ed. *Encyclopedia of Major League Baseball Teams.* HarperCollins, 1994.

Fleischer, Nat, ed. *An Illustrated History of Boxing.* Carol Pub. Group, 1997.

Garner, Joe. *And the Crowd Goes Wild: Relive the Most Celebrated Sporting Events Ever Broadcast.* Sourcebooks, 1999 [book and audio discs].

Golenbock, Peter. *The Last Lap: The Life and Times of NASCAR's Legendary Heroes.* Macmillan USA, 1998.

Hollander, Zander, ed. *Inside Sports Hockey.* Visible Ink Press, 1998.

Latford, Bob. *A Celebration of 50 Years of NASCAR: Half a Century of High-Speed Drama.* Carlton Books, 1999.

Markel, Robert, and Susan Waggoner, eds. *The Women's Sports Encyclopedia.* H. Holt, 1997.

Myler, Patrick, ed. *A Century of Boxing Greats: Inside the Ring with the Hundred Best Boxers.* Robson/Parkwest, 1998.

NASCAR Trials and Triumphs: True Stories of NASCAR Men and Women Who Overcame Tough Obstacles to Find Success. HarperEntertainment, 1999.

Oglesby, Carole A., ed. *Encyclopedia of Women and Sport in America.* Oryx Press, 1998.

Osborn, Kevin, ed. *Scholastic Encyclopedia of Sports in the United States.* Scholastic Reference, 1997.

Pollak, Mark, ed. *Sports Leagues and Teams: An Encyclopedia, 1871 Through 1996.* McFarland, 1998.

Riley, James A., ed. *The Biographical Encyclopedia of the Negro Baseball Leagues.* Carroll and Graf/Richard Gallen, 1994.

Roberts, James B., ed. *The Boxing Register: International Boxing Hall of Fame Official*

Record Book. McBooks Press, 1997.

Rutledge, Rachel. *Women of Sports*. Millbrook Press, 1998–1999 [series].

Siddons, Larry. *The Olympics at 100: A Celebration in Pictures*. Macmillan, 1995.

Smith, Ron, ed. *The Ultimate Encyclopedia of Basketball: The Definitive Illustrated Guide to the NBA*. Carlton Books, 1996.

Thorn, John, ed. *Total Baseball: The Official Encyclopedia of Major League Baseball*. 6th ed. Total Sports, 1999.

Wallechinsky, David. *The Complete Book of the Summer Olympics*. Little, Brown, 1996.

ARTICLES

"The 50 greatest sports figures of the century from each of the 50 states." *Sports Illustrated*, Dec. 27, 1999.

Hoffer, Richard. "Our favorite feats." *Sports Illustrated*, Dec. 27, 1999.

Mallozzi, Vincent M. "The last champions of the century." *New York Times*, Dec. 26, 1999.

"The *Sports Illustrated* 20th Century sports awards." *Sports Illustrated*, Nov. 29, 1999.

VIDEORECORDINGS

America's Greatest Gymnasts. National Broadcasting Company, 1996.

Golden Greats of Horse Racing. Front Row Video, 1989.

100 Years of Olympic Glory. Turner Home Entertainment, 1996.

WEBSITES

American Sportscasters Association, http://www.americansportscasters.com/

Basketball Hall of Fame, http://www.masslive.com/bballhof/inductees.html

CNN/Sports Illustrated Online, http://www.cnnsi.com/

International Boxing Federation/US Boxing Association, http://www.ibf-usba-boxing.com

International Gymnastics Hall of Fame, http://www.ighof.com/

International Olympic Committee [IOC], http://www.olympic.org

Ladies Professional Golf Association [LPGA], http://www.lpga.com

NASCAR Online, http://www.nascar.com/

National Basketball Association [NBA], http://www.nba.com/

National Museum of Racing and Hall of Fame, http://www.racingmuseum.org/ [horse racing]

Official Site of Major League Baseball, http://www.majorleaguebaseball.com/

Professional Golfers' Association [PGA], http://www.pga.com/

"Top North American Athletes of the Century." *ESPN.com*,

http://espn.go.com/sportscentury/athletes.html

United States Soccer Federation, http://www.us-soccer.com/

United States Tennis Association [USTA], http://www.usta.com

USA Basketball, http://www.usabasketball.com/

USA Swimming, http://www.usa-swimming.org/

USA Track and Field, http://www.usatf.org/

Women's National Basketball Association [WNBA], http://www.wnba.com/

INDIVIDUAL ATHLETES

AARON, HENRY

Aaron, Hank. *I Had a Hammer*. HarperCollins, 1991.

Hank Aaron: Chasing the Dream. Turner Broadcasting, 1995 [videorecording].

Hirshberg, Albert. *Henry Aaron; Quiet Superstar*. Putnam, 1969.

AGASSI, ANDRE

Agassi, Andre. *Agassi*. Collins Publishers, 1997.

Bauman, Paul. *Agassi and Ecstasy: The Turbulent Life of Andre Agassi*. Bonus Books, 1997.

Christopher, Matt. *On the Court with Andre Agassi*. Little, Brown, 1997.

AKERS, MICHELLE

Akers, Michelle. *Standing Fast: Battles of a Champion*. JTC Sports, 1997.

Miller, Marla. *All American Girls: The U.S. Women's National Soccer Team*. Archway, 1999.

Michelle Akers Soccer Page, http://www.michelleakers.com/

ALI, MUHAMMAD

Ali, Muhammad. *The Greatest, My Own Story*. Random House, 1975.

Hauser, Thomas. *Muhammad Ali: His Life and Times*. Simon and Schuster, 1991.

Remnick, David. *King of the World: Muhammad Ali and the Rise of an American Hero*. Random House, 1998.

"Muhammad Ali." *International Boxing Hall of Fame*, http://www.ibhof.com/ali.htm

ALLEN, MEL

Gould, Stephen Jay. "A voice with heart." *New York Times*, June 26, 1996.

"1978 Ford C. Frick Award Winner Mel Allen." *National Baseball Hall of Fame*, http://www.baseballhalloffame.org/hofers_and_honorees/frick_bios/allen_mel.htm

"1985 Hall of Fame Inductee Mel Allen." *American Sportscasters Association*, http://www.americansportscasters.com/people/allen.htm

ANDRETTI, MARIO

Andretti, Mario. *Andretti*. Out of print.

Andretti, Mario. *What's It Like Out There?* H. Regnery, 1970.

Prentzas, G. S. *Mario Andretti*. Chelsea House, 1996.

ARCARO, EDDIE

Golden Greats of Horse Racing. Front Row Video, 1989 [videorecording].

Nack, William. "The headiest horseman." *Sports Illustrated*, Nov. 24, 1997.

ARMSTRONG, HENRY

Armstrong, Henry. *Gloves, Glory, and God; an Autobiography*. F. H. Revell, 1956.

"Henry Armstrong." *International Boxing Hall of Fame*, http://www.ibhof.com/armstrng.htm

ARMSTRONG, LANCE

Abt, Samuel. *A Season in Turmoil*. Velo Press, 1995.

Wilcockson, John. *Lance Armstrong and the 1999 Tour de France*. Velo Press, 1999.

Lance Armstrong Online, http://www.lancearmstrong.com/

ASHE, ARTHUR

Arthur Ashe: Citizen of the World. HBO Sports, 1994 [videorecording].

Ashe, Arthur. *Days of Grace: A Memoir*. Alfred A. Knopf, 1993.

Weissberg, Ted. *Arthur Ashe*. Chelsea House, 1991.

ASHFORD, EVELYN

Bondy, Filip. "Ashford gives successors winning handoff in 400." *New York Times*, Aug. 9, 1992.

Connolly, Pat. *Coaching Evelyn: Fast, Faster, Fastest Woman in the World*. HarperCollins, 1991.

AUSTIN, TRACY

Atkin, Ross. "Tracy Austin's return is smashing." *Christian Science Monitor*, Mar. 2, 1993.

Austin, Tracy. *Beyond Center Court: My Story*. W. Morrow, 1992.

Burchard, S. H. *Tracy Austin*. Harcourt Brace Jovanovich, 1982.

AZZI, JENNIFER

Rhoden, William C. "They're ambassadors of the women's game." *New York Times*, July 21, 1996.

"Jennifer Azzi." *Women's National Basketball Association [WNBA]*, http://www.wnba.com/playerfile/jennifer_azzi.html

BAILEY, DONOVAN

Longman, Jere. "In the duel of the fastest, Bailey runs alone." *New York Times*, June 2, 1997.

Donovan Bailey Official Site, http://donovanbailey.com/

BANKS, ERNIE

Banks, Ernie. *"Mr. Cub."* Follett, 1971.

Bjarkman, Peter C. *Ernie Banks*. Chelsea House, 1994.

BEAMON, BOB

Beamon, Bob. *The Man Who Could Fly: The Bob Beamon Story*. Genesis Press, 1999.

"Bob Beamon." *Olympic Hall of Fame*, http://www.olympic-usa.org/games/ga_2_5_11.html

BENCH, JOHNNY

Sabin, Louis. *Johnny Bench, King of Catchers*. Putnam, 1977.

Shannon, Mike. *Johnny Bench*. Chelsea House, 1990.

BERRA, YOGI

Berra, Yogi. *The Yogi Book*. Workman Publishing, 1998.

Berra, Yogi. *Yogi: It Ain't Over*. McGraw-Hill, 1989.

Yogi Berra: An American Original. Sports Publishing, 1998.

BIONDI, MATT

Bondy, Filip. "It's Popov who defeats Biondi, Jager." *New York Times*, July 31, 1992.

"Guest Webmaster: Matt Biondi" [interview]. *USA Swimming*, http://www.usa-swimming.org/biondi.htm

BOGGS, WADE

"After being honored, Boggs sets up winner." *New York Times*, Sept. 4, 1999.

Boggs, Wade. *Boggs!* Contemporary Books, 1986.

Clark, Steve. *Wade Boggs: Baseball's Star Hitter*. Dillon Press, 1988.

BOLTON-HOLIFIELD, RUTHIE

Morgan, Terri. *Ruthie Bolton-Holifield: Sharpshooting Playmaker*. Lerner Publications, 1999.

"Ruthie Bolton-Holifield." *Women's National Basketball Association [WNBA]*, http://www.wnba.com/playerfile/ruthie_bolton-holifield.html

BONDS, BARRY

Muskat, Carrie. *Barry Bonds*. Chelsea House, 1997.

Savage, Jeff. *Barry Bonds: Mr. Excitement*. Lerner Publications, 1997.

Woods, Bob. *Barry Bonds, Roberto Alomar*. East End, 1994.

BORG, BJORN

Borg, Bjîrn. *My Life and Game*. Simon and Schuster, 1980.

Cavanaugh, Jack. "Connors, as intense as ever, is now getting the best of Borg." *New York Times*, Aug. 12, 1997.

BRETT, GEORGE

Born to Hit: The George Brett Story. Random House, 1982.

Brett, George. *George Brett: From Here to Cooperstown*. Addax, 1999. Twyman, Gib.

BUDGE, DON

Hart, Jeffrey. "The lively ghosts of Wimbledon." *National Review*, July 15, 1996.

Schwartz, Larry. "In big matches, he wouldn't budge." *ESPN.com*, http://espn.go.com/sportscentury/features/00014130.html

CAMPANELLA, ROY

Campanella, Roy. *It's Good to Be Alive*. University of Nebraska Press, reprint 1995.

Macht, Norman L. *Roy Campanella: Baseball Star*. Chelsea House, 1996.

CANSECO, JOSE

Aaseng, Nathan. *Jose Canseco: Baseball's 40–40 Man*. Lerner Publications, 1989.

Ling, Bettina. *Jose Canseco*. Raintree/Steck Vaughn, 1996.

CARAY, HARRY

Caray, Harry. *Holy Cow!* Villard Books, 1989.

Stone, Steve. *Where's Harry? Steve Stone Remembers Harry Caray*. Taylor, 1999.

CHAVEZ, JULIO CESAR

Dolan, Terrance. *Julio César Ch†vez*. Chelsea House, 1993.

Smith, Timothy W. "De La Hoya sends Chavez to corner." *New York Times*, Sept. 20, 1998.

CITATION

Durso, Joseph. "Close, but no Citation: Jones has his say on Cigar." *New York Times*, July 14, 1996.

"Thoroughbred Champions: Top 100 Racehorses of the 20th Century." *Blood-Horse Magazine Online*, http://www.bloodhorse.com/tb_champions/top_100_list.html

CLEMENS, ROGER

Clemens, Roger. *Rocket Man: The Roger Clemens Story*. Penguin, 1988.

Devaney, John. *Sports Great Roger Clemens*. Enslow Publishers, 1990.

Korman, Gordon. *Roger Clemens*. Chelsea House, 1998.

CLEMENTE, ROBERTO

Roberto Clemente: Puerto Rican Baseball Great. Schlessinger Video Productions, 1995 [videorecording].

Rudeen, Kenneth. *Roberto Clemente*. HarperTrophy, 1996.

Walker, Paul Robert. *Pride of Puerto Rico: The Life of Roberto Clemente*. Harcourt Brace Jovanovich, 1988.

COBB, TY

Bak, Richard. *Ty Cobb: His Tumultuous Life and Times*. Taylor, 1994.

Cobb, Ty. *My Life in Baseball, the True Record*. Doubleday, 1961.

Stump, Al. *Cobb: a Biography*. Algonquin Books, 1994.

COE, SEBASTIAN

Coe, Sebastian. *Running Free*. St. Martin's Press, 1981.

Lidz, Franz. "Sebastian Coe." *Sports Illustrated*, Mar. 15, 1993.

Miller, David. *Sebastian Coe: Born to Run*. Out of print.

COMANECI, NADIA

Burchard, S. H. *Nadia Comaneci*. Harcourt Brace Jovanovich, 1977.

Calkins, Laurel Brubaker. "10 again." *People Weekly*, July 15, 1996.

Comaneci, Nadia. *Nadia: The Autobiography of Nadia Comaneci*. Proteus Books, 1981.

CONNER, BART

Conner, Bart. *Winning the Gold*. Warner Books, 1985.

"Bart Conner." *USOC Online*, http://www.olympic-usa.org/olympians/meet/bios/gymnastics/conner.html

CONNOLLY, MAUREEN

Krull, Kathleen. *Lives of the Athletes: Thrills, Spills (And What the Neighbors Thought)*. Harcourt Brace Jovanovich, 1997.

Schwabacher, Martin. *Superstars of Women's Tennis*. Chelsea House, 1997.

"The story of >Little Mo.'" *Dallas Tennis Association*, http://www.dta.org/officers/little_mo.htm

CONNORS, JIMMY

Cavanaugh, Jack. "Connors, as intense as ever, is now getting the best of Borg." *New York Times*, Aug. 12, 1997.

Litsky, Frank. "Connors, U.S. Open hero, struts into Hall of Fame." *New York Times*, July 12, 1998.

Sabin, Francene. *Jimmy Connors, King of the Courts*. Putnam, 1978.

COOPER, CYNTHIA

Cooper, Cynthia. *She Got Game: My Personal Odyssey*. Warner Books, 1999.

"Cynthia Cooper." *Women's National Basketball Association [WNBA]*, http://www.wnba.com/playerfile/cynthia_cooper.html

COURT, MARGARET SMITH

Court, Margaret Smith. *Court on Court, a Life in Tennis*. Dodd, Mead, 1975.
Schwabacher, Martin. *Superstars of Women's Tennis*. Chelsea House, 1997.

CRENSHAW, BEN

Bamberger, Michael. "Moment of truth; the wildest comeback in Ryder Cup history." *Sports Illustrated*, Oct. 4, 1999.

"Ben Crenshaw." *ESPN/GOLFonline*, http://www.igolf.com/profiles/

Ben Crenshaw Official Website, http://www.bencrenshaw.com/

DAVIES, LAURA

Dorman, Larry. "Davies drives far, fast and to her own rhythm." *New York Times*, May 12, 1996.

"Who's number one?" *Golf Magazine*, Sept. 1997.

"Laura Davies." *ESPN/GOLFonline*, http://www.igolf.com/profiles/

DAY, PAT

"Day, Pat." *Current Biography*, Oct. 1997.

Durso, Joseph. "Race no. 2 becomes no. 7,000 for Day." *New York Times*, Aug. 26, 1997.

"Pat Day." *Blood-Horse Magazine Online*, http://www.bloodhorse.com/bc99/profiles/pat_day.html

DE LA HOYA, OSCAR

Kawakami, Tim. *Golden Boy: The Fame, Money, and Mystery of Oscar de La Hoya*. Andrews McMeel, 1999.

Taylor, Robert. *Oscar de La Hoya: Boxing's Boy Wonder*. Rourke Enterprises, 1993.

Torres, John Albert. *Sports Great Oscar de la Hoya*. Enslow, 1999.

DEMPSEY, JACK

Dempsey, Jack. *Dempsey*. Harper and Row, 1977.

Kahn, Roger. *A Flame of Pure Fire: Jack Dempsey and the Roaring '20s*. Harcourt Brace Jovanovich, 1999.

Roberts, Randy. *Jack Dempsey, the Manassa Mauler*. Louisiana State University Press, 1984.

DEVERS, GAIL

Gutman, Bill. *Gail Devers*. Raintree/Steck-Vaughn, 1996.

"Gail Devers." *USATF [USA Track and Field]*, http://www.usatf.org/athletes/bios/devers.shtml

DIDRIKSON–ZAHARIAS, MILDRED "BABE"

Cayleff, Susan E. *Babe: The Life and Legend of Babe Didrikson Zaharias*. University of Illinois Press, 1995.

Freedman, Russell. *Babe Didrikson Zaharias: The Making of a Champion*. Clarion Books, 1999.

Knudson, R. Rozanne. *Babe Didrikson, Athlete of the Century*. Viking Kestrel, 1985.

DIMAGGIO, JOE

Durso, Joseph. *DiMaggio, the Last American Knight*. Little, Brown, 1995.

Stout, Glenn. *DiMaggio: An Illustrated Life*. Walker, 1995.

Where Have You Gone, Joe DiMaggio? HBO Home Video, 1997 [videorecording].

"Yankee legend dead at 84." *CNN/SI Online*, http://cnnsi.com/baseball/mlb/news/1999/03/08/dimaggio_obit/

DONOVAN, ANNE

"Anne Donovan." *Basketball Hall of Fame*, http://www.masslive.com/bballhof/inductees.html

"Donovan named interim coach." *Women's National Basketball Association [WNBA]*, http://www.wnba.com/news/indy_donovan.html

DUROCHER, LEO

Durocher, Leo. *Nice Guys Finish Last*. Simon and Schuster, 1975.

Eskenazi, Gerald. *The Lip: A Biography of Leo Durocher*. W. Morrow, 1993.

DUVAL, DAVID

Brown, Clifton. "Woods triumphs in match made in (TV) heaven." *New York Times*, Aug. 3, 1999.

Diaz, Jaime. "Out of the woods." *Sports Illustrated*, Aug. 30, 1999.

"David Duval." *ESPN/GOLFonline*, http://www.igolf.com/profiles/

EARNHARDT, DALE

Latford, Bob. *A Celebration of 50 Years of NASCAR: Half a Century of High-Speed Drama.* Carlton Books, 1999.

Lucido, Jerome. *Racing with the Hawk: The Man Behind Dale Earnhardt.* F. H. Revell, 1998.

Vehorn, Frank. *The Intimidator: The Dale Earnhardt Story.* Down Home Press, 1994.

EDWARDS, TERESA

"Edwards, Teresa." *Current Biography*, Mar. 1998.

"Teresa Edwards added to U.S. national team." *Women's National Basketball Association [WNBA]*, http://www.wnba.com/news/usa2000_edwards.html

EMERSON, ROY

"Roy Emerson." *Tennis Magazine Online*, http://www.tennismagazine.com/gss/emerson.htm

"The wisdom of Emmo." *Tennis*, Mar. 1997.

EVANS, JANET

"Evans, Janet." *Current Biography*, July 1996.

Litsky, Frank. "In the pool, opposites attract gold medals." *New York Times*, Sept. 26, 1988.

Wilstein, Steve. "Janet Evans takes last laps." *Washington Post*, July 26, 1996.

EVERT, CHRIS

Evert, Chris. *Chrissie, My Own Story.* Simon and Schuster, 1982.

Lupica, Mike. "Martina was second to one." *Tennis*, June 1995.

Schwartz, Larry. "Evert: Grit, grace and glamour." *ESPN.com*, http://espn.go.com/sportscentury/features/00014187.html

FINGERS, ROLLIE

Knisley, Michael. "Winning the waiting game." *Sporting News*, Aug. 10, 1992.

Sexton, Joe. "Seaver, Fingers elected to shrine." *New York Times*, Jan. 8, 1992.

FLOOD, CURT

Chass, Murray. "Remembering the courageous Curt Flood, a man for all seasons." *New York Times*, Jan. 21, 1997.

Flood, Curt. *The Way It Is.* Trident Press, 1971. Out of print.

Lipsyte, Robert. "Baseball's last martyr." *New York Times Magazine*, Jan. 4, 1998.

FORD, WHITEY

Ford, Edward [Whitey]. *Slick: My Life In and Around Baseball*. W. Morrow, 1987.

Ford, Edward [Whitey], and Mickey Mantle. *Whitey and Mickey: A Joint Autobiography of the Yankee Years*. Viking Press, 1976.

FOREMAN, GEORGE

Foreman, George. *By George: The Autobiography of George Foreman*. Villard Books, 1995.

Mailer, Norman. *The Fight*. Vintage Books, reprint 1997.

FOYT, A. J.

Foyt, A. J. *A. J.* Times Books, 1983.

Wilker, Josh. *A. J. Foyt*. Chelsea House, 1996.

FRAZIER, JOE

Frazier, Joe. *Smokin' Joe: The Autobiography of a Heavyweight Champion of the World, Smokin' Joe Frazier*. Macmillan USA, 1996.

Lipsyte, Robert. "25 years haven't softened the blows." *New York Times*, Mar. 3, 1996.

Nack, William. "The fight's over, Joe." *Sports Illustrated*, Sept. 30, 1996.

FU MINGXIA

Eskenazi, Gerald. "Fu, at 13, eclipses elders to win gold." *New York Times*, July 28, 1992.

Montville, Leigh. "Fu's gold." *Sports Illustrated*, Aug. 12, 1996.

GARVEY, STEVE

Garvey, Cynthia. *The Secret Life of Cyndy Garvey*. Doubleday, 1989.

Garvey, Steve. *Garvey*. Times Books, 1986.

GEHRIG, LOU

Bak, Richard. *Lou Gehrig: An American Classic*. Taylor, 1995.

The Pride of the Yankees. CBS/FOX Video, 1990 [videorecording].

Robinson, Ray. *Iron Horse: Lou Gehrig in His Time*. W. W. Norton, 1990.

GIBSON, ALTHEA

Biracree, Tom. *Althea Gibson*. Chelsea House, 1989.

Davidson, Sue. *Changing the Game: The Stories of Tennis Champions Alice Marble and Althea Gibson*. Seal Press, 1997.

Gibson, Althea. *I Always Wanted to Be Somebody*. Harper, 1958.

GIBSON, JOSH

Holway, John. *Josh and Satch: The Life and Times of Josh Gibson and Satchel Paige*. Meckler, 1991.

Ribowsky, Mark. *The Power and the Darkness: The Life of Josh Gibson in the Shadows of the Game*. Simon and Schuster, 1996.

Riley, James A., ed. *The Biographical Encyclopedia of the Negro Baseball Leagues*. Carroll and Graf/Richard Gallen, 1994.

GORDON, JEFF

Brinster, Richard. *Jeff Gordon*. Chelsea House, 1997.

Gordon, Jeff, and Bob Zeller. *Jeff Gordon: Portrait of a Champion*. HarperCollins, 1998.

Mair, George. *Natural Born Winner: The Jeff Gordon Story*. Ballantine Books, 1998.

GRAF, STEFFI

Finn, Robin. "Graf, still near top of tennis, leaves it behind." *New York Times*, Aug. 14, 1999.

Knapp, Ron. *Sports Great Steffi Graf*. Enslow, 1995. Monroe, Judy. *Steffi Graf*. Crestwood House, 1988.

GREENE, MAURICE

Clarey, Christopher. "Johnson and Greene run into history." *New York Times*, Aug. 30, 1999.

Layden, Tim. "Gold standard: Once going nowhere fast, sprinter Maurice Greene has found his stride." *Sports Illustrated*, June 28, 1999.

GRIFFEY, KEN, JR.

Griffey, Ken, Jr. *Junior: Griffey on Griffey*. CollinsPublishers, 1997.

Gutman, Bill. *Ken Griffey, Sr., and Ken Griffey, Jr.: Father and Son Teammates*. Millbrook Press, 1993.

Ken Griffey Jr.: Adventures in Baseball. ABC Video, 1996 [videorecording].

GRIFFITH, YOLANDA

Brewer, Jerry. "Driving the lane, not hot-wiring cars; a 10-year-old daughter is all the motivation needed." *New York Times*, July 6, 1999.

"Yolanda Griffith." *Women's National Basketball Association [WNBA]*, http://www.wnba.com/playerfile/yolanda_griffith.html

GRIFFITH-JOYNER, FLORENCE

Aaseng, Nathan. *Florence Griffith Joyner: Dazzling Olympian*. Lerner Publications, 1989.

Brennan, Christine. "So fast, so cool." *New York Times Magazine*, Jan. 3, 1999.

Connolly, Pat. "An athlete to remember, for a variety of reasons." *New York Times*, Sept. 27, 1999.

GWYNN, TONY

Gwynn, Tony, and Jim Rosenthal. *Tony Gwynn's Total Baseball Player*. St. Martin's Press, 1992.

Rains, Rob, ed. *Tony Gwynn: Mr. Padre*. Sports Publishing, 1999.

HAMM, MIA

Christopher, Matt. *On the Field with Mia Hamm*. Little, Brown, 1998.

Hamm, Mia. *Go for the Goal: A Champion's Guide to Winning in Soccer and Life*. HarperCollins, 1999.

Miller, Marla. *All American Girls: The U.S. Women's National Soccer Team*. Archway, 1999.

HENDERSON, RICKEY

Bauleke, Ann. *Rickey Henderson: Record Stealer*. Lerner Publications, 1991.

Henderson, Rickey. *Off Base: Confessions of a Thief*. HarperCollins, 1992.

HINGIS, MARTINA

Finn, Robin. "Hingis is no. 1, but Davenport has her number." *New York Times*, Nov. 23, 1999.

Shaughnessy, Linda. *Martina Hingis*. Dillon Press, 2000.

Teitelbaum, Michael. *Grand Slam Stars: Martina Hingis and Venus Williams*. Harper-Active, 1998.

HOGAN, BEN

Gregston, Gene. *Hogan: The Man Who Played for Glory*. Prentice-Hall, 1978.

Sampson, Curt. *The Eternal Summer: Palmer, Nicklaus, and Hogan in 1960, Golf's Golden Year*. Taylor, 1992.

Sampson, Curt. *Hogan*. Rutledge Hill Press, 1996.

HOLDSCLAW, CHAMIQUE

Battista, Judy. "Holdsclaw a sure thing as Mystics' no. 1 choice." *New York Times*, May 4, 1999.

"Chamique Holdsclaw." *Women's National Basketball Association [WNBA]*, http://www.wnba.com/playerfile/chamique_holdsclaw.html

HOLMES, LARRY

Holmes, Larry, and Phil Berger. *Larry Holmes: Against the Odds*. St. Martin's Press, 1998.

Remnick, David. "Larry Holmes tries a comeback in a sport on the ropes." *New Yorker*, Aug. 11, 1997.

HOLYFIELD, EVANDER

Hoffer, Richard. "Triumph of timidity." *Sports Illustrated*, Nov. 22, 1999.

Holyfield, Evander, and Bernard Holyfield. *Holyfield: The Humble Warrior*. Thomas Nelson, 1996.

HORNSBY, ROGERS

Alexander, Charles C. *Rogers Hornsby: A Biography*. H. Holt, 1995.

Finlayson, Ann. *Champions at Bat; Three Power Hitters*. Garrard, 1970.

Kavanagh, Jack. *Rogers Hornsby*. Chelsea House, 1991.

HUNTER, JIM "CATFISH"

Burchard, S. H. *Jim "Catfish" Hunter*. Harcourt Brace Jovanovich, 1976.

Hunter, Jim. *Catfish: My Life in Baseball*. McGraw-Hill, 1988.

Stambler, Irwin. *Catfish Hunter: The Three Million Dollar Arm*. Putnam, 1976.

INKSTER, JULI

Brown, Clifton. "Out of the spotlight, but in the Hall." *New York Times*, Sept. 29, 1999.

"Juli Inkster." *ESPN/GOLFonline*, http://www.igolf.com/profiles/

JACKSON, "SHOELESS" JOE

Frommer, Harvey. *Shoeless Joe and Ragtime Baseball*. Taylor, 1992.

Gropman, Donald. *Say it Ain't So, Joe: The True Story of "Shoeless" Joe Jackson*. Carol Pub. Group, 1992.

Kinsella, W. P. *Shoeless Joe*. Houghton Mifflin, 1999 [fiction].

JACKSON, REGGIE

Allen, Maury. *Mr. October: The Reggie Jackson Story*. Times Books, 1981.

Going, Going, Gone! Karol Video, 1984 [videorecording].

Jackson, Reggie. *Reggie*. Villard Books, 1984.

JARRETT, DALE

Huff, Richard M. *The Jarretts*. Chelsea House, 1998.

Nobles, Charlie. "Jarrett reaches goal after staying put." *New York Times*, Nov. 17, 1999.

JENNER, BRUCE

Jenner, Bruce. *Finding the Champion Within: A Step-by-Step Plan for Reaching Your Full Potential.* Simon and Schuster, 1997.

Jenner, Bruce. *The Olympics and Me.* Doubleday, 1980.

JOHNSON, JACK

Fradella, Sal. *Jack Johnson.* Branden, 1990.

Jakoubek, Robert E. *Jack Johnson.* Chelsea House, 1990.

Johnson, Jack. *Jack Johnson—In the Ring and Out.* Citadel Press, 1992.

JOHNSON, MICHAEL

Clarey, Christopher. "Johnson and Greene run into history." *New York Times,* Aug. 30, 1999.

Johnson, Michael. *Slaying the Dragon: How to Turn Your Small Steps to Great Feats.* Regan Books, 1996.

JOHNSON, WALTER

Kavanagh, Jack. *Walter Johnson: A Life.* Diamond Communications, 1995.

Thomas, Henry W. *Walter Johnson: Baseball's Big Train.* Phenom Press, 1995.

JONES, BOBBY

Matthew, Sidney L. *Life and Times of Bobby Jones.* Sleeping Bear Press, 1995.

Miller, Dick. *Triumphant Journey: The Saga of Bobby Jones, and the Grand Slam of Golf.* Holt, Rinehart and Winston, 1980.

Price, Charles. *A Golf Story: Bobby Jones, Augusta National, and the Masters Tournament.* Atheneum, 1986.

JONES, MARION

Clarey, Christopher. "Back spasms make Jones fall short of her dream." *New York Times,* Aug. 26, 1999.

Stewart, Mark. *Marion Jones, Sprinting Sensation.* Children's Press, 1999.

JOYNER-KERSEE, JACKIE

Cohen, Neil. *Jackie Joyner-Kersee.* Little, Brown, 1992.

Green, Carl R. *Jackie Joyner-Kersee.* Maxwell Macmillan, 1994.

Joyner-Kersee, Jacqueline. *A Kind of Grace: The Autobiography of the World's Greatest Female Athlete.* Warner Books, 1997.

KALINE, AL

Butler, Hal. *Al Kaline and the Detroit Tigers.* Regnery, 1973. Out of print.

Puscas, George. "Al Kaline's star rose at 20, kept soaring." *Knight-Ridder/Tribune News Service,* April 3, 1994.

KING, BETSY

Brown, Clifton. "King shows she is not the retiring type." *New York Times*, July 31, 1998.

"Betsy King." *ESPN/GOLFonline*, http://www.igolf.com/profiles/

KING, BILLIE JEAN

King, Billie Jean. *Billie Jean*. Viking Press, 1982.

Lannin, Joanne. *Billie Jean King: Tennis Trailblazer*. Lerner Publications, 1999.

Lipsyte, Robert. "Helping others before helping herself; the mother of modern sport now champions health and youth issues." *New York Times*, July 12, 1998.

KORBUT, OLGA

Calkins, Laurel Brubaker. "10 again." *People Weekly*, July 15, 1996.

Coffey, Wayne R. *Olga Korbut*. Blackbirch Press, 1992.

Montville, Leigh. "Olga Korbut." *Sports Illustrated*, Sept. 19, 1994.

KOUFAX, SANDY

Grabowski, John. *Sandy Koufax*. Chelsea House, 1992.

Hano, Arnold. *Sandy Koufax: Strikeout King*. Putnam, 1964.

Sanford, William R. *Sandy Koufax*. Crestwood House, 1993.

KRONE, JULIE

Callahan, Dorothy M. *Julie Krone, a Winning Jockey*. Dillon Press, 1990.

Krone, Julie. *Riding for My Life*. Little, Brown, 1995.

Savage, Jeff. *Julie Krone, Unstoppable Jockey*. Lerner Publications, 1996.

LAMOTTA, JAKE

Anderson, Chris. *Raging Bull II: Continuing the Story of Jake La Motta*. Lyle Stuart, 1986.

La Motta, Jake. *Raging Bull: My Story*. Da Capo Press, 1997.

LASORDA, TOMMY

Friend, Tom. "Lasorda retires, ending an era in the Dodgers' dugout." *New York Times*, July 30, 1996.

Lasorda, Tommy, and David Fisher. *The Artful Dodger*. Arbor House, 1985.

LAVER, ROD

Laver, Rod, and Bud Collins. *The Education of a Tennis Player*. Simon and Schuster, 1973.

Shmerler, Cindy. "The road back." *Tennis*, Sept. 1999.

LEMOND, GREG

Abt, Samuel. *A Season in Turmoil*. Velo Press, 1995.

Gutman, Bill. *Greg LeMond*. Raintree/Steck Vaughn, 1998.

Porter, A. P. *Greg LeMond: Premier Cyclist*. Lerner Publications, 1990.

LENDL, IVAN

Eliot, Chip. *Ivan Lendl*. Crestwood House, 1988.

Finn, Robin. "Back spasms end Lendl's career." *New York Times*, Dec. 21, 1994.

LENZI, MARK

Longman, Jere. "A matter of balance; Lenzi learning to keep life and Olympics in perspective." *New York Times*, Apr. 26, 1996.

Springer, Karen, and Mark Starr. "Ups and downs." *Newsweek*, June 24, 1996.

LEONARD, SUGAR RAY

Burchard, S. H. *Sports Star, Sugar Ray Leonard*. Harcourt Brace Jovanovich, 1983.

Gloeckner, Carolyn. *Sugar Ray Leonard*. Crestwood House, 1985.

Toperoff, Sam. *Sugar Ray Leonard and Other Noble Warriors*. McGraw-Hill, 1986.

LESLIE, LISA

Christopher, Matt. *On the Court with Lisa Leslie*. Little, Brown, 1998. Dougherty, Terri. *Lisa Leslie*. Abdo, 1999.

"Lisa Leslie." *Women's National Basketball Association [WNBA]*, http://www.wnba.com/playerfile/lisa_leslie.html

LEWIS, CARL

Aaseng, Nathan. *Carl Lewis: Legend Chaser*. Lerner Publications, 1985.

Lewis, Carl. *Inside Track: My Professional Life in Amateur Track and Field*. Simon and Schuster, 1992.

LIEBERMAN-CLINE, NANCY

Jones, Betty Millsaps. *Nancy Lieberman, Basketball's Magic Lady*. Harvey House, 1980.

Lieberman-Cline, Nancy, and Debby Jennings. *Lady Magic: The Autobiography of Nancy Lieberman-Cline*. Sagamore Publishing, 1991.

"Nancy Lieberman-Cline." *Women's National Basketball Association [WNBA]*, http://www.wnba.com/shock/coach.html

LISTON, SONNY

Josches, Nick. *The Devil and Sonny Liston*. Little, Brown, 2000.

Lipsyte, Robert. "Decades pass, and what's new under the sun?" *New York Times*, Feb. 25, 1994.

LOBO, REBECCA

Lobo, RuthAnn, and Rebecca Lobo. *The Home Team: Of Mothers, Daughters, and American Champions*. Kodansha America, 1996.

"Rebecca Lobo." *Women's National Basketball Association [WNBA]*, http://www.wnba.com/playerfile/rebecca_lobo.html

LOPEZ, NANCY

Brown, Clifton. "Lopez back on prowl seeking past glory." *New York Times*, May 14, 1998.

Lopez, Nancy. *The Education of a Woman Golfer*. Simon and Schuster, 1979.

"Nancy Lopez." *ESPN/GOLFonline*, http://www.igolf.com/profiles/

LOUGANIS, GREG

Louganis, Greg. *Breaking the Surface*. Random House, 1995.

Louganis, Greg, and Betsy Sikora Siino. *For the Life of Your Dog: A Complete Guide to Having a Dog in Your Life*. Pocket Books, 1999.

LOUIS, JOE

Barrow, Joe Louis. *Joe Louis: 50 Years an American Hero*. McGraw-Hill, 1988.

Louis, Joe. *Joe Louis, My Life*. Ecco Press, 1997.

Mead, Chris. *Champion: Joe Louis, Black Hero in White America*. Scribner, 1985.

LUKAS, D. WAYNE

Durso, Joseph. "Lukas gets his turn, and enters the Hall." *New York Times*, Aug. 10, 1999.

Nack, William. "Broken dream: Charismatic's Triple Crown bid came to a terrible end." *Sports Illustrated*, June 14, 1999.

MACK, CONNIE

Jordan, David M. *The Athletics of Philadelphia: Connie Mack's White Elephants, 1901-1954*. McFarland, 1999.

Kashatus, William C. *Connie Mack's '29 Triumph: The Rise and Fall of the Philadelphia Athletics Dynasty*. McFarland, 1999.

Mack, Connie. *My 66 Years in the Big Leagues: The Great Story of America's National Game*. Winston, 1950. Out of print.

MADDUX, GREG

Christopher, Matt. *On the Mound with Greg Maddux*. Little, Brown, 1997.

Macht, Norman L. *Greg Maddux*. Chelsea House, 1997.

Thornley, Stew. *Sports Great Greg Maddux*. Enslow, 1997.

MAN O' WAR

Farley, Walter. *Man O' War*. Random House, 1983 [fiction].

"Man O' War chosen as horse of the century." *Bergen Record Online*, Feb. 23, 1999, http://www.bergen.com/moresports/top10023199902236.htm

"Thoroughbred Champions: Top 100 Racehorses of the 20th Century." *Blood-Horse Magazine Online*, http://www.bloodhorse.com/tb_champions/top_100_list.html

MANTLE, MICKEY

Falkner, David. *The Last Hero: The Life of Mickey Mantle*. Simon and Schuster, 1995.

Ford, Edward [Whitey], and Mickey Mantle. *Whitey and Mickey: A Joint Autobiography of the Yankee Years*. Viking Press, 1976.

Honig, Donald. *Mays, Mantle, Snider: A Celebration*. Macmillan, 1987.

Mantle, Mickey. *My Favorite Summer, 1956*. Doubleday, 1991.

MARCIANO, ROCKY

Nack, Robert. "The Rock." *Sports Illustrated*, Aug. 23, 1993.

Sandomir, Richard. "Marciano docudrama is light on facts." *New York Times*, Apr. 30, 1999.

MARIS, ROGER

Allen, Maury. *Roger Maris: A Man for All Seasons*. D. I. Fine, 1986.

McNeil, William. *Ruth, Maris, McGwire and Sosa: Baseball's Single Season Home Run Champions*. McFarland, 1999.

MARTIN, CHRISTY

Hoffer, Richard. "Gritty woman." *Sports Illustrated*, Apr. 15, 1996.

"Martin, Christy." *Current Biography*, Oct. 1997.

Nieves, Evelyn. "A boxer in a hurry." *New York Times Magazine*, Nov. 3, 1996.

MATHIAS, BOB

Tassin, Myron. *Bob Mathias: The Life of the Olympic Champion*. St. Martin's Press, 1983.

Terrence, Chris. *Bob Mathias: Across the Fields of Gold*. Green Mountain Publishing, 1998.

MAYS, WILLIE

Grabowski, John F. *Willie Mays*. Chelsea House, 1990.

Honig, Donald. *Mays, Mantle, Snider: A Celebration*. Macmillan, 1987.

Mays, Willie. *Say Hey: The Autobiography of Willie Mays*. Simon and Schuster, 1988.

MCCRAY, NIKKI

Guzman, Ed. "Jump to a losing club hasn't fazed McCray." *New York Times*, July 3, 1998.

"Nikki McCray." *Women's National Basketball Association [WNBA]*, http://www.wnba.com/playerfile/nikki_mccray.html

MCENROE, JOHN

Evans, Richard. *McEnroe: A Rage for Perfection*. Simon and Schuster, 1982.

Evans, Richard. *McEnroe, Taming the Talent*. S. Greene, 1990.

Ross, Lillian. "John McEnroe's serve may have slowed down, but his mouth keeps on going." *New Yorker*, Sept. 8, 1997.

MCGRAW, JOHN

Alexander, Charles C. *John McGraw*. Viking, 1988.

Durso, Joseph. *Casey and Mr. McGraw*. Sporting News, 1989.

MCGWIRE, MARK

McNeil, William. *Ruth, Maris, McGwire and Sosa: Baseball's Single Season Home Run Champions*. McFarland, 1999.

MLB: Race for the Record. PolyGram Video, 1998 [videorecording].

Paisner, Daniel. *The Ball: Mark McGwire's 70th Home Run Ball and the Marketing of the American Dream*. Viking, 1999.

Rains, Rob. *Mark McGwire, Home Run Hero*. St. Martin's Press, 1998.

MILLER, CHERYL

"Cheryl Miller." *NBA.com OntheAir*, http://www.nba.com/ontheair/00421325.html

"Cheryl Miller." *Women's National Basketball Association [WNBA]*, http://www.wnba.com/mercury/coach.html

MILLER, SHANNON

Green, Septima. *Going for the Gold—Shannon Miller*. Avon Books, 1996.

Miller, Claudia Ann. *Shannon Miller: My Child, My Hero*. University of Oklahoma Press, 1999.

Quiner, Krista. *Shannon Miller: America's Most Decorated Gymnast*. Bradford Book Co., 1996.

MOODY, HELEN WILLS

"An American original." *Sports Illustrated*, Jan. 12, 1998 [obituary].

Engelmann, Larry. *The Goddess and the American Girl: The Story of Suzanne Lenglen and Helen Wills*. Oxford University Press, 1988.

MOSES, EDWIN

"Moses called an inspiration." *New York Times*, July 17, 1996.

"Edwin Moses: Hurdles." *Track and Field Hall of Fame*, http://www.usatf.org/athletes/hof/moses.shtml

MUSIAL, STAN

Grabowski, John. *Stan Musial*. Chelsea House, 1993.

Lansche, Jerry. *Stan the Man Musial: Born to Be a Ballplayer*. Taylor, 1994.

NAVRATILOVA, MARTINA

Blue, Adrianne. *Martina: The Lives and Times of Martina Navratilova*. Carol Pub. Group, 1995.

Navratilova, Martina. *Martina*. Knopf, 1985.

Zwerman, Gilda. *Martina Navratilova*. Chelsea House, 1995.

NELSON, BYRON

Nelson, Byron. *Byron Nelson: The Little Black Book*. Summit Publishing Group, 1995.

Nelson, Byron. *How I Played the Game*. Taylor, 1993.

NICKLAUS, JACK

Jacobs, Timothy. *The Golf Courses of Jack Nicklaus*. Gallery Books, 1989.

Nicklaus, Jack. *Jack Nicklaus: My Story*. Simon and Schuster, 1997.

Sampson, Curt. *The Eternal Summer: Palmer, Nicklaus, and Hogan in 1960, Golf's Golden Year*. Taylor, 1992.

NORMAN, GREG

Creighton, Susan. *Greg Norman*. Crestwood House, 1988.

St. John, Lauren. *Shark: The Biography of Greg Norman*. Rutledge Hill Press, 1998.

Vigeland, Carl A. *Stalking the Shark: Pressure and Passion on the Pro Golf Tour*. W. W. Norton, 1996.

OERTER, AL

Litsky, Frank. "Oerter, 63, is winning the duel with aging." *New York Times*, July 22, 1999.

"Al Oerter: Discus Throw." *Track and Field Hall of Fame*, http://www.usatf.org/athletes/hof/oerter.shtml

OTTO, KRISTIN

Johnson, William, and Anita Verschoth. "Out of the shadows; behind their newly breached wall, East Germany's wondrous athletes relish their greatest prize, freedom." *Sports Illustrated*, Nov. 27, 1989.

Litsky, Frank. "In the pool, opposites attract gold medals." *New York Times*, Sept. 26, 1988.

OWENS, JESSE

Baker, William J. *Jesse Owens: An American Life*. Free Press, 1986.

Jesse Owens: Champion Athlete. Schlessinger Video Productions, 1994 [videorecording].

Owens, Jesse. *Blackthink; My Life as Black Man and White Man*. Morrow, 1970.

Owens, Jesse. *Jesse: The Man Who Outran Hitler*. Ballantine Books, 1983.

PAIGE, SATCHEL

Holway, John. *Josh and Satch: The Life and Times of Josh Gibson and Satchel Paige*. Meckler, 1991.

Paige, Leroy. *Maybe I'll Pitch Forever: A Great Baseball Player Tells the Hilarious Story Behind the Legend*. University of Nebraska Press, 1993.

Ribowsky, Mark. *Don't Look Back: Satchel Paige in the Shadows of Baseball*. Simon and Schuster, 1994.

PALMER, ARNOLD

Hauser, Thomas. *Arnold Palmer: A Personal Journey*. Collins Publishers, 1994.

Palmer, Arnold. *A Golfer's Life*. Ballantine Books, 1999.

Sampson, Curt. *The Eternal Summer: Palmer, Nicklaus, and Hogan in 1960, Golf's Golden Year*. Taylor, 1992.

PATTERSON, FLOYD

Anderson, Dave. "Five champions, past and present, debate boxing's curse." *New York Times*, Apr. 5, 1998.

Brown, David, et al. "Boxing's last gentleman." *New Yorker*, July 31, 1995.

Patterson, Floyd. *Inside Boxing*. Regnery, 1974. Out of print.

PELÉ

Hahn, James. *Pelé! The Sports Career of Edson do Nascimento*. Crestwood House, 1981.

Pelé. *My Life and the Beautiful Game: The Autobiography of Pelé*. Doubleday, 1977.

Pelé: The Master and His Method. Magnetic Video, 1981 [videorecording].

PERROT, KIM

Balleza, Maureen. "Kim Perrot, 32, leader of WNBA. champions." *New York Times*, Aug. 20, 1999 [obituary].

"A short but bright life; Kim Perrot 1967–1999." *Women's National Basketball Association [WNBA]*, http://www.wnba.com/features/perrot_tribute.html

PETTY, RICHARD

Bongard, Tim. *The Cars of the King: Richard Petty*. Sports Publishing, 1997.

Petty, Richard. *King Richard I: The Autobiography of America's Greatest Auto Racer*. Macmillan, 1986.

Vehorn, Frank. *Farewell to the King*. Down Home Press, 1992.

REESE, PEE WEE

Golenbock, Peter. *Teammates*. Harcourt Brace Jovanovich, 1990.

Schoor, Gene. *The Pee Wee Reese Story*. J. Messner, 1956. Out of print.

RETTON, MARY LOU

Calkins, Laurel Brubaker. "10 again." *People Weekly*, July 15, 1996.

Retton, Mary Lou. *Mary Lou: Creating an Olympic Champion*. McGraw-Hill, 1986.

Washington, Rosemary G. *Mary Lou Retton: Power Gymnast*. Lerner Publications, 1985.

RICKEY, BRANCH

Frommer, Harvey. *Rickey and Robinson: The Men Who Broke Baseball's Color Barrier*. MacMillan, 1982.

Polner, Murray. *Branch Rickey: A Biography*. Atheneum, 1982.

Rickey, Branch. *Branch Rickey's Little Blue Book: Wit and Strategy from Baseball's Last Wise Man*. Macmillan, 1995.

RIGGS, BOBBY

Bobby Riggs: Ageless Tennis. Academy Entertainment, 1988 [videorecording].

Finn, Robin. "Bobby Riggs, brash impresario of tennis world, is dead at 77." *New York Times*, Oct. 27, 1995.

Garner, Joe. *And the Crowd Goes Wild: Relive the Most Celebrated Sporting Events Ever Broadcast*. Sourcebooks, 1999 [book and audio discs].

RIPKEN, CAL, JR.

Campbell, Jim. *Cal Ripken, Jr.* Chelsea House, 1997.

Ripken, Cal. *The Only Way I Know*. Viking, 1997.

Rosenfeld, Harvey. *Iron Man: The Cal Ripken, Jr. Story*. St. Martin's Press, 1995.

RIZZOTTI, JENNIFER

Cavanaugh, Jack. "A season of losing and learning; Rizzotti bringing in fans but not victories as a pro." *New York Times*, Feb. 20, 1997.

"Jennifer Rizzotti." *Women's National Basketball Association [WNBA]*, http://www.wnba.com/playerfile/jennifer_rizzoti.html

ROBINSON, JACKIE

Falkner, David. *Great Time Coming: The Life of Jackie Robinson, from Baseball to Birmingham*. Simon and Schuster, 1995.

Frommer, Harvey. *Rickey and Robinson: The Men Who Broke Baseball's Color Barrier*. MacMillan, 1982.

Jackie Robinson. A&E Home Video, 1994 [videorecording].

Rampersad, Arnold. *Jackie Robinson: A Biography*. Knopf, 1997.

ROBINSON, SUGAR RAY

Anderson, Dave. "The legacy of Sugar Ray Robinson." *New York Times*, Mar. 7, 1993.

Gutman, Bill. *Pro Sports Champions*. Pocket Books, 1990.

Robinson, Sugar Ray. *Sugar Ray*. Da Capo Press, 1994.

ROSE, PETE

Klein, Frederick C. "Should baseball gamble on Pete Rose?" *Wall Street Journal*, Nov. 1, 1999.

Rose, Pete. *Pete Rose: My Story*. Macmillan, 1989.

Sokolove, Michael Y. *Hustle: The Myth, Life, and Lies of Pete Rose*. Simon and Schuster, 1990.

RUDOLPH, WILMA

Krull, Kathleen. *Wilma Unlimited: How Wilma Rudolph Became the World's Fastest Woman*. Harcourt Brace Jovanovich, 1996.

Sherrow, Victoria. *Wilma Rudolph: Olympic Champion*. Chelsea House, 1995.

Wilma Rudolph. Schlessinger Video Productions, 1995 [videorecording].

RUTH, BABE

Babe Ruth: The Life Behind the Legend. HBO Home Video, 1999 [videorecording].

Creamer, Robert W. *Babe: The Legend Comes to Life*. Simon and Schuster, 1992.

McNeil, William. *Ruth, Maris, McGwire and Sosa: Baseball's Single Season Home Run Champions*. McFarland, 1999.

Ruth, Babe. *The Babe Ruth Story*. Signet, 1992.

Shaughnessy, Dan. *Curse of the Bambino*. Penguin USA, reprint 1991.

RYAN, NOLAN

Gutman, Bill. *Pro Sports Champions*. Pocket Books, 1990.

Rappoport, Ken. *Nolan Ryan—The Ryan Express*. Maxwell Macmillan International, 1992.

Ryan, Nolan. *Miracle Man: Nolan Ryan, the Autobiography*. G. K. Hall, 1993.

SALES, NYKESHA

Huntington, Ann Seaton. "The shot heard round the wrangle." *New York Times*, Mar. 1, 1998.

"Sales, Nykesha." *Current Biography*, June 1999.

"Nykesha Sales." *Women's National Basketball Association [WNBA]*, http://www.wnba.com/playerfile/nykesha_sales.html

SAMPRAS, PETE

Branham, H. *Sampras: A Legend in the Works*. Bonus Books, 1996.

Miller, Calvin Craig. *Pete Sampras*. Morgan Reynolds, 1998.

Sherrow, Victoria. *Sports Great Pete Sampras*. Enslow, 1996.

SCULLY, VIN

Sandomir, Richard. "Chairside with Vin Scully, for maybe a final call." *New York Times*, Oct. 24, 1997.

"1992 Hall of Fame Inductee Vin Scully." *American Sportscasters Association Hall of Fame*. http://www.americansportscasters.com/people/scully.htm

SEATTLE SLEW

Cady, Steve. *Seattle Slew*. Out of print.

Golden Greats of Horse Racing. Front Row Video, 1989 [videorecording].

"Thoroughbred Champions: Top 100 Racehorses of the 20th Century." *Blood-Horse Magazine Online*, http://www.bloodhorse.com/tb_champions/top_100_list.html

SEAVER, TOM

Macht, Norman L. *Tom Seaver*. Chelsea House, 1994.

Seaver, Tom. *The Art of Pitching*. W. Morrow, reissue 1994.

Sexton, Joe. "Seaver, Fingers elected to shrine." *New York Times*, Jan. 8, 1992.

SECRETARIAT

Golden Greats of Horse Racing. Front Row Video, 1989 [videorecording].

"Thoroughbred Champions: Top 100 Racehorses of the 20th Century." *Blood-Horse Magazine Online*, http://www.bloodhorse.com/tb_champions/top_100_list.html

SELES, MONICA

Layden, Joseph. *Return of a Champion: The Monica Seles Story*. St. Martin's Paperbacks, 1996.

Seles, Monica. *Monica: from Fear to Victory*. HarperCollins, 1996.

SHOEMAKER, WILLIE

Golden Greats of Horse Racing. Front Row Video, 1989 [videorecording].

Phillips, Louis. *Willie Shoemaker*. Crestwood House, 1988.

Shoemaker, Bill. *Shoemaker*. Doubleday, 1988.

SMITH, KATIE

Bondy, Filip. "A Larry Bird of women's basketball in Final Four." *New York Times*, Apr. 3, 1993.

"Katie Smith." *Women's National Basketball Association [WNBA]*, http://www.wnba.com/playerfile/katie_smith.html

SNEAD, SAM

Snead, Sam. *The Game I Love: Wisdom, Insight, and Instruction from Golf's Greatest Player*. Ballantine Books, 1997.

Snead, Sam. *Slammin' Sam*. Donald I. Fine, 1986.

SNIDER, DUKE

Bjarkman, Peter C. *Duke Snider*. Chelsea House, 1994.

Honig, Donald. *Mays, Mantle, Snider: A Celebration*. Macmillan, 1987.

Snider, Duke. *The Duke of Flatbush*. Kensington, 1988.

SORENSTAM, ANNIKA

Morfit, Cameron. "More reign forecast for Sorenstam." *Sports Illustrated*, Sept. 28, 1998.

"Annika Sorenstam." *ESPN/GOLFonline*, http://www.igolf.com/profiles/

SOSA, SAMMY

Duncan, Patricia J. *Sosa! Baseball's Home Run Hero*. Simon and Schuster, 1998.

Gutman, Bill. *Sammy Sosa: A Biography*. Pocket Books, 1998.

McNeil, William. *Ruth, Maris, McGwire and Sosa: Baseball's Single Season Home Run Champions*. McFarland, 1999.

MLB: Race for the Record. PolyGram Video, 1998 [videorecording].

SPINKS, MICHAEL

Berger, Phil. "Graceful and grateful, Spinks calls it quits." *New York Times*, July 28, 1988.

"Catching up with...Michael Spinks, champion boxer." *Sports Illustrated*, Aug. 9, 1999.

SPITZ, MARK

Edelson, Paula. *Superstars of Men's Swimming and Diving*. Chelsea House, 1998.

Garner, Joe. *And the Crowd Goes Wild: Relive the Most Celebrated Sporting Events Ever Broadcast*. Sourcebooks, 1999 [book and audio discs].

Olsen, James T. *Mark Spitz: The Shark*. Children's Press, 1974.

STALEY, DAWN

Rhoden, William C. "A hometown hero, who is always at home." *New York Times*, Apr. 13, 1996.

"Dawn Staley." *Women's National Basketball Association [WNBA]*, http://www.wnba.com/playerfile/dawn_staley.html

STARBIRD, KATE

Araton, Harvey. "Make no mistake: Women in the Final Four are genuine athletes." *New York Times*, Mar. 30, 1997.

"Kate Starbird." *Women's National Basketball Association [WNBA]*, http://www.wnba.com/playerfile/kate_starbird.html

STEDING, KATY

Gogol, Sara. *Katy Steding: Pro Basketball Pioneer*. Lerner Publications, 1998.

Katy Steding Basketball Academy, http://www.katysteding.com/

STENGEL, CASEY

Creamer, Robert W. *Stengel: His Life and Times*. Simon and Schuster, 1984.

Nicholson, Lois P. *Casey Stengel*. Chelsea House, 1995.

Stengel, Casey. *Casey at the Bat: The Story of My Life in Baseball*. Random House, 1962.

STEWART, PAYNE

Arkush, Michael. *I Remember Payne Stewart: Personal Memories of Golf's Most Dapper Champion by the People Who Knew Him Best*. Cumberland House, 2000.

Reilly, Rick. "A colorful life: Living well was as important as playing well." *Sports Illustrated*, Nov. 1, 1999.

"Payne Stewart." *ESPN/GOLFonline*, http://www.igolf.com/profiles/

SWOOPES, SHERYL

Burby, Liza N. *Sheryl Swoopes, All-Star Basketball Player*. Rosen Pub. Group, 1997.

Swoopes, Sheryl. *Bounce Back*. Taylor, 1996.

"Sheryl Swoopes." *Women's National Basketball Association [WNBA]*, http://www.wnba.com/playerfile/sheryl_swoopes.html

THOMPSON, TINA

"Tina Thompson." *USA Basketball*, http://www.usabasketball.com/usa_bios/tina_thompson.htm

"Tina Thompson." *Women's National Basketball Association [WNBA]*, http://www.wnba.com/playerfile/tina_thompson.html

THORPE, JIM

Coffey, Wayne R. *Jim Thorpe*. Blackbirch Press, 1993.

Lipsyte, Robert. *Jim Thorpe: 20th-Century Jock*. HarperCollins, 1993.

Updyke, Rosemary K. *Jim Thorpe, the Legend Remembered*. Pelican Publishing, 1997.

TILDEN, BILL

Deford, Frank. *Big Bill Tilden: The Triumphs and the Tragedy*. Simon and Schuster, 1976.

Voss, Arthur. *Tilden and Tennis in the Twenties*. Whitston, 1985.

TYSON, MIKE

Berger, Phil. *Blood Season: Tyson and the World of Boxing*. Morrow, 1989.

Heller, Peter. *Bad Intentions: The Mike Tyson Story*. New American Library, 1989.

Hoffer, Richard. *A Savage Business: The Comeback and Comedown of Mike Tyson*. Simon and Schuster, 1998.

UNSER, AL, JR.

Bentley, Karen. *The Unsers*. Chelsea House, 1996.

Nobles, Charlie. "Unser learns some things in IROC while showing how to win." *New York Times*, Feb. 15, 1997.

Siano, Joseph. "2 families in 24-hour Daytona race." *New York Times*, Jan. 27, 1991.

UNSER, AL, SR.

Bentley, Karen. *The Unsers*. Chelsea House, 1996.

Siano, Joseph. "For Unser, nearing 55 is a sign to retire." *New York Times*, May 18, 1994.

Siano, Joseph. "2 families in 24-hour Daytona race." *New York Times*, Jan. 27, 1991.

VAN DYKEN, AMY

Araton, Harvey. "Lesson by the poolside: Life's more than a gold." *New York Times*, July 21, 1996.

Longman, Jere. "Van Dyken swims to history with 4th gold." *New York Times*, July 27, 1996.

WAGNER, HONUS

DeValeria, Dennis. *Honus Wagner: A Biography*. H. Holt, 1996.

Hittner, Arthur D. *Honus Wagner: The Life of Baseball's "Flying Dutchman."* McFarland, 1996.

Kavanaugh, Jack. *Honus Wagner*. Chelsea House, 1994.

WILLIAMS, SERENA

Howard, Johnette. "Bragging rights." *Tennis*, Nov. 1999.

Price, S. L. "Father knew best." *Sports Illustrated*, Sept. 20, 1999.

"Serena Williams wins at U.S. Open; first black female champion since 1958." *Jet*, Sept. 27, 1999.

WILLIAMS, TED

Curry, Jack. "Williams and Fenway still click." *New York Times*, July 14, 1999.

Linn, Edward. *Hitter: The Life and Turmoils of Ted Williams*. Harcourt Brace Jovanovich, 1993.

Williams, Ted. *My Turn at Bat: The Story of My Life*. Simon and Schuster, 1988.

WILLIAMS, VENUS

Aronson, Virginia. *Venus Williams*. Chelsea House, 1999.

Howard, Johnette. "Bragging rights." *Tennis*, Nov. 1999.

Teitelbaum, Michael. *Grand Slam Stars: Martina Hingis and Venus Williams*. HarperActive, 1998.

WOODS, TIGER

Brown, Clifton. "Woods triumphs in match made in (TV) heaven." *New York Times*, Aug. 3, 1999.

Rosaforte, Tim. *Tiger Woods: The Makings of a Champion*. St. Martin's Press, 1997.

Tiger Woods: Son, Hero and Champion. CBS Video, 1997 [videorecording].

Woods, Earl. *Playing Through: Straight Talk on Hard Work, Big Dreams, and Adventures with Tiger*. HarperCollins, 1998.

YOUNG, CY

Browning, Reed. *Cy Young: A Baseball Life*. University of Massachusetts Press, 2000.

Macht, Norman L. *Cy Young*. Chelsea House, 1992.

Glossary

acclimated To become used to a new situation; to adapt to new living arrangements or a new environment.

accolade An award or expression of praise; in this context, for performing well in a sporting event.

Achilles tendon The tendon joining the muscles in the leg calf to the bone of the heel; a particularly common area of injury in athletic competition.

all-around competition In gymnastics, the winner of the all-around is the gymnast who gains the highest combined score in several events. In women's gymnastics, the four events are floor exercise, vault, uneven bars, and balance beam. In men's gymnastics, the events are floor exercise, pommel horse, vault, rings, parallel bars, and the horizontal bar. In most gymnastics matches or tournaments, there is an award for the team with the best all-around score and the individual with the best all-around score.

alliterative When two or more words or syllables in a sentence or phrase start with the same initial letter. For example, "Mickey Mantle mashed a monster moonshot," is alliterative because of the way five of the words begin with the letter "m." It's also a clever way of saying that Mantle hit a long home run.

Amateur Athletic Union (AAU) A large, nonprofit, volunteer organization that oversees amateur sports programs throughout the United States. The group concentrates on preparing athletes for Olympic competition and follows the motto, "Sports for all, forever." It was founded in 1888.

amyotrophic lateral sclerosis (ALS) A neurological disorder characterized by progressive degeneration of motor neuron cells in the spinal cord and brain, which ultimately results in paralysis and death. The disease, also known as Lou Gehrig's disease, takes its less-scientific name from Lou Gehrig, a baseball player with the New York Yankees in the late 1920s and 1930s, who was forced to retire in 1939 as a result of the loss of motor control caused by the disease.

anemia Condition in which the body is lacking in red blood cells.

anterior cruciate ligament The front ligament of the two ligaments in the knee which cross one another and help stabilize the joint; this ligament is often injured in athletic competition. "Blowing out the ACL" has become one of the most common phrases in all of sports.

antic Zany, good-natured, playfully funny.

aplomb Good-natured in spirit and action; unflappable..

apocryphal Description of quoted statements that are of questionable authenticity, and/or wrongfully attributed.

appendectomy A surgical procedure in which a person's appendix is removed. The appendix is a small tube attached to the large intestine that has no known medical use—a person can live without an appendix with no complications. Most appendectomy's are emergency in nature—the appendix becomes blocked, which causes it to swell and its tissue to die. It will burst if not removed, which can be fatal.

apprentice An individual who learns a craft or trade by practical experience under the supervision of an expert.

Aryan Term used in Nazi Germany to describe a member of the so-called "master race" of non-Jewish Caucasians with Nordic features.

ascent An upward climb, either literally, as in climbing a mountain slope, or figuratively, as in moving upward in a social situation.

assist Action of a team athlete who passes a ball or puck to a teammate who then scores a goal, or makes a putout; statistical measure utilized to recognize such actions.

asthma A disease that causes a constriction in the lungs, which makes it very difficult to breath and often causes coughing and shortness of breath. It can range from very mild to severe cases that can be fatal.

autocratic Operating with absolute power or authority; a ruler who operates with complete power and authority is an autocratic leader.

bar examination Exhaustive test given to recent graduates of law school who attempt to pass in order to gain license to practice law in the individual state administering the exam.

barnstorm To travel from one location to the next, stopping in cities and towns along the way to play a game against local competition. Most often used in reference to baseball teams in early twentieth century America, but also still used today to describe amateur and semipro teams that travel the United States seeking challenges.

battery In baseball, the term used to describe a pitcher and catcher of a baseball team.

belied To have given a false impression or to have actually proved something false.

bonus babies Term used for outstanding draftees of professional athletic teams who are paid large sums of money for signing a contract.

breaking horses Young horses (and wild horses) are unaccustomed to humans and do not like to be ridden. A horse will buck and fight as hard as it can to keep a human from putting a saddle on and riding it. It is up to a trainer to "break" the horse—to acclimate him to human beings and to make him calm enough to accept saddle and rider without putting up even the slightest fight.

brooding To dwell on something and view it in a negative manner, to ponder gloomily.

bullpen The area on a baseball field where pitchers who are waiting to go into a game warm up by throwing to a catcher. The pitchers who wait in the bullpen are known as relief pitchers; they replace the starting pitcher when he gives up too many hits or runs or is injured.

cadence A rhythmic flow or sequence of words and/or sounds in language.

cascaded Poured or rushed, as if in a waterfall. In this context, the announcer's words filled every part of the stadium.

cavorting Engaging in extravagant social behavior.

chauvinist Description of an individual who holds feelings of superiority over the opposite sex. Most often used in the phrase "male chauvinist pig," which became famous when aging male tennis player Bobby Riggs challenged top female player Billie Jean King to a match in the 1970s. King won the match easily.

chemotherapy A common medical treatment, most often for cancer, that involves administering closely regulated doses of powerful drugs designed to kill cancer cells. The drugs are so strong that, while they do kill cancer cells, they can sometimes have negative side effects on the person taking them, such as nausea, fatigue, and hair loss.

clutch In motor vehicles with a manual transmission (as opposed to an automatic transmission), the clutch is the mechanism that allows the driver to shift from one gear to the next.

coiffed Hair that is properly styled by combing, brushing, or curling.

color barrier The unofficial policy of segregation in Major League Baseball that barred nonwhites from competing until 1947, when Jackie Robinson broke the barrier by playing for the Brooklyn Dodgers of the National League.

contusion A bruise or other injury to the skin that does not involve a cut.

Cy Young Award Given annually to the best pitcher in the American League and the best pitcher in the National League. The award is named after Denton "Cy" Young, who is the winningest pitcher in Major League Baseball. He won 515 games in his career that spanned the 1890s and into the 1900s.

demeanor The manner or way that you present yourself to others. A "calm demeanor" demonstrates cool under fire and shows anyone who is watching that you can remain outwardly calm no matter what emotions are present under the surface.

denigrating Insulting and belittling.

designated hitter In baseball, a player who bats in place of the pitcher and who does not play a position in the field. Pitchers are traditionally weak hitters, so designated hitters are used to generate more offense. The DH, as it is known, is a source of great debate because it is used in the American League of Major League Baseball but is not used in the National League. Baseball purists continue to fight the DH rule, saying it takes away from the way the game was meant to be played, but many fans support the DH and the increased offense

diabetes A common disease characterized by the inadequate production of insulin and excessive amounts of sugar in the blood and urine. The disease can be caused by hereditary and environmental factors and causes damage to the kidneys.

diligent Steady and exuberant effort towards achieving a goal; hardworking, steady.

diphtheria A contagious disease characterized by the forming of a false membrane, usually in the throat; produces a toxin which inflames the heart and nervous system.

discus A plastic or wood disc that is thick in the center and thrown for distance in track and field events.

dismount In gymnastics, the dismount is the move gymnasts make to end their routine by leaving the apparatus they are on, such as the balance beam, uneven bars, rings, and others. The dismount move is usually one of the most difficult in the entire routine, and a gymnast must execute the dismount flawlessly to have any hope of receiving a perfect score of 10.

dissipations Intemperate living; overindulging in alcohol consumption or immoral behavior.

doubles In tennis and other racquet sports, doubles competition involves two players against another pair of players in a match.

draft The process by which individuals from high school and college are selected by the organizations and clubs of professional athletic leagues for the purposes of acquiring contract rights to individual players. Also, a system formerly used to select young men for mandatory service in the U.S. Army.

draft evasion Avoiding mandatory service in the United States military by refusing to register for the draft, which determines which people who are required to report for active duty, or by leaving the country or otherwise not reporting for duty once one has already been drafted. Draft evasion played a significant role in the Vietnam War during the 1960s and 1970s; boxer Muhammad Ali refused to fight on religious grounds and was convicted of draft evasion.

earned run average (ERA) Baseball statistic measuring performance of pitchers; calculated by dividing the total of earned runs scored against a pitcher by the total number of innings pitched, then multiplying that number by nine.

ecumenical A general extent of influence; encompassing, including, or representing a variety of religious persuasions.

equestrian Refers to sporting events that involve horseback riding. This includes such events as steeplechase, dressage, and the modern pentathlon.

expansion team A team that joins a professional athletic association or league well after the group of originally chartered teams was established.

farm system Network of teams affiliated with major league clubs that develop younger players' skills and abilities at minor league levels until they are deemed ready for major league play.

Fireman of the Year Annual award given to the outstanding relief pitcher in each league of Major League Baseball, so named because relief pitchers often "save" ballgames for their teams in precarious situations and thus "put out the fire."

flaunting Making a flashy or ostentatious display of wealth, success, or good fortune.

fluke A stroke of luck or an unexpected and perhaps dubious result in an athletic competition when a lesser team or performer defeats a much more skilled and talented opponent.

foaled Gave birth to, in horse terms. Young horses are known as foals.

free agent A professional athlete whose current contract has expired, making him or her free to negotiate and sign with any other professional team.

free throw An unguarded shot in basketball taken from the free throw line, which is 15 feet from the basket. A player is awarded a free throw, which is worth one point, when a player on the opposing team commits a personal foul (a rules violation that involves contact between players) or a technical foul (a procedural foul and/or misconduct).

gangly Loose-limbed and awkward in appearance, often characterized by long arms and legs and a skinny body.

garish Excessively vivid and bright coloring.

genesis The beginning of an event or a seminal point of action.

girth The measurement around a person's body. An overweight person might be said to have a large girth.

Gold Glove Annual Major League Baseball award bestowed upon one individual at each fielding position in the American and National Leagues. The award honors the person who is judged to be the best fielder at that position as determined by a vote of coaches and managers. The award was started in 1957 by the Rawlings Sportings Goods company in conjunction with *The Sporting News* magazine.

Grand Slam (golf) The Grand Slam of men's is made up of four tournaments that are each known as "Major" tournaments on the professional tour. They are, in order that they are held each year, the Masters, in April; the U.S. Open, in June; the British Open, in July; and the PGA Championship, in August. The British Open is the oldest of the four events, having first been held in 1860, while the Masters, which rewards its winner the famous Green Jacket, is the most famous. Since the Masters was first held in 1934, no man has won all four Majors in one year. Prior to the Masters, when the Grand Slam included the U.S. and British Open and the U.S. and British Amateur championships, Bobby Jones was the only man to win all four in a single year, achieving the feat in 1930. The women's Grand Slam of golf includes the U.S. Women's Open, the LPGA Championship, the Colgate Dinah Shore Tournament, and the du Maurier Ltd. Classic.

Grand Slam (tennis) Tennis's Grand Slam is made up of the top four tournaments on the professional tour. They are, in order that they are held each year, the Australian Open, the French Open, Wimbledon, and the U.S. Open. The most famous of the four is Wimbledon, which is played on grass each year at the All England Lawn Tennis and Croquet Club in Great Britain. Only two men—Don Budge (1938) and Rod Laver (1962 and 1967) have won all four tournaments in the same year. Three women—Maureen Connolly (1953), Margaret Smith Court (1970), and Steffi Graf (1988)—have accomplished the feat.

Great Depression Period in the United States between the stock market crash of 1929 and the beginning of World War II; marked by poor economic conditions, high unemployment, and low economic and social confidence.

green, the Area of a golf course at which the hole is located and where players utilize the club known as the putter to strike the ball. The green is mowed much shorter than the other parts of a golf course and the ball moves much faster on the short-cut surface.

ground strokes A type of stroke used to hit the ball in tennis, most often made from the baseline (the line at the very back of the court). The ground stroke can be forehand or backhand; shots hit as a ground stroke most often travel from one baseline all the way to the opponent's baseline.

grueling A physically punishing athletic competition or event that drives an athlete to the point of exhaustion.

hamstring Any of three muscles at the back of the thigh that control flexion and rotation in the leg. Hamstring injuries are very common in sports, as the sudden start and stop motions required in most sports, as well as the intense stress put on the muscles, often lead to painful tears and strains.

heavyweight A boxing classification determined by weight, usually being at least 198 pounds and without limit.

hit-and-run In baseball, the hit-and-run play involves the batter at the plate and any baserunners who are on base at the time. The play occurs when, as the opposing pitcher makes his pitch to the batter, the baserunner(s) take off running before the ball reaches the batter. If the play works correctly, the batter hits the ball safely for a base hit, allowing the baserunner(s) to keep running for one (or more) extra bases. Some experts prefer to call the play the "run-and-hit" since the running occurs first.

Home Run Derby Event in which baseball players engage in a home run-hitting contest; annual event at the Major League Baseball All-Star festivities in which players swing at pitches thrown by a batting practice coach to determine who can hit the most home runs.

iconic Description of a person or thing given great deference and largely uncritical respect. An icon is a person who has reached legendary status.

incarnate Made manifest and comprehensible.

incentive An inducement to perform or act in a certain manner; many professional athletes have clauses in their contracts that promise more money for reaching particular levels of individual or team achievement.

incompetent Inadequate for the situation that is at hand; lacking talent or knowledge.

incumbent In political terms, a person who occupies a title or office. In sports, the term is used to refer to a person or team who already occupies a position that another person or team desires. For example, a person who wins a tennis tournament is the incumbent champion when the tournament is held the following year—other players try to defeat that player and win the championship he or she once held.

indefatigable Untiring; unflagging; unable to be beaten down, no matter how bad a situation seems.

indicted To be charged with a crime after the finding of a grand jury.

ingrate Ungrateful person.

Jazz Age Period in the 1920s in which the national economy was very successful and jazz music first came to prominence in the United States; "The Roaring '20s."

laurels A laurel is actually an evergreen tree that features leaves, flowers and berries. At some point, a crown was made using laurel branches and that crown was awarded as a symbol of excellence. Thus, someone who wins a sporting event or receives praise of some kind is said to receive laurels.

length A unit of measure in horse racing describing distances between horses. One length is meant to represent the approximate length of the average horse.

malicious Mean-spirited, or intending to cause harm or pain to another individual without a good reason for doing so.

mare A female horse at a fully mature or breeding age.

milestone A significant event in a person's life, or in this case, sports career. These are often tied to statistical achievements in sports—hitting 500 home runs, winning 300 games, and so on.

misanthrope A person who hates mankind and everything it stands for.

mitochondrial myopathy A form of muscular dystrophy, usually diagnosed in children, that makes the body unable to use oxygen rapidly enough to provide sufficient energy for athletic (or even everyday) activities. The cause of the disease is unknown.

mixed doubles Match in tennis in which each side consists of one man and one woman playing together as a team.

muckrakers Members of the media who try to stir up trouble by digging up facts or stories from people's backgrounds. Most often used in reference to journalists who cover politics.

mythos Patterns of belief often expressing symbolic attitudes in a culture.

NASCAR Acronym of the National Association of Stock Car Auto Racing. NASCAR is the governing organization that oversees the most popular auto racing series in the United States, the Winston Cup. Drivers compete in racing versions of regular automobile models—the Chevrolet Monte Carlo and the Ford Taurus, to name two. This is what the term "stock car" refers to—the first cars driven in NASCAR races were stock factory models with few modifications. Today's race cars look the same on the outside, but the interior and the engines of the NASCAR racers are very different from the cars found on America's freeways. With more than 30 races across the United States and popular drivers such as Jeff Gordon and Dale Jarrett leading the way, NASCAR races have become the largest spectator sport in the United States.

National Collegiate Athletic Association (NCAA) The governing body for collegiate athletics in the United States. It includes more than 1,200 schools, conferences, and other groups who have an interest in college sports. The NCAA monitors rules regarding who is eligible to play college sports and also oversees officiating and the rules of play for each sport it oversees. The main NCAA offices are located in Indianapolis, Indiana.

nucleus In scientific terms, the nucleus is the center of an atom, which is the tiny piece of matter that all things in the universe are made of. In sports terms, the nucleus of a team is the group of players who are most important to that team's success. Take away any one member of a team's nucleus—by injury or trade, for example—and it's likely that the team will not win as many games as it expected before the player was lost.

nutritionist A scientist or other professional who specializes in the study of food and it's effects on the human body.

paraglider A combination parachute/fan-driven glider that was used by a man calling himself "Fan Man" to fly into the ring before the start of the November 1993 fight between Evander Holyfield and Riddick Bowe that was held outdoors in Las Vegas, Nevada.

penalty kicks A soccer term for a kick taken from the penalty spot area by a player against the opposing goalie without any players closer than 10 yards away; the shot is completely undefended. Because the shooter scores the vast majority of the time on a penalty kick, it is awarded only for the most serious rule violations, and for fouls committed by the defense within its own penalty area. Penalty kicks are also used to break a tie and decide the final outcome of a game when overtime periods fail to determine a winner. In a tiebreaker, each team takes five penalty kicks, and the team making the most goals is declared the winner.

pennant A flag symbolizing a sports championship; mostly associated with Major League Baseball and the champions of the respective American and National Leagues.

Penrod Trophy Annual award given to the top cyclist in the world based on performance in races over a calendar year..

pentathlon An Olympic sport that has its origins in military service. Competitors are required to participate in shooting, fencing, equestrian, swimming, and cross-country running events.

persistence Continuing to take a course of action despite meeting with interference or difficulty. Battling on despite the fact that the odds might be stacked against you.

personification The representation of a thing or a concept by a person who is very closely associated with that thing or concept. A famous athlete is so involved in his or her sport that he or she comes to represent a physical representation of that sport.

phenom In sports, a young player who shows incredible talent and the potential to be a superstar.

pilloried An individual or group being publicly punished or scorned as a result of particular actions or beliefs by that individual.

pine tar Tar distilled from the wood of a pine tree; used on baseball bats to give the batter a better grip on the bat to improve the striking of the ball.

pitch around In baseball, it is said teams sometimes elect to walk or "pitch around" a particularly skilled batter so as to face a lesser batter instead. The batter will be either be intentionally walked or he will receive garbage pitches that, while not intentional balls, are too far out of the strike zone to hit.

pits Area of an automobile racetrack near the course in which the cars are serviced during qualifying and during the actual race. Cars are said to go in for a "pit stop."

platelets Small, flattened bodies of blood.

playoffs In most team sports, teams compete during the regular season to see which teams will win the most games and qualify for postseason competition, which are known as the playoffs. In the playoffs, the top teams face each other for the right to move on to the next level in the quest for a championship. Using either a single-game elimination or a multi-game series to determine the winner, the playoffs end when one team remains unbeaten and is named the champion of that sport.

pluck Determination and courage in the face of long odds.

point guard position in basketball usually occupied by one of the shorter players on a team, who has the best ability to dribble the basketball up the court on offense, organize offensive plays on the court, and distribute the basketball to teammates most frequently.

posthumously An event that occurs after a person's death. For example, when baseball player Roberto Clemente was killed in a plane crash, he was honored "posthumously" for all the charity work he did while he was alive.

power forward Position in basketball usually occupied by a player much taller than a guard, yet shorter than a center; specializes in rebounding and physical play with the ability to score.

predatory Literally, intending to injure or harm another creature identified as your prey. In sports, it means having the instincts to defeat your opponent when you have them down, to finish them off.

prejudice A negative, preconceived opinion about a person or thing that is formed with no real knowledge of what that person or thing is really like.

promoters Individuals or a group of people who assume the financial responsibilities for boxing matches (and other athletic events), including contracting the opponents, renting the site, and collecting the box office proceeds.

protege Individual who learns a craft or skill under the instruction and advice of a successful individual in that particular field..

protracted Extended in time; an event that goes on and on.

pugnacious A belligerent or combative nature; desiring to argue or quarrel constantly.

reneged Went back on one's word; made an offer and then canceled or backed out on that offer for no good reason. For example, a boxing promoter might set up a fight involving two fighters, then change his mind at the last minute and bring in two different boxers for the actual fight. He reneged on his deal with the first two boxers.

rogue A mischevious person known for dishonesty or unfair play.

runs batted in (RBI) In baseball, runs batted in are the number of runners that are able to score during the course of a player's at bats. The total includes the player himself, so if a batter hits a home run with two runners on base, he gets credit for three RBI—one for each of the runners, and one for himself.

Ryder Cup Trophy given to the winning team in a golf competition between teams comprising players from the United States against a team of European players. The competition is held every two years and alternates between an American golf course and a European one.

Scholastic Aptitude Test (SAT) Standardized test given to most high school students planning on attending a college or university; tests abilities in areas of study emphasized in high school; the results are used as a barometer for admission into college, and for eligibility of collegiate athletes as freshmen.

Senior Tour A series of professional golf tournaments that are only open to those golfers who are age 50 or older. Started years ago as a means of letting older golfers continue their playing careers, the Senior Tour is now extremely popular thanks to the presence of such legendary golfers as Tom Watson, Jack Nicklaus, Hale Irwin, Lee Trevino, Gary Player, and more.

sharecropping System in which a tenant farmer is provided with credit, seed, tools, housing, etc., farms land and shares in the proceeds with the landowner.

short shrift Very little attention or consideration given to a particular subject.

Silver Slugger Award Annual award given in the American and National Leagues of Major League Baseball; the award is given to the player at each position (third base, second base, etc.) who has the highest batting average of all players who play that position.

singles In tennis and other racquet sports, singles competition involves one player against another in a match.

slugging percentage Baseball statistic measuring the ratio of a hitter's total bases reached on base hits to official at bats. Many statisticians feel that this is a more reliable measurement of a batter's performance than is his batting average.

stratospheric Descriptive term signifying outstanding statistical production in particular athletic endeavors.

taciturn Silent, not talkative by nature. Many of today's athletes are taciturn with the media because they do not like to reveal too much about themselves in the newspapers and on television.

tailwind A wind that is moving in the same direction as an athlete or a vehicle. In sports, a tailwind most often affects track and field events, where a strong wind can mean the difference between a world record and a disappointing result. Wind can help a long jumper jump further than ever before, and it can make a sprinter turn in his best time in the 100 meters. Officials at track and field events closely monitor wind speed and direction; if the wind is too strong, any race or long jump results are marked with an asterisk and are said to be "wind-aided."

tam o'shanter A wool cap of Scottish origin with a snug headband and a wide circular top.

technical knockout Point in a boxing match wherein the referee halts the fight when he or she declares one of the participants unable to continue because of injuries sustained as a result of the blows delivered by the other fighter.

thoroughbred An English breed of horses kept for racing purposes; originated from crossing English mares and Arabian stallions.

three-point shot A shot in basketball that, if made, is worth three points because the shooter was behind the three-point line with both feet when the shot was released. One foot behind the line and one foot in the air also counts as a three-point shot.

thyroid gland The largest gland found in the neck, the thyroid's sole function is to create and secrete the thyroid hormone, which has an effect on nearly all tissues in the body because it effects cellular activity. The thyroid regulates a body's metabolism.

ticker tape parade A parade through the streets of a city, most commonly New York City, in which confetti and bits of paper are showered down upon the participants from tall buildings lining the parade route. The ticker tape refers specifically to the paper strip that used to be generated from the telegraphic machines that relayed stock quotes to offices in New York.

Tour de France The most famous bicycling race in the world, the Tour de France is held annually over a three-week span in June and July. The race covers more than 2,300 miles as it winds its way through the French countryside and mountains. The first race was held in 1903 and was won by Maurice Gerin.

tribulations The suffering one goes through when being oppressed or persecuted. Any difficult or negative experiences; the phrase "trials and tribulations" is often used to describe the hardships that a person goes through in life.

Triple Crown (baseball) A batter wins the Triple Crown when he leads his league in batting average, home runs, and runs batted in. The feat has been accomplished 14 times in major league history, the last time by Carl Yazstremski of the Boston Red Sox in 1967.

Triple Crown (horse racing) A horse wins thoroughbred racing's Triple Crown when it wins the three most important races of the year—the Kentucky Derby, the Preakness Stakes, and the Belmont Stakes. The term Triple Crown was first coined in 1930 by sports writer Charles Hatton. Since that time, 11 horses have won racing's top prize, the most recent being Affirmed in 1978. Legendary race horse Secretariat holds the fastest time ever in two of the races—the Kentucky Derby and the Belmont Stakes.

ungainly Awkward or clumsy in appearance. lacking grace or smoothness.

United States Automobile Club (USAC) The most diverse auto racing governing organization in the United States. USAC oversees 10 different racing divisions and sanctions more than 180 races around the country each year. Popular racing classes include sprint and midget cars. Many auto racers begin their racing careers in USAC sponsored races.

unseeded In tennis tournaments and other sporting events, participants are "seeded," or ranked, based on their talent level. The most talented players receive the highest seeds, while less talented players receive lower seeds. Players who are just starting out or who are not talented enough to be ranked are left out of the seedings and are thus said to be unseeded.

Vardon Trophy Trophy given annually by the Professional Golfers Association for the player with the best scoring average over the year.

venues The location in which a sporting event takes place, it can refer to the city or region or, more specifically, to the actual building or stadium where an event occurs.

weight divisions (boxing) These separate boxers into classifications based on their weight so that boxers of nearly the same size end up fighting each other. There are currently 17 weight divisions in boxing that cover boxers weighing 105 to more than 190 pounds. The divisions are, from lightest to heaviest: minimumweight, junior flyweight, flyweight, junior bantamweight, bantamweight, featherweight, junior lightweight, lightweight, junior welterweight, welterweight, junior middleweight, middleweight, super middleweight, light heavyweight, cruiserweight, and heavyweight.

wind-aided Phrase attached to a finishing time in a sprint race or other track and field event when a tailwind going beyond a fixed speed assisted a competitor in achieving a particularly good time or score.

Winston Million Annual NASCAR prize of $1 million awarded to a driver who finishes in the top five of any one of the five "crown jewel" NASCAR events, and subsequently wins the next "crown jewel" event.

World Series The championship of Major League Baseball that matches the team that wins the National League pennant against the team that wins the American League pennant. Also known as "The Fall Classic."

wunderkind German in origin, a wunderkind is a very talented athlete who has succeeded at his or her sport at a very young age. Also applies to nonsporting activities.

yarn A tall tale or story of adventure that is at least partially, and quite possibly completely, fabricated. The world of sports is full of tall tales and stories about legendary performers who never made it to the big leagues.

Yom Kippur The holiest day of the Jewish year, it is observed with fasting and prayer.

Index

Ussala Cut—will speak with the Governor

Greenland and Sandy Beach
Sworn by John Johnson [4], Constable, 25 Aug. 1684.

Anthony Brackett 4
John Brackett 4
James Berry 4
William Berry 4
John Marden 4
Francis Rand Sen. 4
Isaac Herrick
Francis Rand Jr.
Thomas Sevey 4
Nathaniel Drake 4
Wm. Sevey Sen. Jr. 44
George Wallis 4
John Foss 4
William Wallis 4
John Odihorne
James Rendle 2, 4
Henry Beck
Aaron Moses 4
Thomas Creber
John Sherborn, mariner
Ferdinando Hoff
Edward Bickford
—will pay
Joseph Walker
Widow Lear
Sergt. Moses
Richard Sloper
—will pay 4
John Peverley
[Richard] Goss 4
Thomas Beck

Rech: Walden
Charles Allen 4
Edward Fox 4
Clement Harvey
Shadrack Walton 2
Justinian Richards 4
John Johnson 4
Thomas Rand 4
John Berry 4
William Davis 4
Ralph Walsh
Nathaniel Wright
Thomas Read
Philip Lewis 3, 4
Joseph Berry 4
Robert Hinkson
John Filbrick
Jotham Lewis 4
Robert Brain 4
Mathias Hains 4
Samuel Hains Sen. 3, 4
Samuel Hains Jr. 4
Lieut. Neal 4
Sergt. Bruster 4
Thomas Quint
John Westbrook 4
John Sherborn Sen. 4
Andrew Wiggin 3, 4
Thomas Wiggin 3, 4
John Sherborn Jr. 4
Leonard Weeks 4
Samuel Whitten 3, 4

Bloody Point, a Precinct of Dover
Sworn by Anthony Nutter, Constable, 25 Aug. 1684.

William Furber Sr. 3, 4
William Furber Jr. 3, 4
Richard Roe
John Dam Jr. 4
John Bickford Jr. 4
Samuel Rawlins
Ichabod Rawlins
John Hudson
Widow Catter
John Bickford Sr. 4

Mickiel Brawne
Henry Longstaff 4
Widow Trickey
Ephrim Trickey
Joseph Trickey
Isaac Trickey 4
William Shackford 4
Nicholas Harris[on] 4
Joseph Hall
James Rawlins

Oyster River, a Precinct of Dover
Sworn by John Woodman, Constable, 25 Aug. 1684.

James Huckens 3, 4
Edward Leathers 2, 4
George Gove
Widow Jones
James Smith
John Davis Jr. 4
Saml. Burnham 4
Philip Chisley Jr. 4
Robert Smart Jr.
David Denis
John Simons
Joseph Feild 3
William Greves 2
William Durgin
Francis Drue 4
Thomas Edgerly 4
Robert Watson 2

John Wille
John Bickford 3, 4
Charles Adams 3, 4
William Williams Jr.
William Williams Sr.
Thomas Stephenson 4
John Dery 4
John Meder Jr. 4
Edward Smalle 4
William Follett
John Drue 4
Joseph Smith
Barth: Stevenson
John Davis Sen. 3
Nick: Folletts wife refuses
John Meder Sr. 3, 4

Dover Neck (and Cochecho)
Sworn by John Gerrish, (3) Constable, 25 Aug. 1684.

[Cochecho]
Richard Waldron 3, 4
Peter Coffin
John Ham 4
William Horn 3, 4
Zack: Feild
Jenkin Jones 4
Thomas Downes Jr. 3, 4
Benjamin Heard 4
Ezek: Wentworth 4
Paul Wentworth

Elder Wentworth 4
George Ricker 4
Thomas Pain 3
Gersham Wentworth 4
John Heard Sen. 3, 4
John Heard Jr.
Stephen Otis 2
Thomas Hanson 4
Peter Mason 4
Robert Evans 4
Toby Hanson 4

Jonathan Watson
Ralph Twamley 4
Thomas Austin
Humph: Coarney
[Varney]
William Partridg
Thomas Downes Sen. 4
Nathaniel Stephens 4
John Church 4
Mark Giles 4
John Evans 4
Timothy Hanson 4
John Fost
Richard Otis Sen.
John Ellis
Richard Scamon
John Knight 4
Maturim Ricker
John Wingett 3, 4
[Dover Neck]
John Dam Sen. 3,4
John Cox
John Roberts Sen. 4

Thomas Roberts Jr. 4
Widow Tibbetts
Jeremy Tibbetts 4
William Dam 4
Abraham Newt
Philip Cromwell
Thomas Whitehouse 4
John Pinkham
William Wille
John Hall Jr. 4
John Hall Sen. 3, 4
John Tutle 4
Richard Rich
Job Clements
John Roberts Jr.
Joseph Canney 4
Nathaniel Hall 4
James Newtt Sen.
Edward Allen
Thomas Perkins
Thomas Young 4
Thomas Roberts Sr. 3, 4
William Henderson 4

Exeter
Sworn by John Foulsham, 25 Aug. 1684.

William Tailour 4
Edward Gilman 4
Nathaniel Foulsham 4
Nicholas Nores
Joel Jutkins 4
John Yong
Teague Drisco 4
Peter Gorden 4
John Ben 4
Christian Dollor 4
Jeremy Gilman 4
Samuel Dudley 4
Roger Kely 4
George Person
Edward Hilton
Thomas Meakins 4
Robert Smart Sen. 3, 4
Andrew Constable
Samuel Hilton 2
Charles Gredon
James Thomas 4
Edward Row
Robert Smart Jr.
Benjamin York
George Swet
Thomas Tedman
John Barber
John Gilman Esq. 3, 4
Richard Hilton
Charles Rumlets 4
James Kid
Armstrong Horne
William Hutchins 4
Peter Foulsham 3, 4
Moses Gilman Sen. 4
Jonathan Thing 4
Robert Wadley

Humphrey Wilson 4
Samuel Levet · 3
Ralf Hall
John Wadley
Samuel Hall 2, 4
Moses Gilman Jr. 4
Eleazer Alkins 3, 4
David Robinson 4
Widow Savel
Henry Magoon 4
Philip Carter 3, 4
Jeremy Conah
George Jones
Alexander Gordon
Cornelius Lery
Robert Powell
Nathaniel Ladd 4
Ephraim Foulsham 3, 4
Richard Scammon 3, 4
Nicholas Lecon
John Sinclere
John Wedgwood
Edward Smith 4
John Gilman Jr. 3
Widow Gilman
Moses Levet
Jonathan Smith
Richard Morgan
George Roberts
Samuel Foulsham
David Lawrence
Bile Dudley 4
Joseph Hall 3
Thomas & Steven Dudley 44
Thomas Rawlins 4

Hampton
Sworn by John Smith and Nathaniel Bacheler, Constables, 25 Aug. 1684.

Constable John Smith's List

Samuel Colcord 4
John Blake 4
Moses Cox, Ja: Perkins
Abraham Cole 4
Widow Colcord
Thomas Dearborn 3, 4
John Dearborn 4
Henry Dearborn 3, 4
Daniel Dow 4
Gershom Elkins
Josiah Sanborn 4
Thomas Levet 3, 4
Ezrom Levet 3, 4

Aretus Levet 4
John Stockbridge 4
William Marston 2, 4
Isaac Marston
John Hobbs
Thomas Roby
Philip Towle Sen. 3, 4
Jo: Taylor & father 4
John Tuck 3, 4
Widow Wale
Thomas Webster 3, 4
John Garland

Constable Nathaniel Bacheler's List

Jacob Brown
Joseph Cass 4
Samuel Cass 4

Thomas Chace
James Chace
Ben: Cramt 4

Henry Dow	4	
Abr: Drake Jr.	4	
Will Fuler Sen.	3	
Will: Fifield	3, 4	
Ben: Fifield	4	
Samuel Fog	4	
Isaac Green		
Isaac Godfrey	4	
Maurice Hobs Sen.	3, 4	
Nehemiah Hobs	4	
Widow Johnson	4	
John Knowls	4	
John Marston	4	
Ephraim Marston	4	
John Hussey		
Henry Moulton	3, 4	
John Moulton	3, 4	
Joseph Moulton	4	
Benjamin Moulton	4	
Thomas Page	4	
Ebenezer Perkins	3	
Joseph Perkins		
Jonathan Filbrook	4	
Sam: Filbrook		

Thomas Filbrook	4
James Filbrook	4
Jacob Perkins	3, 4
Caleb Perkins	4
Joseph Palmer	4
John Redman Sen.	2
John Redman Jr.	
Will Sanborn	4
Jo: Sanborn Jr.	4
Joseph Sanborn	4
Antony Stanion	
John Stanion	
Benjamin Shaw	4
William Swain	
Daniel Tilton	4
Benjamin Swet	3
Joseph Swet	4
Robert Smith	
Joseph Smith	4
Thomas Sleeper	
Aaron Sleeper	
Widow Ward	
David Wedgwood	
Jonathan Wedgwood	4

Saml. Penhallow, etc.).

Walter Nele (John Pickering Sen., Tobias Langdon, John Partridge, etc.).

Tho: Graffort (John Shipway, Sam: Wentworth, Thomas Wacomb, etc.

John Dery of Oyster River (Joseph Meder, John Willie).

Peter Coffin of Exeter (Moses Gilman, Edw. Gillman, John Foullsam, John Gillman Sen.).

With three columns crowded in:

Great Island, headed by Nath. Fryer (Robert Elliot, Tho. Cobbett, John Hatch, Sidrick Walton, etc.).

Greenland, headed by Charles Allin (John Johnston, John Fos, Tho. Lewis, etc.).

Newington, headed by Henry Langstaff (Richard Roo, John Dam, John Nutter, etc.).

A column in the margin:

Stratham, headed by Andrew Wiggin (Tho: Wiggin, Thomas Reade, Nathaniel Wright, etc.).

A column on the back side:

Hampton, headed by Abraham Drak (John Smith. Humphrey Perkins, Thomas Derbarn, William Lain, Nathl. Bachiler, etc.).

Corrections of N. E. Register viii. 233-5.

233 Alter Christian D to Dalhaar
—— to Thomas Wiggin
William Kelaye to ——
John Dooker to Doolhor
Illegible to P[eter Fol]sa[m]
Willm Catter to Philip [Cartee]
Daniel Beame to Beane
234 David Savane to Larance
Anthony to Armstrong Horn
Beniam Cooke to ——   John Duren to Drew
Isaac Stoke to Stokes   Roger Roscar to Rose
R——h etc. to Nathl Fryer Jr.
Hen Sise to Rise   John Horsh to ——
Richard Walldins to Mattone
Nicholas Dam to Dun   Berian to Beriah Higgens
John to James Buncker   John Pinear to Pinder
Salathiel Derbon to Denbou
Philip Doules to Douly
Tho: Grafton to Graffort
Thomas Naramo to Wacomb
Sylan to Splan Lovell   Thomas Stearns to Stevens
Petter Babt to Ball   William Furber to W. F. Jr.
Thomas Chesly to T. C. Sr.   James Terry to Derry
Cancel Nathaniel James Sr.
Alter Nathaniel James to Lamos
Ed Kasee to [Kater]
235 Thomas Kany to Rand
George Tebby to Tebbs   Wla to Nehe: Partridge
John Sill to Hill   Wm. Deanes to Deaves
Samuel Kears to Keais
Richard Jose [——?] to Richard Jose
John Berry [cancel senyer]
Sem Misroy to Clem Misvoy
Thomas Parkham to Picker[in]
James Casewall to Cazawah
John Quin to Sanborn   John Godfrey add Sr.
Joseph —— to Sanbun
Joseph Ste—— to [Swett]
Thomas Derharn to Derbarn
[? insert Samuel Shaw]
[? insert John Moulton Jr.]
Alter Wm. Field to [Fifield]
John Fowler to Sowter

53 Table of Deputies to General Court of Massachusetts
    — N. H. Prov. Papers i. 369-372.
369 Cancel William Heath.
371 'Mr. Josh. Gilman' [-sic-] must have been John Gilman representing Exeter.

54 Petitions favoring Massachusetts Government by Four Towns, Oct. 22, 1677.
    — N. H. Prov. Papers, xvii. 524-528.
    Corrections by conjecture:
525   **Dover**
For George Bracou read Braun.
For Thomas Cauny read Canny.
For John Hud read Herd.
For Nathaniel Stones read Stevens.
526   **Exeter**
For Samuel Leane read ——
For John Gillen Jr. read Gilman.
For Richard Seaman read Scamon.
For Linsley Hall read Kinsley.
527   **Portsmouth**
For John Dame read [Ham?].
For John Harall read ——
For Ben Hollis read [Reuben Hull?].
For Robert Pariaton read Purinton.
528   **Hampton**
For William Samber read Sanborn.
For Adonias Webster read Thomas.
For Hum Godfray read Isaac.
For Christopher Hassey read Hussey.
For Rob Haye read

55a Talesmen for the Gove Treason Trial, Jan. 1682-3. — N. H. Hist. Coll. viii. 167-168.

55b Grand and Petty Jury Lists for 1684, 1686. — N. H. Hist. Coll. viii. 208-209, N. E. Reg. xxxvi. 395.

56 New Hampshire Constitutional Convention held at Portsmouth, 24 Jan. 1689-90. — Notable Events, pp. 95-96.

57 General Petition of Inhabitants and train soldiers 20 Feb. 1689-90, to Massachusetts, to set up a temporary government. Savage scattered these names through four volumes, often unmindful that the signers might be but boys of 16. It was better printed in the N. E. Register viii. 233 than in N. H. Hist. Coll. 13 years later (viii. 293). Some names now illegible are left as printed in 1854, and insignificant misreadings of spellings are not corrected.
    —Mass. Arch. xxxv. 228.
    The original petition was at first headed in five columns by:
Richard Martyn of Portsmouth (Wm. Vaughan, Richard Waldron, Samuel Keais, Richard Jose,

58 Civil and Military Lists approved in Boston for the Interregnum, 19 March 1689-90. — N. H. Hist. Coll. viii. 299.

59 Civil and Military Lists, 12 Sept. 1692. — N. H. Prov. Papers ii. 71-72.

60 Province Treasurer's Account for 1693. — N. H. Prov. Papers xvii. 621-622.
Mr. Thomas Nuton[-sic-]   Martin Williams [-sic-]

61 Tax Collectors' Districts in 1693. — N. H. Prov. Papers xvii. 623.